AF290365

ARCHAEOLOGY AT THE WATERFRONT
1: INVESTIGATING LIVERPOOL'S HISTORIC DOCKS

Richard A Gregory, Caroline Raynor, Mark Adams,
Rob Philpott, Christine Howard-Davis, Nick Johnson,
Vix Hughes, and David A Higgins

Contributions by
Adrian Jarvis and Michael Stammers

Illustrations by
Marie Rowland, Anne Stewardson, and Susie White

2014

Published by
Oxford Archaeology North
Mill 3
Moor Lane Mills
Moor Lane
Lancaster
LA1 1QD
(*Phone:* 01524 541000; *Fax:* 01524 848606)
(*website:* http://oxfordarchaeology.com/)

Distributed by
Oxbow Books Ltd
10 Hythe Bridge Street
Oxford
OX1 2EW
(*Phone:* 01865 241249; *Fax:* 01865 794449)

Printed by
Berforts Information Press, Oxford, UK

© Oxford Archaeology Limited 2014

ISBN 978-1-907686-18-4
ISSN 1345-5205

Series editor
Rachel Newman
Indexer
Marie Rowland
Design, layout, and formatting
Marie Rowland

Front cover: *Excavations of the Mersey Railway Company's Pumping and Ventilation Station, at Mann Island*
Rear Cover: *Excavations at the new Museum of Liverpool site, Mann Island (top right); Excavations of the Countryside Neptune site, Mann Island (top and bottom left)*

LANCASTER
IMPRINTS

Lancaster Imprints is the publication series of Oxford Archaeology North. The series covers work on major excavations and surveys of all periods undertaken by the organisation and associated bodies.

Contents

List of Illustrations

Figures

Plates

Tables

Contributors

Mark Adams
Museum of Liverpool, Pier Head, Liverpool Waterfront, Liverpool L3 1DG

Richard A Gregory
Oxford Archaeology North, Mill 3, Moor Lane Mills, Moor Lane, Lancaster LA1 1QD

David A Higgins
Honorary Research Fellow, School of Archaeology, Classics and Egyptology, The University of Liverpool, 10-12 Abercromby Square, Liverpool L69 3BX

Chris Howard Davis
Oxford Archaeology North, Mill 3, Moor Lane Mills, Moor Lane, Lancaster LA1 1QD

Vix Hughes
Oxford Archaeology South, Janus House, Osney Mead, Oxford OX2 0ES

Adrian Jarvis
Centre for Port and Maritime History, School of Histories, Language and Culture, The University of Liverpool, Liverpool L69 3BX

Nick Johnson
(formerly of) Oxford Archaeology North, Mill 3, Moor Lane Mills, Moor Lane, Lancaster LA1 1QD

Rob Philpott
Museum of Liverpool, Pier Head, Liverpool Waterfront, Liverpool L3 1DG

Caroline Raynor
(formerly of) Oxford Archaeology North, Mill 3, Moor Lane Mills, Moor Lane, Lancaster LA1 1QD

†Michael Stammers

Glossary

Counterfort   A strengthening buttress set at right-angles to a retaining wall

Lucam   A structure that projects out from a building's roof, protecting a hoist, and allows this to winch up goods clear of the building

Abbreviations

BM	Boat Museum (Ellesmere Port)
CWT	Centum Weight (Hundredweight)
GWR	Great Western Railway
LHPC	Liverpool Hydraulic Power Company
LLC	Leeds and Liverpool Canal
LMR	Liverpool and Manchester Railway
LNWR	London and North Western Railway
LORC	Liverpool Overhead Railway Company
LUAU	Lancaster University Archaeological Unit
LVRO	Liverpool Record Office
LYR	Lancashire and Yorkshire Railway
MAS	Merseyside Archaeological Service
MDC	Merseyside Development Corporation
MDHB	Mersey Docks and Harbour Board
MMMMAL	Merseyside Maritime Museum, Maritime Archives and Library
MPTE	Merseyside Passenger Transport Executive
MRC	Mersey Railway Company
NMLFAU	National Museums Liverpool Field Archaeology Unit
NWSIAH	North Western Society for Industrial Archaeology and History
OA	Oxford Archaeology
OS	Ordnance Survey
SURCC	Shropshire Union Railway and Canal Company
SWL	Safe Working Load
UNESCO	United Nations Educational, Scientific, and Cultural Organisation
WHS	World Heritage Site

Summary

Liverpool's historic waterfront forms an internationally significant area, which holds importance for the eighteenth- and nineteenth-century development of world trade, commerce, and the mass movement of people, as evidenced by the United Nations Educational, Scientific, and Cultural Organisation (UNESCO) inscribing World Heritage Status on a *c* 3.5 km stretch of the historic dock system in 2004. Between 2006 and 2008, Oxford Archaeology North and the National Museums Liverpool Field Archaeology Unit conducted extensive programmes of archaeological investigation, both within and adjacent to the World Heritage Site, funded by Countryside Neptune, the National Museums Liverpool, BAM Nuttall Ltd, Balfour Beatty Civil Engineering Ltd, Pierse UK, and British Waterways.

This investigation comprised detailed historical research, excavation, and building survey, which examined parts of the historic dock system that had been progressively created during the eighteenth and nineteenth centuries to the north of Liverpool's first dock (the Old Dock). These focused on two adjacent areas at Mann Island (centred on SJ 3403 9008 and SJ 3394 9004). These areas lay directly north of Canning Dock and the Canning Graving Docks and were examined as a prelude to the construction of a large commercial development (Countryside Neptune site) and also the new Museum of Liverpool. The work provided an unique insight into the establishment of the Dry Dock (later Canning Dock), which opened in 1739, and associated eighteenth-century land reclamation which resulted in the creation of Nova Scotia and Mann Island, an area that historically was known as 'Sailor-town'. This scheme of excavation also uncovered significant evidence relating to George's Dock Passage, constructed in 1775, several eighteenth-century warehouses and slipways, and also late eighteenth-century land reclamation associated with the formation of both Manchester Basin and Chester Basin, which formed two adjacent tidal basins used by a distinctive type of sailing barge, known as a Mersey flat. In addition, the excavations allowed the subsequent sequence of early nineteenth-century land reclamation to be discerned, which led to the extension of Mann Island and the conversion of Manchester Basin initially into a half-tide dock, and later into a fully impounded wet dock, with a double-gated river entrance. Manchester Dock was infilled between 1928 and 1936, apparently leaving the dock intact, since the excavations uncovered the walls of the nineteenth-century dock and river lock, as well as the *in situ* inner lock gates and their opening/closing mechanisms. The excavations across this area, and to the east of George's Dock Passage, also produced evidence for the form and workings of the adjacent quaysides during the nineteenth and early twentieth centuries. This evidence comprised remains relating to warehouses, cranes, bridges, and hydraulic-power systems, as well as other features associated with the policing and maintenance of the docks, and the operation of the George's Dock Pumping and Ventilation Station, which served the Mersey Railway Company's tunnel.

In addition to the Mann Island development sites, the programme of archaeological investigation also extended to a detailed examination of the footprint of the extension to the Leeds and Liverpool Canal, which extended for 2.5 km between Stanley Dock and Canning Dock (SJ 3382 9211 to SJ 3408 9003). This involved historical research and excavation across the Mann Island section of the canal extension, which complemented that work completed at the Countryside Neptune and Museum of Liverpool sites, and also within its Pier Head (centred on SJ 338 904) and Central Docks sections (centred on SJ 334 914). The Pier Head section produced evidence for late eighteenth- and early nineteenth-century land reclamation and the construction of river walls associated with the progressive extension of the western and northern quays of George's Dock; remains of George's Dock Dry Basin, which opened in 1771; elements of a late eighteenth-century pier associated with George's Dock; and early nineteenth-century remains associated with the remodelling and extension of Chester Basin. Moreover, the scheme produced evidence for twentieth-century activity directly adjacent to the 'Three Graces', which forms the centrepiece of the World Heritage Site. Similarly, the Central Docks section of the canal extension allowed an examination of the waterfront's nineteenth- and twentieth-century remains, such as those associated with Prince's Dock, which opened in 1821, and a quay between Victoria and Trafalgar Docks.

Aside from the structural remains, a large collection of artefacts was also recovered during the archaeological investigations across Mann Island and along the Leeds and Liverpool Canal extension. This material principally comprises pottery and fragments of clay tobacco pipe and these, along with the other elements of material culture recovered during the Oxford Archaeology North excavations, are summarised, in order to build an impression of Liverpool's growing industry and its trading contacts throughout the eighteenth and nineteenth centuries.

This volume also summarises the archaeological investigations undertaken by Oxford Archaeology North and the National Museums Liverpool Field Archaeology Unit in other parts of the historic waterfront, prior to 2009. It therefore contains summary details of the excavations completed at Duke's Dock (centred on SJ 3335 3891), Rochdale Basin (centred on SJ 3413 8938), Queen's Dock entrance lock (centred on SJ 3446 8916), Canning Dock (centred on SJ 3423 8996), and at Pier Head (centred on SJ 3379 9022). More significantly, there is a summary of the archaeological work undertaken at the Old Dock (centred on SJ 3437 8997), which represents the world's first commercial wet dock, opened in 1715.

Acknowledgements

The archaeological investigations undertaken on Mann Island and along the Leeds and Liverpool Canal extension owe their success to many individuals, and also the close co-operation between the archaeological contractors and the various companies involved in the redevelopment of Liverpool's waterfront. With regard to the work at the Countryside Neptune site, on Mann Island, Oxford Archaeology North would like to thank Countryside Neptune for commissioning the archaeological investigation, and in particular Ian Bradshaw, Stephen Osuhor, and Tim McCormac for their interest and enthusiasm. In addition, thanks are extended to Dave Hodgkinson and Helen Martin-Bacon, of Wardell Armstrong, who acted as the archaeological consultants for Countryside Neptune. The archaeological investigation at the Countryside Neptune site would not have been possible without the help and support of the principal contractor, BAM Nuttall Ltd, and especially the support of their site team, which included Neil Millward, Peter Marner, David Mahoney, John-Luke Smith, Eamonn Murphy, and Dave Hanlon. During the fieldwork at the Countryside Neptune site, on-site support was provided by Terry Mason, and his team, from Tidale, the demolition contractors, whilst a debt of gratitude is extended to the machine-plant operators, from both Boundary and Mahers plant hire, for their patience and professionalism in undertaking the machining. Hylift operator Des Alcock, of Hylift Access Hire, must also be thanked for his assistance in capturing aerial photographs of the bulk excavation across the Countryside Neptune site as it progressed.

The archaeological evaluation and excavation work at the Countryside Neptune site was undertaken by Vix Hughes, Andy Lane, and Caroline Raynor, with the assistance of Ric Buckle, Caroline Bulcock, Ged Callaghan, Tim Christian, Pascal Eloy, Will Gardner, Fiona Gordon, Annie Hamilton-Gibney, Joanne Hawkins, Pip Haworth, Paul Holmes, Gemma Jones, Andrea Kenyon, Tom Mace, Dave Lamb, Des O'Leary, Mark Oldham, Kieran Power, Andy Proctor, Elizabeth Murray, and Claire Riley. The watching brief work in 2009 was undertaken by Des O'Leary and Ric Buckle, and the watching brief work in 2011 was undertaken by Caroline Raynor. The fieldwork was managed by Jamie Quartermaine, whilst the post-excavation process was managed by Jamie Quartermaine and Murray Cook.

The other excavations along the waterfront include those at the site of the Museum of Liverpool and within the footprint of the Leeds and Liverpool Canal extension. The scheme of archaeological work at the site of the new Museum of Liverpool was undertaken by the National Museums Liverpool Field Archaeology Unit. It was funded and sponsored by the National Museums Liverpool, and the assistance of Sharon Granville and Janet Dugdale is gratefully acknowledged. Fieldwork was managed by Mark Adams, and the project was supervised by Clare Ahmad, assisted by Helen Jones. Site Assistants were Sarah Pevely, George Luke, Ron Gurney, and Jeff Speakman, with volunteers Kathy Jason, Chris O'Brien, and Anys Price. Plant was provided by the main contractor, Galliford Try/PIHL. Post-excavation reporting was managed by Rob Philpott.

The investigation along the canal extension was undertaken by Oxford Archaeology North and formed three separate pieces of commissioned work. The investigation on the Mann Island section was commissioned by BAM Nuttall Ltd and British Waterways; the work at Pier Head was commissioned by Balfour Beatty Civil Engineering Ltd and British Waterways; whilst that within the Central Docks was commissioned by Pierse UK and British Waterways. The Mann Island scheme of work would not have been possible without the on-site support and assistance of the BAM Nuttall Ltd construction team, including Terry Nuttall, Tony Wilkes, Dan Davies, and Alan Bennett. Similarly, sincere thanks go to all of the Balfour Beatty construction team, for support and assistance during the Pier Head excavations, especially Jon Galloway, Mick Rurnmens, Matthew Storr, Stefan Smith, Jonathan Giles, Philip Kelly, and Johnstone Cummings, and the Pierse construction team, for on-site support during the Central Docks fieldwork, particularly Richard Driver, Ronnie Griffith, Pete Ridgeway, Steve Jones, Steve Thiem, and Aled Gary Roberts. Many thanks are also offered to all the British Waterways staff involved in the Mann Island, Pier Head, and Central Docks sections of the canal link, particularly Tim Brownrigg, Charles Wilsoncroft, and Ian Thomas. We especially thank Tony Orme, Clerk of Works for British Waterways, for his infinite patience, advice, and good humour throughout all phases of the excavation, and Richard Longton, for his support after Pierse UK went into liquidation. Thanks also go to the ARUP team of Richard Summers, Lyndsay Hammond, and Miles Wilkinson, whilst the skilled staff of PP O'Connor, Maher, and Clonfin Plant Hire must be thanked for their patience while working alongside the archaeological team.

The evaluation and excavation work on these three sections of the canal extension was undertaken by Vix Hughes, Caroline Raynor, and Andy Lane, with the assistance of Alex Beben, Jeremy Bradley, Ric Buckle, Caroline Bulcock, Tim Christian, Pascal Eloy, Claire Gardner, Will Gardner, Joanne Hawkins, Pip Haworth, Paul Holmes,

Andrea Kenyon, Tom Mace, Dave Lamb, Des O'Leary, Kieran Power, Rebekkah Pressler, Andy Proctor, and Elizabeth Murray. The fieldwork was managed by Jamie Quartermaine, who, along with Murray Cook, also managed the post-excavation assessment and analysis.

More generally, the post-excavation process has been greatly assisted by Rachel Newman (Oxford Archaeology North's Senior Executive Officer: Research and Publication), who edited individual reports and also this volume. In addition, as part of the post-excavation analysis, David Higgins is particularly grateful to Ron Dagnall of Rainford for providing him with transcriptions of documents relating to Thomas Hayes, Jan van Oostveen for his help with dating the Gouda stem stamp, and to Susie White, who prepared the majority of the archival pipe illustrations. Jeff Speakman, National Museums Liverpool Field Archaeology Unit, commented most helpfully on the report on the pottery recovered from Mann Island and from along the Leeds and Liverpool Canal extension.

The majority of the maps and images used in the volume, as well as the documentary sources consulted, are held in the Liverpool Record Office, the University of Liverpool Library, and the Merseyside Maritime Museum, Maritime Archives and Library, and the help and assistance of David Stoker and Roger Hull, Liverpool Libraries, the staff of the Special Collections, the University of Liverpool, and John Moore, Merseyside Maritime Museum, is gratefully acknowledged. Thanks are also extended to Richard Hawes for permission to use a map extract held in his collection. A debt of gratitude must be extended to Sarah-Jane Farr, the former Merseyside Archaeological Officer, who provided information and considerable support throughout the course of all of the archaeological excavations detailed in this volume. Finally, thanks are given to all the members of the public who showed an interest in the archaeological excavations as they progressed along both the canal extension and across Mann Island.

In memory of Mike Stammers

(1943-2013)

Extract from the Buck brothers' 1728 view
of Liverpool from the River Mersey

Figure 1: Liverpool's historic waterfront and the position of extant and buried docks (© Crown copyright 2014 Ordnance Survey 100005569)

1

INTRODUCTION

Richard A Gregory

The Port City and its Historic Waterfront

The development of Liverpool, like many of the world's major port cities, has been conditioned and shaped by its maritime and mercantile history. This important phase of Liverpool's history began in the early decades of the eighteenth century, and reached a zenith between the mid-nineteenth and early part of the twentieth century, when Liverpool functioned as one of the world's premiere general-cargo ports (Milne 2006, 257). During this period, the dock system extended for approximately 9 km along the Mersey foreshore, between Herculaneum Dock in the south and Hornby Dock in the north (Fig 1), and it was argued by Liverpool's protagonists that it represented the 'second city of the empire' (Pike 1911, 13), with trading links to every world port of any importance (Baines 1852, 840). In terms of the people of Liverpool, the incorporation of the city within the global maritime network has also been profound. Whilst at one level, it has largely influenced their economic circumstances, it has also been important in forging a shared cultural, civic, and commercial identity. Indeed, as it has been noted, being part of a global maritime network has, in many respects, been 'central to the way Liverpool thinks of itself' (Milne 2006, 258). Moreover, this view may partly explain the modern restoration and redevelopment of Liverpool's historic docks, an area which the Merseyside Development Corporation (MDC) viewed as paramount for signifying the start of Liverpool's urban renaissance (Murden 2006, 439).

Given these factors, it comes as no great surprise to find the pervading influence of Liverpool's maritime and mercantile history embedded within both Liverpool's upstanding architectural fabric and also its buried archaeological remains, which is most prominent within the surviving edifices defining its historic waterfront and immediate hinterland. Accordingly, the importance of this area, to both Liverpool and to the historic development of world trade, commerce, and the mass movement of people, was recognised by the United Nations Educational, Scientific, and Cultural Organisation (UNESCO),

which inscribed World Heritage Site (WHS) status on portions of the city in 2004 (UNESCO 2014). The WHS, designated as the 'Liverpool - Maritime Mercantile City', encompasses six inter-linked areas (Liverpool City Council 2005, 20), three of which, the Pier Head, Albert Dock, and Stanley Dock Conservation Areas, hold direct relevance to the work outlined in this volume (Fig 2).

Together these portions of the WHS cover a *c* 3.5 km stretch of the historic waterfront, and contain extant docks, warehouses, ancillary buildings, and also several of Liverpool's more iconic commercial buildings and monuments (*ibid*). From south to north, the extant docks within the WHS include Wapping Dock; Wapping Basin; Duke's, Salthouse, Albert, and Canning Docks; Canning Half-tide Dock; Canning Graving Docks Nos 1 and 2; Prince's Half-tide and East Waterloo Docks; Clarence Graving Docks; and Salisbury, Collingwood, Stanley, Nelson, and Bramley-Moore Docks (Fig 2). In addition, the Albert Dock Conservation Area also contains the site of the Old Dock, Liverpool's first dock, which was the world's first commercial wet dock (Jackson 1983, 46-7). This important development, constructed within a natural inlet known as the Pool, was infilled in the nineteenth century and is now partially covered by a modern building, located at the corner of Strand Street and Canning Place, and forming part of Liverpool One. However, following archaeological excavation (*Ch 2, p 37*), part of the dock's retaining wall can now at times be viewed within an information centre at the north-eastern corner of the former dock (Pl 1).

Other important components within the WHS comprise several structures, directly associated with the historic dock system and waterfront, which have been designated as Listed Buildings (Fig 3). These include two mid-nineteenth-century swing bridges, associated with Canning Dock (both Grade II; Liverpool City Council 2005, 58), cyclopean granite river walls in the vicinity of Albert Dock, Canning Island, and Salisbury Dock (all Grade II; *op cit*, 59, 68), and four mid-nineteenth-century granite canal locks linking Stanley Dock with the Leeds and Liverpool Canal (LLC) (Grade II; *op cit*, 69). They

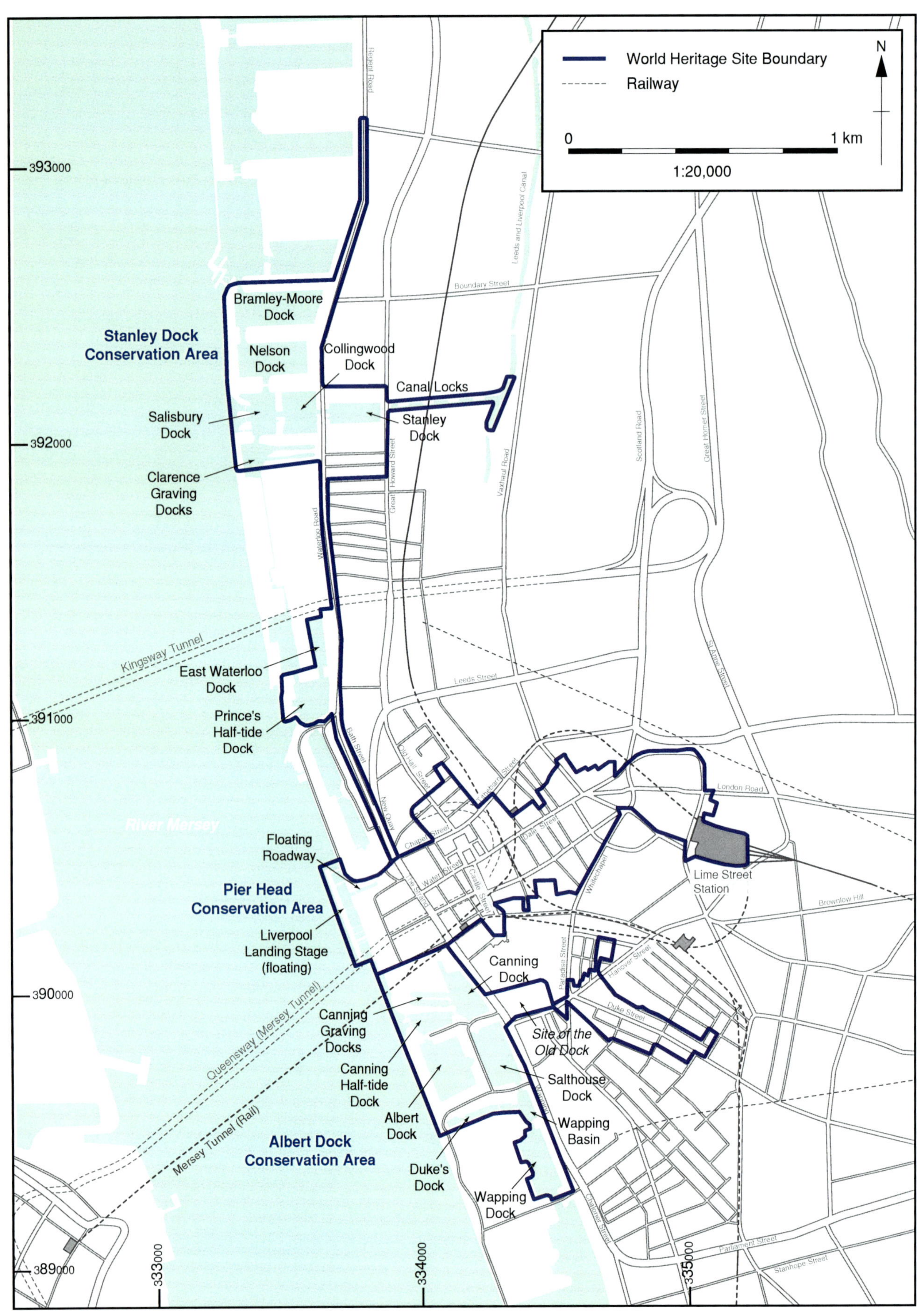

Figure 2: Liverpool's Maritime Mercantile City World Heritage Site and extant docks within its boundaries (© Crown copyright 2014 Ordnance Survey 100005569)

Plate 1: The retaining wall of the Old Dock, as seen in the Old Dock Information Centre

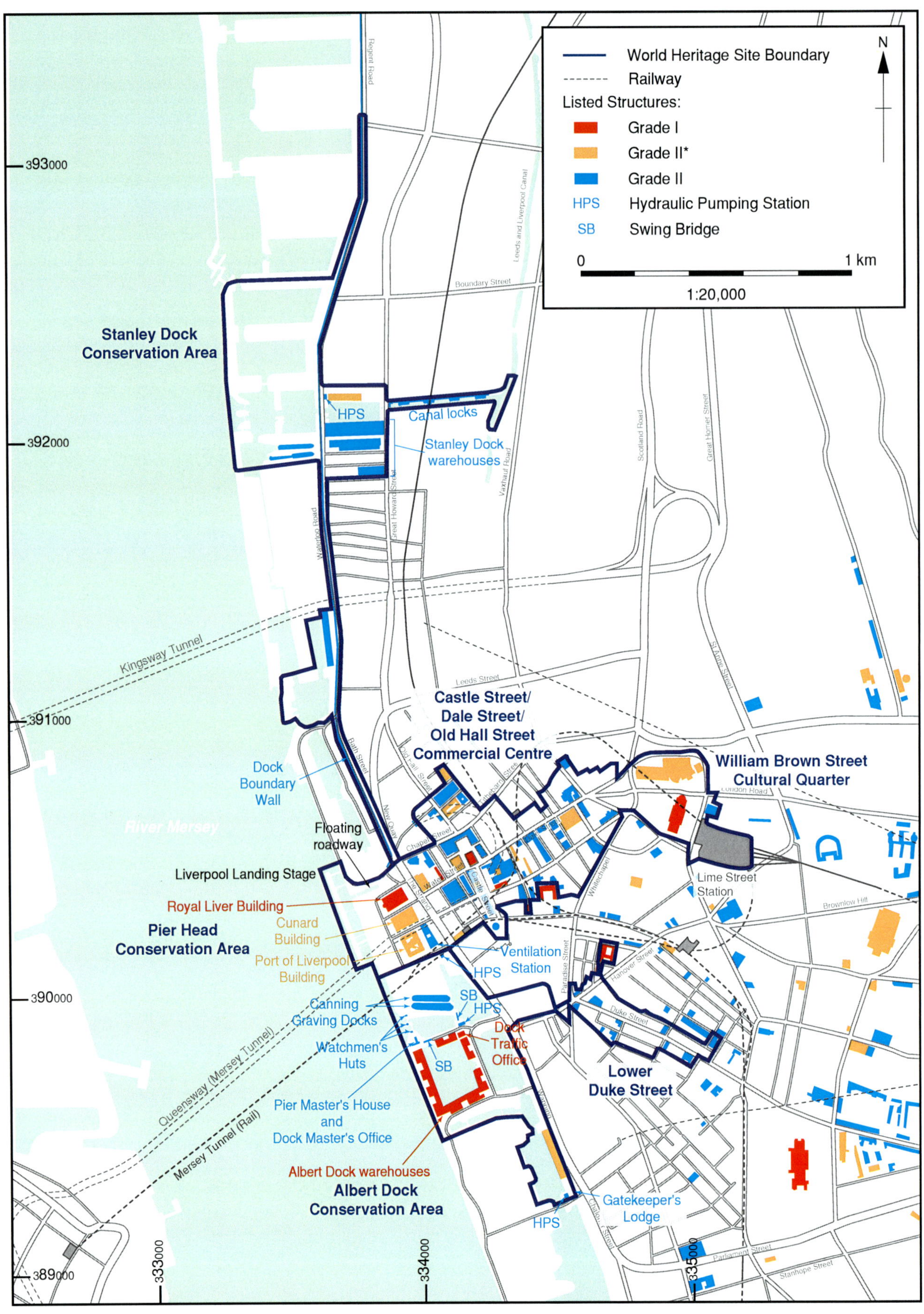

Figure 3: *Liverpool's Maritime Mercantile City World Heritage Site and Listed Buildings within its boundaries (© Crown copyright 2014 Ordnance Survey 100005569)*

4

Plate 2: The dock boundary wall close to the rear of Prince's Dock

also include the massive Dock Boundary Wall and its associated gateways (Grade II; *op cit*, 66), extending from Prince's Dock to Huskisson Dock (Pl 2). This monumental structure was successively built during the early and mid-nineteenth century by several of Liverpool's prominent dock engineers and was designed to separate the dock estate from the city, in order to curtail smuggling and theft (*op cit*, 65).

The Pier Head, Albert Dock, and Stanley Dock Conservation Areas are also characterised by significant upstanding buildings, which hold Listed status, and have a direct association with the historic waterfront. Pier Head holds particular significance to Liverpool's maritime history in that from the mid-nineteenth century onwards it served as an embarkation and arrival point for local ferries and passenger shipping, notably those carrying emigrants to the New World (Cossons and Jenkins 2011, 21). This was made possible by the construction of floating landing stages, that were variously replaced and modified between the mid-nineteenth century and the 1970s, and also through a floating roadway, opening in 1874, which joined with the landing stage (Liverpool City Council 2005, 53). Arguably, Pier Head also contains the more significant of the upstanding buildings along the historic waterfront, at least in terms of Liverpool's external image and former commercial identity (Cossons and Jenkins 2011, 101). Architecturally, this area is dominated by the 'Three Graces' (Pl 3), which form the centrepiece of the WHS, and which partly overlie George's Dock,

Plate 3: The 'Three Graces', from Mann Island

Plate 4: The Royal Liver Building

an infilled eighteenth-century dock, constructed in 1771 (*Ch 3, p 70*). These iconic buildings comprise the Port of Liverpool Building (Grade II*; Liverpool City Council 2005, 50-1), completed in 1907 as the head office of the Mersey Docks and Harbour Board (MDHB), the Cunard Building (Grade II*; *op cit*, 50), finished in 1916 as the head offices and terminal of the Cunard Steamship Company, and the Royal Liver Building (Grade I; *op cit*, 49-50), completed in 1911, as the head office of the Royal Liver Friendly Society (*op cit*, 49-51).

In term of English architecture, the Royal Liver Building is unique (Pl 4). Its more prominent features

Plate 5: The grain warehouses at Waterloo Dock, as depicted on an 1877 engraving (LVRO and Liverpool Libraries Hf 942.721 GRA)

include two clock towers surmounted by two copper Liver Birds, that represent 'the biggest in the city and which to many people are the very identity of Liverpool' (*op cit*, 50). However, although the Royal Liver Building may be more architecturally noteworthy, taken together the 'Three Graces' create an impressive waterfront and an instantly recognisable skyline, when approaching the city by ship (*op cit*, 49). It is also claimed that they have provided architectural inspiration for several buildings within the USA and also Shanghai (Belchem 2006, 20), and the Royal Liver Building may well have acted as inspiration for the Seven Sisters in Moscow and the Manhattan Municipal Building in New York (Cossons and Jenkins 2011, 102). In addition to the 'Three Graces', Pier Head is also the site of another significant Listed Building (Grade II), the Ventilation Station. This curious structure was constructed between 1931 and 1934 to serve the Mersey Road Tunnel; architecturally, it falls within the Art Deco tradition, and is heavily influenced by the architecture of ancient Egypt (Liverpool City Council 2005, 51). This distinctive building is composed of a central ventilation shaft, in the form of an obelisk, with surrounding offices, and was designed by the architect Herbert J Rowse (*ibid*). Furthermore, it is decorated with notable relief sculptures symbolising civil engineering, construction, architecture, and decoration (Sharples 2004, 72).

The other important upstanding buildings are located in the Albert Dock and Stanley Dock Conservation Areas and comprise numerous warehouses lining parts of Liverpool's historic docks (Fig 3). These warehouses, along with those located in the immediate commercial hinterland situated in the Castle Street/ Dale Street/Old Hall Street part of the WHS, were integral to Liverpool's success as a global port

(Liverpool City Council 2005, 47), and they include a significant group surrounding Albert Dock, which form the largest collection of Grade I Listed Buildings in England (*op cit*, 56). These fireproof bonded warehouses, which originally held imported goods, date to the mid-nineteenth century and were designed by the pre-eminent dock engineer Jesse Hartley who, by surrounding Albert Dock with these buildings, and also a perimeter wall, created the world's first secure dock (*ibid*; Cossons and Jenkins 2011, 13). They also hold further significance in that they incorporate the world's first hydraulic cargo-handling installation, used to raise goods from the quayside (Liverpool City Council 2005, 56).

To the south of Albert Dock, another Jesse Hartley-designed warehouse is found fronting Wapping Dock (Grade II*; *op cit*, 62), whilst to the north, in the Stanley Dock Conservation Area, other significant upstanding warehouses include Waterloo Warehouse (Grade II), built in *c* 1868, adjacent to East Waterloo Dock (Pl 5), and a group surrounding Stanley Dock. This group consists of two mid-nineteenth-century warehouses on the northern (Grade II*) and southern (Grade II) sides of the dock, a mid-nineteenth-century bonded tea warehouse (Grade II) positioned between Dublin Street and Dickinson Street, and the Stanley Dock Tobacco Warehouse, which was built in 1901 and then formed the world's largest tobacco warehouse (*op cit*, 70-1).

In addition to the warehouses, other historically significant upstanding buildings can be found in the Albert Dock and Stanley Dock Conservation Areas (Fig 3), which were designed with varying functions in mind. They include the mid-nineteenth-century Dock Traffic Office (Grade I; *op cit*, 57); hydraulic pumping stations at Canning Half-Tide Dock (Grade II; *ibid*), Mann Island (Grade II; *op cit*, 61), Wapping Dock (Grade II; *op cit*, 62), and close to Stanley Dock (Grade II; *op cit*, 71); the Pier Master's House (Grade II; *op cit*, 58) and Dock Master's Office (Grade II; *ibid*) at Albert Pier Head; the Watchmen's Huts at the entrance to Canning Dock (Grade II; *op cit*, 59); and the Gatekeeper's Lodge at Wapping Dock (Grade II; *op cit*, 62).

Archaeological Investigations

Liverpool's historic waterfront and dock system, both within, and immediately adjacent to, the boundaries of the WHS, have witnessed several archaeological investigations over a 33-year period, extending between 1976 and 2009. Significantly, this body of work has generated substantial quantities of stratigraphic and structural data, and also a large assemblage of artefacts. Taken together, these add to an understanding of the form, technology, and chronology of some of Liverpool's most notable maritime engineering structures, associated quayside buildings, and areas of domestic occupation, as well as allowing the role of particular items of material culture to be discerned in early patterns of production and trade.

Early investigations

The earliest of these archaeological investigations was undertaken in 1976 and 1977, immediately prior to the construction of the Courts of Law, and involved the excavation of two comparatively small areas (Davey 1977; Davey and McNeil 1985; Fig 4). One of these lay at the northern end of the demolished South Castle Street, directly south-east of the former castle, within the core area of Liverpool's pre-eighteenth-century settlement. It also lay on the suspected line of the medieval road from the castle to the Pool, a natural inlet, which existed prior to the eighteenth century and gave Liverpool its name (*Ch 2, p 23*). This excavation uncovered features dating to the seventeenth and early eighteenth centuries, which had been heavily disturbed by late eighteenth- and nineteenth-century remains (Davey and McNeil 1985, 3). The other area was positioned at the southern end of South Street

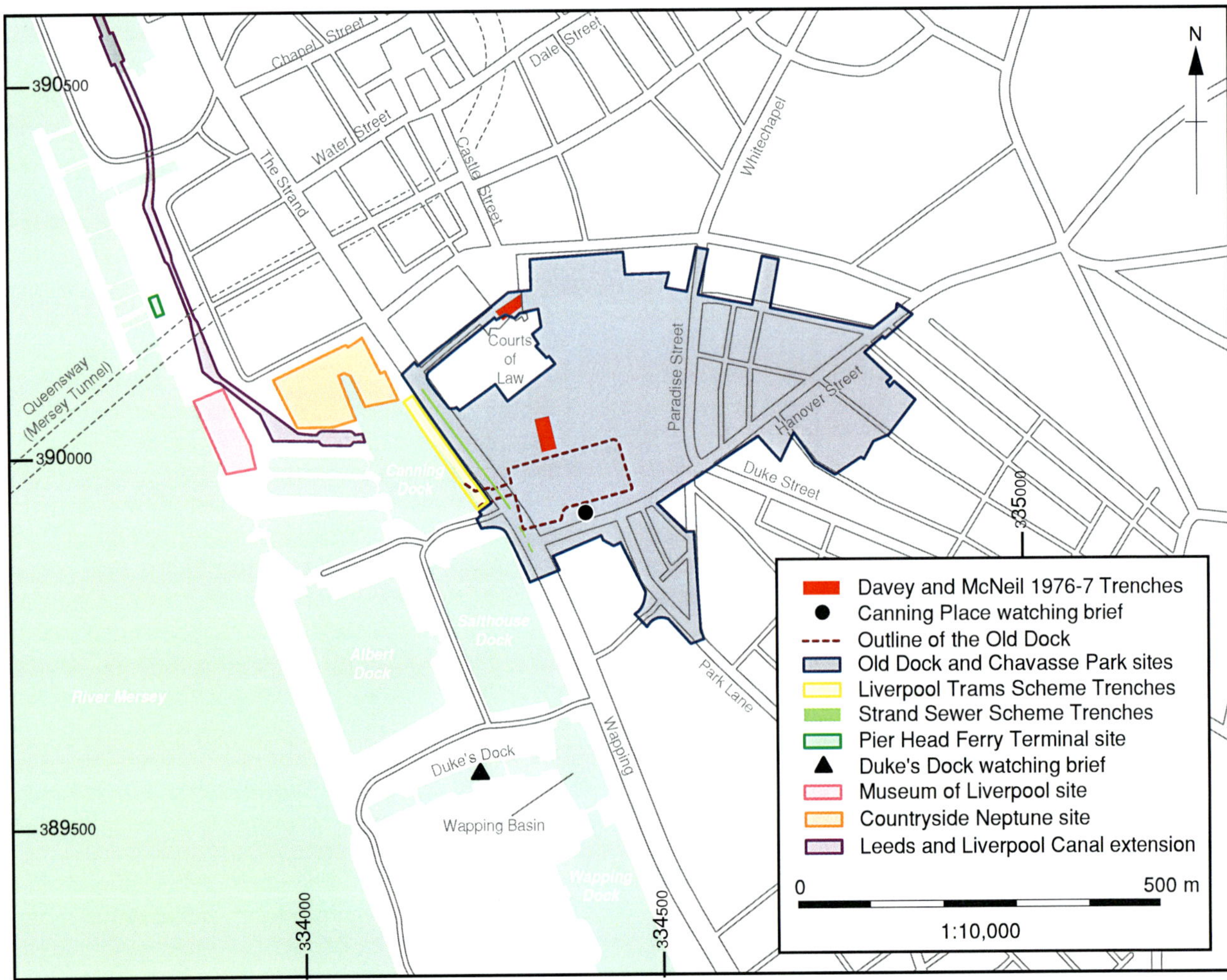

Figure 4: Location of archaeological investigations at the Old Dock and its environs, and across Mann Island and Pier Head (© Crown copyright 2014 Ordnance Survey 100005569)

and, significantly, in terms of Liverpool's maritime development, it was immediately north of the site of the Old Dock, within an area formerly occupied by the Pool (*op cit*, 5). This revealed evidence for infilling and levelling of this inlet dating to the seventeenth and eighteenth centuries (*ibid*).

In 1980, an archaeological watching brief was undertaken by the Archaeological Survey of Merseyside, which observed construction works in Canning Place. Again, this holds some, albeit minor, significance for Liverpool's maritime history, as part of the wall of the Old Dock was uncovered and recorded (Nicholson 1981, 3; Jarvis 1996, 7).

The Old Dock and Chavasse Park

More recently, Oxford Archaeology (OA) North (and in its earlier guise as the Lancaster University Archaeological Unit (LUAU)) completed archaeological fieldwork within the environs of the 1976-7 excavations along South Castle Street and the 1980 watching brief at Canning Place (*see above*). This fieldwork focused on an area bounded by Paradise Street, Hanover Street/Canning Place, The Strand, and the Courts of Law, and was undertaken prior to the construction of Liverpool One (Fig 4; Pl 6). The fieldwork was extensive, both in duration and scope, running between 2001 and 2006, and included archaeological evaluation trenching, open-area excavations, and

archaeological watching briefs, and also building survey of six properties fronting Hanover Street (LUAU 2001; OA North 2005a; 2005b; 2005c; 2006a; 2006b; 2006c; 2006d; 2009a; Fig 5).

The evaluation trenching and open-area excavations focused on several interconnected areas and significantly some of these lay within that part of the WHS which contained the site of the Old Dock. Across this area, 19 evaluation trenches were excavated around the perimeter of this former dock in order to investigate its walls and quayside (OA North 2009a; Fig 5). In addition, two larger trenches were excavated at the north-eastern corner of the dock, at the site now occupied by the Old Dock Information Centre, and these, along with the evaluation trenches, provided important details concerning the construction and history of Liverpool's first dock. Excavation was also undertaken immediately to the north of the Old Dock and across the backfilled area of this dock, which revealed the foundations of Liverpool's early nineteenth-century Customs House (*ibid*).

The other areas explored by this programme of fieldwork were positioned north of the Old Dock, in an area that was covered by Chavasse Park. Within these areas, two large open-area trenches were excavated, which exposed the remains of three former streets (South Castle Street, Traffords Wient, and Litherland

Plate 6: Excavation in progress at Old Dock/Chavasse Park

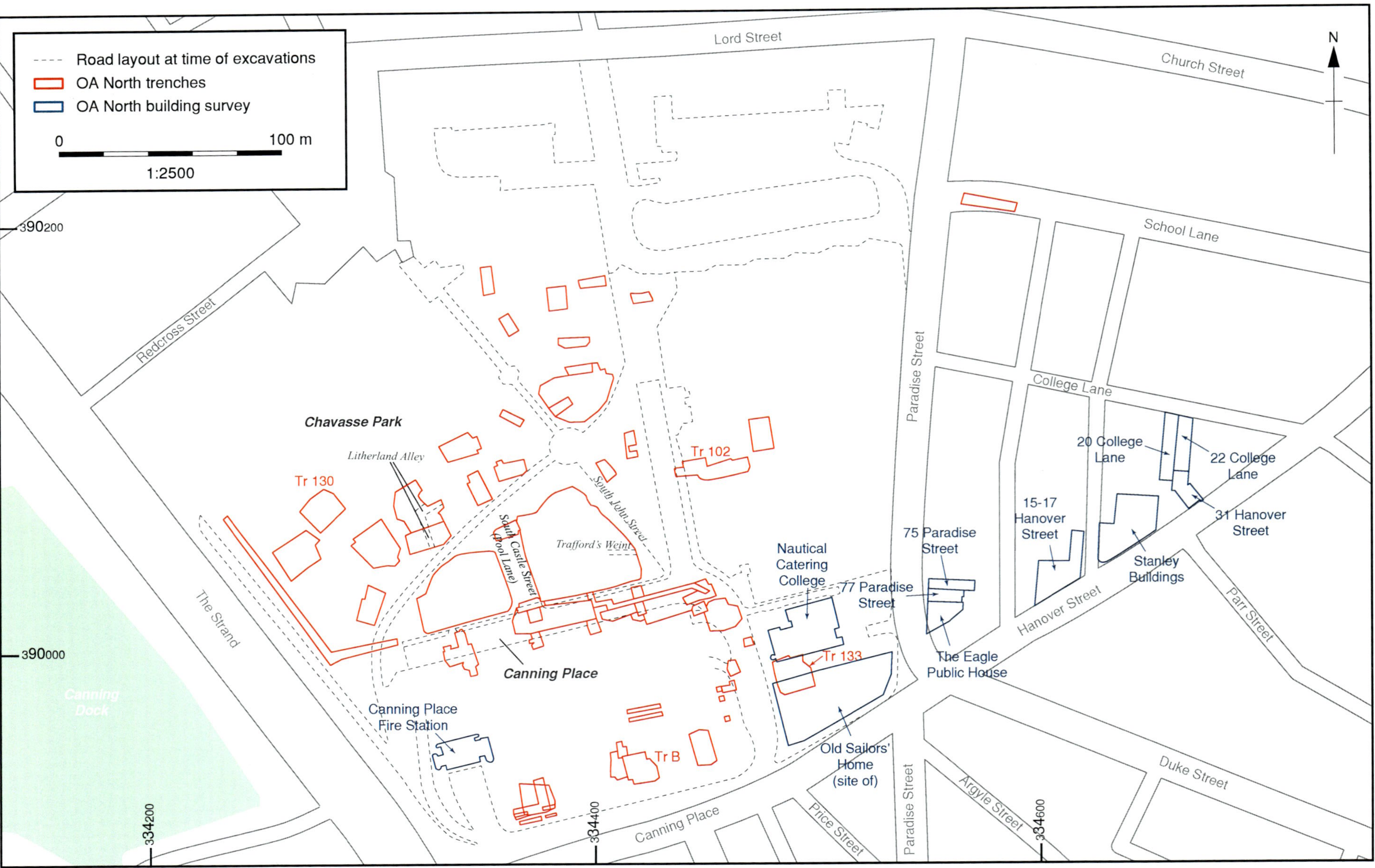

Figure 5: *Archaeological trenches and building surveys in the area of the Old Dock and Chavasse Park, overlaid on modern Ordnance Survey mapping (pre-2008)*
(© Crown copyright 2014 Ordnance Survey 100005569)

Alley) and cellars forming elements of eighteenth- and nineteenth-century properties. Further to the north, 22 evaluation trenches of varying sizes were also excavated, and these produced similar evidence for eighteenth- and nineteenth-century activity, and also buried soils and shallow ditches dating to the medieval period (*ibid*). Although it is anticipated that the full results from this work will form the subject of a separate publication, an outline summary of the pre-industrial remains (*Ch 2, p 27*) and also those relating to the Old Dock (*Ch 2, p 37*), as well as those remains relating to its early nineteenth-century abandonment and infilling (*Ch 4, p 132*), are presented in this volume.

Liverpool Trams Scheme

Concurrent with the Old Dock and Chavasse Park excavations, OA North completed another programme of archaeological evaluation in 2004-5 (OA North 2005d; 2005e; 2005f). This work targeted areas on the Strand (Strand Sewer Scheme) and immediately adjacent to the Canning Dock entrance to the Albert Docks, in advance of work for the proposed Liverpool Trams Scheme (*ibid*; Fig 4). Significantly, this discovered evidence for both the Old Dock and the Dry Dock/Canning Dock wall, which formed an early/mid-eighteenth-century addition to the Old Dock (*Ch 3, p 54*). This evaluation also exposed sandstone walling, dating to the nineteenth century, which had been used to block the entrance to the Old Dock. As with results obtained from the Old Dock and Chavasse Park excavations (*see above*), the results from the excavations in advance of the proposed Liverpool Trams scheme are summarised in the present volume (*Ch 3, pp 56-7; Ch 4, pp 133-4*).

Pier Head Ferry Terminal Building

Within the Pier Head portion of the WHS, OA North also completed an archaeological excavation at a site which is now covered by the Mersey Ferries Pier Head Terminal (OA North 2008; Fig 4; Pl 7). This site lay immediately adjacent to the present-day waterfront, and next to the monument of Edward VII, a Grade II Listed Building, which is strategically placed between the Mersey and the Cunard Building (Liverpool City Council 2005, 52). The excavation uncovered a small portion of George's Ferry Basin, dating to the early nineteenth century. In addition, the investigation also exposed a small element of George's Baths. This saltwater bathhouse, lying directly adjacent to the waterfront, was opened in 1828, and represents the first public baths in Britain (Ashpitel 1851, 2-14). The results of this work are summarised in the present volume (*Ch 4, p 129*).

Plate 7: The Mersey Ferries Pier Head Terminal, with the Leeds and Liverpool Canal (LLC) extension in the foreground

Duke's Dock

In 2007, the National Museums Liverpool Field Archaeology Unit (NMLFAU) completed another archaeological investigation within the WHS. This consisted of an archaeological watching brief undertaken on either side of Duke's Dock, during the excavation of two test pits in advance of piling (Adams 2007; Fig 4). During this work, eighteenth-century reclamation deposits were recorded and also the remains of a late nineteenth-century warehouse, the results of which are summarised in this volume (*Ch 3, p 69*; *Ch 5, p 160*).

Arena and Conference Centre

Another archaeological investigation was completed in 2006, by the NMLFAU, immediately south of the WHS in the area formerly occupied by King's Docks and an associated dry basin, which also served Queen's Dock (Fig 6). The investigation entailed an archaeological watching brief during the construction of an arena and conference centre, and also an electricity sub-station that lay to the south-east (Adams 2006). This work focused on late eighteenth- and early to mid-nineteenth-century remains and recorded parts of a swing bridge, probably dating to the mid-nineteenth century, and elements of a small tidal basin, built between 1805 and 1810, which lay at the northern end of King's Dock western pier. The results of this work are also summarised in the present volume (*Ch 4, pp 130, 148*).

Mann Island and the Leeds and Liverpool Canal (LLC) extension

Between 2006 and 2008, a large scheme of archaeological fieldwork was undertaken across Mann Island and also along a 2.5 km-long extension to the Leeds and Liverpool Canal (LLC), between Stanley Dock and Canning Dock (Pl 7). This extension, known as the Liverpool Canal Link, was created to provide a navigable route for inland leisure craft, along the city's historic waterfront, which would allow access into Liverpool's south docks.

Fieldwork

Mann Island forms an area of reclaimed land sandwiched between the Port of Liverpool building,

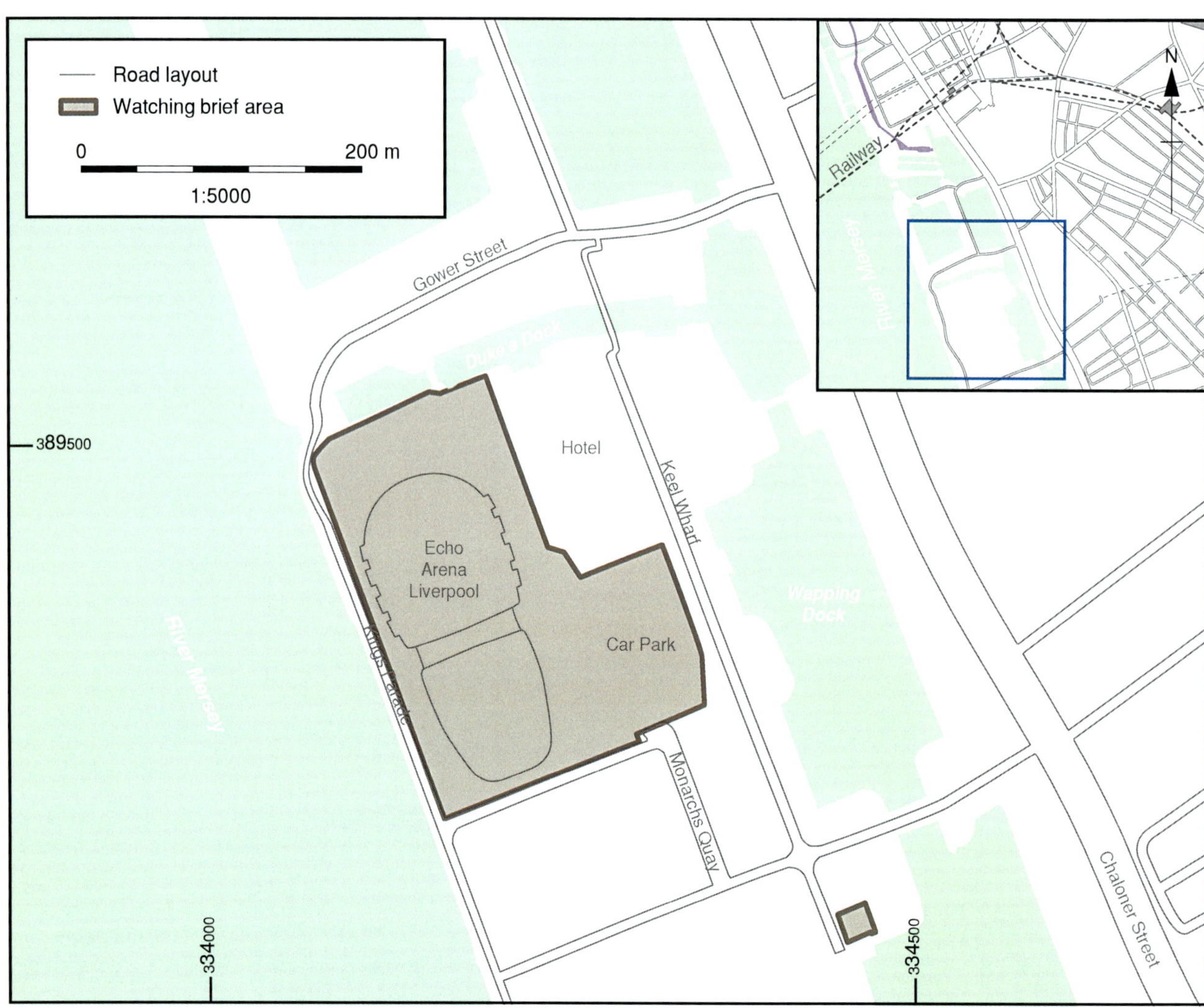

Figure 6: Watching brief areas across the former site of King's Dock and its dry basin (© Crown copyright 2014 Ordnance Survey 100005569)

Strand Street, Canning Dock and its associated graving docks, and the river frontage, within the WHS and also the Albert Dock Conservation Area. This area holds great relevance for comprehending the development of the historic waterfront, due, in part, to the progressive schemes of land reclamation that led to the creation of this area. This process dates from the mid-eighteenth century onwards and began during the creation of the Dry Dock, which opened in 1739, partly designed to ease access into, and congestion within, the Old Dock (*Ch 3, p 54*). Land reclamation was later associated with the construction of Manchester Basin (*Ch 3, pp 74-5*), and its sister structure, Chester Basin (*Ch 3, pp 87-8*), in the late eighteenth century, and also Manchester Dock, the early nineteenth-century successor to Manchester Basin (*Ch 4, p 103*), which was backfilled between 1928 and 1936 (Ritchie-Noakes 1984, 36). In addition, this area also contains other significant buried remains, including George's Dock Passage, which linked Canning and George's Dock, and various eighteenth-century and later buildings, positioned in areas which were known as Nova Scotia and Mann Island. These latter two areas represented a central hub within the early dock system, where victuallers, merchants, artisans, and sailors congregated to provide the necessary skills and supplies vital to the early mercantile endeavours of the city (Belchem 2006).

The archaeological fieldwork across Mann Island constituted three separate investigations, undertaken by both OA North and the NMLFAU. One of these was completed within a 1.1 ha area of land that lay directly north of Canning Dock, as a prelude to the construction of a large commercial development (Fig 4). This work was funded by Countryside Neptune and followed on from an Environmental Statement prepared by Wardell Armstrong, in which the archaeological value of the remains of the dock and river walls, and ancillary structures, was recognised (Wardell Armstrong 2006). Initially, the work involved a building survey of a transit shed, constructed in 1921 to serve the needs of Canning and Manchester Docks, and also a building survey of the Voss Garage (*ibid*). This latter building was a steel-framed commercial structure, designed in the style of Herbert J Rowse (R G McDonald *pers comm*), who was responsible for the nearby Mersey Tunnel Ventilation Station (*p 7*).

In February 2006, the building survey was then followed by an archaeological evaluation across areas that might contain important below-ground remains. This work entailed the excavation of five trenches, which identified the substantive survival of Manchester Dock (*Ch 4, p 103*), along with warehouses under the transit sheds, which correspond to the former area of Nova Scotia (*Ch 3, p 80; Ch 4, p 142*). In addition, cobbled surfaces and structures relating to the remains of the Mersey Railway Pumping and Ventilation Station and the Dock Police Station were also discovered (OA North 2006e). Following evaluation, a programme of open-area excavation, combined with an archaeological watching brief, was then completed, between May 2007 and May 2008, which recorded all buried remains that would be affected during the course of the construction of the new building (OA North 2012; Pl 8). However,

Plate 8: Excavation in progress at the Countryside Neptune site, revealing an early eighteenth-century river wall

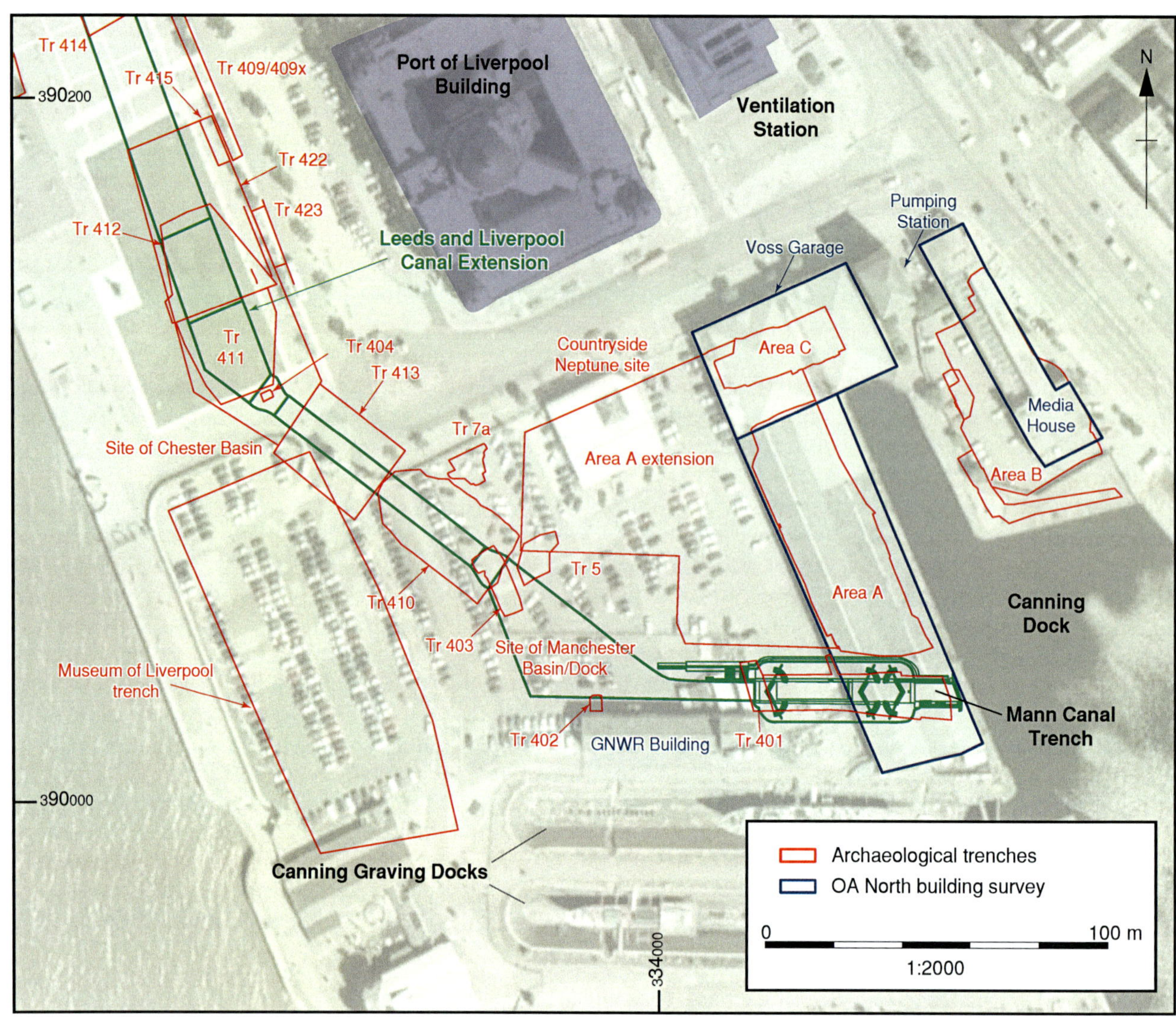

Figure 7: Excavation areas on Mann Island, overlaid on an aerial image taken in 2008 (© Google, Tele Atlas, Infoterra Ltd & Bluesky)

this programme of work paid particular attention to those features considered significant for enhancing knowledge of the historical development of the Liverpool docks and waterfront, and also those remains which might provide evidence for the development of trade and industry, and the social history of the area (OA North 2006f).

Two principal areas were therefore investigated at the northern end of the present Canning Dock, which lay on either side of the former George's Dock Passage (Fig 7; Areas A/C and B; OA North 2012). One of these areas (Areas A/C) centred on the former Transit Shed and Voss Garage (*Ch 5, p 173*), whilst the other (Area B) was positioned across the site of the former Media House, adjacent to The Strand. Together, these uncovered the remains of the Dry Dock (*Ch 3, p 55*), George's Dock Passage (*Ch 3, p 74*), Manchester Basin/Dock (*Ch 3, p 74; Ch 4, p 101*), and also three successive river walls (*Ch 3, pp 58-9*), and deposits and artefacts (*Ch 6*) associated with

land reclamation. In addition, extensive remains of the ancillary buildings serving the docks, such as warehouses, and dwellings, were discovered across the former area of Nova Scotia.

Immediately to the south of this site, OA North also undertook the second archaeological investigation on Mann Island within the footprint of the extension of the LLC, between Canning Dock and Stanley Dock (Fig 7). This work was funded by BAM Nuttall Ltd and followed an impact assessment, prepared by Wardell Armstrong (2003), in which the archaeological value of the potential remains traversed by the canal link was recognised. Initially, the work consisted of the excavation of three evaluation trenches (Tr 401-3) in July 2006, positioned to assess the survival of the former Manchester Dock (OA North 2006g). Within these, Tr 401 revealed the eastern wall of the Manchester Dock (*Ch 4, p 103*), while the southern and northern walls of this feature were respectively uncovered

Plate 9: Excavation in progress within the Mann Island section of the Leeds and Liverpool Canal (LLC) extension

in Tr 402 and Tr 403. In all three cases, survival was excellent, with the top course of the dock wall extant, close to the present ground surface. Furthermore, ancillary structures and fittings were also identified, including the east gable of one of several buildings owned and operated by the Great Western Railway (GWR) on the north side of the dock (Ritchie-Noakes 1984, 35, pl 23; *Ch 5, p 162*), a lamp-post base, and a dock ladder.

This was then followed in August 2007 by the excavation of a single open-area trench (Mann Canal Trench; Fig 7; Pl 9). This subsumed Tr 401 and focused on those structures considered to hold significance for understanding the historic development of Liverpool's waterfront (OA North 2006h). The trench exposed both an early river wall (*Ch 3, p 58*) and a slip wall (*Ch 3, pp 62-3*). Deposits and artefacts associated with land reclamation were also identified, as well as the remains of Manchester Dock (*Ch 4, p 103*), and an associated warehouse (*Ch 4, p 147*). Furthermore, buttresses were uncovered that were used to support the wall of Canning Dock (*Ch 4, p 136*).

The third campaign of fieldwork on Mann Island was completed by NMLFAU, and lay to the south of the canal link, in a parcel of land formerly used as a car park (Fig 4). This work was completed

between January and April 2007 and comprised an archaeological investigation, funded by the National Museums Liverpool (Fig 7), undertaken during the groundworks for the construction of the new Museum of Liverpool. The work resulted from recommendations made in an archaeological desk-based assessment (Harthen and Adams 2005), and entailed observation, excavation, and recording within a *c* 110 x 50 m area, forming the footprint for the new museum, which extended to a depth of *c* 3.5 m beneath the present ground level (Pl 10). Significantly, this work exposed an early nineteenth-century river wall, land reclamation deposits, and the inner entrance lock gates and sandstone walls of Manchester Dock, along with its lock-gate mechanism and sluices, all of which were in an excellent state of preservation (*Ch 4, pp 107-21*). Two subterranean chambers to the north-west of the lock were also identified that were probably part of the hydraulic system used to power cranes situated within the dock, and the foundations of some of this plant survived within the excavated area (*Ch 5, pp 164-5*). In addition, the southern wall of Chester Basin was located at the northern end of the site (*Ch 4, p 125*), whilst brick foundations of nineteenth-century warehouse structures were uncovered, along with cobbled surfaces and roadways (*Ch 4, p 121; Ch 5, p 165*). Finally, the groundworks exposed the well-

Plate 10: Excavation in progress at the new Museum of Liverpool site

preserved remains of an engine house on Manchester Dock's south-east quayside (*Ch 5, p 165*), as well as discrete artefactual dumps, dating to the early nineteenth century.

In addition to the investigations on Mann Island, the extension of the LLC also resulted in further archaeological investigations along its route, across Pier Head, to the west of the 'Three Graces', and within the Central Docks, between Pier Head and Stanley Dock (Fig 8). This work was funded by Balfour Beatty Civil Engineering Ltd, Pierse UK, and British Waterways, and, as with the Mann Island section of the canal, it was preceded by an impact assessment (Wardell Armstrong 2003); in the first instance, it again involved an archaeological evaluation and limited watching brief, undertaken in 2006.

The evaluation entailed the excavation of four trenches (Tr 404-7) in the Pier Head section of the canal (Fig 9). This is an area which holds particular significance for Liverpool's maritime history in that, in terms of below-ground remains, it contains the sites of eighteenth- and early nineteenth-century river walls, as well as portions of Manchester Basin/ Dock (*Ch 3, p 74; Ch 4, p 101*), George's Dock and George's Dock Basin (*Ch 3, p 70*), and Chester Basin (*Ch 3, p 87*). George's Dock and Basin were opened in 1771, though George's Dock Basin was closed

in 1871 and infilled prior to the construction of the floating roadway, which linked with the floating landing stages, whilst George's Dock was closed in 1900, to be later replaced by the 'Three Graces' (Ritchie-Noakes 1984, 28). Similarly, Chester Basin was also constructed in the late eighteenth century and was infilled in the 1930s (*op cit*, 36). Significantly, the evaluation trenches uncovered the well-preserved wall of Chester Basin (Tr 404), while further north a brick-built culvert was discovered (in Tr 405) at the site of a suspected former sea wall. A former sea wall was revealed in several of the trenches at Pier Head (*Ch 3, p 88*), whilst the edge of George's Dock Basin was also exposed (*Ch 3, p 72*). Further to the north, the evaluation was also supplemented by information acquired during a limited watching brief undertaken by OA North and the Merseyside Archaeological Service (MAS 2006), adjacent to Prince's Dock.

The evaluation and watching brief was then followed by a further phase of archaeological investigation across Pier Head, in August 2007, involving the excavation of 13 open-area and smaller trenches (Fig 9; Tr 408, Tr 409/409x-416, Tr 416x, and Tr 422-4). These trenches uncovered the remains of several river walls, deposits, and artefacts associated with land reclamation, as well as the walls of Manchester Dock and Chester Basin, and adjacent buildings and structures (*Ch 4, pp 103, 120-1*).

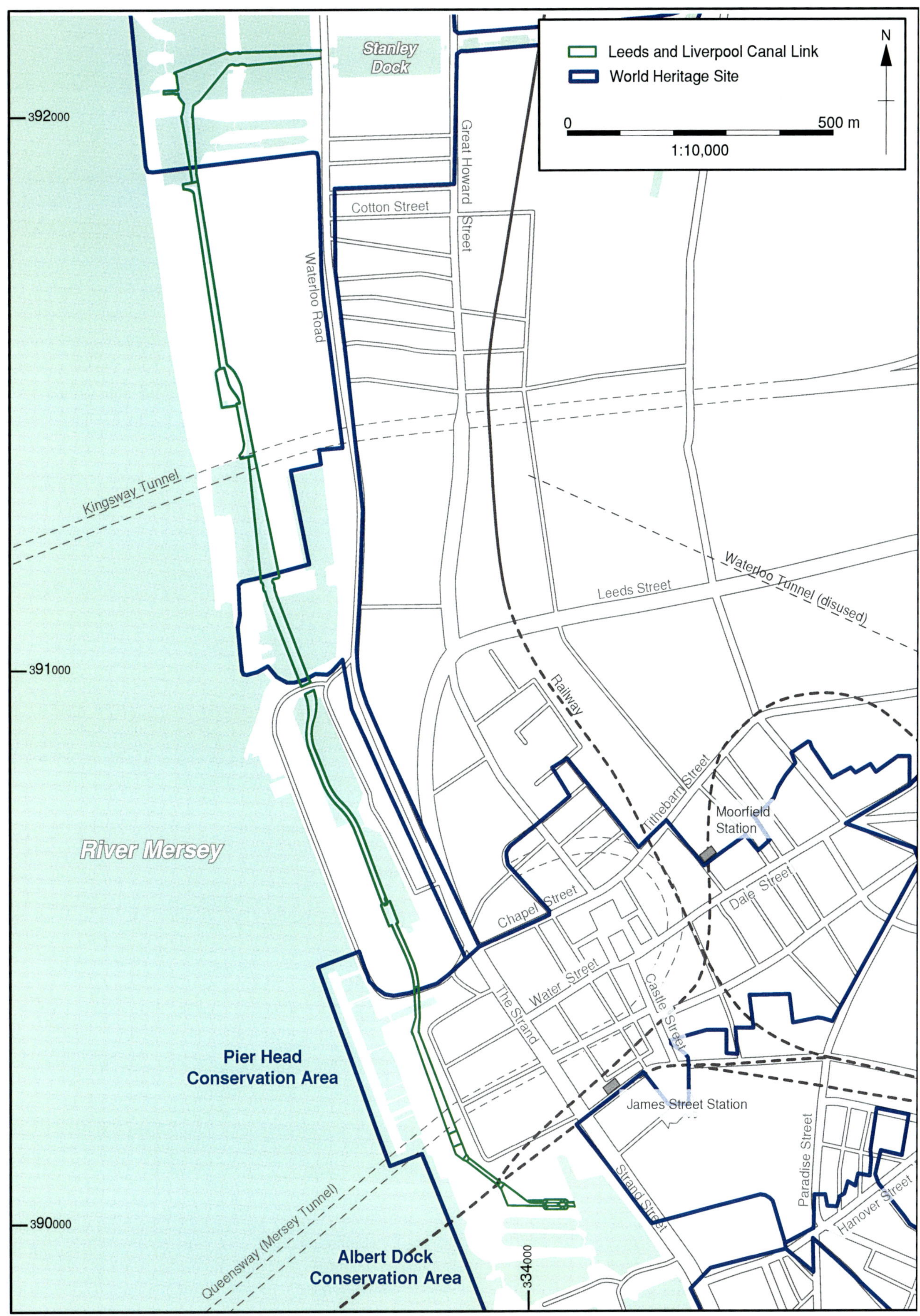

Figure 8: The route of the Leeds and Liverpool Canal (LLC) extension between Mann Island and Stanley Dock
(© Crown copyright 2014 Ordnance Survey 100005569)

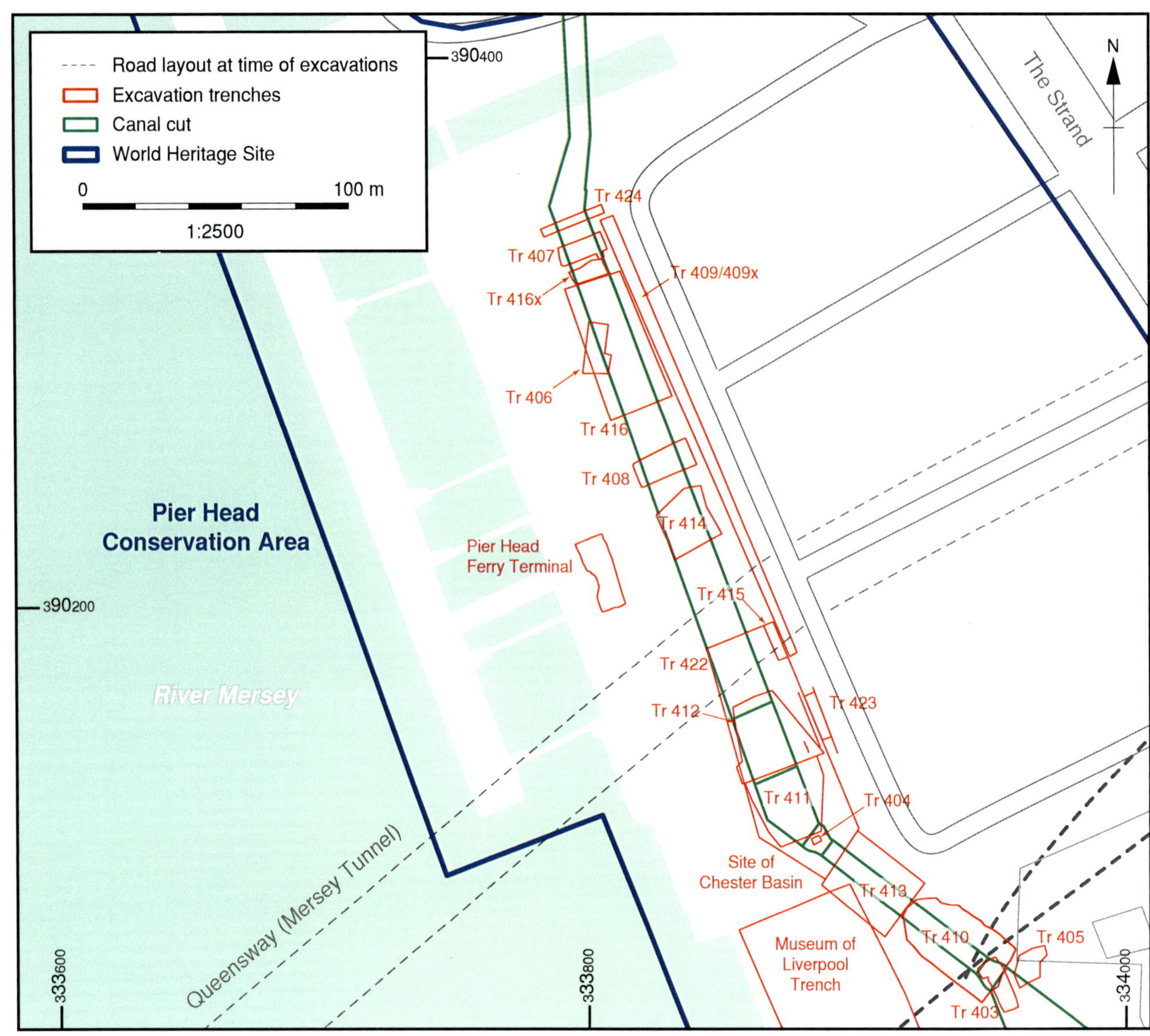

Figure 9: Archaeological investigations in the Pier Head section of the Leeds and Liverpool Canal (LLC) extension (© Crown copyright 2014 Ordnance Survey 100005569)

In addition to the work on Pier Head, two sites were also examined between March and June 2008, within an area just outside the boundaries of the WHS. This work involved targeted excavation, combined with an archaeological watching brief, in the Central Docks section of the canal link, to the north of Pier Head (Fig 10). One of the sites lay immediately north of Pier Head, sandwiched between St Nicholas Place and Prince's Dock, which opened in 1821 (Jarvis 1991a, 230). At this site, the remains of George's Dock Basin were uncovered, as well as an eighteenth-century sea wall and land reclamation deposits (*Ch 3, p 72*). The southern wall of Prince's Dock was also examined, as well as ancillary features and structures to the south (*Ch 4, p 136*). The other site was positioned further to the north, covering an area which originally lay between, and that fell partially within, Trafalgar and Victoria Docks (*Ch 4, p 139*). These docks were opened in 1836 and were backfilled in the early 1970s (McCarron and Jarvis 1992, 90, 94). The excavation

uncovered the walls associated with both of these docks, as well as brick-built structures and culverts.

Excavation and recording methodology
The excavation and recording methodology employed was largely comparable across all areas examined as part of the OA North archaeological works completed at the Countryside Neptune site and along the LLC extension. This entailed the mechanical removal of overburden, followed by manual and, where appropriate, mechanical, excavation of archaeological structures, features, and deposits (Pl 11). All of the areas were accurately surveyed, tied into the Ordnance Survey (OS) datum, and plotted on an up-to-date 1:1250 OS base map, whilst all archaeological features were accurately located on a site plan and recorded by photographs, scale drawings, and written descriptions. In addition, the artefacts recovered during the mitigating works along the route of the canal and at the development site were retained for

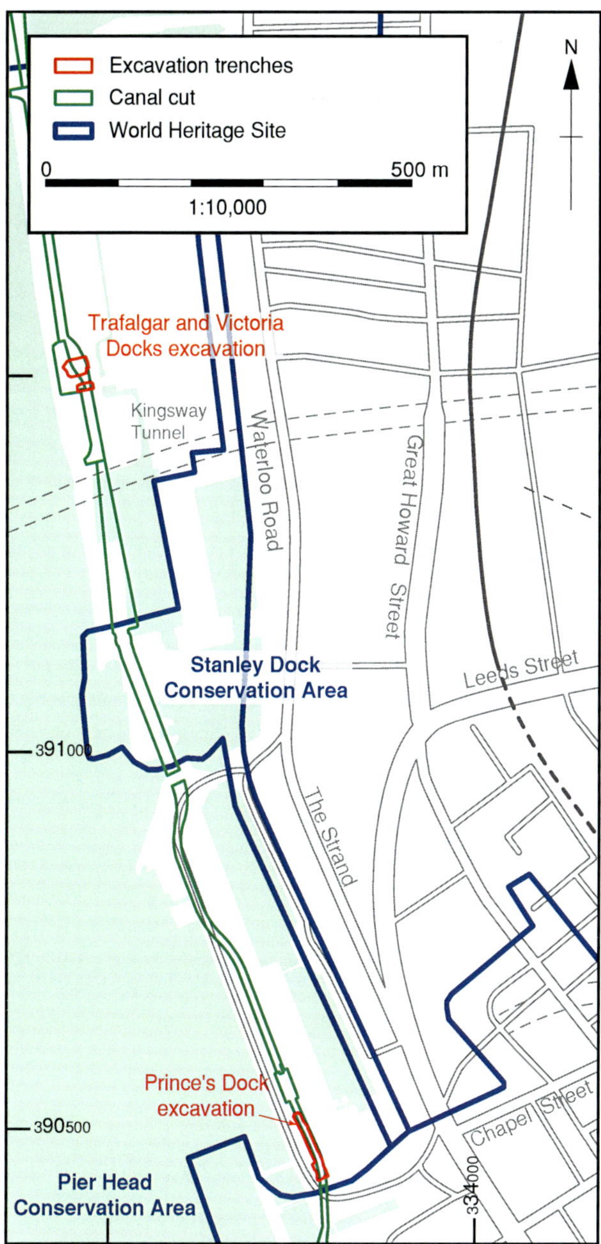

Figure 10: Archaeological investigations in the northern
section of the Leeds and Liverpool Canal (LLC) extension
© Crown copyright 2014 Ordnance Survey 100005569)

Plate 11: Mechanical excavation of land-reclamation
deposits to the north of Manchester Dock

processing and analysis, whilst a proportion of the exposed dock and river walls was recorded with a three-dimensional laser scanner.

The excavation and recording methodology employed by NMLFAU at the Museum of Liverpool site necessitated a slightly different approach to that employed by OA North. Initially, this entailed monitoring the machine stripping of the tarmac in the former car park at this site, which led to the exposure of dock walls and quayside structures. It also exposed entrance shafts leading to sandstone-lined chambers and the tunnels which housed the chains for opening and closing Manchester Dock's lock gates. All of these features were photographically recorded, with views taken from a 60 m mobile-access platform. These images were then rectified to quasi-vertical photography and used as the basis of detailed site plans, which were created in AutoCAD.

A second stage of excavation then focused on the entrance shafts. These were partially excavated by a mechanical mini-excavator and the remaining spoil removed by hand to reveal the worked sandstone blocks lining the chambers and tunnels. The clean and uniform sandstone rubble fill of Manchester Dock was excavated using a mechanical excavator. The walls of Manchester Dock and the southern wall of Chester Basin were recorded using a three-dimensional laser scanner in order to produce a detailed digital model of the surface, which was then linked to video footage and digital images. The walls were also recorded using photography and written records. Rubbings were taken of tool marks and masons' marks.

Following the recording of the quayside, four test pits were excavated across the site in an unsuccessful attempt to locate the Dock revetment wall, which was first recorded on a map dating to 1803 (*Ch 4, p 103*). Subsequently, this revetment wall was identified and recorded when the whole area was reduced in level. The final stage of the watching brief saw the monitoring of machine excavation to formation level for the new Museum of Liverpool, from which point all excavations were constantly monitored by NMLFAU staff.

Across Mann Island and along the LLC extension, full *in situ* preservation of the dock walls was not considered a viable option, but only some sections of Manchester Dock and its associated structures were removed during the groundworks for the new Museum of Liverpool. During this work, six slots (four in the northern wall and two in the southern wall) were cut through the dock walls, using specialist masonry-cutting equipment and a mechanical excavator to remove the excess sandstone blocks. Further slots, which were shallow but had a large surface area, were also removed from the top of the dock wall, using a circular saw and mechanical excavator with hammer attachment. All these slots were monitored throughout the cutting and subsequent removal. Some fittings associated with the dock were also removed prior to the demolition of the walls, including an iron access ladder affixed to the northern dock wall, a timber depth gauge, a roller mechanism for the lock gates, and the upper part of the lock gates, which were cut and removed at formation level. These gates are currently on display within the Museum of Liverpool.

Post-excavation assessment and analysis
With the completion of the archaeological fieldwork on Mann Island and along the LLC extension, several separate programmes of post-excavation assessment and analysis were completed (*cf* OA North 2010; 2011a; 2011b; 2011c; 2012; Philpott *et al* 2011). Importantly, these schemes were structured according to a series of research aims. In general terms, the work aimed to: understand how the environment of the Mersey foreshore and its human use developed over time; comprehend the changing post-medieval layout and character of the individual sites and areas examined by the fieldwork; explore the evidence for post-medieval trade and industry; examine the evidence for developments in dock engineering; and, where possible, consider the evidence for understanding the social history of post-medieval Liverpool.

The results of this work, which form the basis of this volume, entailed stratigraphic analysis, and the subsequent construction of site narratives, which were closely allied with the historical information derived from documentary and cartographic sources. In addition, the post-excavation programme of assessment and analysis also considered the artefacts recovered from all of the areas examined by the archaeological excavations and watching briefs. This entailed the initial separation of the assemblage into specific categories of finds (pottery, ceramic building material, clay tobacco pipe, metalwork, glass, and animal bone), an assessment of significance, and, where appropriate, analysis, which was undertaken by a recognised specialist.

The Structure of the Volume

This volume deals specifically with the archaeological excavations completed across Mann Island, by both OA North and NMLFAU, and along the LLC extension, which were undertaken by OA North. In addition, it also contains summaries of some of the more relevant evidence recovered during the other OA North excavations and NMLFAU's work that have been completed along the waterfront prior to 2009. In terms of its structure, the monograph is conditioned by the historical development of Liverpool's waterfront, and it thus adopts a chronological approach to the excavated evidence. *Chapter 2*, which acts as a prelude, initially outlines the form of medieval and early post-medieval Liverpool. This is then followed by a brief discussion of one of the key events pertinent to Liverpool's maritime history, namely the construction of the Old Dock in the early part of the eighteenth century. The creation of Liverpool's first dock was to have a profound influence on the development of the port-city and, given this importance, *Chapter 2* contains summary details of OA North's excavations within the Old Dock/Chavasse Park area and also those undertaken as part of the Liverpool Trams Scheme.

Chapter 3 then discusses the eighteenth-century expansion of Liverpool (1715-1800) and directly considers the emerging dock system, waterfront features, and areas of reclaimed land that were examined as part of the OA North and NMLFAU excavations on Mann Island, and the OA North excavations along the LLC extension. It also details the eighteenth-century evidence uncovered during the Liverpool Trams Scheme excavations, which holds relevance to the archaeology of the eighteenth-century waterfront, and NMLFAU's work at Duke's Dock. In terms of structure, the excavated remains are described in chronological order and, within each individual section, the relevant historical and cartographic evidence is initially presented, which is then followed by descriptions of the archaeology. Similarly, *Chapters 4 and 5* discuss, in turn, the early- and mid-nineteenth-century (1800-60) and the late nineteenth- and twentieth-century (1860-1950) form of the waterfront. They therefore describe the structural remains uncovered during those excavations undertaken on Mann Island, by OA North and NMLFAU, those undertaken by OA North along the LLC extension, at the Pier Head Ferry Terminal, at the Old Dock, as part of the putative Liverpool Trams Scheme, as well as NMLFAU's work at the Arena and Conference Centre, and Duke's Dock. As with *Chapter 3*, following a general overview of the development of the nineteenth- and early-mid-twentieth-century dock system and waterfront, these chapters describe the excavated evidence chronologically, with each individual section initially outlining the historical background, which is then followed by a discussion of the archaeological remains.

Chapter 6 represents an overview of the artefacts recovered during the OA North excavations on Mann Island and along the LLC extension, many of which have clear intrinsic value. More specifically, it includes discussions of the large assemblages of pottery and clay tobacco pipes, as well as the smaller collection of metalwork, glass, and other items of material culture. A more detailed analysis of some of these finds, particularly the important assemblage of clay tobacco pipes, along with those finds recovered during the NMLFAU excavations at Mann Island, will form the subject of a separate monograph, published by the National Museums Liverpool (Philpott in prep). A final chapter (*Chapter 7*), presents a synthesis of this evidence, which is structured in terms of the evolution of the port-settlement; dock building and land reclamation; warehouses and transit sheds; late eighteenth-/early nineteenth-century domestic occupation; miscellaneous nineteenth-century quayside buildings; dock ancillary features; and material culture.

There are also three appendices at the end of the volume. *Appendix 1* discusses the Mersey Flats, a distinctive type of sailing barge, which used both the Manchester and Chester Basins; *Appendix 2* provides further details about the hydraulic machinery at Manchester Dock; whilst *Appendix 3* presents a timeline outlining the key dates of the openings of and modifications to Liverpool's historic docks, basins, and selected ancillary features.

Archive

The project archive includes all of the data and material gathered during the course of the archaeological investigations on Mann Island and along the route of the British Waterways' canal extension. This combined archive has been collated and indexed in accordance with accepted guidelines (English Heritage 1991; UKIC 1984), and it will be deposited with National Museums Liverpool.

2

EARLY LIVERPOOL AND THE OLD DOCK

Richard A Gregory, Caroline Raynor, and Vix Hughes

Medieval Liverpool

Liverpool's history, as a settlement, extends back to at least the medieval period, and its location on the eastern bank of the Mersey played a significant role in its development, first as a small fishing hamlet and later as an emerging port. The first evidence for the presence of the settlement of Liverpool is a reference to '*Liuerpol*', in a charter of 1190-4 (Nicholson 1981; Kermode *et al* 2006, 59). This name is undoubtedly a reference to the natural tidal inlet known as the Pool, and it probably means 'the pool with the thick water' (Ekwall 1922, 117). Although the precise location, form, and size of the nascent settlement are not clear, it is quite possible that it formed a small rural hamlet, close to the Pool, which lay within the hundred of West Derby (Liverpool City Council 2005, 104). However, at a regional level, this unassuming settlement held little significance. For instance, at Liverpool, the Mersey presented certain problems for sea-borne vessels in that the river had rapid currents, contained numerous sand spits, and had a considerable tidal range of *c* 10 m (MacLeod 1982, 3). Moreover, during this period sea-borne trade undoubtedly entered the area through Chester, at the mouth of the River Dee, the region's major port and capital (Higham 2004, 169), whilst the beachhead site at Meols, on the Wirral peninsula, also appears to have acted as a port and long-distance trading centre during the earlier part of the medieval period (Griffiths *et al* 2007). At a more local level, the administrative and ecclesiastical role of early Liverpool was, at best, non-existent, with administrative control lying at West Derby, whilst the district's ecclesiastical centre lay at Walton-on-the-Hill (Kermode *et al* 2006, 60).

At the beginning of the thirteenth century, Liverpool's fortunes were radically lifted when, in 1207, King John founded the royal borough of Liverpool, after acquiring the land around the Pool from Henry Fitzwarin (Liverpool City Council 2005, 104). The founding of this borough, on a greenfield site, represented a speculative investment by John (Kermode *et al* 2006, 61), but it appears that its creation partly resulted from its potential benefits as a west-coast port. In John's mind, this new town could therefore provide a convenient point of embarkation to Ireland, where he had, in his youth, been set up as king by his father, Henry II, and had extensive land and trade interests (Hudson 2006, 40-2). Moreover, the use of this west-coast port also provided him with a base from which to pursue his military ventures in both Wales and Scotland (Liverpool City Council 2005, 104; Kermode *et al* 2006, 61) and, importantly, was one that was free from outside interference, particularly from Ranulf de Blondeville, earl of Chester, who by this date held significant independence, power, and influence within the region (Liverpool City Council 2005, 104; Kermode *et al* 2006, 63).

This freedom, coupled with burgage tenure, a degree of self-governance, and the payment of a fixed annual rent to the King, also provided the correct environment for commercial and economic growth (Kermode *et al* 2006, 63). Royal boroughs, such as Liverpool, were attractive locales for early entrepreneurs, and John's letters patent, effectively the borough's charter, recruited a new urban population drawn from a wide area, a small proportion of which were presumably engaged in trading. At its core were those people drawn from the nearby demesne manor of West Derby (*op cit*, 61), the majority of which probably retained interests in local agriculture and fishing (Hyde 1971, 1; Higham 2004, 184).

The conditions for economic and commercial growth, and self-governance, were initially advanced by John's son, King Henry III. In 1229, Henry, for a fee, granted the town a merchant's guild, a council to organise trade, exemption from outside tolls, and also the right to levy tolls, and he also fixed the town's yearly rent at a manageable level (Kermode *et al* 2006, 63). However, later in 1229, Henry was forced to grant the town to the earl of Chester, after which Liverpool was subject to direct control by a series of feudal lords (*op cit*, 65). Initially, these included the Ferrers, the earls of Derby, and then, from 1266, the earls of Lancaster, following the acquisition of the Ferrers' estates by Henry's son, Edmund, the first Earl of Lancaster (*ibid*). This shift in control was in some way detrimental to the emerging town, particularly as it did not have its own body of officials to promote and argue its claims (*ibid*).

Geographically, the medieval town was laid out along the Mersey foreshore, *c* 3 km west of the high sandstone ridge of Everton Brow and Edge Hill, which acted as a significant natural barrier (Hyde 1971, 1, 12; Fig 11). The original foreshore lay some 280 m back from the present waterfront, and today its position is roughly marked by the course of The

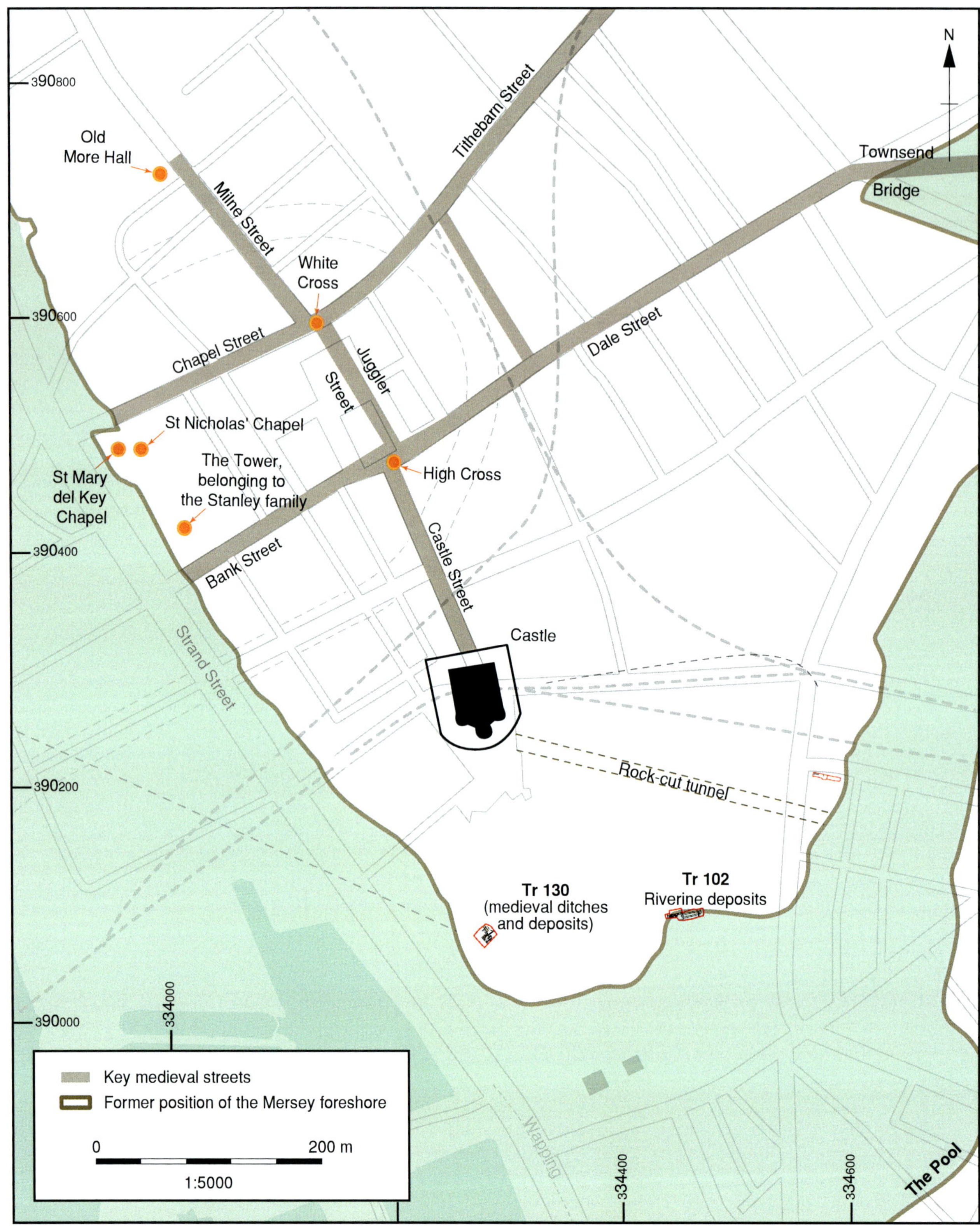

Figure 11: The original position of the Mersey foreshore, the Pool, and Liverpool's medieval core, overlaid on modern Ordnance Survey mapping (pre-2008). Possible medieval features and deposits uncovered by archaeological excavation are also indicated (© Crown copyright 2014 Ordnance Survey 100005569)

Strand, New Quay, Bath Street, Waterloo Road, and Regent Road (Fig 2). Geologically, this early foreshore consisted of superficial deposits of alluvium and intermixed silts and sands, and these were encountered during the excavations at the Countryside Neptune site (*Ch 1, p 12*). There, natural alluvial silts and gravels were identified that were devoid of archaeological finds, and which represent the original Mersey foreshore, prior to the massive phases of land reclamation and dock building which occurred from the eighteenth century onwards (*Chs 3* and *4*). Significantly, the furthest of these deposits lay more than 150 m out into the Mersey from the edge of former shoreline, and its depth and location indicates that the pre-eighteenth-century foreshore was extensive and gently sloping (*p 23*).

By the late thirteenth century, the morphology of the medieval town had been largely established. It consisted of seven streets, arranged in an H-formation, which were probably fronted by timber buildings contained within burgage plots (Liverpool City Council 2005, 104; Fig 11). The streets included two parallel routes, which ran directly to the Mersey foreshore. One of these streets, named Bank Street, followed the course of present-day Water Street and continued uphill into Dale Street. This latter street continued up to a stream, which fed into the Pool (*p 26*), and crossed this watercourse via a stone bridge (the Townsend Bridge). This route then exited the town and, in doing so, formed the main route into and out of the settlement (Ritchie-Noakes 1984, 17; Liverpool City Council 2005, 105; Kermode *et al* 2006, 73).

The second street, running down to the foreshore, was named Chapel Street in its south-western section, and Tithebarn Street in its north-eastern stretch, and these routes still survive in Liverpool's modern-day street plan (*ibid*). Set between and linking these two streets, parallel to the foreshore, was Juggler Street (later High Street). This street then joined with Milne Street at its north-western end, and Castle Street at its south-eastern end, which was a slightly later addition to the medieval street plan, being added following the established of Liverpool's castle (Higham 2004, 183).

The castle lay at the southern extreme of the town, situated on a rocky ledge, and was constructed in *c* 1235 by the Ferrers (Kermode *et al* 2006, 65; Pl 12). Importantly, it was designed to house the constable and a small garrison, and represented a potent symbol of lordly power (*ibid*). The thirteenth-century settlement also contained three mills and the chapel of St Mary del Key (*op cit*, 63), which lay at the far south-western end of Chapel Street, adjacent to the foreshore. Other notable features within the thirteenth-century town included two market crosses, High Cross and White Cross, which stood at either end of Juggler Street. These acted as the foci for the weekly market, held on Saturdays, and the annual fair, which by the early fourteenth century was held in November (*ibid*). A large hall, Old More Hall, residence of the More family from 1296, also stood at the northern end of Milne Street (*op cit*, 69), whilst immediately outside the town lay enclosed land in the possession of the

Plate 12: Late nineteenth-century reconstruction of Liverpool Castle, by W G Herdman (1878, pl I), as it would have appeared in 1689 (by courtesy of the University of Liverpool Library SPEC Y87.5.41v1)

Plate 13: Tr 102, excavated during the investigations at the Old Dock and Chavasse Park, showing riverine deposits of clay at the northern edge of the Pool

burgesses, and beyond these, pastures and waste, where the burgesses had grazing rights and could also cut turf (Hyde 1971, 2).

Significantly, the new town was built next to the Pool, a prominent topographical feature and inlet which also defined its southern limits. This natural creek was fed by a stream, the Moss Lake, rising further north; it was nearly 1.5 km long at high tide, and its mouth lay across the area now occupied by Strand Street and Wapping (Stewart-Brown 1932, 88; Ritchie-Noakes 1984, 17). Its complete extent, although far from clear, was partially determined by the archaeological investigations in the vicinity of the Old Dock and Chavasse Park (*Ch 1, p 9*). This work uncovered riverine deposits of clay (for instance, in Tr 102; Fig 11), which denoted the northern side of the Pool (OA North 2009a; Pl 13). This excavation also uncovered evidence for a small stream on the northern side, which presumably fed into the Pool to the south (*ibid*).

In terms of the medieval and later town, this inlet served as Liverpool's haven, or proto-port, where, in theory, seagoing vessels could shelter, ships' cargoes could be unloaded, and small ships could be careened and repaired. However, its use as a harbour was problematic in that it was awkward to enter from the Mersey, and was probably shallow and silt-laden

(Bird 1963, 280). In addition, the Mersey's tidal range (*p 23*) meant that ships entering the Pool had to be beached on its foreshore in order to discharge and load cargo (*ibid*). It is therefore probable that, whilst the Pool may have been partly used, a proportion of the ships using Liverpool were also beached on its gently sloping foreshore, which lay immediately west of the medieval core (Jackson 1983, 46).

During the thirteenth and early part of the fourteenth centuries, the settlement expanded from 168 burgages in 1296 to 196 in 1346, though the population was probably more than halved from the ravages of plague in the latter part of the fourteenth century (Kermode *et al* 2006, 61, 69). In consequence, the form of the town remained fairly static, though the period did witness the construction of the chapel of St Nicholas. This was consecrated in 1362 and lay at the south-western end of Chapel Street, directly adjacent to both the foreshore and the earlier chapel of St Mary del Key (*op cit*, 69; Liverpool City Council 2005, 106; Fig 11).

Unfortunately, in terms of Liverpool's archaeological resource, the evidence for the thirteenth- and fourteenth-century settlement is generally sparse, which is probably a result of later construction, particularly that associated with the building of eighteenth- and nineteenth-century basements. The

Plate 14: Tr 130, excavated during the investigations at the Old Dock and Chavasse Park, showing possible medieval ditches

evidence that has been recovered is confined to the edge of the medieval town, to the south of the former castle. This was examined between 2001 and 2006, during which time three ditches and associated soil horizons of possible medieval date were exposed (within Tr 130; Fig 11; Pl 14), along with a small collection of medieval pottery sherds (OA North 2009a). In addition, it is also possible that a rock-cut tunnel, uncovered during the excavations at the Old Dock (*Ch 1, p 9*), was created during this period (Fig 11). This tunnel led into the Pool, and later was blocked by the construction of the Old Dock (*p 38*). It was orientated towards the castle, and may well have functioned as a drain, allowing effluence from this fortification to drain into the Pool.

Liverpool's early role as a port was also stimulated during the fourteenth century through its use as a base for the royal fleet, which carried both goods and troops (Kermode *et al* 2006, 68). This, in turn, encouraged trade along the Lancashire coast and also strengthened the pre-existing links with Ireland (*ibid*). The traded goods may have included woollen cloths, iron, oats, barley, and corn, and cattle and hides (*ibid*). In addition to sea-borne trade, the fourteenth century also saw the establishment of the Mersey ferry, one of Liverpool's more iconic symbols. The origins of this service reside in a royal grant dating to 1330, which allowed a ferry to operate, with concomitant collection of tolls, between Liverpool and Birkenhead, on the Wirral (Liverpool City Council 2005, 107). The ferry allowed easy access to the Benedictine Priory, which was founded at Birkenhead in *c* 1170, and it probably stimulated both business and commercial activity within Liverpool (*ibid*).

The fourteenth century also holds significance in that it witnessed the emergence of Liverpool's first entrepreneurial families, and the establishment of the offices of mayor and bailiffs (*op cit*, 66, 71). These latter posts probably boosted the process of self-governance, though their influence and duties are not particularly clear (*op cit*, 71). Further advances in self-governance were also made in 1357. In this year, the Liverpool burgesses were granted, for a fee, the town's lease, by the earl of Lancaster, which gave them control over 'the management of markets and fairs, the ferries, mills, collection of rents and income from the courts' (*op cit*, 70).

During the fifteenth century, Liverpool continued to function as a regional centre, with a port and small fleet of ships and mariners, whose trade links continued with Ireland and the Lancashire coast, and very occasionally with France and Spain (*op cit*, 71). However, the town struggled due to economic

Plate 15: The Tower, by W G Herdman (1878, pl III), as it appeared in the early nineteenth century (by courtesy of the University of Liverpool Library SPEC Y87.5.41v1)

recession, and was subjected to periodic feuding between some of the town's more influential families. One of these was the Molyneux family, who gained the possession of the town's constableship and, in turn, residence of the castle, in the mid-fifteenth century (Liverpool City Council 2005, 106). Significantly, the Molyneux family retained possession of this title across the late medieval and post-medieval periods and they had a significant influence on the growth and development of Liverpool.

Another of the town's more influential families, who violently clashed with the Molyneux family in 1424, were the Stanley family (Kermode *et al* 2006, 72). Their main residence lay to the north-east of Liverpool at Lathom House, and they held extensive land holdings in Lancashire and Cheshire (Liverpool City Council 2005, 106). From the beginning of the fifteenth century, they were also the Lords of the Isle of Man and this connection resulted, in 1406, in Sir John Stanley gaining permission from Henry IV to fortify his Liverpool residence (*ibid*). This led to the construction of a substantial stone building, known as the Tower, effectively a military base, which was adjacent to the Mersey foreshore at the bottom of Bank Street (later Water Street; Fig 11). This building became a prominent and enduring feature of the early town (Pl 15), and survived until 1821, when it was eventually demolished (Kermode *et al* 2006, 71). Significantly, in terms of the early history of Liverpool, it allowed the Stanley family, who in 1485 acquired the earldom of Derby, a foothold to intervene directly in the affairs of late medieval and post-medieval Liverpool.

The Early Post-medieval Town and Haven (1500-1660)

In the sixteenth and first half of the seventeenth centuries, Liverpool remained a small regional town, the form of which was in many ways comparable to its medieval predecessor (Pl 16). Therefore, for much of this period, the town was still dominated by the seven major streets that had been established during the thirteenth century, and it was not until the early part of the seventeenth century that three smaller streets were probably added (*p 32*). Moreover, during the earlier medieval period, the two chapels of St Nicholas and St Mary del Key, the castle, and the Tower represented the only stone-built buildings, and these were surrounded by timber-built dwellings, which lay within the town's burgage plots (Kermode *et al* 2006, 72, 75, 97). However, during the sixteenth century, the significance of the majority of these stone buildings had waned, as the castle was no longer garrisoned, and was in a very dilapidated state, whilst the Tower was also rarely used (*op cit*, 75). In addition, the chapel of St Mary del Key was closed in the 1540s, and was used as a common warehouse (*ibid*), and this complemented another common warehouse on Juggler Street, which also functioned as the town gaol (*op cit*, 76).

During the early part of the seventeenth century, the history of the town is, in some measure, dominated by various outbreaks of plague and also conflict, as a direct result of the English Civil Wars (1642-51). During this conflict, control of the town fluctuated between the Royalist and Parliamentary forces on several occasions, as both sides recognised the significance of Liverpool as a strategic west-coast port (*op cit*, 102). This conflict also appears to have caused some damage to the fabric of the seventeenth-century town and led to the creation of a series of Civil-War fortifications, consisting of trenches and earth ramparts surrounding the town and castle, constructed by Parliamentary forces in 1644, with later additions by the Royalists, also in 1644 (*op cit*, 104-5).

The inhabitants of the sixteenth- and early seventeenth-century town included a small community of merchants and traders, craftsmen, such as leather workers, blacksmiths, woodworkers, weavers, and textile workers, millers, and butchers (*op cit*, 77-9). However, many of those engaged in these professions were also dually employed in farming, which remained an important element of Liverpool's economy throughout this period (*op cit*, 81). The products produced by some of these professions were sold at the weekly market, which also acted as a venue for outside traders, who largely sold agricultural products, but also coal, derived from the Prescot area (*op cit*, 82). Maritime trade was also significant (*Ch 3, p 50*) and fostered some prosperity, though the increasing wealth it did generate became concentrated into the hands of the small community of merchants and traders, several of which were elected as the town governors (Hyde 1971, 4). This, in turn, created a significant connection between Liverpool's governors and the town's mercantile wealth, a connection which was to persist for the better part of two centuries, up

Plate 16: Conjectural plan of Liverpool in 1650, produced by Charles Okill and published in The Stranger in Liverpool (Kaye 1829)

until the reform of the municipal corporations in 1835 (Longmore 2006, 113). However, although this mercantile group formed Liverpool's wealthy elite during the sixteenth and early part of the seventeenth century, they were not particularly wealthy in comparison with those merchants found in other urban centres (Kermode *et al* 2006, 77). In terms of Liverpool's governance, during the seventeenth century a charter, granted by Charles I in 1626, incorporated and confirmed the status of the royal borough, and also granted the right of the burgesses to hold a court under the Statute of Merchants (*op cit*, 99). This said, the early seventeenth-century town was still heavily under the sway of the powerful land-owning families of the region, such as the Stanley family, as earls of Derby, and the Molyneux family, who had purchased the Crown rights over Liverpool in 1632 (*ibid*).

During the early post-medieval period, there are various references to the site of Liverpool's harbour, the Pool. The earliest of these date to the mid-sixteenth century, and significantly indicate that a breakwater had been established at the mouth of the Pool (Ritchie-Noakes 1984, 18; MacLeod 1982, 3). This feature would have provided additional shelter and protection for those ships entering and mooring within the inlet, and presumably increased the effectiveness of the proto-port. Indeed, the effectiveness of this breakwater for Liverpool's trade appears to have been clearly recognised by the town's Corporation, which, following the destruction of this feature by a storm in 1560, called on the townspeople to contribute free labour to its rebuilding and realignment in order to create a new haven (Stewart-Brown 1930, 89). In addition, during the early post-medieval period, it appears that the shallow draught of the Pool, and in turn Liverpool's maritime trading capabilities, was addressed through the installation of sluice gates on the stream feeding the Pool. These sluices, which had certainly been installed by 1635, would have provided a means of scouring out accumulations of silt from the inlet and would also have maintained an open channel for shipping entering and leaving the port (Ritchie-Noakes 1984, 18). Furthermore, during the earlier part of the seventeenth century, Liverpool was also served by a quay, where goods could be unloaded and handled (Jackson 1983, 46). However, the location of the quayside is far from clear, and it is possible that it lay outside the Pool, directly on the Mersey foreshore, as was the case with a new quay constructed by the Corporation in 1665 (Ritchie-Noakes 1984, 18; *p 34*).

The volume of ships using Liverpool was comparatively small, though. For example, historical records dating to the late sixteenth century indicate that, during 1558, only 13 ships were sailing from Liverpool, which decreased to ten ships in 1582, though by 1601 20 ships are documented as sailing from the harbour (Kermonde *et al* 2006, 84). These ships appear to have included ocean-going vessels of 30-6 tons, and also less than 20 tons, as well as smaller fishing boats, ranging between six and eight tons (*ibid*).

The main focus of Liverpool's early post-medieval trade was the Irish Sea basin. Within this trading zone, Liverpool shipping transported foodstuffs and iron along Britain's western coastline, between north Wales and Cumbria. This early trade also included the transportation of salt (*op cit*, 85). Initially, this commodity, which was largely used for agricultural purposes, was acquired from Brittany, and then re-exported, though by the latter stages of the sixteenth century, Liverpool's merchants began to exploit more local sources, and were trading in Cheshire, rather than Breton, salt (Hyde 1971, 2). The Isle of Man also formed another important trading destination, bolstered by the earls of Derby's connection with this area (*p 28*), though the main focus of maritime commerce during the latter part of the sixteenth century was with Ireland (Kermode *et al* 2006, 85-6). This trade saw Liverpool ships sailing to the Irish ports of Dublin and Drogheda, and to a lesser extent those at Dundalk, Carlingford, Carrickfergus, Waterford, and Wexford (*op cit*, 86; Hyde 1971, 3). These ships were involved in the transportation of foodstuffs, hides and fells, flax, wool, and linen yarn, from Ireland, whilst exported goods included foodstuffs, textiles, salt, iron, copper, metalwork, and a selection of luxury items, such as clothing, glass vessels, spices, dyes, combs, and soap (*ibid*). In addition to the transportation of these general trade goods, importantly, Liverpool also formed a point of embarkation for English troops crossing to Ireland, which eventually led to Liverpool ships transporting men and supplies to Ireland 'on a shuttle basis' (Kermode *et al* 2006, 87).

In the later sixteenth century, Liverpool ships also traded outside the Irish Sea region, with connections in French and Spanish ports, and occasionally received cargoes from Denmark and Hamburg (Hyde 1971, 3). Incoming international goods included iron, copper, tar, resin, and whale oil, as well as exotic foodstuffs. These latter products comprised Spanish sherry, figs, dates, spices, French wine, as well Danish and German grain. In return, Manchester textiles were exported to Continental Europe (*ibid*). However, these trading forays were often risky ventures, and there are numerous records of Liverpool ships being attacked by pirates in French and Spanish waters (Kermode *et al* 2006, 85). These attacks were probably exacerbated by the difficult political relations between Spain and England which typify the late sixteenth century, and, after 1585, war between the two nations eventually led to the end of direct trading contacts (*op cit*, 87).

Although the early to mid-seventeenth century can be characterised by outbreaks of disease and conflict (*p 28*), this period proved extremely significant for Liverpool's maritime history, witnessing both increases in trade and prosperity. The period up to 1660 is characterised by increasing prosperity, due to the continued exploitation of the Irish Sea trade routes that had been developed in the preceding century (*op cit*, 98). This resulted in Liverpool rivalling Chester as the region's most significant port, which was, in part, exacerbated by the rapid silting of Chester's harbour, situated at the mouth of the River Dee, and also by Liverpool's lower customs duties (*ibid*). As in the latter part of the sixteenth century (*p 31*), Liverpool was principally trading with the Irish ports, along with those on the Isle of Man, and along the Lancashire and Cumbrian coastlines. The main commodities traded during the early to mid-seventeenth century included Manx wool, coal, and foodstuffs, Manchester cottons, Lancashire metalwares, and salt. During this period, this latter commodity was also partly derived from Liverpool, following the establishment of a saltworks in the town in 1611 (Hyde 1971, 3). In addition to the Irish Sea trade, Liverpool sent arms and ammunition to Plymouth and there also appears to have been trade with France (Kermode *et al* 2006, 98).

Significantly, this period also marks the beginnings of transatlantic trade with the West Indies and North America (*op cit*, 99), following the foundation of colonial Virginia in 1606, New England in 1620, and Barbados in 1625 (Liverpool City Council 2005, 108). This trade probably began in the late 1630s, and was furthered in the 1640s when Liverpool ships were used to carry emigrants, in the form of political prisoners and refugees, and various religious factions, to the West Indies and North America (Hyde 1971, 5; Liverpool City Council 2005, 108). In 1648, the first shipment of American tobacco arrived in Liverpool (Longmore 2006, 115), and this was to establish an important trade precedent, whereby English supplies, exported from Liverpool, were exchanged for North American and West Indian products (Liverpool City Council 2005, 108).

Between the late 1660s and first decade of the eighteenth century, significant changes were made to the layout and form of Liverpool, with the town entering a phase of impressive urban growth, spurred on demographically by increasing levels of immigration (Kermode *et al* 2006, 109). By 1670, Liverpool's street pattern (Fig 12) had therefore been expanded and modified, through the addition of Fenwick Street, parallel to Castle Street, and Moor Street, which ran

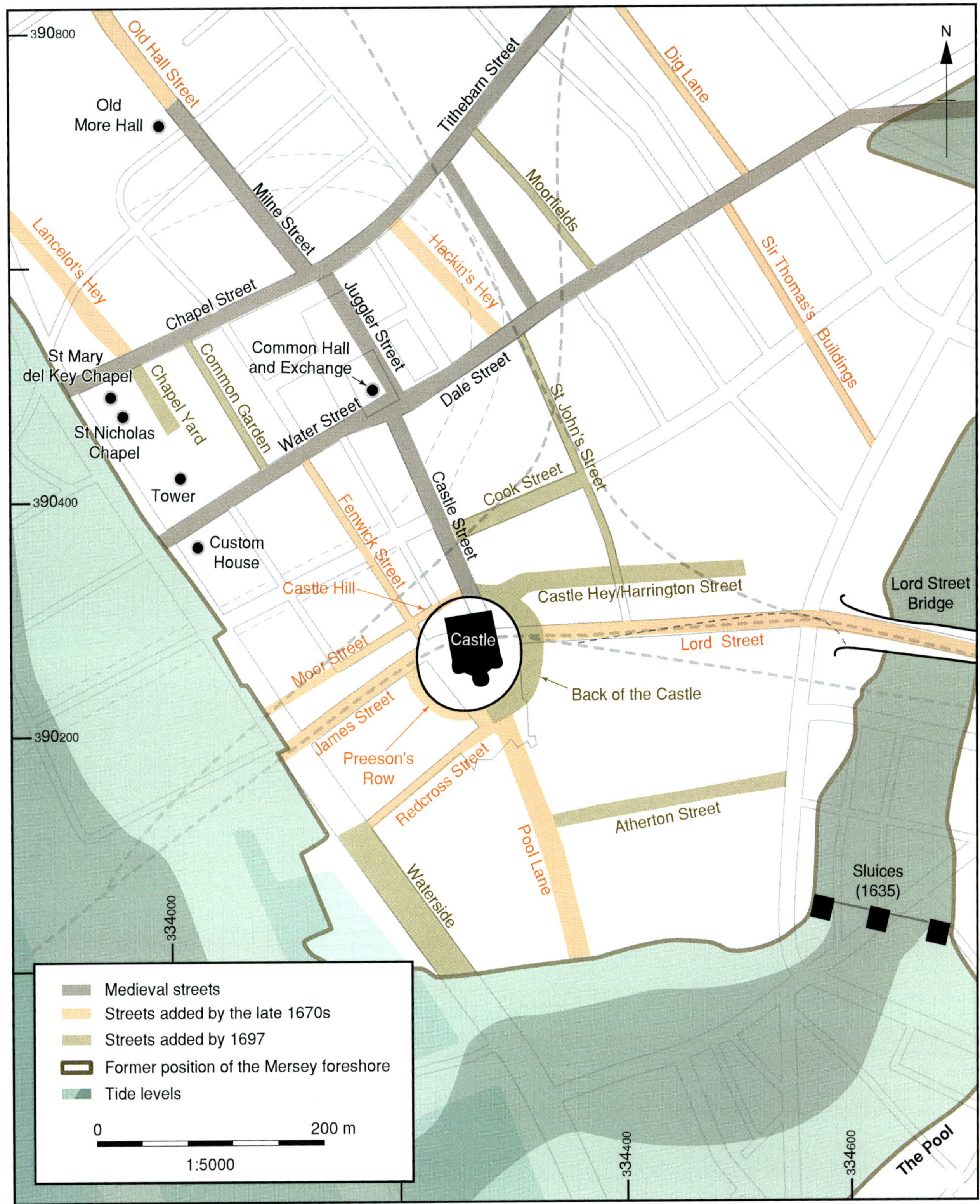

*Figure 12: Liverpool's late seventeenth-century urban morphology, overlaid on modern Ordnance Survey mapping (pre-2008)
(© Crown copyright 2014 Ordnance Survey 100005569)*

Plate 17: View of Liverpool from the River Mersey in 1680, by R P Herdman, based on an original painting held by Ralph Peters (LVRO and Liverpool Libraries Local Collection 506)

from Fenwick Street down to the Mersey (Hyde 1971, 5). In addition, the lines of Old Hall Street, which continued on from Milne Street, and Lord Street (later Church Street), named after Lord Molyneux, were in the process of being established (*ibid*). This latter street ran through the Castle orchard up to the Pool and then across the Pool to the common land beyond (Liverpool City Council 2005, 108), and its creation holds particular significance for Liverpool's subsequent history (*p 33*). Lesser streets that had probably been laid out in the early part of the seventeenth century included Dig Lane, between Tithebarn Street and Dale Street, and Pool Lane (later South Castle Street), which continued the line of Castle Street up to the Pool, and also a street running towards the Pool, which became known as Sir Thomas's Buildings (Hyde 1971, 4-5). By 1677, six new streets had been established, including Lancelot's Hey, Hackin's Hey, Castle Hill, Preeson's Row, Redcross Street, and James Street, whilst, by 1697, a further nine streets had been created (*op cit*, 6; Fig 12). These latter streets included Chapel Yard, Common Garden, Moorfields (Moor Street), Back of the Castle, St John's Street, Castle Hey/Harrington Street, Cook Street, Atherton Street, and Waterside (Strand Street) (*ibid*).

Within the town, the older, more significant, buildings remained, namely the castle, the Tower, and the chapels of St Mary del Key and St Nicholas, and Old More Hall, though these were very dilapidated, or, in the case of the castle, ruinous. The functions of some of these buildings had also shifted. The

chapel of St Mary del Key, following its use as a common warehouse (*p 28*), had been converted into a free school, whilst the Tower was leased by the Corporation, and was used as the town's gaol during the latter part of the seventeenth century (Kermode *et al* 2006, 71, 105). Similarly, the castle was also leased from the Crown by the Corporation in the late seventeenth century (*ibid*).

Although the form and architectural type of the majority of the town's buildings during the late seventeenth century is not particularly clear, it is possible that the majority were now constructed in stone, and had replaced those timber buildings constructed in the medieval and early post-medieval periods (Pl 17). However, this replacement of the older housing stock with more 'modern' urban buildings is not peculiar to Liverpool, but is a feature of some of the other large urban centres within the North West during the late seventeenth century (McNeil and Newman 2006, 153). In addition, whilst many of these late seventeenth-century buildings were constructed in more durable materials, they would have ranged in size and quality, based on the respective wealth of their inhabitants; some of the larger and noteworthy residences included the stone-built house occupied by William Blundell on Tithebarn Street, and Thomas Blundell's brick-built house on Dale Street. Moreover, this period also witnessed the construction of a new Common Hall and Exchange, built in stone in 1675 on Water Street, which would form the most prominent of the

Plate 18: Nineteenth-century reconstruction of the Old Exchange, by W G Herdman (1878, pl XXIV, 2; by courtesy of the University of Liverpool Library SPEC Y87.5.41v1)

late seventeenth-century buildings (Hyde 1971, 7; Kermode *et al* 2006, 109; Pl 18).

Some indications of the form and growth of the late seventeenth-century town are also provided by contemporary descriptions, particularly those made by the author, traveller, and social commentator, Daniel Defoe, who visited Liverpool in 1680 and again in 1690. Defoe (1726, 541) notes that,

> ... the town was, at my first visiting it, about the year 1680, a large handsome, well built and increasing or thriving town. At my second visit, anno 1690, it was much bigger than at my first seeing it, and, by the report of the inhabitants, more than twice as big as it was twenty years before that...

The late seventeenth century and first decade of the eighteenth century also witnessed several key events that were to have important ramifications for Liverpool's subsequent maritime and mercantile development. Perhaps the most significant of these involved a legal dispute between Liverpool's Corporation and Lord Molyneux over claims to an area of common land, on the southern side of the Pool (Hyde 1971, 9; Kermode *et al* 2006, 105). In 1668, Caryl Molyneux wished to bridge the Pool and build Lord Street over this area of common land (Fig 12). This was vigorously opposed by the Corporation, which felt that it was it that held the rights over this area, and in 1672, a compromise was reached. In hindsight, this compromise firmly worked in the Corporation's favour, as it involved Molyneux selling all of his rights to the overlordship of Liverpool, with the exception of the ferries and burgage rents, on a lease of 1000 years, at a rent of £30 per year (*ibid*). The importance of the acquisition of these rights was fourfold. First, they provided the Corporation with an important level of autonomy, allowing it to dictate the subsequent pattern of urban growth and expansion across the Pool, wastes, and common land (Jarvis 1991a, 5); second, the Corporation directly gained rents and fines from any leasehold properties constructed outside Liverpool's medieval and early post-medieval core, which formed an important source of revenue (Hyde 1971, 9); third, it allowed the Corporation to levy Town Dues on goods passing through the nascent port, which acted as a stimulus for further investment in port and dock facilities (Jarvis 1991a, 5); finally, the acquisition of the Pool, and its surrounding environs, provided the Corporation with an ideal site for the construction of Liverpool's first system of docks (*p 35*).

The expansion of Liverpool's trade and its advantages over other English ports represents a second key feature of the late seventeenth century and first decade of the eighteenth century. This can be assessed, in some measure, by the available shipping figures, which indicate that, between 1672 and 1702, the tonnage of goods entering Liverpool had risen from 2600 to 8600 tons, and this then increased to 14,600 tons by 1709 (Longmore 2006, 116). Furthermore, by 1702, Liverpool represented the third largest trading port in England, behind London and Bristol, with 102 vessels and 1101 seamen (Liverpool City Council 2005, 108). The reasons for this expansion are manifold, but, in one sense, Liverpool benefited from the economic potential of, and developments within, its immediate hinterland, which provided the required goods for export. Liverpool was, for instance, geographically well positioned to receive raw materials from the South Lancashire coalfields and also was adjacent to the Cheshire salt industry which, itself, greatly benefited from the discovery of large deposits of rock salt in the 1670s (Longmore 2006, 116). Moreover, the importance of salt to Liverpool led to the establishment of John Blackburne's salt refinery within the town in 1696, where salt could be processed immediately prior to export (*op cit*, 127). Liverpool also developed important links with the textile industries of Manchester and, in addition, it had access to the industrial products of the Midlands (*op cit*, 115).

In turn, the goods from Liverpool's economic hinterland were principally used, as during the sixteenth and early seventeenth centuries, for trade within the Irish Sea zone. However, they also fuelled the continued expansion in transatlantic trade, with a particular emphasis on the exchange of metal goods, foodstuffs, and textiles, for tobacco and sugar, which by 1704 included imports of 600 tons and 760 tons per year respectively (Kermode *et al* 2006, 107; Longmore 2006, 116). Importantly, the importation of this latter product also led to the establishment of Liverpool's first sugar refinery in 1667, by London merchants, and this heralded the beginnings of one of Liverpool's more enduring and important industries (Longmore 2006, 115).

During this period, overseas trade also continued with France and Spain, through the importation of wine, and links were also forged with the Baltic, which would become an important source of timber (Kermode *et al* 2006, 107-8). Late seventeenth-century overseas trade to Liverpool was also boosted by the Anglo-French war of 1689-97, as French privateers disrupted trade with the east-coast ports and London (Longmore 2006, 115). This disruption led, in turn, to the practice of transatlantic

ships discharging in the north-western ports, which ultimately resulted in both Liverpool and Glasgow supplanting London as the principal recipients of the tobacco trade (Davis 1962, 270). In addition, Liverpool's merchants were not constrained by precedent, guilds, or chartered companies, and as entrepreneurs were willing to seek and employ new methods to exploit new markets (Jackson 1983, 27-8; Longmore 2006, 118). In 1699, Liverpool's trading potential was further enhanced through the establishment of a Custom House, positioned on the Mersey foreshore, at Back Goree at the corner of Water Street, immediately east of the Tower, which provided the town with its own official custom's administration (Hyde 1971, 9; Longmore 2006, 116; Pl 19; Fig 12). The construction of the first dedicated Custom House, therefore, represents an important event in Liverpool's commercial history. Prior to this, its customs men were subject to administration from the rival port of Chester and they were first housed within the Old Town Hall, which stood on Juggler Street, and then temporarily housed on Moor Street (Fig 12), following the construction of the new Common Hall and Exchange in 1675 (*p 32*; Rideout 1928).

In terms of the vessels using the late seventeenth-/ early eighteenth-century harbour and port facilities, many involved in transatlantic trading were 'probably two-masted brigs or snows of between 50 and 200 tons', whilst many smaller craft were engaged in the inshore trade (Longmore 2005, 116; *Appendix 1*). In order to load and unload cargo, these vessels would have been grounded close to the Mersey foreshore, as Collins' (1693, 8) contemporary account indicates, and in doing so were probably served by an insubstantial quay, lying directly on the foreshore, which was rebuilt in 1665 (Ritchie-Noakes 1984, 18; Jackson 1983, 46). Collins' (1693, 8) account also indicates that ships laying up for extended stays could use the Pool, an area which also appears to have been the focus of boat- and shipbuilding, as evidenced by the increasing references to ship's carpenters and shipbuilders during the last two decades of the seventeenth century (Stewart-Brown 1932, 89-92). However, the form of this inlet, and presumably its effectiveness as a haven, and hence for trade, appears to have been gradually transformed, and limited, over the latter part of the seventeenth century. This was due in part to the practice of tipping rubbish into this inlet, and also to the numerous encroachments onto its foreshore by private landowners, which followed on from fairly piecemeal reclamation during the late sixteenth century (MacLeod 1982, 6).

During the later seventeenth-century, reclamation was encouraged by the cheap rentals that were offered on Pool lands, and there was also an obligation to reclaim adjacent areas (Stewart-Brown 1932, 103-4). This reclamation is evidenced on early nineteenth-

Plate 19: View of the Old Custom House, with the Tower and Castle, by W G Herdman (1878, pl II, 1), based on an etching by Daniel King (1780; by courtesy of the University of Liverpool Library SPEC Y87.5.41v1)

century maps, such as Charles Okill's plan of 1828 (Pl 16), and evidence for it has also been encountered during archaeological excavation. More specifically, during excavation along South Castle Street (formerly Pool Lane; *Ch 1, p 8*), various reclamation deposits were encountered, composed of soil, crushed sandstone, and stones, dating to the mid- to late seventeenth century (McNeil 1985, 27-8). Although in the seventeenth century the use of the Pool for trade appears to have, therefore, been limited, its economic potential was recognised by at least one of Liverpool's largest landowners, Sir Edward Moore (Hyde 1971, 8). Moore, writing in the mid-seventeenth century, astutely suggested to his son, regarding the land, or closes, adjacent to the inlet, that 'if ever the Pool be cut and become navigable,…there being no other place in Liverpool the like for cellars and warehouses,…the shipping must be all along those closes and the trade will be all in them of the whole town. You may have building here worth more than £20,000' (Moore 1899, 104). It was not, however, until the second decade of the eighteenth century that Moore's predictions would finally be realised, following the construction of the Old Dock, the world's first commercial wet dock.

The Old Dock

During the latter part of the seventeenth and first decade of the eighteenth century, the number of ships entering Liverpool's port increased fairly dramatically (*p 34*)

and, in terms of transatlantic trade, this was associated with larger vessels (Longmore 2006, 121). However, Liverpool's port facilities were severely lacking (*p 34*). For example, the fast-flowing waters and tidal nature of the Mersey were problematic for shipping and this was exacerbated, close to Liverpool, by the depth of the foreshore, which had been progressively reduced through the practice of tipping rubbish and ballast from moored ships (Liverpool City Council 2005, 109). The use of the adjacent inlet, the Pool, was no good alternative, as its size and depth had been dramatically reduced by land reclamation (*p 34*), meaning that it was inadequate to accommodate the pronounced surge in shipping. Given these factors, it is therefore unsurprising that, in 1699, the Corporation convened to consider what improvements and management of the waterfront and Pool would be appropriate, to encourage and promote growth and secure future trade (MMMMAL MDHB/MP/25, 2).

At the start of the eighteenth century, discussions were therefore opened between the Corporation, and the prominent civil engineer, George Sorocold, who may well have designed the Howland Great Wet Dock at Rotherhithe on the River Thames, which was constructed between 1697 and 1700 (Jackson 1983, 43). The aim was to develop an enclosed wet dock within the area of the Pool, where water could be impounded, allowing vessels to float regardless of the height of the tidal waters (Ritchie-Noakes 1984, 3, 19). While the creation of an artificial dock was a considerable innovation, it is important to recognise that it was driven by the needs of traders, rather than speculation; dock-building was expensive and, for years to come, was directed at existing, rather than future, trade (Jackson 1983, 46).

Sorocold's initial proposal was to canalise part of the stream feeding the Pool and to create an artificial harbour (*op cit*, 47), though the Corporation abandoned both this scheme, and Sorocold, and commissioned Thomas Steers, another prominent civil engineer, to create Liverpool's first artificial dock (*ibid*). Significantly, Steers probably worked alongside George Sorocold at the Howland Dock (MacLeod 1982; Clarke 1993) and so came to Liverpool with a level of experience and knowledge, which would have been vital to the success of this ambitious project (Stewart-Brown 1932). It is also possible that Steers was suggested for the project by the earl of Derby, who may have appreciated his talents during military campaigns (Clarke 1993, 9).

With the sponsorship of two leading Liverpool tobacco merchants and MPs, Thomas Johnson and Richard Norris, a Dock Act was passed by Parliament in 1709, permitting the Corporation to proceed and empowering them as the trustees of the dock to levy dues on the ships entering the harbour (Ritchie-Noakes 1984, 19). Shortly afterwards, the process of raising the necessary finance to construct what became known as the Old Dock was initiated (*ibid*). The construction process began in 1710 and, initially, £6000 was borrowed to fund this scheme, though this proved inadequate, and the scheme once completed probably cost somewhere between £15,000 and £30,000 (Jackson 1983, 47; Longmore 2006, 121-2).

The construction of the dock was certainly a formidable task, particularly as it was built entirely by hand. As one of the design novelties was that it lay within a pre-existing tidal creek, as opposed to being positioned on dry land, the building work had to be undertaken in a sea-lake, the coffer-dam for which was constantly hammered by tidal currents, and from water flowing down into the Pool from the streams off the high ground of Moss Lake (MacLeod 1982, 12). The ground was also unstable and Picton (1873, 640) notes that, '...the site was soft mud, through which the walls had to be carried down a considerable depth to reach the rock'.

The Old Dock was partially opened for shipping in 1715 and Nicholas Blundell recorded on 31 August of that year that he had seen the first three ships in the dock, the Mulbury, the Batchlor, and the Robert (Tyrer 1970, 145). One of the major advantages of this new dock was that, if necessary, ships could now unload in one-and-a-half days, rather than the 12-14 days previously, reducing the cost of handling cargo compared to other ports (MacLeod 1982, 13).

The size and form of the Old Dock can be seen on eighteenth-century mapping, specifically Chadwick's map of 1725 (Fig 13). This map indicates that the long axis of the dock was orientated east/west, measuring 179 m long by approximately 85 m wide, and covering an area of 13,750 m². In addition to the main dock, several additional elements were also included in its design, which are also depicted on Chadwick's map. These included a 1½ acre octagonal tidal entrance basin, which provided short-term berthing and safe access to the dock, and a graving dock off the north side (Ritchie-Noakes 1984, 19). Chadwick's map also indicated that the dock was provisioned with a single set of lock gates, and later mapping, such as Lightoller's plan of 1765, indicates that these were inward-facing mitre gates. This, in turn, indicates that passage into the Old Dock was only possible at the top half of the tide and that it therefore functioned

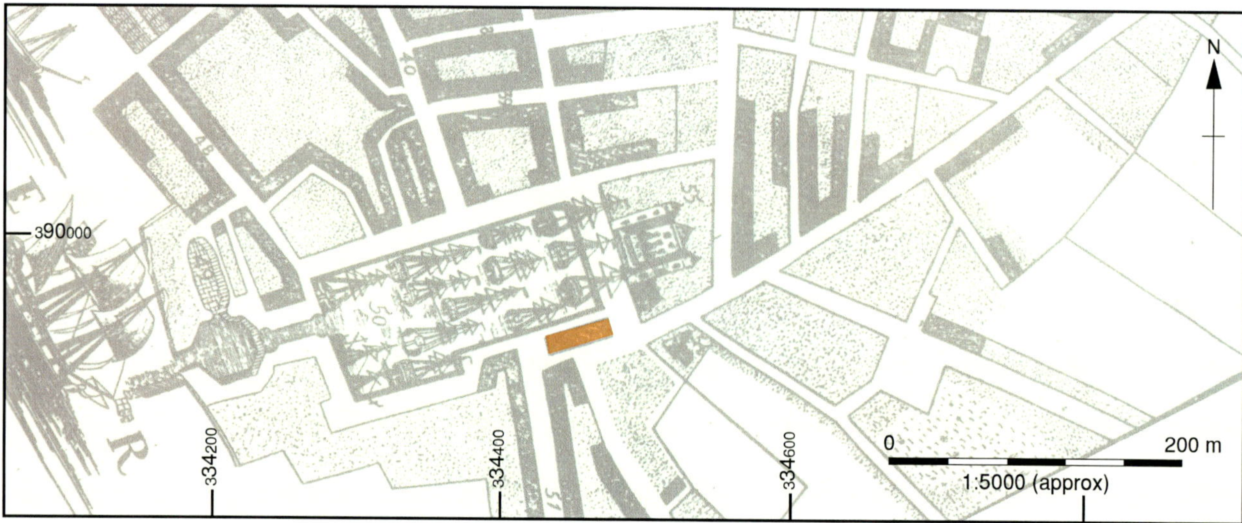

Figure 13: Extract from Chadwick's map of 1725, showing the Old Dock, associated features, and the position of the excavated building (highlighted)

as a half-tide dock. This would set a precedent for accessing the larger of Liverpool's docks, which would only be altered following the introduction of half-tide basins in the early part of the nineteenth century (*Ch 4, p 95*).

Although the Old Dock was in use by 1715, the Minutes of the Common Council suggest that those elements that would have completed the dock were still not in place by as late as 1731. The records of 5 January 1731 state that '... all monies raised by leasing the ground around the dock be applied to finishing the dock' (MMMMAL MDHB/MP/25, 32). Further to this, the records from 1726 onwards make it abundantly apparent that the Old Dock was already proving to be problematic from the perspective of maintenance, as it was prone to silting, which dramatically reduced the depth of the basin, causing problems for the passage of larger vessels.

The Archaeology of the Old Dock

The process and methods employed during the construction of the Old Dock were not recorded in detail at the time, and only limited mention is made to the building of the dock in the records of the Common Council. It is often assumed, however, that stone used to construct the Old Dock was derived from St James' Mount or Brownlow Hill, and some might also have been salvaged from the ruined medieval castle (Ritchie-Noakes 1984, 19). Based on documentary records, it was suspected that the walls of the Old Dock were not particularly substantial, due to the fact that 'shipbuilders are said to have pulled down sections of the wall when they wished to launch their vessels into the dock' (*ibid*).

Fortunately, two programmes of archaeological investigation have specifically targeted elements of the Old Dock. This work includes that undertaken at the site of the Old Dock and Chavasse Park (*Ch 1, p 9*), and also an investigation completed as part of the Liverpool Trams Scheme (*Ch 1, p 11*). Together, this work involved the excavation of 20 evaluation trenches around the perimeter of the Old Dock (Fig 14) in order to investigate its walls and quayside, and also the excavation of two trenches across the walls of the dock, during the construction of the Old Dock Information Centre (OA North 2005d; 2009a).

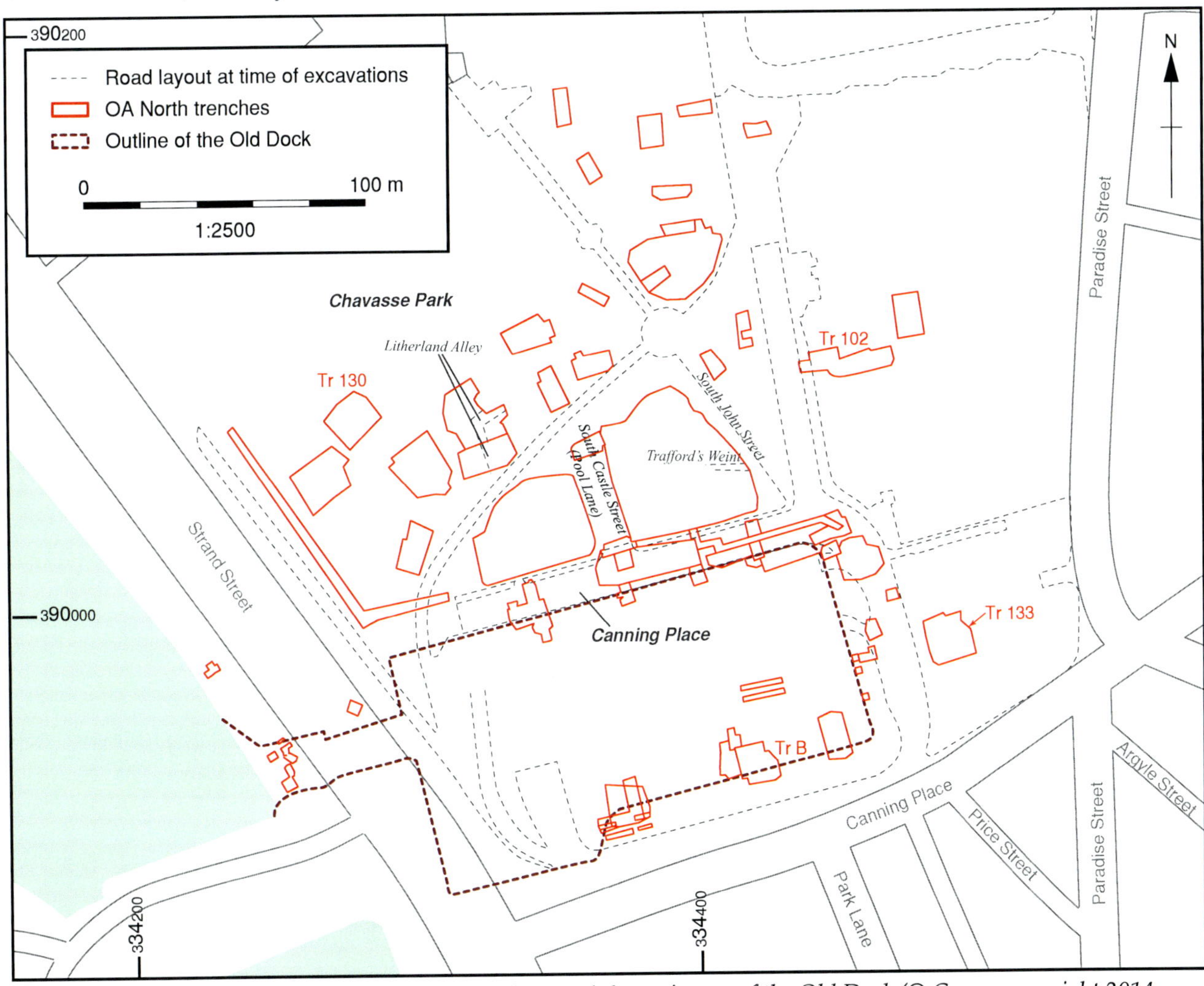

Figure 14: Archaeological trenches excavated around the perimeter of the Old Dock (© Crown copyright 2014 Ordnance Survey 100005569)

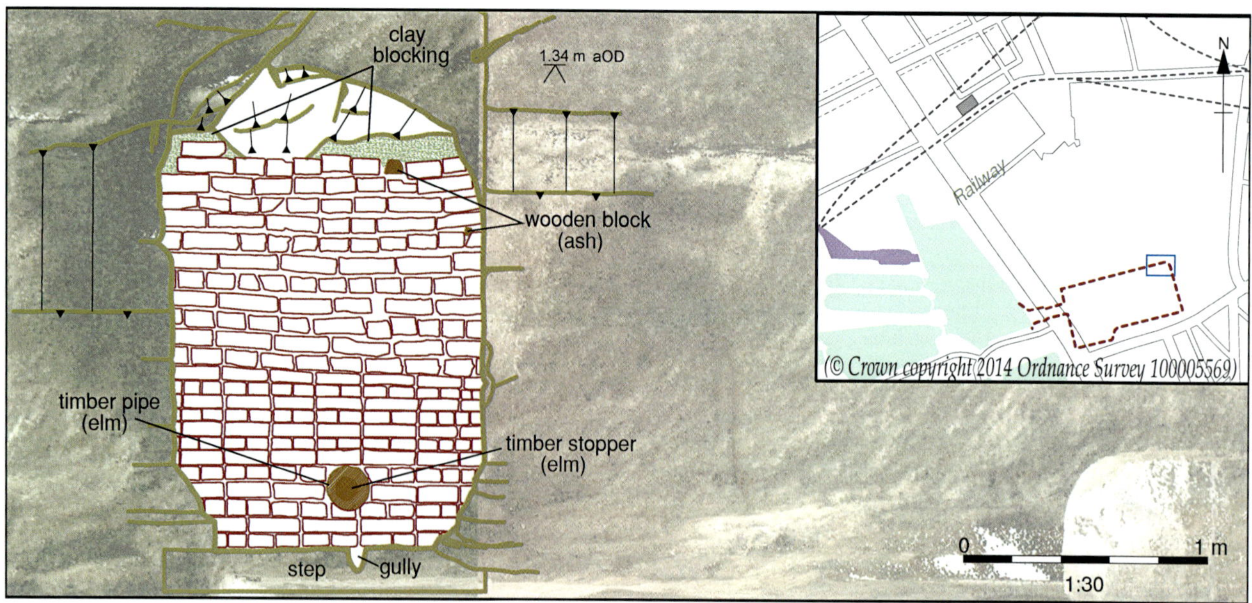

Figure 15: The blocked tunnel entrance revealed during excavations at the Old Dock

These excavations indicated that well-preserved remains of the Old Dock were present below the ground, and that the positions of these remains tallied well with the layout of the Old Dock as depicted on John Chadwick's map of 1725 (Fig 13). Significantly, the excavations indicated that the lowest portion of the northern side of the dock consisted of bedrock, that had been cut and modified to create the base of the dock, on top of which a brick wall had been constructed. There were also indications of large sandstone blocks used for the lower courses on the eastern side of the dock. The base of the southern side was not reached, but it is possible that in this area the basal construction was slightly different, since it was within the deeper, central part of the Pool, while the northern part lay along the edge of the Pool, where the bedrock was at a higher level. Along this northern section, it was also evident that, during the construction of the Old Dock, the rock-cut tunnel, that was perhaps medieval in date (*p 27*), was blocked (Fig 15). The blocking comprised a wall of handmade bricks, which had a narrow-diameter timber (*Ulmus* (elm) species) pipe protruding from it, perhaps initially to facilitate the draining of any residual effluence from the tunnel. However, this pipe was subsequently blocked by the insertion of a timber stopper.

The main element of the dock wall, as it survived, was a continuous, unbroken construction of handmade red bricks, bonded with lime mortar, at least 3 m in height and over 1.25 m wide (Pl 20). This vertical wall was then capped with yellow sandstone blocks, which would have been contiguous with the quayside (Pl 21). The upper clays behind this wall were clearly backfill, beneath which were layers of crushed and fragmentary brick waste. The backfilled

clay was almost identical to the Pool deposits but lacked the laminations evident in the natural silts. This demonstrates that the clay had been moved in bulk, probably stored, and then used as backfill once the wall was complete. The clay was particularly suited for this purpose as it provided a watertight seal for the dock.

The other main discovery was that large horizontal timbers had been inserted into the rear face of the north wall during construction, and possibly after some partial backfilling. These timbers consisted of long tree trunks, with minimum trimming, laid horizontally, perpendicular to the back of the wall, and in several examples vertical stakes had been employed in order to anchor these timber supports (Pl 22). Most of the timbers were found in the north and north-eastern sections of the dock, although

Plate 20: Results of a three-dimensional laser-scan survey of the Old Dock, showing the landward face of the Dock wall, with a sluice in the centre

Plate 21: Remains of the brick retaining wall forming the north-eastern corner of the Old Dock, with two yellow sandstone capping blocks

Plate 22: The arrangement of timbers running from the rear face of the Old Dock wall

timber exposed in one of the evaluation trenches appears to imply that the timber supports were also present on its southern side.

In addition to the retaining walls of the Old Dock, the remains of a contemporary building were uncovered on it southern quay. These remains consisted of a north/south-aligned wall, which was keyed into the quayside, the position of which equated with a building that is depicted on Chadwick's map of 1725 (Fig 13). The wall was of the same yellow sandstone as the quayside; four courses remained and below these were what appeared to be wooden foundations sitting on the clay backfill (Pl 23). This suggests that, once the lower part of the dock wall had been built and partial backfilling had taken place, the foundations for the building were put in and the quayside was constructed before completing the backfilling.

Plate 23: The Old Dock wall, and the sandstone foundations of a contemporary building

The Significance of the Old Dock

The opening of the Old Dock occurred 53 years ahead of the first commercial wet dock at Bristol, 63 years before the example at Kingston upon Hull, and almost 90 years prior to the establishment of London's first commercial wet dock, which opened in 1802 (MacLeod 1982, 1). In terms of the development of Liverpool, it appears to have affected its maritime commerce fairly rapidly and, in turn, the prosperity and wealth of the town. For example, Daniel Defoe (1726, 541), who visited the town for a third time in 1724, following the opening of the Old Dock, comments that

> I was surprised at the view, it was more than double what it was at the second [visit in 1690]; and I am told that it still visibly increases both in wealth, people, business and buildings. What it may grow to in time, I know not.

Defoe also states that the town had an opulent, flourishing, and increasing trade, although he does emphasise that this trade was not a rival to Bristol (*ibid*). Defoe's perceptions were probably accurate at this stage, as the Old Dock had only been open for just over a decade and its full impact was yet to be felt. However, he goes on to note of the Liverpool Merchants that,

> They trade round the whole island [Britain], send ships to Norway, to Hamburgh [*sic*] and to the Baltick [*sic*], as also to Holland and Flanders; so that in a word, they are almost become like the Londoners, universal merchants (*ibid*).

This high praise indicates that, even as early as 1724, the transformation of the developing maritime mercantile town of Liverpool was substantial, with a rapid development of infrastructure, and also merchant dwellings/warehouses, ancillary works, and other substantial buildings. In essence, the Old Dock was to the form the hub of the later dock system for the best part of a century, and its positioning would greatly influence the urban morphology of the eighteenth-century and later town.

3

EIGHTEENTH-CENTURY EXPANSION (1715-1800)

Richard A Gregory, Caroline Raynor, Nick Johnson, Vix Hughes, and Mark Adams

The Eighteenth-century Town

Following the opening of the Old Dock in 1715, Liverpool entered an unprecedented phase of expansion for the remainder of the eighteenth century. This expansion included a dramatic enlargement of the town's population, which rose from 5145 inhabitants in 1700 to approximately 77,000 at the close of the eighteenth century (Longmore 2006, 169). This demographic explosion was, in turn, associated with an increase in the town's size, a remodelling and extension of the town's early post-medieval core, and also the construction of several important civic buildings.

In determining the growth and form of the eighteenth-century town, it is fortunate that, more generally, this period is characterised by a rise in high-quality cartography depicting some of England's larger urban centres (Delano-Smith and Kain 1999, 204). Relevant eighteenth-century maps, which highlight both Liverpool's expansion and its progressive urban morphology, include those produced by the cartographers John Chadwick in 1725, John Eyes in 1765 and 1768, George Perry in 1769, Charles Eyes in 1785, John Stockdale in 1795, and John Gore in 1796. To these may also be added a plan of the town reputedly produced in 1729, by an unknown cartographer, which appears as an inset in a map published in 1833 by the Society for the Diffusion of Useful Knowledge (Pl 24), and several other valuable sources of illustrative evidence.

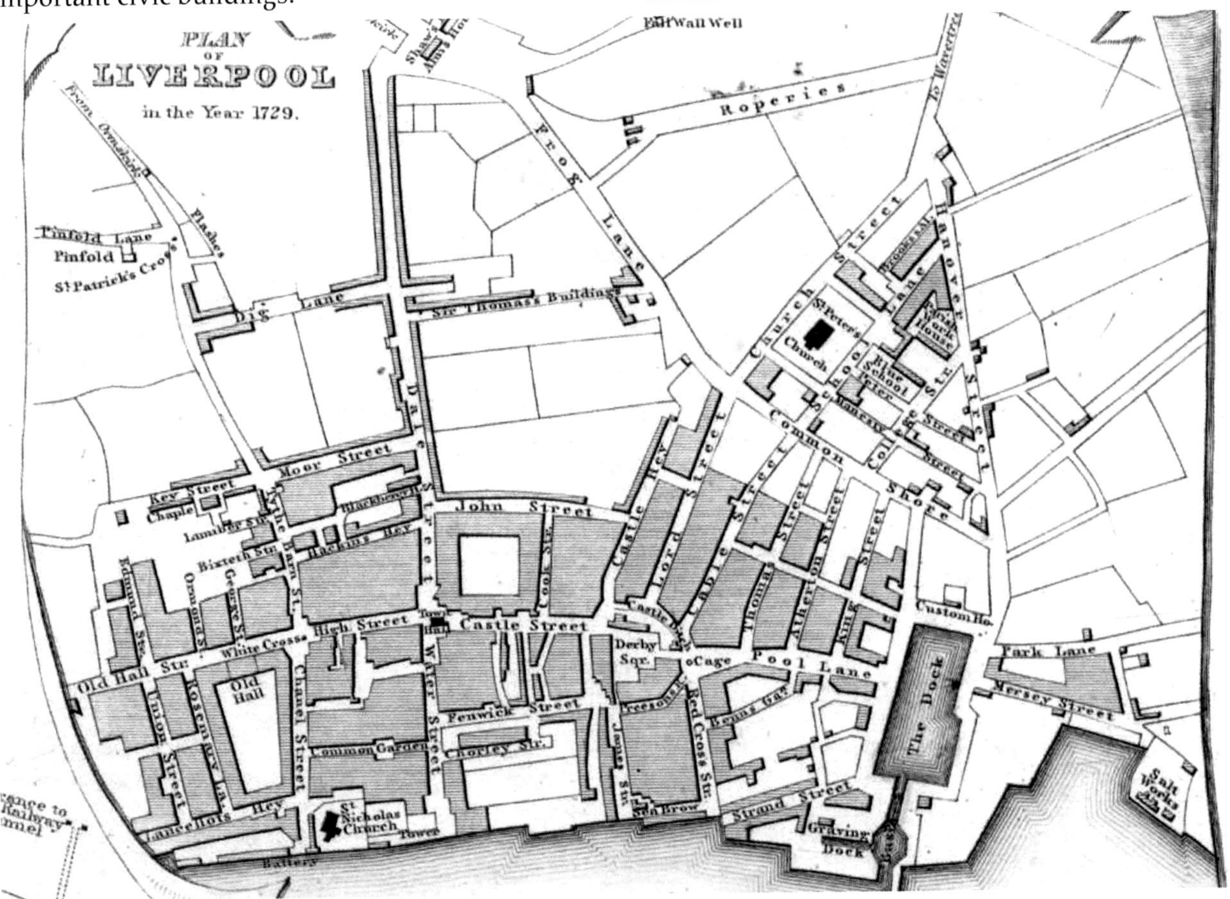

Plate 24: Early eighteenth-century Liverpool, as depicted on a plan reputedly produced in 1729, and reproduced in the Society for the Diffusion of Useful Knowledge's 1833 map of Liverpool

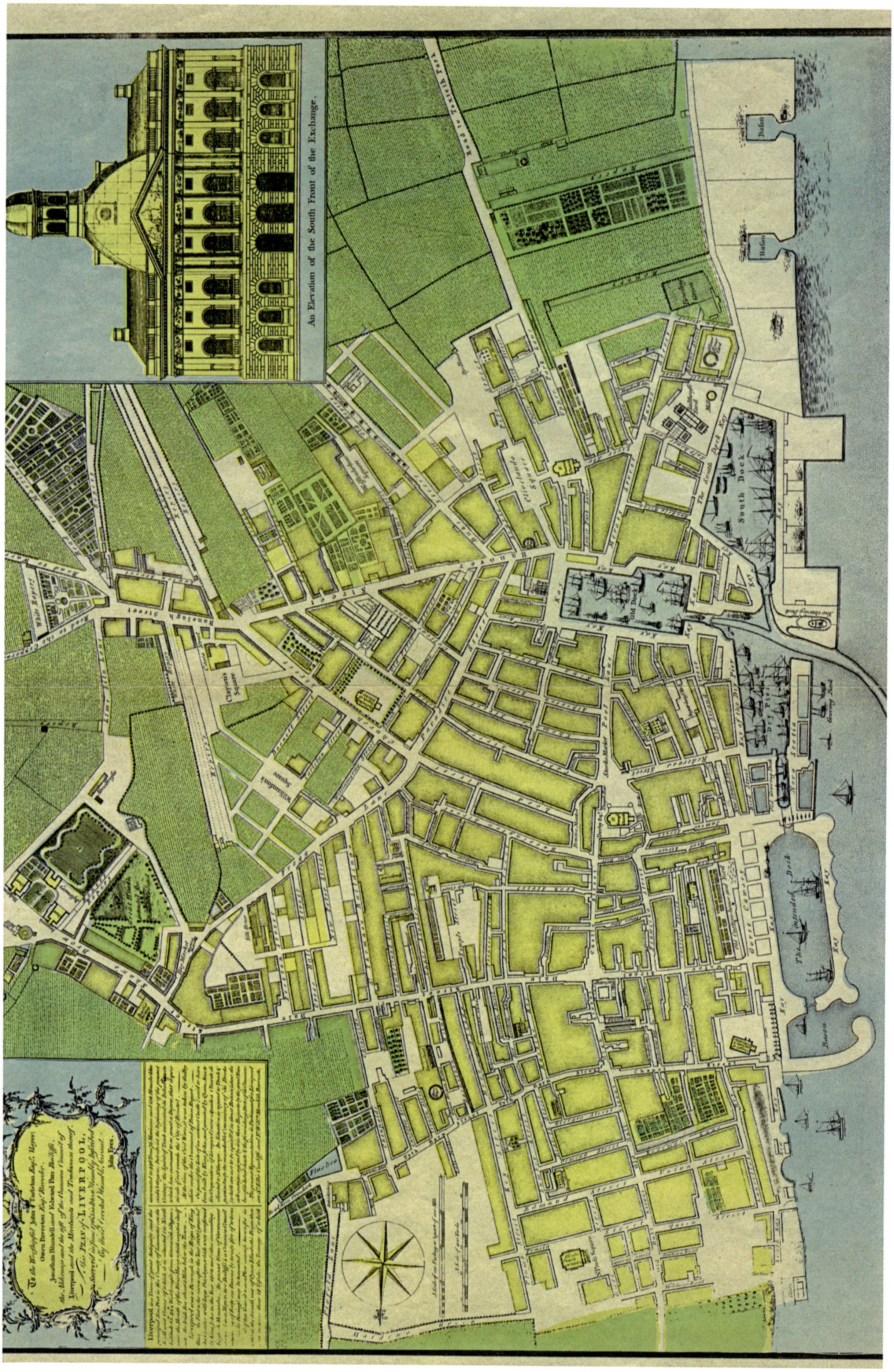

Plate 25: John Eyes' plan of Liverpool from 1765

Importantly, this latter material includes perspective drawings and engravings produced by Nathaniel and Samuel Buck, showing the town in 1728, as part of their series of long prospects of English and Welsh sea-ports (Hyde 1994).

Together these sources indicate that, initially, following the infilling of the Pool and the creation of the Old Dock, the town expanded southwards and eastwards, through the creation of several principal routes, which were fronted by properties. These are all depicted on Chadwick's map of 1725 and the 1729 map, and amongst the major routes were Common Shore (later Paradise Street)/Frog Lane (later White Chapel), which followed the line of the infilled Pool, Hanover Street, running eastwards from the Old Dock, and Park Lane and Mersey Street, running from the south-eastern corner of the Old Dock. Between these main streets, and several of the pre-eighteenth-century streets, such as Pool Lane and Lord Street, a smaller system of minor streets, and associated properties, was also created in the early part of the eighteenth century. Chadwick's map of 1725 and that of 1729 also indicate that several streets, albeit largely without concomitant properties, had been laid out further to the south, extending from Hanover Street. From west to east, these included Argyle Street, Duke Street, Wolstenholme Street, and Wood Street. In addition, some more minor expansion had occurred at the northern end of the town, within an area bounded by two of the pre-eighteenth-century streets, Tithebarn Street and Old Hall Street, and the newly established Key Street, which extended the line of Moor Street (Pl 24) northwards.

Further expansion of the town, and also of the docks and waterfront (*p 53*), then occurred, and by the mid-eighteenth century the town is known to have possessed a total of 222 streets (Hyde 1971, 22). This expansion is visible on John Eyes' map of 1765 (Pl 25) and Perry's of 1769, which indicate that streets and properties had been established to the east of the post-medieval core, across a triangular area of land sandwiched between John Street, Dale Street, and Frog Lane. In addition, streets and properties, as well as two squares (Williamson and Clayton), had been constructed to the south of this area between Church Street and Frog Lane. A similar pattern of development had also occurred in the southern part of the eighteenth-century town, which is again depicted on Eyes' map of 1765. This involved the construction of properties along those streets off Hanover Street, which had been established in the early eighteenth century (*see above*), along with the construction of further streets, squares (Wolstenholme and Cleveland), and associated properties in this area. Over the next 20 years, the southern portion of the town was further developed. This is evidenced on Charles Eyes' map of 1785, which plots a series of streets and associated properties to both the east and west of Park Lane, Duke Street, and Bold Street.

Some impression of the character of the early eighteenth-century town can be gained from an illustration produced by the Buck brothers', showing the town in 1728 (Pl 26). This presents a view of the town, from the Mersey, immediately prior to the expansion of its dock system and port facilities in the mid-eighteenth century (*p 53*). The Old Dock forms one of the more prominent features on the Buck brothers' drawing, and is depicted laden with ships, with a timber pier extending from its mouth into the river. Other smaller vessels can also be seen beached on the Mersey foreshore, suggesting that this area still held some maritime importance. Although by the time of this engraving the last remains of Liverpool castle had just been removed, in 1727 (*p 44*), the Tower and the church of St Nicholas, and former chapel of St Mary del Key, still remained, forming the more prominent vestiges of Liverpool's medieval and early post-medieval architectural fabric.

Plate 26: The Buck brothers' 1728 view of Liverpool from the River Mersey (LVRO and Liverpool Libraries Local Q912.42253 BUC)

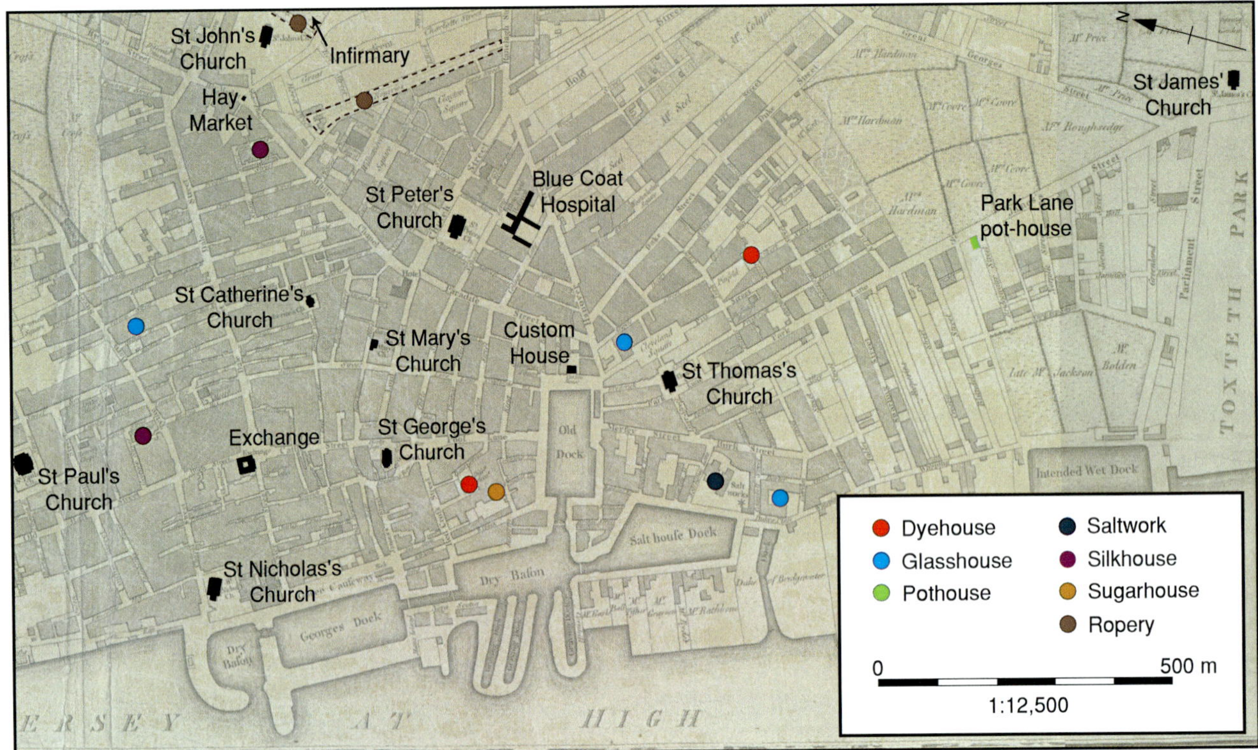

Figure 16: Extract from Charles Eyes' map of 1785, showing the positions of churches, the Custom House, the Exchange, the Blue Coat Hospital, and industrial sites important to the functioning of the eighteenth-century town, which are depicted on John Eyes' earlier map of 1765

The Buck brothers' drawing and the successive eighteenth-century maps indicate, however, that several other prominent buildings, some of which held important civic functions, were constructed in the course of the eighteenth century (Fig 16). Principal amongst these was a series of churches, which gradually appeared during this period. The earliest of these was St Peter's Church, on Church Street, consecrated in 1704, which functioned as Liverpool's first parish church (Sharples 2004, 179), and St George's Church, with its classical tower and spire, was built between 1726 and 1734, being designed by the dock engineer, Thomas Steers (*ibid*). This latter church holds particular significance, as it was constructed by the Corporation across the site of the medieval castle; it had secured the rights to demolish it from Lord Molyneux in 1704 (Liverpool City Council 2005, 110; Longmore 2006, 148). The demolition of this manorial edifice and its replacement with a Corporation church is significant, in that it symbolises 'the final shift in the balance of local political power', away from the manorial Lord and into the hands of a mercantile oligarchy (Longmore 2006, 149). The construction of St George's Church was then followed by four other eighteenth-century churches of note, which appear on the mid- and late eighteenth-century maps of Liverpool. These include the large and visually impressive stone-built and domed church of St Paul, opened in 1769 at the northern end of the town (Colvin 1954, 521; Sharples 2004, 179), St John's Church, on

the town's eastern fringe, consecrated in 1767 and completed in 1784, St Thomas's Church, consecrated in 1750, and St James's Church, built in 1774-5; both these latter were in the southern part of the town (Lancashire Online Parish Services nd).

Significantly, the sites of the churches of St Peter, St Paul, and St Thomas have been subjected to archaeological investigation. On the eastern edge of the site of St Peter's Church, within the former churchyard, five evaluation trenches were excavated in 2006, and in this area it was felt that burials might be encountered (OA North 2009a). One of the trenches produced demolition material, consisting of fragments of yellow sandstone and brick, derived from the church, whilst another trench contained a large flat stone slab, which might represent a grave marker (*ibid*). In addition, this trench also contained fragmentary human remains, clay tobacco pipe bowls and stems, and eighteenth- and nineteenth-century pottery. However, although some evidence for burial was discovered, it was notable that there was an absence of articulated human remains within the churchyard, which undoubtedly relates to an earlier programme of exhumation. In 1868, for example, some 2000 burials from St Peter's Church were removed to Anfield Cemetery in advance of the widening of Church Street (Lewis 2001). Furthermore, with the decommissioning of the church, over 6000 wooden boxes filled with disarticulated human remains were removed and reinterred in Rice Lane Cemetery in 1921-2 (*ibid*).

Similarly, at St Paul's Church, six trial trenches were excavated in 2005, which exposed yellow and white sandstone walls, of ashlar construction, probably parts of the church's foundations (OA North 2005g). Intriguingly, only one burial, the partially articulated remains of a young adult, was discovered, and there was a general absence of burials in the church and churchyard areas. This, along with a layer of redeposited natural clay overlying the foundations of the walls, indicates that the site had been systematically cleared of burials, probably when the church was demolished in 1931 (*ibid*). The few finds included a painted sandstone tile, probably from the church, a sherd of late-eighteenth- to twentieth-century earthenware with a blue transfer print, and five fragments of bone, including a juvenile human femur (*ibid*). Further work was carried out at the site of St Paul's Church in 2006 and 2009, which revealed a series of structures, including 22 brick barrel-vaulted crypts (OA North 2006i; 2009b). The crypts had all been emptied prior to the demolition of the church, but numerous fragments of human bone, gravestones, and coffin wood and furniture were recovered during the excavation (*ibid*).

At St Thomas's Church, the archaeological work consisted of a watching brief across the former church and churchyard. At the site of the church, several well-preserved sandstone walls were recorded, which formed the foundations for its north, west, and south walls. Within the churchyard, the investigation was specifically designed to determine the survival of the graves and also to locate an eighteenth-century brick-vaulted tomb (OA North 2009a). This tomb was known to contain the remains of the influential Tate family and also the philanthropist, Joseph Williamson, who in the 1800s created a series of underground tunnels in Edge Hill (Murden 2006, 480). In total, 43 late eighteenth- and early nineteenth-century graves were uncovered in the churchyard. Most of the grave markers were horizontal sandstone slabs, 1.66 x 0.97 m in size, and aligned east/west, with the inscription at the western end of the stone. During excavation, it was evident that some of the backfill around the graves was derived from the demolition of the church, as bricks with an intricate green and white pattern were recovered. These would have formed part of the church's mosaic floor. The Tate vault was also identified. The vault, containing six inhumations, was overlain by a standard stone slab, without embellishment or decoration (Pl 27). The inscription read:

> To the memory of Richard Tate who departed this life 7th May 1787 in the 51st year of his age. Also Ann Tate the

Plate 27: The Tate family vault, as found during the watching brief

> mother of the above Richard Tate died 6th day of October 1791 in the 76th year of her age. Hannah Tate the wife of Richard Tate died 29th July 1793 aged 59 years. Also the remains of Elizabeth daughter of Richard and Hannah Tate and the wife of Joseph Williamson of Edgehill who departed this life the 3rd day of October 1822 aged 56 years.
>
> Also the remains of Richard the youngest son of the above Richard and Hannah Tate who died 7th June 1826 aged 56 years.
>
> Also the remains of Joseph Williamson of Edgehill who died the 1st May 1840 aged 71 years.

This inscription tallied with that recorded in 1886 in a hand-written record produced for the council (LVRO Hf 352 CEM 1/17/2), and it was also engraved with the original plot number (260) along the base. Within the vault, the outline of the sides of a lead-lined coffin was also revealed, with limited survival of the woodwork on the outside of the lead sheet. Despite the complete survival of the sides, there was no evidence for a coffin lid.

The watching brief at St Thomas's church also identified a brick path, which ran around the south side of the church, dividing it from the graveyard, and a substantial yellow sandstone wall, which was one-course wide, two-courses high, and orientated north-west/south-east. This latter wall was set in the north-eastern corner of the graveyard, and was evidently its boundary wall. This yellow sandstone was typical of that in use in Liverpool in the eighteenth century (Ritchie-Noakes 1984, 37) and its use at St Thomas's Church would have been contemporary with the original construction of the church.

Aside from the churches, several other important civic buildings were also built in the eighteenth-century town, some of which are depicted by the Buck brothers and the eighteenth-century cartographers. Perhaps the most important of these was the Exchange, situated at the heart of the town's historic core, the elevation of which appears as a small vignette on Charles Eyes' map of 1785 (Pl 25). This impressive civic building was constructed between 1749 and 1754 on the site of the earlier Common Hall and Exchange that had been constructed in 1675 (*Ch 2, p 32*; Pl 18). It was designed by the pre-eminent Georgian architect, John Wood the Elder, who, most famously, was responsible for several of Bath's more important buildings (*cf* Mowl and Earnshaw 1988). The Exchange represented an important symbol of civic power and, accordingly, the Corporation, in 1780, commissioned another pre-eminent Georgian architect, James Wyatt, to design its extension (Colvin 1978, 722; Longmore 2006, 148). Following a fire in 1795, which damaged the interior of the Exchange, Wyatt was also commissioned to design the reconstruction of this important building, which is considered by many to represent an outstanding architectural achievement (Longmore 2006, 148; Sharples 2004, 48).

At the eastern end of the Old Dock was another important eighteenth-century building, which holds particular significance for Liverpool's maritime history. This was the new, or second, Custom House (Fig 16), replacing the earlier Custom House at the corner of Water Street (*Ch 2, p 34*). Again, Liverpool's second Custom House can be partially seen on the Buck brothers' drawing and the eighteenth-century maps, and it is also depicted more clearly on a drawing made by W G Herdman in the early nineteenth century (Herdman 1856, 52; Pl 28). This three-storey brick-built building was designed by Thomas Ripley and opened in 1722 (Ritchie-Noakes 1984, 22), and a small portion of it was exposed during the archaeological excavations in the vicinity of the Old Dock (OA North 2009a). During this programme, one trench uncovered a series of steps, descending downwards from east to west, with a sandstone pillar on their southern side (Pl 29), which formed a minor element of the second Custom House.

Plate 28: An early nineteenth-century view of the Custom House at the eastern end of the Old Dock, drawn by W G Herdman (1856, pl 18; by courtesy of the University of Liverpool Library SPEC Y87.5.35 V5)

Plate 29: The yellow sandstone steps of the early eighteenth-century Custom House

Two other important buildings of note, depicted on the eighteenth-century town plans, were the Blue Coat Hospital, sandwiched between Hanover Street and Paradise Street (Fig 16), and the Infirmary (Pl 25), situated at the far eastern limits of the town, adjacent to Hay Market (Fig 16). The former was a charity school, which housed and educated poor children. It opened in 1718, and was largely financed by Bryan Blundell, one of Liverpool's wealthy merchants, and may even have been designed by Thomas Steers, the civil engineer responsible for the Old Dock (*Ch 2, p 36*), who also designed the 1740s playhouse on Drury Lane (Longmore 2006, 142, 149). The Infirmary was a later manifestation, opened in 1749, the construction of which was dependent on both a Corporation lease and funding by a large number of its members (Longmore 2006, 151). Significantly, this hospital was designed to serve both Liverpool's inhabitants and also people from outside the town, suggesting that, by this date, and by virtue of its maritime connections, Liverpool contained a mixed and transient population (*ibid*). In terms of Liverpool's maritime significance, this location held further significance, as the Seamans' Hospital was built, in 1752, directly adjacent to the Infirmary. This institution functioned as a retirement home for ex-sailors and was funded through contributions obtained from all of Liverpool's seamen (*ibid*).

The eighteenth-century cartographic sources also indicate that the town housed numerous industries, the majority of which were directly linked to Liverpool's growth in maritime trade (*see below*). These included roperies on the eastern and southern fringes of the town, whilst the area between Castle Street/Pool Lane and the foreshore was home to numerous industries connected with ship building and maintenance, and with the packaging and movement of goods (Liverpool City Council 2005, 111; Jarvis 1991a, 6; Fig 16). Food processing also occurred in this area, with numerous open-fronted slaughterhouses fronting Pool Lane, which would have created a fairly insalubrious and rank environment (Jarvis 1991a, 7). The mid-eighteenth-century town also contained eight sugar-houses (Longmore 2006, 135), but the precise location of only one can be discerned from eighteenth-century mapping (Fig 16). Within these works, imported sugar would have been refined, prior to regional and national redistribution. In addition, the town contained two silk-houses and a dye house, which were potentially producing fabric for export (Longmore 2006, 135). The saltworks, established in 1696 (*Ch 2, p 34*), which lay to the south of the Old Dock, also continued to refine salt ready for export. This works also formed a dominant feature of the eighteenth-century townscape, particularly as contemporary accounts (Moss 1796), and the Buck brothers' engraving (Pl 26), indicate that its chimney belched out large quantities of offensive smoke.

Glass production, another of Liverpool's prominent eighteenth-century industries, would have been reliant on salt from the saltworks, and would also have further contributed to airborne pollution across the town. John Eyes' map of 1765 indicates that, by the mid-eighteenth-century, the town contained three glassworks (Fig 16). One of these was to the south of the Old Dock, adjacent to the saltworks, one lay at the far southern end of Hanover Street, whilst the other was located close to Tithebarn Street.

In addition to the glassworks, Eyes' map plots the position of a 'pot-house' on Park Lane. The Park Lane Pot-House formed one of the potteries known to have existed in the eighteenth-century town, prior to the establishment in 1796 of the Herculaneum Pottery, which was Liverpool's most prominent pottery (Hyland 2005). Indeed, during the early-mid-eighteenth century, Liverpool contained a thriving pottery industry, which was initially centred on the production of tin-glazed earthenwares and tile, and later the manufacture of Creamwares and porcelain (*Ch 6, pp 186, 189-92*). Other early-mid-eighteenth-century potteries within the town were present at Shaws Brow; at the east ends of Dale Street (Haymarket Pottery), Lord Street, and Duke Street; at the corner of Flint and Parliament Street (Flint Mug Works); and on Brownlow Hill and Islington. Numerous smaller, less prominent, works also existed that were exclusively engaged in the production of tin-glazed wares (Ray 2000, 5; Hyland 2005, 5, 7, 9; *Ch 6, p 186*). Another component of Liverpool's mid-eighteenth-century pottery industry was ceramic printing, which was pioneered by the Liverpool printer, John Sadler, in 1756 (Hyland 2005, 11). Sadler, in conjunction with Guy Green, subsequently established a ceramic print works on Harrington Street, which was in operation between the 1760s and 1799 (*ibid*). This print works was under an exclusive contract to Josiah Wedgwood, the pre-eminent Staffordshire potter, and glazed and fired pots were therefore sent from Staffordshire for printing, and were then returned to a Wedgwood warehouse or sent back to Wedgwood's Staffordshire pottery (*ibid*).

In addition to domestic pottery production, several eighteenth-century ceramic works, such as the Mould Works, near the Infirmary (Smith 1970), were engaged in the manufacture of sugar wares, which were essential for sugar refining (*Ch 6, p 207*). Furthermore, by the late eighteenth century, numerous clay tobacco-pipe works were also scattered across the town, transforming Liverpool into a major pipe-production and export centre (*Ch 6, p 206*). A final industry associated with the early-mid-eighteenth-century town was milling, and unsurprisingly the Bucks' engraving shows numerous windmills, used for milling corn, peppering Liverpool's early skyline (Pl 26).

From the Buck brothers' drawing, it is also clear that by the early eighteenth century the town was dominated by two- and three-storey buildings, the majority of which functioned wholly, or partly, as dwellings. Within Liverpool's historic core, these would have included those stone-built residences which had been constructed in the late seventeenth century (*Ch 2, p 32*), and also other stone-built houses, constructed in the early eighteenth century, as evidenced by Daniel Defoe's (1726, 541) comment that, 'many of the houses are all of free stone, and completely finished'. In addition, the early eighteenth-century town would have contained numerous brick-built dwellings, again witnessed by Defoe (*ibid*), during his visit in 1724, who notes that, aside from the stone-built houses, 'all the rest (of the new part I mean) (are) of brick, as handsomely built as London it self'. These more 'handsome' dwellings continued to be constructed throughout the eighteenth century and undoubtedly housed the more affluent sections of Liverpool's society, lining the new streets and squares established in the southern and eastern parts of the town. For example, one such route was Hanover Street, running eastwards from the Old Dock, and on the basis of information contained within Liverpool's first street directory, this was originally the home to a high proportion of its wealthy merchants (Gore 1766).

Although, as noted by Defoe and the mid-eighteenth-century street directories, there were undoubtedly wealthy and well-built houses, which were concentrated in the south-eastern part of the town and around the Town Hall and Exchange, the waterfront and central areas appear to have housed the mass of poorer groups, many of which were associated with Liverpool's maritime economy (Pooley 2006, 176). The dwellings of the poor would have been insalubrious in character, and from the 1780s onwards distinct types of workers' housing emerged, across both Liverpool and the other industrialised urban centres of the North West (*cf* Sharples 2004, 8; Roberts 1993). In Liverpool, as with other urban centres, these types of dwelling consisted of high-density, small double-depth terraced houses, and smaller single-depth back-to-back and blind-back terraced housing, which would continue to house the urban poor well into the early part of the nineteenth century (Sharples 2004, 8). Moreover, the back-to-back and blind-back houses were often constructed within vacant plots located to the rear of pre-existing buildings and were situated around small cramped and insanitary courtyards, that could only be accessed via covered alleyways (Sharples 2004, 8; Trinder 1982, 123). From the late eighteenth century, a proportion of the urban poor were also housed in the cellars of the earlier and later eighteenth-century properties. Although not specific to Liverpool, it appears that this type of dwelling was significant, and by 1790 there were 1728 known cellar dwellings, housing 12.6% of the total population of the town (Sharples 2004, 10).

The character of Liverpool's poorer late eighteenth-century areas may also be gleaned from contemporary accounts. One such, dating to 1780, was by the Salem merchant Samuel Curwen, who visited Liverpool *en route* on a tour of Britain and Europe. Within his diary Curwen notes that,

> ...houses are by a great majority in middling and lower style, few rising above that mark; streets long, narrow, crooked, and dirty in an eminent degree. During our short abode here, we scarcely saw a well-dressed person, nor half a dozen gentlemen's carriages...The whole complexion nautical, and so infinitely below all our expectations, that nought but the thoughts of the few hours we had to pass here rendered it tolerable...The docks however are stupendously grand...(Atkinson Ward 1842, 246).

Although Curwen did not specify which streets in Liverpool he was describing, it is likely that he was exposed to the areas around George's Dock, Mann Island, and the Old Dock. These areas were overly populous, ill-maintained, and represent an area that would become known as 'Sailor-town', a place filled with public houses and victuallers to serve the needs of the itinerant maritime populace (*ibid*). As Milne (2006, 301) notes, the concept of a 'Sailor-town' was common to many ports, and these were usually viewed as areas of urban depravity.

Archaeological excavation provides a direct link with the eighteenth-century dwellings, housing both the rich and poor, and allows their form and construction to be examined, as well as providing some details of the types of artefacts used by these respective socio-economic groups. In Liverpool, whilst some of the eighteenth-century dwellings, specifically several potential cellar dwellings, have been archaeologically examined at Mann Island, close to the present-day waterfront (*p 80*), other eighteenth-century dwellings were also uncovered during the excavations in Chavasse Park (OA North 2009a; *Ch 1, p 9*).

The most coherent area examined lay immediately north of the Old Dock, at the southern end of Pool Lane, an area which had contained buildings from the early part of the eighteenth century, as evidenced on Chadwick's 1725 plan of the town (Fig 12). In this area, an inter-linked complex of cellars was uncovered on either side of Pool Street. These cellars were associated with buildings dating from the eighteenth century, which were successively modified/rebuilt over the course of the nineteenth and twentieth centuries (Pl 30). The majority of the cellars survived almost intact, to the level of the ground floor, and were up to 3 m deep. They varied in size and contained a range of features, including fireplaces, wells, lift shafts, stairwells, floors,

Plate 30: A view of the eighteenth- and nineteenth-century cellars exposed at Chavasse Park

doorways, storage areas, alcoves, and barrel-vaulted ceilings. All showed several phases of construction and alterations, and the earlier phases, presumably dating to the eighteenth century, were constructed in stone, whilst the later phases were constructed in brick (OA North 2009a). More specifically, within this area, and also immediately to the north, it appeared that the earliest street frontages, probably dating to the eighteenth century, were built of yellow sandstone, which were then realigned and constructed in brick, in the mid-nineteenth century (*ibid*).

In addition to the dwellings, the eighteenth-century town also contained numerous warehouses, which were essential for the storage of goods, especially those which were perishable (Ritchie-Noakes 1984, 131). Initially, many eighteenth-century merchants used the cellars of their residences for storage, though during this period the practice emerged whereby small brick-built warehouses were constructed that were attached to the merchant's dwelling (Giles and Hawkins 2004, 14; Sharples 2004, 205). These private warehouses were normally sited inland, away from the publicly owned waterfront, and formed 'one of the most characteristic building types of this period' (Sharples 2004, 205).

In addition, several private eighteenth-century warehouses stood directly adjacent to the docks and waterfront. These included those early-mid-eighteenth-century warehouses that were established around the Old Dock, and the quayside warehouse, built in 1783, at Duke's Dock (*p 69*) which, along with the dock, was built on land that had been leased by the Duke of Bridgewater in 1765 (Ritchie-Noakes 1984, 22, 31).

Furthermore, several small private warehouses were established at Nova Scotia and Mann Island (*p 80*), and around Salthouse, and King's, and Queen's Docks during the late eighteenth century (*op cit*, 139).

In form, the eighteenth-century warehouses were largely comparable and were anywhere between four and ten storeys in height, with gabled fronts, and were usually long and narrow in plan. Distinctively, they often had a central pulley below the gabled roof, with the loading doors for each floor positioned below (*ibid*). They were also generally plain and of utilitarian design, containing all the necessary service facilities, but little or no architectural embellishment (Giles and Hawkins 2004, 23-9).

At end of eighteenth century, massive, and imposing, warehouses began to be constructed, which were to set the pattern of nineteenth-century warehouse development, particularly within the dock estate (Sharples 2004, 98). One of these was the Goree Warehouses, built by the Corporation, at the end of Water Street, close to George's Dock, which opened in 1793 (Liverpool City Council 2005, 113). Significantly, its name reflects the trade links with Goree Island, off Senegal, which was probably the largest slave-trading centre on the African coast (*op cit*, 123). This was then followed by the King's Dock Tobacco Warehouse, also built by the Corporation, which stood immediately north-east of King's Dock (*p 54*), next to Wapping. This warehouse was completed in 1792, was designed to contain 7000 hogsheads of tobacco, and formed one of the largest buildings in the town, prior to its partial demolition in 1824, and its eventual replacement by Wapping Dock in the mid-nineteenth century (Ritchie-Noakes 1984, 38, 57, 155; Jarvis 1991a, 60; *Ch 4, p 100*).

The Growth of Maritime Trade and the Development of Liverpool's Hinterland

The reasons behind the dramatic expansion of the eighteenth-century town and port facilities (*see below*) were intimately linked to the growth of eighteenth-century trade, and the expansion of production, which, within Liverpool's immediate hinterland, was spurred on by the advent of the industrial revolution. The increase in Liverpool's trade, particularly in the latter half of eighteenth century, is certainly exemplified by the available figures relating to the combined tonnage of shipping entering and leaving the port. For instance, this initially rose from 36,400 tons, following the completion of the Old Dock, to 60,900 tons in 1752, and then to a massive 450,000 tons at the close of the eighteenth century (Hyde 1971, 235-6).

Trade during the eighteenth century continued to connect Liverpool with local inland and coastal markets, the Irish ports, and also those international markets found in Africa, the Americas, the West Indies, the Mediterranean, and the Baltic. However, the ships used were probably relatively small and of comparable size (up to 200 tons) to those used at the beginning of the eighteenth century (*Ch 2, p 34*). This contrasts markedly with the larger eighteenth-century ships (*c* 400 tons) operating on the east coast between London and Newcastle (Barker 2011, 119). Prominent eighteenth-century goods entering Liverpool's trading network, and being carried by these comparatively small vessels, included salt, coal, textiles, iron, lead, and cheese, derived from its hinterland. Of these goods, coal and salt held particular importance to Liverpool's commercial success (Longmore 2006, 127; Hyde 1971, 27). The export of salt, for example, which was an important feature of the town's late seventeenth-century economy (*Ch 2, p 30*), and which was derived from both the Cheshire saltfields and Liverpool itself, had reached 48,000 tons by 1790, and was mainly sent to America and Ireland (Hyde 1971, 28). Textiles, specifically cotton goods derived from the south Lancashire textile industry, would also prove important in the latter part of the eighteenth century (Longmore 2006, 127). In this instance, the production of cotton goods from the 1780s onwards was a direct result of the industrial revolution, which witnessed the implementation of the factory-based system, most notably in the urban centres of Manchester, Salford, Stockport, Oldham, Rochdale, Bury, and Bolton (Farnie 1992).

Significantly, the expansion of production and concomitant trade within Liverpool's hinterland resulted in various schemes designed to improve the inland routes of communication across Lancashire, Cheshire, and the Midlands, which would again be vital to Liverpool's commercial success. This focused on waterborne transport, and the earliest of these were specifically concerned with improving the navigability of existing natural waterways (Fig 17). Initially, these included improvements to the River Weaver, leading to the opening of the Weaver Navigation in 1732 (Hadfield and Biddle 1970, 40-1), and the Mersey and Irwell Navigation Act of 1720, which by 1734 had connected Manchester with Liverpool (George and Brumhead 2002). Whilst the transportation of salt from the Cheshire saltfields was the dominant driving force behind the development of the Weaver Navigation, this route also allowed the transportation of coal to the Cheshire saltworks from the south-west Lancashire coalfields, which was required for the evaporation of the brine, and, importantly, stimulated pottery production in North Staffordshire (Longmore 2006, 127). Indeed, the rise of the North Staffordshire pottery industry would directly contribute to Liverpool's success as, from the mid-eighteenth century onwards, it acted as the chief port supplying ceramics to the North American colonies (*ibid*).

In contrast, the Mersey and Irwell Navigation was largely instigated by Manchester's textile merchants. These merchants required improved communications for commercial expansion and accordingly they commissioned Liverpool's Old Dock engineer, Thomas Steers, to undertake the preliminary survey of the route (George and Brumhead 2002). Another early scheme, involving improvements to a natural watercourse, was the Sankey Navigation. This opened in 1757 and its implementation was driven by the need to transport coal more efficiently from the St Helens' coalfields to Liverpool, which had previously been via a turnpike road (Barker and Harris 1954, 11-23). Indeed, a cheap supply of coal to Liverpool was paramount to Liverpool's success, as it was required by the majority of the town's eighteenth-century industries (*p 47*). Hence, it is not surprising to find that financial backing for the Sankey Navigation was largely derived from Liverpool's Corporation (*ibid*). Significantly, goods were transported along these early navigations by a specific type of vessel, which became synonymous with Liverpool's maritime history. These are known as the Mersey flats, which were also used to deliver and collect cargoes between the ports along the Irish Sea coast (*Appendix 1*).

The completion of the Sankey Navigation was then immediately followed by the construction of several true canals (Fig 17). The earliest of these was the Bridgewater Canal, constructed between 1759 and

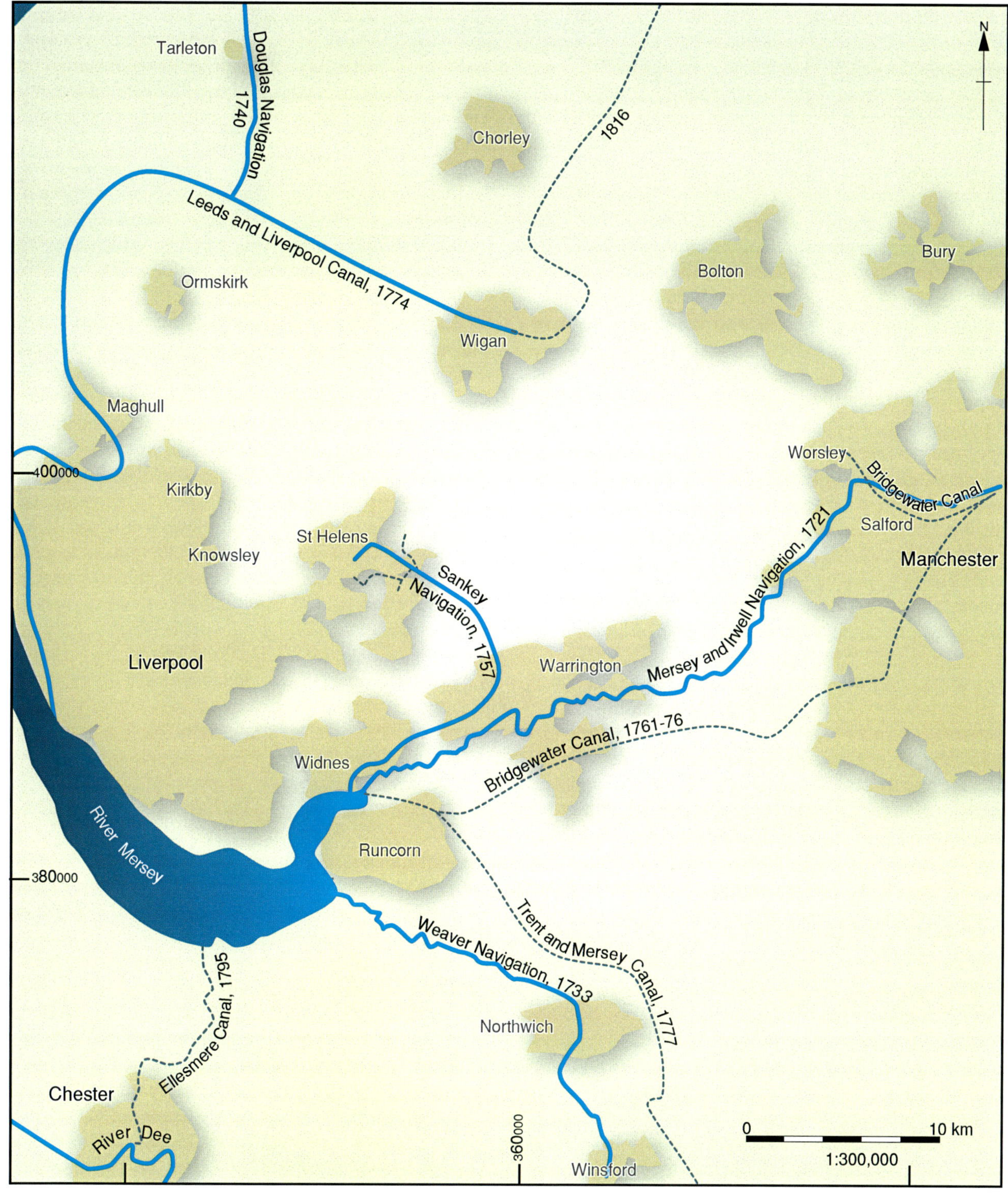

Figure 17: Eighteenth-century river navigations and canals within Liverpool's regional hinterland

1761, which originally extended between the Duke of Bridgewater's coalmines in Worsley and Manchester, though it was later lengthened to link Manchester with Runcorn, and, in turn, the port at Liverpool (Malet 1977). It therefore formed a valuable commercial link between the two emergent centres, which would be vital to their later growth and commercial success. Similarly, the opening of the Trent and Mersey Canal in 1777, which joined with the Bridgewater Canal, formed another important commercial link, this time connecting Liverpool with the Midland potteries and iron industry (Lindsay 1979).

The Leeds to Liverpool Canal scheme was also proposed in the late eighteenth century, and was once again driven by the desire to supply Liverpool with a cheap source of coal, this time derived from the Wigan and West Yorkshire collieries (Longmore 2006,

128). Although the entire scheme was not completed until 1816, the route between Liverpool and Wigan was opened in 1774 (Hadfield and Biddle 1970, 73-4), and its terminus, and associated coal wharf, at the far northern end of the town can be seen on Charles Eyes' map of 1785. The Liverpool to Wigan section of canal also incorporated the earlier Douglas Navigation (*ibid*). This navigation had been promoted by Thomas Steers, the Old Dock engineer, and, when opened in 1742, allowed the movement of coal from Wigan to North Lancashire (*op cit*, 61-2). A final canal forming another component of Liverpool's inland trading network, created in the late eighteenth century, was the Ellesmere Canal, which opened in 1795, between the rivers Mersey and Dee (Wilson 1975). It was originally envisaged that this canal would form part of a larger canal link, which would join the rivers Mersey and Severn, and allow Liverpool access to the coalfields of north-east Wales and the manufacturing centres of the West Midlands. Although this proposed system was never completed, the Ellesmere Canal was joined with the Chester Canal, which eventually led to the formation of the Ellesmere and Chester Canal Company in 1813, and in the mid-nineteenth century both of these became branches of the Shropshire Union Canal (*ibid*; Emery 2005).

Turning to the overseas goods, which formed another significant part of Liverpool's eighteenth-century trade network, these included Baltic timber, linen yarn from Ireland, and a suite of products/items from the West Indies, North America, and also Africa (Hyde 1971, 26; Longmore 2006, 129). In addition, licenced piracy, or privateering, involving the capture of French and Spanish vessels, brought some minor wealth into the eighteenth-century town (Longmore 2006, 130). Of the transatlantic products, sugar, from the West Indies, and tobacco, from North America, were highly significant and the eighteenth-century trade in these commodities built upon the pre-existing trading patterns, which had been established in the late seventeenth century (*Ch 2, p 34*). The importance of the sugar and tobacco trade to the eighteenth-century town cannot be over-estimated since, between 1704 and 1711, the importation of tobacco increased from 600 tons to 1600 tons, with sugar increasing from 760 tons to 1120 tons, whilst 'between 1785 and 1810, annual imports of sugar rose from 16,600 to 48,000 tons, and those of tobacco from 2500 to 8400 tons' (Hyde 1971, 26). It should be stressed, however, that the trade in tobacco did experience a short-lived collapse in the 1720s and 1730s (Longmore 2006, 129).

In addition to sugar and tobacco, there were 23 other principal commodities imported from the West Indies in the eighteenth century (Hyde 1971, 34). Cocoa, coffee, dyewood, and rum formed the more valuable of these and, as with sugar and tobacco, the imports of these commodities into Liverpool increased dramatically in the late eighteenth century (*ibid*). During that century, the West Indies also supplied the main bulk of cotton entering Liverpool, with some imports also arriving from the Mediterranean, though by the early nineteenth century, a large proportion of cotton was instead derived from North America (*ibid*). The importation of cotton was vital to the success of the Lancashire textile industry, and between 1780 and 1800 imports of raw cotton into Lancashire had increased from 5-6,000,000 lb to 50,000,000 lb *per annum*, much of which was via Liverpool's port (Deane and Cole 1962, 52).

During the 1730s and 1740s, the transit of slaves also became a feature of Liverpool's maritime economy. This involved a triangular pattern of trade, whereby Liverpool ships sailed to West Africa to collect slaves, which were then transported to the West Indies and North American colonies, in exchange for colonial products (Hyde 1971, 32). Some indication of the extent and growth of this trade, prior to the abolition of the slave trade in 1807, is provided by the number of known slave traders in the town. For example, in 1730, Liverpool contained 15 known slave traders, which then rose to around 101 in 1753, following the collapse of an earlier monopoly held by the Royal African Company (Longmore 2006, 131-2). The influence of slave trading on Liverpool has been much debated, but it is clear that it permeated the eighteenth-century town, creating wealth, albeit often limited in amount, for its investors, as well as stimulating manufacturing within Liverpool and its hinterland, in order to produce a proportion of the commodities required for the acquisition of slaves (*op cit*, 135; Hyde 1971, 32). In addition, at least some eighteenth-century households in Liverpool contained African servants, and by the 1780s and 1790s, a black population had become firmly established in the town (Belchem and MacRaild 2006, 322).

Although Liverpool's maritime trade, particularly in the period after 1750, increased dramatically, this did mean that the town was subject to the ebbs and flows inherent in global, as well as local, markets. Overseas conflict was one possible source of fluctuation, due to its potential disruptive effects on trade, and also more directly on the port's security. One such conflict was the American War of Independence (1775-83), which appears to have preoccupied the thoughts and actions of Liverpool's Corporation. Moreover, the Corporation appears to have recognised the potential threat to Liverpool as a prominent west-coast transatlantic port, particularly after June 1779, when Spain joined the war. This resulted in the acquisition and stockpiling of gunpowder, and the manning of George's and Queen's Batteries (MMMMAL MDHB/MP/25, 138). Pilots were also sent out into the river to gather intelligence from incoming ships and a light-based warning system was established at Bidstone lighthouse (*ibid*). However, although precautions were taken, this conflict appears to have had limited influence on maritime trade, and between the early 1770s and early 1780s there was still a 60% increase in the amount of ships using Liverpool's port (Ritchie-Noakes 1984, 37). The later French Revolutionary War (1793-1802) also had a similar, limited, effect on the volume of maritime trade entering the port, which between 1793 and 1801 also dramatically increased (*cf* Hyde 1971, 236-7). Although trade was not markedly curtailed between the 1770s and 1800, these two conflicts, particularly the latter, would have constrained, and extended in duration, those civil-engineering projects associated with the eighteenth-century waterfront (*p 54*). For example, they created a shortage of manpower, and increased the price, and reduced the availability, of horses (Jarvis 2011). Supplies of timber also became scarce during these conflicts, and this again made construction of the late eighteenth-century docks problematic, as timber was needed for temporary falsework and cofferdams (*ibid*).

During the late eighteenth century, the town was also subject to two major financial crises. One of these dates to 1793 and was a result of high levels of speculation in foreign produce (Hyde 1971, 36). This led to the bankruptcy of several merchant firms, the closure of one of the town's largest banks, and a halving in the amount of imported raw cotton. This crisis was only finally resolved through the Corporation issuing its own banknotes (*ibid*). The second financial crisis to blight the town dates to 1797, and this followed the restoration of the gold standard in France. Again, as with the earlier crisis, this affected the importation of raw cotton and also the export of piece-goods, and led to bankruptcy (*ibid*).

The 1715-1800 Dock System and Waterfront

General historical development
Throughout the eighteenth century, several new docks and waterfront features were established under the auspices of Thomas Steers (dock engineer 1710-50), Henry Berry (dock engineer 1750-89), and Thomas Morris (dock engineer 1789-99), in response to the rapid increases in maritime trade (Ritchie-Noakes 1984, 95-6). However, it is important to stress that this was not a speculative venture, but was instead based on existing, rather than anticipated, volumes of trade (Jackson 1983, 47). Indeed, as Ritchie-Noakes (1984, 3) notes, 'dock building in the eighteenth century barely kept up with the demands of trade, as the provision of each new dock fed commercial pressures for yet further accommodation'.

Following the construction of the Old Dock, the sequence of reclamation and dock building (Fig 18)

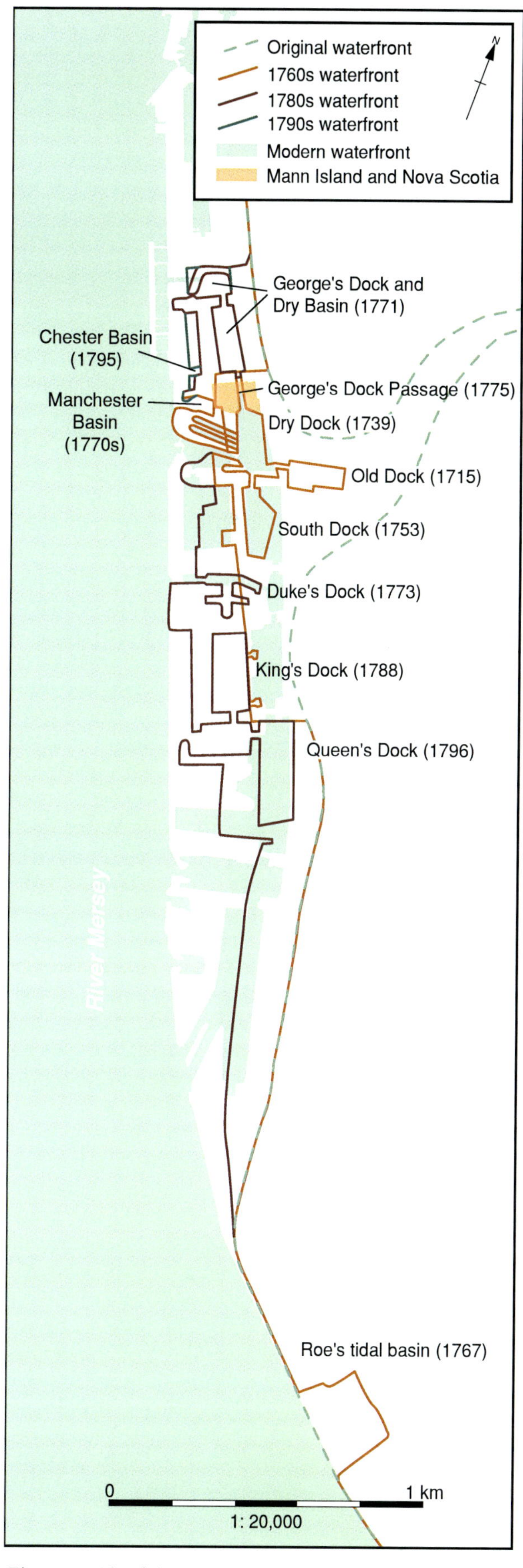

Figure 18: The eighteenth-century dock system and waterfront (© Crown copyright 2014 Ordnance Survey 100005569)

initially began with the establishment of the Dry Dock (later Canning Dock; *p 55*; *Ch 4, p 134*), which opened in 1739 (*op cit*, 19), and the creation of an area of reclaimed land, known as Nova Scotia (*p 60*). A graving dock was also attached to the north-western corner of the Dry Dock in 1746 (*ibid*), which was subsequently converted into George's Dock Passage (*p 71*). This graving dock was now required as the earlier graving dock, attached to the Old Dock's original tidal basin (*Ch 2, p 36*), had been destroyed during the creation of the Dry Dock.

To the south-east of the Old Dock, a second wet dock, known as South Dock (later Salthouse Dock), was then constructed. This opened in 1753, being finally completed in 1754, and was created by the dock engineer Thomas Steers, though, following his death in 1750, it was probably completed by his successor, Henry Berry (*op cit*, 23). This dock was designed to serve John Blackburne's salt refinery, which had been established at the end of the seventeenth century (*Ch 2, p 34*), and it had a slightly irregular plan, enclosing 1.8 ha (4½ acres; *ibid*). An area of reclaimed land located immediately to its west served as a pier and also contained several small buildings which are depicted on Charles Eyes' map of 1785 (Fig 16; *op cit*, 23). However, by the mid-nineteenth-century, this area had been destroyed, following the construction of Albert Dock.

With the completion of South Dock, Liverpool was effectively committed to a further scheme of dock building, in response to the rapid increase in trade in the latter half of the eighteenth century (Jackson 1983, 48). This, therefore, led to a fairly prolific period of dock construction and land reclamation in the 1760s and 1770s (Fig 18). This included the construction of three graving docks (Nos 1-3 Graving Docks), which were added to the western side of the Dry Dock. One of these was constructed around 1756 (Ritchie-Noakes 1984, 23), though it was later obliterated during the construction of Canning Half-tide Basin in the mid-nineteenth century (*Ch 4, p 99*). The other two (later referred to as Canning Graving Docks Nos 1 and 2) were constructed in the late 1760s (*op cit*, 19). In 1762, work also began on the construction of a third wet dock, George's Dock (*p 70*), though, due to unforeseen delays, this dock was not finished until 1771 (*op cit*, 27). This new dock was also associated with a dry, tidal, basin, known as George's Basin, that allowed access into the wet dock from the river (*ibid*), and was later linked to the Dry Dock by George's Dock Passage (*p 71*). This passage utilised the earlier graving dock that lay at the north-western corner of the Dry Dock (*see above*), and also split the area of reclaimed land, known as Nova Scotia, into two (Fig 18).

To the south of the mid-eighteenth-century docks, John Eyes' map (1765) also depicts an area of reclaimed land and two tidal basins, to the south of South Dock (Pl 25). This reclaimed land and also the tidal basin would later be subsumed during the construction of King's and Queen's Docks (*see below*). To the south of these, a small, privately owned, tidal basin was also constructed by Charles Roe in 1767 to serve his copper-smelting works (*op cit*, 61; Fig 18). In the late eighteenth century, this basin was acquired by the Herculaneum Pottery, and would later form the site of Herculaneum Dock (*Ch 5, p 155*). The construction of Roe's basin was then followed by the establishment of Liverpool's first privately owned dock, as opposed to a tidal basin. This was Duke's Dock, which opened in 1773, immediately to the south of South Dock (*p 69*). Other schemes which came into fruition during the 1770s included the beginning of a scheme of land reclamation immediately west of Nova Scotia, which created both Mann Island and Manchester Basin (*p 74*), a precursor to Manchester Dock (*Ch 4, p 103*). As with Duke's Dock, Manchester Basin was designed to cater for inland trade, this time carried by the flats (*Appendix 1*) along the Mersey and Irwell Navigation (*p 50*).

The final phase of eighteenth-century waterfront development occurred during the 1780s and 1790s. In the 1780s, plans were drawn up to construct two new wet docks to the south of Duke's Dock (Fig 18). These, known as the King's and Queen's Docks, were opened in 1788 and 1796 respectively (*op cit*, 37). The larger of these was Queen's Dock, enclosing 3.1 ha (7¾ acres), which was designed by the dock engineer Thomas Morris, and, in the late eighteenth century, had a quay on its eastern side, next to Wapping (*op cit*, 37, fig 28). In contrast, King's Dock enclosed 2.5 ha (6¼ acres) and was the work of Morris's predecessor, Henry Berry (*op cit*, 37). During the 1790s, a large tobacco warehouse (*p 49*) lay to its east, whilst timber yards were established on an area of reclaimed land between it and the river (*op cit*, fig 28). Both docks were also linked to a dry basin, on the southern side of which were two graving docks and a timber yard (*ibid*). The 1790s also saw the creation of Chester Basin (*p 87*), which lay immediately north of Manchester Basin (*see above*). In a similar manner to its sister structure, Chester Basin was a tidal structure, designed to serve inland trade, and it was constructed in response to the opening of the Ellesmere Canal (*p 52*).

The archaeology of the eighteenth-century waterfront

The archaeological investigations on Mann Island (*Ch 1, p 12*) and along the LLC extension (*Ch 1, p 12*) uncovered numerous remains relating to the eighteenth-century docks and waterfront, and these may be allied with the evidence derived from the Liverpool Trams scheme (*Ch 1, p 11*). All of these remains fall within an area lying to the north of the Old Dock and they form elements of the Dry Dock,

George's Dock, and Manchester Basin, and river walls relating to eighteenth-century land reclamation and the creation of quaysides. In addition, they also include remains relating to the occupation of Nova Scotia and Mann Island, an area of reclaimed land between George's Dock and the Dry Dock.

The Dry Dock (late 1730s)

Historical background

By 1737, the Common Council was under increasing pressure from local merchants and ship owners to continue the expansion of the dock estate. Most tellingly, a strongly worded entry from the records of the Common Council, dated 11 January 1737, states that,

> It having been heretofore and is now again represented to this council that there is an absolute necessity to have an addition made to the present dock or bason for light ships to lye in whilst refitting and other necessary uses and a convenient pier to be erected in the open harbour on the north side of the entrance into the present dock, towards Red Cross street... (MMMMAL MDHB/MP/25, 41).

The dock engineer Thomas Steers provided a plan and estimate for the work, which he completed in January 1737. His new plan was for a dock which would encompass at least seven acres (2.83 ha) of waste ground (*op cit*, 41). In 1738, an Act of Parliament was issued which authorised the developments petitioned for by local merchants and ship owners (*op cit*, 73). These initially consisted of further land reclamation, to allow the construction of what was variously called the Dry Dock, the New Pier, and the Dry Pier, which would effectively extend the entrance basin to the Old Dock (Pl 31; *op cit*, 53; Hyde 1971, 73-4; Ritchie-Noakes 1984, 21).

The Committee of Works for the construction of the Dry Dock largely comprised merchants and ship owners, who probably had only a limited knowledge of the techniques required to construct a new dock. However, Thomas Steers was listed as being a member of the committee and it is likely that he played a key role in the proceedings, ensuring the correct implementation of his design. The committee was not only responsible for managing the finances of the project, but was required to source and purchase the necessary materials and also a suitably skilled workforce. With this in mind, advertisements were placed in the public newspapers in Chester and Manchester, for persons willing to undertake mason's work at the Dry Dock (MMMMAL MDHB/MP/25, 48). The records show that the outward wall of the Dry Dock was constructed by Mr Edward Litherland, who proposed,

> to undertake the building of said outward wall and to build the same of Quarry Hill stone at five shillings for every cubical yard sufficiently and workmanlike and to find all (services excepted)... (*ibid*).

The Dry Dock opened in 1739 and, although being a tidal dock, which was dry at low tide, it made it easier for ships to leave the Old Dock and provided protection for shipping during the winter months, when vessels were normally laid up (Jackson 1983, 43). It also provided protection for those ships waiting for favourable conditions to leave the port, and for those waiting to enter the Old Dock, which could only be accessed at high tide (Ritchie-Noakes 1984, 21). Moreover, it alleviated crowding within the Old Dock and, in turn, mitigated against the risk of fire, which would easily spread between ships that were moored at close quarters.

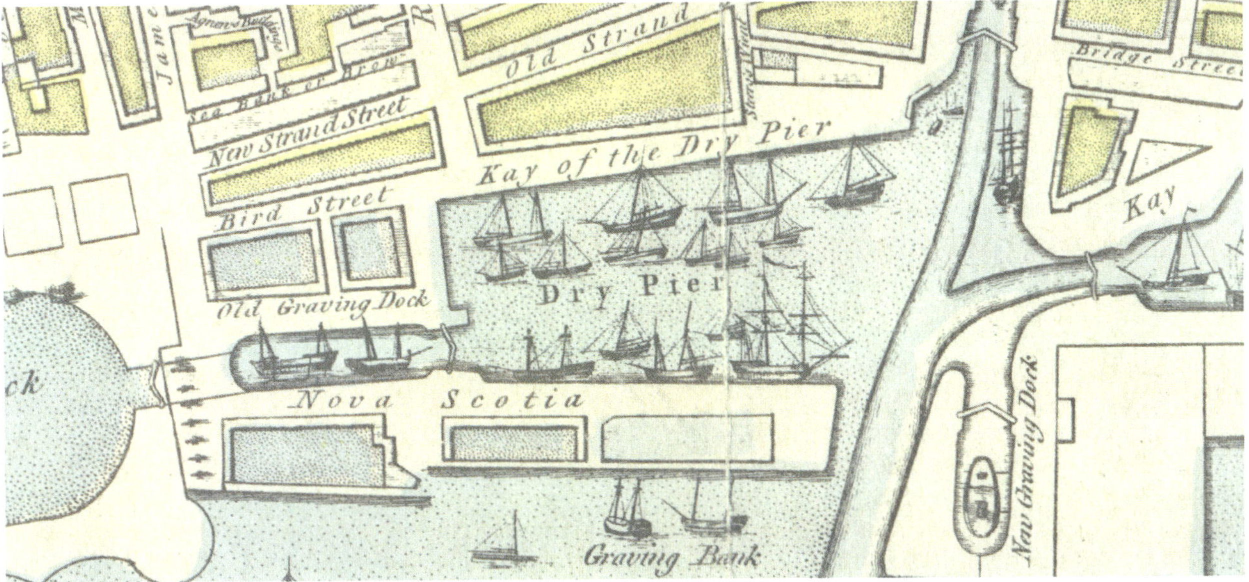

Plate 31: Extract from John Eyes' map of 1765, showing the position and form of the Dry Dock, associated graving docks, and Nova Scotia

The excavations at the Countryside Neptune site on Mann Island (*Ch 1, p 13*) identified a single section of walling (**5270**) which formed the north wall of the Dry Dock (Fig 19). This well-built wall lay beneath the quayside of Canning Dock, which represents a later reconstruction of the Dry Dock dating to the early nineteenth century (*Ch 4, pp 134-5*). The wall was composed of locally quarried yellow sandstone blocks and was 1.35 m wide, with a vertical seaward face. Furthermore, it consisted of a mixture of large rectangular blocks and smaller square blocks, laid irregularly, some of which were bonded with a sandy lime mortar (Pl 32). No coping stones were found, suggesting that the wall had been reduced in height and that some of the upper courses, including the coping stones, had been removed for

reuse elsewhere. The south-facing elevation also had, in places, a series of masons' marks, which were largely geometric in form.

Significantly, the wall exposed at Mann Island was similar to another section of the Dry Dock wall, which was discovered during an archaeological evaluation completed as part of the Liverpool Trams Scheme (*Ch 1, p 11*). Within one of the evaluation trenches (Tr 142; Fig 20), on Strand Street, to the south-east of Mann Island, the rearward side of a yellow sandstone wall (**2325**) was encountered, which formed the back of the eastern wall of the Dry Dock. This wall was constructed of rectangular sandstone blocks, which had also been bonded with a soft yellowish sandy lime mortar. The blocks within this wall were also stepped out with each course

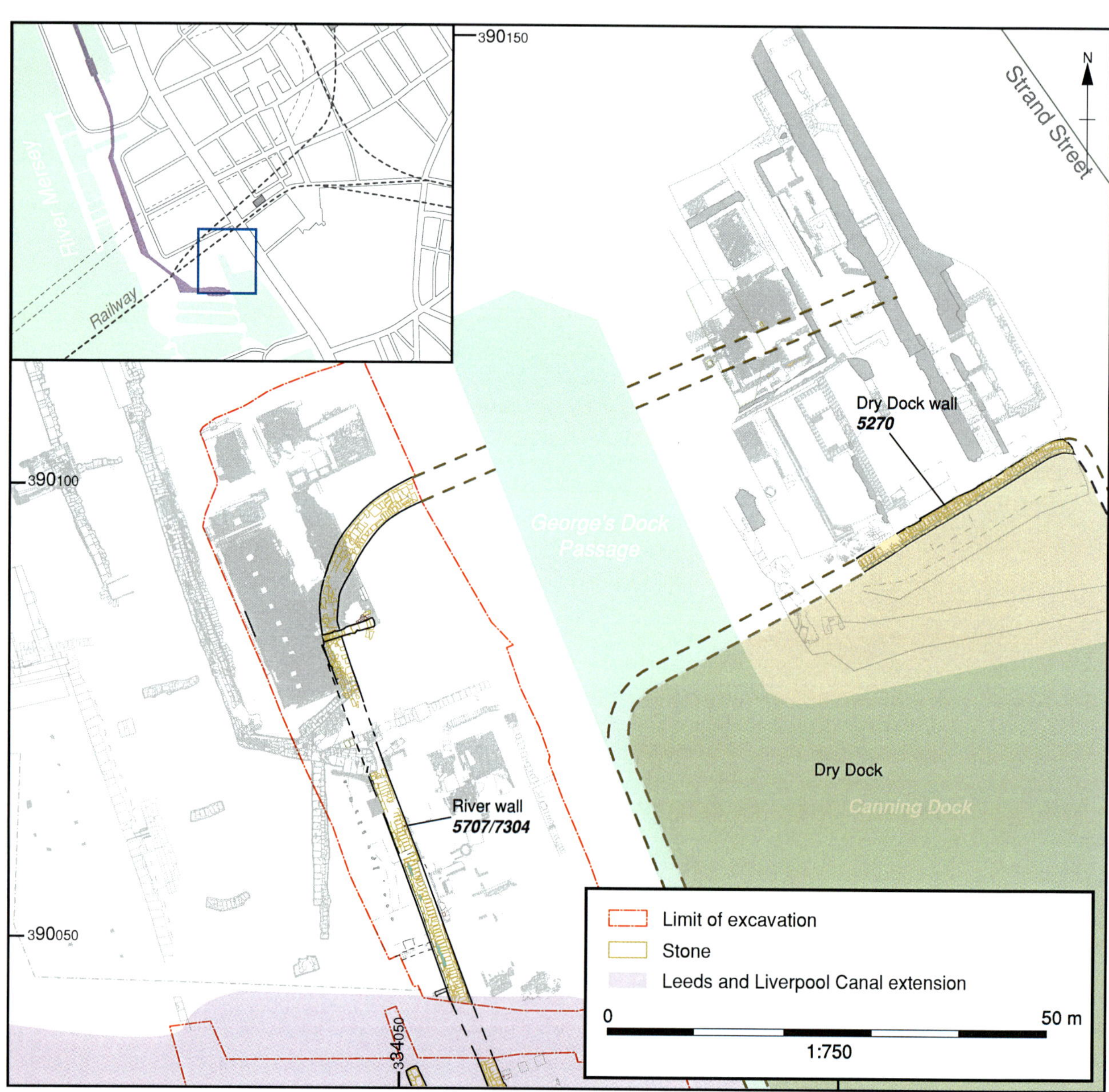

*Figure 19: The position of the Dry Dock wall (**5270**) and river wall (**5707/7304**) at the Countryside Neptune site and within the Leeds and Liverpool Canal (LLC) extension (© Crown copyright 2014 Ordnance Survey 100005569)*

Plate 32: West-facing view across the northern wall of the Dry Dock at the Countryside Neptune site

down, indicating that the wall widened towards its base. Furthermore, another sandstone wall (*2317*) overlay this section of the Dry Dock wall, indicating that it had been rebuilt at a later date. This rebuilding probably dates to the early nineteenth century, and was connected with the creation of Canning Dock (*Ch 4, pp 134-5*).

Although clearly certain sections of the Dry Dock wall survived as below-ground features, it is perhaps significant that no other *in situ* remains of its retaining walls were discovered within the Countryside Neptune site, even though the projected line of the Dock's wall lay within another of the areas (Area A; Fig 7) examined during this excavation. It is therefore possible, at its northern end at least, that during the construction of Canning Dock the majority of the Dry Dock's retaining walls were removed, with stone, perhaps, being reused. Indeed, some support for this was seen during an excavation undertaken across the western wall of Canning Dock, completed as a prelude to the extension of the LLC (*Ch 4, p 135*). This excavation exposed the landward (*ie* west) face of the Canning Dock wall and identified several yellow sandstone blocks within it. These were comparable to those used in the construction of the north wall of the Dry Dock, and may well have been recycled from the western wall of the earlier dock.

Apart from northern wall of the Dry Dock, another substantial yellow sandstone wall (*5707/7304*;

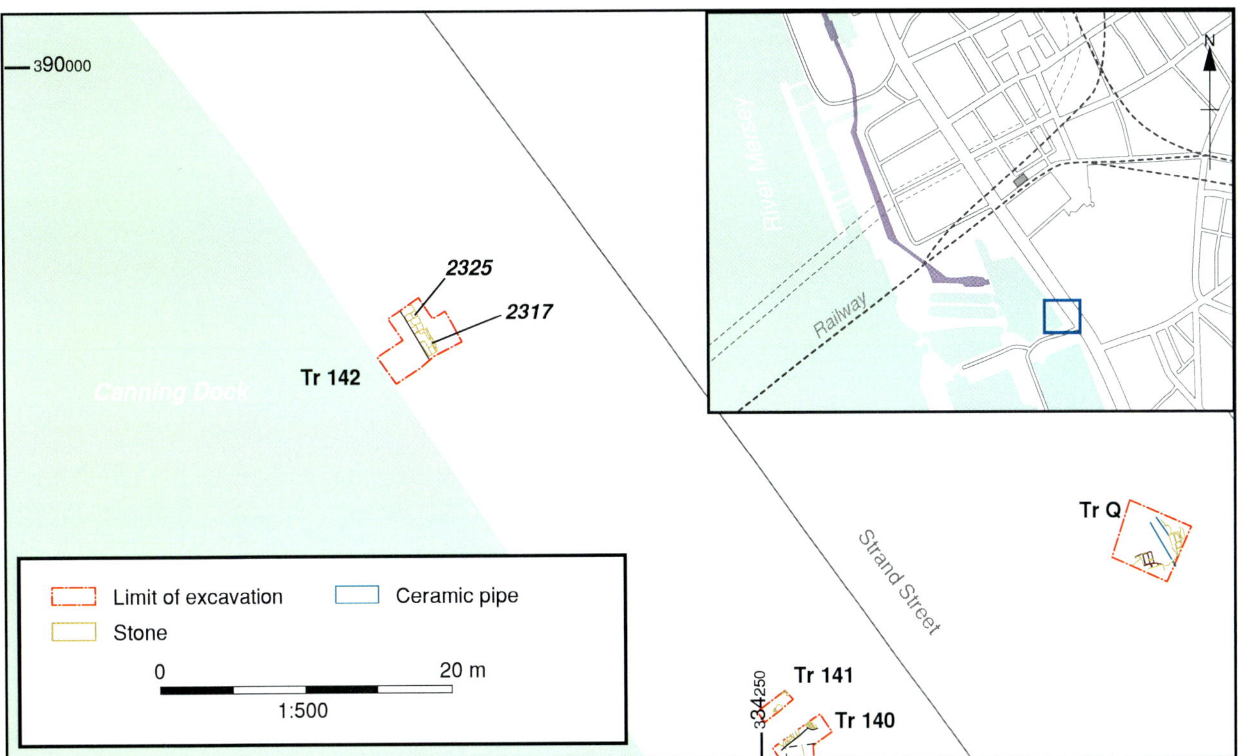

Figure 20: The evaluation trench (Tr 142) excavated close to Canning Dock, as part of the Liverpool Trams Scheme (© Crown copyright 2014 Ordnance Survey 100005569)

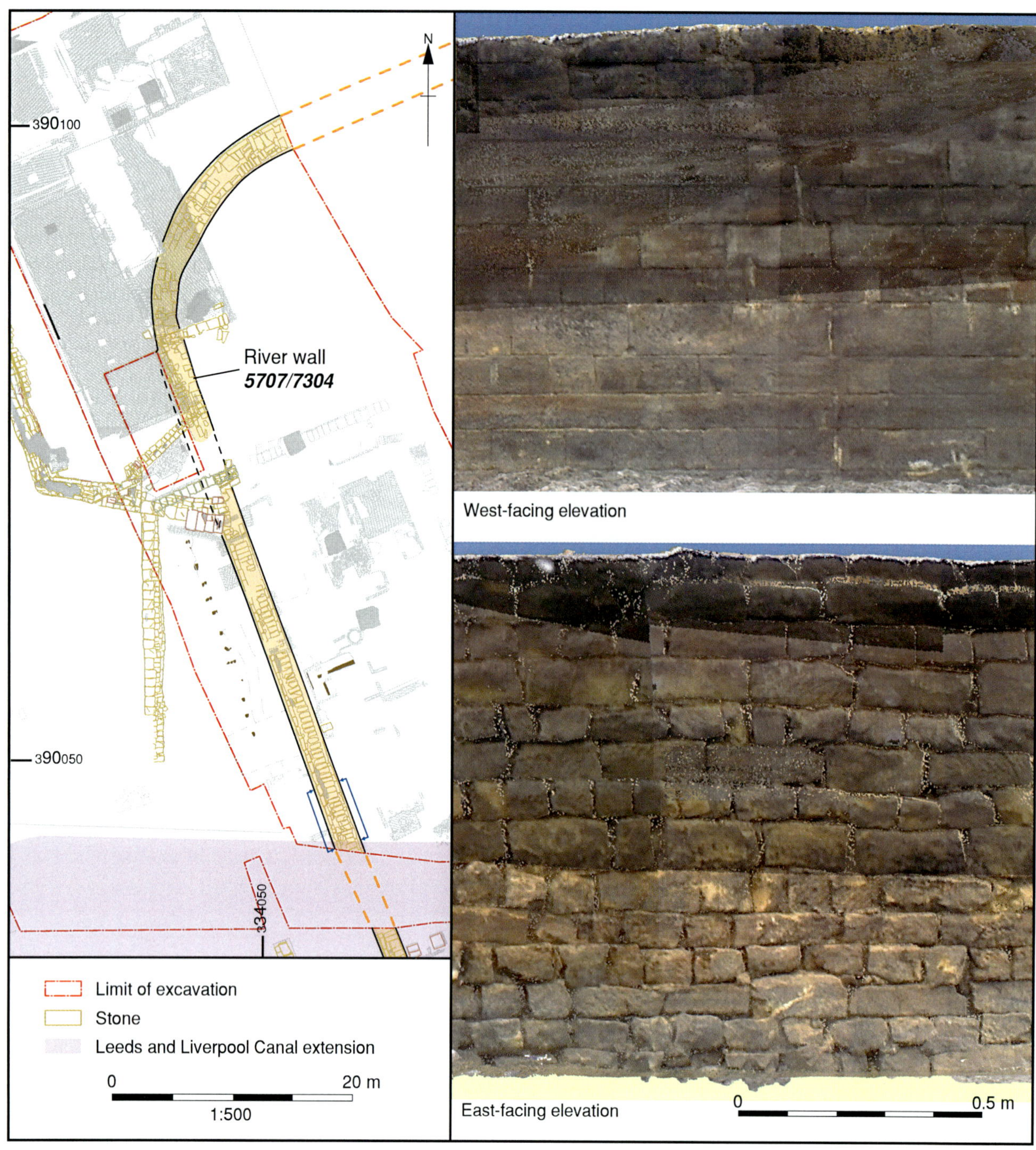

Figure 21: Laser scan of elevations of river wall **5707** *(© Crown copyright 2014 Ordnance Survey 100005569)*

Fig 21) was encountered during the excavations on Mann Island, which was contemporary with the construction of the Dry Dock (Fig 19). This was a river wall, behind which lay an area of reclaimed land, later forming part of Nova Scotia (*p 60*). Moreover, this wall is an excellent early example of a river defence in the newly developed dock system. Indeed, in many respects, it seems to have set the standard for construction and design of the later river-defence walls, which, where uncovered, proved to be close copies.

A north/south-orientated section of this wall (**5707**) was exposed at the Countryside Neptune site, approximately 26 m west of the western wall of Canning Dock. At its northern end, this wall also curved to the east on a radius of approximately 14.3 m, after which it continued eastwards, but beyond the limit of excavation (Pl 33). However, a projection on this east/west alignment demonstrates that it may have lain approximately 31 m north of the north wall (**5270**) of the Dry Dock (Fig 19). The river wall survived some 0.5 m below the ground surface, and was exposed to a depth of 13 courses (Fig 21). The wall was trapezoidal in profile, and was 1.5 m wide at the top, widening to just over 2 m at the bottom of the excavation. The stonework

*Plate 33: River wall **5707**, at the Countryside Neptune site, showing the curving return to the east*

was well-tooled, to a near-flat finish, on the western, waterside elevation, but was only roughly squared on the eastern, construction face. As with the northern wall of the Dry Dock, the west-facing elevation of **5707** was found to have a number of masons' marks (Fig 22). These were mostly geometric in pattern and included crosses, 'L' shapes, triangles, and rotated 'E' shapes, and some were a repeat of the marks used on the stones of the Dry Dock wall. The river wall continued to a depth of at least 1.4 m beneath the formation level of the site and a limited portion of this was examined within a sondage, which was sunk to establish its true depth. The construction technique and bond were found to be the same as in the upper part of the wall but, as a result of water ingress, it was not possible to establish whether or not the wall was sited on top of timber piles, which was a possible foundation technique.

Another section of this north/south-orientated wall (**7304**) was exposed close to Canning Dock, during excavations along the LLC extension (Pl 34). This section of the river wall stood to a height of 5.45 m, though its base was not revealed. The riverward, west-facing, elevation was vertical, and finished to a very high standard. Each block was perfectly faced and laid in a regular bond. A series of masons' marks was identified, but there were no fixings such as mooring pins, nor space for timber fenders. The rear, east, face

*Figure 22: The four main types of masons' marks visible on river wall **5707***

of the wall was much rougher, and was irregularly stepped, such that its lower cross-section was wider, giving it greater structural strength.

Backfilling to create the reclaimed land between the river wall (**5707/7304**) and the west wall of the Dry Dock probably occurred concurrently with the construction of the walls, and would have provided much-needed support for these structures. In Area A of the Countryside Neptune site (Fig 7), this backfilled material comprised layers of coarse sands, silty clays, and coarse, crushed pink sandstone, from which no artefacts were recovered. Tiplines were, however, visible within these backfilled deposits, sloping downwards from east to west. These suggested that, while much of the material was dumped in bulk, there were smaller localised episodes of deposition, which contributed to the land that became part of Nova Scotia (*p 60*). Although some of this material, such as

*Plate 34: River wall **7304**, within the Leeds and Liverpool Canal (LLC) extension, from the west*

the crushed sandstone and coarse sand, may represent quarry waste, it is also possible that originally it was used as ballast and was, in turn, derived from the eighteenth-century ships arriving at the port.

Nova Scotia and Bird Street (1740-72)

Historical background

The area named Nova Scotia on John Eyes' map of 1765 (Fig 16) and Perry's of 1769 would eventually form the heart of 'Sailor-town', a part of Liverpool which housed its largely itinerant maritime population (*p 48*). In terms of its slightly unusual name, this was possibly derived from the Canadian colony of Nova Scotia, particularly as it seems that there was a close connection with this area in the mid-eighteenth century, shown by the founding of a settlement there, in 1759, named 'Liverpool', also situated on a river named the Mersey (Fergusson 1967, 362-3).

The Nova Scotia on Eyes' and Perry's maps may well have begun life as a small island, or bank, of unstable land, created through the repeated dumping of ships' ballast at the outside wall of the intended Dry Dock, following orders made by the Common Council in July 1738 (*op cit*, 50). However, following a meeting of the Common Council on 18 October 1740, this area, to the west of the Dry Dock, was enlarged (*op cit*, 56). This enlargement was through further land reclamation, which created a more useful space, particularly as a

point of disembarkation for cross-river ferries and also for smaller boats unloading locally acquired cargoes which, in turn, helped to reduce traffic moving in and out of the Old Dock.

Initial improvements to this enlarged area occurred in the early 1740s when the northern side of the Dry Dock was partially paved by its landowners, Joseph Bird and Owen Pritchard, with a view to creating a suitable quay (*op cit*, 57). Bird and Pritchard represent the area's first residents and entrepreneurs, and were men of some standing, being involved in the early establishment of the Old Dock and the developing dock estate. Moreover, both served as aldermen and Owen Pritchard was mayor in 1744-5, whilst Joseph Bird took up this position for the years 1746-7. Similarly, both were also heavily involved in the slave trade and held shares in numerous voyages, as well as financing voyages in their own right (Williams 1897, 82). In addition, in 1754 Joseph Bird was formally appointed as superintendent of the Dry Dock and was awarded a wage of 15 guineas *per annum* for carrying out this work (MMMMAL MDHB/MP/82). This role was equivalent to that of the later Dock Master, and Bird's role would have included superintending the docking and sailing of ships, appointing them berths within the dock for the receiving and unloading of cargo, and attending to the dock gates, associated with a new graving dock (*p 61*).

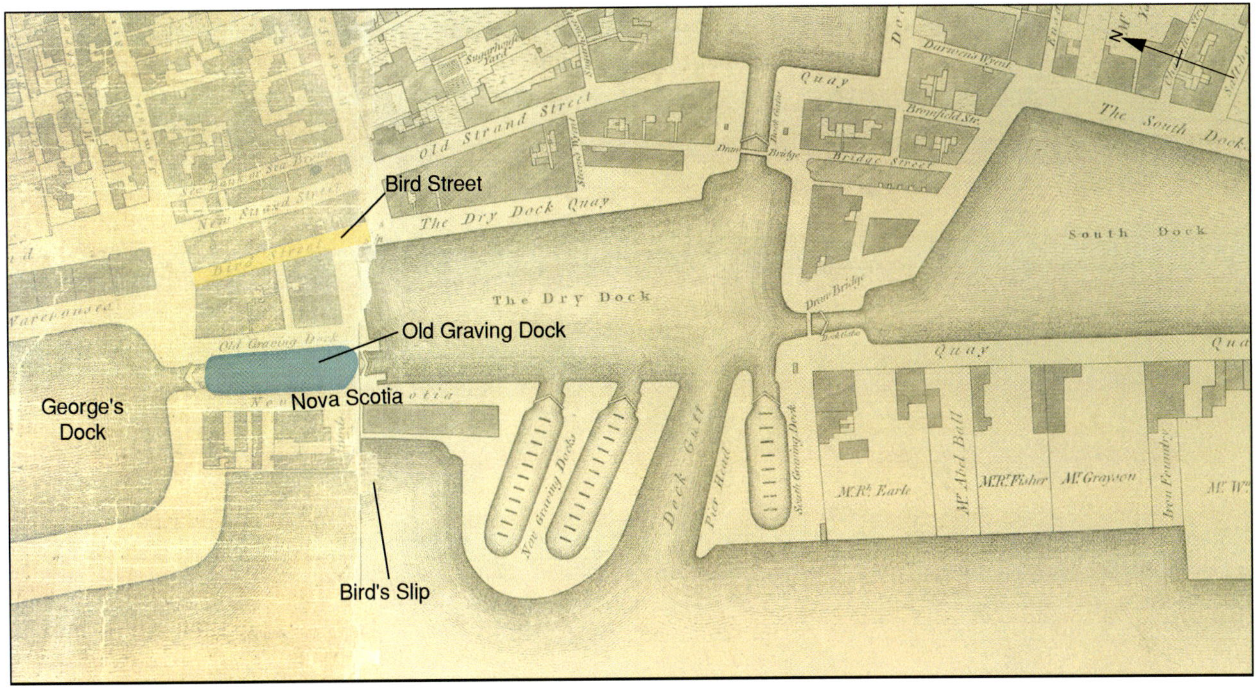

Figure 23: Extract from Perry's map of 1769, showing Nova Scotia and the position of Bird's slip

The dock engineer Thomas Steers was the driving force behind the next stage of the 1740s improvements within this area. On 18 August 1743, Steers entreated the council to pave further areas to the east of Nova Scotia, which was referred to as the 'new pier', and this scheme of work was completed by February 1744 (*op cit*, 61). In 1746, Nova Scotia then became the site of a new graving dock, which opened off the north-western side of the Dry Dock. This was constructed by the Town Corporation and formed a replacement for the Old Dock's original graving dock, which had been destroyed during the construction of the Dry Dock (Ritchie-Noakes 1984, 19). The construction of the new graving dock was again overseen by Thomas Steers, who was supported by a committee of merchants and aldermen. Dock gates would have separated the graving dock from the Dry Dock and would also have acted as a footbridge, allowing access between the areas now found to both the east and west of the graving dock. The area to the west of the graving dock saw further development in 1749 through the addition of a wall and cart road from the slipway at Nova Scotia down to the graving bank (MMMMAL MDHB/MP/25, 69). This bank formed an area of foreshore that was accessible at low tide and its position is denoted on John Eyes' map (1765) as lying immediately west of Nova Scotia (Pl 31).

Fortunately, with reference to the late 1750s and 1760s, the cartographic sources allow a partial insight into the layout and morphology of the two areas on either side of the 1746 graving dock. For example, Perry's map of 1769 indicates that two blocks of properties existed between the graving dock and Bird Street (Fig 23), which was presumably named after the landowner and local resident, Joseph Bird. These properties were separated by a small street. Perry's map also depicts several irregular-shaped buildings contained within two separate plots in the area to the west of the graving dock. These properties were separated by a small street named Irwell Place on later mapping (*cf* Gage's map of 1836). To the south of these properties, Perry's map also shows a linear range fronting Nova Scotia, which was perhaps replaced during the latter part of the eighteenth century by a row of terraces that are depicted on Horwood's map of 1803 (*p 80*). In addition to the properties, Perry's map depicts a small private embayment, known as 'Bird's Slip', again presumably named after the landowner Joseph Bird. Moreover, it is probable that this slip is that mentioned in 1749 (*see above*).

With regard to the function, and also occupancy, of the properties depicted on Perry's map, some details may also be gleaned from documentary sources. For instance, during the 1750s, the area is known to have contained properties which functioned as dwellings, as an advert from the *Liverpool Chronicle and Marine Gazetteer*, dating to 12 June 1757, indicates that Bird Street was the site of

> A new well-built messuage or dwelling house situate(d) on the east side of the graving dock and fronting not only said dock but also a street or alley leading to Bird Street; containing to the front towards the dock about six yards and to the said street or alley about twelve yards and two feet... (*ibid*).

An additional two properties, both previously belonging to Owen Pritchard, are also described as messuages or dwelling houses in the late 1750s, with the first being on the east side of the graving dock and the second on the west side of Bird Street. Both were to be let for 15 guineas *per annum* (*ibid*).

However, a clearer indication of the occupancy of the area is available from the mid-1760s onwards, as a result of the publication of successive street directories. The first of these, Gore's *Liverpool Directory* of 1766, lists six persons as living and working on Bird Street and five persons living and working in Nova Scotia. Many of the trades and occupations listed for the residents reflect the nearness of the dock and seafaring connections; Robert Breckell was a ship's carpenter, Thomas Davis a pilot, and John Robinson, an anchor smith. Joseph Bird is also listed in the 1766 directory as owning properties to the east of the graving dock. One of these properties was his home, whilst the other was a mug warehouse, listed under the ownership of Bird and Jones. A mere three years later, Gore's *Liverpool Directory* of 1769 lists 39 persons as living and working within the area of Nova Scotia and Bird Street. This record clearly highlights the types of people there, and the businesses being conducted in the area, although it does not provide an address for each individual, merely stating which street the person lived/worked on. Persons listed as living in Nova Scotia tend to be those involved in shipping; for instance, John Bibby and Henry Brewer both resided in Nova Scotia and are listed as pilots. William Chapman, a mariner, lived on the west (the Nova Scotia side) of the graving dock, as did Robert Lee, a ship's pilot. Persons living and working on Bird Street tended to be those employed in trades or manufacture: for example, Thomas Clucas (tailor); Cope and Wright (ironmongers); Richard Hill (tobacconist); John Lawrence (flax dresser); and William West (ship's broker).

In *c* 1772, a further development within the area of Nova Scotia included the establishment of a quay by Henry Berry (Ritchie-Noakes 1984, 35). Although the position of this quay is not depicted on eighteenth-century mapping, it is known to have been situated to the west of the Dry Dock, close to the area that would later form Manchester Basin (*ibid; p 74*). Documentary evidence also indicates that it acted as a coal wharf and contained a weighing engine (*ibid*).

Archaeological evidence
The documentary evidence suggests that, following the construction of the Dry Dock, further land reclamation was undertaken during the 1740s (*p 61*). Significantly, direct evidence for this was uncovered at the Countryside Neptune site. This evidence took the form of a yellow sandstone river wall (**7638**), which bounded the reclaimed land dating to this period (Fig 24). This wall was, on the whole, orientated north-north-west/south-south-east, though its southern end was angled eastwards to enable it to join to the earlier river wall (**5707**), whose construction was contemporary with the Dry Dock (*pp 57-8*). John Eyes' map (1765; Pl 31) suggests that river wall **7638** extended approximately 90 m north from the point where it joined wall **5707**, and then turned eastwards in order to bound a small area of reclaimed land. This land was to the north of the graving dock, which had been constructed in *c* 1746 (*p 61*), and the presence of arrows on Eyes' map suggests that it sloped downwards to the north, to form a ramp. This ramp and, by implication, the northern part of wall **7638** were subsequently subsumed during the construction of the quay at the south-western corner of George's Dock (*p 70*).

Wall **7638** was constructed from well-tooled yellow sandstone blocks, arranged in an irregular bond without any evidence of mortar, and was backed by a mixture of stepped rubble and ashlar stone walling in the same material (Pl 35). Invariably, the ashlar masonry at the back face of the wall was not as cleanly worked as the stones comprising the face; however, many stones presented evidence of neat lines of toolmarks and squared-off edges. The narrow, rough steps at the back face of the wall created a rudimentary and continuous counterfort. The space between it and its predecessor (**5707**) was filled with layers of coarse sands, silty clays, and possible sandstone quarry waste, and again it is likely that some of this material may have been obtained by the carefully directed discharge of ships' ballast as they put into port. Some of this reclamation material was industrial waste, indicated by a sizable dump of pottery, consisting of 47.74% by weight of the total assemblage of sugar wares recovered from the Countryside Neptune site (*Ch 6, p 207*).

Wall **7638** also exhibited numerous repairs, one of which, approximately 12 m from the northern limit, was quite substantial, with a much more irregular bond type, suggesting that at some point a section of the wall, measuring around 8 m in length (and through its full thickness), had been breached. It is not known whether this repair was carried out after storm damage, or as maintenance to an area which had suffered badly from the long-term effects of water and mechanical erosion.

Another eighteenth-century wall (**7735**; Fig 24; Pl 36) was also discovered at the Countryside Neptune site, which butted against river wall **7638** (Pl 37). This wall appears to have formed an element of Bird's Slip, a small private embayment, which is marked on

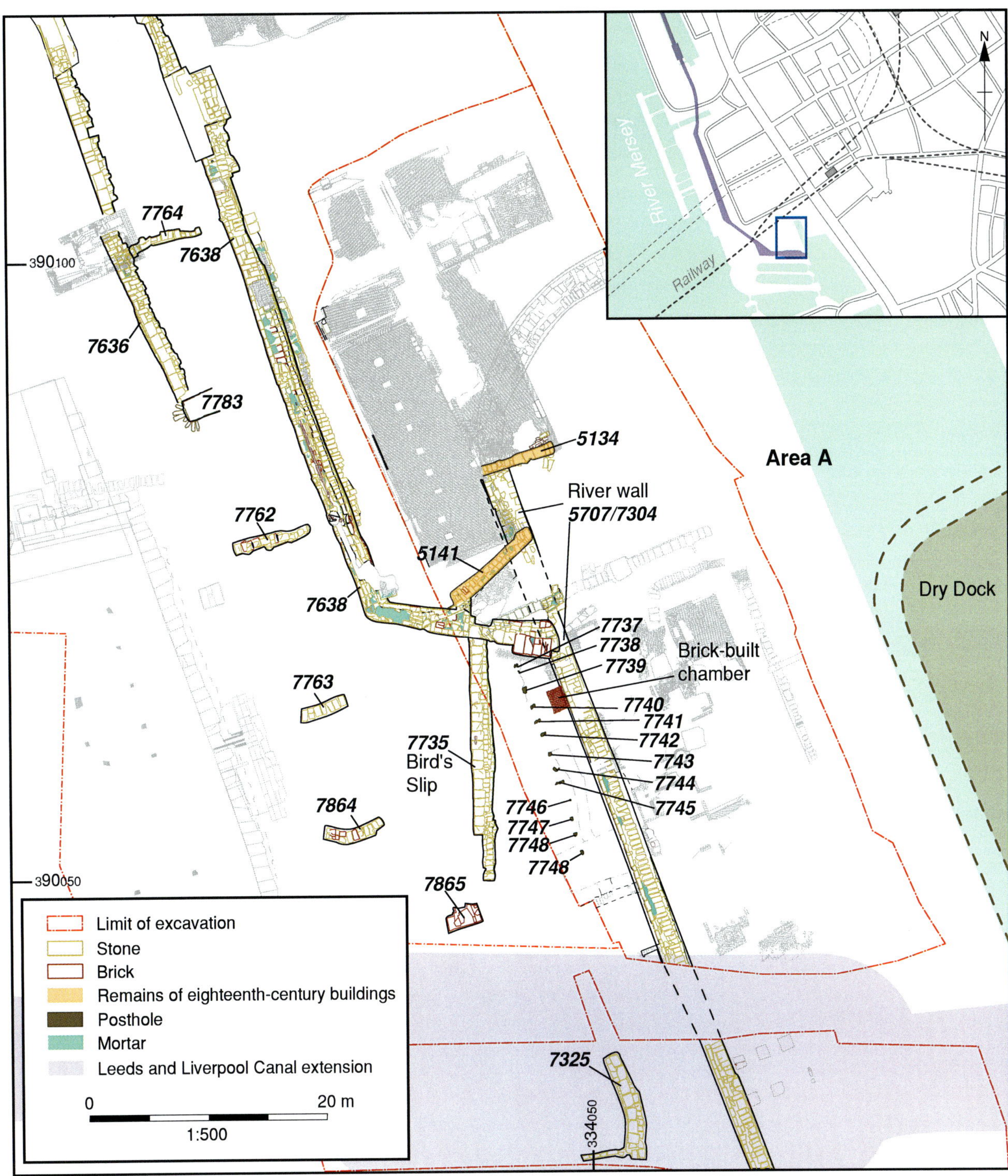

Figure 24: Mid- to late eighteenth-century features at the Countryside Neptune site and within the Leeds and Liverpool Canal (LLC) extension (© Crown copyright 2014 Ordnance Survey 100005569)

John Eyes' map of 1765 and Perry's of 1769 (Pl 31; Fig 23), and which is also mentioned in 1749 (*p 61*). This wall sloped downwards from north to south, was *c* 1.6 m wide at the limit of excavation (Pl 38), and was probably intended to facilitate unloading from the foreshore.

A further, southerly, element of Bird's Slip was also uncovered during the excavations completed during the extension of the LLC. This element comprised a yellow sandstone wall (**7325**; Fig 24), which was constructed upon a layer of compact, grey, gritty sand of undetermined depth, probably forming part of the foreshore. The sandstone blocks used in its construction, especially the coping stones, were generally crudely finished and irregular in size and coursing (Pl 39). The west-facing elevation provided examples of a few, but varied, masons' marks, including one in the shape of an anchor.

*Plate 35: West-facing elevation of river wall **7638**, at the Countryside Neptune site*

*Plate 36: West-facing elevation of slip wall **7735**, at the Countryside Neptune site*

*Plate 37: The Countryside Neptune site, showing the interface of sea walls **5707**, **7636**, **7735**, and **7638***

Plate 38: Three-dimensional laser-scan survey of Bird's Slip

*Plate 39: Wall **7325**, within the Leeds and Liverpool Canal (LLC) extension, from the east*

In addition to the walling of Bird's Slip, a line of vertical wooden posts (**7737-49**) was also discovered, which were aligned parallel to river wall **5707**, rather than the slipway (Fig 24; Pl 40). In total, 18 posts were identified and all appeared to have been roughly hewn. Removal of two of the timbers, from the northern end of the group, showed that their bottoms had been shaped into four-sided points to facilitate driving them into the river bed. The line of timbers was not found to continue to the north of the line of

Plate 40: The alignment of posts associated with Bird's Slip, at the Countryside Neptune site, from the south-west

*Plate 41: Wall **7636** and structure **7783**, from the west*

wall *7638*, suggesting that the timbers were put in place following the construction of this wall. The presence of this wall also created a sheltered area to the north of the graving bank (*p 61*) and would have presented a useful place to moor smaller ships and river-based traffic that were not destined for the Old Dock. Bird's Slip, constructed a short time after the completion of river wall *7638*, provided additional shelter to this mooring as well as a slipway for foot traffic, enabling the movement of goods arriving and departing from the numerous boathouses which sprung up on Nova Scotia in the 1760s. Both features are of a scale and character appropriate for estuarine or small-scale coastal trading (*cf* Stammers 2007, 37-49).

To the north-west of Bird's Slip, another wall (*7636*) was discovered, during the excavation at the Countryside Neptune site, parallel with river wall *7638* and some 7 m west (Fig 24). Although this wall does not appear on any of the historical maps, it was seemingly constructed between the production of Perry's map in 1769 and that of Charles Eyes in 1785. Given its position in relation to those features plotted on Perry's map (Fig 23), it is likely that it joined with the quayside positioned at the far south-western corner of George's Dock (*p 70*). This was confirmed, in some measure, by a slight westwards curve that was evident at the far northern end of the wall, which suggests that it joined with an area of reclaimed land that lay to the north-west of the Countryside Neptune site.

The wall was composed of yellow sandstone and extended for almost 40 m. Its construction was similar to wall *7638*, with a well-tooled finish to the regularly coursed stone blocks of the riverward face, and a less even rubble build on the landward side. At its southern end, its toe terminated in an earth-filled rectilinear wooden construction (*7783*; Fig 24), consisting of oak planks set on edge, varying in width from 0.2 m to 0.54 m (Pl 41). The function of this structure was not determined; however, it appeared to be poorly constructed and was likely to be an incidental or temporary construct.

In terms of its function, it seems likely that wall *7636* was a slipway, leading to the quay at the south-western corner of George's Dock, that allowed vessels, with some effort, to take on and discharge cargo at all levels of the tide. Moreover, one possibility is that it was constructed in *c* 1772 by Henry Berry and related to the establishment of a quay, which functioned as a coal wharf (*p 62*). However, this quay was a short-lived feature and its putative slipway was seemingly subsumed, probably in the mid-1770s, during land reclamation associated with the creation of Manchester Basin and Mann Island (*p 74*).

Between walls *7636* and *7638*, a row of yellow sandstone blocks (*7764*) was revealed beneath the backfill, which was aligned perpendicular to both walls, and was no more than 0.7 m wide (Pl 42; Fig 24). This was one of a series of such

*Plate 42: The row of sandstone blocks (**7764**) between river wall **7638** and slip **7636***

implies that they post-date the second river wall (*7638*), and pre-date slip wall *7636*. Their closely comparable alignment, construction, and orientation suggests they were related and all fulfilled a similar purpose. Although this purpose was not entirely apparent, it is possible that they were somehow connected with the construction of slip wall *7636*. A further possibility is that these parallel lines of sandstone were used as hard standings or supports for the laying down of timbers, which then allowed a safe footway out onto the graving bank at low tide. Essentially, they may have provided the basis for a temporary roadway, which would have allowed timbers and other material to be carried safely across the soft silts to the graving bank, where ships were careened for repair. Once the process was completed, or at the rising tide, the timber boards could be lifted, leaving behind the stone platforms.

To the east of river wall *7638*, the partial, heavily truncated, remains of eighteenth-century buildings were also exposed during the excavation undertaken at the Countryside Neptune site, and these appear to equate with some of those buildings which are first plotted on John Eyes' map of 1765 (Pl 31). These remains comprised two lengths of walling (*5134* and *5141*), constructed in yellow sandstone, comparable to the material used to construct the adjacent river walls (Fig 24; Pl 43). Indeed, given the variations in

constructions, with four more revealed to the south (*7762*, *7763*, *7864*, and *7865*), at no fixed interval, but all on the same east/west alignment and on the same north/south axis. The level of the upper surfaces of these features was comparable with the base of the first and second river walls, although their position

*Plate 43: The northern end of Nova Scotia and the early angled yellow sandstone wall, **5141** (centre left), from the south-east*

levels and the missing coping stones, it is not unlikely that, as the river walls were superseded and fell out of use, through the progression of the land-reclamation process, the top courses of stone were reused for local construction. Perry's map of 1769 (Fig 23) suggests that wall *5134* formed the southern gable wall of an irregular-shaped building, which lay within the central block of properties on Nova Scotia during this period, and which also fronted the graving dock. Similarly, John Eyes' and Perry's maps suggest that wall *5141* defined the southern end of an adjacent eighteenth-century building, which directly fronted Bird's Slip. With regard to this latter building, it is also possible that river wall *7638* formed the foundation course for its western wall, and this would certainly explain the unusual appearance of its upper course. In addition, this building may well have been ravaged by fire, which led to its later reconstruction in the latter part of the eighteenth century (*p 82*).

Duke's Dock (1765-1773)

Historical background

Duke's Dock formed a private dock that was owned by Francis Egerton, the third Duke of Bridgewater. Initially, in 1765, the Duke leased a small parcel of land to the south of Salthouse Dock, which was then expanded westwards, across the Mersey foreshore, through the process of land reclamation. This phase of reclamation was completed under the supervision of John Gilbert, who acted as the Duke's resident canal engineer during this period (Malet 1977, 38; Ritchie-Noakes 1984, 31). The dock itself was largely constructed within this area of reclaimed land and was probably also designed by John Gilbert (Ritchie-Noakes 1984, 31). It was finally completed in 1773, under the supervision of Thomas Wallwork (*ibid*).

Duke's Dock formed a half-tide dock, which was entered through a tidal passage (Pl 44). It had a narrow rectangular form and therefore, in this respect, it was more akin to a canal terminus and wharf, as opposed to a maritime dock (*ibid*). It was designed to serve inland trade, specifically that carried via the Bridgewater and Trent and Mersey canals (*p 51*), and its main focus was on the transportation of cotton and foodstuffs, notably grain, which was brought to

Duke's Dock from the surrounding maritime docks (*ibid*). Once the products had been transferred to this canal dock, they were loaded onto the Duke's own flats and barges, which were slightly smaller in size than the Mersey flats (*Appendix 1*), measuring about 45 ft (13.7 m) in length and carrying *c* 30 tons of cargo (*op cit*, 33). In order to assist the process of transportation, a quayside warehouse was built at Duke's Dock by Peter Hewitt & Co. This opened in 1783 and represented an early example of such a warehouse that was not separated from the dock by a public thoroughfare (*op cit*, 31; *p 49*). In addition to this, from its inception Duke's Dock was also flanked by timber yards, which

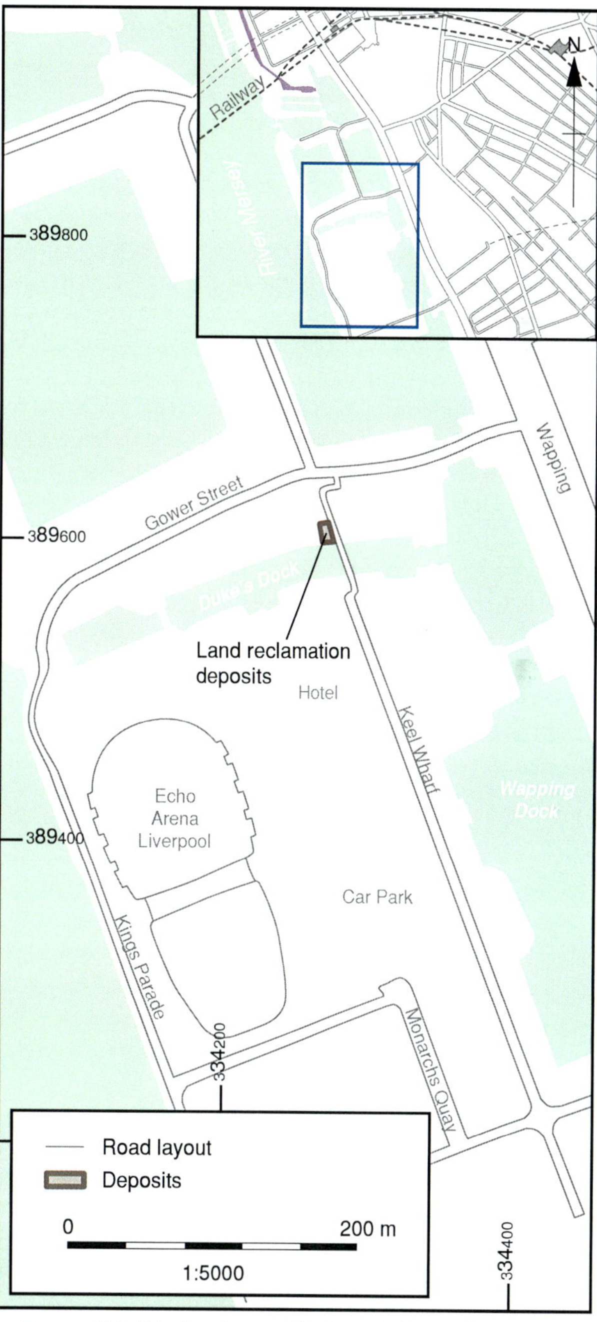

Figure 25: The location of the late eighteenth-century land reclamation deposits identified at Duke's Dock (© Crown copyright 2014 Ordnance Survey 100005569)

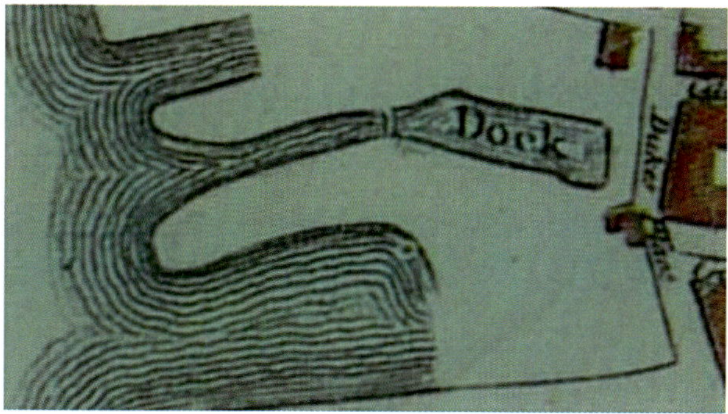

Plate 44: Extract from Stockdale's map of 1795, showing Duke's Dock

stored imported timber received from the adjacent docks, ready for inland transportation.

Archaeological evidence
During the watching brief at Duke's Dock (*Ch 1, p 12*), a land-reclamation deposit was recorded on its northern quayside (Fig 25), which was probably laid down between 1765 and the early 1770s. It comprised a *c* 2 m-thick deposit of sand, sandstone rubble, and occasional handmade brick fragments, which overlay a black silty sandy gravel. This gravel represents a natural deposit that lay at the early waterfront, indicating that the foreshore in this area was originally gently sloping, which would undoubtedly have assisted in the process of eighteenth-century land reclamation.

George's Dock (late 1760s-79)
Historical background
From 1766 onwards, the north-facing aspect of the port underwent radical alterations, with Henry Berry overseeing further expansion of the dock estate. The next major development of the docks was the construction of a new river wall, known as 'Sea Strand' (MMMMAL MDHB/MP/25, 109), with reclamation behind it, to permit work to build Townside Dock, which would later be known as St George's Dock, and latterly as George's Dock. There is very little certain evidence for the condition of the Mersey foreshore prior to this, since John Eyes' map of 1765 interpolates the conjectured layout of the new dock. Indeed, the inclusion of proposed works is not an uncommon feature of Liverpool's historical mapping, particularly at such times of great change and expansion.

The construction work immediately encountered a number of difficulties, including serious storm damage,

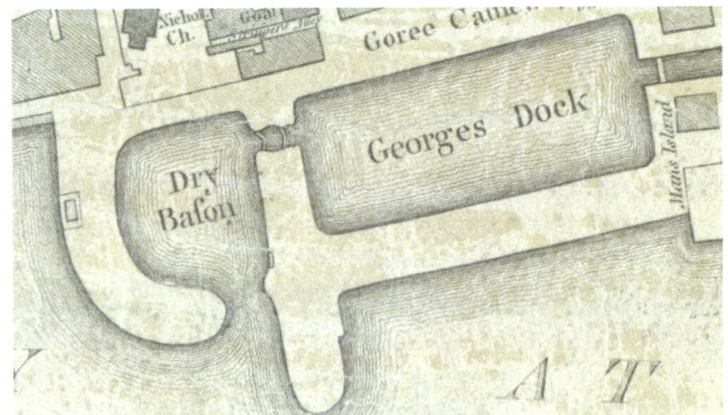

Plate 45: Extract from Charles Eyes' map of 1785, showing George's Dock and Basin, and George's Dock Passage

which destroyed the new river wall, and forced a delay in further works until 1767 (Hyde 1971, 74-5; Ritchie-Noakes 1984, 27). In 1770, the Common Council ordered that a draft view and estimate be made for enclosing a parcel of land (the area now known as Pier Head) to the west of the new dock from out of the sea or river (MMMMAL MDHB/MP/25, 109); following this, Henry Berry was authorised by the council to lease a piece of ground at Quarry Hill to fulfil the construction needs of the latest public works (*ibid*).

The completed dock was eventually opened in 1771 at a cost of £21,000, and despite the expense, this dock now offered an expansive 2460 square yards (2249.4 m^2) of enclosed water, with a quay measuring 700 yards (640 m) long (Lewis 1831, 101). The new dock did not stand alone at the northern limit of the port, as it was paired with a spacious Dry Basin. This latter feature is depicted on Charles Eyes' map of 1785 (Pl 45), and is also visible on a nineteenth-century engraving, which is a copy of a drawing dating to 1797 (Herdman 1878, 18; Pl 46).

Plate 46: A 1797 view of George's Dock Basin and the north-west quay of George's Dock, reproduced by W G Herdman (1878, pl IX; by courtesy of the University of Liverpool Library SPEC Y87.5.41v1)

In 1775, the Minutes of the Common Council note that a committee had been formed to oversee 'the destroying of one Dry Dock for the use and making of a passage or entrance from out of the Dry Pier (the Dry Dock) and into the new or George's Dock (MMMMAL MDHB/MP/25, 129), indicating that George's Dock was not originally linked to the Dry Dock. The new link was formed by reusing the channel formerly created by the graving dock at the northern end of The Dry Dock, and became known as George's Dock Passage (Ritchie-Noakes 1984, 19, 27). During its construction, land to the west of George's Dock was also paved to a width of 14 ft (4.26 m) to increase the quay and landing space for goods (MMMMAL MDHB/MP/25, 130).

In 1779, further land reclamation took place, extending the pier just to the south of the entrance to George's Dock Basin (*op cit*, 137), which was probably intended to create a sheltering promontory to protect the ships as they turned into the open basin. The form of this completed pier is depicted on Charles Eyes' map of 1785 (Pl 45).

Archaeological evidence
Although no actual remains of George's Dock, or the 'Sea Strand' river wall complementing it, were uncovered, as these lay beyond the limit of the route of the LLC extension, small portions of George's Dock Dry Basin and George's Dock Passage were revealed. In addition, several structures were excavated which

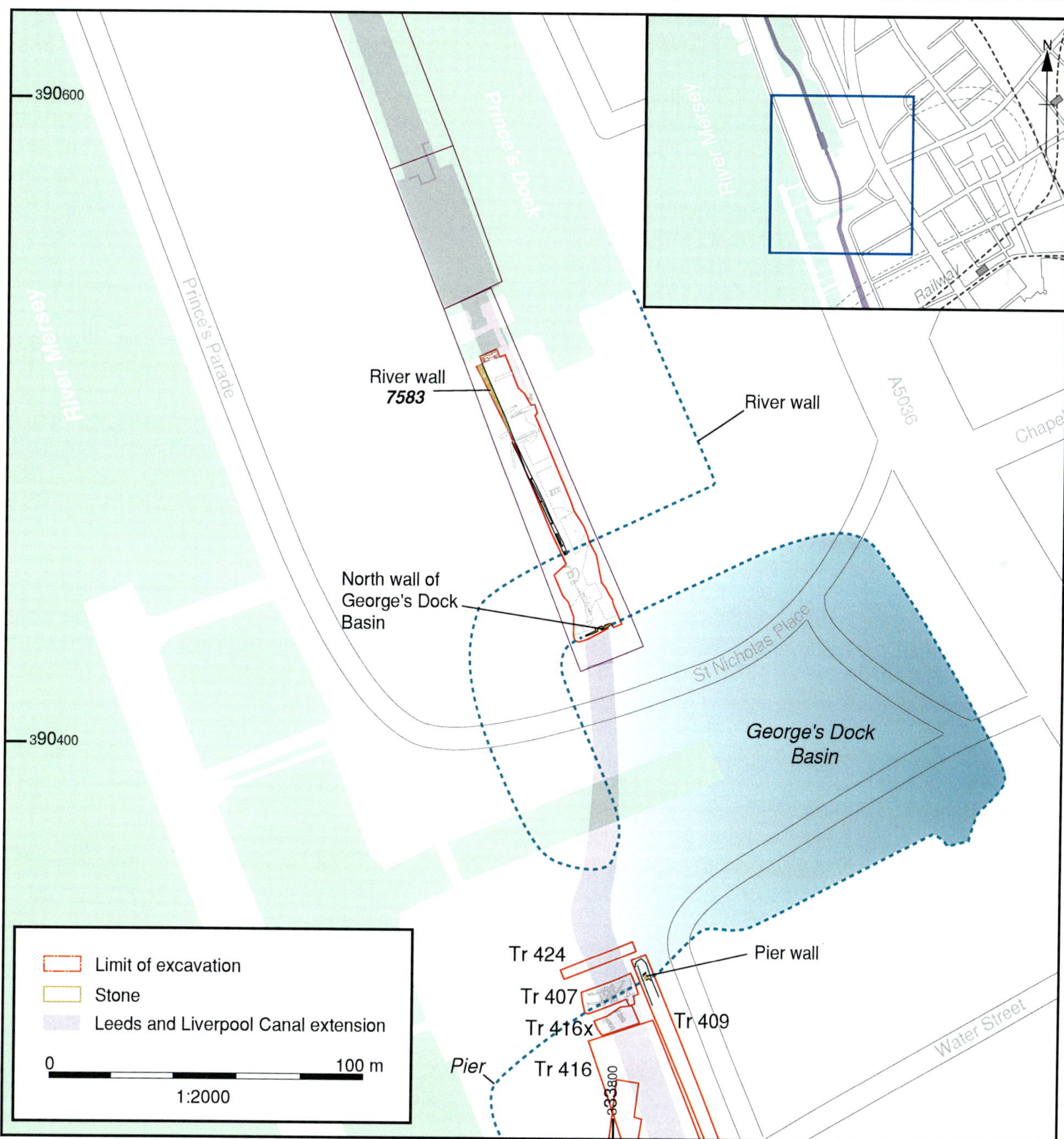

Figure 26: Eighteenth-century features in the Leeds and Liverpool Canal (LLC) extension between Pier Head and Prince's Dock
(© Crown copyright 2014 Ordnance Survey 100005569)

Plate 47: The northern wall of George's Dock Basin and its recess, in the Leeds and Liverpool Canal extension (LLC), from the south

appear to have formed elements of the pier that was added in 1779 to the south of the entrance to George's Dock Basin (*p 71*).

The element of George's Dock Dry Basin that was exposed during excavation along the extension to the LLC, between Pier Head and Prince's Dock, formed the north wall of the basin (Fig 26). This wall was partly composed of yellow sandstone blocks, forming its original elements. However, on the whole, it was constructed in pink sandstone, suggesting that it had been repaired at a later date, and this might have been undertaken during the rebuilding of the walls of George's Dock in the early 1820s (*Ch 4, p 97*). To its rear, deposits of red sandstone fragments, of unknown origin, were present, forming backfill dumped during the construction of the basin. In addition, a sandstone- and brick-built recess was revealed within one section of this wall and, although there was no clear evidence of its purpose, it may have served to protect a ladder for access to the lower levels of the

basin at low tide (Pl 47). The foot of the rear face of the wall was stepped out, indicative of improved engineering (Pl 48). It was not entirely certain that this was an original build, although this is implied by the execution of the lower levels in yellow sandstone, similar to the rest of the wall.

Other remains associated with George's Dock Dry Basin included a yellow sandstone wall exposed in Tr 407 and Tr 409, excavated within and adjacent to the footprint of the LLC extension, which defined the northern side of the 1779 pier (Fig 27). Intriguingly, immediately south of this wall, two parallel dry-stone walls (**5520** and **5521**) were also revealed in Tr 416x, which were orientated north-west/south-east. These were both constructed from yellow sandstone ashlar masonry, and may well have acted as buttresses to the walls of the 1779 pier (Pl 49). Although the decision leading to their installation has not been recorded, given that the pier projected into the tidal stream, there is a clear engineering imperative for their presence.

Plate 48: The rear face of the northern wall of George's Dock Basin, in the Leeds and Liverpool Canal extension (LLC), from the north

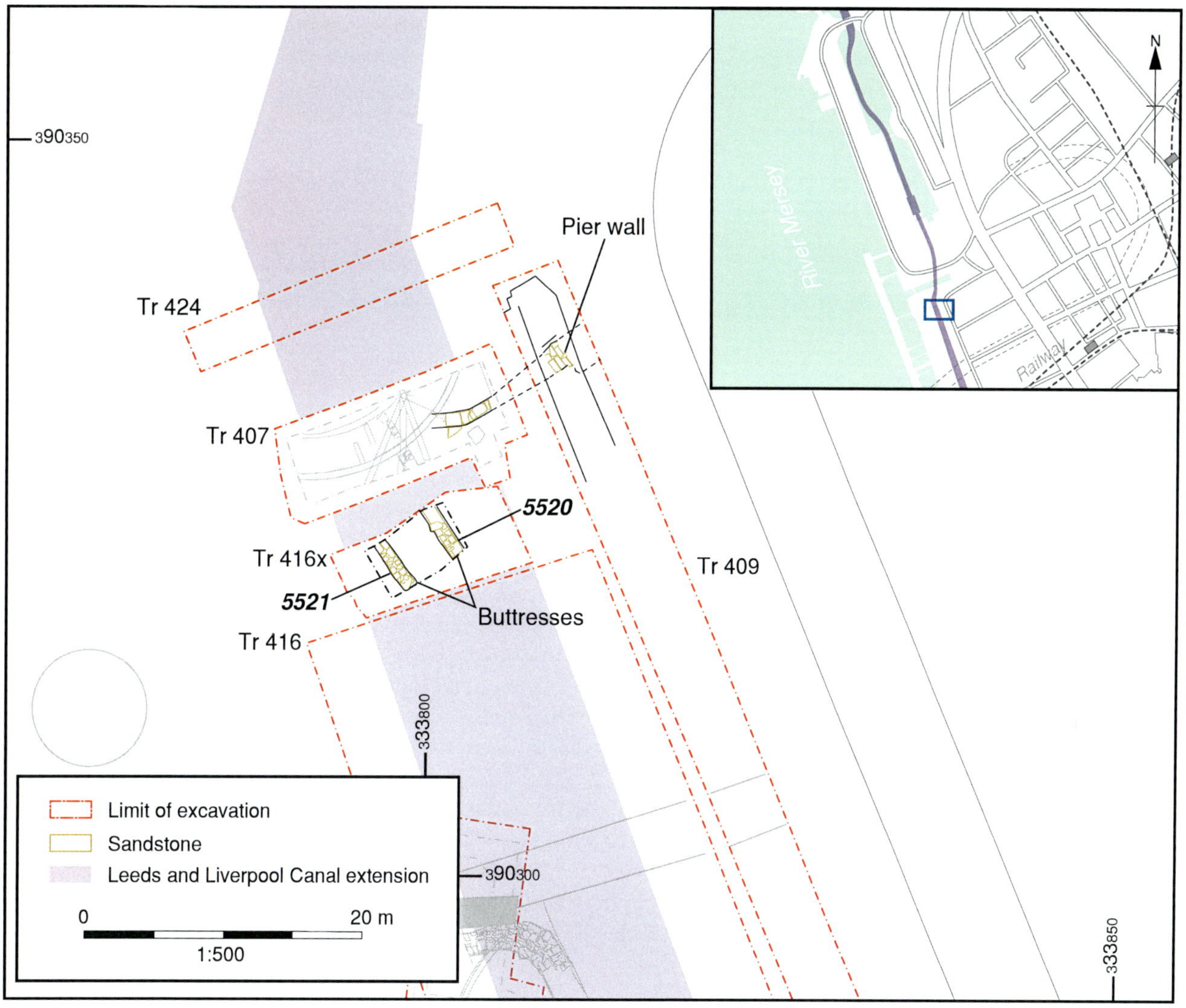

Figure 27: The eighteenth-century walls in Tr 407 and Tr 416x (© Crown copyright 2014 Ordnance Survey 100005569)

Plate 49: The buttress walls in Tr 416x, from the south

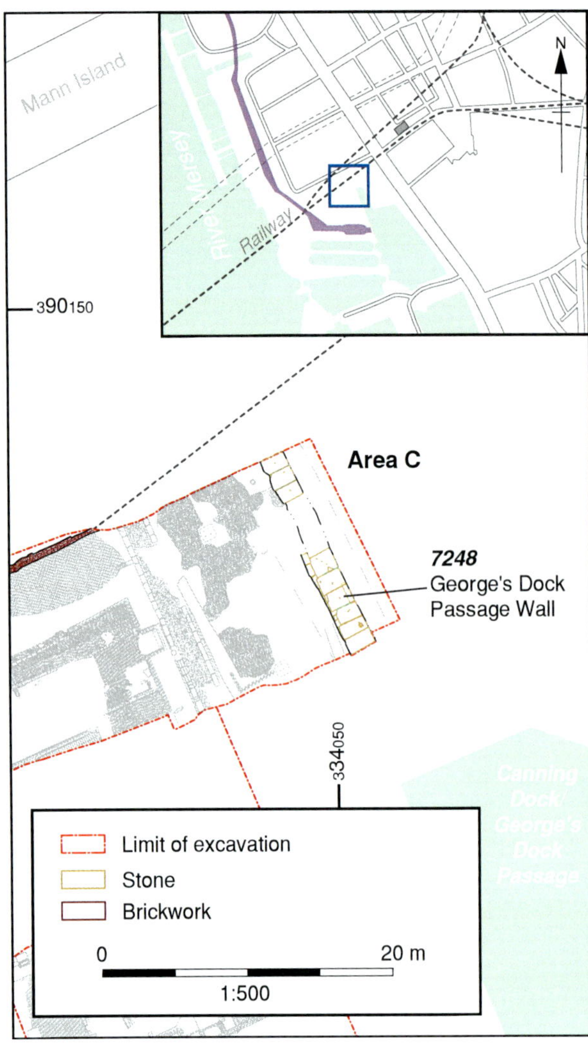

Figure 28: The western side of George's Dock Passage at the Countryside Neptune site (© Crown copyright 2014 Ordnance Survey 100005569)

Apart from the remains of George's Dock Basin and its associated pier, a short length of eighteenth-century wall (7248; Fig 28) was exposed at the Countryside Neptune site on Mann Island (Ch 1, p 13). This wall formed the west side of George's Dock Passage, which was constructed in 1775 in order to provide a direct link between George's Dock and the Dry Dock (p 71). The upper three courses of this, otherwise yellow, sandstone wall were executed in the more resilient pink sandstone (Pl 50) that was typically used after 1785 (Ritchie-Noakes 1984, 37), and this probably suggests that the wall had been repaired at some stage. The walls of George's Dock Passage were also identified during a programme of landscaping undertaken as part of the LLC extension. These walls were constructed entirely of yellow sandstone, with the blocks being large and coarsely hewn, though the coping stones were missing. The size of the yellow sandstone blocks might also suggest that some of these originally formed part of the earlier graving dock, which was constructed in 1746 (p 54), the presence of which dictated the position of George's Dock Passage.

Plate 50: South-facing view of the western wall of George's Dock Passage

Manchester Basin and the creation of Mann Island (mid-1770s-c 1800)

Historical background

The establishment, or at least the conception, of Manchester Basin, a precursor of Manchester Dock (Ch 4, p 103), probably dates to the mid-1770s (p 75). It was built by Liverpool's Corporation and it appears to have superseded a quay that was built by Henry Berry in c 1772 (Ritchie-Noakes 1984, 35), elements of which were potentially uncovered during the excavation at the Countryside Neptune site (p 67). During the late eighteenth century, it was a tidal basin that was used by the Mersey and Irwell Navigation Company's inland flats (*Appendix 1*), which operated between Manchester and Liverpool (*ibid*). In addition, other vessels, specifically small sailing packets, ferries, and perhaps wherries, also used Manchester Basin in the late eighteenth century. For example, in 1777, the Dublin packet office received the *Duke of Leinster* packet into Manchester Basin, and the Castle Quay office and the Old Quay office both had small boats putting into port in this area to provide services to Dublin, the Wirral, and Manchester (Gore 1777). Similarly, Gore's *Liverpool Directory* for the year 1790 provides a list of ships berthing in the Basin (Table 1).

Ship	Captain
Duke of Leinster	John Buah
St Patrick	John Basely
Hibernia	James Hayes
Viceroy	William Wood
Prince of Orange	William Letman
Earl of Charlemont	James Cane
Hawke	James Sibbald

Table 1: Ships berthing in the Manchester Basin, based on Gore's Directory of 1790

The creation of Manchester Basin was dependent on land reclamation west of Nova Scotia (*p 60*), and also of the Dry Dock, in the area occupied by its two graving docks, which were added in the 1760s (*p 54*). Eighteenth-century mapping indicates that, whilst the graving docks and the surrounding areas of reclaimed land had been fully extended between the time of Perry's survey of 1769 and that by Charles Eyes in 1785, the reclamation of land to the west of Nova Scotia was more piecemeal in nature. In this area, the cartographic sources indicate that, between 1769 and 1785, the land reclamation extended west, and that by the time of Charles Eyes' survey, the river wall bounding the quayside area had a stepped plan (Pl 51). On this map, this reclaimed land and quayside is denoted as 'Man's Island'. Significantly, the place-name 'Mann Island' is first mentioned in Gore's *Liverpool Directory* of 1774, implying that this initial phase of land reclamation had occurred by this date.

Manchester Basin, as depicted on Charles Eyes' map, appears as an open basin, which may well have been relatively shallow, with no associated infrastructure (Pl 51), though documentary evidence indicates that it was provided with retaining walls (MMMMAL MDHB/MP/25, 147). However, at first these walls appear to have been fairly inadequate, as at high tide they were often swamped, which resulted in the flooding of the quay. Therefore, in order to deal with this, in 1785 it was ordered that the height of the wall be raised to prevent flooding (*ibid*). By the time of Stockdale's map (1795), the Mann Island quayside had also been extended slightly westwards, through additional land reclamation, and it had a slight breakwater extending to the south (Pl 52). This map names the quay as 'Manchester Old Quay', which was owned by the Mersey and Irwell Navigation Company, and documentary evidence indicates that sheds, cranes, and accommodation had been established on this quayside in 1789 (Ritchie-Noakes 1984, 35; Hayman 2003, 81). These features, in turn, allowed cargo transported by the Mersey flats (*Appendix 1*) to be stored, and loaded and unloaded. During the early years of the nineteenth century, further land reclamation occurred, and this period also witnessed the modification of the late eighteenth-century tidal basin, through the creation of new retaining walls (*Ch 4, p 104*).

Archaeological evidence
The area formerly occupied by Manchester Basin was examined during the excavations undertaken at the site of the new Museum of Liverpool (*Ch 1, p 15*) and the Countryside Neptune site (*Ch 1, p 13*), and also those on the LLC extension (*Ch 1, p 14*). Although *in situ* evidence for the revetment walls of the late eighteenth-century basin was largely absent, a fragmentary wall was exposed at the Countryside Neptune site, which may well represent the basin's

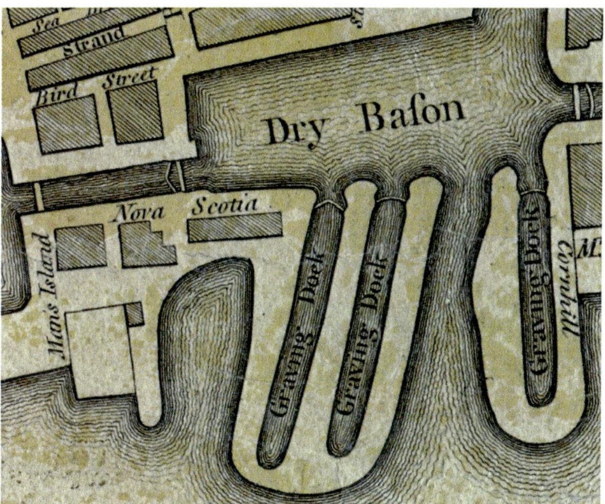

Plate 51: Extract from Charles Eyes' map of 1785, showing Nova Scotia, Mann Island, and Manchester Basin

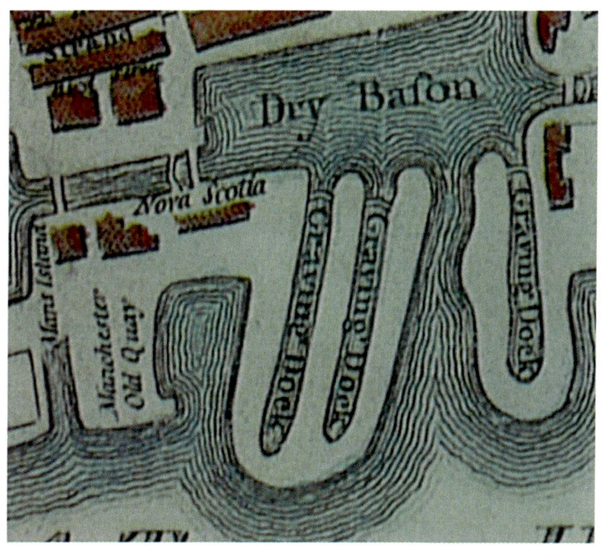

Plate 52: Extract from Stockdale's map of 1795, showing Nova Scotia, Mann Island, and Manchester Basin

original retaining wall (Fig 29). This was parallel to the north wall of the later dock, constructed during the basin's conversion into Manchester Dock (*Ch 4, p 103*). The wall had been largely destroyed and was defined by three discrete lines of yellow sandstone blocks. These defined a *c* 1 m-wide wall (Pl 53), which had seemingly been robbed as part of the early nineteenth-century modifications to the basin (*Ch 4, p 108*). Presumably, elsewhere the original late eighteenth-century basin walls had been removed entirely, and some of the stonework was probably recycled and incorporated into the later retaining wall associated with Manchester Dock (*Ch 4, p 108*).

In addition to the fragmentary retaining wall, evidence was also discovered relating to the progressive phases of late eighteenth-century land reclamation immediately north of the basin, which both

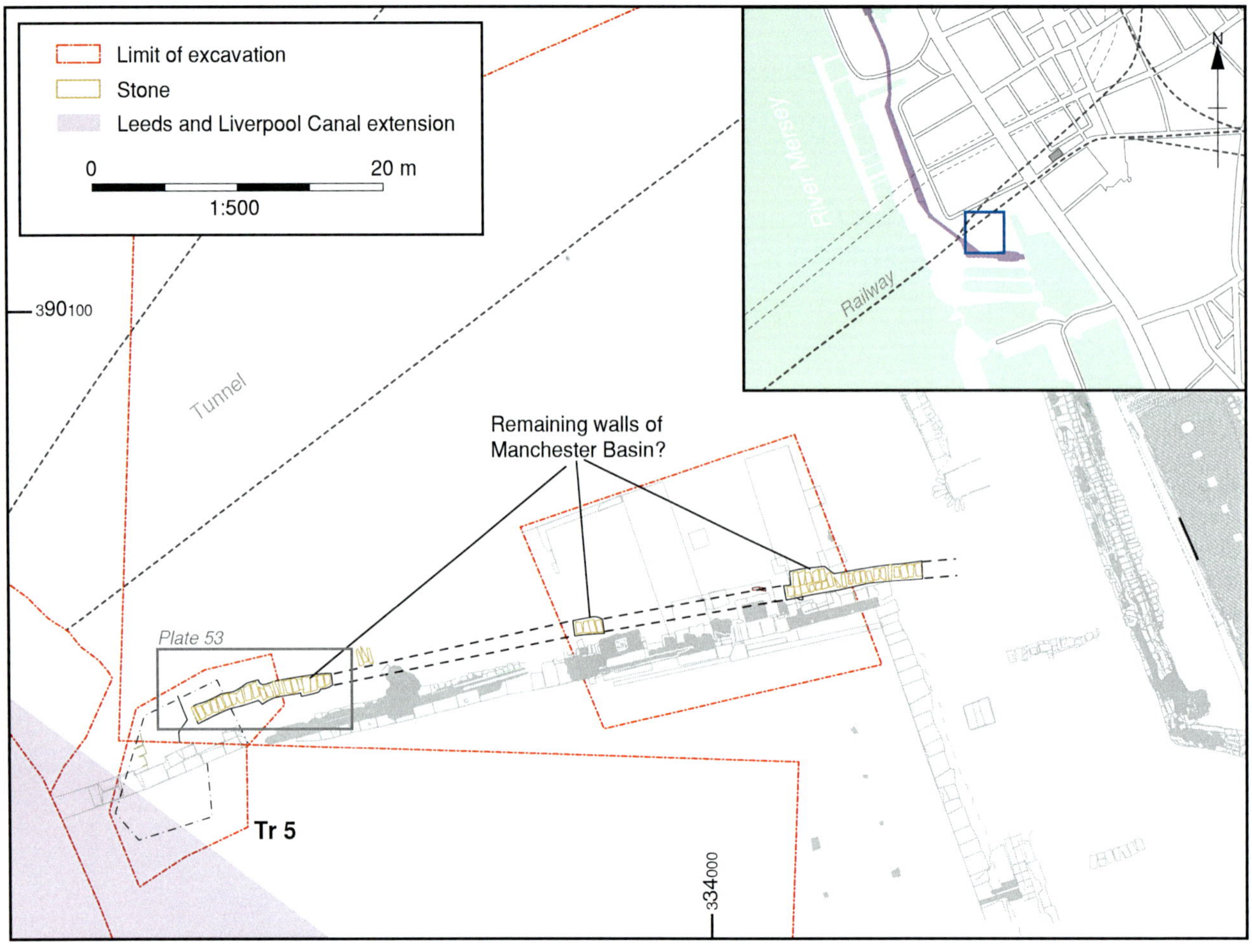

Figure 29: The potential remains of Manchester Basin, at the Countryside Neptune site (© Crown copyright 2014 Ordnance Survey 100005569)

contributed to its creation and also the extension of Nova Scotia and Mann Island. This evidence consisted of two sections of river wall and backfill deposits, which had been dumped in order to create new areas of land surrounding and defining Manchester Basin.

The river walls (**3504** and **3544**) were exposed in Tr 410, excavated within the footprint of the LLC extension (Fig 30). The earlier of these (**3504**) was composed of unmortared yellow sandstone blocks and was aligned north-east/south-west, roughly parallel to the retaining walls of Manchester Basin. Its north side was composed of dressed blocks, laid in regular courses, and this clearly faced the water (Pl 54). In contrast, the south side was a construction face, which was originally backed by

Plate 53: The possible base of Manchester Basin's retaining wall

76

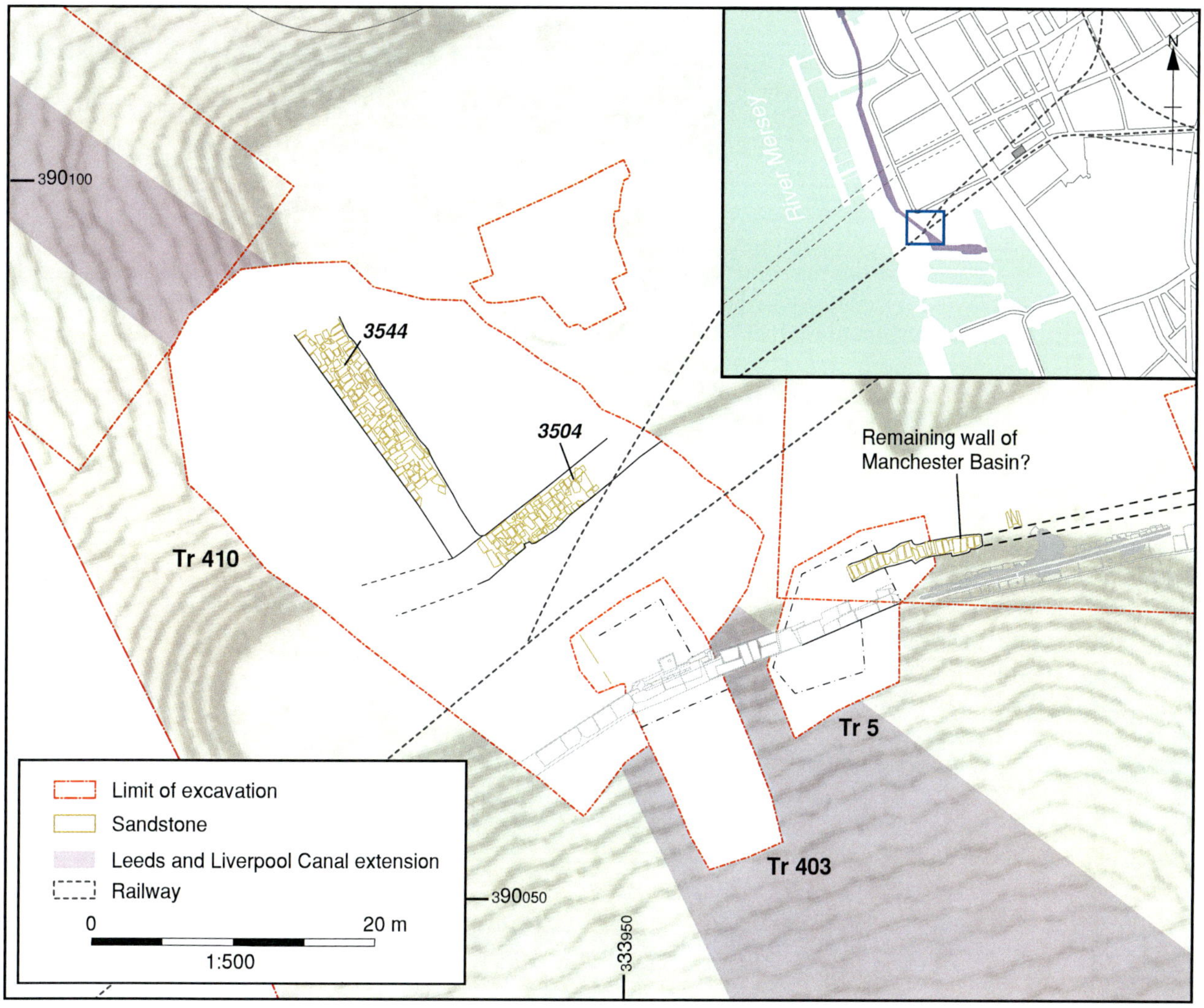

*Figure 30: Tr 410 and river walls **3504** and **3544**, superimposed on Charles Eyes' 1785 map (© Crown copyright 2014 Ordnance Survey 100005569)*

*Plate 54: River wall **3504** in Tr 410, from the north*

land-reclamation material. The presence of this wall indicates that, initially, a narrow finger of reclaimed land lay immediately north of Manchester Basin. Significantly, the form of this narrow parcel appears to have been preserved as a later land boundary, which is depicted on Charles Eyes' map (Pl 51). The other river wall (*3544*) was later in date, though it too was constructed in a comparable manner to its predecessor. This wall was aligned north-west/south-east and it defined the far western edge of land that had probably been reclaimed in the 1780s. This parcel of land lay immediately north of the earlier finger of reclaimed land and is again depicted on Charles Eyes' map.

One early area of backfilling, associated with the establishment of Manchester Basin, probably lay immediately west of the river walls dating to the late 1730s and 1740s (*5707* and *7638*; Fig 24). This area also lay immediately west of Nova Scotia and contained Bird's Slip (*p 61*); it is possible that backfilling in this area began in the late 1770s and it may have occurred at a similar time to the construction of river wall *3504*, which lay to the north-west (*see above*). This backfilled area was examined by the excavations undertaken at the Countryside Neptune site and also along the Mann Island section of the LLC extension, which identified a sequence of backfill layers that sealed the remains of Bird's Slip. The layers were composed of tipped quarry waste and ships' ballast, sloping gently downwards from east to west. They also contained large dumps of industrial waste, which were visible as discrete tip lines within the sterile ballast and quarry-waste deposits.

Significantly, this industrial waste included five clay tobacco-pipe kiln dumps. Moreover, one of these dumps (*5747*; Ch 6, pp 201-3) contained in excess of 33,500 fragments of clay tobacco-pipe, as well as more than 1000 pieces of kiln supplements, and represents the largest yet recovered from Liverpool. This material was derived from the workshops of William Morgan (I) and Thomas Hayes (II), two of Liverpool's more prominent late eighteenth-century pipe manufacturers (Ch 6, p 197). The pipe dumps probably date to the 1780s and they therefore suggest that backfilling in this area, at least, was a fairly protracted process. It is probable, however, that backfilling had been completed by the close of the eighteenth century, as evidenced by a brick-built chamber against the western elevation of river wall *5707* (Fig 24). This had been cut into the uppermost layers of backfill and contained several early nineteenth-century coins (Ch 6, p 209).

Other backfill deposits were exposed on the LLC extension to the east of wall *3544* (Fig 30). These

also comprised successive layers of quarry waste and ballast, indicative of incremental deposition. The tip lines evident within these deposits sloped from south to north, indicating that material had been carted and dumped from the narrow finger of land that lay on the northern side of Manchester Basin (*see above*).

Land reclamation to the north of George's Dock dry basin (1796- *c* 1800)

Historical background

Following the opening of George's Dock in 1771, further late eighteenth-century land reclamation occurred to the north. The cartographic evidence indicates that this took place in the final years of the eighteenth century, between 1796 and 1803, since its form is visible on Horwood's map of 1803 (Pl 55).

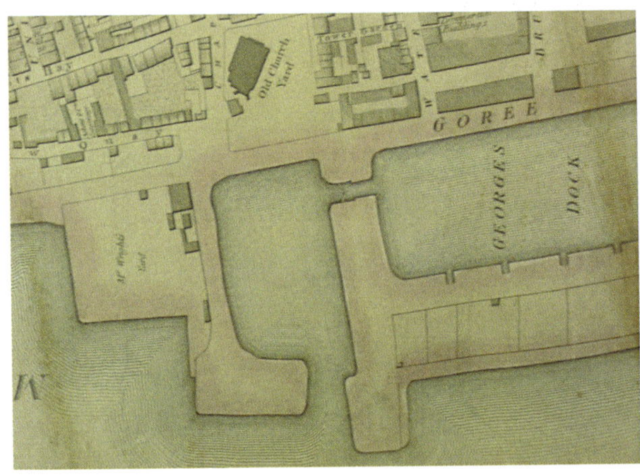

Plate 55: Extract from Horwood's map of 1803 (© Trustees of National Museums Liverpool), showing George's Dock and Basin, and land reclamation to the north

Archaeological evidence

Evidence for this reclamation was identified along the LLC extension, close to Prince's Dock. This comprised a 0.6 m-wide north/south-aligned river wall (*7583*; Fig 26; Pl 56) and, although this wall does not coincide with the westward extent of the new land shown on Horwood's map, it probably marks an early stage in the process of land reclamation.

This wall was constructed in yellow sandstone and was identical to the river walls revealed during excavations further south at Mann Island (*p 62*). Only a single course of the wall survived and this suggested that it had been reduced in height during later, more expansive, land reclamation. This is the earliest example of the dismantling of a river wall during land reclamation, and suggests that there had been a change in the value of finished sandstone.

*Plate 56: Remains of river wall **7583**, associated with late eighteenth-century land reclamation to the north of George's Dock Basin*

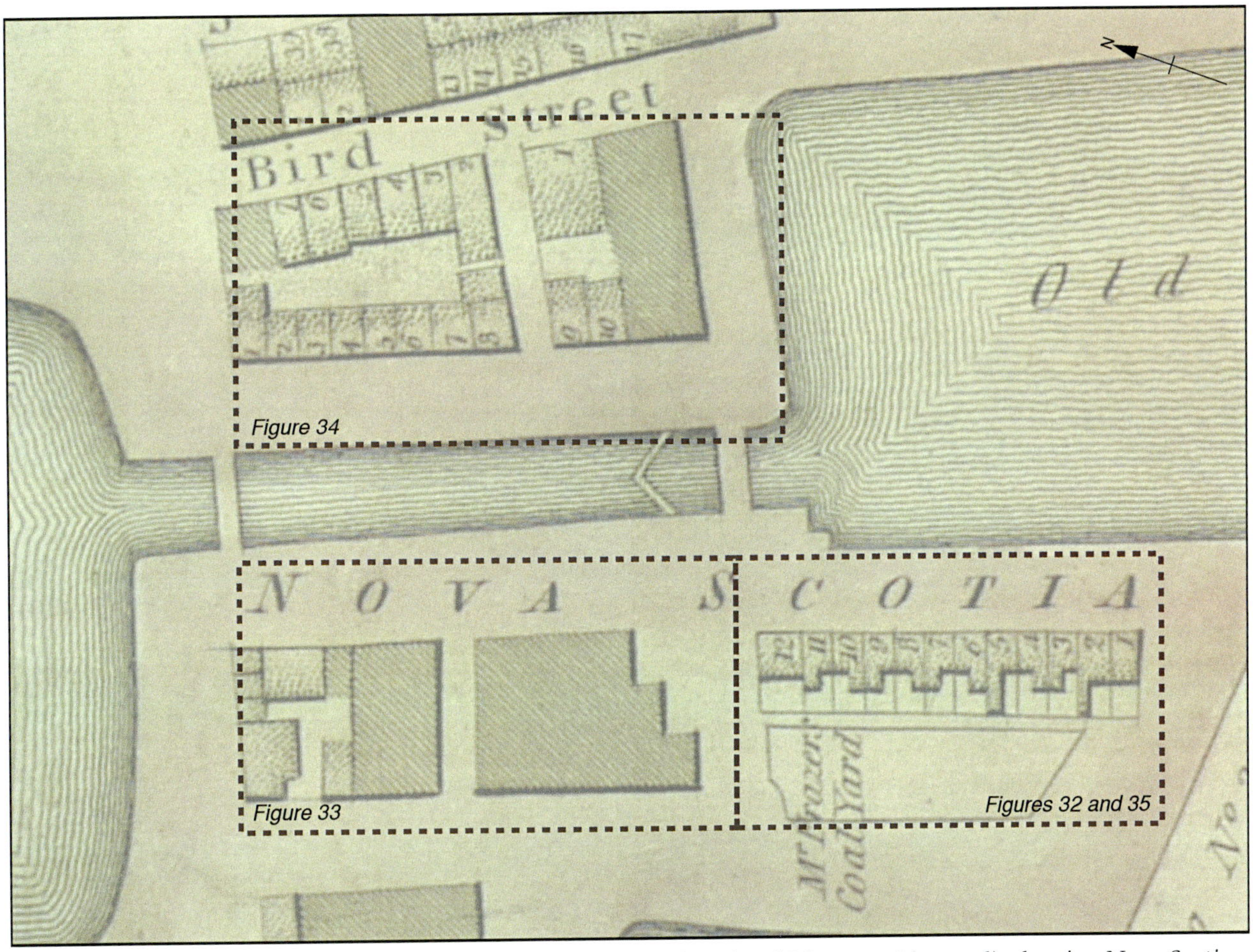

Figure 31: Extract from Horwood's map of 1803 (© Trustees of National Museums Liverpool), showing Nova Scotia and Mann Island

Nova Scotia and Mann Island in the late eighteenth century

Historical background

Following the initial creation of Mann Island in *c* 1774 (*p 74*), this land and the adjacent area of Nova Scotia were continually occupied throughout the late eighteenth century. This occupation involved the construction of new buildings, some of which were constructed across the footprints of the earlier eighteenth-century buildings on the site (*pp 68-9*). Significantly, Charles Eyes' map of 1785 (Pl 51) and Horwood's map of 1803 (Fig 31) allow the form of those buildings present in the latter decades of the eighteenth century to be discerned to some degree. These, particularly Horwood's map, indicate that the area between Bird Street and George's Dock Passage contained two blocks of properties, which lay within those areas occupied in the mid-eighteenth century (*p 61*). These include a row of terraced double-depth properties fronting Bird Street, with a larger building, perhaps a warehouse, facing the Dry Dock, with smaller, single-depth properties facing George's Dock Passage.

On the western side of George's Dock Passage, two plots, containing adjoining properties, are also depicted on Horwood's map. Slightly later mapping, dating to the early nineteenth century (*eg* Gage's map of 1836; Pl 57), indicates these properties varied in size and form, and that the two plots were bounded by three major routes, named Mann Island, Nova Scotia, and Irwell Street, and also by two smaller streets, named Irwell Place and Murray Place. In addition, a nineteenth-century photograph indicates that, of these, the large rectangular property immediately north of Irwell Place was a substantial five-storey warehouse, with cellars, and overhead hoists (Pl 58; Stammers 1999, 101). As these properties were extant in the late nineteenth century, further details regarding their form can also be gained through reference to a Goad's Insurance Plan of 1890 (1890; sheet 32;

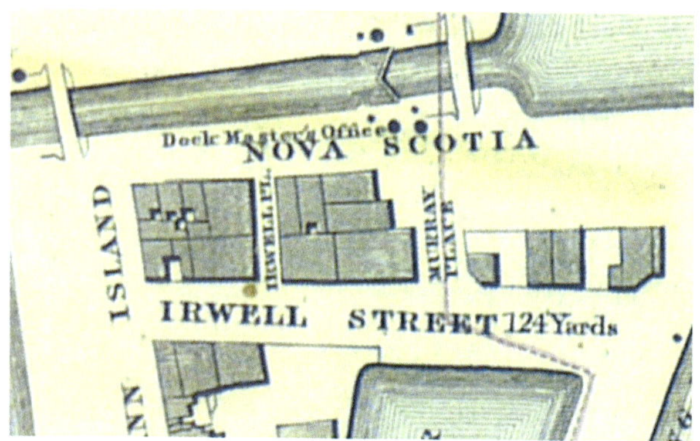

Plate 57: Extract from Gage's map of 1836 (© Trustees of National Museums Liverpool), showing Nova Scotia and Mann Island

Plate 58: Late nineteenth-century photograph of Nova Scotia, showing the late eighteenth-century buildings facing George's Dock (MMMMAL Archives Collections; © Trustees of National Museums Liverpool)

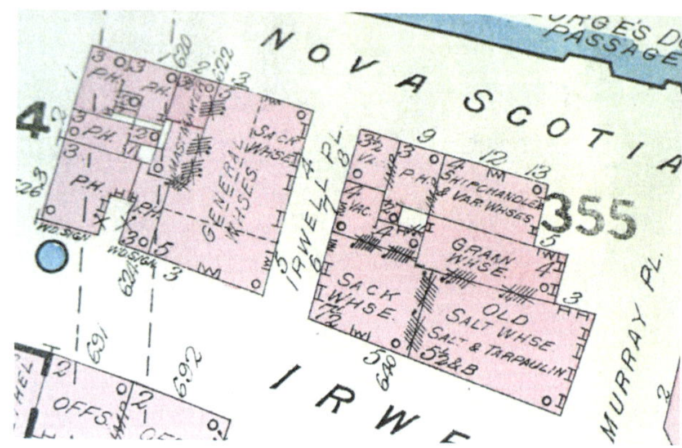

Plate 59: Extract from an 1890 Goad's Insurance Plan

Pl 59). This indicates that the smaller properties fronting Mann Island, and at the corner of Mann Island and Nova Scotia, were three- and three-and-half-storey buildings. The properties at the corner of Irwell Place and Nova Scotia were of a similar height and size, whilst the remaining larger properties in this block, between Irwell Place and Murray Place, were larger in size and consisted of four adjoining warehouses. Two of these were four storeyed, whilst the two warehouses fronting Irwell Street had seven-and-half and five-and-half storeys.

To the west of these properties, a linear building is depicted on Horwood's map that might represent a warehouse, whilst, to the south, fronting the Dry Dock, Horwood depicts a row of single-depth terraces with outshuts and yards to the rear (Fig 31). These properties appear to have replaced an earlier linear range, which is first depicted on John Eyes' map in 1765 (Pl 31), and, by at least the early years of the nineteenth century, to their rear lay 'Mr Frazer's Coal Yard'.

With regard to the occupants and businesses in this area, the late eighteenth-century street directories provide valuable details, which, from 1774 onwards, give street numbers for individual properties. Considering the information contained within the directories, Gore's *Liverpool Directory* of 1774 holds particular significance because it contains the first historical reference to the place-name 'Mann Island' (*p 75*). It also suggests that at this date the area contained only a few residents. For instance, only two persons are listed, these being William Jones, a flax dresser, at No 5 Mann Island, and John Mann, an oilstone dealer, and possibly the person after whom the parcel of land was named, living at No 3 Mann Island. Although there are only two people listed, the fact that the properties are numbered three and five suggests that numbers one, two, and four had already been applied to other parcels of land, or that other properties already existed, but the occupants chose not to be included within the directory for that year. This directory also provides details of those occupying Nova Scotia (Table 2), the majority of whom were associated with shipping.

This directory also lists nine people living on Bird Street, four persons on the east side of the graving dock, one on the west side of the dock (adjacent to, but not part of, Nova Scotia), and one on the northern side of the Dry Dock (east of Bird Street).

By 1781, the street directories indicate that small shipping companies operating from Mann Island and Nova Scotia had been firmly established in the area. Captain Joseph Connor had an office at Packet House, 12, Nova Scotia (Fig 32), from which all the departures of the Dublin Packets were overseen. Arrayed along the old quay at Nova Scotia were the boat houses which served the local ferries; the Rock boathouse was operated by Joseph Williams, the New Ferry boathouse by Mrs Cherry, and the Woodside boathouse by Mrs Barton (Gore 1781, 132).

Although, from 1774 onwards, street numbers are provided by the directories, attributing numbers to the properties depicted on Horwood's map is problematic, as the numbering system was altered through the years. This said, it is possible to relate the information contained in the Gore's *Liverpool Directory* of 1800 to the row of single-depth terraced properties fronting Nova Scotia (Fig 32). These

Name	Address	Occupation
John Barnes	Nova Scotia	Victualler
Henry Brewer	Nova Scotia	Pilot
Captain William Chapman	1, Nova Scotia	Ship's Captain
G Cherry	8, Nova Scotia	Boatman and Victualler
Captain John Evans	7, Nova Scotia	Newry Trader
Richard Gore	Nova Scotia	-
Daniel Hadkinson	17, Nova Scotia	Liquor merchant
William Hall	Nova Scotia	Carter
Hind, Wilson, and Hopwood	15, Bird's Slip, Nova Scotia	Coal Office
Thomas Holt	6, Nova Scotia	Flax Dresser
Hunter and Kirkhams	16, Nova Scotia	Sail Room
John Lacy	5, Nova Scotia	Pilot and Victualler
Naylor and Co	Nova Scotia	Tar warehouse
Alice Pilmore	2, Nova Scotia	Pilot and Victualler
Captain Richard Pritchard	7, Nova Scotia	Ship's captain
Thomas Williams	Nova Scotia	-
Edward Winstanley	14, Bird's Slip, Nova Scotia	Smith
Thomas Briggs	Nova Scotia	Coal Office
Castic Quay office	Bird's Slip, Nova Scotia	-
Old Quay office	Bird's Slip, Nova Scotia	-
Tyres and Roberts	Bird's Slip, Nova Scotia	Coal Office

Table 2: Residents in Nova Scotia listed in Gore's Directory *of 1774*

indicate that, by this date, this row of properties functioned as public houses, victuallers, and also housed several small shipping companies.

Archaeological evidence
Excavation on Mann Island, at the Countryside Neptune site, revealed two blocks of late eighteenth-century properties, which originally lay between Mann Island and Murray Place, separated by Irwell Place (*p 80*). These buildings were probably constructed in the latter decades of the eighteenth century, and appear to have replaced those buildings established in the mid-eighteenth century. Indeed, it is quite possible that at least one of these mid-eighteenth-century buildings, the gable walls of which were exposed during the excavation (*pp 68-9*), was partially, or wholly, destroyed by fire (*p 83*). The later eighteenth-century buildings are first depicted on Charles Eyes' map of 1785 and also in more detail on several nineteenth-century maps, such as Gage's map of 1836 (Pl 57), the large-scale OS town plans

(OS 1864a; 1864b), and a Goad's Insurance Plan (1890; Pl 59).

The southern block of properties, between Murray Place and Irwell Place, was defined by several substantial cellars (Fig 33; Pl 60). The positions of these tallied with five of the six properties depicted on Gage's map (Pl 57), though it is clear from the cartographic evidence, and also the excavated remains, that two of these properties, at the corner of Irwell Place and Nova Scotia, had been modified and subdivided between 1836 and *c* 1850. Most of the extant walling and flooring of the cellars was executed in red brick, though sandstone was used to provide bases, in two of the cellars, for columns supporting upper floors. Moreover, three of the cellars were filled at an unknown date with carefully stacked loose bricks. While a large proportion of the cellars appeared to have served as storage space throughout their existence, the discovery of at least one fireplace indicated the possible provision of domestic accommodation. This fireplace was

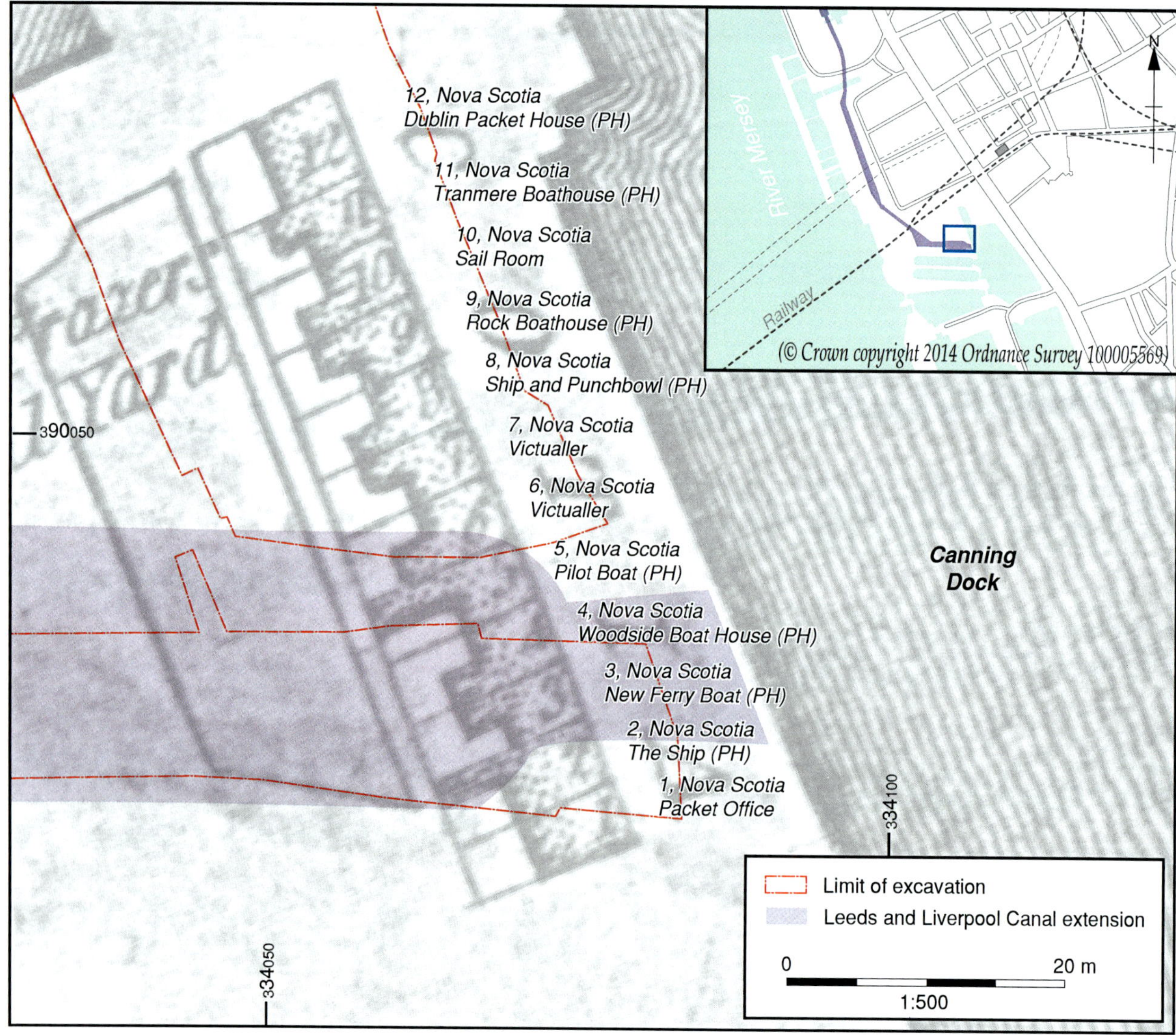

Figure 32: Extract from Horwood's map of 1803 (© Trustees of National Museums Liverpool), showing the terrace on Nova Scotia, with information on occupancy derived from Gore's 1800 Liverpool Directory

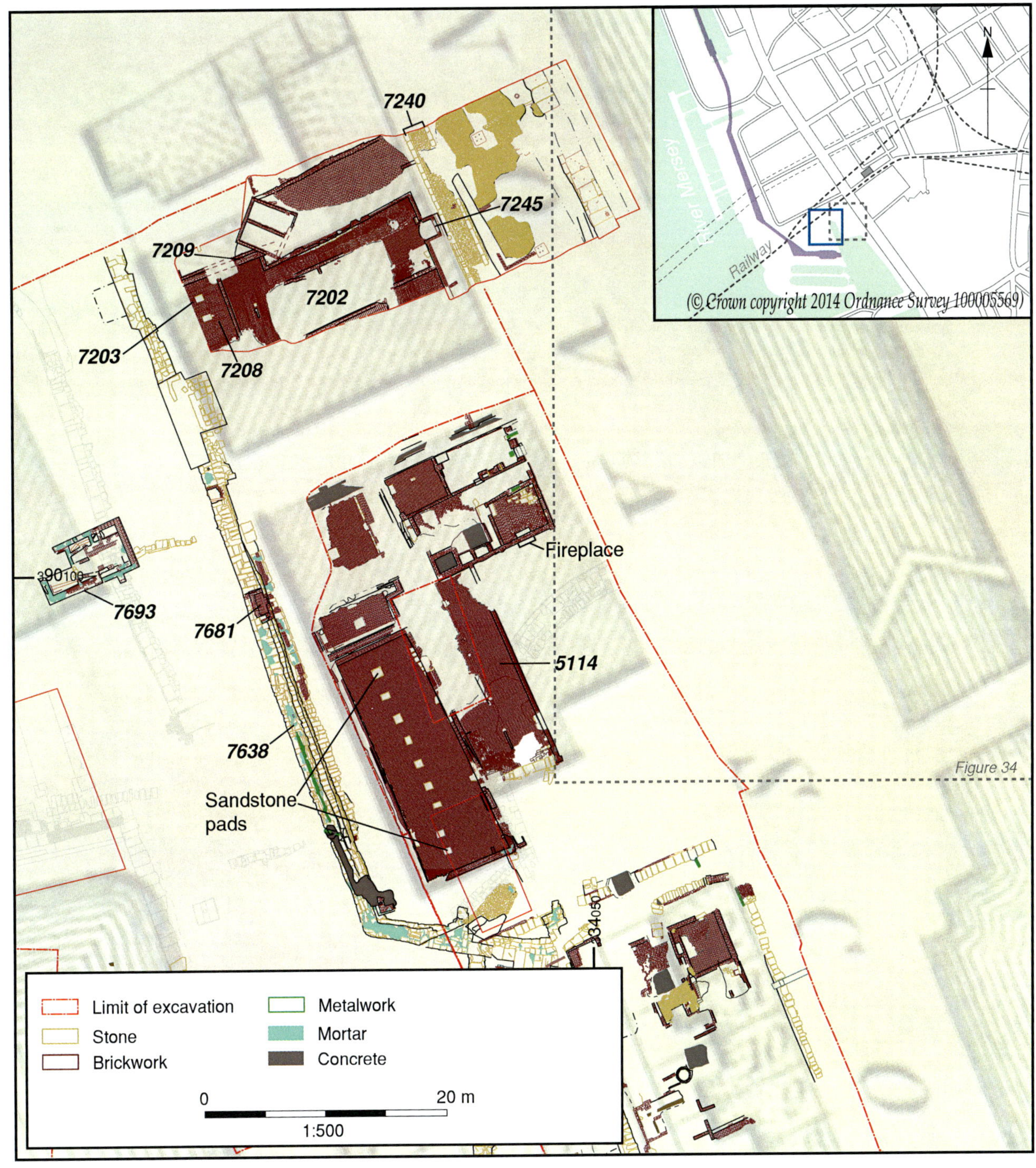

Figure 33: The excavated buildings between Murray Place and Mann Island, superimposed on Horwood's map of 1803 (© Trustees of National Museums Liverpool)

positioned on the southern cellar wall of a double-depth property that fronted Nova Scotia, suggesting that it may have contained a late eighteenth-century cellar dwelling. However, by the mid-nineteenth century, this property had been modified and functioned as a public house, named 'Legs of Man' on the large-scale OS map (OS 1864b; *Ch 4, p 140*).

Significantly, a burnt layer was found beneath the brick flooring of the central property (*5114*; Fig 33), from which eighteenth-century artefacts were recovered.

It is possible that this layer relates to a fire within an earlier building, perhaps that established in the mid-eighteenth century, the remains of which partially survived (*pp 68-9*). Moreover, this fire may, in turn, have resulted in construction or reconstruction, and might partly explain why 'new' buildings were established in this area during the latter decades of the eighteenth century.

In addition to the cellars, the red brick west walls of the late eighteenth-century buildings fronting Irwell

Plate 60: The excavated cellars between Irwell Place and Murray Place, from the north

Street partially survived above an earlier river wall (**7638**; *p 62*), presumably because it was regarded as a firm foundation. A typical loading well (**7681**) for a warehouse, lined and floored in brick, was cut into the upper course of the river wall, to serve the west-facing property immediately south of Irwell Place (Pl 61), which the Goad's Insurance Plan (1890) indicates was a seven-and-half storey building (Pl 59).

The northern block of properties, between Irwell Place and Mann Island, was also defined by cellars, though these were more partial than those located to the south, and they had been altered by later development (Fig 33; Pl 62). The cellars which could be firmly dated to the late eighteenth century were located at the southern end of this block, and these formed elements of a substantial five-and-a-half-storey warehouse (*p 80*). They included two separate cellars (**7202** and **7203**), which were bounded by handmade brick walls and contained brick floors. The larger of these (**7202**) measured *c* 14 x 5 m and on its eastern wall was a *c* 1.5 m square access well (**7245**) to permit easy movement of goods in and out of this cellar, using a hoist. This access well was also constructed of handmade brick.

Within the interior of this cellar, an internal brick wall was identified parallel with its northern wall (**7209**). The wall was set *c* 1 m to the south of the northern wall of the cellar and it probably supported a wooden stairs leading down from the ground floor. The cellar to its west (**7203**), which also lay within the warehouse,

Plate 61: Warehouse loading well, cut into sea wall **7638**, *from the north-east*

Plate 62: The excavated cellars between Mann Island and Irwell Place, from the east

was of similar construction. It was *c* 5 m wide and its western frontage probably directly overlay the earlier river wall (**7638**). This room also contained a well-preserved brick floor (**7208**), and this contained the foundations of two yellow sandstone pillars, with square recessed sockets, for supporting the floor above. Immediately to the east of the warehouse, the yellow sandstone kerbs of a pavement, and the large river-rolled cobbles forming a road (**7240**) survived, which demarcated the line of the pedestrian area along the quay at Nova Scotia. The loading quay itself was also exposed and this was constructed of river-rolled cobbles, although these were much smaller and had been laid in a more haphazard and less-regular manner.

In addition to the buildings positioned between Mann Island and Murray Place, other possible late eighteenth-century structures were identified to the west, east, and south during excavations at the

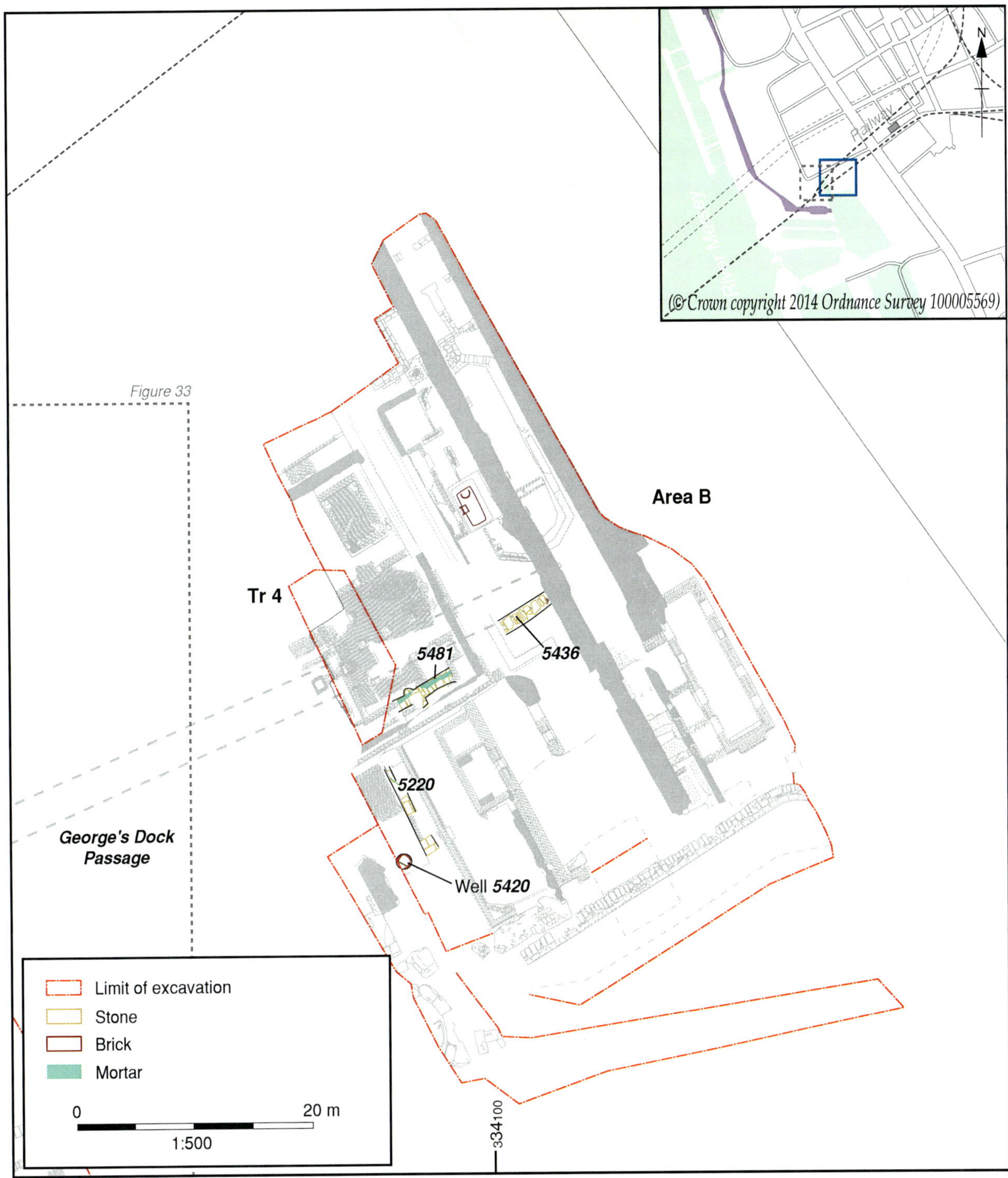

Figure 34: Remains of late eighteenth-century buildings to the east of George's Dock Passage, superimposed on Horwood's map of 1803 (© Trustees of National Museums Liverpool)

Countryside Neptune site. To the west, a possible late eighteenth-century building (*7693*) was identified, which was positioned opposite the west entrance to Irwell Place (Fig 33). This building partly bisected an earlier river wall (*7636; p 67*); its surviving remains were 4.3 x 8 m and appear to have formed three small adjoining rooms. Its eastern wall was constructed in English Cross Bond (Ching 2011), and was the equivalent of four-bricks wide. The eastern room contained a brick-built floor, beneath which were several sections of 'walling', one of which housed a drain. Although no artefacts were recovered to confirm its date or indicate its purpose, it is possible that this building formed part of a north/south-aligned linear range, perhaps a warehouse, which is depicted on Horwood's map of 1803 (Fig 31). It is also possible that this building was demolished in the 1830s, as Gage's map indicates that it had been replaced by another building by 1836.

To the east, short lengths of stone footings were uncovered, *5220*, *5436*, and *5481*, in yellow and pink sandstone (Fig 34), and these may represent all that remains of a large rectangular building shown in this area on Horwood's map of 1803 (Fig 31). This building was probably a late eighteenth-century warehouse that stood at the northern end of the Dry Dock. No finds were in association with these structural remains, although artefacts dating from the late eighteenth century onwards were recovered from the fill of a well (*5420*) to the west of one of the buildings.

The final late eighteenth-century buildings were uncovered to the south of the properties between Mann Island and Murray Place and included the remains of a row of terraced properties that fronted Nova Scotia (Fig 31). These comprised four cellars, each *c* 3.8 x 3.8 m, which formed elements of two properties located at the far northern end of the terraced range (Fig 35), which functioned as public houses in 1800 (Gore 1800). The cellars were all constructed from brick, and two were floored in the same material, while a third had a cobbled floor,

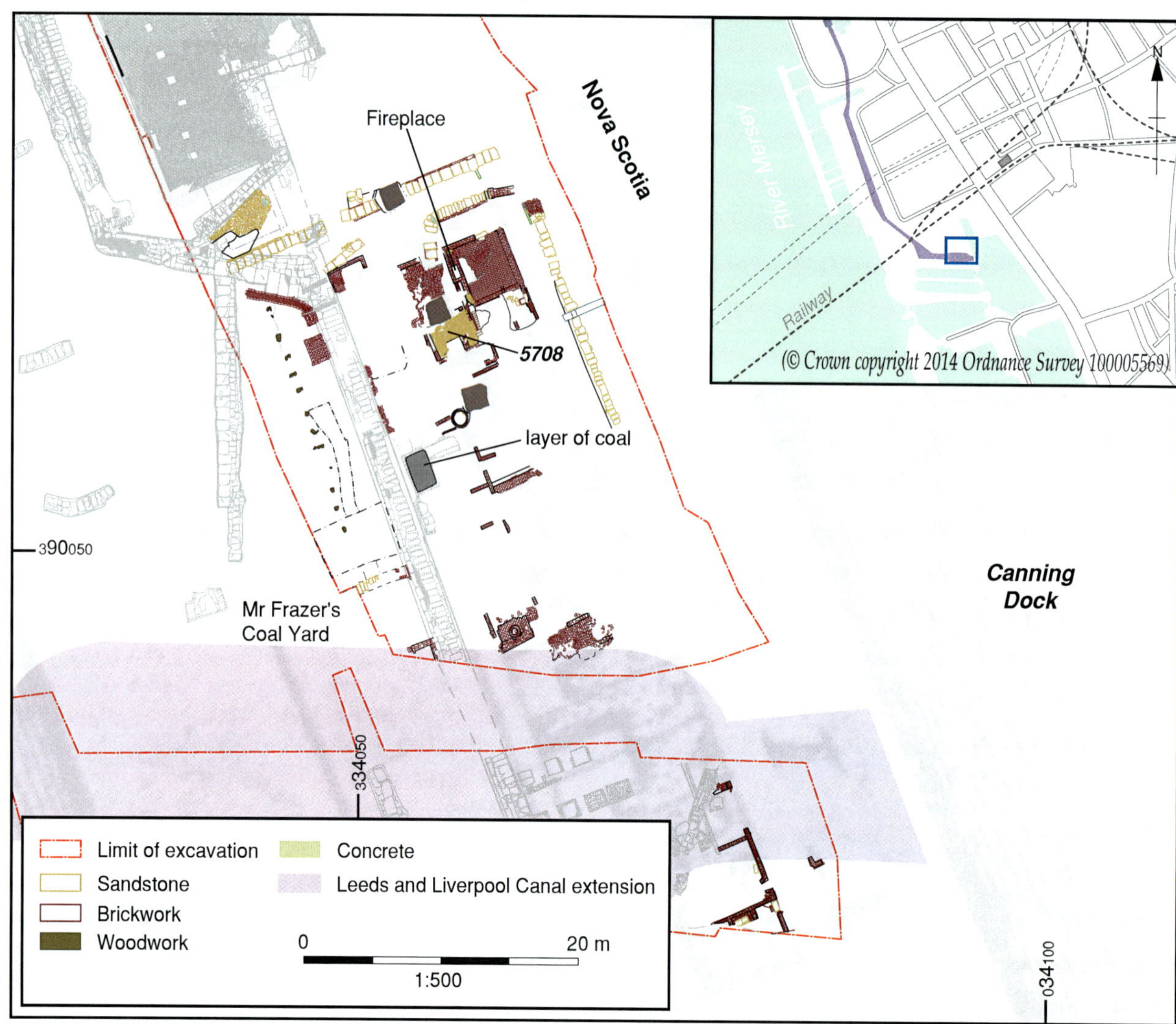

Figure 35: Remains of the late eighteenth-century terraced properties fronting Nova Scotia, superimposed on Horwood's map of 1803 (© Trustees of National Museums Liverpool)

5708, from which a penny of 1799 was recovered. In addition, other artefacts were also recovered from floor *5708*, sufficient to suggest domestic use, ranging in date from the late eighteenth through to the nineteenth century. This may therefore suggest that this formed a cellar dwelling. A fireplace, in the west wall of the north-eastern cellar, similarly suggests domestic accommodation, and it is quite possible that this was a second cellar dwelling. Fragments of other walls, of comparable style and appearance, were revealed to the south of this group, and probably represent the insubstantial remains of similar cellars, complementing the line of properties shown on Horwood's map of 1803. The cartographic evidence indicates that these properties had been demolished by 1836 and a small warehouse was then constructed in this area during the mid-nineteenth century (*Ch 4, p 143*).

In addition to the cellars, a layer of coal was also exposed to the rear of the terraced properties, and this may well have been derived from Mr Frazer's coal yard (Fig 35).

Chester Basin and the extension of George's Dock quayside (1795)

Historical background

Chester Basin was a sister structure to Manchester Basin, to its north, which in the late eighteenth-century was designed to serve the Mersey flats belonging to the Ellesmere Canal Company and the Chester Canal Company (*Appendix 1*). In a similar manner to its southerly counterpart, it was a tidal basin and is first depicted on Stockdale's map of 1795 (Fig 36). A construction date of 1795 has also been given for this narrow basin (Ritchie-Noakes 1984, 35).

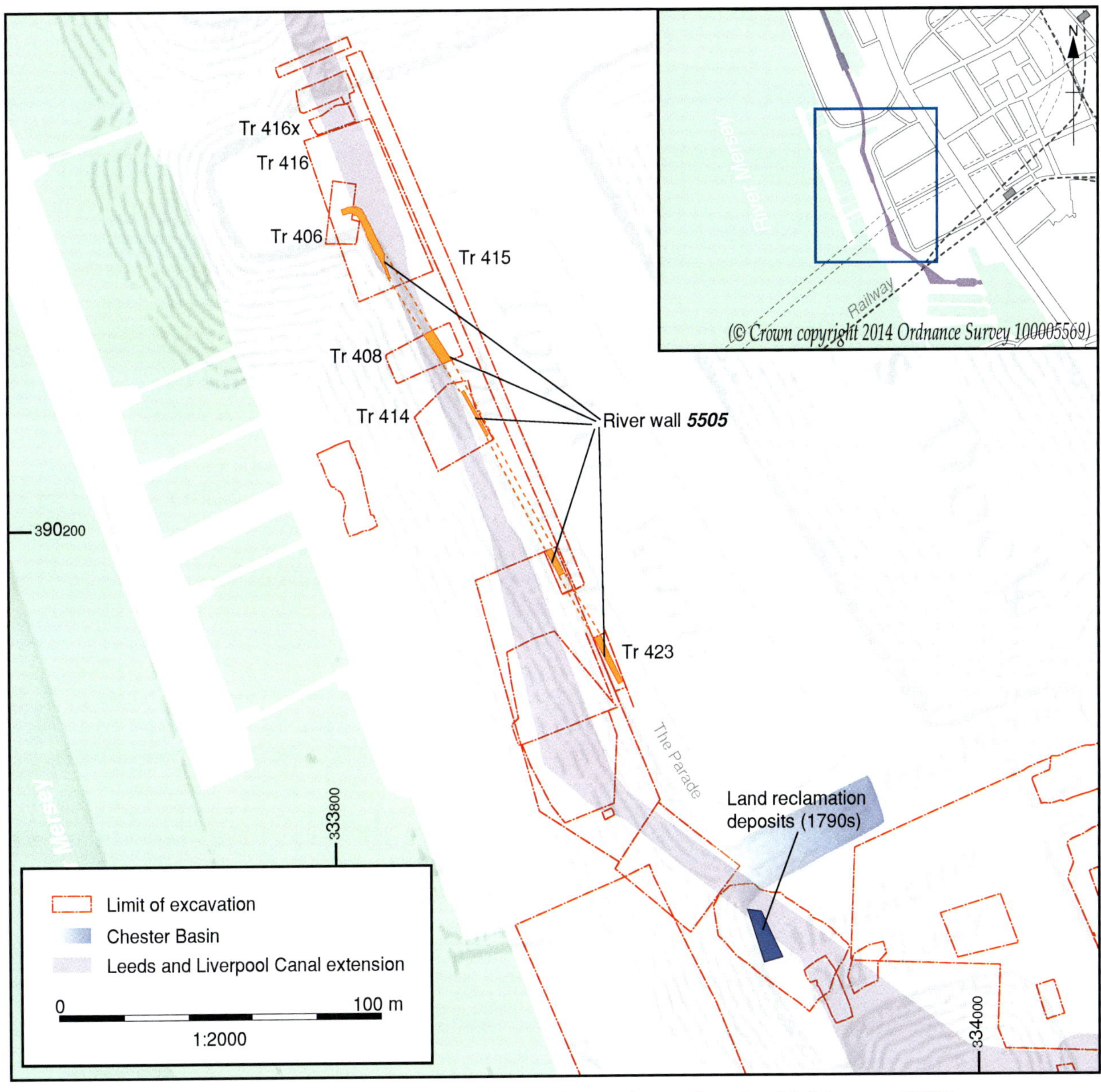

Figure 36: Excavation trenches on Pier Head, superimposed on Stockdale's map of 1795

The construction of this basin was coincident with the that of a river wall, immediately west of George's Dock, also depicted on the 1795 map, which extended its quayside *c* 25 m further west. The cartographic evidence also indicates that construction of this new river wall probably resulted in modifications to the pier extending to the south of George's Dock Basin (*p 71*). The 1795 plan indicates that this new quayside contained a timber yard, whilst the portion directly adjacent to the waterfront is named as 'The Parade' (Fig 36).

Archaeological evidence
During excavation along the Pier Head section of the canal link, remains of Chester Basin were uncovered. However, these walls were probably constructed in the early nineteenth century when the basin was modified

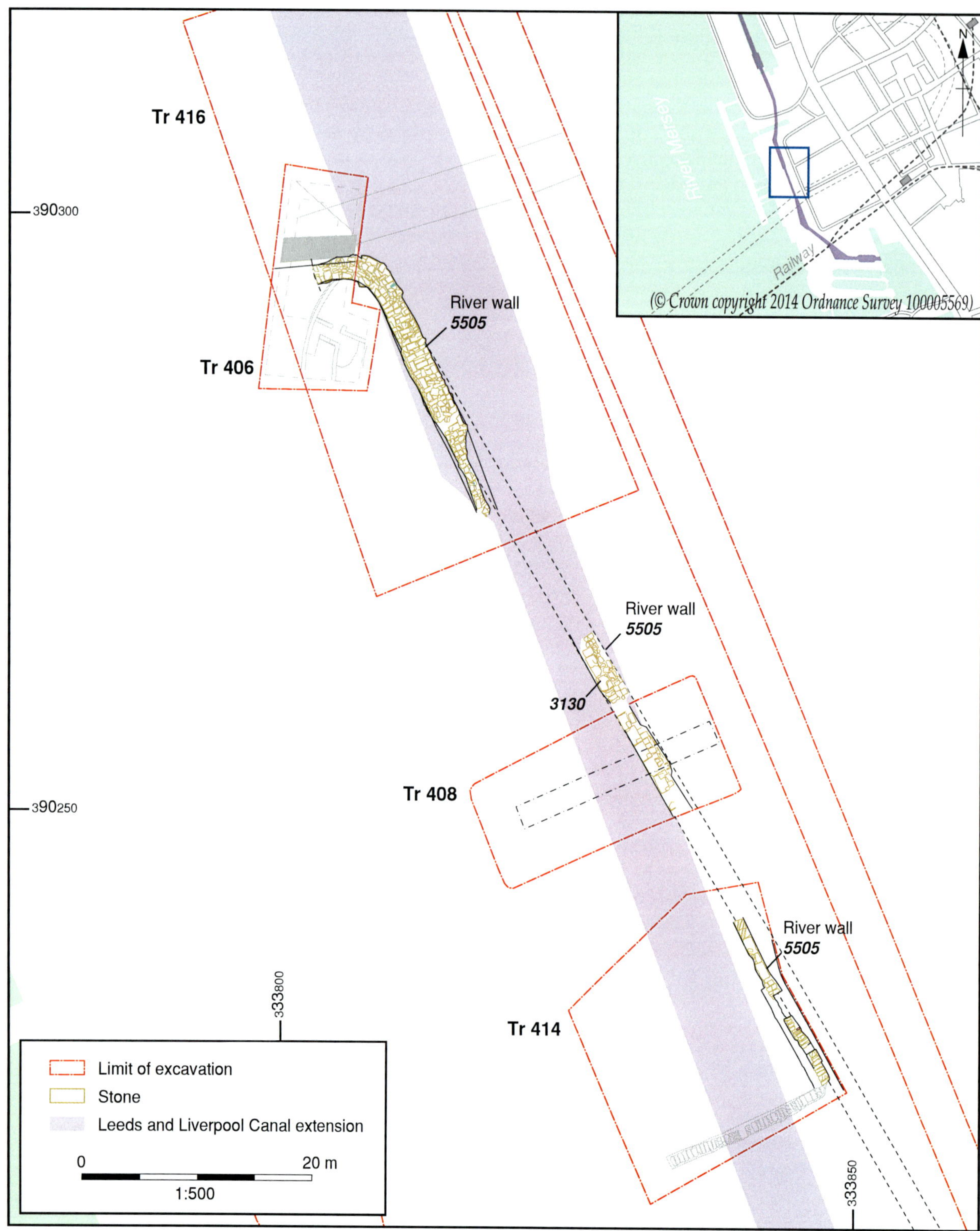

Figure 37: The late eighteenth-century river wall, as seen in Tr 406, Tr 408, Tr 414, and Tr 416

and extended (*Ch 4, p 122*). Although no clear evidence for the eighteenth-century remains of Chester Basin was located, evidence for an associated phase of land reclamation was uncovered immediately to the south of the basin during excavation along the LLC extension. This evidence took the form of reclamation deposits (Fig 36) that were present immediately west of an earlier river wall (*3544*; Fig 30), which defined Manchester Basin's quay in the 1780s (*p 78*). These deposits were probably laid down as part of the scheme of work designed to create Chester Basin and may thus date to the late 1790s. These consisted of quarry waste and ballast that contained discrete deposits of industrial waste. Within this latter material were two clay tobacco-pipe kiln dumps (*3519* and *3543*; *Ch 6, pp 203-4*), both derived from the workshops of Thomas Hayes (II), who was active between *c* 1780 and 1800. Given the date of the reclamation deposits, the material within these dumps probably dates to *c* 1795.

In addition to this land reclamation, evidence was also present to the north relating to the extension of the quayside of George's Dock. This took the form of a river wall (*5505*; Fig 37) that was revealed in several of the trenches (Tr 406, Tr 408, Tr 414, Tr 416, and Tr 423) excavated along the Pier Head section of the LLC extension. Significantly, the position of this wall equates with the river wall depicted on the 1795 map (Fig 36). It was constructed from yellow sandstone ashlar, without mortar, with a horizontal timber fender, in a style closely comparable to earlier river walling found during the excavations at the Countryside Neptune site (*p 62*). Although for much of its length this wall was aligned parallel with the present-day waterfront, it exhibited one right-angled turn in Tr 416 (Fig 37). Within this trench, the wall turned westwards, towards the Mersey, and defined the southern side of the modified pier near the entrance to George's Dock Basin (*p 88*).

4

THE EARLY-MID-NINETEENTH-CENTURY DOCKS (1800-60)

Richard A Gregory, Mark Adams, Caroline Raynor, Rob Philpott, Nick Johnson, and Vix Hughes

The Growth in Maritime Trade and the Early- and Mid-nineteenth-century Town

During the early and mid-nineteenth century, Liverpool once more entered an unprecedented phase of commercial and urban growth, laying the foundations for the creation of the modern port-city (*Ch 5*). In many respects, this growth was a result of Liverpool's dynamic community of traders who, between 1800 and 1860, exploited the full potential of both local and global trading links, expanding those which had been forged in the eighteenth century (*cf* Milne 2000; *Ch 3, pp 50-3*). Significantly, this occurred in tandem with several major technological advances. These included improvements in inland communication, through the development of the nineteenth-century rail and road networks, and the rise of textile manufacturing and other associated industries in Liverpool's immediate hinterland.

In terms of maritime trade, this period was also extremely significant, due to important advances in naval technology. These advances, which would influence the form of Liverpool's nineteenth-century docks and waterfront, initially resulted in the use of paddle steamships, ferries, and tugs (*Appendix 1*) that, along with more traditional seagoing sailing ships, and smaller inland craft, were a common sight in the Liverpool docks during the early years of the century, until the advent of screw-propelled steamers in the mid-nineteenth century (Canney 1998; Greenhill 1980). In addition, the Crimean War (1854-5), which was the first conflict to make use of steam troopships, injected income into the hands of the Liverpool shipowners, and this encouraged the building of larger steamships which, in this instance, were utilised in Mediterranean trade (Milne 2006, 260).

By the mid-nineteenth century, iron-hulled ships were also common. With regard to seagoing vessels, the use of iron hulls was greatly stimulated following the launch of the iron-hulled sailing vessel, the *Iron Sides*, in 1838, which was built in Liverpool (McCarthy 1985,

220). Their use was then further stimulated following the successful launch of the steamship the *Great Britain*, which represented the most significant iron-hulled vessel of the age (McCarthy 2002, 8). However, smaller iron-hulled vessels used for inland transport also proliferated, and some of these were built in Liverpool from 1829 onwards (McCarthy 1985, 220).

The period 1800-60 has therefore been viewed as one characterised by adaptation and expansion, and one where Liverpool acted as an interface between 'the world of raw materials and that of manufacturing' (Milne 2006, 259). It was a period when raw materials, most notably cotton, entered the port, via sailing ships, largely from North America, in order to supply the booming textile-manufacturing industry of north-west England. However, as Milne (*ibid*) notes, the rapidly expanding urban economies of the North West also required other overseas materials and goods. These included foodstuffs, timber, and other commodities, which were partly derived from those areas which formed the focus of eighteenth-century trade, such as North America, West Africa, the West Indies, and Ireland (*Ch 3, p 52*), and also from increasingly diverse global locations, such as India, China, and Central and South America (Hyde 1971, 35).

The reasons behind the rise in early nineteenth-century trade, and in particular the expansion and diversification of Liverpool's global trading network, is complex, but it appears to have been partly stimulated by specific historical events. One of these was the movement against slavery, resulting in an Act of Parliament in 1807, which effectively abolished the slave trade (HL/PO/PU/1/1807/47G3sIn60). Although many merchants operating in Liverpool asserted that the town would be ruined by the process of abolition (Clarkson 1830, 39), it is clear that those engaged in the slave trade anticipated its demise. Therefore, prior to its cessation, they actively developed suitably diverse interests abroad to ensure that the development of their businesses continued almost unimpeded, albeit with a loss of trade from West Africa (Hyde 1971, 35). Similarly, warfare within the Atlantic, as a result of the continuing Napoleonic

Wars (1803-15) and the Anglo-American war of 1812, led many of Liverpool's merchants to seek out new markets, particularly focusing on those in India and China. In addition, during the Napoleonic Wars, Napoleon's *Blocus Continental* (Continental Blockade) policy against Britain resulted in a dramatic increase in the tonnage of ships entering Liverpool between 1806 and 1810, and this war also eventually resulted in the collapse and disintegration of the French and Spanish navies (Jarvis 1991b, 11). Following this, Liverpool's trading connections with India and China were further stimulated as a result of the partial removal of the East India Company's monopolies in 1813, and their complete removal in 1833 (Mountfield 1965, 19).

An indication of the dramatic expansion in early and mid-nineteenth-century trade can be gained from the available shipping figures, which reveal that the average tonnage of shipping using the port had increased from *c* 450 tons in 1800 to *c* 4100 tons by 1855 (Hyde 1971, 237). Naturally, this increase in trade and commerce had a dramatic influence on both Liverpool's waterfront and also the expansion of the town. This influence is, in some measure, reflected in the dramatic demographic expansion during that period, as evidenced in the nineteenth-century censuses. For instance, although by 1801 Liverpool could lay claim to be the largest provincial town in England, with around 78,000 inhabitants, its population had spectacularly risen to around 376,000 by the time of the 1851 census (Pooley 2006, 174, 248).

Accordingly, this dramatic expansion led to the progressive physical expansion and development of the town, which can be clearly seen from the nineteenth-century cartographic sources. It resulted in the creation of housing, directly surrounding the eighteenth-century core, which included a swathe of high-density dwellings to the north of the city centre (*op cit*, 207). Within the eighteenth-century core, the area known as 'Sailor-town' also still existed (*Ch 3, p 48*), although it was complemented during the nineteenth century by a second 'Sailor-town', which lay behind Prince's Dock (Milne 2006, 301). During this period, the majority of the higher-density housing, in which the poorer sections of society lived, consisted of double-depth terraces, and smaller back-to-backs and blind-backs. These were types of dwellings which had first emerged in the late eighteenth century, and were often arranged around insalubrious courtyards (Sharples 2004, *Ch 3, p 48*; Pl 63).

In addition, the early nineteenth century was also characterised by the continued and increasing use of cellars for domestic occupation, and also the subdivision and occupation, by Liverpool's lower social classes, of many of the larger eighteenth-century residences, following the relocation of their former

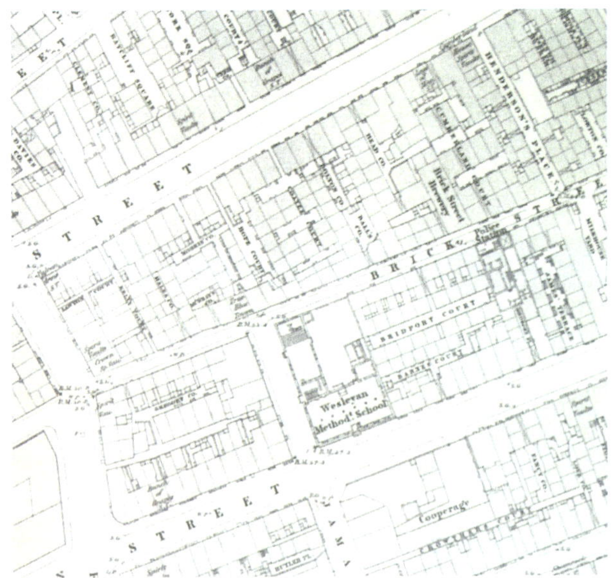

Plate 63: Extract from the Ordnance Survey 1864 5 ft: 1 mile town plan (1864c), showing the typical form of high-density, lower-class, housing between Norfolk and Jordan Streets, immediately east of Queen's Dock

higher-status occupants to the suburbs (Pooley 2006, 207). The more salubrious suburbs, and their associated higher-status residences, were located to the east of Liverpool's historic core and included several notable squares, such as Great George Square, Abercromby Square, and Falkner Square, which were surrounded by high-status terraces (Sharples 2004, 14; Pl 64).

However, within the poorer areas, housing conditions were slightly improved in the 1840s, following the 1842 Liverpool Building Act and the Liverpool Sanitary Act of 1846, although courts and poorly constructed houses continued to be a feature of the mid-nineteenth-century town (*op cit*, 25). This period also witnessed other advances in health care, such as the appointment, in 1847, of the country's first Medical Officer of Health (Liverpool City Council 2005, 116), and also the establishment of the world's first public wash-house (*ibid*) and public baths (*p 123*).

Plate 64: Early nineteenth-century high-status terraced housing on the southern side of Abercromby Square

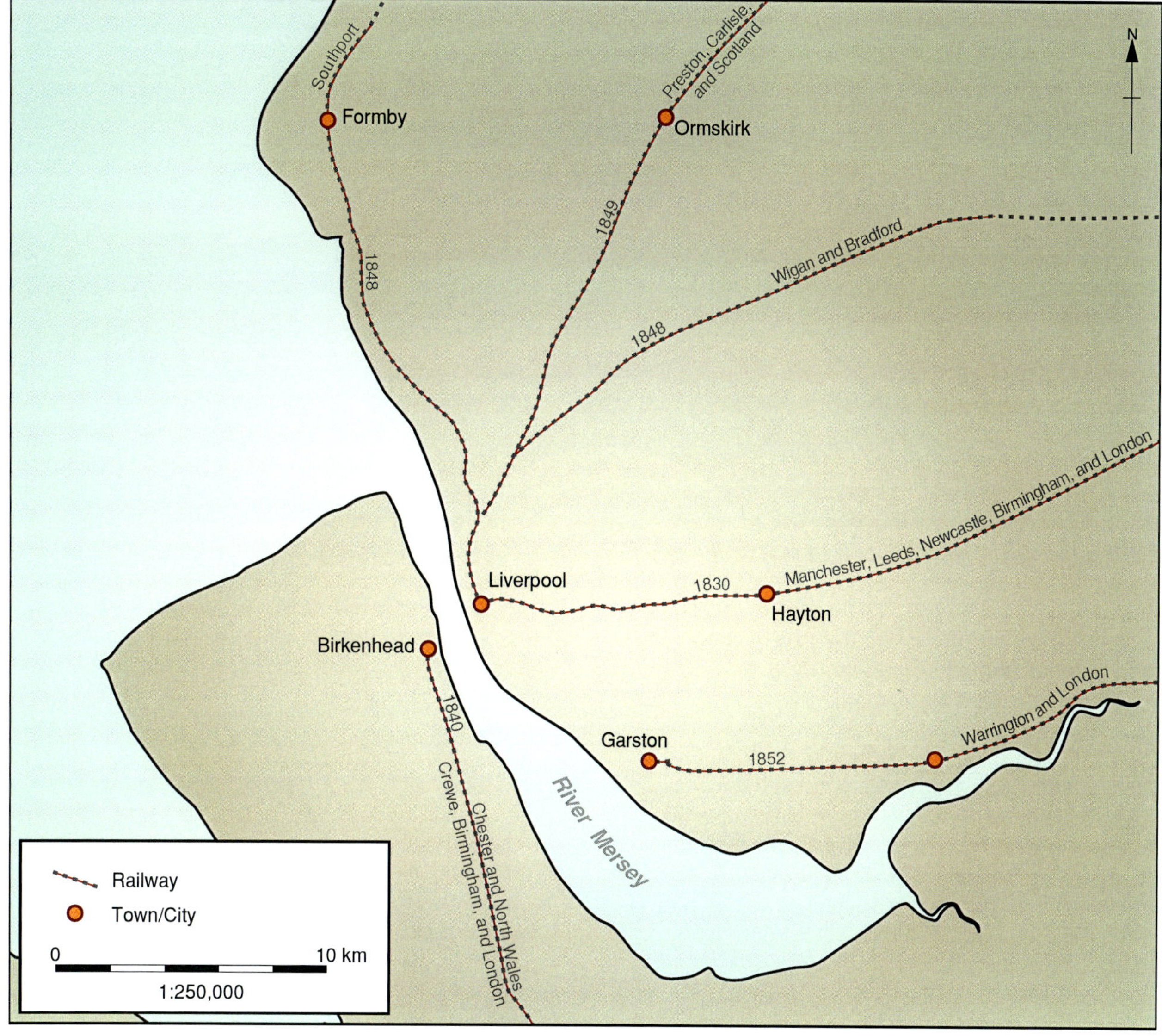

Figure 38: The mid-nineteenth-century railway network across Merseyside

During the first half of the nineteenth century, as well as housing many of Liverpool's poorer inhabitants, the historic core was also increasingly utilised by commercial concerns. Furthermore, the expanded town, and the historic core, contained numerous hospitals and schools (Hyde 1971, 45), many of which were established from the 1840s onwards (Liverpool City Council 2005, 116), as well as places of worship. These included several grand early Gothic-revival-style churches and a plethora of smaller Non-conformist chapels and Roman Catholic churches, many of which served Liverpool's large migrant population (Sharples 2004, 13, 23; Pooley 2006, 186). In addition, the historic core also housed many commercial concerns and private warehouses, which were comparable in form to those established in the late eighteenth century (Sharples 2004, 205; *Ch 3, p 49*). The more notable surviving examples include the Clarence Warehouses, sandwiched between Dublin Street and Dickson Street, which date to *c* 1844 (*op cit*, 126). From the 1840s onwards, architecturally

impressive office buildings and mixed-use properties, combining both offices and storage facilities, also became an increasing feature of the town (*op cit*, 18, 21; Liverpool City Council 2005, 115).

The early nineteenth century held great significance, in addition, for the creation of the Liverpool and Manchester Railway (LMR), the world's first public railway, which heralded a dramatic transformation in the transportation of both goods and people (Fig 38). The line was opened to the public in 1830 and the volume of passengers and freight was large from the outset, with 71,951 passengers and 4063 tons of cargo being carried in the first year alone (Marriner 1982, 25). Originally, the Liverpool to Manchester passenger line terminated just north of the town centre at Crown Street; however, by 1832, the construction of a central passenger terminus at Lime Street was under way, which was completed in 1836, and was originally fronted by a monumental neo-classical screen (Sharples 2004, 188).

Plate 65: St George's Hall, opposite Lime Street Station

Following the success of the LMR, the railway network was expanded in the 1840s and 1850s, linking Liverpool with both southern and northern England, and also Scotland (Pooley 2006, 185). In terms of commerce and trade, the development of the LMR, and the subsequent expansion of the mid-nineteenth-century railways, were to have a marked impact, in that they allowed for the more efficient transportation of goods entering and leaving the port of Liverpool (Milne 2006, 269). For instance, from its initiation, the LMR line was designed to link with the docks, and it included a branch line, running within a tunnel, which terminated at Wapping Goods Station, close to Queen's Dock (Ritchie-Noakes 1984, 165; Sharples 2004, 188).

The first half of the nineteenth century was also an era when 'the town began to assume a more gracious and elegant aspect and its physical features were conforming to the wealth and taste of its principal inhabitants' (Hyde 1971, 45). The earliest of these 'elegant' buildings included several libraries, such as the Lyceum on Bold Street, completed in 1802, which was designed by the esteemed architect Thomas Harrison (Sharples 2004, 11). Other early libraries were contained in the Athenaeum, on Church Street, which opened in 1799, and the Union News Room, which opened in 1800, on Duke Street (*op cit*, 11-12). Following the establishment of these libraries, several other prominent cultural buildings were constructed, the majority of which were, architecturally, products of the Greek Revival. The most significant and iconic of these was St George's Hall, perhaps one of the grandest and finest neo-classical buildings of the age, which was designed by Harvey Lonsdale Elmes (*op cit*, 13; Pl 65). This visually imposing building, which opened in 1854, was designed to reflect the thriving nature of the town, and was accordingly placed adjacent to Lime Street station, on a prominent plateau overlooking the town (*op cit*, 49), a position that had formerly been occupied by the eighteenth-century Infirmary (*Ch 3, p 47*).

The 1800-60 Dock System and Waterfront

Historical development

In tandem with the flourishing town, the increasing levels of trade and maritime activity naturally resulted in the development and expansion of Liverpool's waterfront. Significantly, this process led to the creation of many of the docks, which now characterise the southern and central waterfront area, during the tenureships of the dock engineers, John Foster (in 1799-1824), who consulted the engineers, William Jessop and John Rennie, and Jesse Hartley (dock engineer 1824-60), who, importantly, was responsible for all aspects of dock engineering (Jarvis 1996, xi).

Initially, during the first two decades of the nineteenth century, development of the waterfront involved modification of several of the docks, tidal basins, and graving docks, which had been established in the eighteenth century (Pl 66). These works were overseen by John Foster and included modifications to Manchester Basin in the early years of the nineteenth century, which initially converted it into a half-tide dock (*p 105*); the lengthening of the graving docks, attached to the Dry Dock, in 1813 (Liverpool City Council 2005, 60); the slight enlargement of George's Dock, between 1810 and 1815 (Ritchie-Noakes 1984, 27); and modifications to King's and Queen's Docks, at the southern end of the dock estate. This latter scheme appears to have been

94

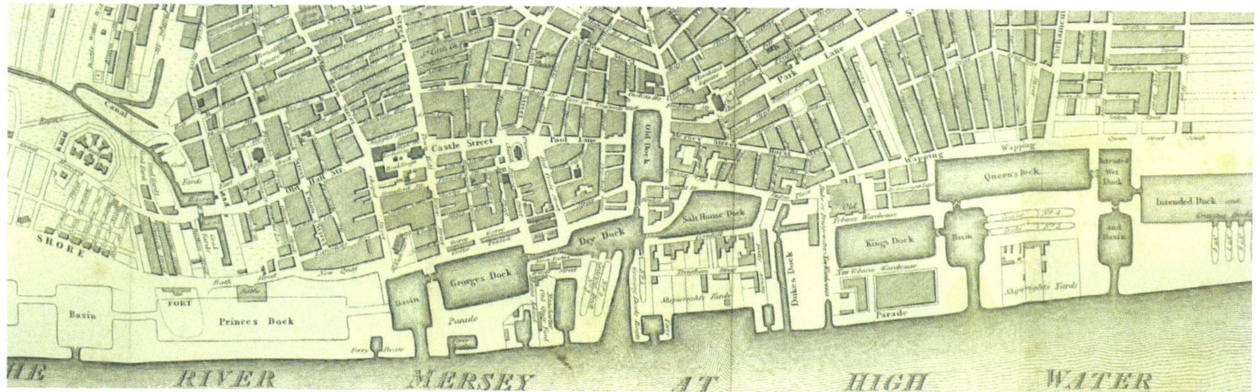

Plate 66: The early nineteenth-century docks and waterfront, as depicted on Thomas Kaye's map of 1815

partly driven by the problems of silting and also the collapse of dock walls at King's Dock, and initially involved improving sluicing and fitting Queen's Dock's cloughs with iron paddles (*op cit*, 37). This was then followed by the extension, into the river, of King's Dock's western pier between 1805 and 1810 (*p 131*), followed by the deepening and widening of this dock during the period 1802-10, whilst between 1810 and 1816, Queen's Dock was practically doubled in size (*ibid*).

The phase of land reclamation associated with the extension of the western pier at King's Dock also led to the creation of a small tidal basin, originally known as Rochdale Basin (*p 131*), which is evident on Thomas Kaye's map of Liverpool (1815; Pl 66). In addition, during the second decade of the nineteenth century, land reclamation, dating to 1811, also led to the extension of the river frontage between Duke's Dock and the gut of the Dry Dock (Ritchie-Noakes 1984, 32). This necessitated the extension of the entrance into Duke's Dock and also resulted in the creation of two small tidal basins positioned between a wider embayment, as evidenced on Kaye's map. Other modifications to Duke's Dock dating to this period included the construction of a southern arm to the dock, in order to serve a grain warehouse, with barge holes, which was opened in 1811 (*op cit*, 31). To the north of the Dry Dock's gut, Chester Basin, along with the adjacent quayside, was also extended between 1805 and 1815 (*p 122*), and it was during this time that a small tidal ferry basin, named George's Ferry Basin, was also created (*p 123*).

Union Half-tide Dock and its associated tidal basin, Brunswick Basin (Fig 39), were also opened in 1816 during John Foster's time as dock engineer. These two features lay at the far southern end of the dock estate and functioned as a more efficient entrance into Queen's Dock (*op cit*, 47). Union Half-tide Dock also formed Liverpool's first half-tide entrance dock, allowing access into a wet dock, though their use, in Liverpool, was first proposed by the engineer

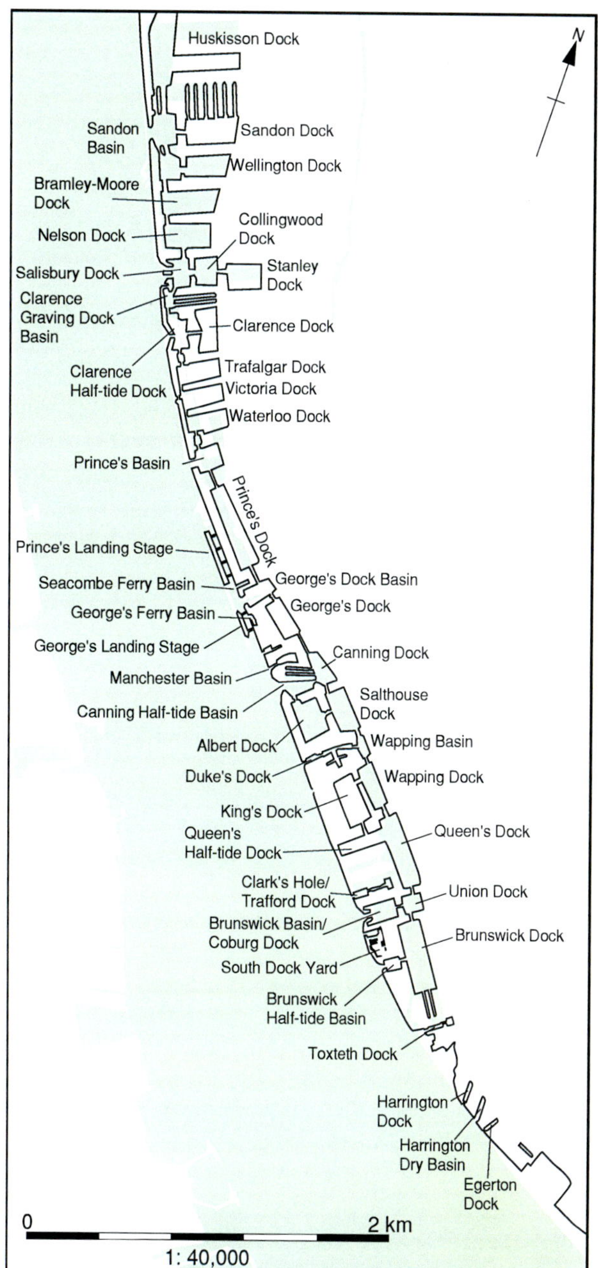

Figure 39: The early- to mid-nineteenth-century docks and waterfront (© Crown copyright 2014 Ordnance Survey 100005569)

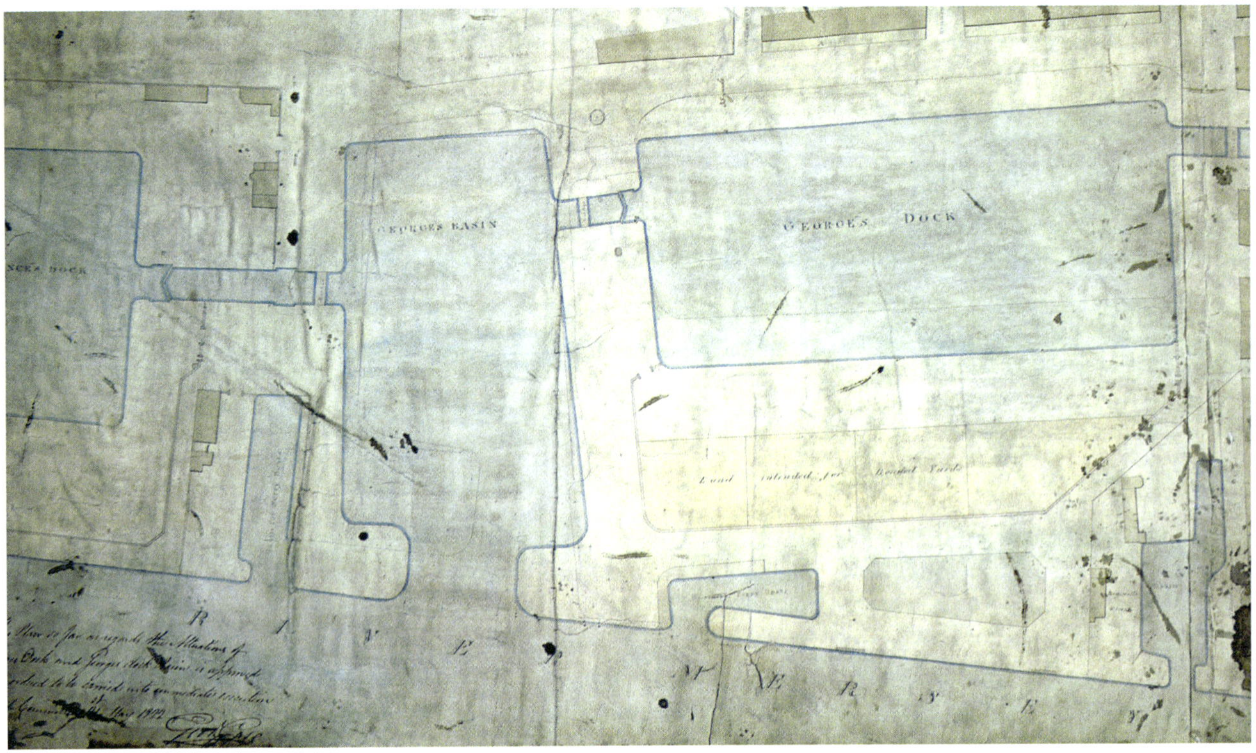

Plate 67: Extract from an 1822 plan of George's Dock, showing George's Dock and Basin, Chester Basin, Seacombe Ferry Basin, George's Ferry Basin, and Prince's Dock (© Trustees of National Museums Liverpool)

William Jessop in 1800 (Sharples 2004, 117). This style of entrance dock would become an increasing feature of Liverpool's evolving dock system, and in essence, they functioned in a comparable way to Liverpool's eighteenth-century docks, and also the early incarnation of Manchester Dock (*p 103*), whereby a vessel approaching the half-tide dock would enter it at high tide and the river gates would then be closed (*ibid*). However, in the case of a half-tide entrance dock, in a similar manner to a canal lock, following the closure of the river gates, and the impounding of water, the inward-facing gates to the wet docks could then be opened and the vessel could berth at the wet dock's quayside (Jarvis 1991a, 70). The use of half-tide docks, which were only opened at high tide, also alleviated the build-up of silt, which was a particular problem within the ungated tidal basins (*ibid*).

During the second decade of the nineteenth century, the construction of Prince's Dock and its basin (Prince's Basin) were initiated (Fig 39). Both the dock and basin finally opened in 1821 (*p 136*), and these were again overseen by John Foster, though the basin was deepened in 1825, during Jesse Hartley's second year as resident dock engineer (Jarvis 1991b, 11; 1991a, 144). This dock was principally designed to receive transatlantic vessels engaged in the importation of cotton, and transportation of emigrants to the New World (Liverpool City Council 2005, 127). During the construction of Prince's Dock, it is also probable that Seacombe Ferry basin was established, which

lay between Prince's Dock and George's Dock Basin, particularly as this is depicted on a plan of George's Dock dating to 1822 (MMMMAL 182/1/2; Pl 67).

During this period, two other small tidal basins used by the Mersey ferries and flats were also constructed in the southern docks. One of these was South Ferry Basin, which lay to the south of Brunswick Basin, and opened in 1823, whilst the other was known as Clark's Hole, lying to the north of Brunswick Basin, which opened in 1825 (Ritchie-Noakes 1984, 38, 47; Fig 39). In addition to these, to the north of Clark's Hole, two further tidal basins are also shown, which had associated slipways (Pl 68). The mid-1820s also hold further significance in that, in 1825, it appears

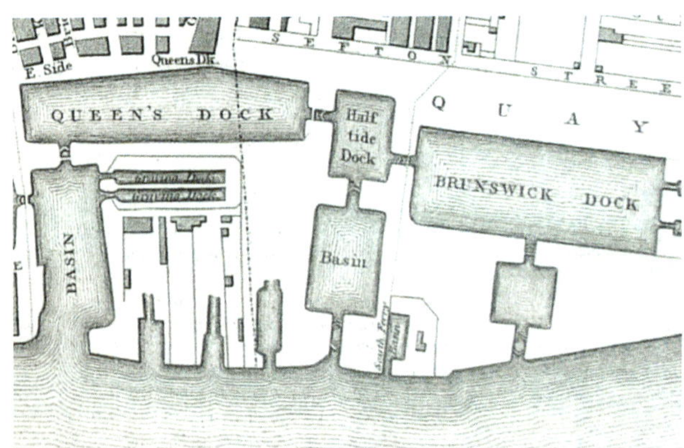

Plate 68: Extract from Austin's map of 1836, showing the southern docks, along with South Ferry Basin, Clark's Hole, and two additional small tidal basins

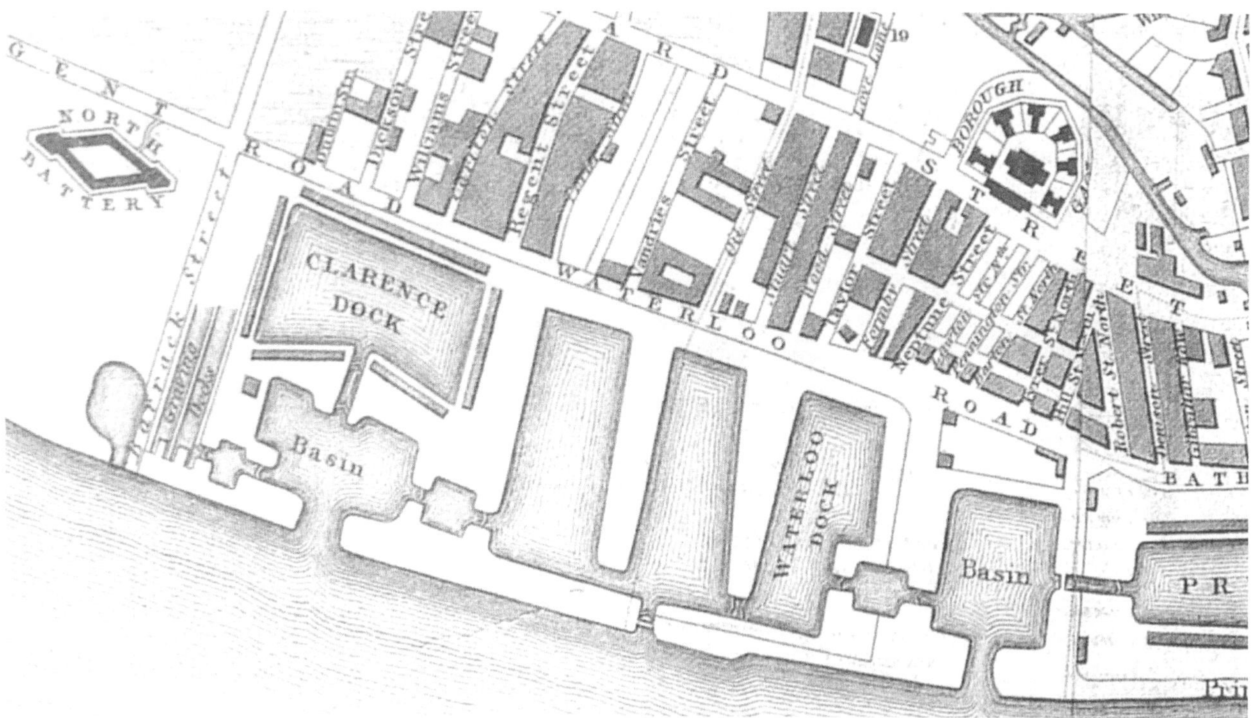

Plate 69: Extract from Austin's map of 1836, showing the early nineteenth-century dock system to the north of Prince's Dock

that Manchester Dock was converted into a fully impounded wet dock (*p 104*), whilst 1826 witnessed the infilling of the Old Dock (*p 132*), though this had actually been sanctioned 15 years earlier (*op cit*, 21). Other minor dock modifications dating to *c* 1820 occurred at Duke's Dock and these led to the creation of two canal arms, appended to the southern arm of the dock, that served the grain warehouse (*p 95*). The cartographic evidence indicates that these features had been constructed between 1815 and 1823 (Kaye 1815; Walker and Walker 1823).

The 1820s also represent a period that, again, involved the major modification of pre-existing tidal basins and docks. For instance, in 1822, work began, under John Foster, on replacing the walls of George's Dock and enlarging the dock, which was finally completed under the supervision of Jesse Hartley in 1825 (Ritchie-Noakes 1984, 27; MMMMAL 182/1/2; Pl 67). Under Jesse Hartley, the Dry Dock (*Ch 3, p 55*) was also modified to form Canning Dock (*p 134*).

During the 1830s, a series of docks was then opened to the north of the pre-existing docks, which were ambitious undertakings, adapted to meet changes in trade and the merchant fleet (Jarvis 1991a; Pl 69). These were designed by Jesse Hartley, Liverpool's pre-eminent dock engineer, who effectively expanded the dock estate from 45 to *c* 210 acres (Ritchie-Noakes 1984, 97). The earliest of Hartley's docks was Clarence Dock and its associated half-tide basin (Clarence Half-tide Dock), which opened in 1830 (Jarvis 1991a, 9).

This dock was specifically designed to accommodate paddle steamships, and hence was deliberately sited by the Corporation's Dock Committee some distance from the pre-existing docks, as a solution to the risk of fire (Jarvis 1991b, 29-30). Two substantial east/west-aligned graving docks were also constructed immediately to its north, which were accessed from the Clarence Graving Dock Basin. This basin lay to the west of the graving docks and to the north of Clarence Half-tide Basin, which provided its point of access via a short entrance lock. Clarence Dock also holds further significance in that it was during the construction of this dock that Jesse Hartley used granite for the first time as the wall facing (Sharples 2004, 96).

Following the construction of Clarence Dock, Hartley soon filled the intervening gap between it and the southern docks, through the construction of Waterloo, Victoria, and Trafalgar Docks, which opened between 1834 and 1836 (Jarvis 1991a, 9; Pl 69). Of these docks, Victoria and Trafalgar Docks were multifunctional, in that they were not designed for a specific trade, whilst Waterloo Dock was initially designed to accommodate the largest sailing ships then in service, and also to relieve overcrowding at Prince's Dock (Jarvis 1991a, 145). However, especially following the repeal of the Corn Laws in 1846, this latter dock gradually began to specialise in the import of grain, which led to construction of associated grain warehouses (McCarron and Jarvis 1992, 103). These three uniform docks were also inter-linked via passages. Although they could originally be accessed from the river via an entrance running from Victoria Dock, and also via Prince's Basin or Clarence Half-tide Dock, in 1836 the Victoria Dock entrance was closed and blocked (*op cit*, 72). These were the last three docks that were specifically built to provide berthing and quaysides for sailing ships. While sailing vessels continued in widespread use until the turn of the nineteenth century (Greenhill 1980), and experienced a brief resurgence during the First World War (*op cit*, 49-52), the purpose of every dock constructed in Liverpool from *c* 1840 was the accommodation of increasingly large steamships (McCarron and Jarvis 1992, 94).

In addition to the construction of those docks defining the northern end of the early nineteenth-century estate, dock building also occurred at the far southern end of the dock estate during the late 1820s and early 1830s (Pl 68). Specifically, this entailed the construction of Brunswick Dock, and its half-tide basin, which opened in 1832, along with two associated graving docks, a river wall, and a passage that linked this dock with Union Half-tide Dock (Ritchie-Noakes 1984, 44). This dock was used exclusively by the timber trade and had been provisioned with angled dock walls, akin to slips, in order to facilitate the discharge of timber (Jarvis 1991a, 75). However, shortly after its opening it required rebuilding, due to the failure of its wall foundations (Ritchie-Noakes 1984, 44). Immediately south of Brunswick Dock, the Dock Trustees then constructed a small half-tide dock for river craft in the late 1830s, which was named Toxteth Dock (*op cit*, 67). To the south of this, several small privately owned docks were also established in the late 1830s (Pl 70). These included Egerton Dock, owned by the Bridgewater Trustees, which was fitted with a gate and was designed to receive river craft carrying timber, and Harrington Dock and Harrington Dry Basin (*ibid*). These latter two docks, one of which was fitted with a river gate, were built by the Harrington Dock Company, and followed the designs of the dock engineer, Jesse Hartley, and his son, John (*ibid*). Finally, the 1830s also saw the creation of Liverpool's first floating landing stage, which was built in 1833 and was possibly designed by Marc Brunel (*op cit*, 30; Liverpool City Council 2005, 127). The precise location of this landing stage is not known, though it is quite possible that it lay in the vicinity of George's Dock (*p 123*).

A series of additional docks was then constructed by Hartley during the 1840s and 1850s, along with associated modifications to pre-existing docks, in order to meet the increases in commerce and trade. Within the central hub of the dock estate, work began on Albert Dock in 1841, which was finally opened in 1845 (Ritchie-Noakes 1984, 50-1). Significantly, it formed Liverpool's first secure dock, as it was surrounded

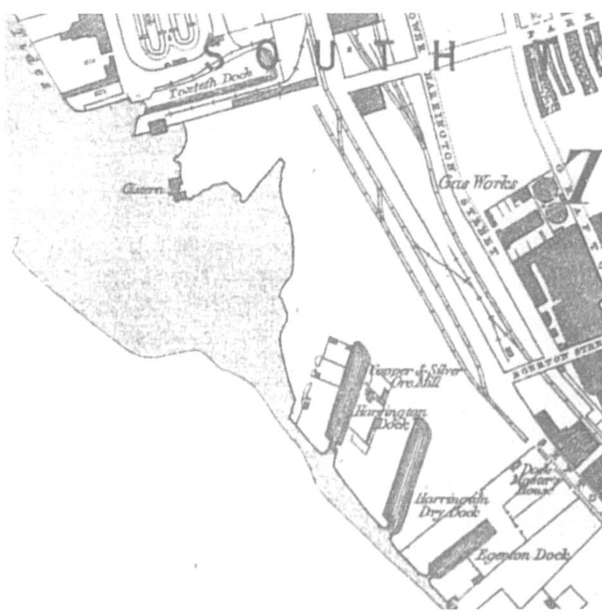

Plate 70: Extract from the Ordnance Survey 1850 6": 1 mile map (1850a), showing the Toxteth, Harrington, and Egerton Docks

by bonded warehouses, which formed an integral element of the dock's design (*p 101*). The construction of Albert Dock also led to the remodelling of the adjacent docks and the construction and modification of several associated features (Pl 71). For example, during the early 1840s, Salthouse Dock (earlier known as South Dock; *Ch 3, p 54*) was deepened, its dock

Plate 71: Extract from the Ordnance Survey 1893 25": 1 mile map (1893a), showing Albert Dock and its environs

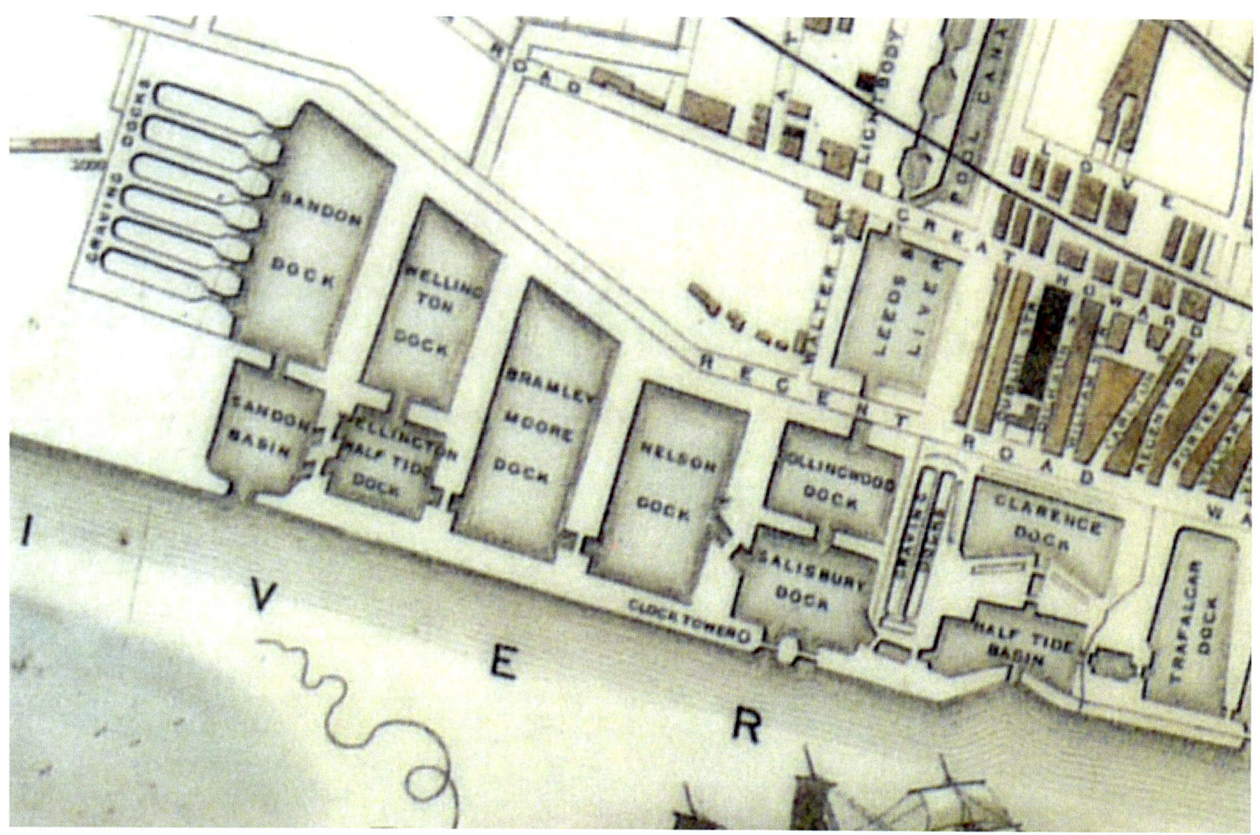

Plate 72: Extract from Tallis & Co's map of 1851, showing Hartley's northern docks

walls rebuilt, and it was provided with a second entrance, which linked it with Albert Dock (*op cit*, 23). During this period, iron swing bridges were also constructed across both of the entrances to this dock (*ibid*). Similarly, Canning Dock was deepened and Canning Half-tide Basin was constructed (*op cit*, 41). This basin lay across the former gut of the Dry Dock and had a double river entrance, whilst its other entrance, which led to Canning Dock, was traversed by a swing bridge (*op cit*, 50). Duke's Dock was also modified, as part of the works associated with the construction of Albert Dock, and this took the form of the creation of a new river entrance and half-tide basin, as well as the establishment of an adjacent area of reclaimed land, bounded by a new river wall, which was designed to function as a parade (*op cit*, 32, 50). Moreover, during the construction of Albert Dock, one of the eighteenth-century graving docks originally attached to the Dry Dock (*Ch 3, p 55*) was infilled, whilst the two remaining graving docks were rebuilt and deepened in 1842, and were then named as Canning Graving Docks Nos 1 and 2 (*op cit*, 41; Liverpool City Council 2005, 60).

Other docks that were established in the 1840s by Jesse Hartley lay at the northern end of the dock estate and included Stanley, Salisbury, Collingwood, Nelson, and Bramley-Moore (Pl 72). These docks all opened in 1848 and are viewed as incorporating all of the features which now define and typify Hartley's

dock-building career (Jarvis 1991a, 72-3). They formed an inter-linked system of small docks, which were accessed from the river through a double half-tide entrance at Salisbury Dock (*op cit*, 74). In addition, Salisbury Dock, as well as Collingwood and Stanley Docks, was provided with small locks, which were used by the Mersey flats and other smaller vessels (*op cit*, 74-5), whilst Stanley Dock was linked to the LLC by four canal locks, which allowed berthed ships to load or discharge cargoes directly to canal boats (*op cit*, 77). This latter dock also represents the only Liverpool dock which was constructed in a dry-land location (Jarvis 2003, 6). During this period, the Clarence Graving Dock Basin (*p 97*) was also enlarged (Jarvis 1991a, 230).

In 1840, Brunswick Basin (*p 98*), at the southern end of the dock estate, was also modified, which involved fitting gates onto its entrance and thus converting it into a wet dock (Ritchie-Noakes 1984, 47). The remodelled dock was subsequently named Coburg Dock (Pl 73) and, significantly, its wide entrance was designed to receive ocean-going paddle steamers; it thus complemented Clarence Dock, Liverpool's other steamship dock, at the northern end of the dock estate (*p 97*). Immediately to the south of this new dock lay the Dock Yard, which was the main depot of the dock engineer, containing offices, workshops, and equipment, which up until the early part of the twentieth century represented the 'largest establishment of its kind in the world' (Jarvis

2003, 3). The 1840s also witnessed the construction of additional facilities for the Mersey flats and ferries in the southern part of the dock estate. This specifically involved the construction of a lock and dock for inland traffic, named Trafford Dock, off Clark's Hole basin (*p 96*), adjacent to Coburg and Queen's Dock (Ritchie-Noakes 1984, 38; Pl 73) and, in 1847, the opening of George's Landing Stage, at Pier Head, which was designed for ferry boats (Cossons and Jenkins 2011, 21), and was adjacent to George's Ferry Basin (*p 123*). This landing stage may well have replaced that established in the 1830s (*p 98*).

The 1850s witnessed the completion of several inter-linked docks at the northern end of the dock estate. Of these, Wellington Dock opened in 1850 (Pl 72; Ritchie-Noakes 1984, 169), which was accessed from the river via a half-tide basin, provided with a double half-tide entrance. This was followed in 1851 by the opening of Sandon Basin and Sandon Dock, which had five graving docks on its northern side, and Huskisson Dock, which opened in 1852 (Pl 74; *ibid*). This latter dock was accessed from Sandon Basin via two locks, and was provided, at this date, with a single branch dock. In 1853, Clarence Half-tide Dock was also enlarged (Jarvis 1991a, 231).

In the southern docks, one major scheme of dock construction also occurred during the 1850s. This involved the construction of Wapping Dock and Basin, which were completed in 1855 (Ritchie-Noakes 1984, 169; Pl 71). These were positioned inland, between Salthouse, Duke's, King's, and Queen's Docks, and

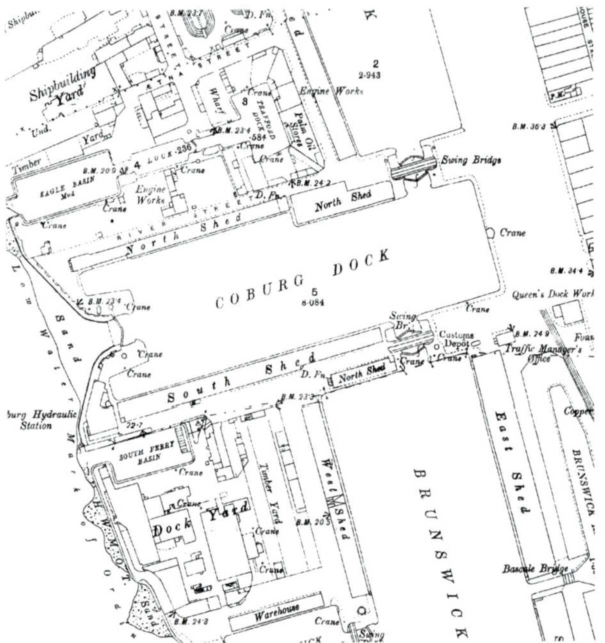

Plate 73: Extract from the Ordnance Survey 1893 25": 1 mile map (1893b), showing Coburg Dock and its environs

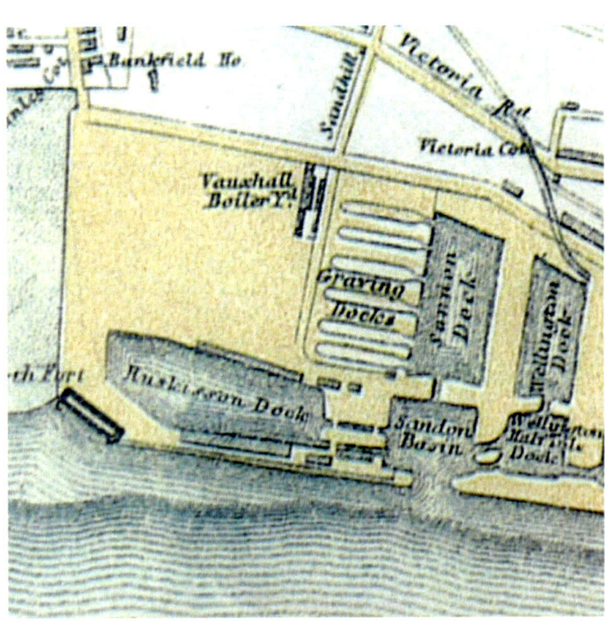

Plate 74: Extract from Bartholomew's map of 1855, showing the northern docks

were principally designed as a means of linking these with the system of docks to the north (*op cit*, 57). In order to facilitate this link, both Wapping Dock and Basin were designed with three entrances (*ibid*), and, as part of this scheme of works, several of the surrounding docks were modified. For instance, Salthouse Dock was enlarged by realigning its eastern quay (*op cit*, 24), whilst in 1851-2 the dry basin serving King's and Queen's Docks (*Ch 3, p 54*) was converted into a half-tide dock, which was then renamed Queen's Half-tide Dock; this opened in 1856 (*op cit, 37; p 148*). In addition, this latter scheme of work also included the further deepening of Queen's Dock and the rebuilding of its dock walls (*ibid*).

Significantly, in 1857, the Liverpool Corporation lost control of the docks and waterfront, following the issuing of an Act of Parliament, and control of the docks instead fell to an independent non-profit-making body, termed the Mersey Docks and Harbour Board (MDHB; Mountfield 1965, 12). In terms of the physical development of the dock system, following the creation of the MDHB, the first of the docks that opened was Canada Dock and its basin in 1858. These were specifically built to serve the timber trade, and the eastern side of Canada Dock was provided with a slip to aid the unloading of timber (*ibid*). Canada Dock, at 6.9 ha (17 acres), represents Hartley's largest dock and it was linked to Huskisson Dock by two entrance gates, whilst a sizable angled lock lay on its northern side, which linked it to Canada Basin (Jarvis 1991a, 100; Pl 75). Significantly, this latter feature represents the first large angled river lock used within the Liverpool Docks, and it was designed to allow steamships to enter the docks at most levels of the tide (Sharples 2004, 117).

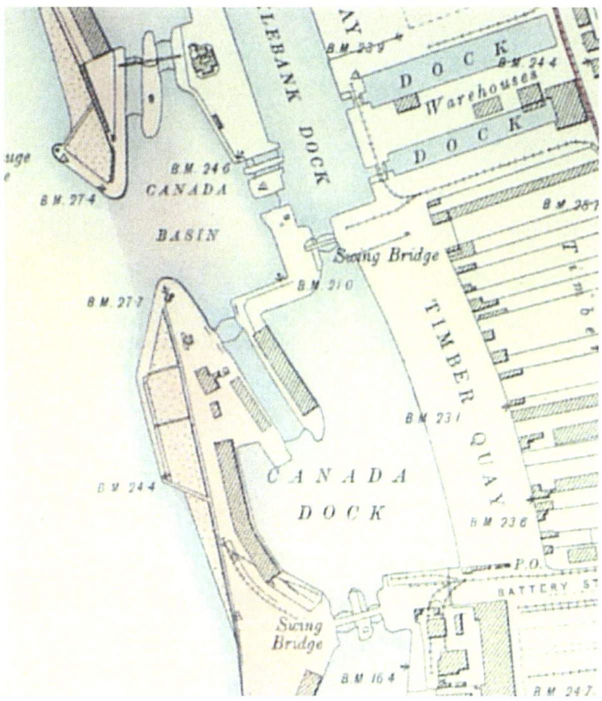

Plate 75: Extract from the Ordnance Survey 1894 6": 1 mile map (1894a), showing Canada Dock and its environs

Immediately following the formation of the MDHB, additional improvements were also made to the southern docks between 1857 and 1858. These included the joining and enlargement of Coburg and Union Docks, which were then named Coburg Dock, and the widening of the passages between this enlarged dock and Brunswick and Queen's Docks (*op cit*, 47). In 1857, Prince's Landing Stage, adjacent to Prince's Dock, was also opened, which formed another floating landing stage designed to serve passenger ships and transatlantic liners (Cossons and Jenkins 2011, 21).

The first half of the nineteenth century is also typified by the development of a series of buildings and structures within the dock estate, which were integral to the functioning of the docks. For example, this period witnessed the continued construction of warehouses directly within the dock estate, similar in form to those that had emerged at the end of the eighteenth century (*Ch 3, p 49*). Notable amongst these was a large single-storey tobacco warehouse, designed by John Foster, on the western side of King's Dock, which opened in 1814 (Ritchie-Noakes 1984, 38; Pl 76). However, within the dock estate, the construction of other nineteenth-century warehouses was specifically influenced by the 1803 Warehousing Act, which was extended to Liverpool in 1805 (Sharples 2004, 98). This act led to the creation of bonded warehouses, within which unloaded goods were stored until excise duty was paid on them (*op cit*, 98, 205). The advantage of this system was that goods could be unloaded without the presence of excise

men and the immediate levying of duties; cargoes could be sorted on the quayside; and merchants did not have to pay duties on their goods until they were sold (Ritchie-Noakes 1984, 49).

For security reasons, the 1803 Act required the adoption of a closed-dock system, such as that in London, built at the beginning of the nineteenth century, and initially, security at Liverpool's waterfront was considered insufficient by the Board of Customs and Excise (*ibid*). Moreover, many of Liverpool's merchants were opposed to the implementation of public, as opposed to private, warehouses, and the system was not fully adopted until the early 1840s, when Hartley constructed Albert Dock. This dock was specifically designed as a closed dock, surrounded by fireproof bonded warehouses (Pl 77), and now represents the country's finest surviving example of this style of maritime warehousing (*Ch 1, p 7*). Following the success of Albert Dock, Hartley also partly conceived Stanley and Wapping Docks as specialised docks, respectively opened in the 1840s and 1850s (*p 99*), to receive bonded goods. Accordingly, both docks were fringed with bonded warehouses, similar in style to those at Albert Docks, and those at Stanley Dock were designed for rail and hydraulic power (Ritchie-Noakes 1984, 58; Sharples 2004, 124).

Other buildings that fringed and characterised the early and mid-nineteenth-century docks and quaysides were transit sheds, which were designed

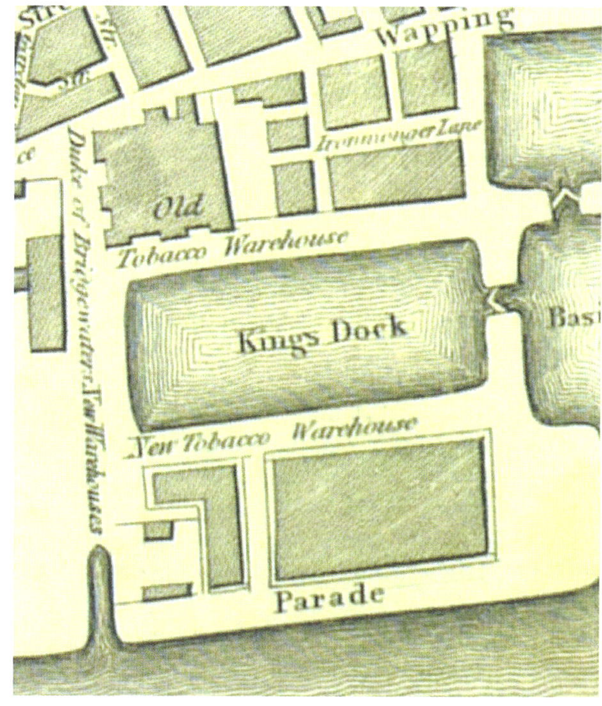

Plate 76: Extract from Thomas Kaye's map of 1815, showing the Old Tobacco Warehouse, built in 1793, and the New Tobacco Warehouse, built between 1811 and 1814

Plate 77: Bonded warehouses surrounding Albert Dock

temporarily to hold goods (Sharples 2004, 99). These narrow, linear buildings, extending along the length of the quayside, were initially constructed in wood, with cast-iron sheds appearing from 1818, though, following Hartley's appointment as dock engineer, these sheds were constructed in both iron and wood (Ritchie-Noakes 1984, 132-3). Mid-nineteenth-century mapping indicates that they were a common component of the docks (*ibid*).

Other notable early and mid-nineteenth-century structures included hydraulic towers and accumulators, gatekeeper's and policemen's huts, houses/offices, depots, and swing bridges, designed by both Rennie and Hartley, which, along with cranes, capstans, and dock gates, utilised hydraulic power from the 1850s onwards (Sharples 2004, 115). Several other significant buildings were also constructed close to Waterloo Dock. These comprised the northern Custom House, which was much smaller than the main offices at Canning Place (*p 132*). This new Custom House lay on the south side of the dock, along with a new fish market. In addition, Liverpool's second observatory was built in 1844 on the south side of this dock. This superseded the smaller observatory on St James Mount and played a central role in helping to fix the longitude of Liverpool (Jarvis 1991a, 146).

The opening of the Wapping Goods Station in 1830 also allowed the development of the dock's railway (Ritchie-Noakes 1984, 165; Fig 40). This railway network first appeared in 1842, and ran to the north of Salthouse Dock, though it was initially developed as a means of speeding up dock construction (*ibid*). The network was then extended in the 1850s and created links with Wapping Goods Station, Queen's Dock, and Canning Dock, with branch lines extending to Brunswick Dock and Wapping Warehouse (*op cit*, 166). By 1850, additional goods stations had been constructed, adjacent to the waterfront, and, from

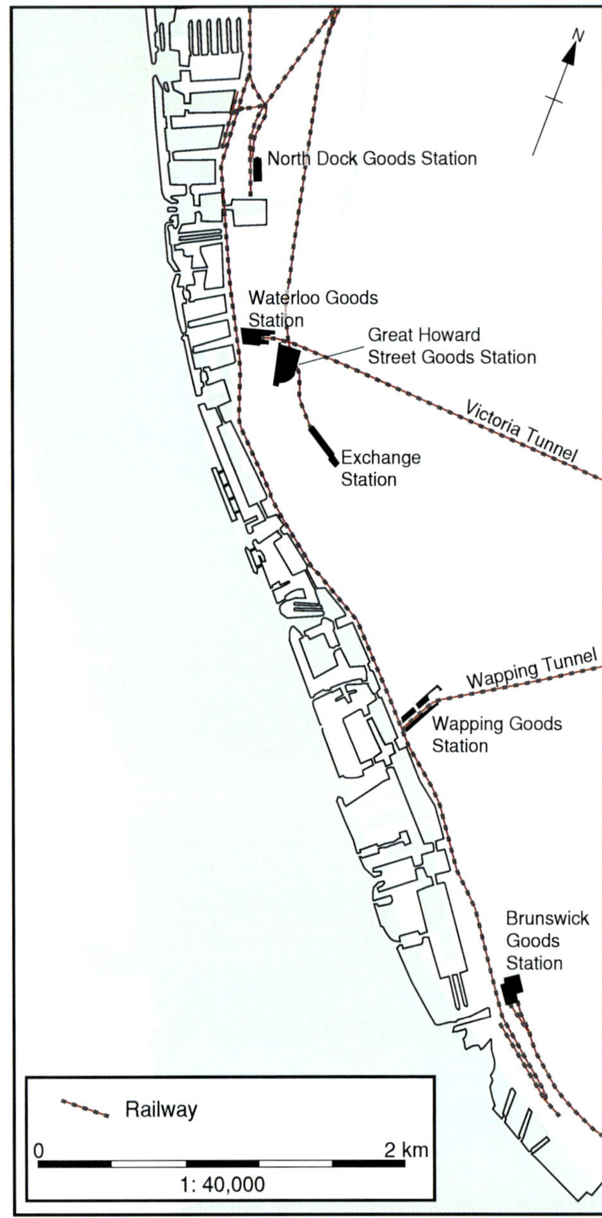

Figure 40: The mid-nineteenth-century dock-railway system and associated stations (© Crown copyright 2014 Ordnance Survey 100005569)

north to south, these included North Dock Goods Station; Waterloo Goods Station; Great Howard Street Goods Station, and Brunswick Goods Station. In 1850, Exchange Station, adjacent to the waterfront on Tithebarn Street, was also opened, which served as the terminus for the Lancashire and Yorkshire Railway (LYR; Sharples 2004, 26).

A final major feature of the early- to mid-nineteenth-century dock estate was the perimeter wall (*Ch 1, p 5*; Pl 2), which was specifically designed to enclose portions of the estate following the 1803 Warehousing Act, and to protect against trespass and pilfering (*p 101*). This wall initially enclosed Prince's Dock in the early nineteenth century and was then extended both northwards and southwards by Hartley in the mid-nineteenth century, forming a 'physical and psychological barrier' separating the docks from the town (Sharples 2004, 123).

The archaeology of the early-mid-nineteenth-century waterfront

The investigations on Mann Island (*Ch 1, p 12*) and along the LLC extension (*Ch 1, p 14*) uncovered various archaeological remains which hold relevance to the early- and mid-nineteenth-century waterfront and docks. In addition, investigations as part of the Liverpool Trams Scheme (*Ch 1, p 11*), and the Old Dock and Chavasse Park developments (*Ch 1, p 9*) also produced evidence relevant to this period, as did the development of the Pier Head Ferry Terminal Building (*Ch 1, p 11*) and the Arena and Conference Centre (*Ch 1, p 12*).

The archaeological remains specifically relate to the conversion and adaptation of particular eighteenth-century waterfront features, such as the Dry Dock, the entrance lock to Queen's Dock, and the Manchester and Chester Basins, and the construction of several new docks to the north, which formed part of John Foster's, and then Jesse Hartley's, dock-building schemes. In addition to the docks and associated land reclamation, archaeological remains relating to nineteenth-century activity were uncovered on Mann Island and Nova Scotia, as well as further north, along the route of the LLC extension, that were associated with the operation and infrastructure of the early- and mid-nineteenth-century docks.

Manchester Basin and Dock, and the extension of its northern quay (*c* 1800-60)

Historical background

One of the earliest nineteenth-century developments within Liverpool's waterfront relates to the modifications of Manchester Basin, which was created in the late eighteenth century by the Corporation (*Ch 3, p 74*). These modifications eventually led to the creation of Manchester Dock, and the sequence of

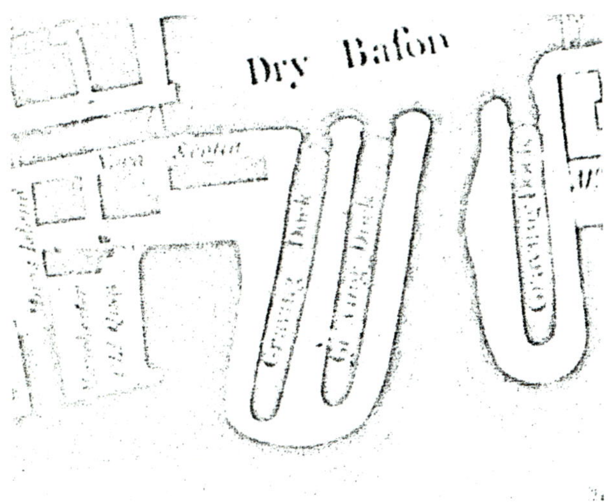

Plate 78: Extract from John Gore's map of 1796, showing Manchester Basin

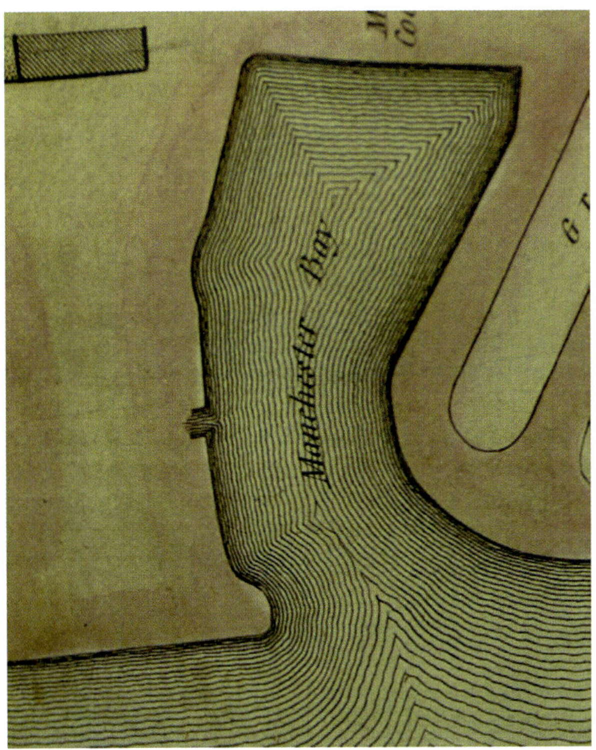

Plate 79: Extract from Horwood's map of 1803 (© Trustees of National Museums Liverpool), showing Manchester Bay

alteration is evident through consideration of the late eighteenth- and early nineteenth-century cartographic sources. These indicate that, between the time of Gore's map of 1796 (Pl 78) and Horwood's map of 1803 (Pl 79), the shape of the basin had been slightly altered, probably through the construction of new retaining walls. In addition, Horwood's map indicates that these modifications involved a further phase of land reclamation on the northern side of the basin, which extended the quayside further westwards. The form of the basin and northern quay as depicted

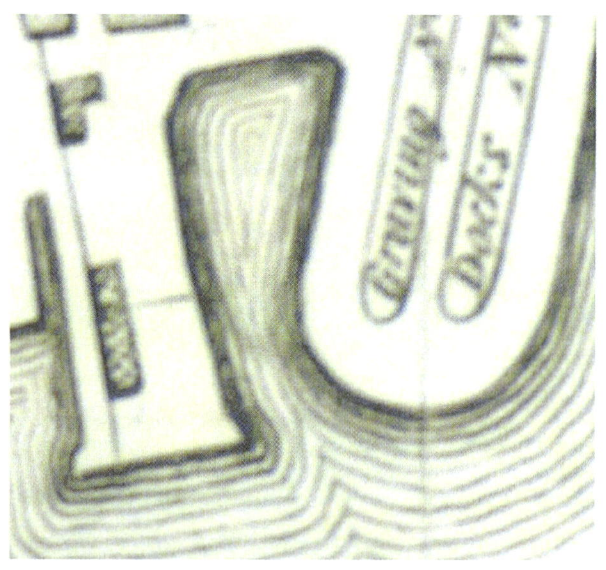

Plate 80: Extract from Jones' and Woodward's map of 1805, showing Manchester Bay (by courtesy of the University of Liverpool Library)

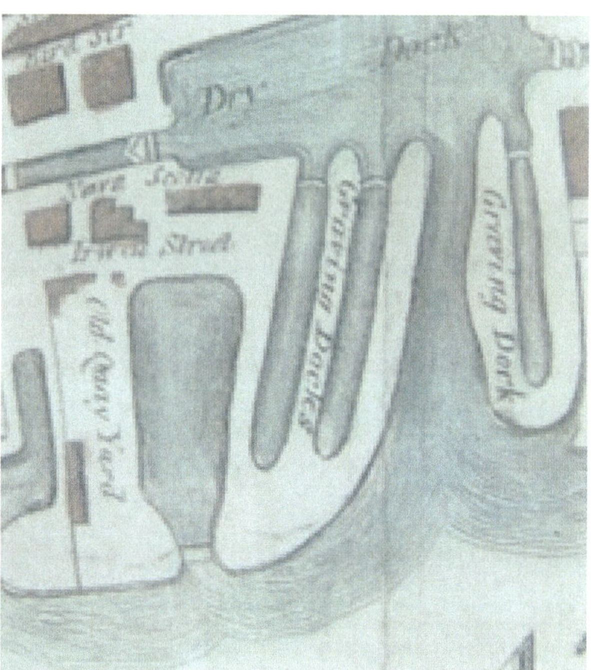

Plate 81: Extract from Gore's map of 1806, showing the conversion of Manchester Bay into Manchester Dock

The next stage of early nineteenth-century modification relates to the entrance of the basin and specifically to those works that were designed to convert Manchester Basin into a dock. Based on the cartographic evidence, this probably occurred between 1805 and 1806 (*contra* Picton 1873, 646; Rees 1991, 7; Hutchinson 1978, 3; Ritchie-Noakes 1984, 35). For example, the entrance is not depicted on Jones' and Woodward's map, dating to 1805 (Pl 80), though the walls of the entrance lock had certainly been finished by the time of Gore's survey of 1806 (Pl 81). Moreover, this completion date is confirmed by a Liverpool Dock Committee minute (MMMMAL MDHB/MP/25), dated 16 March 1807, which contains a reference to a '...wall and pierhead....on the south side of their [*ie* the Mersey and Irwell Navigation Company's] new basin'. The reference to a 'new basin' therefore implies that the lock had been finished by this time. In addition, this scheme of work also involved a further stage of land reclamation, which led to the westwards extension of the Manchester Basin's / Dock's northern quay. This appears to have been the last stage of land reclamation in this part of Liverpool and is again depicted on Gore's map of 1806.

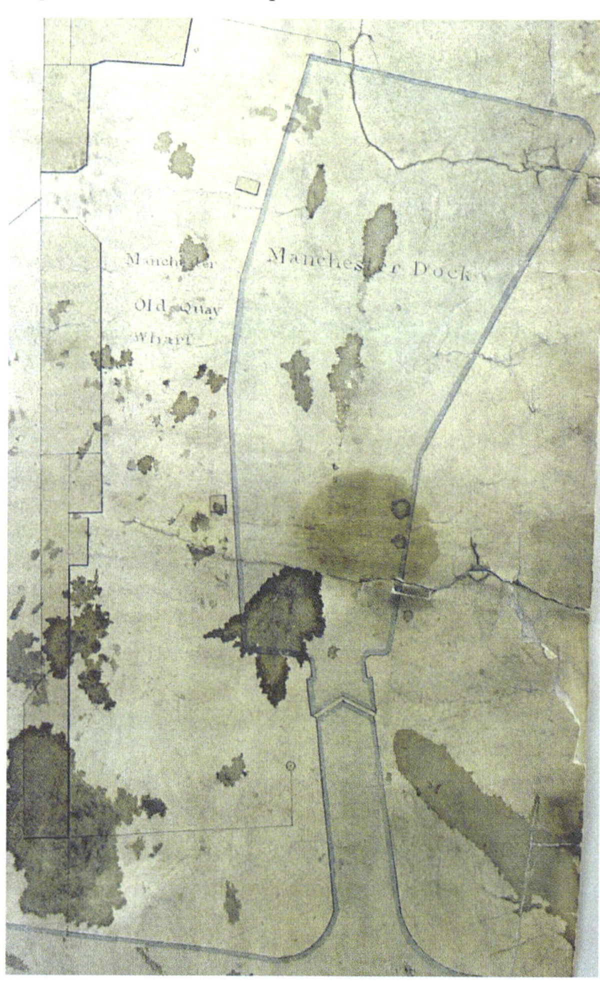

Plate 82: Extract from an 1822 plan of George's Dock (MMMMAL 182/1/2; © Trustees of National Museums Liverpool), showing Manchester Half-tide Dock

on Horwood's map is also replicated on Jones' and Woodward's plan (Pl 80). Although this modified basin, named 'Manchester Bay', remained a tidal basin, as it still possessed a wide entrance, the archaeological evidence suggests that the walls defining this, and also the quay to the north, were never completed (*p 111*). In terms of chronology, this therefore suggests that these features were being constructed at the time of Horwood's survey, and thus date to *c* 1803, and that they were still a work in progress in 1805 when Jones and Woodward surveyed the waterfront.

With regard to the provision of lock gates within the entrance lock, Sherwood's plan of 1821 depicts one pair of inward-facing mitre gates, positioned at the eastern end of the entrance lock. However, this arrangement is more clearly depicted on a plan of Manchester Dock produced by the Dock Committee, which dates to 21 May 1822 (MMMMAL 182/1/2; Pl 82). The presence of one set of gates is significant, as these indicate that Manchester Dock began life as a half-tide dock. However, by the time of Gage's map of Liverpool (1836), the entrance lock possessed two inward-facing mitre gates, indicating that by this date it functioned as a fully impounded wet dock (Pl 83). Documentary evidence indicates that the insertion of the second lock gates, and thus the conversion of Manchester Dock into a wet dock, as opposed to a half-tide dock, may well have occurred in 1825. The documentary sources specifically relate to the evidence presented against the first Liverpool and Manchester Railroad (*sic*) Bill (HL/PO/JO/10/8/685). Within this Bill, Mr Earle, presenting the case of the Mersey and Irwell Navigation Company, notes that works to make the entrance of Manchester Dock operable at all states of the tide are well advanced. A plan, accompanying this Bill, suggests that this work entailed the construction of the recesses for the outer lock gates, which had not yet been fitted. If this supposition is correct, the conversion of Manchester Dock into a fully impounded wet dock is much later than previously believed, and can probably be accurately placed late in 1825.

The quayside of Manchester Dock lay to its north, which, along with the area to the east, was owned

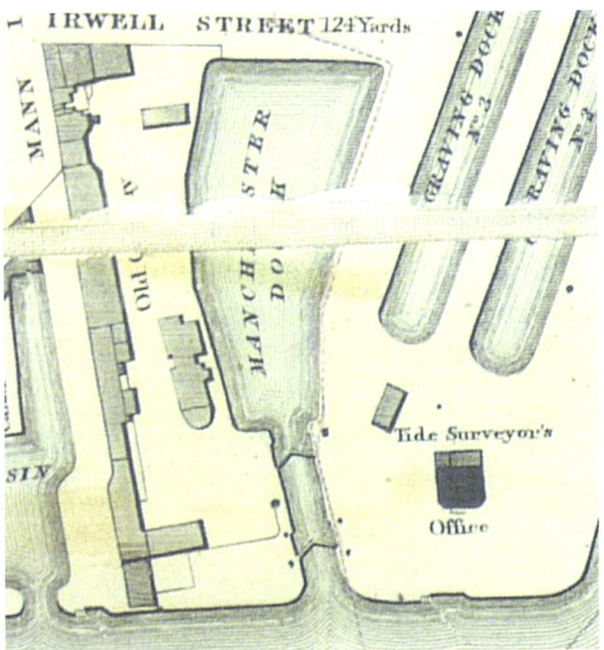

Plate 83: Extract from Gage's map of 1836
(© Trustees of National Museums Liverpool), showing Manchester Dock

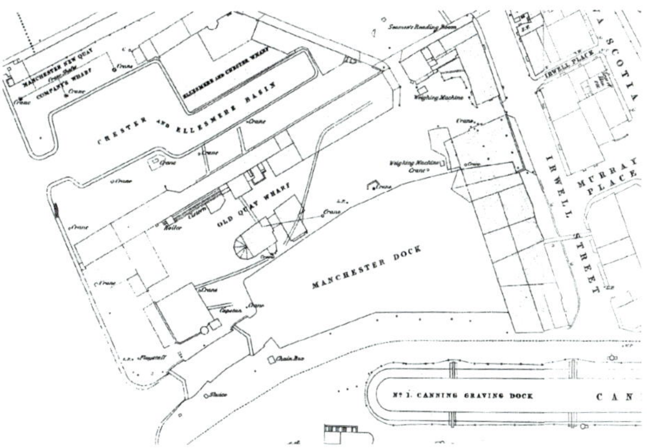

Plate 84: Extracts from the Ordnance Survey 1864
5 ft: 1 mile town plans (1864a; 1864b), showing Manchester Dock

during the early nineteenth century by the Mersey and Irwell Navigation Company. The cartographic evidence indicates that these areas were developed in the early nineteenth century through the progressive construction of ancillary buildings (Pl 84). These buildings had largely been constructed by 1822, when Manchester Dock functioned as a half-tide dock and comprised a range of offices, warehouses, and agents' residences along the northern side of the quay. These formed a range which, according to a Goad's Insurance Plan dating to 1890 (1890), had two storeys and an L-shaped range. This latter range stood at the corner of Mann Island and Irwell Street, and the Insurance Plan indicates that it comprised two, two-storeyed, terraces, a small seafarers' chapel, or bethel, and a small office. During the twentieth century, the cartographic evidence indicates that the range and other buildings were progressively demolished between the 1920s and early 1960s, and by 1980 only the two terraced properties fronting Irwell Street were extant, one of which was used by the Traffic Manager of the Dock Board, along with the small office building to their rear (Moss and Stammers nd, 17-18).

By the time of Gage's survey (1836; Pl 83), when the dock functioned as a wet dock, some small additions had been added to the early nineteenth-century buildings on the northern side of the quay, and two buildings had also been constructed directly adjacent to the northern side of the dock. However, these latter two buildings were demolished in *c* 1872 (Ch 5, p 161).

Following the construction of the early- and mid-nineteenth-century buildings, two weighing machines were constructed on the northern quay, and a warehouse/transit shed was also constructed. All of these features are depicted on the OS large-scale town plans of 1864 (1864a; 1864b; Pl 84). The warehouse is probably the 'shed' that was erected in 1841 by the Mersey and Irwell Navigation Company to attract independent traders to the dock (Ritchie-Noakes 1984, 35). It overhung the east end of Manchester Dock and its overhanging section formed three covered loading bays, or 'barge holes' (Moss and Stammers nd, 17). This warehouse was, however, partially destroyed by fire in 1890 and was subsequently rebuilt (*Ch 5, p 162*). Other smaller features depicted on the 1864 OS town plans include several cranes, weighing machines, and short sections of rail track (Pl 84).

In 1844, the Mersey and Irwell Navigation Company sold their undertakings to the Bridgewater Trustees, whilst in 1851 the Dock Trustees acquired Manchester Dock from the Corporation (*ibid*). With the establishment of the MDHB in 1858 (*p 100*), both Manchester Dock and Chester Basin were placed in its ownership (A Jarvis *pers comm*).

In terms of trade passing through Manchester Dock during the early nineteenth century, this predominantly consisted of the movement of coal and manufactured goods to Liverpool, and corn and cotton back inland, and it is estimated that it handled an average of 1000 tons per day (Ritchie-Noakes 1984, 36). However, from the mid-nineteenth century, Manchester Dock was used for lighterage, in conjunction with the railway companies (*ibid*), and this resulted in the construction of several buildings on the dock's southern quay. These included a two-storey, brick-built, office building, which was constructed in *c* 1854 for use by the London and North Western Railway (LNWR) Company, and still stands (Moss and Stammers nd, 17, 20; Pl 85). The construction

of this office appears to have entailed the demolition and modification of the far southern end of the 1841 warehouse/transit shed that lay at the eastern end of the dock (*p 105*). A warehouse/transit shed was also constructed, which was attached to the western side of the office and extended along Manchester Dock's southern quay, and also contained a covered berth. In 1860, this warehouse, along with the more southerly of the covered bays contained within the 1841 warehouse, was used by the Birkenhead Railway Company (Ritchie-Noakes 1984, 36). However, as with the 1841 warehouse, the transit shed on the southern side of the quay was partially destroyed by fire in 1890 and was then largely rebuilt (Moss and Stammers nd, 17).

Archaeological evidence
During the various archaeological investigations on Mann Island, as a prelude to the construction of the Countryside Neptune development (*Ch 1, p 13*) and the new Museum of Liverpool (*Ch 1, p 15*), and also within the footprint of the LLC extension (*Ch 1, p 14*), significant early- and mid-nineteenth-century remains were uncovered. More specifically, these related to the gradual conversion of Manchester Basin into Manchester Dock, and also included evidence for structures and buildings situated on the adjacent quayside.

The eastern half of the area formerly occupied by the basin and dock was examined during excavations on the Countryside Neptune site and also those completed along the line of the LLC extension. During these campaigns of excavation, the northern

Plate 85: The London and North Western Railway offices, dating to 1854, and transit sheds, which were rebuilt in 1890 following a fire

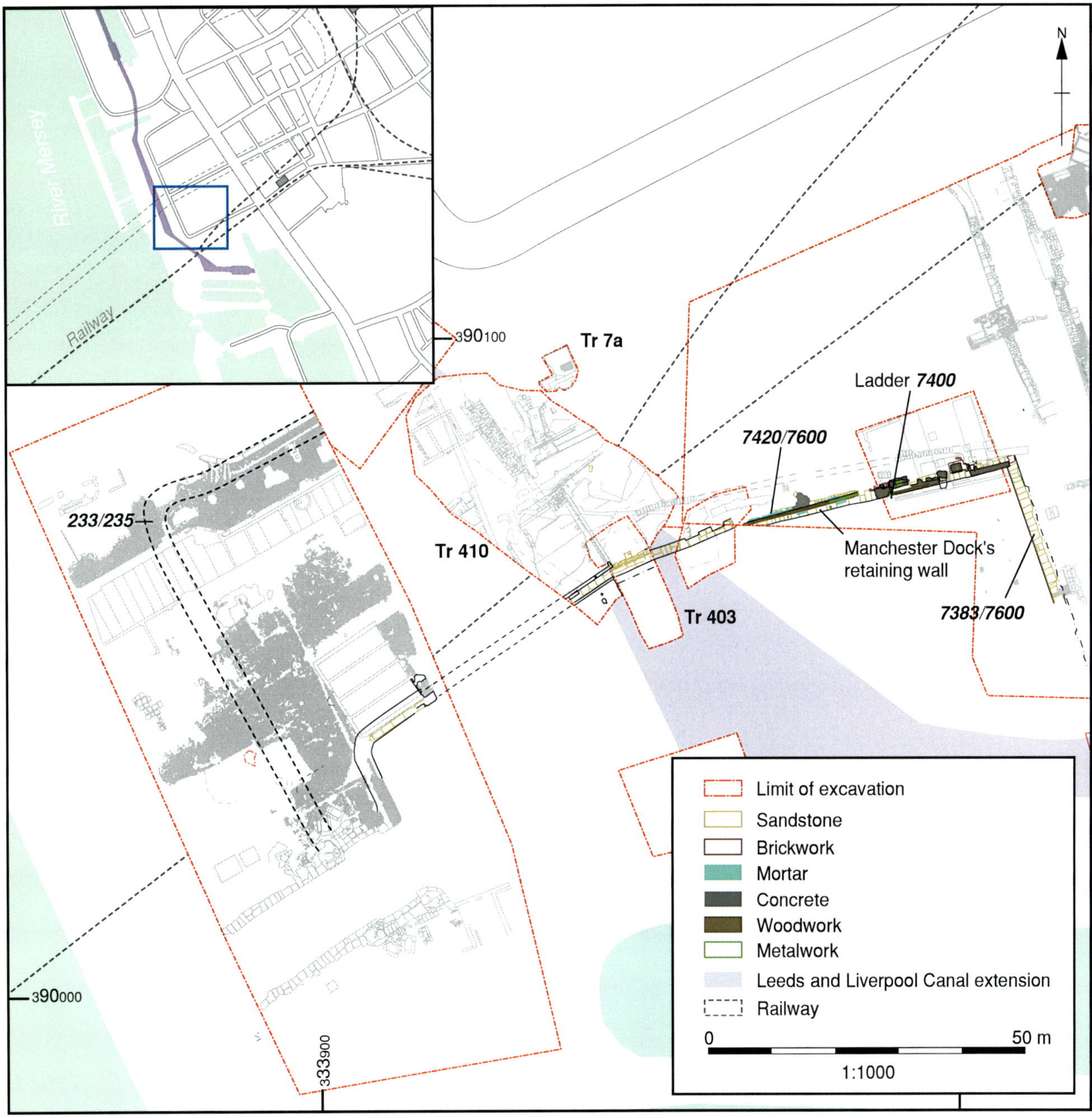

Figure 41: The early nineteenth-century remains (c 1803-7) of Manchester Basin (© Crown copyright 2014 Ordnance Survey 100005569)

(**7420/7600**) and eastern (**7383/7600**; Fig 41) walls of the basin were exposed, and these appear to be the retaining walls depicted on Horwood's map of 1803 (*p 103*). Indeed, these walls were probably constructed around 1803 (*p 103*) and they replaced the earlier retaining walls of Manchester Basin; they also altered its shape. Excavation indicated that these walls, which defined the eastern half of the basin, were retained throughout the nineteenth century and therefore formed part of Manchester Dock, first in its incarnation as a half-tide dock and also following its conversion into a fully impounded wet dock (*p 105*).

The visible waterside elevations of these walls were composed of pink sandstone ashlar, which, more generally, was used in dock construction after *c* 1785 (Ritchie-Noakes 1984, 37). These ashlar blocks were laid in irregular courses and were originally bonded with lime-based mortar, but were later repointed with grey cement mortar (Pl 86). They were also decorated with masons' marks, which included crosses, lozenges, and 'A', 'H', and '1' symbols (Fig 42). Although the source of this pink sandstone is not known, it is probable that, as with Prince's Dock, under construction from *c* 1810 (*p 136*), it was derived from quarries at Runcorn (Jarvis 1991b, 12). These retaining walls also stepped out towards their bases, providing a more substantial foundation, which was recorded by laser scanning. Moreover, in some places it appeared that the bases of the walls were situated upon a series of vertical timber piles, although it was

*Plate 86: The interior face of Manchester Dock's northern retaining wall (**7600**)*

Figure 42: The main types of masons' marks visible on Manchester Dock's retaining wall

not possible to expose these during the excavation. Where examined, the composition of the rear face of the basin/dock wall was, however, slightly different, in that it used both pink and yellow sandstone, the latter probably recycled from the walling of the earlier Manchester Basin (Pl 87; *Ch 3, p 74*). The upper section of the eastern wall (**7383/7600**) of the dock featured T-shaped metal pins to secure a timber fender. In addition, mooring pins and rings were visible along this wall, and also on the northern dock wall (**7420/7600**), which was also associated with a metal ladder (**7400**; Pl 88; Fig 41).

A short section of the basin's retaining wall was also uncovered to the west during excavations at the Museum of Liverpool site (Fig 41; Pl 89). The position of this wall equates with that depicted on Horwood's map of 1803, which was at the entrance of the basin. However, this wall differed from the retaining walls defining the eastern half of the basin in that it was constructed using alternate courses of brick and sandstone. A horizontal piece of timber had also been set into the wall, sandwiched between sandstone blocks and brick, presumably to act as reinforcement. The reasons for the difference in construction are not entirely clear, though it does appear that this wall was never completed, due to a subsequent change in design, which resulted in the insertion of an entrance lock (*p 111*).

Within the Museum of Liverpool site, immediately to the north of the wall close to the basin's entrance

*Plate 87: The rear face of Manchester Dock's northern retaining wall (**7600**)*

Plate 88: The metal ladder associated with Manchester Dock's northern quay

Plate 89: The early section of retaining wall identified at the entrance of Manchester Basin

(*p 108*), a fragmentary north-south-aligned river wall (**233/235**; Fig 41; Pl 90) was also uncovered, the position of which equates to the western end of the basin's northern quay as depicted on Horwood's map (1803; Pl 79) and Jones' and Woodward's map (1805; Pl 80). This wall formed a continuation of that at the entrance of the basin, was 3.8 m thick, and in one section it survived to a height of *c* 2 m. This upstanding section was composed of masonry blocks of yellow sandstone, with a chiselled / punched finish, laid in regular courses. The west-facing (external) side of this wall was finished to a high standard, while the east-facing section was more roughly coursed. The blocks used to construct the wall varied in size,

Plate 90: River wall **233/235**, from the west

Plate 91: Backfill deposits sealing wall **233/235**, from the west

the largest measuring c 1 m square, and they were very similar in character to those used for the rear elevations and core of the lock to Manchester Dock (*p 111*). This suggests that dismantled sections of this wall were reused in order to create the slightly later entrance lock.

Significantly, it appears that the river wall (*233/235*) and, by implication, the basin-retaining wall close to the entrance were never raised to their full height, and hence represent abandoned works that were never completed. This was evidenced by later infill deposits (*p 113*), which sealed portions of the incomplete river wall, and extended to both its east and west (Pl 91). If this is correct, this implies that, in common with many contemporary mapmakers, Horwood and Jones and Woodward seem to have shown works that were intended, or only partly constructed, in the same style as existing elements of the waterfront.

The reasons for the abandonment of the river wall defining the western side of the basin's northern quay, and the retaining wall at the entrance to the basin, probably relate to the decision, during construction, to provide the basin with an entrance lock in order to convert it into a half-tide dock. This also entailed the further westward extension of Manchester Basin's northern quay. The cartographic evidence indicates that this new design was completed by 1806 (*p 104*).

Significantly, the walls (*2* and *3*) of this entrance lock, along with the adjoining dock walls defining the western end of the dock, were exposed during the excavations at the Museum of Liverpool site (Fig 43). These walls were in an excellent state of preservation and were faced entirely in fine-grained pink sandstone

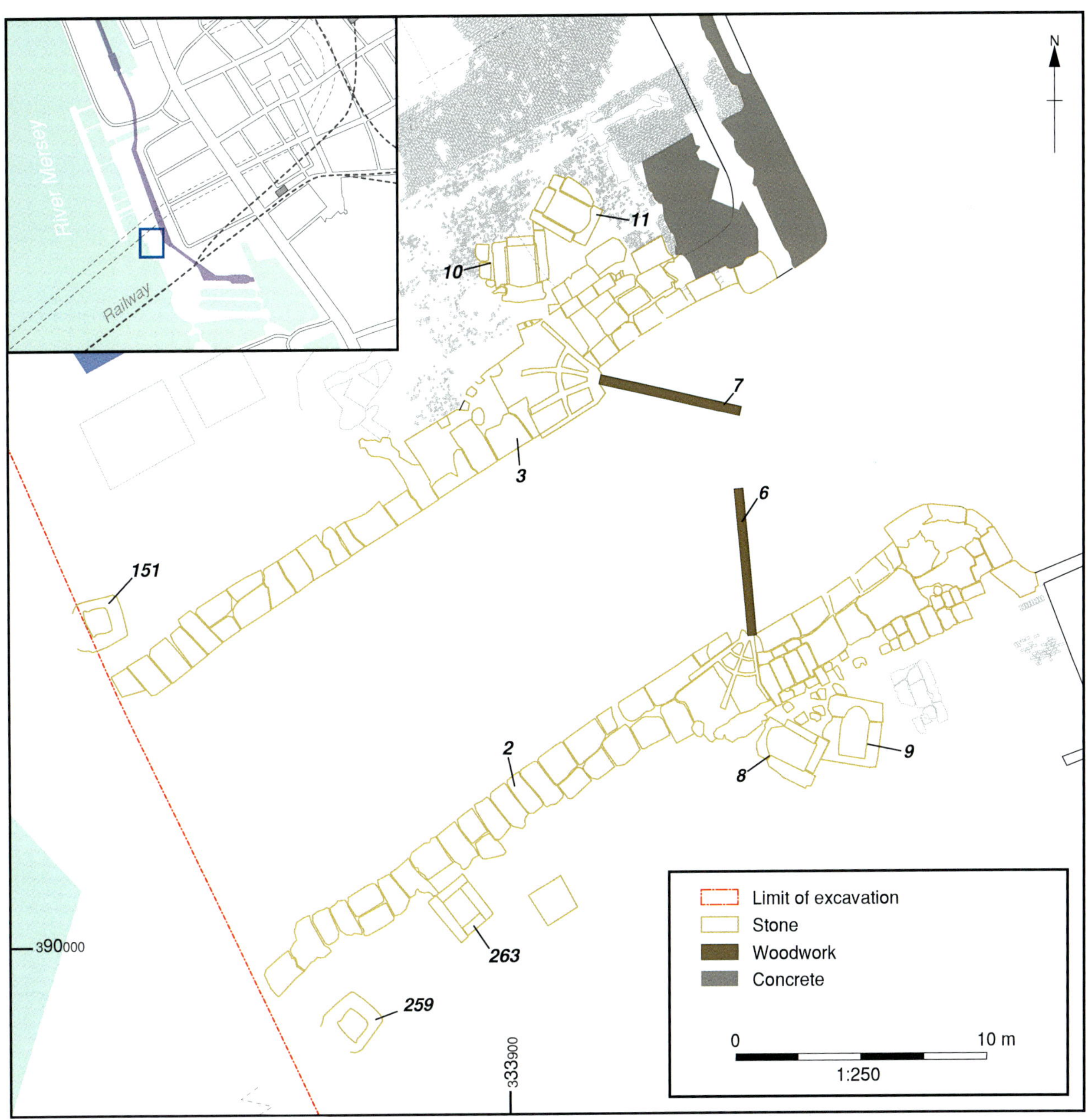

Figure 43: The eastern lock gates of Manchester Dock (© Crown copyright 2014 Ordnance Survey 100005569)

*Plate 92: The Museum of Liverpool excavation, showing the partially excavated entrance lock walls, **2** (left) and **3***

ashlar masonry, with occasional repairs in brick or granite (Pl 92). The masonry facing used at the entrance was therefore comparable to that employed in the slightly earlier dock walls exposed to the east at the Countryside Neptune site (*p 107*). Within the northern dock wall (**3**) were lengths of timber, aligned north-south through the eastern part of the wall, approximately 3 m below the original ground level. Although these appear to have provided additional support for the wall, no similar timbers were apparent in the southern dock wall (**2**).

The well-preserved curved recesses for the lock gates were also present and were constructed using

masonry of a significantly better quality than that used within the rest of the lock (Pl 93). However, it was not possible to determine if these recesses were original features or a result of rebuilding. Masons' marks were observed throughout the entrance lock and included letters, numbers, and symbols such as arrows and diamonds. The predominant mason's mark was the letter 'T', which had been used at varying sizes in the southern lock-gate recess. Other masons' marks included 'G', 'H4', and triangular symbols (Fig 44).

*Plate 93: Curved recesses for the lock gates, associated with entrance lock wall **3***

Figure 44: Masons' marks on the entrance-lock walls

Apart from the dock and river walls relating to the conversion of Manchester Basin into a dock, evidence was also recovered for associated land reclamation. Reclamation deposits were examined at the Museum of Liverpool site, and they relate specifically to that phase of land reclamation which resulted in the further extension of the dock's northern quay. The cartographic evidence indicates that this phase of work dates to between 1805 and 1806 and formed part of the scheme of works designed to convert Manchester Basin into a half-tide dock. It also represents the final phase of land reclamation in this part of Liverpool (*p 104*). The archaeological remains associated with this consisted of infill deposits, some containing artefacts, which sealed the earlier unfinished river wall (**233/235**; Fig 41), dating to *c* 1803 (*p 109*). It is

also possible that many of these deposits represent dumped ships' ballast, which in this instance was carted from the surrounding docks for deposition in this area (A Jarvis *pers comm*).

To the west of the earlier river wall, the lowest of the later reclamation deposits encountered were composed of red-brown clays, becoming greyer with depth. However, these deposits could not be fully investigated as their surfaces coincided with the formation level. Detailed examination of the upper reclamation deposits was made possible through the excavation of four evaluation trenches (Tr 2-5; Fig 45). Tr 2 contained an upper layer of rubble, which sealed deposits that included layers of black clinker and very clean, pale sand, below a reddish-brown sandy clay.

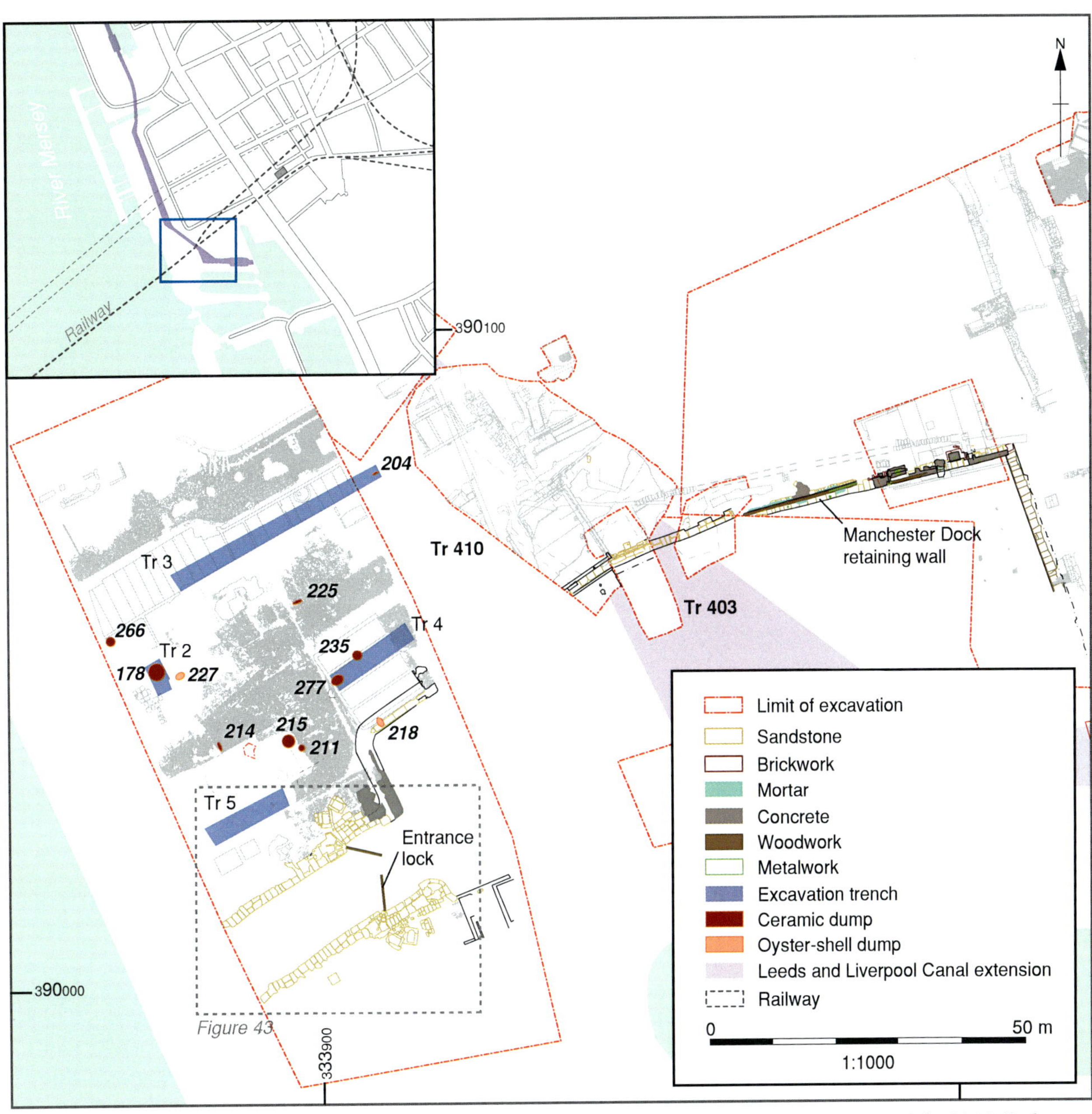

Figure 45: The early nineteenth-century (post-1806) remains of Manchester Dock (© Crown copyright 2014 Ordnance Survey 100005569)

Plate 94: Reclamation deposits associated with the conversion of Manchester Basin into a dock, at the Museum of Liverpool site

The clinker and pale sand deposits both contained large dumps of sugar-mould fragments (*178*). Other finds included fragments of syrup jars, dark-glazed earthenwares, china, and animal bone. Similarly, in Tr 3, a deposit of rubble and brown sand extended for a depth of *c* 1.2 m, above yellow sand. This latter deposit sealed a black silty clay. Finds from this trench included clay tobacco-pipe fragments from a small discrete deposit of grey ashy material (*204*). In addition, a two-brick wide wall was identified at the base of the trench. Although the function of this wall was not clear, it might represent a temporary river wall used during this phase of land reclamation. To its north, a small collection of sugar-mould fragments was recovered. Within Tr 4, the upper fill deposits consisted of layers of sand and sandy gravel set above layers of clay. One deposit of brown sand also contained sugar-mould and syrup-jar fragments (*277*). Only one land-reclamation deposit was encountered in Tr 5: a layer of sand containing large fragments of yellow sandstone.

Other reclamation deposits were examined during the watching brief. Tip lines within these deposits suggest that those at the northern end of the site had been dumped from the riverside, probably after transportation up-river, whilst elsewhere tipping appeared to be from the landward side. Generally, these deposits consisted of horizontal layers of red and yellow crushed sandstone, and clean white sands, possibly from river dredgings, and also, in places, more mixed material. Significantly, within these reclamation deposits were lenses composed, almost entirely, of broken artefacts, as well as molluscs, and clinker (Pl 94). This material included late eighteenth-/early nineteenth-century pottery, with a small number of residual seventeenth- or earlier eighteenth-century sherds. The later pottery predominantly consists of fine wares, such as pearl and cream ware, with smaller quantities of glazed earthenwares.

Two of the more significant pottery dumps (*215* and *235*; Fig 43) contained mainly fragmentary pieces of Staffordshire pottery, although some whole cups, lids, and figurines were present. A few cross-joining sherds were also identified within these two dumps, indicating that they were probably derived from a single source, such as a substantial tip of discarded pottery from one of the town's warehouses.

Plate 95: Lock-access ladder on the southern wall (2) of the entrance lock

Plate 96: Timber depth gauge on the northern dock wall

Extensive deposits of clinker and sand containing sugar-mould fragments and syrup jars were also uncovered across the whole site, though one deposit (**214**), on the western periphery, contained only syrup jars. In addition, three large dumps of clay tobacco pipes (**211**, **225**, and **266**), associated with kiln furniture, were present in the northern part of the site, along with several smaller deposits. Finally, two large deposits of oyster shells (**218** and **227**) had been deposited during this phase of land reclamation. These probably represent waste shells derived from the early nineteenth-century sale and consumption of oysters in the town.

The entrance lock and adjoining dock walls were associated with several *in situ* fittings. Within the lock, a set of access ladders was present on the southern wall (**2**), which consisted of wooden rungs, attached to the wall with iron bolts and brackets (Pl 95). This set had not survived particularly well and partly collapsed during excavation. Directly opposite, another set of timber access-ladders was evident on the northern wall (**3**), associated with a slot cut into the sandstone wall, which had, at a later date, been repaired with concrete.

A timber depth gauge (Pl 96) was also exposed on the inner face of the northern dock wall (**3**), adjacent to gate **6** (*see below*). This gauge was at a depth of 0.85 m below the dock wall, and recorded water levels in feet, beginning with '20' at the top, with the numbers carved into the wood and painted over in white. The base of the gauge was not reached, since it was only exposed to a maximum depth of 2.4 m (10 ft) before the water table was met. It had been fastened to the dock wall with iron brackets at regular 1 m intervals, and traces of a bituminous coating were also visible. The upper part of the gauge was removed at the 10 ft mark by conservators from the National Museums Liverpool. Other *in situ* dock fittings included cast-iron bollards, iron rope-tie rings, and heel-post strap anchors for securing the lock gates.

The inner lock gates (**6** and **7**; Fig 43) within the entrance were also present. These were in a closed position, their tops being encountered at a depth of *c* 0.75 m below the original ground surface (Pl 97), and they had a slight curve or arch to the front (Pl 98), which fitted into a similar curve in the gate recesses, a design that was described by Troughton in 1810 (Troughton 1810, 278). Although the top of the heel posts and iron brackets securing the gates to the stays had been removed during the filling of the dock in the 1920s (*Ch 5, p 162*), one of the heel-post heads was recovered from this backfill. Its upper section was faceted, probably to allow fixing of the bearing (Pl 99).

Plate 97: The in situ *lock gates*

Plate 98: The curved front of the lock gates

116

Plate 99: Heel-post pad for one of the lock gates

The east-facing sides of the gates were clad with vertically aligned, *c* 0.26 m-thick, softwood planks, which were in a very poor condition, with a large number of holes where the wood had rotted away (Pl 97). Various iron fittings remained *in situ* on this side of the gates, including rods, brackets, and a pair of staples for securing the operating chains. The main structural elements were in a much better condition and were clearly visible on the western faces of the gates, consisting of two short, horizontal softwood fenders, although very badly decayed, attached to the second and sixth horizontal beams from the top of the gates. It is possible that these fenders may have been recycled boat masts. The visible section of the frame was composed of six horizontal timbers, *c* 0.24 m thick, bolted to two upright timbers on either side (Pl 100). In addition, iron brackets on the third and fourth horizontal beams were also attached to the upright nearest the walls. Diagonal braces had been added between horizontals on both gates as strengtheners, apparently fixed in place using a lap joint. Gate *6* had one diagonal joint missing between the fifth and sixth horizontal, although it was unclear whether it had been removed or had rotted away. The three lower beams on both gates were in slightly better condition, probably as a result of more favourable burial conditions, and had not been covered in bitumen like all the other timber used in the gates. Compacted grey clay with pockets of sand was found in between the horizontal timbers, though it was not present between the first and second timbers. It is unlikely that this was an original component of the gate, though it was not clear whether the clay had naturally silted up against the gates or if it had been deliberately packed in to seal them before backfilling.

The inner lock gates were built of the tropical hardwood, Guyanese Greenheart (*Ocotea rodaei*). This timber was in use in the North West by 1830, as it was employed in the construction of the LMR Warehouse at Liverpool Road Station, Manchester (Greene 1995), and it appears to have been used in Liverpool for the construction of dock gates during the 1830s (Jarvis 1996, 197). This might, therefore, suggest that the excavated dock gates were not the original set, but were perhaps replacements dating to the 1830s, once Greenheart timber became readily available. In terms of construction, Greenheart was preferred over oak or other timbers as it possesses organic durability and toughness, and is resistant to rot and marine worms, and was also available in long lengths, making it eminently suitable for lock gates (Jarvis 1996, 197-200; Scholfield and Smith 1999, 56). Indeed, this durability is evidenced by those Greenheart gates which were installed in Canada Dock in 1856 and were still in use in 1950 (Scholfield and Smith 1999, 56).

Plate 100: The west-facing side of the lock gates

*Plate 101: Timber stop pinned to dock wall **3**, and the exit hole for the sluice-gate mechanism, provided with iron rollers*

0.23 m thick. The outer core of each timber was in a relatively poor state of preservation, probably due to the decay of their relatively soft sapwood.

Each of the inner lock gates was opened and closed by a combination of four gate-operating mechanisms, two for each gate, based on the four-engine system (Jarvis 1996, 200-1). Each set worked in opposition, one for opening and one for closing the gates, and they were operated using winches. These winches would have been situated above four square chambers (*see below*), constructed under the quayside, which were connected to the lock by inclined shafts through the dock walls. Originally, these shafts housed ropes or chains, the latter of which were in use in the Liverpool docks from April 1808 (Phillips 1983, 14), and these would have connected to staples on the gates. Winding in one set of chains would therefore have caused the gates to open or close. A photograph of the entrance lock, taken in *c* 1928 (Ritchie-Noakes 1984, 35), suggests that these were Type 4.2 (W2) winches (Phillips 1983, 14), which had two horizontally mounted axles; the lower axle was mounted at, or just above, ground level and carried the chain drum between a large gear wheel and a brake wheel. The upper axle carried a small cog, which meshed with the large gear, whilst a removable crank handle turned the winch, with a friction show acting on the brake wheel.

In addition to the dock gates, two timber stops (Pl 101) were present, which were pinned to the dock wall at the eastern corner of each recess with two iron nuts and bolts, though these were probably late nineteenth- or twentieth-century replacements. These timber stops had been sawn to lengths of 0.9 m and 1 m, and were

Although the winches and chains had been removed prior to filling the dock, all four winch chambers (**8-11**; Fig 43) were present. These were rectangular in plan with an apsidal end pointing towards the dock (Pl 102). However, this latter feature had probably been created as a result of thinning the stonework, caused

*Plate 102: Winch chambers **8** and **9**, to the south of the lock gates*

*Plate 103: Winch chambers **10** and **11**, to the north of the lock gates*

by abrasion from the chain used to operate the gate. The chambers were arranged symmetrically, with two (*8* and *11*) aligned south-east/north-west and the other two (*9* and *10*) north-east/south-west (Pl 103). Although constructed using similar methods and materials, each chamber was slightly different in size and in the details of its construction. This may be a consequence of each having been built by different work parties working to a general plan, rather than from detailed drawings.

Although only one of the shafts (*10*) had not been filled, their general character was established. The internal walls of the shafts were lined with high-quality sandstone masonry, finished with punched chisel marks. The roof of each shaft had a series of grooves worn into the softer sandstone by constant wear from the chains (Pl 104). In contrast, however, the floors were constructed of granite, and this durable stone was probably used to reduce friction and to prevent erosion as a result of wear from the chain. Significantly, the use of granite and punch drafting is more commonly associated with Jesse Hartley's time as dock engineer, and this implies that the shafts were repaired after 1826 (A Jarvis *pers comm*).

All of the shafts were fitted at either end with cast-iron rollers, to aid the passage of the chains and protect the surrounding masonry from further erosion. Therefore, each had a horizontal roller in the main chamber, whilst each of the shaft's exits had been provided with a horizontal and vertical roller, the positions of

which varied, depending on the orientation of the shaft in relation to the gate (Pl 101). The horizontal roller was designed to stop the chains dropping onto the sandstone walls, whilst the vertical roller protected the shaft's most vulnerable edge. Little survived of the winch mechanisms, though their housings were probably mounted on iron bars that were set into holes on the upper edge of the winch chambers. In addition, the scarring from the lower axle and drum of one of

*Plate 104: The roof of winch chamber **10**, and its associated horizontal roller*

Plate 105: The in situ *sluice gate and attached chain, in sluice housing* **259**

the winches was just visible, on the side wall of one of the chambers, as an arc of corrosion product.

A similar sandstone block-constructed chamber (**151**; Fig 43) was discovered adjacent to the outer lock gates.

However, this was constructed differently from the winch chambers associated with the inner lock gates, as there did not appear to be a shaft from the chamber into the lock and, furthermore, there were no signs of any exit tunnel within the lock. The function of this feature is therefore not particularly clear.

In addition to the lock-gate mechanisms, two sluice housings (**259** and **263**), constructed in red sandstone ashlar, were also evident just to the south of the entrance lock (Fig 43). One of these (**263**) was only partially excavated, as it had been destroyed above formation level. However, the second (**259**) survived beneath a concrete and paved walkway at the extreme western edge of the site. This housing contained an *in situ* sluice gate, complete with chain attached (Pl 105).

At the far eastern end of Manchester Dock, remains relating to a warehouse were also exposed during the excavation at the Countryside Neptune site (Fig 46). This warehouse was probably erected in 1841, though it was partially rebuilt following a fire in 1890 (*p 106*). It was designed to overhang the dock, and had three covered loading bays for ease of discharge and loading. Within the dock, the remains of the timbers (**7645**) that supported the overhanging section of the warehouse

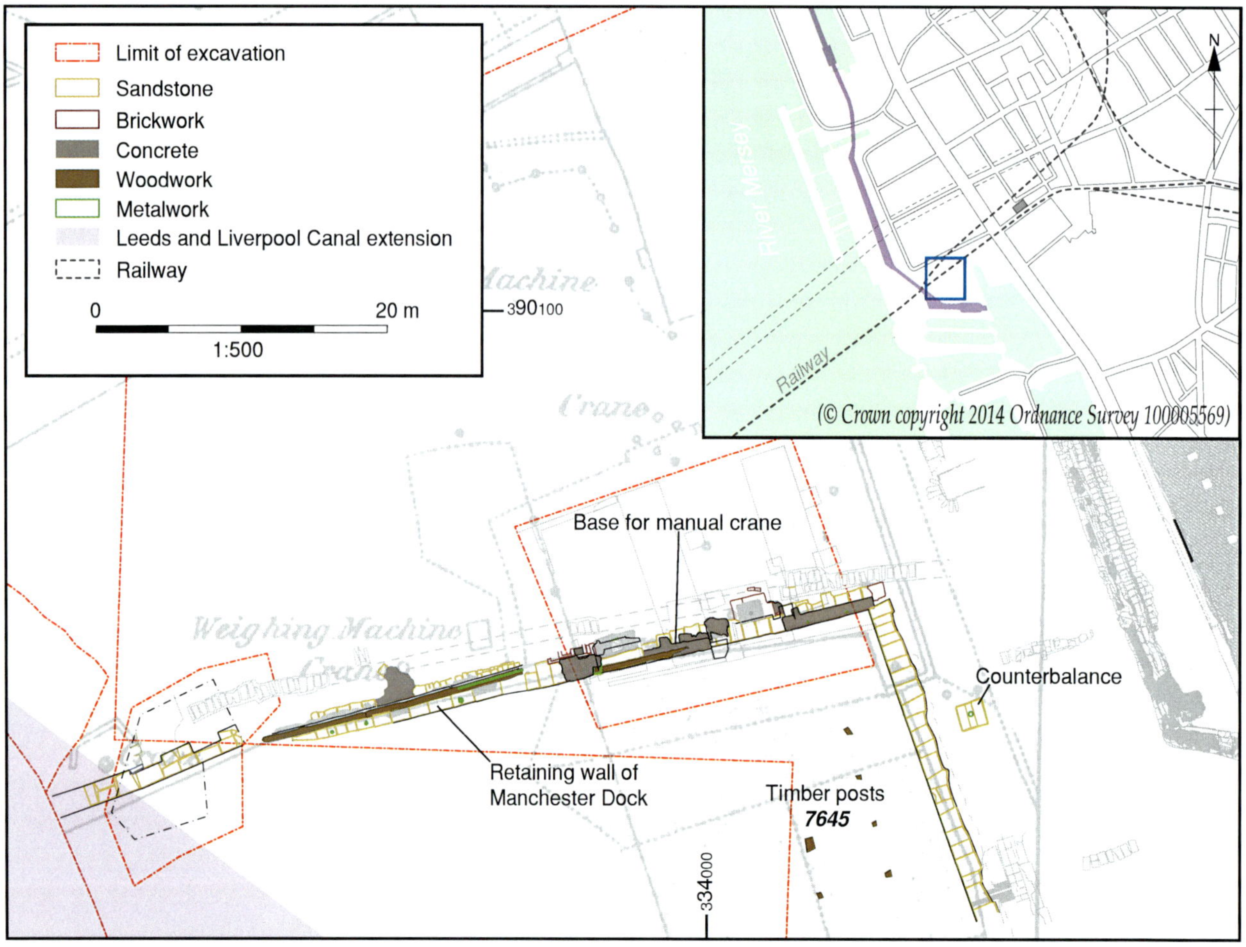

Figure 46: Remains of the 1841 warehouse overhanging the eastern end of Manchester Dock, superimposed on the Ordnance Survey 1864 5 ft: 1 mile town plans (1864a; 1864b)

Plate 106: The interior of Manchester Dock, showing the remains of timber piers protruding from the sandstone backfill

were evident, and it is possible that these formed elements of the original building, thus dating to 1841. These comprised a series of eight vertical and four horizontal timber supports (made from pitch pine), projecting out of the infill of the dock (Pl 106). The bottom of these timbers was not reached, however, as they lay below the formation level for the development, nor was it possible to see what sort of deposits they were embedded in. However, it was clear that the timbers had been squared off, with chamfered edges, and were fitted with large iron bolts and chains, which contributed to the structural integrity of the piers. A large sandstone counterbalance was another structure associated with this warehouse (Fig 46). This counterbalance lay to the rear of the dock wall and presumably it aided in securing the warehouse's overhanging framework, which was probably composed of iron and timber, in a similar manner to the other transit sheds dating to this period (Ritchie-Noakes 1984, 132). Another early- or mid-nineteenth-century structure, relating to the functioning of Manchester Dock, was identified on the eastern quayside at the Countryside Neptune site. This consisted of the sandstone base for a manually operated crane, which probably pre-dates the construction of the 1841 warehouse.

The footings for another early- to mid-nineteenth-century warehouse/shed were also exposed on Manchester Dock's northern quay during the excavations at the Museum of Liverpool site. These were composed of handmade brick and could be directly related to the range plotted on Gage's map of 1836 (Pl 83), which bounded the northern quayside of Manchester Dock (Fig 47).

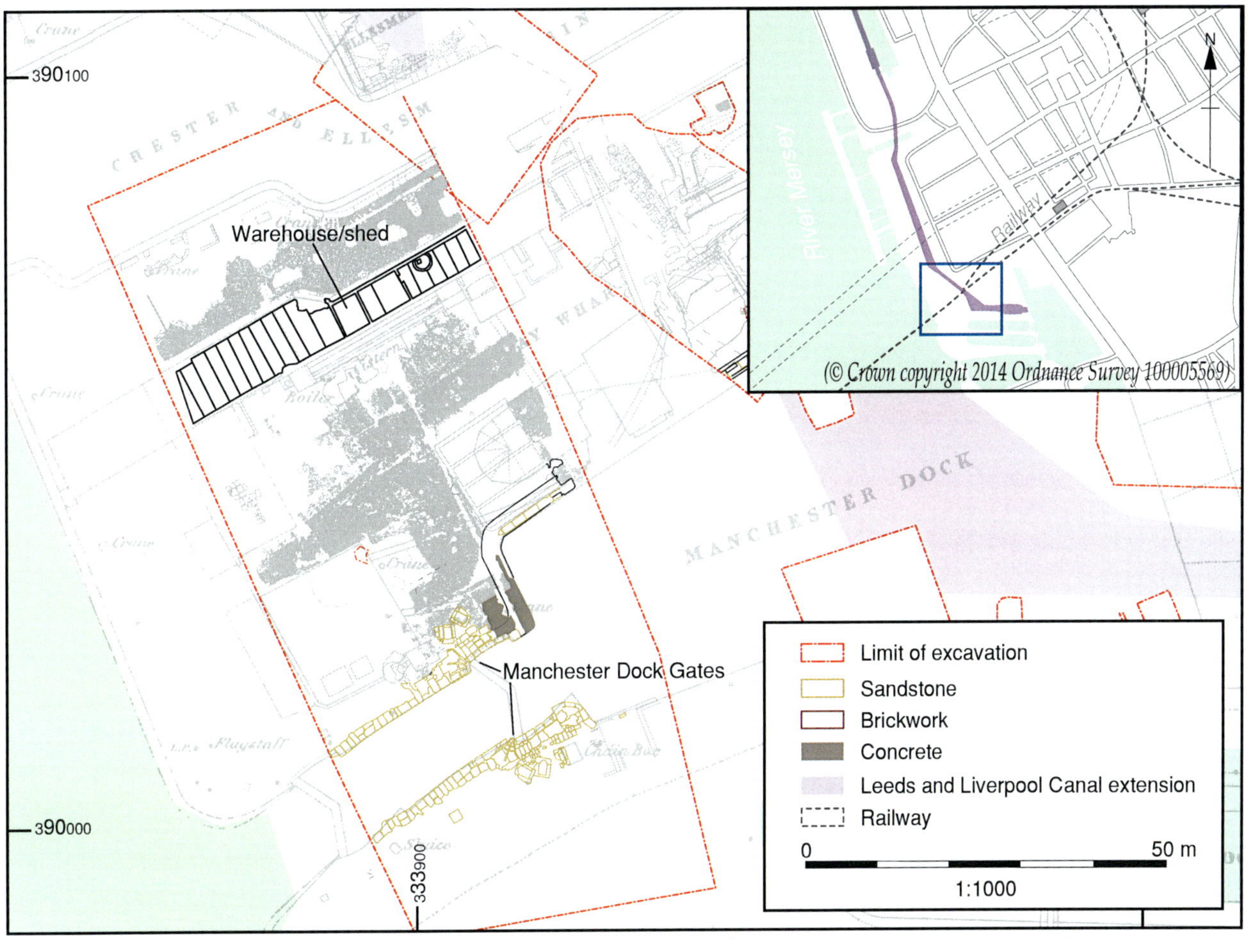

Figure 47: Remains of the early nineteenth-century warehouse/shed on Manchester Dock's northern quay, superimposed on the Ordnance Survey 1864 5 ft: 1 mile town plan (1864a)

Chester Basin, George's Ferry Basin, and George's Baths (1803-20s)

Historical background

As part of the early nineteenth-century scheme of land reclamation, which extended Manchester Dock's northern pier (*p 109*), its sister structure, Chester Basin, was also modified and extended westwards and northwards. In addition, this work included a programme of land reclamation, immediately to the north, which extended the eighteenth-century quay to the west of George's Dock (*Ch 3, p 70*). The modifications to Chester Basin, and the concomitant scheme of land reclamation to the north, appear to have occurred over a fairly protracted period. Jones' and Woodward's map of 1805 (Pl 107) suggests that initially this involved the construction of a projecting finger of reclaimed land immediately to the north; it is denoted 'wharf' on Gore's map of 1806 (Pl 108). Further reclamation had taken place by the time of Gore's map, which resulted in the northward extension of Manchester Dock's northern pier. By September 1807, Troughton's map indicates that the modifications to and extension of Chester Basin were still ongoing (Pl 109). For instance, he denotes Chester Basin as an 'intended basin', and it appears from this map that work was progressing on the construction of a new river wall to the north, in order to extend the eighteenth-century quayside to the west of George's Dock. However, this combined scheme of work had certainly been completed by 1815, as evidenced by Kaye's map (Pl 110).

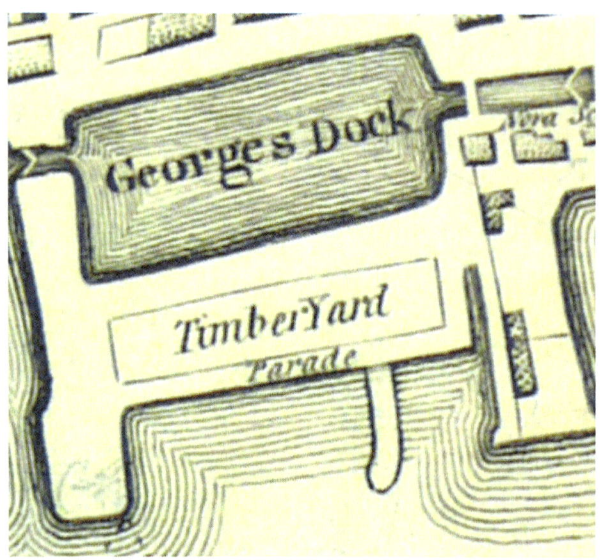

Plate 107: Extract from Jones' and Woodward's map of 1805, showing Chester Basin and the extended quayside adjacent to George's Dock (by courtesy of the University of Liverpool)

Plate 109: Extract from Troughton's map of 1807, showing the initial modifications to Chester Basin and the early scheme of land reclamation to its north (by courtesy of the University of Liverpool)

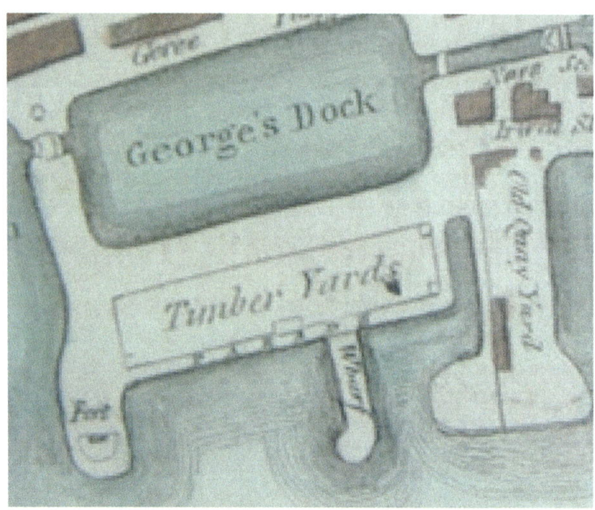

Plate 108: Extract from Gore's map of 1806, showing the initial modifications to Chester Basin and the early scheme of land reclamation to its north (by courtesy of the University of Liverpool)

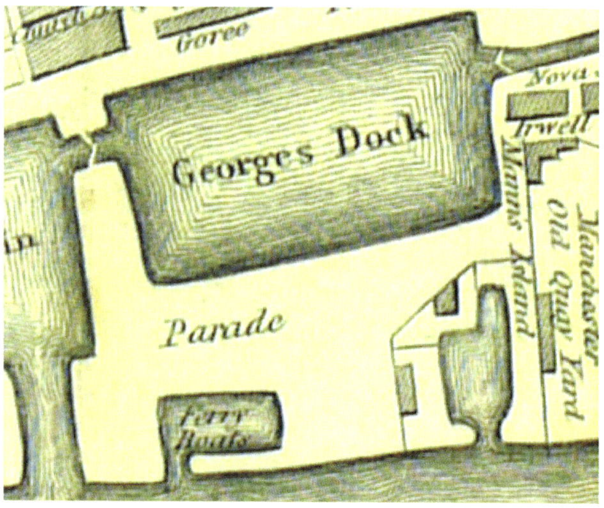

Plate 110: Extract from Thomas Kaye's map of 1815, showing Chester Basin, George's Dock western quay, and George's Ferry Basin (by courtesy of the University of Liverpool)

It is evident from mapping and documentary sources that the new section of expanded quayside to the west of George's Dock was used by the Mersey ferries, which during the late eighteenth century sailed from the dock, its basin, and also the adjacent foreshore (Ritchie-Noakes 1984, 29). Access to this was initially via wooden drawbridges that spanned the northern entrances to George's Dock, which were replaced by iron swing bridges in 1821 (*op cit*, 30). During the early nineteenth century, there was, however, an increase in the number of ferries using this locale (*ibid*) and, probably as a consequence, George's Ferry Basin was created as part of the scheme of land reclamation to the west of George's Dock. This small basin is depicted as an intended feature on Troughton's map of 1807 (Pl 109) and had been completed by the time of Kaye's survey (1815; Pl 110), when it would probably have been used by steam-powered ferries, which were operating from 1815 onwards (*ibid*). In the latter half of the nineteenth century, this basin was described as

> a place of shelter and for river-boats; has a water-area of 1,344 yards, and a quayage of 160 lineal yards; and includes an incline slip for the landing and shipping of goods out of and into ferry-vessels…(Wilson 1870-2, 123).

It is also possible that in 1833 a floating landing stage was opened adjacent to this basin, designed by Marc Brunel, which allowed access/egress from the Mersey ferries, regardless of the tidal levels (Ritchie-Noakes 1984, 30). This putative landing stage was then replaced by a second landing stage in 1847, known as George's Landing Stage (Cossons and Jenkins 2011, 21).

George's Baths was also constructed on this quayside, immediately south of the ferry basin, and is depicted as an intended feature on Troughton's plan (Pl 109). Sea-bathing along Liverpool's foreshore had a relatively long ancestry, with the earliest references dating to the beginning of the eighteenth century when, more generally, bathing became a fashionable pursuit. These early references are found in a Rate Assessment Book of 1708 (Aughton 1993), which records a Mr James Gibbons, who lived at 'ye bagniall' (bathing place) in Water Street. Another early reference dates to 1709, when the antiquarian Nicholas Blundell wrote of his wife and children taking to the water along Liverpool's foreshore (Tyrer 1970). However, Liverpool's first purpose-built sea-baths were those depicted on Charles Eyes' map of 1785, which were in an area of the late eighteenth-century foreshore that was later subsumed by the construction of Prince's Dock (*p 136*). These baths appear, however, to have been used by wealthier members of society, who bathed in the river under the protection of stalls and a canopy (Aughton 1993). These baths were demolished in 1811 when work began on the construction of Prince's Dock (*p 136*), and this led to the establishment in 1816 of a floating baths, off George's Dock quay (*ibid*; Pl 111).

This was then followed by the construction of George's Baths, on the quayside. These saltwater baths, constructed by Liverpool's Corporation, represent the country's first public baths, opened in 1828 (Metcalfe 1877, 3). Contemporary illustrations and mapping indicate that the baths had an E-shaped plan, with a central clock tower and chimney. The baths also possessed a stone-built façade, with a colonnade

Plate 111: The 1816 floating baths, by W G Herdman (1878, pl XXI), originally moored off George's Quay (by courtesy of the University of Liverpool Library SPEC Y87.5.41v1)

Plate 112: An 1829 watercolour of George's Baths by G and C Pyne (LVRO and Liverpool Libraries Hq 942.7204 Col)

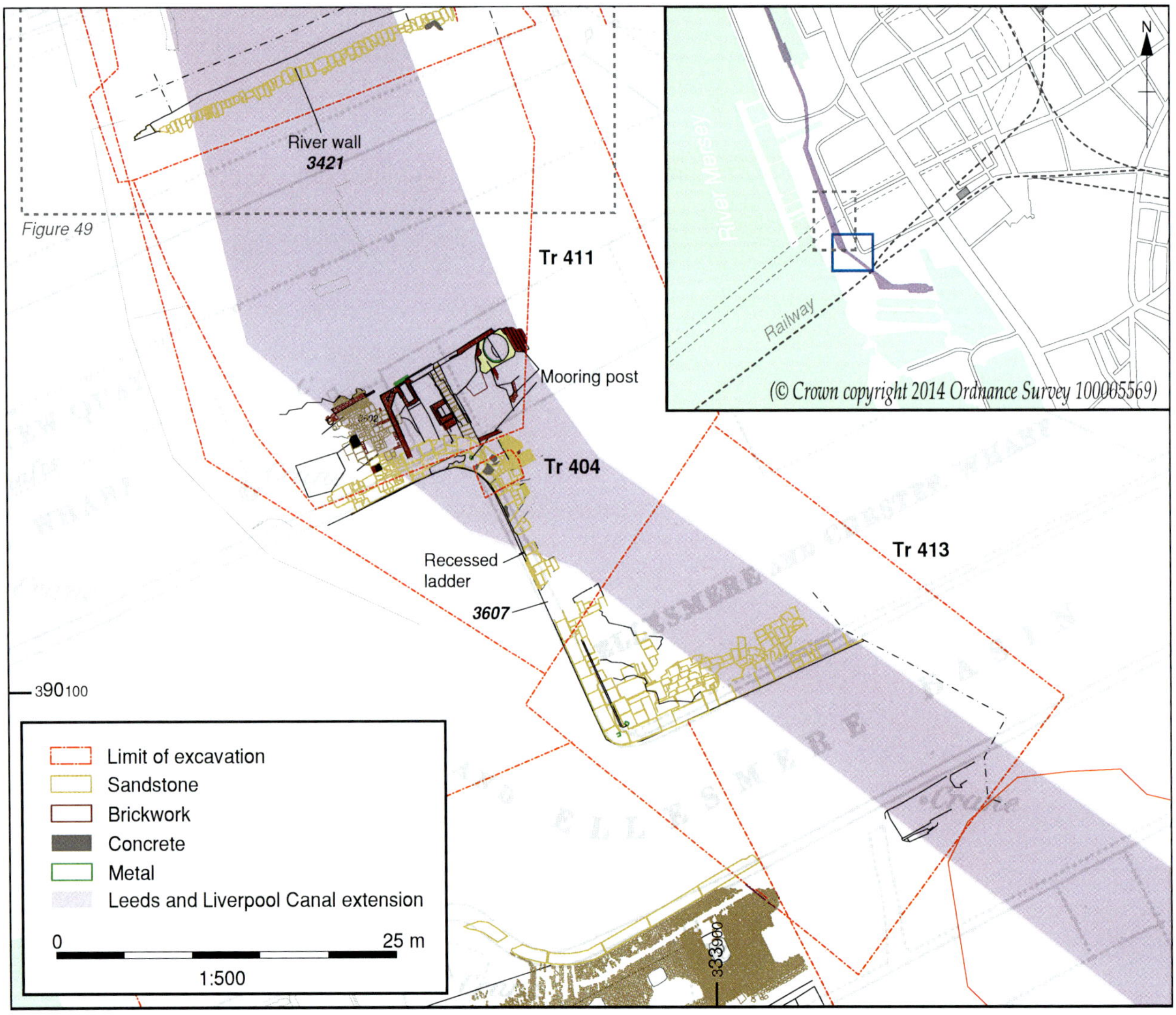

Figure 48: The excavated walls of Chester Basin, superimposed on the Ordnance Survey 1864 5 ft: 1 mile town plan (1864a)

positioned on either side of the central tower (Pl 112). To the north and south of this central tower, the colonnade was also bounded by two small rooms, positioned respectively at the northern and southern ends of the baths.

Archaeological evidence
During the archaeological investigation at the site of the Museum of Liverpool (*Ch 1, p 15*), the southern wall of Chester Basin was encountered (Fig 48). This was aligned north-east/south-west and was constructed of pink sandstone, though the upper coping stones had been replaced by concrete (Pl 113). The position of this wall lay at the far western end of the eighteenth-century basin (*Ch 3, pp 88-9*) and it also defined the northern side of Manchester Basin/Dock's northern quay. Moreover, its position corresponds to that depicted on Gore's map of 1806 (Pl 108). Based on this plan, and Jones' and Woodward's slightly earlier map (Pl 107), it is probable that this river wall was constructed between 1805 and 1806. As the wall was uniform throughout, with no changes in construction, it appears to have been built in a single phase, which, in turn, suggests that the retaining walls of the original eighteenth-century basin were replaced as part of this scheme of land reclamation. During demolition, an octagonal timber was visible in section at the western

Plate 113: The southern wall of Chester Basin, from the north

extreme of the wall, which probably represents a 'filler' used during its construction. It measured approximately 1.5 m in length and 0.5 m wide, and was set vertically into the sandstone wall around 1 m below the nineteenth-century ground level.

A dog-legged length of wall (*3607*), which originally defined the northern side of Chester Basin, was also exposed within Tr 411 and Tr 413, excavated within the footprint of the LLC extension (Fig 48; Pl 114).

Plate 114: The northern wall of Chester Basin within the Leeds and Liverpool Canal (LLC) extension, from the south-west

Significantly, its position partly equates with the southern wall of the projecting wharf depicted on Jones' and Woodward's map of 1805 (Pl 107), and this implies that it was built between 1803 and 1805, and formed part of the extension/rebuilding of Chester Basin. The wall also appears to have replaced those of the original eighteenth-century basin and was constructed of pink and yellow sandstone ashlar,

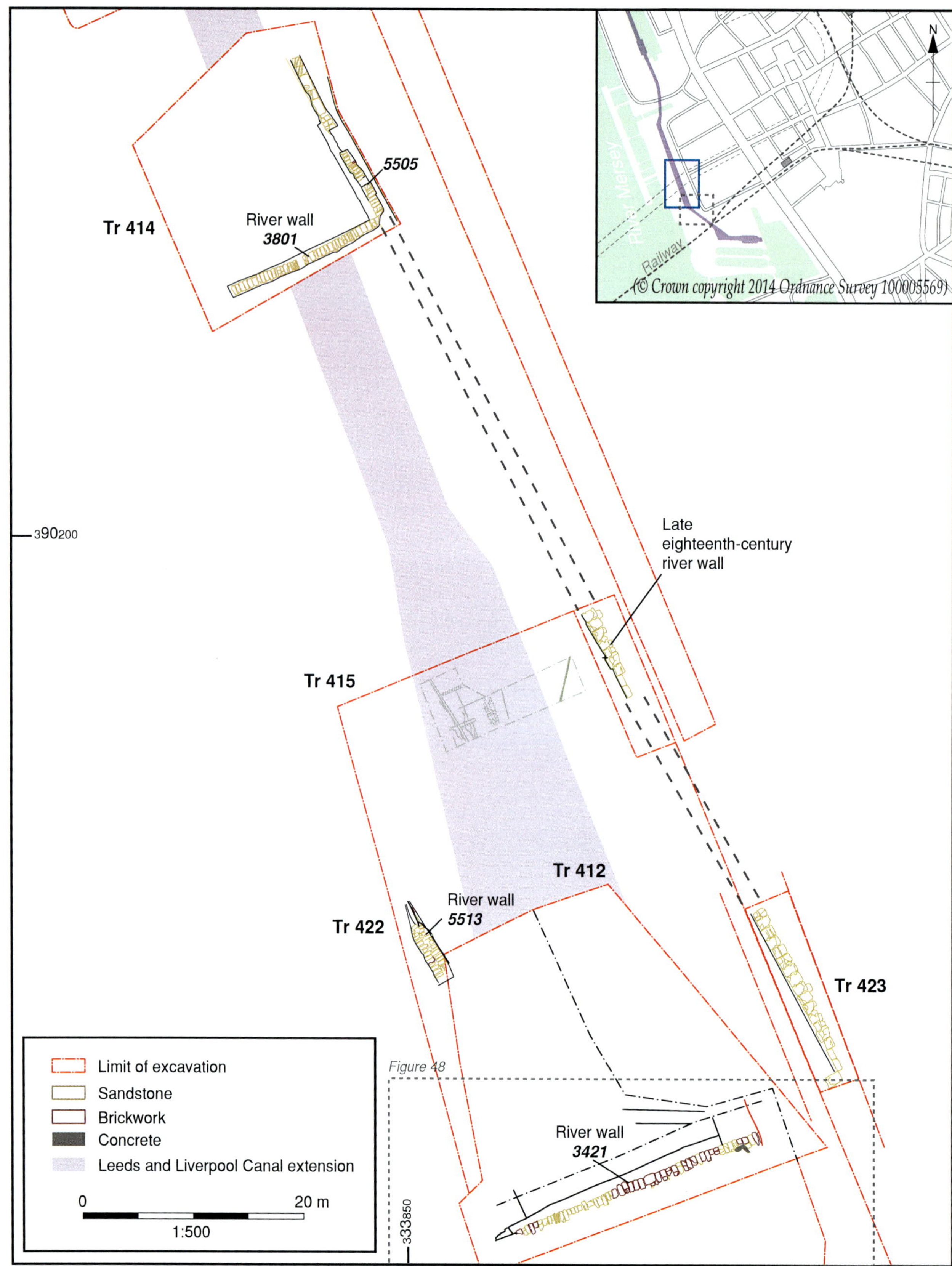

Figure 49: Temporary land-reclamation walls, dating to between 1803 and 1815, to the north of Chester Basin

*Plate 115: The north face of temporary river wall **3421** in Tr 412*

mixed with more roughly hewn blocks of the same material. The harder, pink stone was used for the waterside face. A small retaining wall, and also a vertical square shaft acting as a sluice, was uncovered on the eastern wall of the basin, whilst a sandstone flagged surface surrounded this basin.

To the north of Chester Basin, evidence was uncovered along the LLC extension relating to land reclamation adjacent to the western pier of George's Dock. This evidence took the form of a substantial yellow sandstone wall (**3421**), aligned east/west, which was present at the southern end of Tr 412 (Fig 49). Significantly, the position of this wall suggests that it formed the northern side of the projecting wharf depicted on Jones' and Woodward's map (Pl 107). If this is correct, this wall can accurately be dated to between 1803 and 1805, based on its presence on Jones' and Woodward's

map and its absence from Horwood's map (1803). Importantly, the character of this dry-stone wall indicates that the projecting wharf was only intended as a temporary feature within this scheme of early nineteenth-century land reclamation, as it was constructed entirely from recycled masonry (Pl 115). The recycled sandstone varied in style but included decorated pieces, depicting Lancashire roses carved in relief, and parts of a Corinthian capital, lintels for windows, and voussoir stones, which would have formed part of an arched aperture, either for a window or large door. This material appears, therefore, to have been removed from a demolished building of some pretension. The wall also had a 5° batter, designed to resist pressure from the layers of made-ground to its south.

Another similar east-west-aligned wall (**3801**) was exposed *c* 85 m north of wall **3421**, at the southern end of Tr 414 (Fig 49; Pl 116). This was composed of yellow sandstone blocks, and the cartographic evidence suggests that it dates to between 1806 and 1815 (*p 122*). It appears therefore to have formed another temporary river wall that was thrown up as part of the scheme of early nineteenth-century land reclamation in this section of the waterfront.

A short section of wall (**5513**) was also uncovered in Tr 422 (Fig 49), though this was aligned north-west/south-east, parallel with the waterfront. This wall was constructed from yellow sandstone blocks, without mortar, and lay *c* 23 m west of the quayside

*Plate 116: The west-facing elevation of late eighteenth-century river wall **5505** and the north-facing elevation of temporary river wall **3801**, in Tr 414*

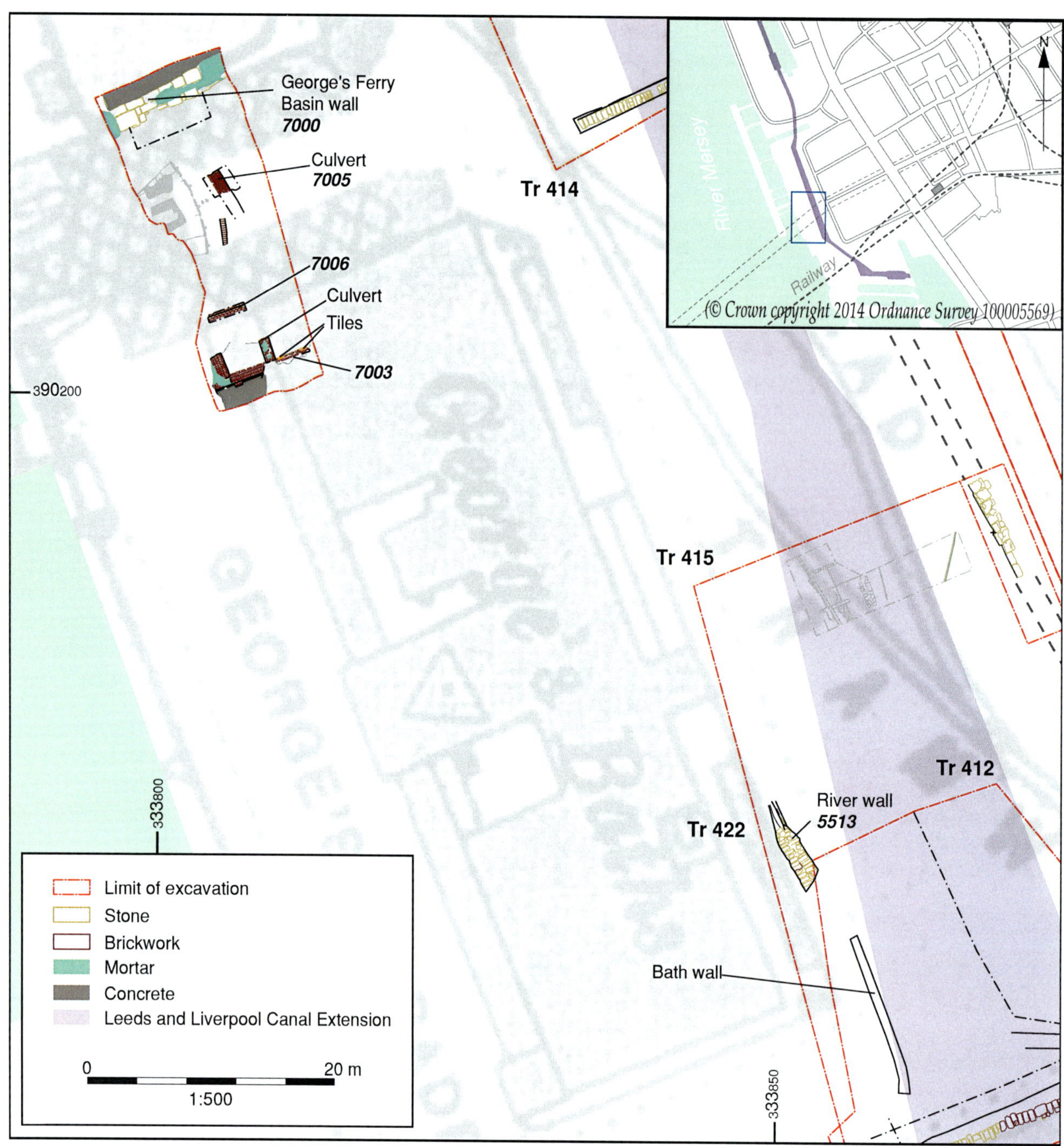

Figure 50: Remains of George's Ferry Basin and George's Baths, superimposed on the 1893 Ordnance Survey 25": 1 mile map (1893a)

wall that defined the western side of the late eighteenth-century quay associated with George's Dock (*Ch 3, p 88*). Although only the landward side was revealed, it may also represent a temporary river wall that was erected as part of the early nineteenth-century scheme of reclamation in this area. To its rear, deposits containing many artefacts and other debris were exposed, and these related to the infilling of the area in order to create the extended early nineteenth-century quayside. This material included a substantial proportion of organic and timber debris, in two lower layers, which were sealed by backfill deposits containing pottery, clay pipes, and glass. The pottery formed the largest proportion of the

artefacts, and its date, on the cusp of the eighteenth and nineteenth centuries, is consistent with the historical documentation of construction and reclamation. The fragments of clay pipes and glass probably represent waste material from industrial production, and are indicative of the significance, at this date, of Liverpool as a production centre in its own right (*Ch 6*).

Apart from the temporary river walls and the walls of Chester Basin, several other features were also uncovered, which formed part of the early- and mid-nineteenth-century quay. These included the partial remains of George's Ferry Basin, which was uncovered

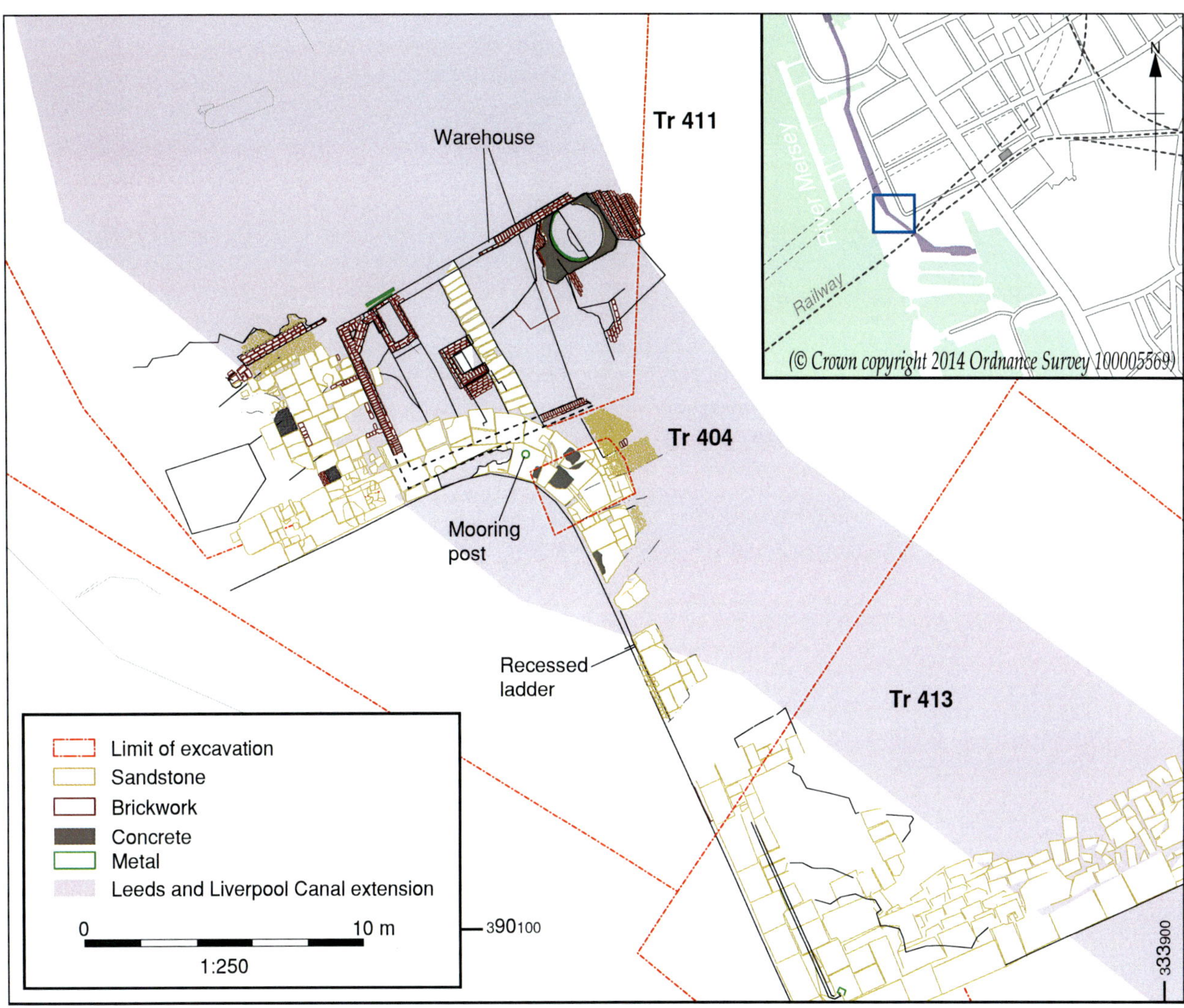

Figure 51: The mid-nineteenth-century quayside building adjacent to Chester Basin

during the excavation at the Pier Head Ferry Terminal Building (*Ch 1, p 11*). This work exposed the southern wall (**7000**; Fig 50) of the ferry basin, which was discovered to be fairly substantial, at 2.2 m wide. It was constructed of pink and yellow sandstone blocks, which were tightly keyed into place, with some evidence of a mortar bond. The southern elevation of this wall also contained a deliberate gap within a worked sandstone block, which was grooved on its western and southern face. This was positioned on the right side of the gap and may have been a fixture for a ladder, or some fitting giving access to the wall.

The partial remains of two buildings were also uncovered, which had stood on the nineteenth-century quay to the north of Chester Basin. One of these buildings, George's Baths (*p 123*), dates to the early nineteenth century and elements of it were uncovered along the canal extension, and also at the Pier Head Ferry Terminal Building site. At the latter site, the remains formed a small rectangular room, or annexe, which lay at the far north-western end of the building, and which also bounded the northern colonnade of the baths (*pp 123-4*).

This room was *c* 5 m across, from north to south, and was defined by two brick walls (**7003** and **7006**; Fig 50). Wall **7006** formed the northern wall of the room, whilst **7003**, which was right-angled in plan, formed part of its southern and western walls. Both were constructed using handmade bricks bonded with a light-grey lime mortar. Within the room, the remains of a brick culvert were also present, and this may well have linked with a similar culvert (**7005**), to the north of the baths, which was aligned north-north-east/south-south-west. This latter culvert was constructed in handmade brick with a domed roof, and it appears to have been designed to remove water from George's Baths, particularly as its floor sloped in a northerly direction. Within the footprint of the LLC extension, the remains of one of the baths was exposed in the far western side of Tr 412. These comprised a *c* 0.7 m-thick brick wall, which was lined with white ceramic tile.

The other building is of a slightly later date, and was present within the footprint of the LLC extension in Tr 411 to the south-east of George's Baths. It lay immediately north of Chester Basin (Fig 51; Pl 117) and

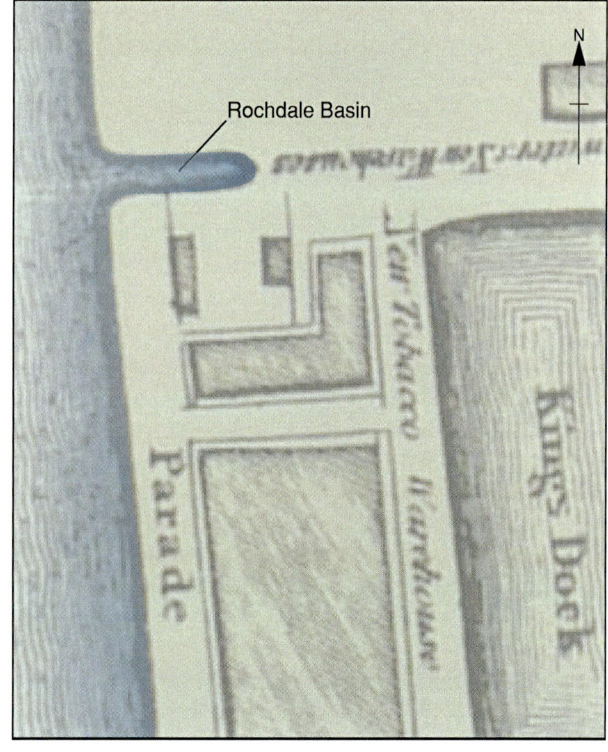

Plate 117: The foundations of a small building contemporary with Chester Basin

its remains comprised a series of poorly constructed handmade brick walls, set above pink sandstone foundations. These defined a small, two-roomed building, which was provided with a cobbled surface to the south. This building is depicted on the large-scale OS town plan of 1864 (1864b) and it was extant until the early part of the twentieth century, since a photograph dating to *c* 1928 provides further details. This shows a two-storey building, which may have originally functioned as a small warehouse (Ritchie-Noakes 1984, 35, pl 24), whilst a Goad's Insurance Plan (1890) indicates that, by this date, it formed part of a 'Crystal Soda Stores'. Artefacts recovered from the footings of this building, and within it, confirm its mid-nineteenth-century date.

Rochdale/Northwich Basin and wharf

Historical background

Another early nineteenth-century development within Liverpool's waterfront occurred in the southern docks and involved the extension of the western pier of King's Dock. This work, which entailed the construction of a new river wall in order to bound an area of reclaimed land, occurred during the first decade of the nineteenth century, as evidenced by cartography. Jones' and Woodward's map of 1805 indicates that at this date the late eighteenth-century pier remained unaltered, though it had been extended by the time of Kaye's map of 1810 (Fig 52). Following the completion of land

Figure 52: King's Dock, its western pier, and Rochdale Basin as depicted on Thomas Kaye's map of 1810

reclamation, the Corporation constructed a large tobacco warehouse on the pier, which was probably designed by John Foster (Ritchie-Noakes 1984, 38). The position of this warehouse is depicted on Kaye's map of 1810, although work on its construction was not completed until 1814 (Ritchie-Noakes 1984, 38).

In addition to the tobacco warehouse, Kaye's map also indicates that, during the extension of the western pier of King's Dock, a small, narrow tidal basin was created for the use of inland craft, which lay at the northern end of the pier, adjacent to Duke's Dock (*Ch 3, p 69*). A plan of Duke's Dock dating to 1899 (*op cit*, fig 22) indicates that originally this basin was known as Rochdale Basin, suggesting that it initially received flats from the Rochdale Canal (*Appendix 1*), though it was subsequently known as both Anderton and Northwich Basin (*ibid*; OS 1893a). This renaming relates to the use of the basin by the Anderton Company of Northwich, in the first half of the nineteenth century, which specialised in the transportation of pottery from Staffordshire to Liverpool, and also of bulk materials from Liverpool to Staffordshire that could be used in pottery manufacture (*op cit*, 33). Moreover, the Anderton Company used

> its own wooden narrow boats with characteristic barrel-shaped sides that enabled them to make the fast trips required by the potters, which were used up until the 1950s (*ibid*).

Early nineteenth-century mapping (*eg* Fig 52) suggests that during this period the Anderton Company operated from an enclosed yard immediately south of the basin, which contained several quayside buildings.

In 1848, the Bridgewater Trustees acquired the Anderton Company and hence would also have acquired Anderton/Northwich Basin, and its associated yard and buildings to the south. After this date the basin would therefore have also served the Duke of Bridgewater's yard, which lay immediately to its north. In consequence, a wharf was established on the northern side of the basin, within the Duke's yard, which by 1850 was associated with several small warehouses that presumably also served the basin (OS 1850a). The form of these buildings are clearly depicted on late nineteenth-century mapping (Fig 53).

Archaeological evidence
During the watching brief at the Arena and Conference Centre site (*Ch 1, p 12*), an east/west-aligned wall was recorded (*9*; Fig 53), which formed the southern wall of Rochdale Basin. A *c* 40 m length of this wall was exposed, which was constructed of substantial pink sandstone blocks *c* 1-2 m long, 1 m wide, and 1 m deep (Pl 118). These were dressed on

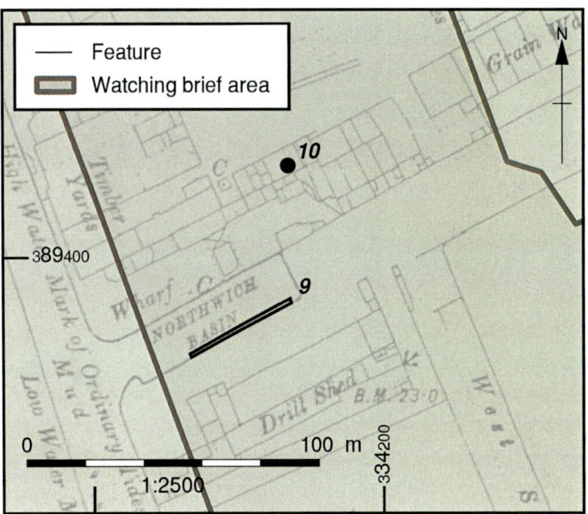

Figure 53: The early nineteenth-century remains at the Arena and Conference site, superimposed on Ordnance Survey 1893 25": 1 mile (1893a)

Plate 118: The coping stones of Northwich Basin's southern wall, from the east

the northern face and heavily worn on the upper surface, and appear to be coping stones.

In addition to the wall, a deposit of crushed early nineteenth-century ceramics (*10*), extending across an area of some 5 x 5 m, was recovered to the north (Fig 53). Although the circumstances of the watching brief meant that it was not possible to establish the relationship of this deposit to those surrounding it, the ceramics included earthenware and blue transfer-printed sherds dating to 1800-20 (Philpott in prep). Moreover, these may represent export pieces destined for the American market that may well have been initially transported to Liverpool by the Anderton Company (*p 131*).

Closure and infilling of the Old Dock, and the construction of the New Custom House (1826-39)

Historical background

One of the more significant events on the waterfront during the early nineteenth century was the closure of Thomas Steers' Old Dock (*Ch 2, p 35*). In comparison to the later docks, the Old Dock was, by the early nineteenth century, land-locked and deemed to be too small, thus representing a potential fire hazard, and too prone to silting to warrant it remaining an integral part of the dock system (Ritchie-Noakes 1984, 21). Indeed, in terms of silting, this was probably a problem almost from the time of the dock's construction. For instance, the first mention of silting appears as early as 1726 in the Minutes of Common Council, and in 1736, John Martindale was officially contracted to clean silt from the dock basin (MMMMAL MDHB/MP/25, 39). In addition, the problem of silting was compounded, as the Old Dock had been used as a popular dumping ground for waste and sewage from the old town during the early nineteenth century (Rennie 1846). In 1810, a survey by the engineer, John Rennie, pointed out that the adjacent quays were too narrow, but that the site of the dock was a suitable location for a new Custom House (Ritchie-Noakes 1984, 21).

An Act of Parliament, the fourth Dock Act, was therefore passed in June 1811, allowing the dock to be filled in as soon as the Queen's Dock and Prince's Dock had been enlarged (*ibid*). However, merchants' opposition to the backfilling caused a long delay, as arguments raged over the lack of space in the new docks and the distance from established businesses (*op cit*, 22). Furthermore, the process of closure was impeded by disagreements between the Corporation and the Dock Trustees, who respectively owned the eastern and western parts of the dock (*ibid*), and it was not until June 1826 that the Old Dock was finally closed. The last ship sailed out from it on 31 August 1826, and the dock was filled in shortly after.

The newly acquired land, created by the filling of the dock, was then given over to the construction of a new Custom House. This imposing neo-classical building, with its I-shaped plan (Pl 119), designed by the architect John Foster Junior, was constructed between 1828 and 1839 (Sharples 2004, 15). During its construction, the walls of the Old Dock continued to act as retainers, while the foundations and basement were built, with the gap between the walls being backfilled once the

Plate 119: A mid-nineteenth-century view of Liverpool, showing the Custom House, adjacent to the docks, which replaced the Old Dock (MMMMAL Archives Collections; © Trustees of National Museums Liverpool)

ground level was reached (MacLeod 1982). Significantly, this constructional practice appears to have set a precedent for the construction of some of Liverpool's later waterfront buildings, specifically the Cunard and Liver Buildings, which lie within the former George's Dock (Cossons and Jenkins 2011, 21).

Archaeological evidence

During the archaeological investigation of the Old Dock (*Ch 1, p 9*), limited evidence was recovered relating to its use during the early part of the nineteenth century, immediately prior to its infilling. This was uncovered on the northern quay and consisted of a north/south-aligned drain, which fed into the Old Dock (Fig 54). The drain was clearly late in date, as a sizable section of the dock wall had been removed during its construction. The destructive, and potentially structurally unsound, manner in which this had been carried out also implies that the dock was falling into a state of disrepair when the drain was built. In terms of its function, given its late date, it is possible that it was designed to carry sewage into the Old Dock, which is known to have occurred during the early nineteenth century (*see above*). The drain was constructed of handmade bricks and it contained a well-preserved grooved wooden frame, which may have secured a small sluice. Furthermore, this appears to have been operated from an aperture in the quayside. The provision of a sluice would have allowed control over the amount of sewage

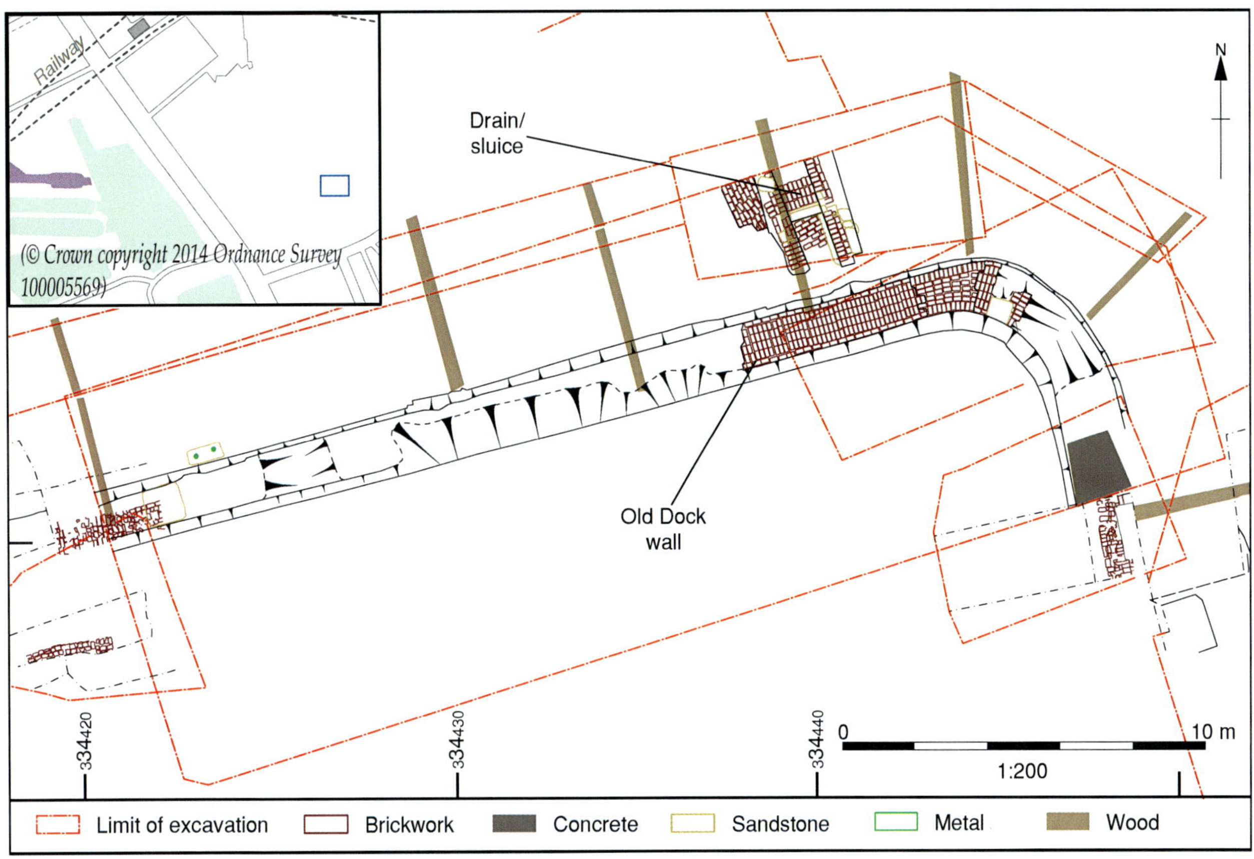

Figure 54: Early nineteenth-century features associated with the Old Dock

entering the dock at any one time, and may also have served to stop a reverse flow of material when the dock was full to capacity. A contemporary, but unrelated, find, the articulated remains of a small horse or pony, was discovered on the western side of this sluice on the quayside.

Further evidence for the drainage of the Old Dock was exposed to the west, during the investigations undertaken as part of the Liverpool Trams Scheme (*Ch 1, p 11*). This evidence took the form of a wall (***1254 / 1222 / 1213 / 1279***; Fig 55), which had been constructed across the entrance to the Old Dock. This

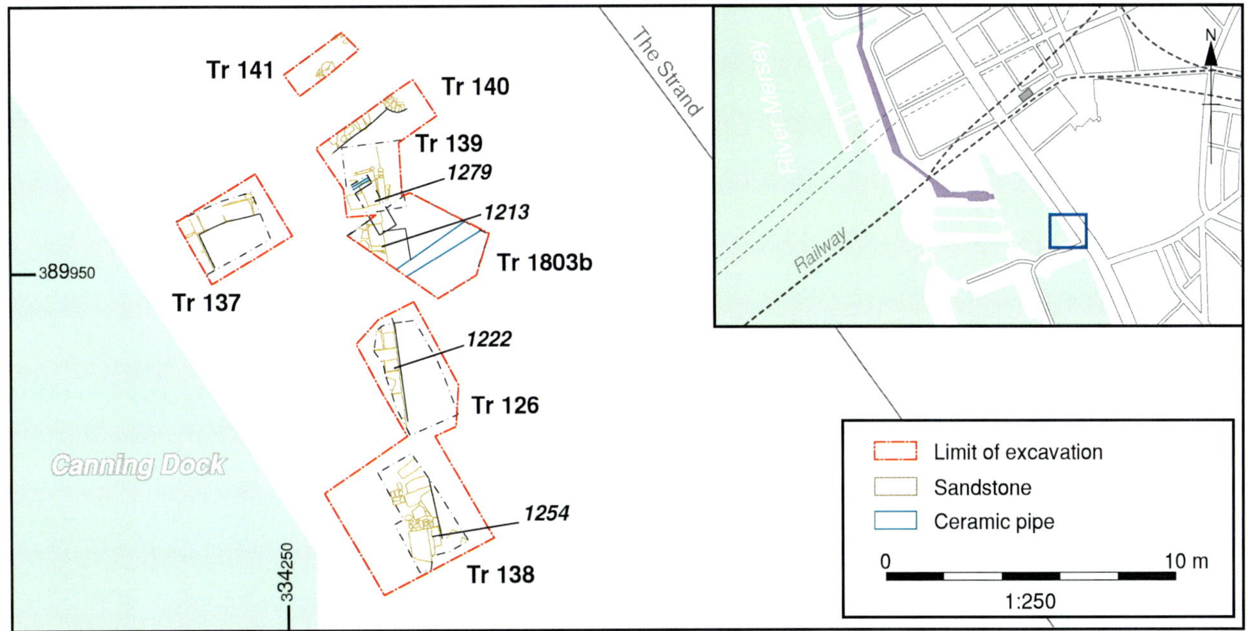

Figure 55: The position of the early nineteenth-century wall across the mouth of the Old Dock (© Crown copyright 2014 Ordnance Survey 100005569)

Plate 120: The sandstone block with inverted Roman numerals discovered at the mouth of the Old Dock

wall probably functioned as a temporary dam and was constructed of roughly shaped yellow sandstone blocks which, in some sections, had been bonded with lime mortar. It also incorporated a sandstone block that had the inverted Roman numerals XVII and XVI marked on its face (Pl 120). The numerals were not complete, but enough survived to suggest that the relevant measurement was in feet. This suggests that this stone originally formed part of a depth gauge set within a dock wall, which was removed and then reused, and set upside down, during the construction of the temporary dam wall. Given this, it is highly likely that this depth-marker stone was originally associated with the Old Dock.

Following drainage, the Old Dock was then infilled and John Foster Junior's Custom House was constructed. Direct evidence for the infilling was again uncovered at the Old Dock site and during the Liverpool Trams Scheme investigation. This took the form of backfill deposits, composed of silt and sand of varying colours and thickness, which were contained inside the Old Dock and had clearly been tipped into it. In addition, in several of the trenches excavated at the Old Dock site, the pink sandstone foundations of John Foster Junior's Custom House were evident. Generally, these walls defined the basement of this building, and also truncated parts of the Old Dock's retaining walls. In places, there was evidence for later repairs to the Custom House, in the form of patches of brick.

Canning Dock (1820-40s)
Historical background
The Dry Dock (*Ch 3, p 55*) was modified during the late 1820s to form Canning Dock, a gated wet dock (Pl 121), which opened in 1829. This new feature

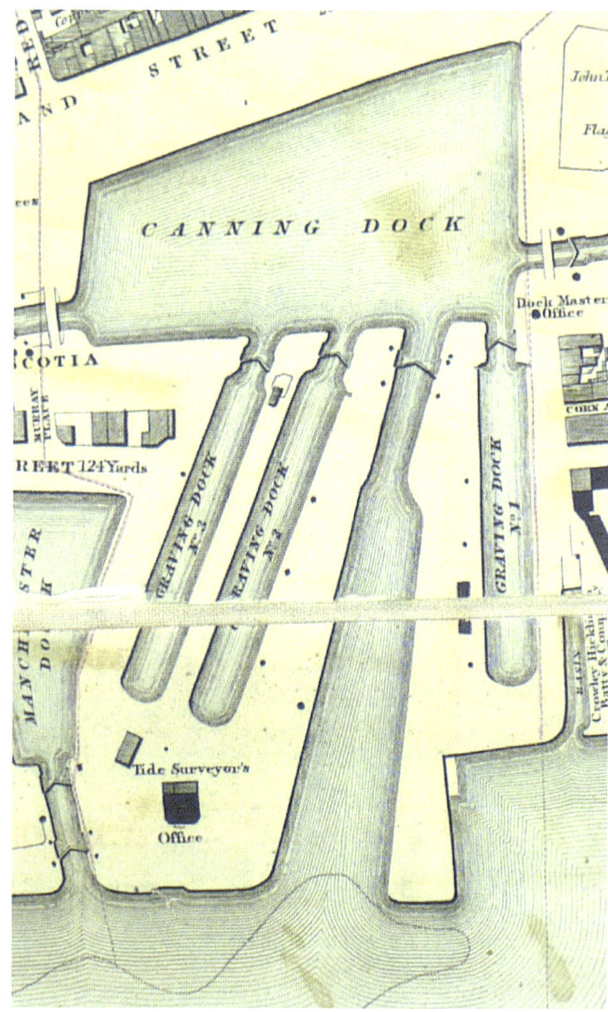

Plate 121: Extract from Gage's map of 1836 (© Trustees of National Museums Liverpool), showing Canning Dock

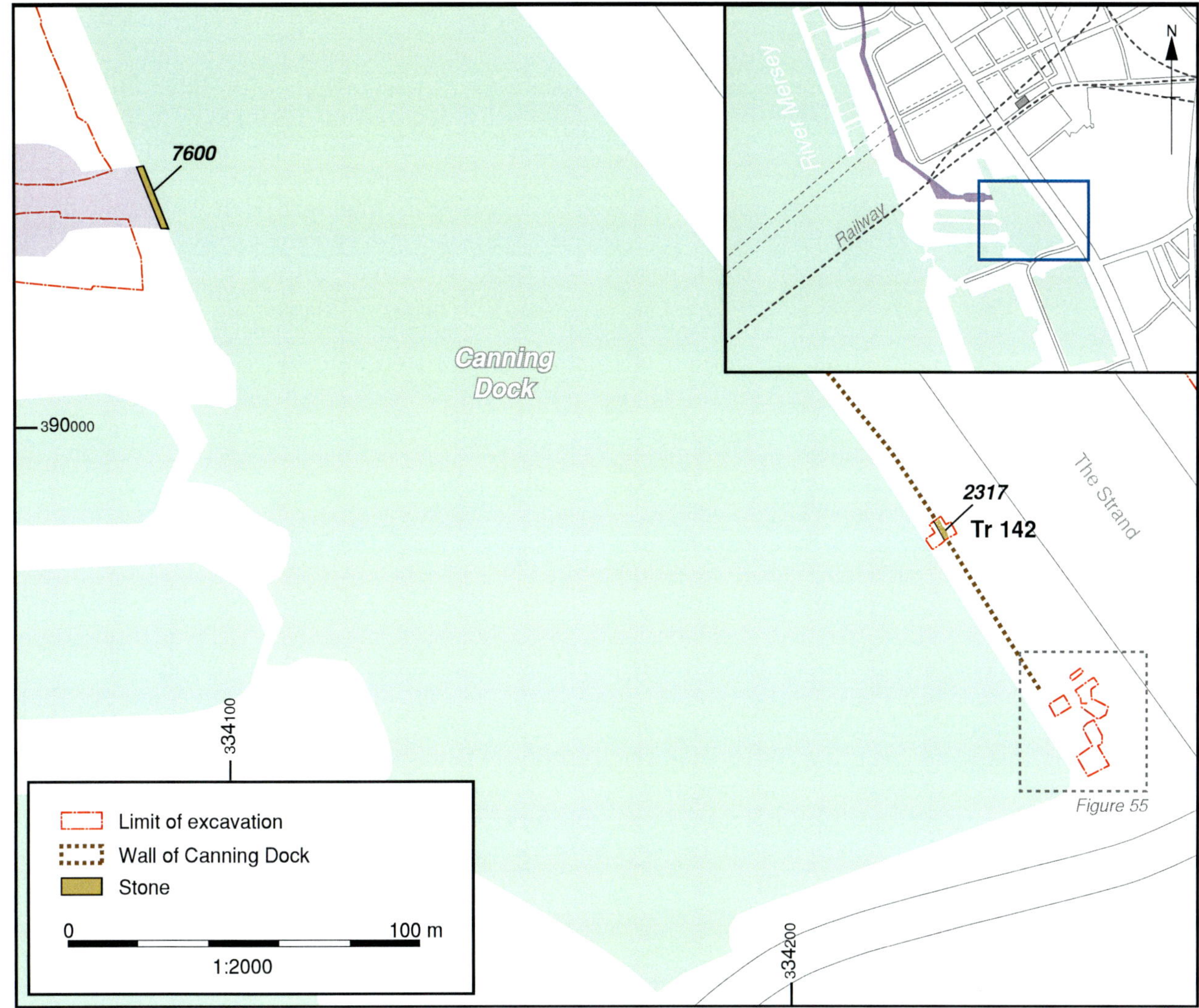

Figure 56: The sections examined of Canning Dock's retaining wall (© Crown copyright 2014 Ordnance Survey 100005569)

reused some sections of the original walling of the eighteenth-century dock, although the angle to the south-east and the location of the northern wall were altered and moved further southwards (Ritchie-Noakes 1984, 41). During this period, the creation of a permanently impounded wet dock meant that the three graving docks, that were originally attached to the western side of the Dry Dock (*Ch 3, p 55*), also required modification. This involved providing each with an iron syphon, to allow them to be drained once a vessel had entered them for repair or maintenance (*ibid*).

During the 1840s, further modifications were made to Canning Dock and its graving docks, as part of the scheme of works that led to the creation of Albert Dock (*ibid*). These modifications included the deepening of the main dock and the construction of a half-tide basin, with a double river entrance, to extend the period when ships could enter and leave the dock system. This basin, which opened in 1844, was constructed in the position of the former Dry Dock gut and also necessitated the infilling of one of

the graving docks (*ibid*). The remaining two graving docks were subsequently rebuilt and deepened, the pier between them lowered, and both were also provided with new gates (*ibid*).

Archaeological evidence

Although Canning Dock is an extant feature, a small section of its western wall was examined prior to its demolition during the construction of the LLC extension (*Ch 1, p 14*). This 14 m-long section (Fig 56) was dismantled by hand to create the entrance to the canal, and some of the stone was retained and used, along with stone derived from Chester Basin, to reface the new entrance.

The east side (waterside; **7600**) of the wall, which was exposed using a cofferdam, had an even, vertical face, constructed from large, rectangular, pink sandstone blocks. The blocks exhibited a variety of masons' marks, as well as small horizontal niches, which may have been used as points to locate timber scaffolding during construction. The wall had clearly suffered much wear and tear, and had been repointed with grey

135

concrete. There was no surviving dock furniture, and the coping stones had been covered with a thick layer of modern concrete, associated with the foundations of the transit sheds on Mann Island. The west-facing, landward elevation of wall **7600** was composed of roughly hewn blocks of pink sandstone, interspersed with yellow sandstone ashlar, and was supported by a single buttress. Significantly, the yellow sandstone blocks were probably derived from an earlier dock wall found at this location, forming the western wall of the Dry Dock (*Ch 3, p 57*), which was dismantled during the works associated with the creation of Canning Dock.

The rear face of the eastern retaining wall of Canning Dock (*2317*; Tr 142; Fig 56) was also uncovered during the investigations undertaken as part of the Liverpool Trams Scheme (*Ch 1, p 11*). This was constructed of pink sandstone blocks, containing small areas of brick, and it extended to a depth of 3.4 m below the present ground surface. Both the sandstone blocks and bricks were bonded with mortar, though that used to bond the stone blocks was a hard grey mortar, whilst that used to bond the bricks was a lime-based mortar. Significantly, this wall lay above another built of yellow sandstone, which had originally formed part of the earlier Dry Dock (*Ch 3, p 57*); this indicates that the upper sections of the Dry Dock's eastern wall were rebuilt during its conversion into Canning Dock.

Prince's Dock and Basin (1821-1900)
Historical background
Prince's Dock opened in 1821 (Pl 122), though it took 11 years to construct and, before this, had been ten years in the planning (Jarvis 1991a, 230; McCarron and Jarvis 1992, 71). Although, at the beginning of the nineteenth century, maritime trade continued to increase (*p 92*), and hence there was sufficient justification and pressure for the construction of a new dock (Jarvis 1991b, 8), the procrastination in the building of Prince's Dock was down to a number of specific factors.

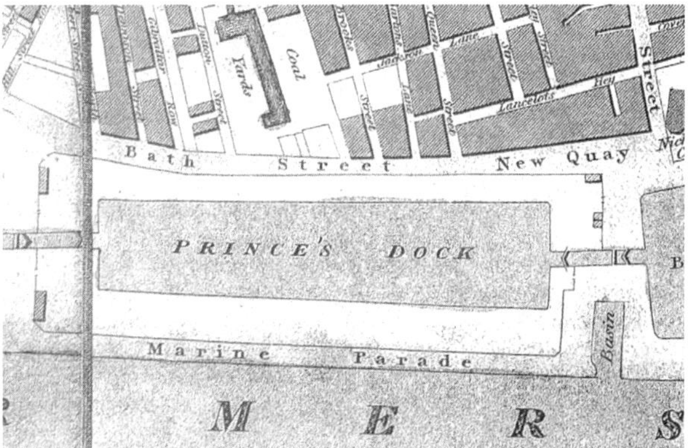

Plate 122: Extract from the Walkers' map of 1823, showing Prince's Dock

One of these initial factors was that the proposed site of Prince's Dock was partly occupied by a fort, established in the late eighteenth century, the position of which is depicted on Charles Eyes' map of 1785. In terms of conflict, at the beginning of the nineteenth century, the French Revolutionary War (1793-1802) was still ongoing, which was immediately followed by the Napoleonic Wars (1803-15), and although these had limited effects on maritime trade entering Liverpool (*p 91*; *Ch 3, p 53*), there was some reluctance to dispense with the fort while the French wars continued (*op cit*, 11). Significantly, these conflicts also resulted in shortages to, and substantial increases in, the costs of both labour and timber (*Ch 3, p 53*), which were essential components of dock construction. Furthermore, the Napoleonic Wars limited the supply of horses, for moving spoil and stone, and fodder for those that were available (Jarvis 1991a, 33). These problems were further compounded by the lack of funds of the Corporation's Dock Committee, following the completion of King's Dock further south, which opened in 1788 (*Ch 3, p 54*). In addition, during the first decade of the nineteenth century, the Dock Committee was unclear about the design and construction of a new dock, particularly following problems occurring at King's Dock, including collapsing walls and silting (*p 95*). Again, this led to a delay, as the Corporation's Dock Committee felt compelled to consult with both William Jessop and John Rennie, two of the leading engineers of the time (Hadfield and Skempton 1979, 249; Jarvis 1991a, 10; 1996, 14).

In his report of 1800, Jessop commented on the silting of those older dock entrances with tidal basins, and proposed the installation of proper locks as a solution, together with improvements to the construction of the retaining walls (Jarvis 1991b, 10). He also rejected the idea that the area of the planned new dock could be advantageously increased by building below the low-water mark, pointing out the considerable increase in cost this procedure would cause (*ibid*). It had been recognised that there were structural flaws in setting sandstone walls directly on the reclaimed ground, as the sheer weight of the walls made them likely to subside. There was also doubt about the choice of stone, as the sandstone from the town quarries was friable and prone to fracture and erosion (Ritchie-Noakes 1984, 37). Rennie reported in 1809 and, although the Dock Committee may have hoped otherwise, he confirmed the necessity to build as Jessop had specified (Jarvis 1991b, 11).

Work on Prince's Dock finally commenced in 1810 (*op cit*, 12), with the intention of making a much smaller dock than originally planned, since the full complement of land remained unavailable. At the same time, the river wall that now forms the boundary of the current Marine Parade was under construction. Stone for these works was shipped across the river from quarries at Runcorn (*ibid*). The Corporation's Dock Committee sought a government loan in 1812 to complete the dock, and at the same time applied for powers to acquire the remainder of the land, including that occupied by the fort (*op cit*, 15). Ironically, the main opponents to the construction of the dock, in the form proposed, were the shareholders of the Leeds and Liverpool Canal Company, who stood to benefit considerably from the increased trade the dock would generate. Specifically, the shareholders objected to the idea that the dock was to be constructed within a walled, secure compound, because the Company had only just extended their basins southwards, with the aim of constructing a set of locks to link with the new dock (Jarvis 1991b, 62).

Aside from the dock, in 1819 construction began on the first buildings around it and its half-tide basin. These included transit sheds, open to the dockside and designed to be dismantled easily and resituated, should the need arise (McCarron and Jarvis 1992, 71). This was then followed, after the opening of the dock (*see below*), by the construction of open-sided transit sheds, lining both of its long sides, which were completed in *c* 1827 and were augmented by closed sheds along the west side in 1843 (Jarvis 1991b, 46). In 1821, work also began on the Dock Wall, which was initially designed specifically to enclose Prince's Dock, separate it from the town, and, in turn, provide security for goods entering the northern dock system (Liverpool City Council 2005, 128; Pl 2).

The dock was officially opened on 19 July 1821, the day of the coronation of King George IV, a full 21 years after it was commissioned (Liverpool City Council 2005, 127). It was accessible from the south, via George's Dock Basin and a linking channel (Pl 122), and from the north, via Prince's Basin. This was originally a 'dry' basin, directly open to the river, and empty at low tide. As such, it was only suitable for manoeuvring into the dock towards the top of the tide, and was otherwise used by small vessels, which could load or unload conveniently in the time allowed by the water level. At the time of its opening, it represented the largest dock in Liverpool and it was designed to receive North America vessels involved in the importation of cotton and the transportation of passengers to America's eastern seaboard (*ibid*).

Significantly, the construction of Prince's Dock had cost ten times as much per acre as King's Dock, its immediate predecessor, and this vastly increased cost appears partly to reside with the dock engineer,

John Foster, who was involved in fraudulent activity during its construction. This became apparent in 1822, following a report by the Audit Commissioners, who were able to show that the amount paid for stone vastly exceeded the quantity delivered. Indeed, the amount of stone paid for 'would have more than sufficed to sink each and every one of the vessels said to have delivered it' (Jarvis 1991b, 20). In addition, the actual stone supplied during Foster's tenure for the construction of Prince's Dock was found to be soft, and had subsequently to be replaced in certain places (Jarvis 1991a, 38).

Archaeological evidence
A small section of Prince's Dock was examined as part of the excavations along the LLC extension (*Ch 1, p 14*). At the southern end of Prince's Dock, a short length of the south quay (Pl 123; **7553**; Fig 57) was revealed, in an area where a 'roll-on/roll-off' facility had been installed in 1967 (McCarron and Jarvis 1992, 72). Although, during the construction of this facility, the wall of the dock had been removed and reinstated, some of the original wall remained *in situ*. This was constructed in pink and yellow sandstone, with a waterside face of pink sandstone ashlar. Backfill deposits to the rear of this wall included quarry waste that was probably derived from the excavation of the dock.

Other below-ground remains were encountered immediately south of Prince's Basin during the work along the canal extension, and comprised a hard surface composed of beach cobbles (Fig 57). The presence of beach cobbles is significant, as during the nineteenth century they formed the cheapest form of hard surfacing and were often employed in areas where cargo was to be placed (Jarvis 1996, 227). Furthermore, their presence indicates that this area was not primarily used by horse-driven vehicles, as horses travelled most effectively on granite-set surfaces, which provided the required grip for the rear edge of the horse shoes, or indeed by hand carts, which required a smooth stone surface (*ibid*).

Plate 123: The south wall of Prince's Dock, from the north

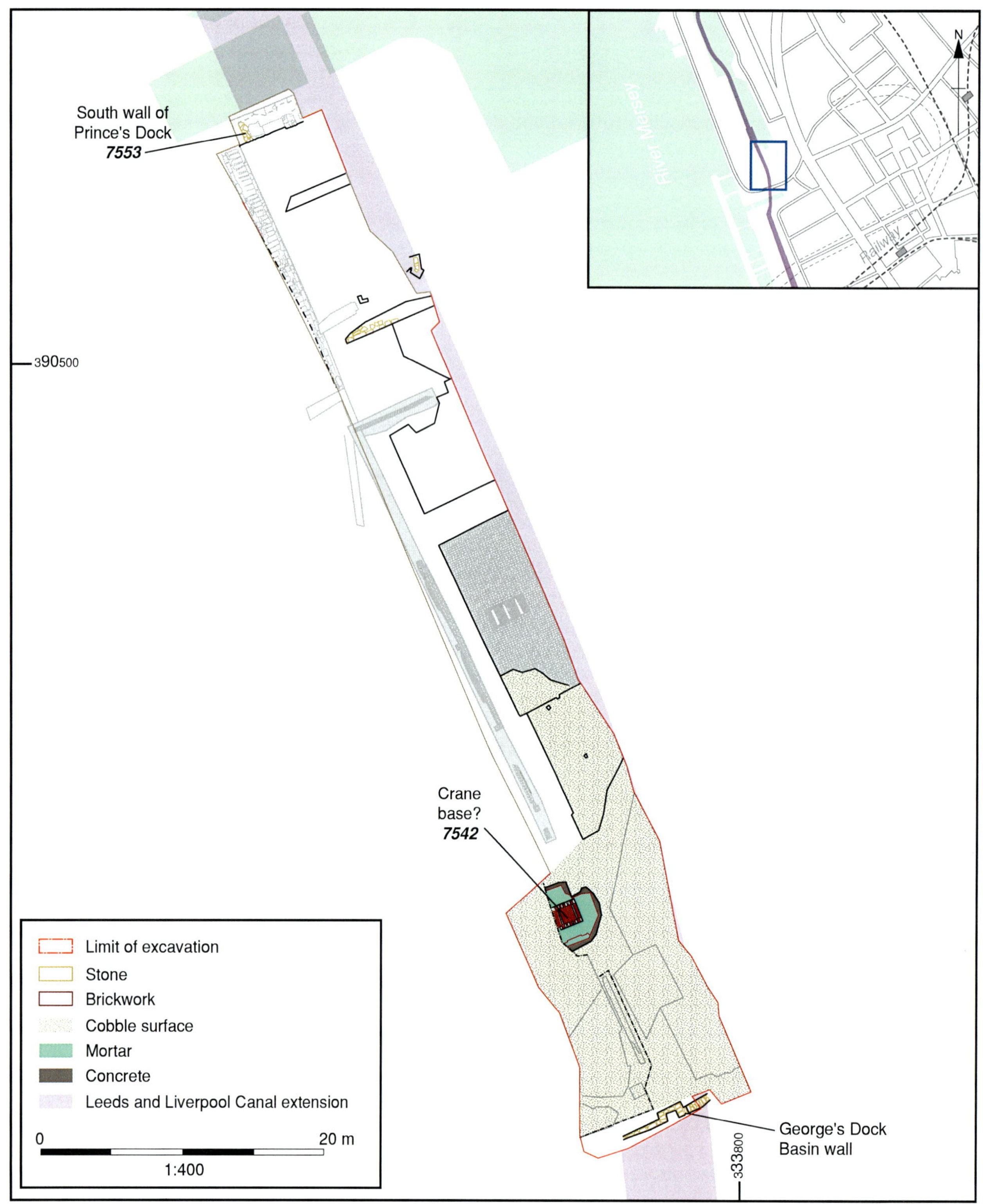

Figure 57: The section examined of the retaining wall of Prince's Dock, and other early nineteenth-century remains (© Crown copyright 2014 Ordnance Survey 100005569)

Historical mapping indicates that this area remained mostly open until *c* 1955, with only a few buildings, relatively small in dockside terms; a cobbled surface, closely resembling the excavated surface, is visible in a photograph, dated *c* 1860, of the north quay of George's Dock Basin (Stammers 1999, 100). Another mid-nineteenth-century feature uncovered in this area was an irregularly shaped brick platform (*7542*; Fig 57). This had a maximum north/south width of 5.5 m, and its centre was a *c* 2.4 m square setting, defined by brick walling. This central setting contained a complex arrangement of recesses, some containing timber, and it is possible that it represents the base for a crane.

Victoria and Trafalgar Docks (1830s)

Historical background

During the 1830s, four docks, Clarence, Waterloo, Victoria, and Trafalgar Docks, were constructed to the north of Prince's Dock (*p 97; Pl 124*), all designed by Jesse Hartley. Clarence Dock was the first to open in 1830, whilst Waterloo dock opened in 1834 (Jarvis 1991a, 230). This was then followed by the opening of both Victoria and Trafalgar Docks in 1836 (*ibid*). Three of these docks, Waterloo, Victoria, and Trafalgar, were specifically designed to provide berthing and quaysides for sailing ships, as opposed to steamships (McCarron and Jarvis 1992). Of these three docks, Victoria Dock covered almost 6 acres, with a gated entrance which was 45 ft (13.7 m) wide. Its river entrance was soon regarded as superfluous, however, and was closed in 1846, after which time access could only be gained through the dock network, either from the north or south, making the Victoria, Trafalgar, and Waterloo system 'the first real examples of spine and branch docks' (*op cit*, 94). The dock was flanked on the south and north by a transit shed, which extended the full length of the quayside (Pl 124).

Trafalgar Dock was a similar size to Victoria Dock, covering 6½ acres. This dock could be accessed either from the Victoria entrance to the south, or the Clarence Half-Tide Basin to the north. In a comparable manner to Victoria Dock, it was not designed for a specific trade, and the quayside was initially occupied by two sets of transit sheds, the larger to the south, and a smaller shed at the east end of the north quay.

Archaeological evidence

During the work along the LLC extension, a quayside area between Victoria and Trafalgar Docks was subjected to archaeological excavation (Fig 58). Both docks were largely infilled in the early 1970s (McCarron and Jarvis 1992, 90, 94) and hence the excavation provided an opportunity to examine their retaining dock walls.

The south quay of Trafalgar Dock was revealed 0.3 m below the present ground surface, in excellent condition (Pl 125). The dock wall was *c* 2 m wide and was constructed from pink sandstone, bonded with pozzolanic-type cement, and capped with granite coping stones, which were maintained in alignment by Jesse Hartley's trademark diamond-shaped locking stones (Liverpool City Council 2005, 56). At the rear, south face, of the wall, a *c* 1.1 m-square stone buttress, or counterfort, was also uncovered. These types of feature were used fairly extensively in Hartley's engineering, and were designed to counteract the tendency of dock walls to rotate and founder (Ritchie-Noakes 1984, 105-6). In addition to the counterfort, two drainage apertures were also present on the rear face of the wall, and these linked to a fairly complex, interconnecting network of culverts (Pl 126), which were originally associated with the transit sheds lining this section of the docks. The culverts were all constructed of brick, with domed roofs, and they had an average width of 0.6 m. The exposed system consisted of a main east/west-aligned culvert, which had three north/south-aligned branches linking to its northern side, and two north/south-aligned branches coming from its southern side.

The wall of Victoria Dock was almost identical to that of Trafalgar (Fig 58), in that it was *c* 2 m wide and was constructed in pink sandstone, with apertures for drainage, and granite coping stones. Again, a large counterfort was also present, 1.1 m square, constructed from pink sandstone against the rear of the wall. The fill behind both dock walls consisted of sandstone waste, coarse and fine sands, with some pea gravel, and shale and shell fragments. The upper levels of the fill behind the wall of Victoria Dock consisted of clay and demolition rubble.

Another feature uncovered in the excavation area was an unusual circular structure revealed at the

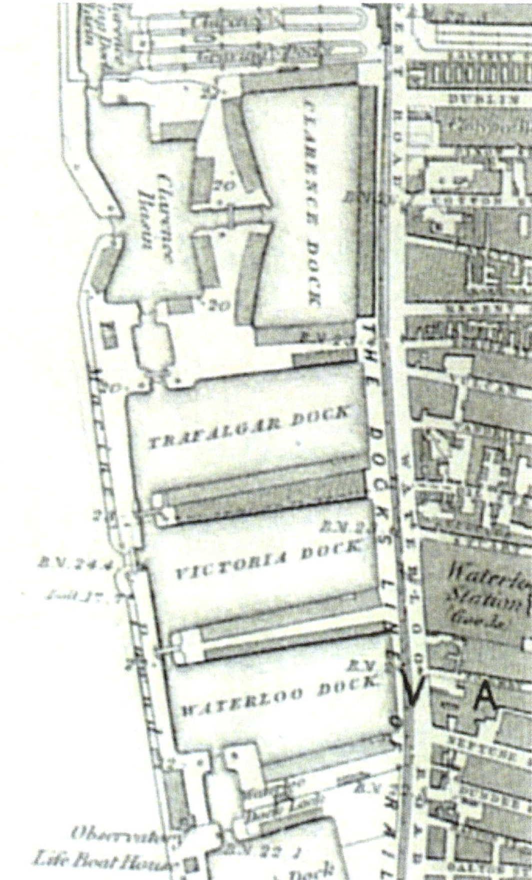

Plate 124: Extract from the Ordnance Survey 1850 6": 1 mile map (1850b), showing Clarence, Waterloo, Victoria, and Trafalgar Docks

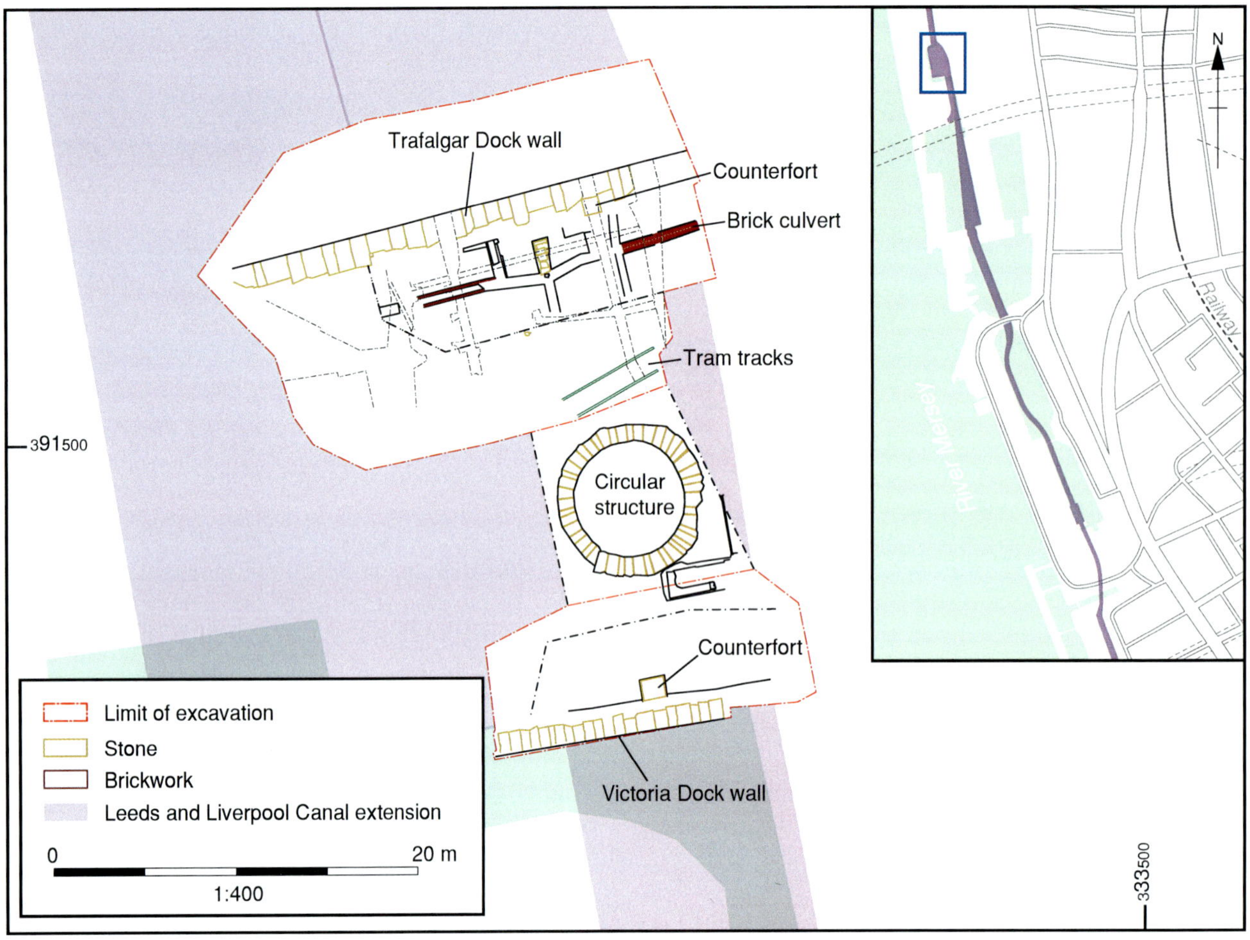

Figure 58: The excavation area at Victoria and Trafalgar Docks (© Crown copyright 2014 Ordnance Survey 100005569)

Plate 125: The south wall of Trafalgar Dock

Plate 126: Brick-built culverts positioned between Trafalgar and Victoria Docks

Plate 127: Yellow sandstone circular structure at Trafalgar Dock

base of the formation level (Fig 58; Pl 127). This had a diameter of 10 m and was formed from a *c* 1.1 m- wide wall built using yellow sandstone ashlar, closely comparable to those employed in the eighteenth-century river walls exposed during excavations at Mann Island (*Ch 3, p 56*). No artefacts were recovered in association with the structure, although it must post-date the 1830s, as, prior to this, the area formed part of the River Mersey. However, nothing that might explain this feature is apparent on any historical mapping, and its chronology and purpose remain unknown.

Nova Scotia and Mann Island (1800-60)

Historical background

Throughout the early- and mid-nineteenth century, historical mapping suggests that the outlines of the majority of the late eighteenth-century buildings between George's Dock Passage and Irwell Street remained mostly unaltered. Several buildings did, however, undergo some minor alterations and some were also replaced by 'new' buildings. These changes and schemes of rebuilding appear to have affected two specific areas. One of these lay at the far north-eastern corner of this block, at the junction of Nova Scotia and Mann Island, where the smaller late eighteenth-century properties were replaced/modified during a scheme of work that also witnessed the construction of additional properties. The other place subjected to minor modification lay at the corner of Irwell Place and Nova Scotia. In this area, two late eighteenth-century properties were subdivided between 1836 (Pl 128) and 1850,

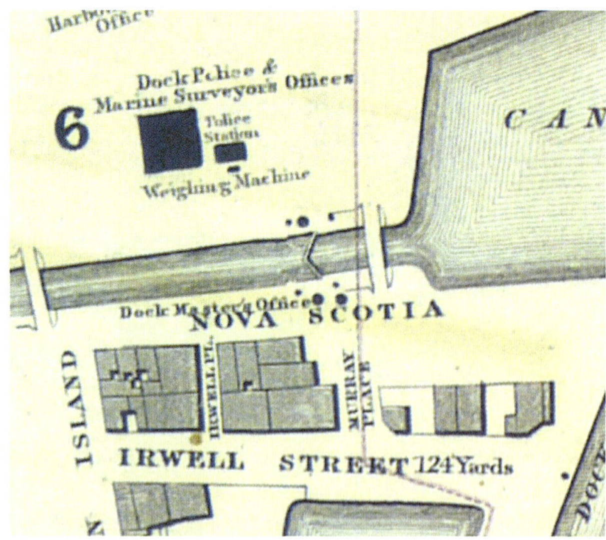

Plate 128: Extract from Gage's map of 1836 (© Trustees of National Museums Liverpool), showing Mann Island and Nova Scotia

in order to create three properties, one of which functioned as a public house named 'Murphy's Boat House' on the large-scale 1864 OS town plan (Pl 129; 1864b).

In contrast, in the area to the south, sandwiched between Manchester and Canning Docks, a more radical scheme of demolition and rebuilding occurred.

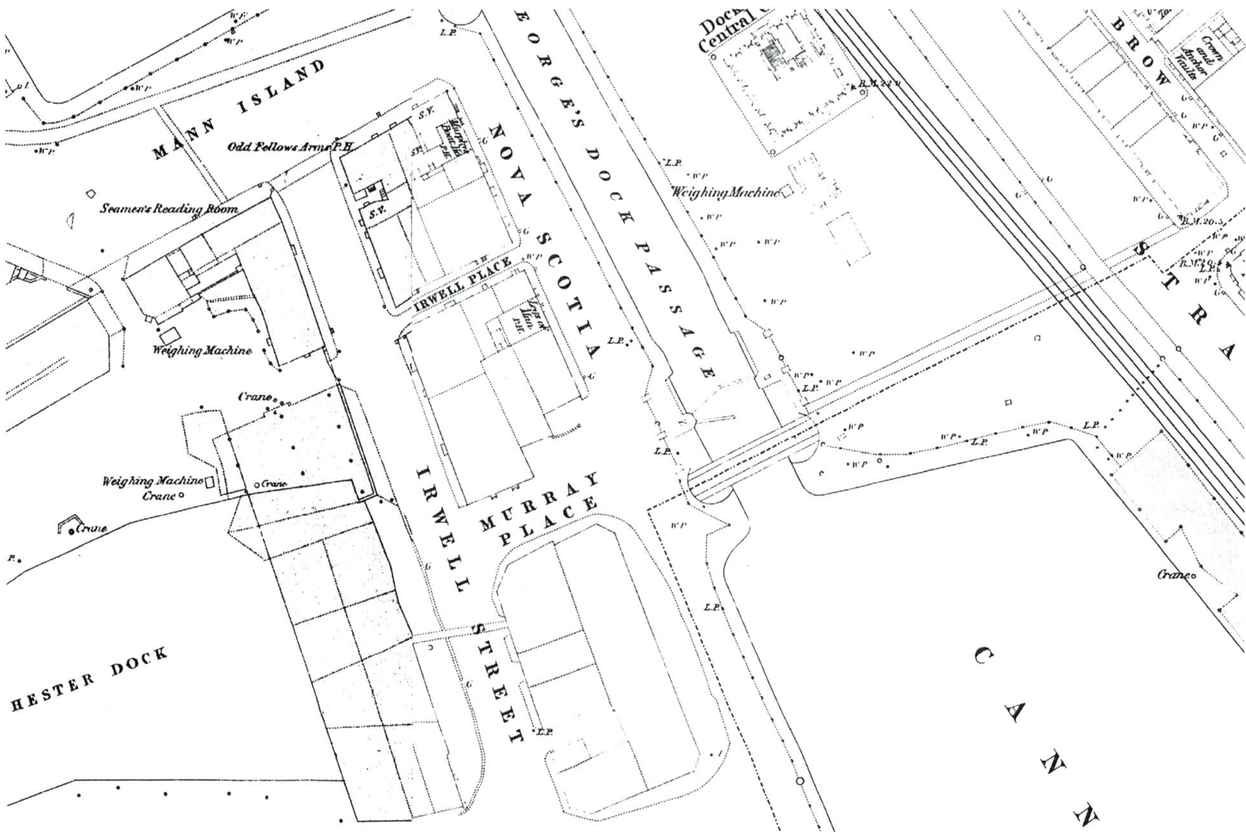

Plate 129: Extracts from the Ordnance Survey 1864 5 ft: 1 mile town plans (1864a; 1864b), showing Mann Island and Nova Scotia

Early nineteenth-century mapping indicates that, there, by 1836, three possible warehouses and a smaller detached building had been constructed across an area formerly used as a coal yard (*Ch 3, p 81*), and that the row of late eighteenth-century terraces to their rear (*Ch 3, p 87*) had been demolished (Pl 128). By 1864, a large range had been constructed in this latter area, which late nineteenth-century mapping indicates contained three adjoining warehouses that faced Canning Dock. A Goad's Insurance Plan (1890) indicates that these warehouses possessed two storeys. By 1864, an additional warehouse had also been built, within the area formerly occupied by the coal yard, at the corner of Irwell Street and Murray Place, which replaced a small detached building (Pl 129; OS 1864b). The Goad's Insurance Plan (1890) indicates that this warehouse was one-and-half storeyed.

Similarly, substantial alterations were made east of George's Dock Passage during the early- and mid-nineteenth century. In this area, buildings and streets were swept away to allow for the construction of the Dock Police and Marine Surveyor's Office. The police office was now required due to the increasing use of police on the waterfront, who prevented plunder and disorder, and also ensured that the relevant import duties were paid, and the numerous rules and regulations which surrounded a ship putting into port were enforced (*cf* Anon 1848, 143). The Liverpool City Police Force was founded in 1836, though prior to this time, a City Watch Committee had successfully policed the town, waterfront, and river (Hellier nd). It is clear from the map evidence that the police station was in place by at least 1836, as it is depicted on Gage's map (Pl 128). Architectural plans (MMMMAL 184/5/1/42) and records (MMMMAL MDHB/JH/117) indicate that the Dock Police and Marine Surveyor's Offices were designed by Jesse Hartley and were constructed in 1834. The structure was described as 'a handsome stone building' (*ibid*), and plans and elevations indicate that it was a three-storey edifice with an ashlar pink sandstone facade, pitched roof, and extensive basement. Each elevation of the building was divided into five bays, with the central one on the principal elevation having an iron framework balcony projecting over the main doorway (Pl 130). The principal entrance was south facing, with a view towards the newly remodelled Canning Dock.

In addition to the police office, Gage's map (1836; Pl 128) also plots the position of a small rectangular building, labelled as 'Police Station', which is shown

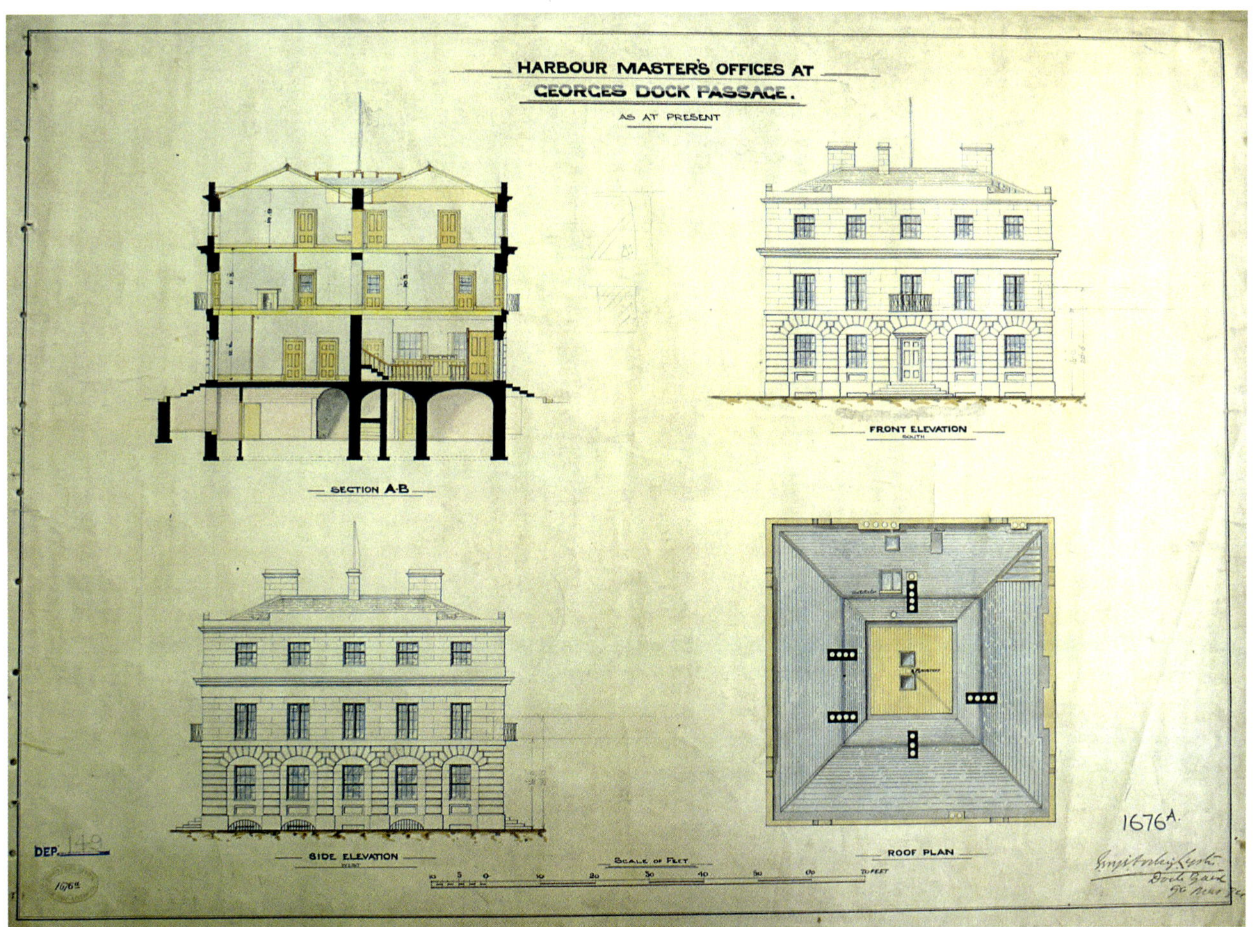

Plate 130: Architectural drawing (MMMMAL 184/5/no ref; © Trustees of National Museums Liverpool), showing the principal elevations, cross-section, and roof plan of Hartley's 1834 Dock Police and Marine Surveyor's Offices

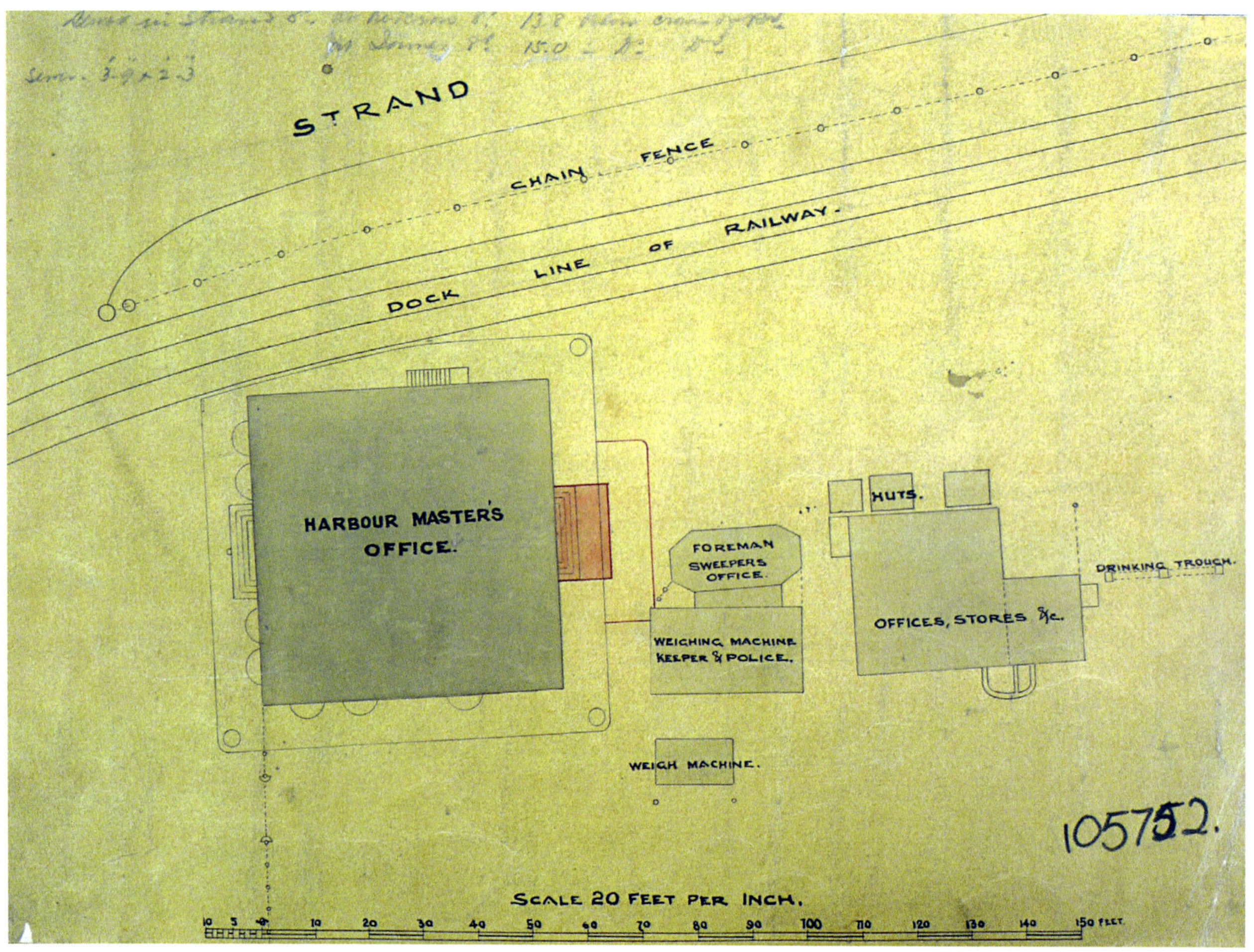

Plate 131: An undated nineteenth-century plan, showing the Dock Police and Marine Surveyor's Offices and their environs (MMMMAL 105/7/52; © Trustees of National Museums Liverpool)

as a two-roomed building on the 1864 OS town plan (Pl 129; 1864b). Gage's and later mapping also indicate that this building was adjacent to a 'Weighing Machine'. Weighing machines had been present within Mann Island and Nova Scotia for a substantial period of time, as they are mentioned in editions of Gore's *Liverpool Directory* dating to 1777 and 1781, when they were managed as personal enterprises. However, it is possible that the weighing machine depicted on Gage's map, given its proximity to the police station, was utilised by the nascent Liverpool City Police Force. The large-scale OS town plan also indicates that, by 1864, an additional small rectangular building had been built adjacent to the police station (OS 1864b), whilst to the south-west, the OS town plan also depicts a swing bridge spanning George's Dock Passage, which appears to have replaced an earlier timber bridge (Pl 129). The swing bridge was undoubtedly constructed of iron and probably dates to the early 1840s, when several of the surrounding docks were provided with comparable bridges (*p 99*).

Following the production of the OS town plan, several other small buildings were established in this area, probably in the middle decades of the nineteenth

century, which are depicted on an undated nineteenth-century plan (MMMMAL 105/7/52; Pl 131). These included a lozenge-shaped structure labelled the 'Foreman Sweeper's Office', and an additional range, and 'huts', which were added onto the eastern side of the small rectangular building next to the police station, and which functioned as offices and stores.

Archaeological evidence
Excavation at the Countryside Neptune site (*Ch 1, p 13*) and within the footprint of the LLC extension (*Ch 1, p 14*) revealed several features and structures which formed elements of early- and mid-nineteenth-century activity on Mann Island and Nova Scotia. Several of these were located in the area immediately east of George's Dock Passage, which was examined during the excavations at the Countryside Neptune site.

Within this area, limited remains of the Dock Police and Marine Surveyor's Offices were present, comprising walling executed in finely tooled pink sandstone. This was *c* 1 m wide and appears to have acted as the foundations for the principal stepped entrance on the south-facing elevation of the

144

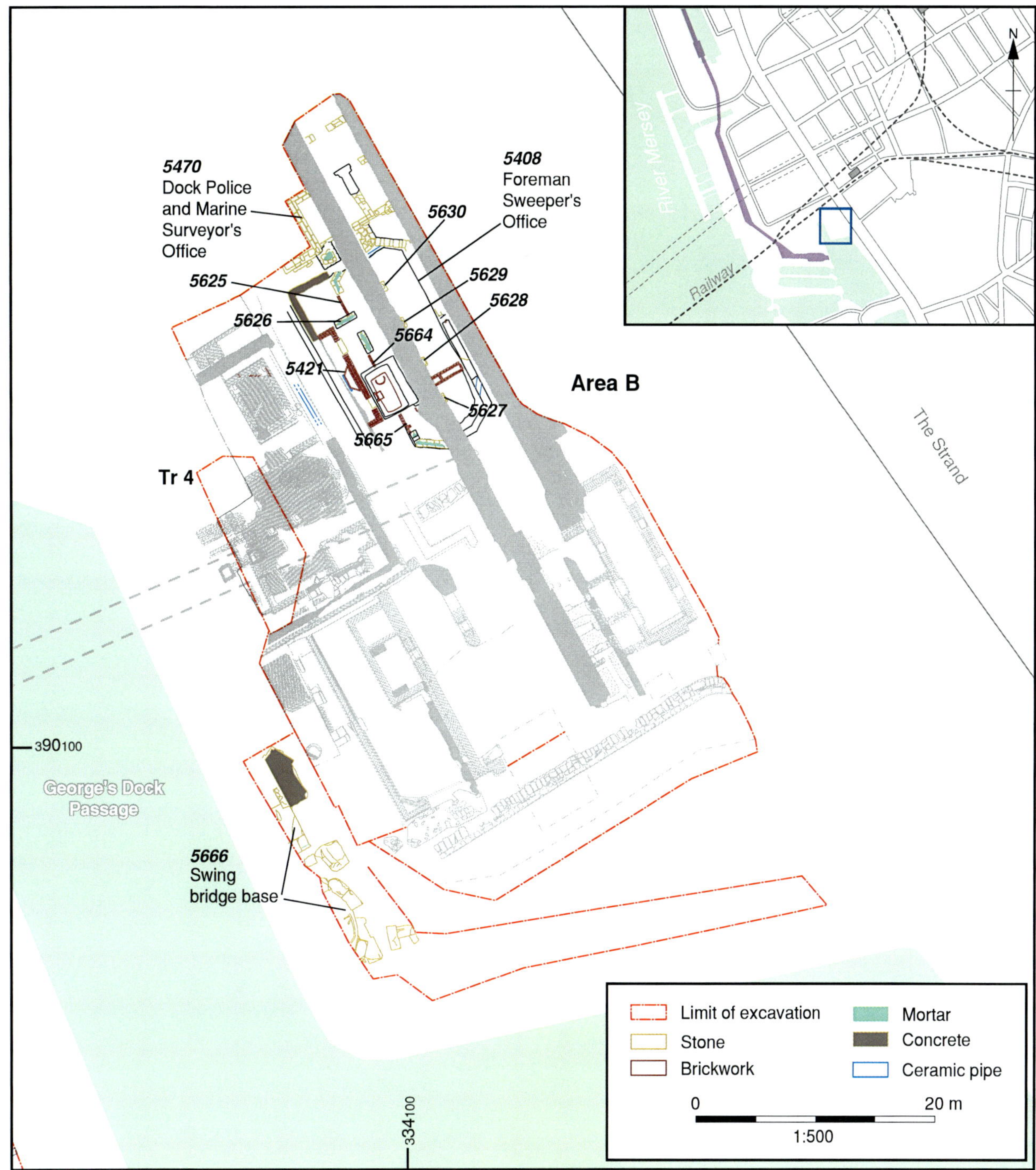

Figure 59: Early- to mid-nineteenth-century remains to the east of George's Dock Passage (© Crown copyright 2014 Ordnance Survey 100005569)

building, spanning a 5 m-wide area (**5470**; Fig 59). Architectural plans (MMMMAL 184/5/1-42) show that the extensive basement of the building extended beneath these steps in order to maximise storage space. The remainder of the offices lay to the north, beyond the limit of the excavation.

Immediately south of the Dock Police and Marine Surveyor's Offices lay a further structure (**5408**), which had been heavily disturbed by the later foundations for Media House (*Ch 5, p 171*). This formed the remains of the 'Foreman Sweeper's Office' (*p 144*) and the surviving evidence comprised finely tooled, well-constructed, pink sandstone walls defining a rectangular building with bayed ends (Fig 59; Pl 132). Within the interior of the building, a set of four hexagonal pink sandstone columns (**5627**, **5628**, **5629**, and **5630**) were also present, along its central, long axis, and these presumably supported the ground floor over an open-plan basement. No finds were recovered from the structure. The precise function of the 'Foreman Sweeper's Office' remains uncertain,

145

Plate 132: The heavily disturbed remains of the 'Foreman Sweeper's Office', from the south

although it is not improbable that the position of Foreman Sweeper was one awarded to the individual in charge of maintaining a level of order and cleanliness on the quays and wharfs around Mann Island, and the surrounding environs. However, why this position warranted such a well-constructed office is unclear. This structure was clearly in use for long enough to be modified, with the blocking of apertures in the west-facing wall (both low-level windows or doorways) at a later date by red-brick infill *5625*, *5664*, and *5665*.

An east/west-orientated sandstone wall (*5626*) extended from the western side of the 'Foreman Sweeper's Office' and butted a contemporary brick structure (*5421*), which appears to have been the eastern wall of the police station, depicted on Gage's map of 1836 (*p 143*). Another structure uncovered during the excavation, to the east of George's Dock Passage, was the eastern housing (*5666*) for the mid-nineteenth-century swing bridge (*p 144*). The housing was constructed in pink

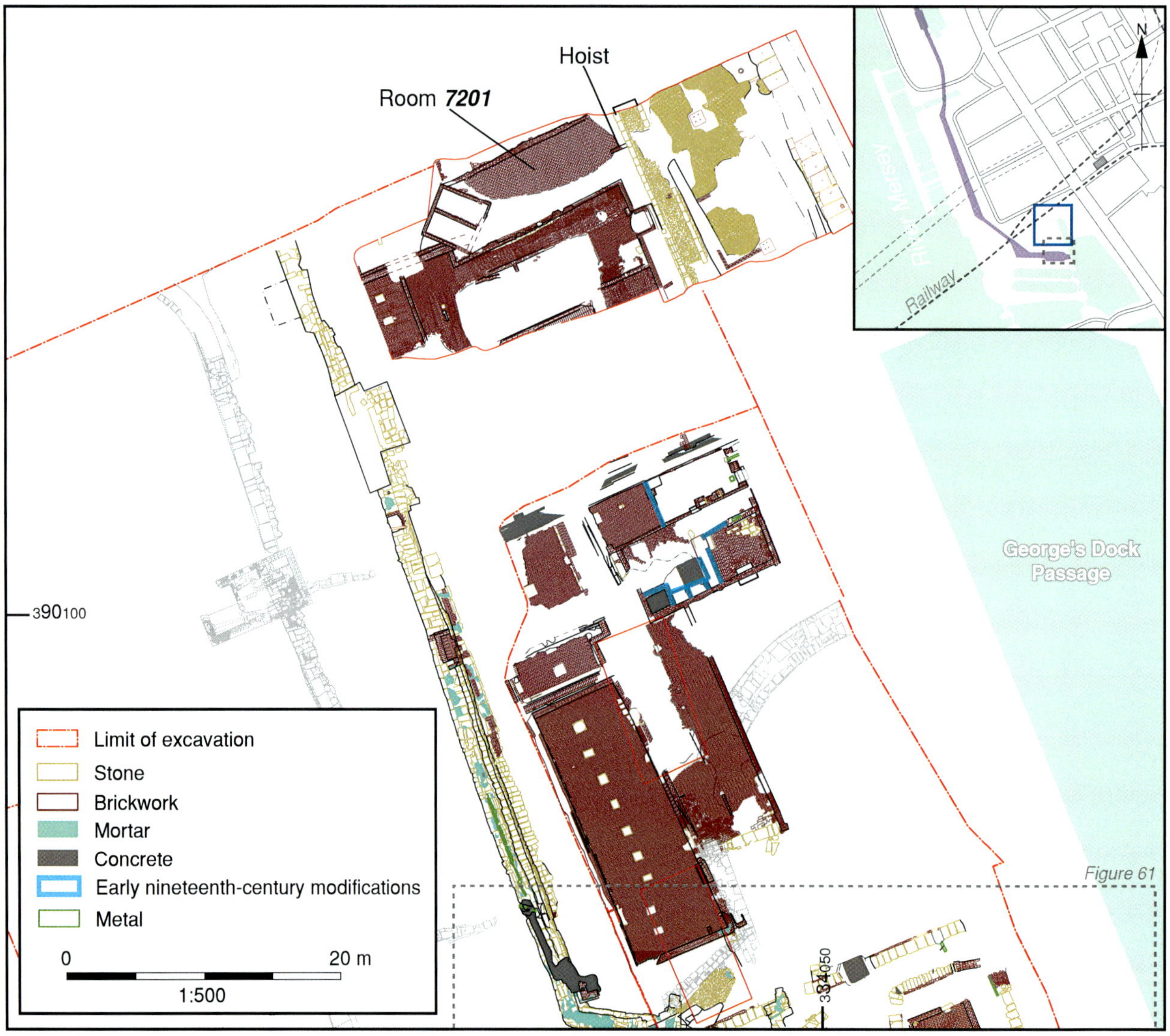

Figure 60: Early nineteenth-century modifications to the late eighteenth-century buildings at Mann Island (© Crown copyright 2014 Ordnance Survey 100005569)

sandstone and covered an area of some 10 x 4.8 m. It also had a curved form and this corresponds to the shape of the housing, as depicted on the mid-late nineteenth-century OS maps (*eg* OS 1864b).

Other nineteenth-century remains were encountered at the far north-eastern corner of Mann Island. The map evidence indicates that, between 1803 and 1836, a small single-depth property adjacent to a substantial five-storey warehouse (*Ch 3, p 80*) was replaced, or modified, to form a larger property. The cellar of this larger property was exposed (Room *7201*; Fig 60), *c* 10 x 4.7 m, containing a brick floor. In addition, the partial remains of an access well for a hoist were evident, allowing the easy movement of goods, which in turn suggests that the property functioned as a small warehouse. To the south, evidence for the subdivision of the late eighteenth-century properties at the corner of Irwell Place and Nova Scotia was also uncovered. This took the form of nineteenth-century handmade brick walls, within the cellars of these properties, which butted onto the original late eighteenth-century walls.

The partial remains of two further warehouses were exposed to the south. These were constructed between 1836 and 1850, on the site of an earlier row of terraces (*Ch 3, pp 80-1*), and they formed the central and southern warehouses within a row of three adjoining buildings that faced Canning Dock. The remains relating to the central warehouse included a handmade brick wall that defined its north-western corner, and also a handmade brick wall which defined a *c* 2.5 m-wide room within this part of the building (Fig 61). Inside this room, a single floorboard was also exposed. A series of 11 substantially constructed bases (*7339*; Pl 133) was exposed at the far southern end of the southern warehouse. These were probably designed to support the flooring and to take some of the load of the roof. Each base consisted of a three-tiered platform, measuring 1.46 x 1.46 m, and 1.22 m high, composed of handmade bricks bonded with a whitish-grey lime mortar. On top of the brick platform was a thin bedding of slate, upon which rested a single large block of reddish-brown sandstone, acting as a plinth; most of these were damaged, with no evidence of mortar or metal fixings. They were probably originally obscured beneath the floor, with only the

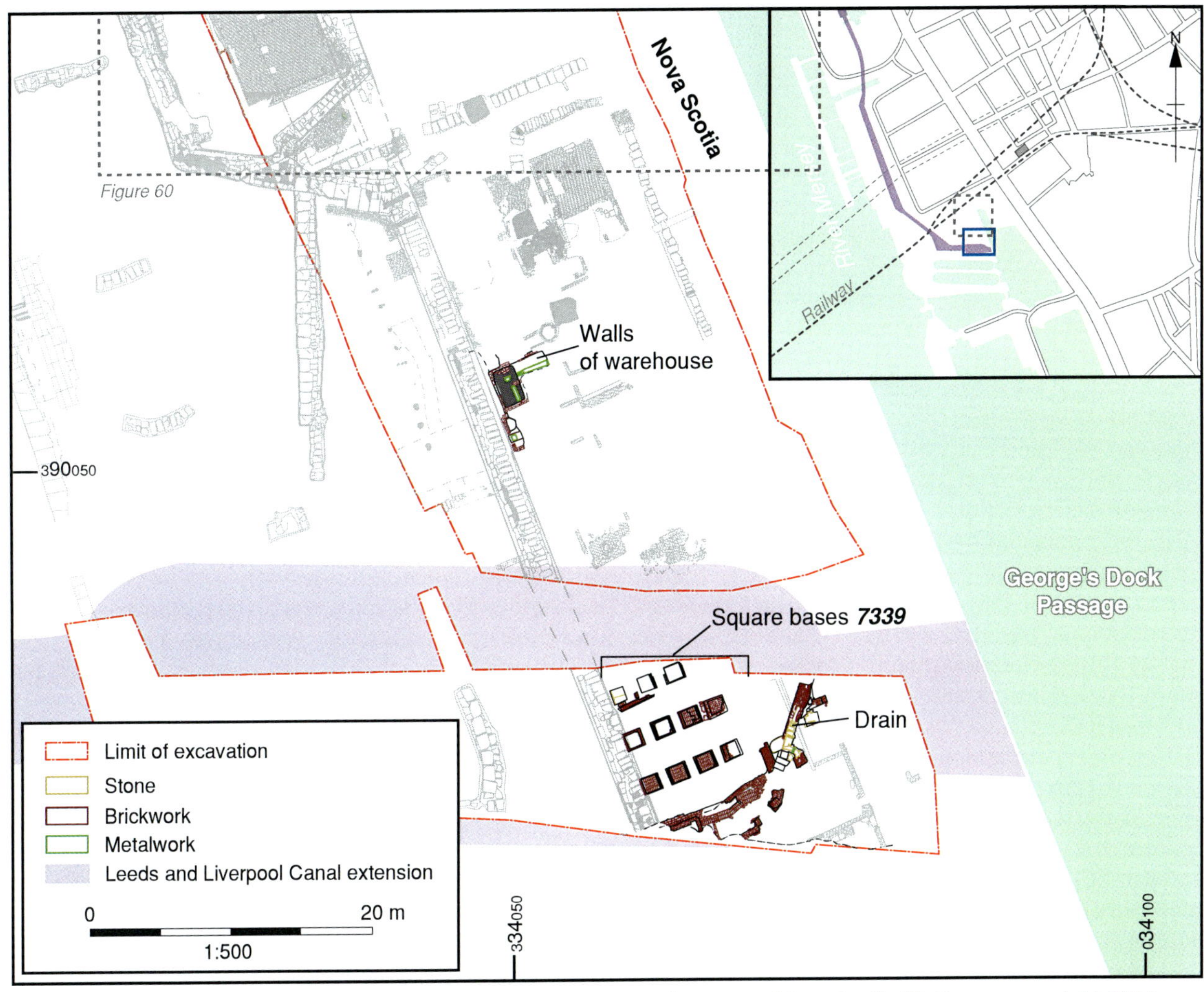

Figure 61: Remains of early- to mid-nineteenth-century warehouses on Nova Scotia (© Crown copyright 2014 Ordnance Survey 100005569)

*Plate 133: Brick and stone bases **7339**, from the south*

columns they supported protruding. Immediately to their south, an angled brick- and stone-built drain was also present, which appears to have come from the warehouse, after which it presumably linked with the nineteenth-century drainage system running down the length of Nova Scotia.

The Entrance Lock to Queen's Dock and Basin
Historical background
Between 1851 and 1852, the dry basin serving both King's and Queen's Docks was converted into a half-tide dock (Ritchie-Noakes 1984, 37). This was achieved by installing two pairs of river gates at the entrance of this basin, which flanked a small island (*ibid*). As part of this work, Queen's Dock was deepened and its walls were rebuilt (*ibid*). The cartographic evidence (*eg* Bennison 1848; OS 1893a) suggests that this work also involved fitting the entrance lock of Queen's Dock with an additional set of outward-opening lock gates, which complemented the pre-existing inward-opening gates. Furthermore, it is likely that at this time a swing bridge was constructed, situated between the lock gates at the entrance of Queen's Dock. This bridge probably replaced an earlier wooden double-leaf drawbridge 'employing massive overhead balance-beams with bar or cable staying' (Jarvis 1996, 212), which is depicted on an illustration dating to *c* 1800 (Ritchie-Noakes 1984, 38, fig 26).

Archaeological evidence
During the watching brief at the Arena and Conference Centre (*Ch 1, p 12*), an examination was made of the former entrance lock between Queen's Dock and Queen's Half-tide Dock. The principal remains recorded formed elements of the northern housing for the swing bridge, which was probably constructed between 1851 and 1852 (*see above*).

This housing was defined by an arcing wall (*1*; Fig 62) *c* 15 m in length, which was predominantly constructed of coursed pink sandstone (Fig 63), though some granite blocks were also present in its build. Although the wall had been partially destroyed by a later concrete bock (*2*), a circular cut (*4*), 0.75 m in diameter, was situated at the north-eastern corner of the wall. This probably housed a manually operated engine, which was used to move the bridge. A sandstone ramp (*3*), sloping downwards from west to east, was also present at the eastern end of the wall, though it was not possible to record this feature fully.

The base of the swing-bridge housing was encountered at a depth of *c* 1.8 m below the top of the wall (Pl 134). Although it was not possible to make a direct examination of this base, it appeared to have been surfaced with a cement render and was constructed of substantial sandstone blocks, some up to 3 m

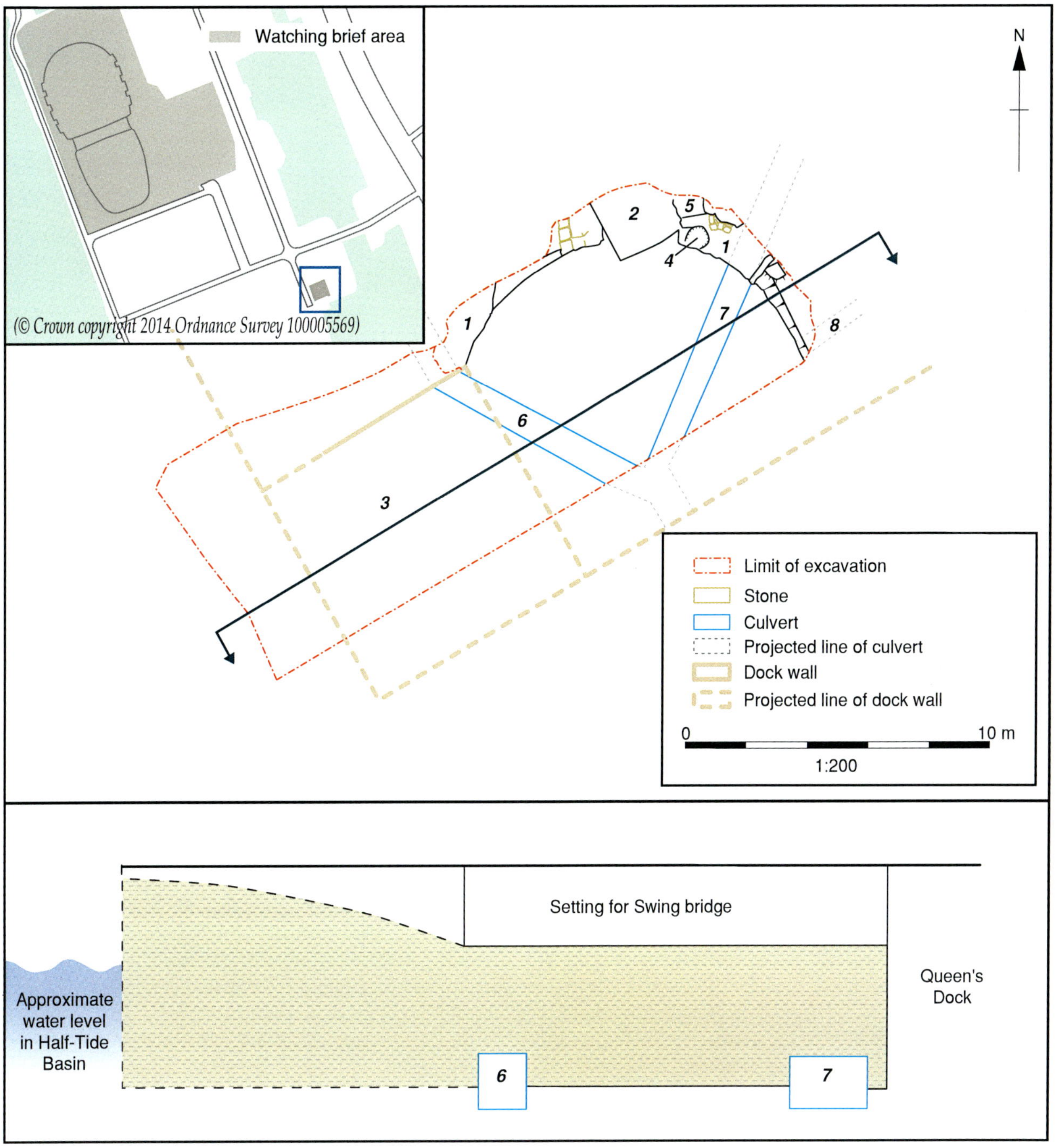

Figure 62: The remains of the swing-bridge housing

Figure 63: Photomontage of the main structural elements of the swing-bridge housing

*Plate 134: Base of the swing-bridge housing and elevation of wall **1**, from the west*

across and secured with wrought-iron clamps, laid two to three-courses deep over bedrock (Fig 62). Two culverts (*6* and *7*) were also set within the base, aligned east/west and north/south respectively and joining at the south-east to form a V-shaped arrangement. At their southern end, both were cut into bedrock to a depth of *c* 1.5 m. Large sandstone and granite capstones covered them, up to 3 m long and 1 m wide, and although the precise function of these features is not clear, they probably related to the filling and draining of the adjacent entrance lock. A third culvert (*8*) entered the housing from the east, though this was at a higher level and contained a wrought-iron shaft connected to cast-iron gears, set within a stone-lined chamber. This mechanism probably formed part of a sluice controlling the flow of water into the culvert.

5

THE LATE NINETEENTH- AND TWENTIETH-CENTURY DOCKS

Richard A Gregory, Caroline Raynor, Rob Philpott, Mark Adams, and Vix Hughes

The Port City 1860-1960

During the late nineteenth and early part of the twentieth century, Liverpool reached a commercial zenith, which resulted in the creation of a modern and global port-city (*cf* Milne 2000). Between 1860 and 1914, commercial activities within the port expanded and this period saw Liverpool flourish as a shipowning and business centre (Milne 2006, 259). Significantly, during this time, Liverpool's maritime economy was greatly influenced by its capacity to embrace, and provide facilities for, increasingly large steam-powered ocean-going passenger ships, and hence it was transformed into the 'world's premier liner port' (*op cit*, 260). In addition, the use of larger goods-carrying steamships allowed easier access to those areas that were traditionally difficult and costly to access via sailing ship, and this led to Liverpool's reconnection with West Africa, which during the late nineteenth century was an important source of palm oil (*op cit*, 261). This transformation was largely the result of entrepreneurship and also luck, brought about by specific global events, particularly those dating to the 1860s (*op cit*, 260). For instance, the American Civil War (1861-5), whilst catastrophic for Lancashire's textile industry, since it resulted in shortages of imported cotton, led to the disappearance of the United States' merchant fleet, allowing Liverpool shipowners to monopolise the transatlantic trade routes (Milne 2000, 36; 2006, 261). Moreover, during this decade, Liverpool's trading capabilities were further bolstered following the opening of the Suez Canal in 1869, which allowed easier access to the Asian markets (Milne 2006, 260).

Given the exploitation and monopolisation of these global trade routes, the steamships operating out of Liverpool continued the earlier trend of importing cotton for Lancashire's textile industry, which during the latter half of the nineteenth century was derived from Egypt, India, the Far East, and America, and, in turn, exporting their products to the global marketplace (*op cit*, 261). Liverpool's maritime economy was also closely tied in with the transportation of migrants to the United States, which greatly increased after 1865, following the collapse of the United States' merchant fleet (*ibid; see above*). During the late nineteenth century, Liverpool effectively functioned as the main European 'gateway' to the United States and hence vast numbers of Irish and European migrants passed through the port-city, the latter mostly entering England via Kingston upon Hull (Liverpool City Council 2005, 117). In addition, the late nineteenth-/early twentieth-century port emerged as a hub for the importation and processing of global foodstuffs and other commodities. These included the more traditional colonial goods, such as sugar and tobacco, and, following the development of prairie agriculture in the Americas, large quantities of grain, meat, and dairy products (*op cit*, 262).

Accordingly, this economic zenith, dating to the latter half of the nineteenth and early part of the twentieth century, greatly influenced the form of the town, which acquired city status in 1882 (Liverpool City Council 2005, 117). Demographically, as with the upsurges dating to the late eighteenth (*Ch 3*) and early- and mid-nineteenth century (*Ch 4*), the town/city once more experienced significant growth, with its population rising from around 376,000, at the time of the 1851 census, to *c* 685,000 by 1901 (Pooley 2006, 248). Consequently, between 1860 and 1913, a series of new residential suburbs emerged, which expanded the physical limits of the city both northwards and eastwards (*op cit*, fig 3.3).

Liverpool's role as a hub for the importation of global foodstuffs, and other commodities, also had a significant influence on the urban morphology of the nascent port-city. For example, the increasing levels of imported goods entering the port led to a rise in the number of warehouses constructed during the late nineteenth century (Milne 2006, 270). These were built of iron and brick, and included grain warehouses, such as those constructed by the dock engineer George Lyster (1861-97), and an abundance of privately owned warehouses that were adjacent to the dock estate, within the

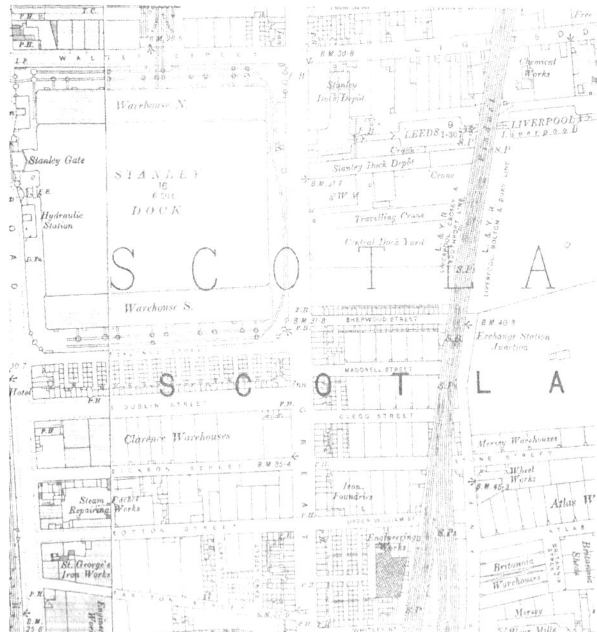

Plate 135: Extracts from the Ordnance Survey 1893 25": 1 mile maps (1893c; 1893d), showing the warehouses and range of industrial works in the vicinity of Stanley Dock

'Dock-side Belt' (*ibid*; Pl 135). Moreover, during this period, the largest warehouse of the age was also constructed within the dock estate, adjacent to Stanley Dock, by the dock engineer Anthony Lyster (1897-1913; Sharples 2004, 125). This is the enormous Tobacco Warehouse (*Ch 1, p 7*), which opened in 1901, and, at this time, formed both the world's largest warehouse, and also brick-built building (Liverpool City Council 2005, 71). In addition to warehouses, during the late nineteenth and early twentieth centuries, the area immediately adjacent to the docks was a busy industrial zone, which contained numerous factories, such as those associated with the processing/refining of grain, tobacco, and sugar, as well as gasworks, goods stations, and a plethora of smaller workshops and factories (Milne 2006, 270).

Liverpool's increasing development as a shipowning and business centre also resulted in the architectural transformation of many areas of the town/city. This involved the remodelling of Liverpool's historic core, which now housed the central business district, through the construction of shops and mixed-use buildings, continuing a process which had been initiated in the mid-nineteenth century (Sharples 2004, 18-26). This area was also home to a range of new offices and commercial buildings that became increasingly larger in size at the close of the nineteenth century (*op cit*, 26). In many respects these buildings, such as the White Star Line buildings on James Street and the Royal Insurance Building on North John Street (*op cit*, 26-7), embody Liverpool's late nineteenth-century commercial success, and this process of

aggrandisement was dramatically concluded at Pier Head, following the construction of the iconic 'Three Graces', which now form the centrepiece of the World Heritage Site (*Ch 1, p 5*; Pl 136). Significantly, these latter buildings also heralded a new phase of modernity, which was strongly associated with American architectural styles, and would develop more fully during the first half of the twentieth century (*see below*).

The twentieth century is dominated by a series of shifts in Liverpool's mercantile character, which eventually resulted in a period of decline within its historic waterfront (*cf* Jarvis 2003; Milne 2006). During the first half of the twentieth century, Liverpool had to contend with many significant global events and transformations, notably two world wars, the economic depression of the 1930s, and shifts in the global markets (Milne 2006, 259). Of these events, the two world wars greatly affected Liverpool's maritime economy, in that they both disrupted trade links and posed serious risks to Liverpool's merchant seamen and ships. Moreover, the port sustained direct damage during the Second World War, particularly at Huskisson and Canada Docks, during the blitz of 1941 (Collard 2001, 13). However, although the two wars undoubtedly undermined Liverpool's economy, during the inter-war years the port still managed to maintain its mercantile character.

This period is characterised by a clear economic switch, whereby the port focused more on the trade of metals and machinery, and the importation of oil, as opposed to its nineteenth- and early twentieth-century preoccupation with cotton, textiles, and foodstuffs (Milne 2006, 264). The inter-war years also witnessed the continued modernisation of Liverpool's central business district. This was through the construction of 'canyon' streets lined with American-influenced office buildings, such as the India Buildings and Martin's Bank, and also the adoption, in other parts of the city, of other modern architectural styles, such as Art Deco (*op cit*, 278; Sharples 2004, 31). Modernisation was not, however, confined to Liverpool's commercial centre, as it also affected residential areas. Indeed, perhaps the greatest visible testament to this was in the construction of large blocks of multi-storey flats, which became a feature of Liverpool's cityscape from the 1930s onwards (Sharples 2004, 32).

Between 1945 and the 1960s, trading patterns at the port once again shifted as mercantile attention focused on consumer goods and high-technology products (Milne 2006, 264). However, some of the port's more 'traditional' activities still held sway and, accordingly, several new features were constructed along the historic waterfront (*p 159*). In addition, in 1948, Liverpool obtained the world's first port radar

Plate 136: Aerial photograph dating to 1923 (LVRO and Liverpool Libraries City Engineer's Image No 4104), showing the 'Three Graces', Pier Head and the landing stages, Manchester Dock, Chester Basin, and Prince's Dock

station, which was at Gladstone Dock, allowing more effective control of shipping utilising the port (Collard 2001, 15). From the late 1960s, Liverpool's maritime economy was greatly influenced by the adoption of containerisation and the advent of readily available air travel, which affected the use of passenger liners (Milne 2006, 264). Containerisation requires large mechanised docks, associated factories, and open spaces, and also ports with substantial hinterlands (*ibid*), and initially, the absence of these elements at Liverpool resulted in a loss of trade, which was absorbed by the container ports established at London, Felixstowe, and Southampton (Collard 2001, 17).

The latter half of the twentieth century also saw the liquidation of the MDHB, which then, through government assistance, was reinvented in 1971 as the Mersey Docks and Harbour Company (MDHC) (*ibid*). Following this, the port's focus was readjusted through the transformation of the far northern end of the dock estate. This involved the construction of the Royal Seaforth container terminal, which opened in 1972 (*op cit*, 18). However, although the construction of this terminal allowed Liverpool to continue to operate as a viable port, and one which now handles more than

65 million tonnes of cargo a year (Peel Ports nd), the very nature of containerisation was to have serious implications for Liverpool's historic system of docks. The effects on this area included 'the loss of most of its waterfront employment, the abandonment of most of its docks and the sudden vanishing of the connection between port and city' (Milne 2006, 264).

Naturally, the decline in portside activities has once more led to transformation, and during the twenty-first century, some of the historic waterfront area, particularly the central part of the former dock estate, has formed the focus for regeneration schemes. Initially, this was undertaken by the Merseyside Development Corporation (MDC), a government-funded body that was established in 1981 (Sharples 2004, 37). Under its auspices, areas of the south docks were redeveloped through the establishment of housing and businesses and, significantly, the Albert Dock warehouses and its environs (*Ch 4, p 98*) were restored. The process of urban regeneration was then further expanded in 1999 through the establishment of Liverpool Vision, the country's first Urban Regeneration Company (Murden 2006, 473). Following its formation,

153

the redevelopment of Liverpool's city centre has continued, with a particular flourish prior to 2008, the year that marked the beginning of the most recent deep economic downturn. This flourish was instrumental in facilitating archaeological exploration, enabling a clearer understanding of Liverpool's historic waterfront.

The Late Nineteenth- and Twentieth-century Dock System and Waterfront

Historical development

The growth of trade and transportation during the latter half of the nineteenth century and the use of increasingly larger steamers, as with those increases in trade and commerce during the first half of the century (*Ch 4*), were to have a profound influence on the form of Liverpool's waterfront (Fig 64). Between 1861 and the advent of the First World War, many of Liverpool's existing docks were modified, and a series of new docks was also established. This work was overseen by the dock engineer, George Fosbery Lyster (1861-97), aided by his son, Anthony George Lyster, from 1889, who eventually succeeded his father as the Board's dock engineer (1897-1913; Ritchie-Noakes 1984, 99-100).

Initially, the work of George Fosbery Lyster involved modifying one of the existing northern features, Huskisson Dock (*Ch 4, p 100*), which he provided with a second branch dock (Pl 137). This was constructed in 1861 and, as with the earlier branch dock to its south, was surrounded by transit sheds (Jarvis 1991a, 231). This was immediately followed in 1862 by the construction of a new dock, known as Canada Half-Tide Basin, which was later renamed Brocklebank Dock (*ibid*). This lay immediately north of, and was linked to, Canada Dock (*Ch 4, p 100*). However, access to Brocklebank Dock from the river was through Canada Dock's Basin (*Ch 4, p 100*), immediately to its east, either through a double set of lock gates, which allowed smaller vessels to enter and leave at any state of the tide, or through a larger inward-facing mitre gate, which was designed to receive larger vessels at high tide. Brocklebank Dock was partly designed for the timber trade and had a timber quay, whilst at its southern end were two small, branch carriers' docks (North and South Carriers' Docks), which were associated with several small warehouses.

In the northern docks, during the late 1860s, sections of the walls of Prince's Dock were relaid and modifications were then made to Prince's Basin in order to convert it into half-tide dock, which opened in 1868 (Jarvis 1991b, 36, 41). This conversion involved constructing a triple river entrance at the mouth of

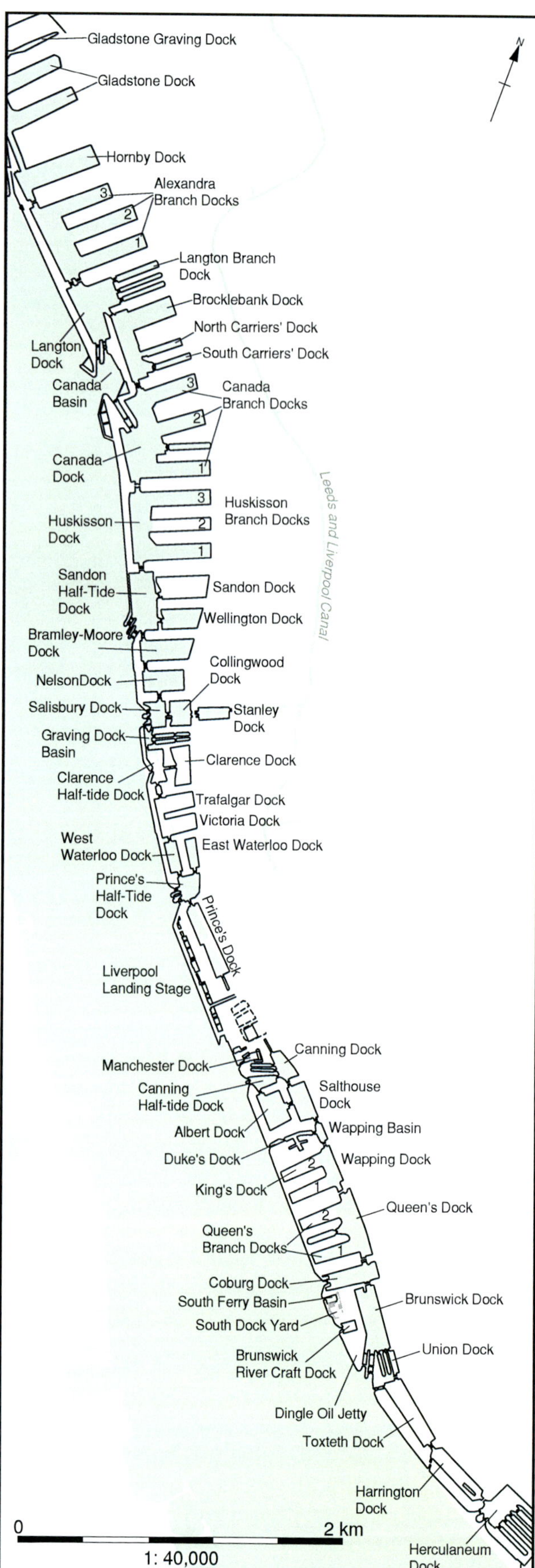

Figure 64: The late nineteenth- and early twentieth-century docks and waterfront (© Crown copyright 2014 Ordnance Survey 100005569)

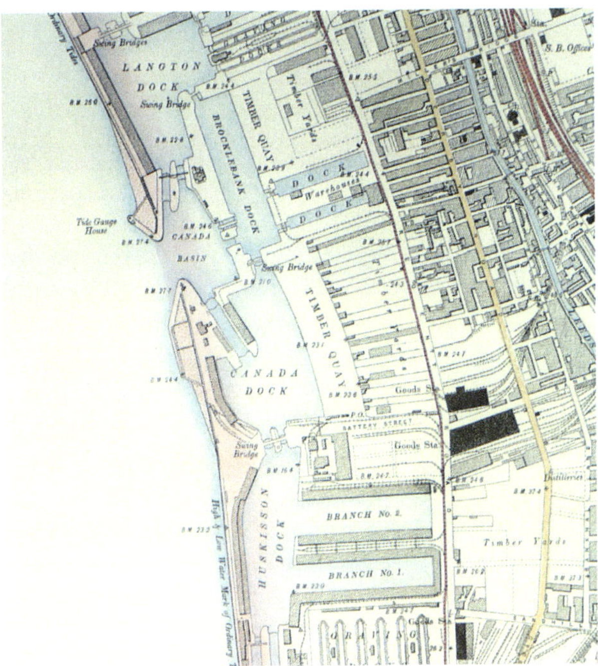

Plate 137: Extract from the Ordnance Survey 1894 6": 1 mile map (1894a), showing Lyster's modifications to the northern docks

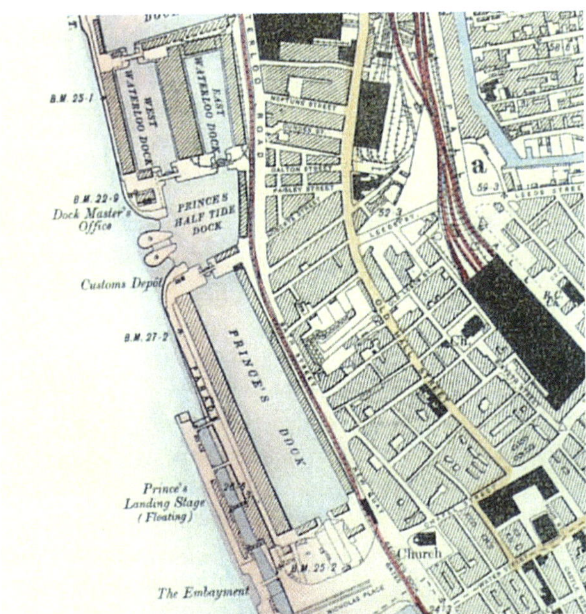

Plate 138: Extract from the Ordnance Survey 1894 6": 1 mile map (1894a), showing Lyster's modifications to Prince's Dock and Basin, and Waterloo Dock

the former basin (Pl 138). This entrance had two large half-tide gates, suitable for larger vessels, sandwiching a smaller river lock, which allowed smaller craft to enter at any state of the tide (*ibid*). Accordingly, the new half-tide basin was predominantly used by the Mersey flats (*Appendix 1*), which, following the construction of a railway transit shed in 1875 at the eastern end of the dock, could unload goods to, and receive goods from, the docks' railway (*ibid*). In conjunction

with the alteration of Prince's Basin, the late 1860s also witnessed modifications to Waterloo Dock, immediately to its north (*Ch 4, p 97*). This involved the construction of an north/south-aligned pier, which subdivided the dock into two (East Waterloo Dock and West Waterloo Dock). These two docks were accessed from the Prince's Half-tide Dock through two separate entrances. These new docks, as with the earlier Waterloo Dock, were designed to receive grain, and a large grain warehouse was constructed on the dividing pier.

In the early 1860s, a large dock was also constructed in the area of the southern docks, representing George Fosbery Lyster's first major dock-building work (Ritchie-Noakes 1984, 61), which formed a separate berth some distance south of Brunswick Dock (*Ch 4, p 98*). This was Herculaneum Dock, named after the Herculaneum Pottery, which had been established in this area during the late eighteenth century, adjacent to a small tidal basin (*Ch 3, p 54*), though by the late 1830s this business had ceased to trade (*ibid*). The dock initially functioned as a half-tide dock, opened in 1866, and was accessed through a double river entrance, containing hydraulic-powered gates (*op cit*, 62; Pl 139). The original edifice was designed for the maintenance and repair of large vessels, and it was accordingly associated with two massive graving docks attached to its southern side. In 1866, work began on the construction of a third graving dock, though this was not completed until the 1870s (*op cit*, 61). In addition, to the north of Herculaneum Dock, a small landing stage was constructed in 1863 off Harrington Dock (*Ch 4, p 98*), which was used by the Mersey River Steam Boat Company (*op cit*, 67).

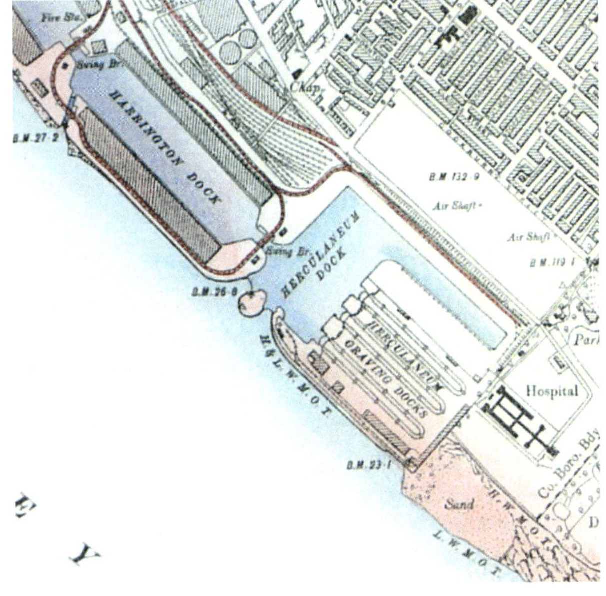

Plate 139: Extract from the Ordnance Survey 1894 6": 1 mile map (1894b), showing Herculaneum and Harrington Docks

It appears, however, that dock construction in the 1860s did little to reduce the growing pressure of increased maritime trade, and during the 1870s the records of the MDHB indicate that the docks were becoming severely congested (Mountfield 1965, 36). During this period, the northern docks were being used by the Cunard and Inman liners, and also Bibby's Mediterranean ships, whilst Bramley-Moore Dock was constantly full of American packet ships. To the south, Albert and Salthouse Docks were full of ships from the East Indies, whilst George's Dock was full of fruit schooners (*ibid*). In addition, South American traders were placing increasing pressure on Prince's Dock, and similarly increased levels of Continental trade were entering King's and Queen's Docks (*ibid*).

In order to ease these pressures, initially a scheme of modification was undertaken in the northern docks. In 1871, this entailed the enlargement of Brocklebank Dock, which was followed in 1872 by the opening of a third branch dock at Huskisson Dock (Jarvis 1991a, 231). An Act of Parliament in 1873 then sanctioned the spending of £4m pounds to carry out a further scheme of dock building and associated works (Mountfield 1965, 37). This entailed the construction of a river wall north of Canada Basin, at the northern end of the dock system, which contained a new group of inter-linked docks, comprising Langton Dock, Alexandra Dock, and Hornby Dock, which respectively opened in 1879, 1880, and 1884 (Ritchie-Noakes 1984, 170; Pl 140). This group could be accessed from Canada Basin through two locks, completed in 1881, which joined with Langton Dock (Jarvis 1991a, 232), and also through a lock on the northern side of Brocklebank Dock. Of these docks, Langton was associated with a branch dock and two graving docks, built for the world's largest

ships, and dealt with general and Mediterranean trade, and by 1893 it was used by the Ellerman and Leyline Lines; Alexandra Dock had three branch docks, and acted as a grain terminal; whilst Hornby was used by the timber trade and therefore incorporated a sloping quay to aid unloading (Liverpool Museums nd; Jarvis 1991a, 143; 2003, 10). By 1893, the firms, Canadian Pacific and the Pacific Steam Navigation Company, also operated out of Alexandra and Hornby Docks (Jarvis 2003, 11).

In addition, during the 1870s and early 1880s, several schemes of improvements and construction were undertaken in the southern docks. At Herculaneum Dock, work on the third graving dock (*p 155*) was finally completed in 1876, which was then followed by the deepening of Herculaneum Dock's entrance in 1881, and the building of a branch dock (Ritchie-Noakes 1984, 61-2; Pl 139). This branch dock was specifically designed to receive vessels carrying barrels of petroleum, which were held in an adjacent store composed of barrel-vaulted chambers cut into the outcropping bedrock. During this period, a small, narrow dock was also constructed, named Brunswick River Craft Dock, which was a replacement for Egerton Dock (*see below*). This opened in 1878 and, as the name implies, was attached to the eastern side of Brunswick Dock by a short passage, and was also designed to accommodate inland vessels (*op cit*, 44; Pl 141).

In the area that had been occupied by Egerton and Harrington Docks, and Harrington Basin, the three privately owned docks established in the early nineteenth century (*Ch 4, p 98*), a major scheme of dock building was also initiated in the 1870s, which would

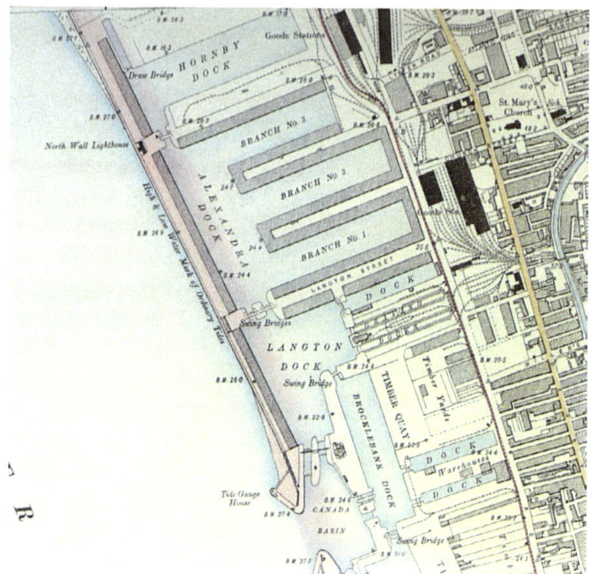

Plate 140: Extract from the Ordnance Survey 1894 6": 1 mile map (1894a), showing Lyster's Langton, Alexandra, and Hornby Docks

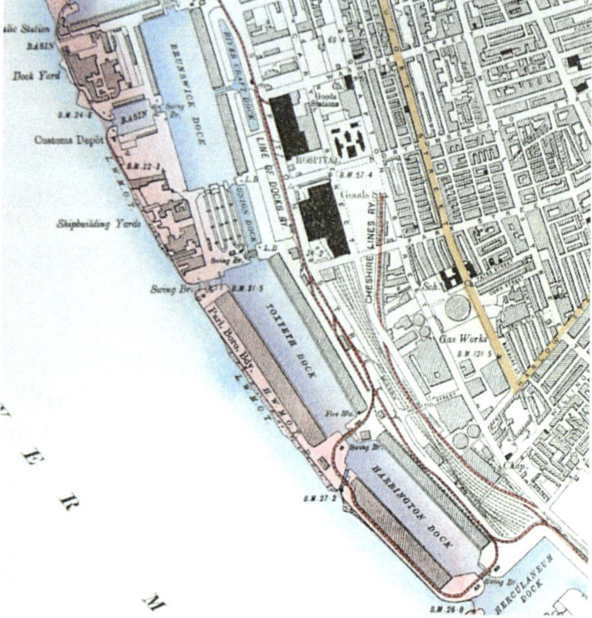

Plate 141: Extract from the Ordnance Survey 1894 6": 1 mile map (1894b), showing Brunswick, Toxteth, and Harrington Docks

result in their destruction (*op cit*, 67). This scheme involved the construction of two large inter-linked docks, known initially as Dock I (later renamed Toxteth Dock) and Dock K (later renamed Harrington Dock), sandwiched between Herculaneum and Brunswick Docks, which opened in 1888 and 1883 respectively (*op cit*, 68; Jarvis 1991a, 232; Pl 141). Access to Toxteth Dock from the river was via a lock, whilst Harrington Dock could only be accessed from either Toxteth or Herculaneum Docks. Both docks were involved in the outbound trade of regionally manufactured metal, textiles, and salt, the latter carried to the docks by the Mersey flats (*Appendix 1*). However, at Toxteth Dock, foodstuffs and manganese ore were discharged from vessels travelling from West Africa, and at Harrington Dock, foodstuffs and cotton were received from vessels that had departed from India, North America, and Brazil (*op cit*, 71). These imported and exported goods were stored in double-storey sheds, which lined the respective quaysides (*op cit*, 70). In 1889, work was also completed on Union Dock, a sizable passage joining Brunswick and Toxteth Docks (*op cit*, 44). This was provided with gates at either end and acted as a lock, which was required because of the difference in the water levels between the two docks (*ibid*).

The 1890s and first decade of the twentieth century witnessed major alterations and improvements to the existing docks. This entailed dock enlargement and modification to the river lock at Canada Dock, in 1895/6, followed by the construction of three large branch docks (Canada Branch Docks Nos 1-3), across the former timber quay, which were completed in 1896, 1903, and 1906 (Jarvis 1991a, 232-4; Pl 142). These new branch docks were subsequently used as berths for the Ismay Imrie, Allan Line, and Leyland Lines shipping companies (Jarvis 2003, 10). In conjunction with this work, substantial alterations were also made to Huskisson Dock and its lock in 1896, 1897, and 1900, which enlarged the size of the dock (Jarvis 1991a, 233). Furthermore, in 1902, an additional branch dock was constructed to the south of the two earlier branch docks (*ibid*), and during this period, these three branch docks were used by Ismay Imrie, Cunard, and Leyline Lines (Jarvis 2003, 10). Immediately to the south of Huskisson Dock, in 1902, Sandon Basin and Wellington Half-tide Basin (*Ch 4, p 100*) were merged and altered, to form Sandon Half-tide Basin (Jarvis 1991a, 233). This could be accessed from the river through two large deepwater locks, which allowed large vessels to enter the basin. These large locks were, however, positioned on either side of a smaller lock, used by lesser inland craft (Jarvis 2003, 10). Another major scheme of alteration was also undertaken at Brocklebank Dock. Initially, this involved the conversion of its South Carriers' Dock (*p 106*) into a graving dock, which opened in 1903 (Jarvis 1991a, 234). This was then followed by the

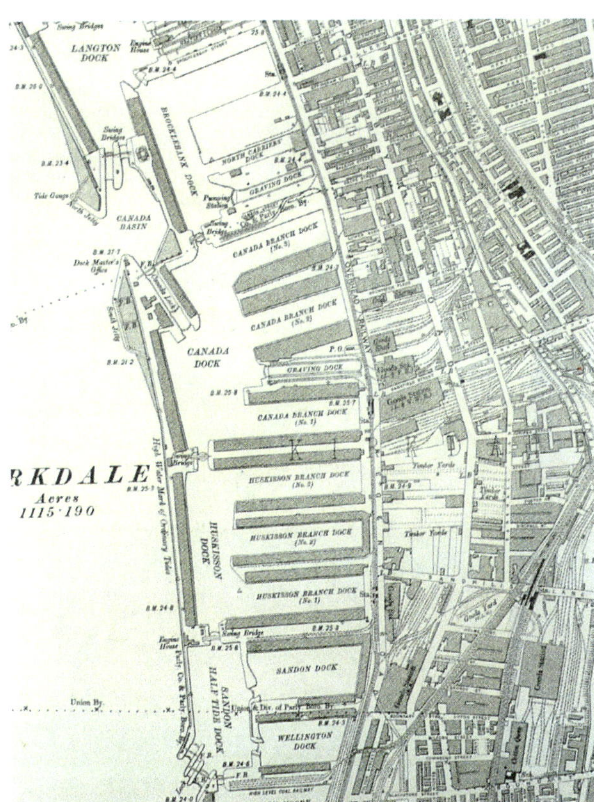

Plate 142: Extract from the Ordnance Survey 1910 6": 1 mile map (1910a), showing the late nineteenth- and early twentieth-century alterations to Canada, Huskisson, and Brocklebank Docks, and Sandon Half-tide Basin, created in 1902

construction of a large branch dock, which opened in 1906, and was built across the area formerly occupied by the Brocklebank timber quay (*ibid*).

In the southern docks, the Mersey Docks (New Works) Act of 1898 allowed for the rebuilding of the group of docks between Wapping Basin and Toxteth Dock (Ritchie-Noakes 1984, 38; Pl 143). This therefore resulted, in 1903, in the construction of two large deepwater river locks, which allowed access into Brunswick Dock, and the construction of a river wall between Coburg and Duke's Docks (*ibid*; Jarvis 1991a, 234; 2003, 3). Behind this wall, substantial alterations were also made to King's and Queen's Docks. These included the enlargement of Queen's Dock through the addition of two branch docks and a graving dock, on its western side, in the area formerly occupied by Trafford Dock (*Ch 4, p 100*), Queen's Half-tide Dock, and its associated graving docks (*Ch 3, p 54*). Similarly, King's Dock was largely rebuilt, and by 1906 it consisted of two east/west-aligned branch docks, which were attached to the western side of Wapping Dock (Jarvis 1991a, 234; 2003, 3). A fourth graving dock was also added to Herculaneum Dock in 1902 (Ritchie-Noakes 1984, 61). Some more minor dock alterations were also made during the period 1897-1906 (Jarvis 1991a, 233-4). These included: the widening of some

Plate 143: Extracts from the Ordnance Survey 1910 6": 1 mile maps (1910b; 1910c), showing the early twentieth-century dock system between Wapping Basin and Toxteth Dock

of the passages linking several of the docks (Hornby and Trafalgar-Victoria); modifications to a number of quaysides (Brunswick and Coburg); and minor alterations to Prince's and Langton Docks.

The late nineteenth, and initial years of the twentieth, century also witnessed several schemes of dock infilling. The earliest of these related to the infilling of George's Dock Basin in the early 1870s, in order to construct the Floating Bridge (*p 175*), a structure designed to provide improved access to the Pier Head landing stages (*see below*). The passage, which once linked the south end of Prince's Dock to George's Dock Basin, was then partly infilled and converted into a graving dock (Jarvis 1991b, 45). This was followed, in 1897, by the partial infilling of Stanley Dock, in order to construct the large Tobacco Warehouse (*p 152*) on its southern quay (Jarvis 1991a, 233). Finally, in 1900, George's Dock was closed, as its presence, as with its basin, was a barrier to the growing amounts of ferry traffic using the floating landing stages (Ritchie-Noakes 1984, 30; *see below*). Following its closure, the dock was infilled and then became the site of the 'Three Graces' (*p 152*).

Although the floating landing stage at Pier Head, serving the Mersey ferries, had been established and

rebuilt in the first half of the nineteenth century (*Ch 4, p 123*), this was destroyed by fire in 1874 (Ritchie-Noakes 1984, 30). It was therefore replaced by another landing stage, constructed in 1875, which retained the name George's Landing Stage (*p 174*), and continued to act as a landing for river ferries (*ibid*; Cossons and Jenkins 2011, 21). To the north of this, Prince's Landing Stage had been constructed in 1857 as access for ocean-going liners (*Ch 4, p 101*). The southern end of this was extended in the mid-1870s during the construction of the Floating Bridge (*p 175*), and this was used as a ferry goods stage. A further significant development then occurred in 1895, with the opening of the Riverside Railway Station (Quick 2001, 249; Fig 65). This, and its line, were operated by the LNWR and it was situated directly adjacent to Prince's Landing Stage, on the western quay of Prince's Dock; it thus afforded rail passengers easy access both to the Irish Packet and transatlantic liners. Immediately following the opening of this station, the landing stage was replaced in 1896 by a new Prince's Landing Stage, which linked with George's Landing Stage (Cossons and Jenkins 2011, 21; Pl 136). It appears that this new landing stage, along with the establishment of the Riverside Railway Station, was principally a response to Cunard's threat to leave Liverpool (Jarvis 1991b, 54-7; Reed 1992, 4).

During the late nineteenth century, the rail infrastructure within the dockside belt was also expanded through the extension of the dock railway and the construction of several new goods stations, designed to serve the evolving dock system (Fig 65). Within the waterfront, the latter decades of the century also saw the construction of two additional lines of communication. The earlier of these was the Mersey Railway Company (MRC) tunnel, which ran beneath the River Mersey from James Street Station, immediately east of George's Dock Passage, across to Green Lane Station in Birkenhead (Maund 2002, 68). The construction of this tunnel had been authorised in 1866, though the project stalled, due to a lack of capital investment (Slaughter 1869, 118). Construction of the MRC tunnel began formally in August 1881, and this led to upheaval in the area to the east of George's Dock Passage (Fox 1886, 40). Although there were problems with the geology, which were not predicted by the engineers, the work progressed steadily, particularly after the acquisition of a special boring machine designed by Colonel Beaumont RE, which moved the work forward at a rate of 150 ft (45.7 m) per week. The tunnel was finally completed in 1886 (Merseyside Passenger Transport Executive (MPTE) 1986, 2). This was followed in 1888 by the formation of the Liverpool Overhead Railway Company (LORC), which by 1893 had constructed a double-track elevated railway along the majority of the length of

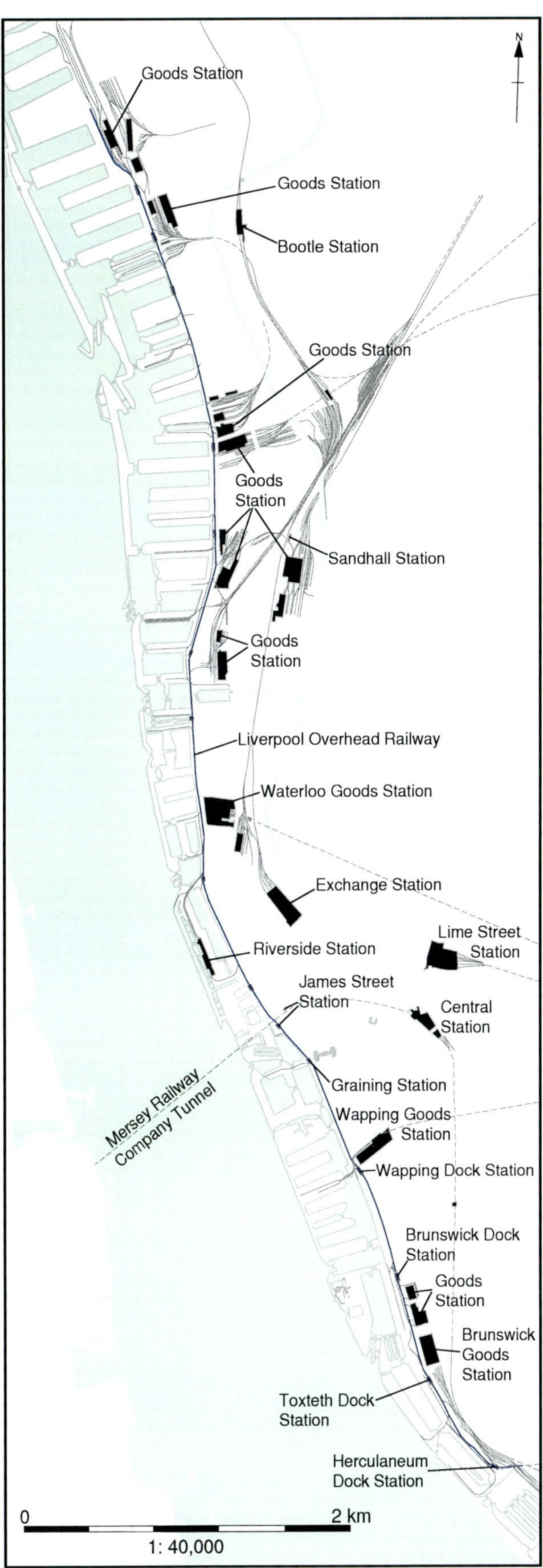

Figure 65: The late nineteenth-century dock railway system and associated stations (© Crown copyright 2014 Ordnance Survey 100005569)

the dock estate, from Alexandra Dock in the north to Herculaneum Dock in the south (Sharples 2004, 100). This line extended for a distance of 14.5 km and was supported on an iron and steel viaduct. It originally had 11 stations designed to serve the various docks along its route (Liverpool City Council 2005, 141), and it was designed for the movement of dock workers. However, it also became a popular tourist attraction, providing the first real view of Liverpool's waterfront (Sharples 2004, 100).

Further developments to the physical and functional character of the dock estate occurred between 1914 and the 1960s. The earlier of these developments included the establishment of Gladstone and Gladstone Graving Docks, which in the early twentieth century formed Liverpool's most northerly docks (Fig 64). Their construction followed a 1906 Parliamentary Act and they were designed by the dock engineer Anthony George Lyster as the world's largest and deepest dock system, that could adequately receive, and also repair/maintain, the largest transatlantic steamers (Collard 2001, 12). The graving dock and massive river entrance were opened in 1913, whilst the main dock was finally completed in 1927 (Jarvis 1991a, 142; Collard 2001, 12). This had two branch docks and a large lock, which connected it with Hornby Dock. At the southern end of the dock estate, the Dingle Oil Jetty was also opened in 1922, adjacent to Herculaneum Dock, reflecting Liverpool's increasing involvement with the importation of oil (Milne 2006, 264). In 1922, Prince's Landing Stage was further extended to become the world's longest floating landing stage (Cossons and Jenkins 2011, 21), whilst the late 1920s also witnessed the closure of Manchester and Chester Basins (*p 162*). These docks were subsequently filled with spoil generated by the excavations associated with the construction of the Mersey Road Tunnel, and they had been completely eradicated by 1936.

Other modifications to the dock system made in the inter-war period included the rebuilding of Clarence Half-tide and Trafalgar Docks (Ritchie-Noakes 1984, 13). During the post-war period, Waterloo, Langton, and Canada Docks were provided with new entrance locks, Victoria Dock was remodelled, while Langton Dock was also given new berths, and a graving dock associated with Prince's Dock was converted into a branch dock (*ibid*; Collard 2001, 13-15). In addition, the improvements at Canada Dock also entailed rebuilding large portions of its basin and widening the passage linking it to Brocklebank Dock (Ritchie-Noakes 1984, 13).

Following the advent of containerisation, several key facilities were established in the late 1960s/early 1970s. These included the Royal Seaforth Dock, which opened in 1972, at a similar time to the closure of Liverpool's south docks to shipping, and the complete infilling of Victoria Dock and partial filling of Trafalgar Dock (Ritchie-Noakes 1984, 14). This large L-shaped dock now forms the hub of Liverpool's present-day port activities and is associated with a large container-stacking area. Access to this dock from the river is from Gladstone Dock via its entrance lock. In addition to the construction of the Royal Seaforth Dock, a smaller container berth was constructed at Hornby Dock to receive trade from Spain, Italy, and Portugal (*op cit*, 18), whilst Canada Dock began to receive containers from North America (Liverpool Museums nd).

The archaeology of the late nineteenth- and twentieth-century docks

During the investigations on Mann Island (*Ch 1, p 12*), along the LLC extension, and also at the sites of the Pier Head Ferry Terminal Building (*Ch 1, p 11*) and Duke's Dock (*Ch 1, p 12*), various late nineteenth- and twentieth-century structures and deposits were identified. These remains specifically relate to the use of Duke's Dock; Manchester Dock, prior to its infilling in the late 1920s, and also the adjacent area of Nova Scotia and Mann Island; the construction of the 1870s landing stage and Floating Bridge at Pier Head; and various twentieth-century modifications made to Pier Head and Prince's, Victoria, and Trafalgar Docks.

Duke's Dock (1860-1900)
Historical background

Following the major scheme of reconstruction in the mid-nineteenth century (*Ch 4, p 95*), the form of Duke's Dock remained unaltered during the latter part of the century (Fig 66). During this period, the Dock was entered from the river through a small half-tide basin, which had been constructed by Hartley (*Ch 4, p 99*) in the 1840s, and was linked to Wapping Basin, which lay immediately to its east, via a river lock that had been constructed in 1855 (*op cit*, 32). Surrounding the dock, the majority of the early and mid-nineteenth- century warehouses and other buildings were also still present, though it is evident from the cartographic evidence (*eg* OS 1850b; 1893a) that several additional warehouses and buildings had been built during the latter half of the nineteenth century (Fig 66).

Archaeological evidence

During the archaeological watching brief at Duke's Dock (*Ch 1, p 12*), a small area, measuring 5 x 2 m was examined on its southern quay. A north/south-aligned brick wall was identified, which dates to the late nineteenth century and formed an element of a small warehouse that is depicted on the 1893 OS map (1893a; Fig 66). This wall was *c* 1 m wide and was constructed in machine-made Ruabon or St Helens brick, laid in an English Garden Wall bond using a hard

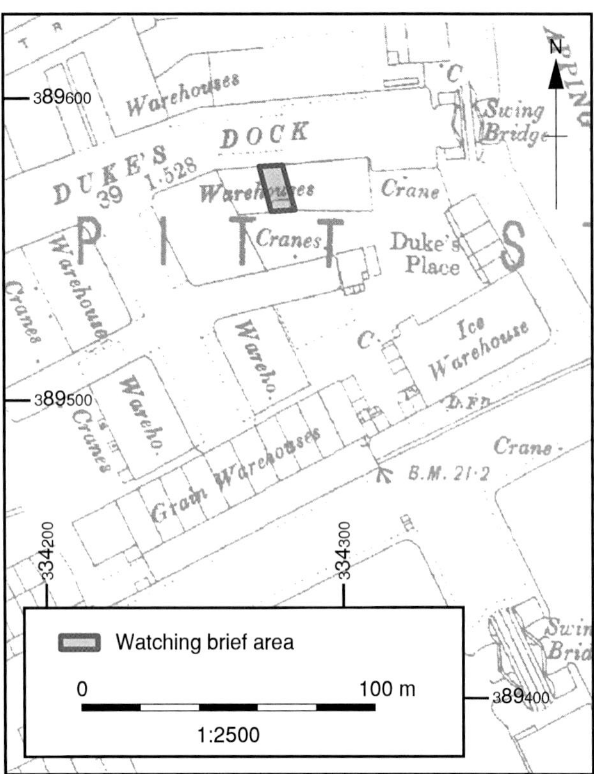

Figure 66: Extract from the 1893 25": 1 mile Ordnance Survey map (1893a), showing Duke's Dock, early/mid- and late nineteenth-century buildings, and the watching-brief area within the late nineteenth-century warehouse

Portland cement mortar. No floors were associated with this feature, which was flanked to east and west by deposits of reddish brown sand containing brick and slate fragments.

Manchester Dock (1860-1960)
Historical background

By 1872, the whole of Manchester Dock was leased to the LNWR Company, which by this date represented the Shropshire Union Railway and Canal Company (SURCC), the GWR, and Birkenhead Joint Lines (Ritchie-Noakes 1984, 36). Moreover, the dock was used as the GWR's foothold on the eastern shore of the Mersey, and this allowed the company to transfer goods into Liverpool from its facilities at Morpeth Dock in Birkenhead (Atkins and Hyde 2000, 139). During the late nineteenth century, the northern quay (Manchester Old Quay; *Ch 3, p 75*) was utilised by SURCC, which partly used it as a coal depot, whilst the southern quay formed a GWR goods depot (Ritchie-Noakes 1984, 36). Both areas contained hydraulic cranes, and documentary evidence indicates that this hydraulic machinery, on the southern quay, was powered by GWR's own hydraulic-power system up until 1919, after which date it purchased power from the Liverpool Hydraulic Power Company (LHPC), via a 3 in (76 mm) main along the length of Irwell Street (*Appendix 2*).

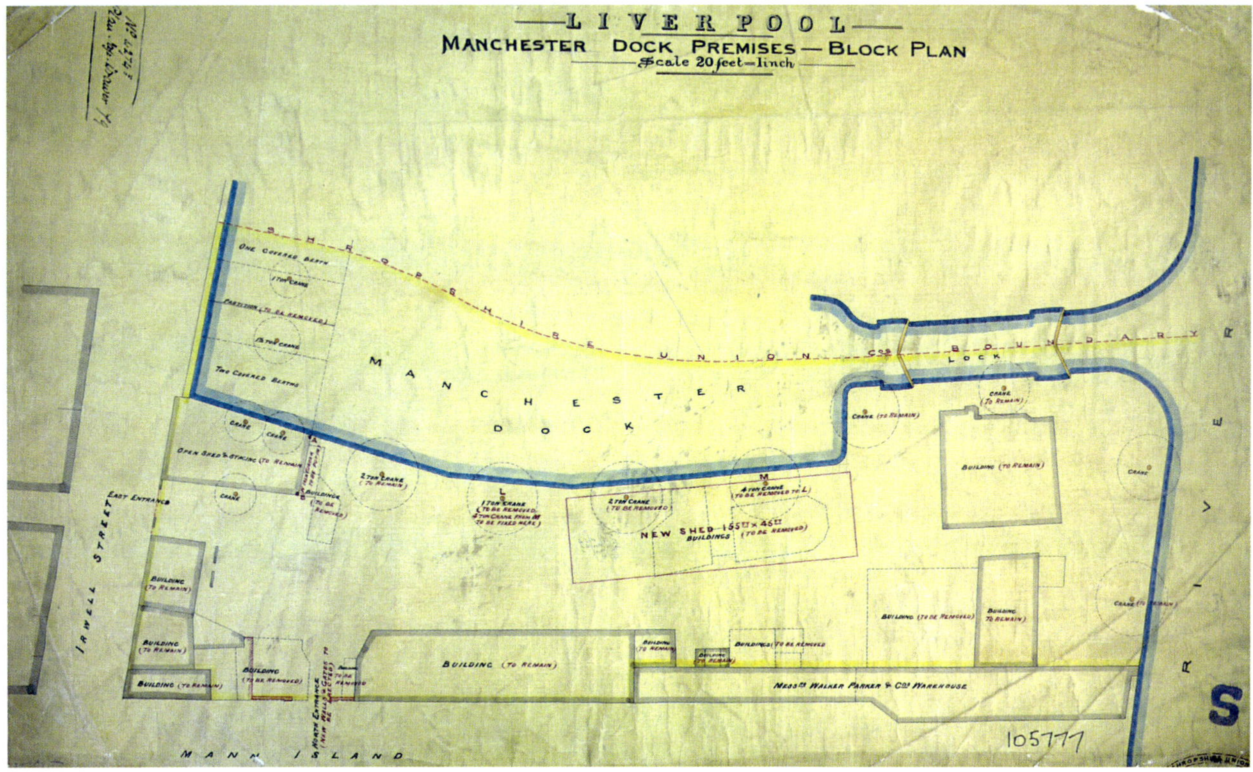

Plate 144: Block plan (MMMMAL 107/1/5; © Trustees of National Museums Liverpool) of the Manchester Dock premises, dating to 7 November 1872

Fortunately, the form of the northern quay during the late nineteenth century can be discerned through reference to several plans and drawings. The earliest of these dates to 7 November 1872 (MMMMAL 107/1/5) and is a block plan, which was produced as a prelude to the construction of a new transit shed (*see below*). This plan (Pl 144) confirms that the northern quay was utilised by SURCC and also indicates that in 1872 the mid-nineteenth-century warehouse at the eastern end of the dock (*Ch 4, p 105*) was divided between SURCC and the GWR, which utilised the southern quay. This plan also plots the position of the quay's early nineteenth-century buildings, which were still in use, and depicts a series of cranes, positioned along the northern quay and waterfront. These included a 1-ton crane, two 2-ton cranes, and a 4-ton crane, as well as seven cranes whose tonnage is not annotated, which may suggest that they were small, manually operated derricks. The plan also indicates that, in 1872, the warehouse at the eastern end of the dock contained a 1-ton and 1½-ton crane, and that the range along the northern side of the quay functioned as a warehouse, occupied by 'Walker, Parker & Co'.

Apart from extant features, the block plan also plots the position of a proposed transit shed directly adjacent to Manchester Dock's northern wall, the construction of which would lead to the demolition of an earlier quayside building and also the removal and relocation of two cranes. This building was constructed in 1873 and a surviving architectural drawing (MMMMAL 184/52/45) indicates that it was single storeyed, with brick walls and a pitched roof, supported by timber trusses, and with glass skylights (Pl 145). The drawing also depicts internal supports and indicates that the shed had a raised storage area at its western end. Furthermore, a photograph dating to *c* 1928 (Ritchie-Noakes 1984, 35, illus 23) shows that it had lucams projecting out over the dockside, though the 1873 architectural drawing suggests that these were not original features, but were added at a later date (*p 145*). Further details regarding the form of Manchester Dock's northern quay can be gleaned from a Goad's Insurance Plan (1890) dating to July 1890 (Pl 146). By this date, the lucams had been added to the 1873 transit shed and the buildings on

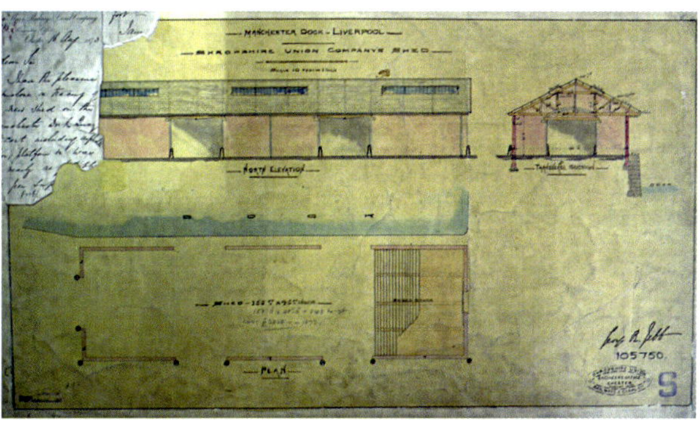

Plate 145: Architectural drawing of the Shropshire Union Railway Canal Company transit shed, constructed in 1873 on Manchester Dock's northern quay (MMMMAL 184/52/45; © Trustees of National Museums Liverpool)

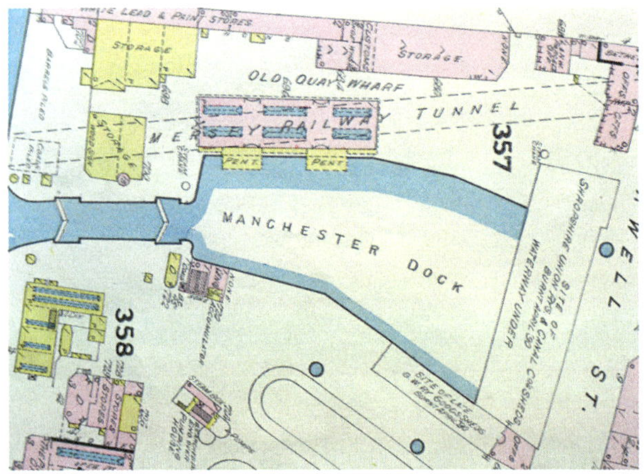

Plate 146: Extract from Goad's Insurance Plan (1890), showing Manchester Dock and its quaysides

the 'Old Quay Wharf' functioned as storage areas, one containing white lead and paint, and a shoe warehouse, alongside a customs and other offices. This plan also indicates that by 1890 three cranes were present on the northern quay, two of which are denoted as 'steam crane'. However, it is evident from the OS survey (1893a) that, in addition to these cranes, five others were also present within this area (Pl 147).

Several structures and buildings were also constructed by the GWR in *c* 1875 on Manchester Dock's southern quay. These included an engine/pump house, 5-ton and 10-ton Vulcan cranes, and a road weigh-bridge (*ibid*; Liverpool City Council 2005, 60-1; Moss and Stammers nd, 17, 20; *Appendix 2*). In terms of the positions of these features, the OS survey published in 1893 (Pl 147) and a Goad's Insurance Plan (Pl 146) both indicate that the engine/pump house stood close to the entrance lock, and that the cranes were between this building and an earlier warehouse/transit shed on the southern quay (*Ch 4, p 106*), whilst the road weigh-

Plate 147: Extract from the 1893 25": 1 mile Ordnance Survey map (1893a), showing Manchester Dock and its quaysides

bridge was at the far southern end of Irwell Street. The Goad's Insurance plan (1890) indicates that the engine was at the eastern end of the engine house and that it was associated with an accumulator, which drove hydraulic machinery (*Appendix 2*). Furthermore, this plan demonstrates that two boilers were employed to power the engine and these lay in the western portion of the engine house. Documentary sources allow further insight into this engine house, and indicate that the boilers were placed at ground level, with the machinery floor elevated to create space below for the heavy pipe work (*Appendix 2*). Immediately to the west of the engine house, an associated building was present, which had a rectangular form, with a curving southern end.

In 1890, a major fire resulted in the destruction of several of the buildings at Manchester Dock (*cf* North Western Society for Industrial Archaeology and History (NWSIAH) 1982-4, 3; Ritchie-Noakes 1984, 36). These fire-damaged buildings are annotated on the Goad's Insurance plan (Pl 146) and included the mid-nineteenth-century warehouse/transit shed on the dock's southern quay. However, following this destruction, a new GWR warehouse was built, directly on the foundations of the earlier building (Moss and Stammers nd, 17). Significantly, this warehouse is still extant, and in 1990 it was, along with the adjoining mid-nineteenth-century railway office building (*Ch 4, p 106*), rehabilitated as museum accommodation (Rees 1991, 7; Pl 85). The 1890 fire also appears to have partly damaged the adjacent warehouse of 1841, on the dock's eastern quay (*Ch 4, p 106*), which required partial rebuilding (Moss and Stammers nd, 17). This rebuilt warehouse was extant in 1980 and was a two-storeyed building, with brick-built external walls and a twin-gabled, slated roof (*ibid*).

As a result of competition, first from the Manchester Ship Canal, which opened in 1894, and later from road hauliers, which contributed to a decline in the use of the inland carriers, Manchester Dock became largely redundant. By the mid-1920s, the SURCC had given up its cross-river lighterage business and the GWR was considering discontinuing the use of Manchester Dock for barging. Furthermore, it is possible that the site was settling dangerously as a result of the MRC tunnel excavations, which had occurred beneath the dock (Ritchie-Noakes 1984, 36). Once the decision had been taken to close it, it became necessary to backfill. Conveniently, during the late 1920s, work began on the construction of the Queensway Tunnel, the first Mersey road tunnel, and accordingly 'between 1928 and 1936 Manchester Dock and Chester Basin were filled with 60,000 tons of spoil from the tunnel works' (*ibid*). The MDHB then paved the site of the former dock with granite setts (NWSIAH 1982-4, 2). However, although infilled, map evidence suggests that the form of the dock was apparent for many years, revealed by the extant buildings around its quayside, and the GWR continued to operate a goods service from its own warehouses on the site during the 1930s (Atkins and Hyde 2000). Following the collapse of the GWR, its successors, the British Transport Commission, became the titleholders of the land around the former Manchester Dock and were in possession of the land until January 1962 (MMMMAL MDHB/2211/M38, 1962).

Archaeological evidence
Excavation at the Countryside Neptune site (*Ch 1, p 13*), at the Museum of Liverpool site (*Ch 1, p 15*), and also within the footprint of the LLC extension (*Ch 1, p 14*) uncovered several features and structures

dating to the latter part of the nineteenth-century. These related to the functioning of Manchester Dock's late nineteenth-century quayside, and included the remains of cranes, the engine house established in 1875, hydraulic-powered features, and also evidence for late nineteenth-century warehousing (Fig 67). In addition, during the various campaigns of excavation, the deposits used to backfill Manchester Dock in the late 1920s were exposed and recorded.

On Manchester Dock's northern quay, remains within the SURCC Depot (*p 160*) were identified. These included the bases of three late nineteenth-century cranes, two of which were uncovered close to the dock's north-eastern corner, within the Countryside Neptune site, which can be linked to those plotted

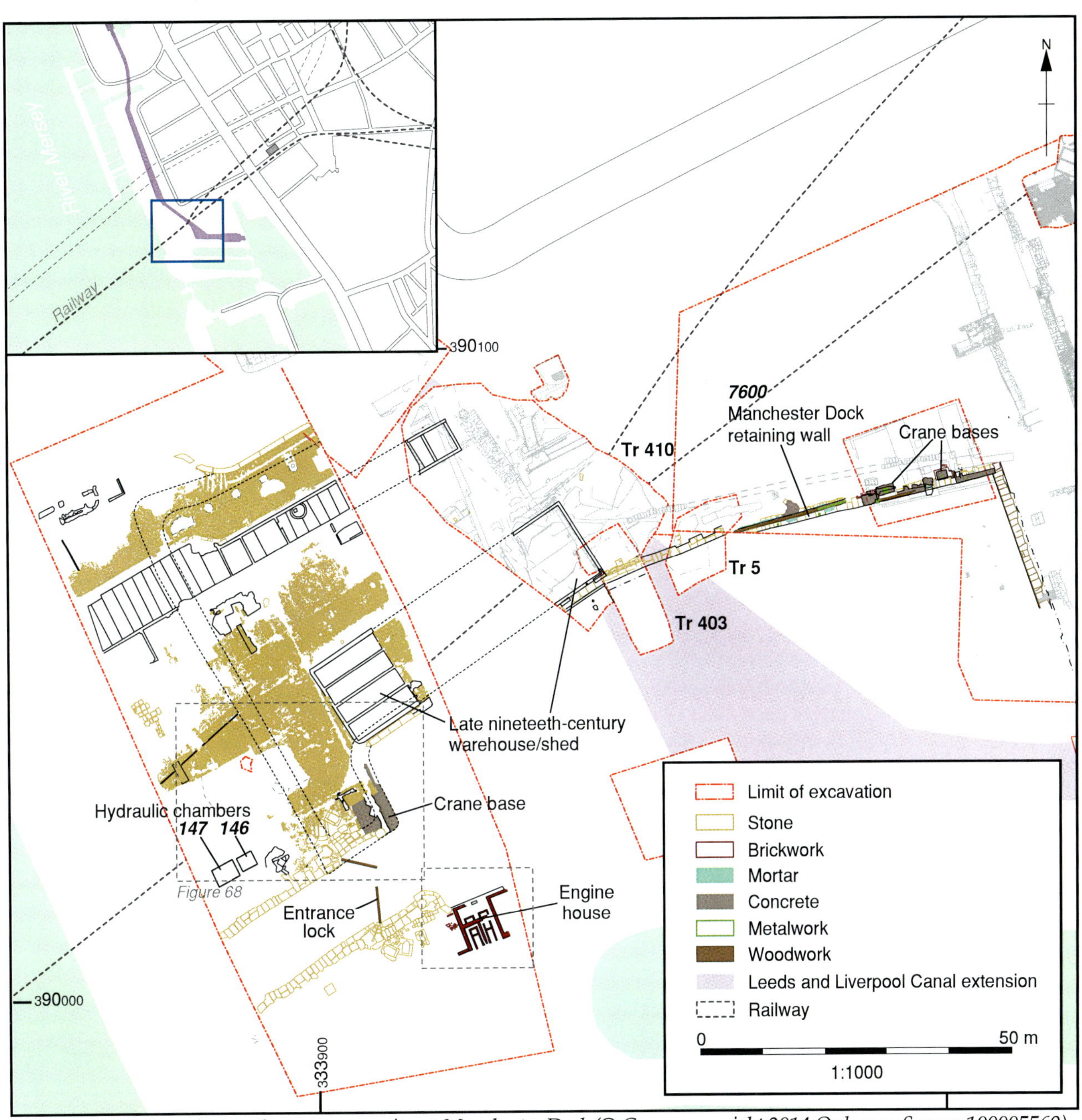

Figure 67: The late nineteenth-century remains at Manchester Dock (© Crown copyright 2014 Ordnance Survey 100005569)

Plate 148: One of the late nineteenth-century crane bases, close to the north-eastern corner of Manchester Dock

on the 1872 block plan (MMMMAL 107/1/5; Pl 144). Furthermore, they were placed within an open shed that formed the northern end of the 1841 warehouse overhanging the eastern end of Manchester Dock (*Ch 4, p 105*). Their remains were comparable in that they both consisted of a 1 m-square metal setting, housed in a brick-lined recess, with a concrete base, measuring *c* 2.5 x 1.5 m (Pl 148). The absence of hydraulic fittings, and their positioning within the shed, may suggest that both were small, manually operated derricks. The remains of the third late nineteenth-century crane base lay at the north-eastern end of the lock (Fig 68), and these were exposed at the Museum of Liverpool site. This base formed elements of an hydraulic crane

depicted on a blueprint dated 10 February 1891 (MMMMAL, no ref) and also visible on a photograph taken in *c* 1910-20 (Ritchie-Noakes 1984, 35, illus 23). The date of this blueprint indicates that this crane replaced an earlier 'steam crane' which is depicted on the 1890 Goad's Insurance Plan (1890; Pl 146). The surviving remains of the crane included its base, which consisted of a *c* 2.8 x 5 m rectangular area of concrete (*24/25*; Fig 68), with a 1.3 m-square, central brick setting (*192*), approximately 0.5 m deep (Pl 149). Below the concrete base, hydraulic fittings and pipes were also present, within brick retaining walls.

On the northern quayside, just north of the northern dock wall, the remains of two subterranean chambers (*146* and *147*; Fig 67) were also exposed during excavation at the Museum of Liverpool site, which were probably associated with an hydraulic-pump mechanism (Pl 150; *Appendix 2*). Chamber *146* was the smaller of the two, measuring 2.65 x 2.30 m, constructed in brick, and its walls and floor were lined with plaster. An iron pipe was also visible at the base of its western wall, whilst a ceramic circular pipe lay flush against the top of the same wall. In contrast, chamber *147* measured 3.75 x 2.80 m, and was constructed from sandstone blocks, with only the walls lined with plaster. Its floor was composed of large sandstone blocks, carved with the masonry mark 'M' or 'W'. Iron pipes were observed at the base and top of its western wall, and these perhaps linked with the adjacent chamber. Both chambers

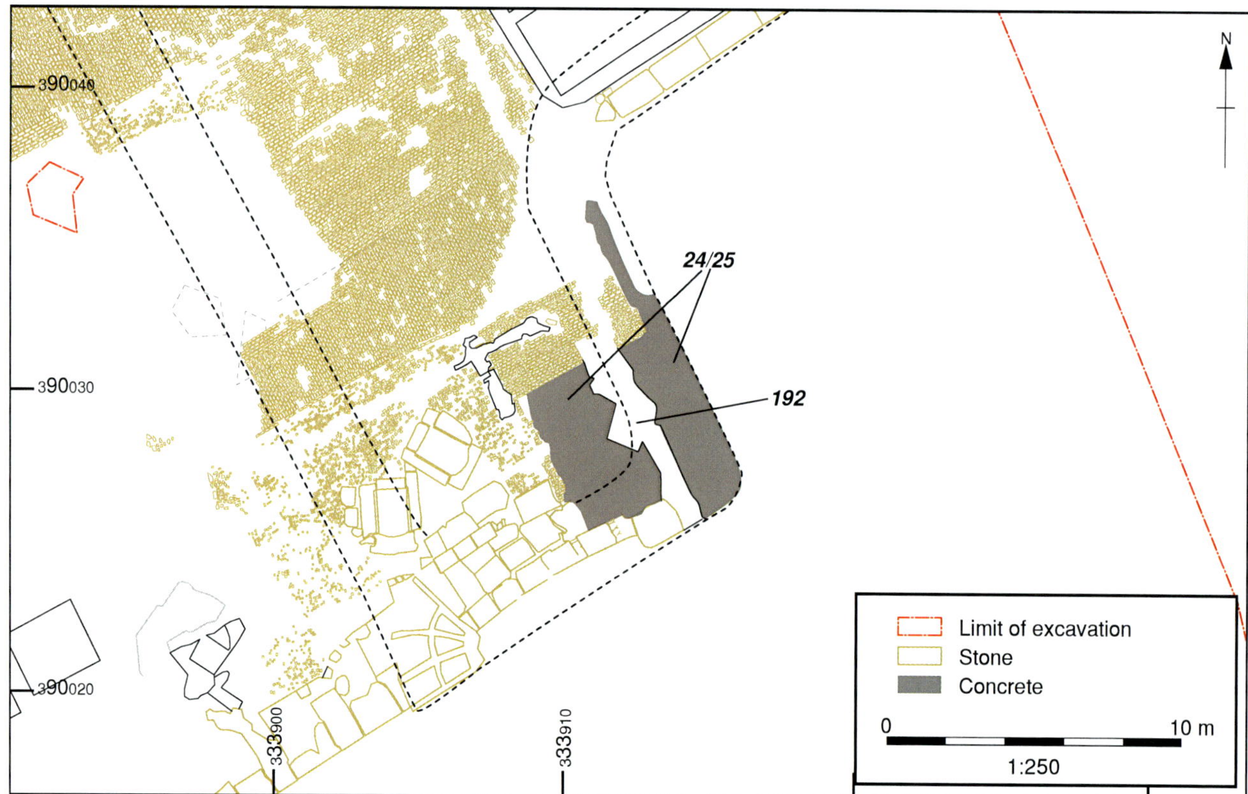

Figure 68: The late nineteenth-century crane base, positioned at the north-eastern end of Manchester Dock's lock

Plate 149: Aerial view of the late nineteenth-century crane base at the north-eastern end of the river lock

Plate 150: The hydraulic chambers at Manchester Dock

had a similar depth of *c* 1.75 m and they had been backfilled with rubble containing large quantities of nineteenth- and early twentieth-century glass-bottle and stoneware-vessel fragments. The backfill from one of the chambers also produced a *c* 0.5 m-long section of hydraulic pipe.

The other remains present on Manchester's Dock northern quay included a series of footings, which were exposed during the excavations at the Museum of Liverpool site and within Tr 403 and Tr 410, excavated within the footprint of the LLC extension (Fig 67). These remains were composed of concrete

Plate 151: Aerial view of the brick footings defining the western end of the 1873 transit shed

and brick, bonded with a cement mortar, and formed the gable and side walls of the 1873 SURCC transit shed (*p 161*). In addition, within this shed, at its western end, three parallel brick walls were also present (Pl 151), which would have supported a raised storage area, which is known to have been present in this part of the transit shed (Pl 145).

As well as the northern quay, part of Manchester Dock's southern quay was also examined during the excavations at the Museum of Liverpool site. There, the excavation uncovered the remains of the boiler room (Fig 69), lying within the engine house constructed in 1875 (*p 162*). The remains comprised brick-built walls defining the north-western corner (**20**) of the engine house, which was partly built over the north-facing dock wall, and also another wall (**187**), which defined the eastern side of the boiler room. Within this room, five blocks of brickwork relating to the boiler settings were exposed. Two of these blocks represented the housings for two separate boilers, whilst the other three appear to have aided in the support of the boilers' external casings (Pl 152). Each of the boilers was also associated with a rectangular brick structure, which lay on their northern sides. In addition, a cast-iron pipe extended from the rectangular brick structure, associated with the more westerly of the boiler settings, to the edge of the dock wall. This pipe was seated on a bed of crushed red brick (**179**) and was overlain by two courses of laid bricks, and beneath the crushed red brick was a solid concrete block surface (**206**), measuring 5.13 x 2.46 m. Another metal fitting recovered from this area, during the

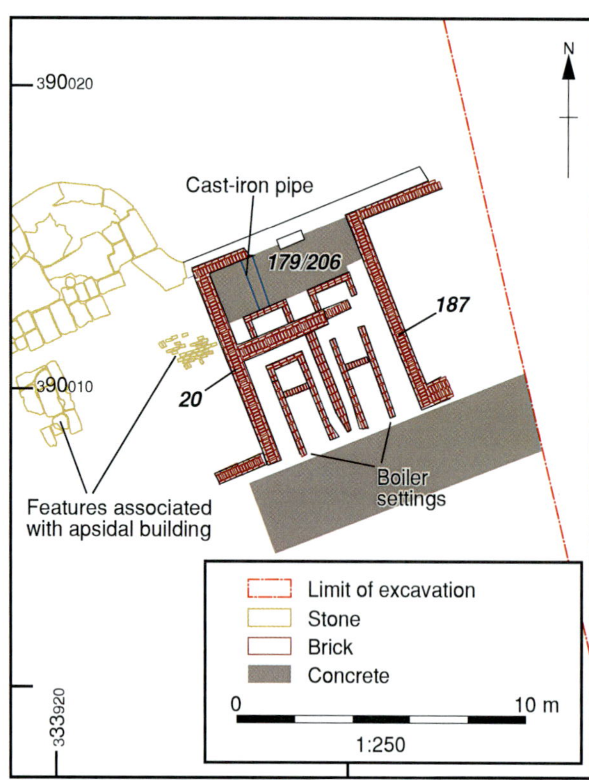

Figure 69: Remains associated with the late nineteenth-century engine/pump house on Manchester Dock's southern quay

An incoherent arrangement of sandstone and brick walls was identified to the east of these boilers. These latter remains were probably associated with the apsidal building plotted on the Goad's Insurance plan (1890; Pl 146) and 1893 OS survey (1893a; Pl 147). Significantly, these remains included a concrete-lined, single-coursed, brick wall, which possibly housed an hydraulic feed, drainage system, or perhaps formed a filterbed for the feedwater (A Jarvis *pers comm*), implying that this building was associated with providing hydraulic power. In addition, a semicircular metal plate was discovered in this area, which lay well below ground level. This may have been associated with an hydraulic ejector used to lift water to the header tank, or was used to clear seepage (A Jarvis *pers comm*).

The watching brief undertaken at the Museum of Liverpool site also recorded a large concrete slab, approximately 5 m in length, on the front of the engine house. This had a width of 2.5 m and a depth of 0.25 m, and appears to represent the foundation for the front of the building. At the extreme eastern end of the building, a large concrete block was also exposed, *c* 2 m wide and *c* 3 m deep, which was overlain by a large sandstone slab. Together these appear to have been a later addition and were perhaps inserted as a solution to subsidence.

watching brief, was a large sheet of metal, lining part of the floor, which presumably related to the boiler seatings.

During the excavations on Mann Island, the material infilling Manchester Dock was exposed. This waste from the excavation of the first Mersey road tunnel

Plate 152: The boiler settings within the 1875 engine house

166

(*p 159*) was largely composed of crushed brownish-red sandstone, containing no artefacts of any kind.

Mann Island and Nova Scotia (1860-1950)
Historical background
The cartographic evidence indicates that only comparatively minor modifications were made during the late nineteenth century to the late eighteenth- and early nineteenth-century buildings (*Ch 4, p 142*) between Irwell Place and Nova Scotia. As evidenced by the late nineteenth-century OS mapping (*eg* 1893a), this appears, on the whole, to have involved the subdivision of some of these properties into smaller units.

With regard to the character of this area, the late nineteenth- and early twentieth-century trade directories indicate that it continued to thrive and was probably also still viewed as forming part of 'Sailor-town' (*Ch 3, p 48*), in that it contained a multitude of public houses. For instance, the area of Mann Island, specifically the northern limit of Nova Scotia with the principal elevations facing George's Dock, was entirely populated by victuallers running public houses. Gore's *Directory of Liverpool and environs* for 1900 indicates that No 1 Mann Island functioned as a public house (although no name is given) run by John Henry Quayle, a victualler. Similarly, No 2 Mann Island is listed as The Old House Public House, run by Francis Gore, and No 3 Mann Island is listed as The Odd Fellow's Arms (no victualler's name is provided). This dense group of public houses is further complemented by the presence of The Old Life Boat Public House at No 1 Nova Scotia, the Packet House at No 1 Irwell Street, and Dicky Sam's Inn at No 8 Nova Scotia (Gore 1900). Aside from public houses, the streets also continued to house small businesses serving the shipping industry, which had been long established. For instance, in 1900, Nos 5 and 7 Irwell Street and No 2 Murray Place housed salt merchants, and had done so since the 1850s (Gore 1850; 1900). The 1891 and 1900 directories also indicate that No 2 Nova Scotia was in use as a saddlers, and No 2A was the premises of a block and mast maker (Gore 1891), whilst a smithy was housed at No 10 Nova Scotia (Gore 1900). The dock gateman lived at No 9 Nova Scotia, directly opposite the gate and bridge over George's Dock Passage (*ibid*).

However, although Mann Island and Nova Scotia formed an important, albeit minor, component of the late nineteenth-century waterfront, the area was now anomalous, partly because of its small-scale domestic architecture and also because it was the only place within the boundary of the dock estate where licenced premises were still allowed to operate. It also appears that during the late nineteenth century the area's dilapidated and run-down character was troubling to some, and from 1891 onwards, a series of letters and correspondence was lodged with the MDHB, indicating that the buildings of Nova Scotia and Mann Island were in a particularly poor state of repair (MMMMAL MDHB/2901/L88). Moreover, in 1903, a group of Justices of the Peace visited the area to assess the state of the buildings there, and the Clerk of City Justices recorded that,

> ...a committee of Justices have visited the public houses [at] Nova Scotia and in view of their dilapidated and insanitary condition and unsuitability for their present purpose, it will be necessary...to consider whether all or any licences should be renewed (*ibid*).

In contrast, in the area to the east of George's Dock Passage, a more radical scheme of building occurred during the late nineteenth century. This was intimately linked to the construction of the MRC tunnel, between 1881 and 1886 (*p 158*). The trains operating on this line were Beyer and Peacock-built steam engines, and this meant that substantial investment was necessary to provide effective ventilation, in addition to the inevitable necessity of removing water from the tunnel (Maund 2002). Two pumping and ventilation stations were therefore set up, at either end of the tunnel, one at Mann Island in Liverpool, and the other on Shore Road in Birkenhead (MPTE 1986, 15). The pumping and ventilation station at Mann Island stood immediately east of George's Dock Passage and south-west of the Dock Police and Marine Surveyor's Offices (*Ch 4, p 143*), which by the 1890s functioned as the Harbour Master's Office, and also contained the Graving Dock Office, Marine Surveyor's, and Public Enquiry Office (Pl 153). The construction of this ventilation also necessitated the demolition of the early nineteenth-century police station, weighing machine, and Foreman's Sweeper's Office, located in this area (*Ch 4, pp 143-4*).

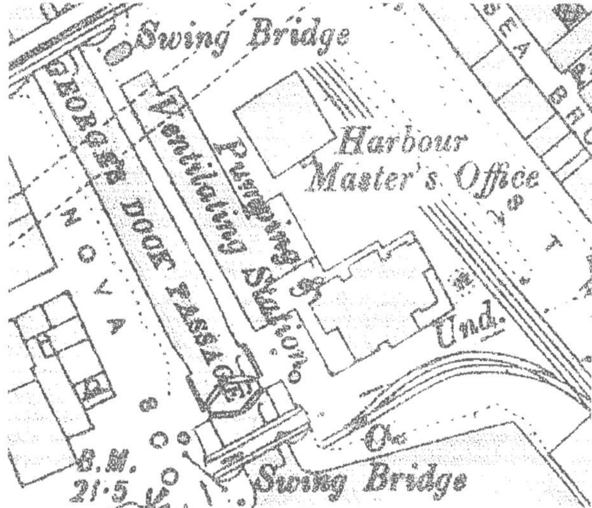

Plate 153: Extract from the 1893 25": 1 mile Ordnance Survey map (1893a), showing the Pumping and Ventilation Station at Mann Island

In terms of the operation of the Mann Island ventilation station, late nineteenth-century documentary evidence indicates that it contained steam-driven pumps that were used to clear water from the railway tunnel's drainage heading. More specifically, these comprised,

> a pair of pumps, 20 inches [0.51 m] in diameter by 6 feet [1.83 m] length of stroke, connected by means of quadrants with a compound-engine manufactured by Messers. Hathorn, Davey and Co., of Leeds…also a pair of pumps 30 inches [0.76 m]…having cylinders 60 inches [1.52 m] and 33 inches [0.84 m] in diameter respectively, and a length of stroke of 10 feet [3.05 m]; and lastly, of one pump 40 inches [1 m] in diameter and 15 feet [4.57 m] length of stroke, driven directly by an overhanging beam-engine, manufactured by Messers. Andrew Barclay and Son, of Kilmarnock (Fox 1886, 42).

The station also contained two Guibal-type fans. These types of fans, with their close-fitting casing, were usually employed to ventilate coalmines (*cf* Percy 1905, 282-3) and, in the case of Liverpool's underground railway, they created a vacuum in the ventilation heading, which allowed fresh air to be drawn through the railway tunnel. The fans at Mann Island had respective diameters of 40 ft (12.2 m) and 30 ft (9.1 m), and were produced by Black Hawthorn & Co, a steam-locomotive manufacturer based in Gateshead (Maund 2002, 6, 15; Jones 2006, 132). It is known that the 30 ft fan ventilated a section of the tunnel lying between James Street Station and the tunnel terminus, and exhausted 120,000 cubic feet of air per minute, whilst the 40 ft fan ventilated the tunnel between James Street Station and the centre of the River Mersey, and exhausted 130,000 cubic feet of air per minute (Fox 1886, 56). These fans were driven by horizontal engines, 'each fan having a compound tandem condensing engine with a horizontal condenser and also a simple high-pressure stand-by engine, coupled direct to the fan shaft' (*op cit*, 55).

The late nineteenth-century cartographic sources and surviving architectural drawings (MMMMAL 689, 691, and 694) indicate that this machinery was housed in two brick-built buildings, which were designed by the architects Grayson and Ould in the Venetian style (Sharples 2004, 112; Moss and Stammers nd, 23). One of these was a pumping station, adjacent to Mann Island, which housed the steam-driven pumps and also covered the pumping shaft. Fortunately, the arrangement of the pumps and position of the shaft can be discerned from a surviving architectural ground plan, which shows the positions of the engine pillars for the 20 inch (0.51 m), 30 inch (0.76 m), and 40 inch (1 m) pumps in relation to the pumping shaft (Pl 154). This ground plan also indicates that the south-eastern end of this building was a boiler house, containing the boilers which presumably powered the pumping engines, and also the engines for the ventilation fans. Moreover, a Goad's Insurance Plan (1888; Pl 155), dating to October 1888, indicates that six boilers were in this area, arranged side by side.

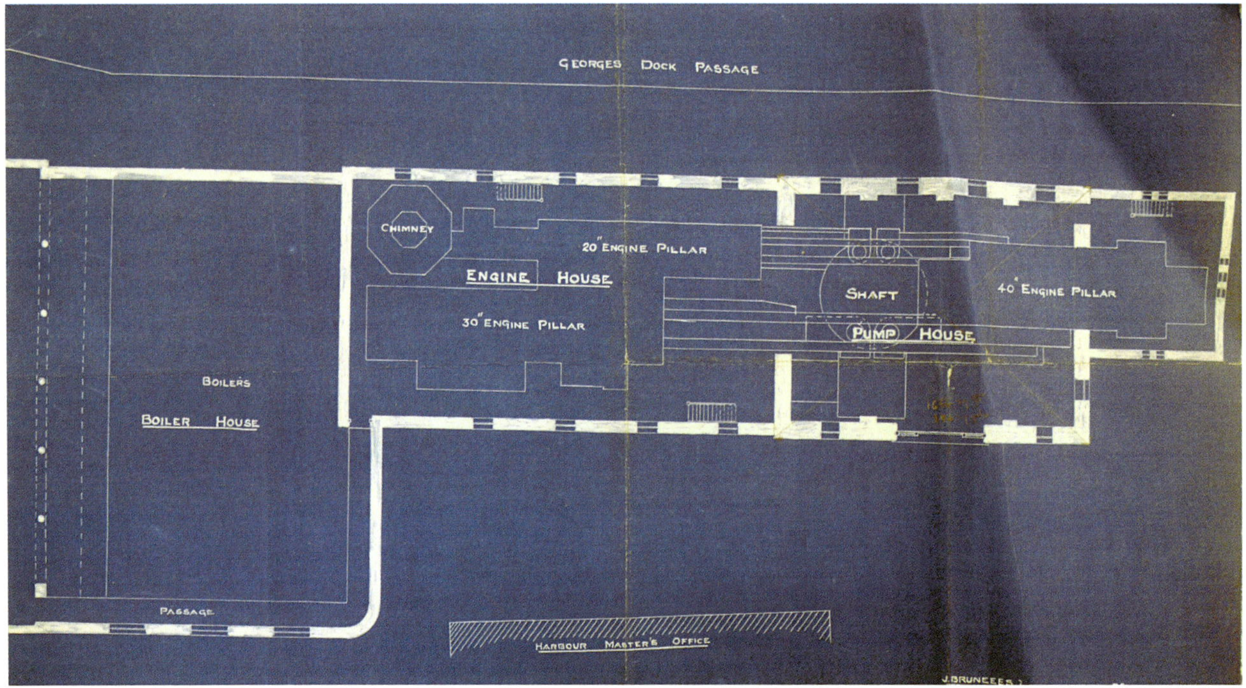

Plate 154: Architectural ground plan of the George's Dock Pumping Station (MMMMAL 691; © Trustees of National Museums Liverpool)

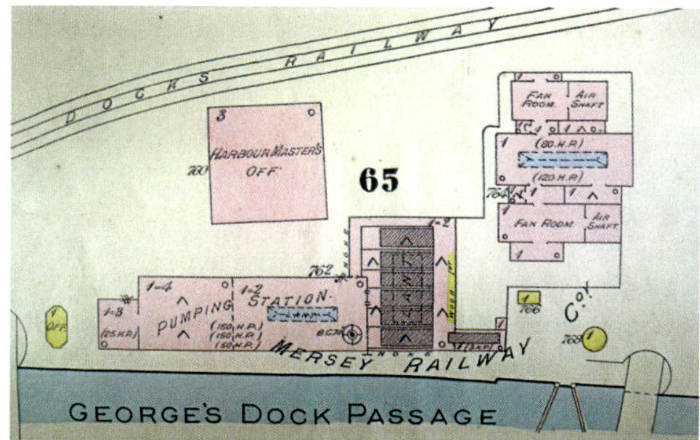

Plate 155: Extract from an 1888 Goad's Insurance Plan, showing the George's Dock Pumping and Ventilation Station

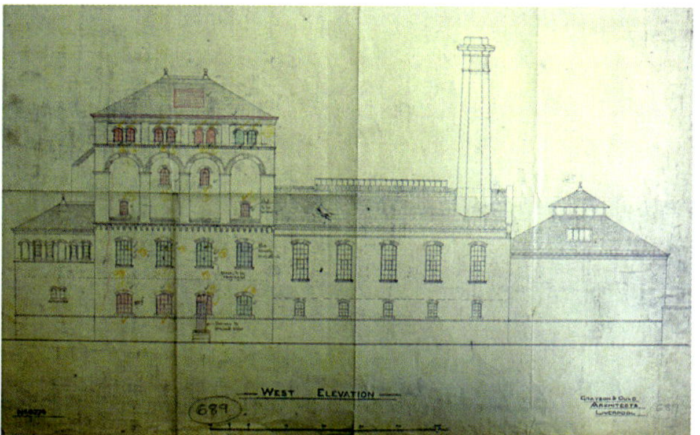

Plate 156: Architectural drawing of the western elevation of the George's Dock Pumping Station (MMMMAL 689; © Trustees of National Museums Liverpool)

This plan also indicates that a 25 horsepower (hp) engine was positioned at the far north-western end of the pumping station, whilst a 3 hp engine lay at its south-eastern end, associated with an additional boiler. The surviving architectural elevations provide further details of the appearance and form of this building, indicating that the area housing the engines was both two- and four-storeyed, and was also provided with an octagonal chimney, whilst the boiler house was single-storeyed (Pl 156). Of these elements, the four-storeyed element of the pumping station is still extant (Pl 157) and is a Grade II Listed Building (Liverpool City Council 2005, 61).

The second building associated with the pumping station housed the ventilation gear and covered, in turn, numerous subterranean chambers housing deep shafts, which descended into the rockhead and opened at a level just above the 1:27 gradient of the tunnel's main line (Maund 2002, 6 and 15; Jones 2006, 132). Significantly, the Goad's Insurance Plan (1888; Pl 155) indicates that this was a single-storey building and it also plots the position of the two fans and their associated airshafts. These shafts, in common with those employed at collieries, formed chimneys with an expanded form, becoming wider at the top, and would

have emitted exhaust gasses derived from the tunnel (Fox 1886, pl 4; Percy 1905, 282, fig 148). The Goad's plan also indicates that, sandwiched between the fans, were two horizontal engines (80 hp and 120 hp) that provided the required motive power.

Despite the inclusion of fans and an intricate ventilation system, the Beyer and Peacock-built steam engines produced far more smoke and soot than the ventilation system could clear. Due to this, and despite the novelty, people returned to using the long-established ferry, especially during the summer months, and the MRC was soon making serious losses that affected the financial viability of the scheme. By 1888, the MRC was declared bankrupt (MPTE 1986, 3), and in 1898, the receivers stated that, 'if the tunnel could be freed from smoke and noxious fumes, the main obstacle to the development of traffic would be removed' (*op cit*, 4). This was eventually achieved in 1903, with the introduction of electrically powered trains on the Mersey Railway, which was possible due to the financial backing of the American industrialist, George Westinghouse (*op cit*, 5).

OS mapping (*eg* 1927) indicates that further changes were made, and schemes of redevelopment initiated, across Nova Scotia and Mann Island during the early- and mid-twentieth century. In the area to west of George's Dock Passage, which itself had been partly

Plate 157: The extant remains of George's Dock Pumping Station

infilled following the closure of George's Dock in 1900 (*p 158*), the late eighteenth- and early nineteenth-century buildings, between Irwell Street and Nova Scotia were finally demolished in 1920. This scheme of clearance was undoubtedly undertaken as a result of the buildings being run-down and anomalous in character, and in a poor state of repair (*p 167*). Initially, in the southern part of this now-vacant plot, a transit shed was constructed, which is plotted on the 1927 25":1 mile OS map and was extant immediately prior to the excavation at the Countryside Neptune site (*Ch 1, p 13*). This was then followed in the 1930s by the construction, at the northern end of the area, of an Art Deco building, which functioned as the Voss Garage. As with the transit shed, this building was also extant immediately prior to the excavation at the Countryside Neptune site.

Changes were also made to the area to the west of George's Dock during the first half of the twentieth century. These were triggered by a 1909 agreement between the MDHB and MRC, which resulted in the

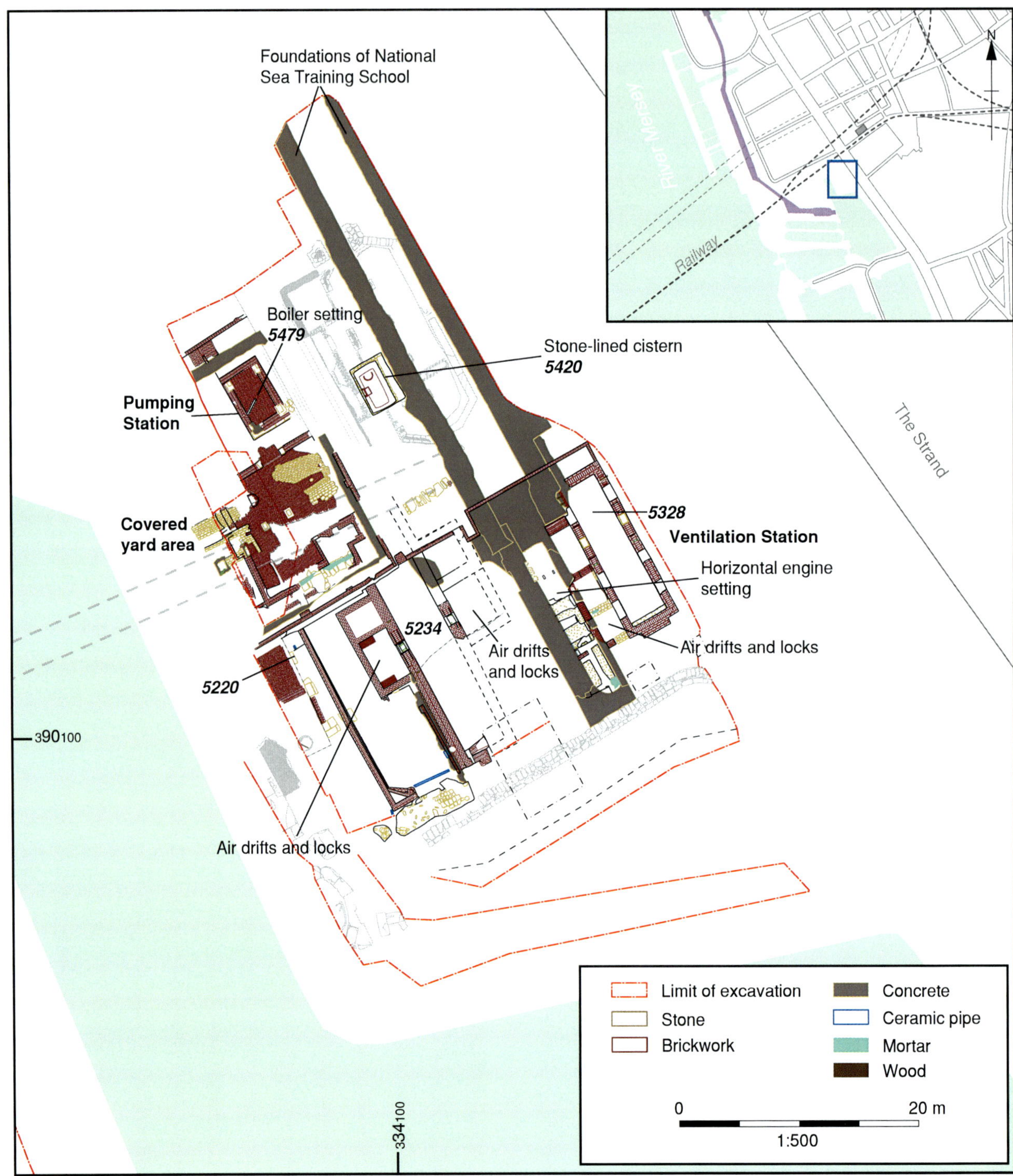

Figure 70: Remains of the Pumping and Ventilation Station (© Crown copyright 2014 Ordnance Survey 100005569)

filling in of some of the vertical shafts associated with the Mann Island ventilation station, following the installation of the electrified line (MMMMAL MDHB/ M51, 2). After this, the MRC also relinquished its lease on this area of land. Accordingly, the cartographic evidence indicates that by the late 1920s the building (*p 169*) containing the ventilation gear had been demolished and replaced by three large buildings. This was followed by the demolition of the linear building attached to the pumping station, which was replaced by a garage. Aside from the pumping station (*p 168*), all of the buildings in this area were demolished in about 1950, and the majority of the site was subsequently occupied by Media House. This building initially functioned as a National Sea Training School and was later used as the offices of a media and printers (Moss and Stammers nd, 23).

Archaeological evidence
Excavation at the Countryside Neptune site (*Ch 1, p 13*) uncovered various fragmentary remains associated with the late nineteenth-century pumping and ventilation station to the east of George's Dock Passage. Principal amongst these were two substantial pits (*5234* and *5328*; Fig 70), housing the two ventilation fans, which were contained within the building with a crenellated plan that is depicted on OS mapping (1893a; Pl 153) and the Goad's Insurance plan (1888; Pl 155). Both pits were lined with brick and were mostly intact, and both contained the mounts for the horizontal axle bearings for the fans. Both bases of the pits were also finished in concrete, and were concave and semicircular, to provide a close fit with the fans themselves (Pl 158).

Plate 159: The remains of the Pumping and Ventilation Station, from the south

Plate 158: Fan housing **5328**

However, although comparable in construction, the size of the pits differed slightly, indicating that the more easterly (*5328*) was designed to house the fan with a diameter of 30 ft (9.1 m), whilst the western pit (*5234*) housed the 40 ft-diameter (12.2 m) fan (*p 168*).

Brick and stone-built shafts were also associated with the fan housings, which formed the air drifts, and probably also an air lock, required to draw air from the railway tunnel (Pl 159). One set of shafts was uncovered on the western side of the smaller of the fans (*5328*), defined by a *c* 10.5 x 2.7 m rectangular setting, which had been divided into two square compartments and one rectangular compartment by transverse brick and stone walling. The larger fan housing (*5234*) was associated with two sets of rectangular shafts. These were identical in form and were found on either side of the housing, at its northern end. They both measured *c* 8 x 3 m and each was subdivided into two compartments by a transverse brick wall.

In between the two shafts was a concrete setting, which contained a *c* 2 m-wide channel, parallel with the fan housings. The setting was also associated with a series of holes, that probably originally secured iron bolts, or restraining rods. Given its form, and the presence of possible restraining rods, it is likely that this setting secured the 80 hp horizontal engine, which drove the eastern fan (*p 169*). The partial remains of a brick-floored room (**5220**) were also present immediately to the west of the fan housings.

Immediately to the north-west of these housings, several contemporary features were also exposed. These included brick walls defining a *c* 13.5 x 14.5 m area situated between the separate buildings housing the pumping and ventilation gear. Late nineteenth-century mapping (OS 1893a; Pl 153) indicates that this area probably formed a yard, and the archaeological remains suggest that it had a protruding recess on its western wall and also a brick floor, into which were set three sandstone pads. These latter features were probably used as the bases for supporting uprights, suggesting that the yard area may have been covered. Immediately to the north-west of this yard, the rear wall of the pumping house's boiler room was also uncovered, which could be entered through a *c* 2 m-wide doorway. A flat, rectangular brick-built structure (**5479**) was found inside this room. This structure measured *c* 6 x 3.6 m, had metal fixing plates at its corners, and marks the position of one of the boilers.

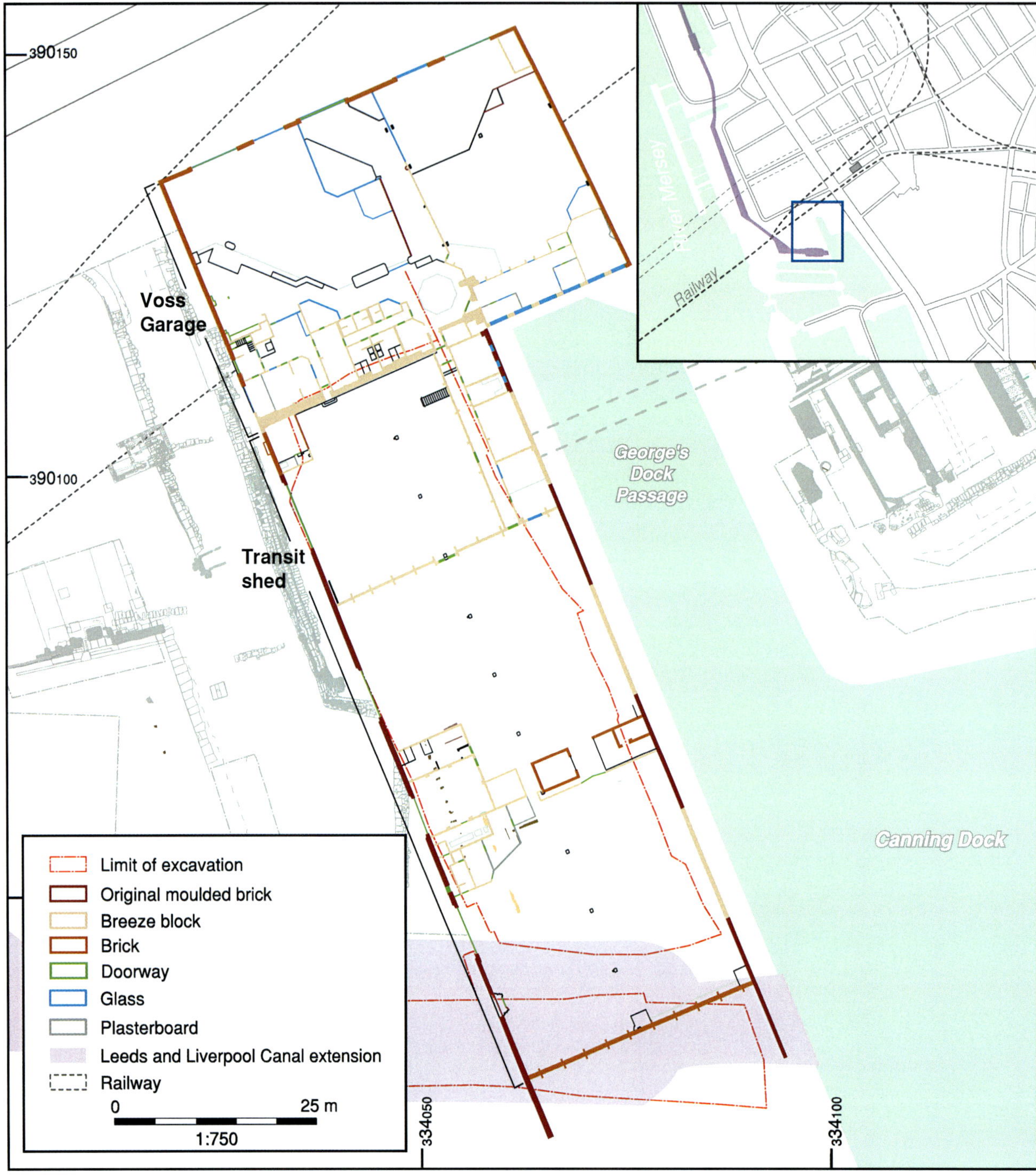

Figure 71: Ground plan of the Voss Garage and the transit shed (© Crown copyright 2014 Ordnance Survey 100005569)

Other features associated with the pumping and ventilation station included a stone-lined cistern (**5420**), encased in clay, which lay to the north of the fan housings and also truncated the earlier Foreman Sweeper's Office (*Ch 4, p 144*). The remaining features within this area were comparatively recent in date and included the concrete foundations for the National Sea Training School, which was constructed around 1950 (*p 171*).

Aside from the excavation at the Countryside Neptune site, the 1920s transit shed and 1930s Art Deco garage to the west of George's Dock Passage were both subjected to survey, prior to demolition (Fig 71). This indicates that originally, prior to later subdivision, the transit shed was a long, single-storey rectangular structure (*c* 110 x 30 m; Pl 160), with a twin-gabled roof, and had extensive steel trusses and

Plate 160: Transit sheds fronting onto Irwell Street in 2007

bracing. Skylights had been set into the corrugated roof as the primary source of light. The building was arranged approximately north-west/south-east and followed the line of the western limit of Canning Dock. The external walls of the transit shed were constructed of red brick, in an English Garden Wall-style bonding, while the south-east wall was dominated by five concertina-type folding doors, which were evidently replacements for large sliding doors that had fitted into tracks, still extant along the base of the wall. With the exception of some minor repairs and the addition of vents and utility access, this wall had not been subject to much alteration. Excavation, following the survey, indicated that the shed had originally had a brick floor.

The Voss Garage was a two-storey building that measured approximately 50 x 45 m (Fig 71; Pl 161), which abutted the northern end of the transit shed. It was aligned south-west/north-east (along its long axis). The rear and eastern elevations looked over Canning Dock, whilst the front faced onto the former offices of the MDHB, and to the west were the remnants of Irwell Street and the infilled Manchester Dock. The external walls of Voss Garage were constructed of red brick, in an English Garden Wall-style bonding, using modern rectangular brick.

The ground floor of the west wall of the Voss Garage contained two doors and three windows, the northernmost of which was a four-light floor-to-ceiling window. Five further windows were incorporated into the first floor of the same elevation. A parapet ran the length of this elevation to the straight joint with the

Plate 161: The principal elevation of the Voss Garage in 2007, overlooking Mann Island

transit shed. The eastern elevation of the Voss Motors building had no features beyond a modern fire door at the northernmost point.

The north façade of the Voss Garage had finer bricks and a better bond, by comparison with the coarser brick of the south-east wall. It also exhibited several Art Deco features, and these characterised the building above all else, particularly since the design was clearly sympathetic to the Art Deco ventilation tower for the Mersey Tunnels, immediately to the north. The northern elevation was five-bays wide, with bays two and four protruding by a single course of brick at the first-floor level (Pl 161). A round window, or possible clock housing, had been blocked at the first-floor level of this elevation. The ground floor of the north wall had floor-to-ceiling segmented rectangular windows in bays two and four, whilst sliding glass doors were fitted into bays one, three, and five, designed to allow vehicle access into the garage/showrooms. A large arched window dominated each of bays two and four, and each was decorated with pronounced mullions and an exaggerated keystone. A parapet, with architrave and cornice, ran the length of the north-west wall and was higher over bays two and four, where it was designed in a classical style, with architrave and ionic volutes.

The internal floor plan of the Voss Motors building had been extensively altered since its construction and it is likely that only the rooms to the south-west were the original offices and welfare rooms for customers and staff. The roof, similar to that of the principal room above the transit shed, was a corrugated sheet-metal construction, and was twin-gabled and hipped at the north and south ends.

George's Landing Stage (1875)
Historical background
In 1874, the mid-nineteenth-century landing stage adjacent to George's Ferry Basin (*Ch 4, p 123*) was destroyed by fire and was subsequently replaced by a new landing stage (Ritchie-Noakes 1984, 30). Late nineteenth-century OS mapping (OS 1893c) indicates that this floating landing stage served the Tranmere Rock and New Ferries companies and was attached to, and accessed from, the quayside by two covered piers.

Archaeological evidence
During excavation at the Pier Head Ferry Terminal Building (*Ch 1, p 11*), remains associated with the more southerly of the piers leading to the landing stage were discovered. These comprised a footing (*7001*; Pl 162), which secured the southern pier to the quayside. This was mainly constructed of large pink sandstone blocks, many of which exhibited toolmarks, with substantial iron plates on the eastern elevation. These were 1.2 m wide by 0.04 m thick, and were

*Plate 162: Pier footing **7001**, from the north*

fitted to the sandstone blocks in an upright position, at intervals, tying them together.

The Floating Bridge (1873-6)
Historical background
In 1871, George's Dock Basin was closed and infilled, and became the site of the Floating Bridge (Pl 163), which was constructed between 1873 and 1876 (Ritchie-Noakes 1984, 28; McCarron and Jarvis 1992, 40; Sharples 2004, 121). This 'bridge' formed a long, hinged ramp, which was able to take the rise and fall of the tide, and provided direct access to the extended portion of Prince's Landing Stage (*p 158*).

Archaeological evidence
Evidence relating to the backfilling of George's Dock Basin was encountered in Tr 407, excavated along the LLC extension. This comprised archaeologically sterile pink sandstone waste, which had been dumped into the basin.

Pier Head in the twentieth century
Historical background
The twentieth century has been characterised by several dramatic alterations to the Pier Head section of Liverpool's waterfront. Initially, this entailed the closure of George's Dock in 1900, as this was proving to be a considerable impediment to the cross-river ferry traffic, which had grown substantially (Ritchie-Noakes 1984, 28, 30). The closure of George's Dock rendered other dock facilities in the locality redundant, and George's Ferry Basin (*Ch 4, p 123*) and George's Dock Passage (*Ch 3, p 72*) were also taken out of service (*op cit*, 28). Following its closure, viaducts to carry Water Street and Brunswick Street down to the waterfront were constructed, and these created three prime building plots, which would contain three buildings that would come to be representative of Liverpool and core elements of its famous skyline. These were the MDHB offices (now the Port of Liverpool Building), the Royal Liver Assurance Building, and the Cunard Building, which together form Liverpool's 'Three Graces' (*Ch 1, p 5*).

During the early twentieth century, the open space west of the 'Three Graces' was occupied by a complex network of tramlines, which are depicted on OS mapping dating to this time (*eg* 1927). Electric trams ran along these lines, which had been introduced to Liverpool in 1898, with services continuing until 1957 (Welbourn 2008, 92-3). Pier Head, with both tram and ferry terminals, became, therefore, the hub of the city's transport system (Stammers 1999, 68). Photographs show that the area was landscaped, with lawns, paths,

Plate 163: Photograph of 1925, showing the Floating Bridge (LVRO and Liverpool Libraries)

175

Plate 164: Photograph of 1928, showing the circular flower beds and tram system to the west of the 'Three Graces' (LVRO and Liverpool Libraries, City Engineer's Image No 6788)

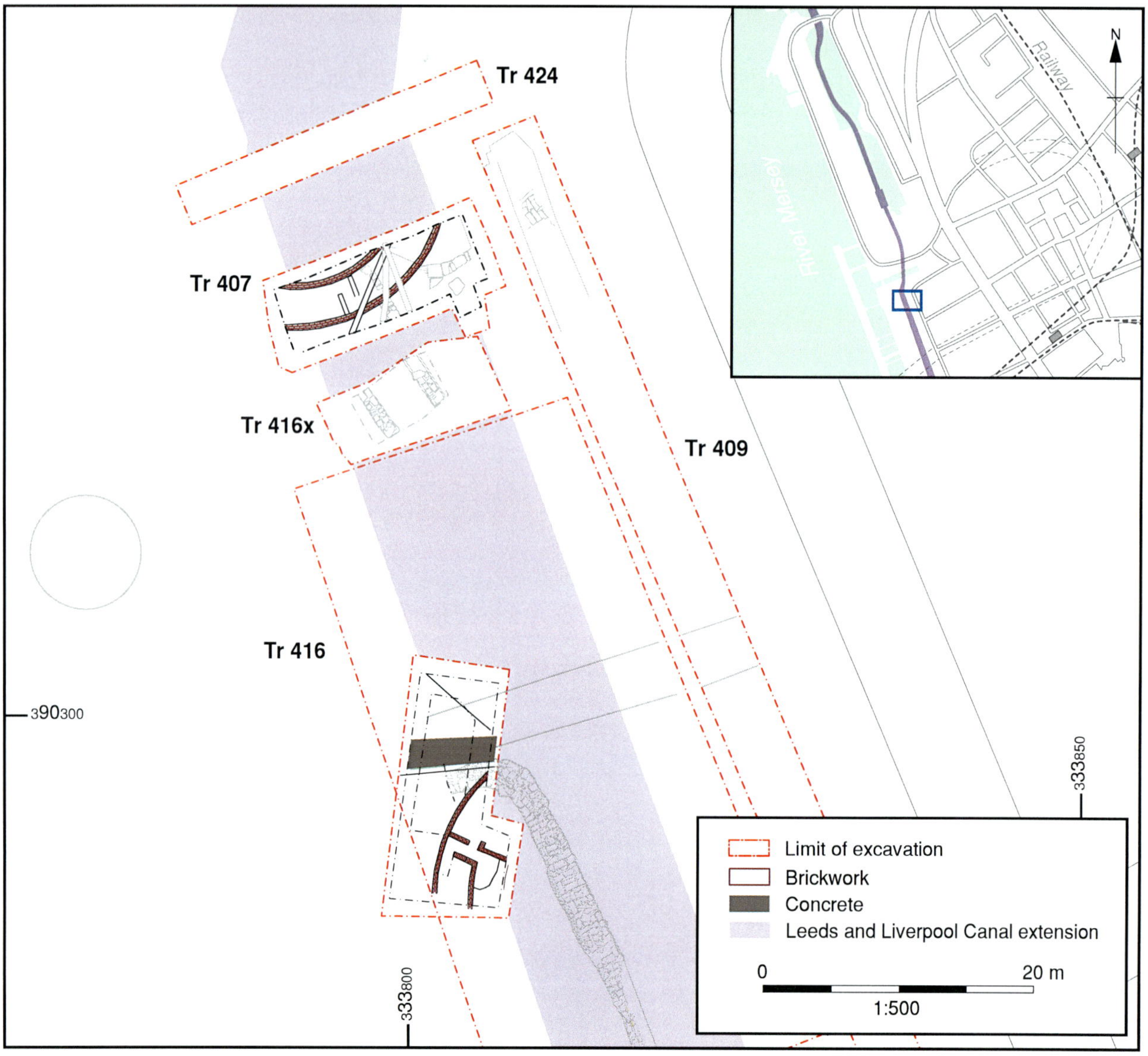

Figure 72: The air-raid shelters at Pier Head (© Crown copyright 2014 Ordnance Survey 100005569)

and flowerbeds, including three large circular beds, around which ran return loops for the trams (Joyce 1983, 16; Pl 164).

Two of the circular beds at Pier Head became the sites of large air-raid shelters during the Second World War, with roofed stairwells forming access visible on both wartime and post-war photographs (Joyce 1983, 131; Jarvis 2001, 84). During the 1960s, following the removal of the tramlines in 1957, Pier Head was remodelled, and a bus station and new ferry terminal were constructed (Sharples 2004, 121). As one of the few public open spaces in Liverpool, the landscaped piazza became a focus for major events, and acquired a number of monuments and memorials (Liverpool City Council 2005, 51-3). Following near-bankruptcy in the 1980s, the Mersey ferry service was relaunched, mainly as a tourist operation, and the terminal was refurbished in 1991 (Sharples 2004, 121).

Archaeological evidence
During excavation along the LLC extension (*Ch 1, p 14*), evidence relating to the circular flowerbeds west of the 'Three Graces' was uncovered. These flowerbeds had been modified in 1939, when they were used as air-raid shelters (*see above*). The remains of two of these shelters were present, defined by twin concentric walls, three bricks thick and *c* 3 m apart, filled between with demolition debris (Fig 72). Both constructions appeared to have been raised on a concrete raft, and there was no evidence for their roofs, which were probably removed by later remodelling.

The central docks (Prince's to Trafalgar Docks) in the twentieth century
The part of the dock estate to the north of Pier Head and south of Clarence Dock also experienced several major alterations during the twentieth century. For instance, at Prince's Dock, by the turn of the century, it was obvious that the dock walling itself was a problem. Designed to accommodate sailing vessels, and ensure long-term stability, its curved, toed-out cross-section was unsuited to steamships with vertical, deep sides and bilge keels, which collided against the lower levels of the wall. Concrete staging was built out over the water to solve this, so that the open area of the dock was significantly reduced. The west side was so treated in 1904-5, and the east in 1928 (Jarvis 1991b, 49-51, 63). In the early twentieth century, Prince's Dock was mainly used by the Belfast Steamship Company (*op cit*, 53) and, in the late 1930s, the pressure from coastal traders led to the conversion of the graving dock at the south end of Prince's Dock to a branch dock, and the construction of a new transit shed on its west quay (*op cit*, 64–5).

In the longer term, the shift to containerisation brought about another change of use. A 'roll-on/roll-off' terminal was installed, and opened in 1967, in the south-west corner of Prince's Dock, for the Irish Packet, but the continuing reduction in passenger numbers and the construction of a new terminal at Victoria Dock combined to make it redundant by 1981 (McCarron and Jarvis 1992, 72). The dock then fell into decline until the 1990s, when a new phase of regeneration used it as the focal point of a waterfront business district.

Waterloo, Victoria, and Trafalgar Docks and their quaysides also experienced twentieth-century alterations. At Waterloo Dock, in 1925, the nineteenth-century warehouses were completely re-equipped for handling oil seeds, and in 1949 an entrance lock was installed (*op cit*, 103). The north warehouse was damaged during the Blitz, and demolished in 1951, while the west warehouse was demolished following redundancy in 1969, although the east warehouse is still extant, having been converted into apartments in 1989-98 (Sharples 2004, 123; Liverpool City Council 2005, 129).

Victoria Dock was remodelled in 1929, which resulted in alterations to the railway access and the clearance of buildings along the north and south quaysides, whilst a new shed was added to the north quay in the mid-twentieth century. The dock was then backfilled for the construction of the British and Irish Steam Packet office and berth in 1972, but was closed in 1988 (McCarron and Jarvis 1992, 94).

As with Victoria Dock, the redevelopment of Trafalgar Dock resulted in the clearance of sheds from the north and south quaysides, and the addition of rail access, depicted on the OS mapping of 1955. At the turn of the nineteenth century, the pier dividing Trafalgar from Victoria Dock was also shortened, and the gate between them was removed, as was the swing bridge crossing from it to the west quay. The west quay shed was also then extended to the south and west, as evidenced from early twentieth-century OS mapping (1927). In common with all the central docks, Trafalgar Dock soon became too small for transatlantic ships engaged in bulk trades, and switched to high-value ocean trades in small vessels, and coastal trading (Jarvis 1991a, 42). It was mostly filled in, and reorientated north/south in 1971, when it became the site for a new coastal container terminal, and a roll-on/roll-off ramp was provided (McCarron and Jarvis 1992, 90).

Archaeological evidence
Early twentieth-century activity (1900-50)
Excavation along the LLC extension uncovered a series of twentieth-century remains in the central docks area. To the south of Prince's Dock, these included the brick foundations, beam slots, and timber sills of a shed,

some 38 m in length (Fig 73). The area west of the graving dock and east of the Irish Sea Packet offices was, for many years, occupied by a timber yard, with an overhead travelling crane, and the foundations seem likely to belong to a large, rectangular, single-storey shed, aligned north/south, which appears on OS maps (*eg* 1955) and in a number of photographs (Welbourn 2008, 126). This shed contained a stone-sett floor and also a concrete base, which was likely to have accommodated a crane or other machinery. No artefacts were discovered in association with this setting, and its only stratigraphic relationship was with the stone setts, into which it had been inserted. It might therefore have been nearly contemporary

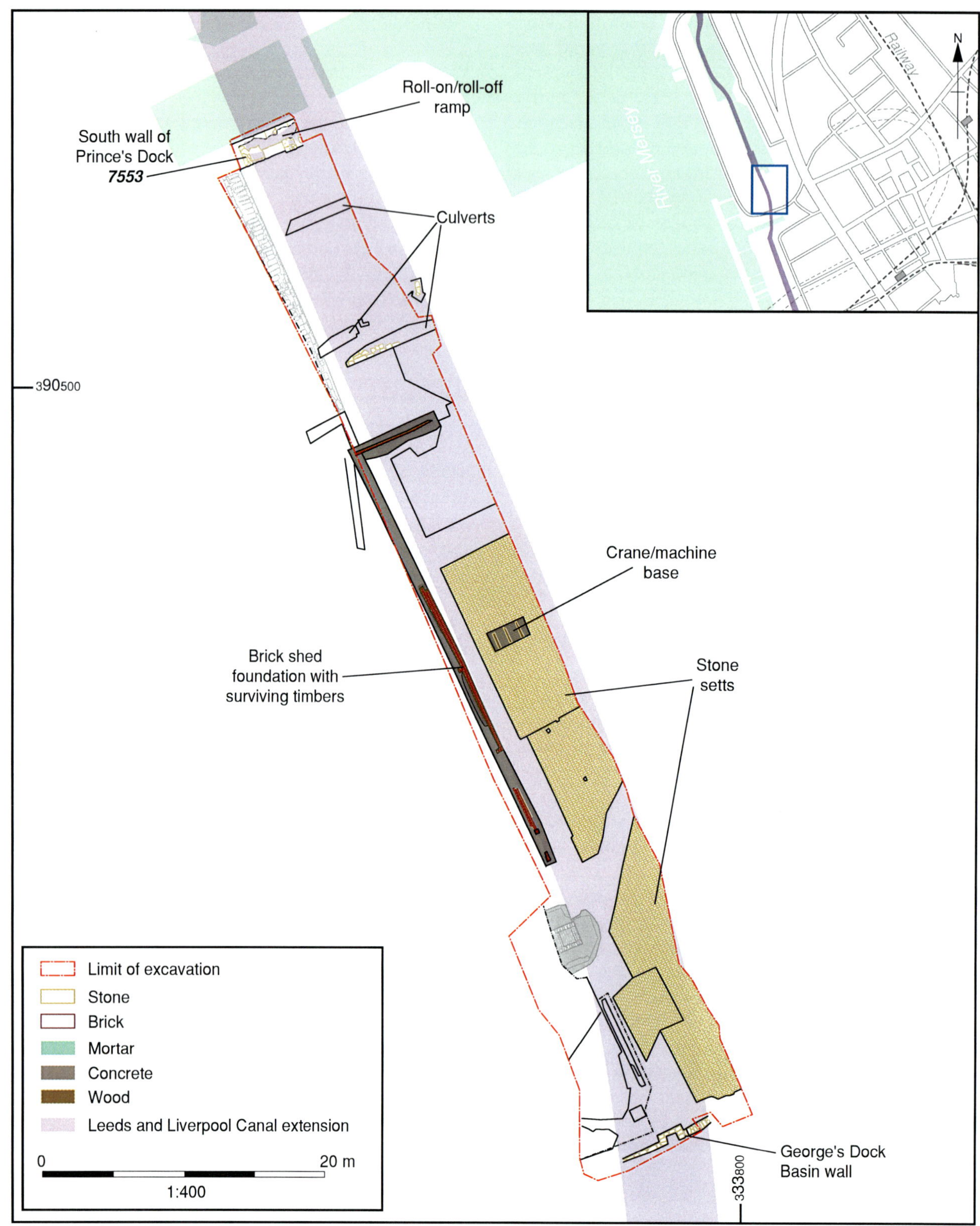

Figure 73: Twentieth-century remains immediately south of Prince's Dock (© Crown copyright 2014 Ordnance Survey 100005569)

with these setts, or it may have been associated with the construction of a new transit shed on this site in the late 1930s (*p 177*).

In addition to remains associated with the timber yard, several east/west-orientated culverts were uncovered to the north of the shed, and it seems likely that the hard surfacing south of Prince's Dock was also altered during the early twentieth century, particularly as this phase of alteration is evident on photographs of other parts of the dock estate (Stammers 1999). At Prince's Dock, the excavation indicated that this alteration involved the replacement of the earlier beach cobbles (*Ch 4, p 137*) with square and rectangular stone setts.

Excavation at Prince's Dock also revealed remnants of the roll-on/roll-off facility, which opened in 1967 (*p 177*). The dock wall (**7553**), that had been cut through to accommodate the ramp, had been restored using concrete and coloured cement render, and backfilled behind with rubble. In addition, there was a substantial, rectangular, concrete structure 0.4 m below the surface, measuring 5.5 x 6 m, and 1.2 m deep. This appears to have been a component of the new dock facility, and is likely to have housed machinery. The ramp was no longer used from 1981, and was demolished shortly after (Jarvis 1991a, 68).

Further to the north, in the area of quayside between Victoria and Trafalgar Docks, excavation revealed a short length of standard-gauge railway line, inset into the hard surfacing of square and rectangular stone setts. The alignment of the railway does not coincide with that shown on the 1955 OS map and it is possible that it dates to the early part of the twentieth century. A cast-iron water main was also uncovered in this area, which cut into one of the counterforts and the edge of the quay of Trafalgar Dock (*Ch 4, p 139*).

Other evidence within this area relates to late twentieth-century activity. For example, a single, two-storey office block, with a 1970s appearance, was extant prior to the work along the LLC extension, and this served the coastal container service which operated from West Waterloo, Victoria, and Trafalgar Docks (*op cit*, 68; McCarron and Jarvis 1992, 94-5). It was also clear that most of the area of the backfilled docks had been capped with concrete during the latter part of the twentieth century. The backfill appeared to be material dredged from the Mersey, and consisted of fine and coarse yellow sand, with pea gravel, shale, and shell fragments. Elements of the methodology recorded for the backfilling of Herculaneum Dock may well have been applied there, with an initial phase during which accumulated silt was removed, probably to ensure later stability, followed by filling with dredged sand (Ritchie-Noakes 1984, 66).

6

FINDS OVERVIEW

Christine Howard-Davis

Despite its size and importance, the amount of formal archaeological investigation undertaken in Liverpool has been limited, and still less analysis has been published to date. Only a handful of the published sites have produced significant artefact assemblages, the most relevant being the South Castle Street excavations undertaken in 1976 and 1977 (Davey and McNeil 1985). The excavations at the Countryside Neptune site and along the LLC extension have both produced sizable assemblages of finds, many of which have the potential to contribute significantly to an understanding of the production and use of pottery, glass, and clay tobacco pipes during Liverpool's later eighteenth- and nineteenth-century period of growth. A fuller analysis will appear alongside that of material from the Museum of Liverpool site and other recent excavations in the city (Philpott in prep).

The finds from the Countryside Neptune (*Ch 1, p 13*) and LLC extension sites (*Ch 1, p 14*) came from a range of contexts; many were dumped during eighteenth- and nineteenth-century land reclamation, and others were from backfill, or from demolition debris levelled for new construction at a later date. Thus, almost none of the artefact assemblage derives directly from the homes and manufactories of eighteenth- and nineteenth-century Liverpool and, in consequence, only the broadest of conclusions about life in the town can be made. As could be predicted, the material comprises all the major finds groups that might be expected from a growing and increasingly wealthy eighteenth-century port, and they also reflect Liverpool's nineteenth-century importance. They include large dumps of pottery (including sugar wares) and clay tobacco pipes, as well as the debris of their manufacture; glass; metalwork; and animal bone and molluscs (Table 3). The amounts recovered are quite substantial, with, for instance, 5476 fragments of pottery, weighing a little over a quarter of a metric ton (257.848 kg), and almost 41,700 fragments of clay tobacco pipe. The dating evidence gained from them confirms and refines the chronology of land reclamation and development along Liverpool's waterfront as it has been reconstructed from the historical sources. In addition, the finds offer rare glimpses into the industries of the growing town, the tastes and aspirations of its inhabitants, and the appearance of its buildings.

Artefact Type	Total fragments
Post-medieval pottery	5476
Ceramic building material	128
Clay tobacco pipe	*c* 41,700
Metalwork	450
Glass	1726
Gunflint	1
Animal bone	*c* 460

Table 3: Totals of finds, by type

Pottery

Before the port: medieval pottery

The small amount of medieval pottery recovered provides very few details on life in medieval Liverpool, and the presence of a handful of early pottery sherds from the Countryside Neptune site can only suggest, in the most general terms, the possibility of medieval activity in the area. They are most probably the result of casual losses or discard along the riverbank, long before the docks were constructed, or they could even have been brought to the site accidentally in material dumped from elsewhere. By the end of this period, and certainly by the late seventeenth century, it is quite likely that pottery was coming from some of the more aspiring Liverpool households, but the highly disturbed nature of the deposits means that none can be directly associated.

The sherds comprise a small out-turned rim (24 g) in a slightly sandy, orange oxidised fabric, with a reduced core reminiscent of local Romano-British fabrics, which was recovered from a feature sealed beneath a brick floor of a possible late eighteenth-century cellar dwelling excavated at the corner of Nova Scotia and Irwell Place (*Ch 3, p 86*). In addition, two small abraded sherds in an unglazed orange-pinkish gritty fabric (together weighing only 22 g) seem likely to be medieval, but were residual in much later deposits, and a small fragment (14 g) in a fine pinkish fabric, with a thin pale-green glaze, is also most likely to be medieval, but came from a nineteenth-century culvert. The fragments are too small and damaged to be assigned to particular ware groups or given more precise dates, but a twelfth- to fourteenth-century range might seem appropriate, as would an origin in the medieval settlement to the north of the Pool (*Ch 2, pp 23-8*). There are no finds in other materials that can be attributed to this early period.

The growth of the port: early post-medieval to mid-eighteenth-century pottery

Although Liverpool's first dock was not operational until 1715 (*Ch 2, p 37*), it is clear that trade through the nascent port had been increasing significantly during the previous century (*Ch 2, p 34*). This was especially the case after the English Civil Wars and it is probable that some of this trade included the export of pottery. For example, by 1674, there were dues to be paid on the shipment of 'mugs, cupps and pipes to foreign parts' (Longworth nd, citing Mayer 1855, 178). A proportion of this pottery undoubtedly derived from the Midlands as, by the third quarter of the seventeenth century, a thriving trade existed in the export, from Liverpool, of Staffordshire pottery to the New World (Longworth nd). The general growth of industry within the town during the early part of the eighteenth century, as a direct result of the expansion in maritime trade, probably also stimulated local pottery production (*Ch 3, p 47*), whilst the export of Staffordshire pottery continued to be a substantial source of income for the port (*ibid*).

Staffordshire slipwares and other imports

There is a small group of fragments of Staffordshire-type slipware within the assemblage, dating from the later seventeenth to the mid-eighteenth century (Barker 1993), mostly from the Countryside Neptune site, which produced 42 fragments (283 g; Table 4). These probably represent no more than a handful of vessels, with the level of disturbance and mixing caused by repeated dumping on the site amply illustrated by the fact that they were distributed between some 20 contexts, most of which also produced later material.

Fabric	No fragments	Percentage total assemblage	Weight (g)	Percentage total assemblage
Tin-glazed wares				
Countryside Neptune site	34	0.62	261	0.1
Mann Island LLC extension	6	0.11	65	0.03
Pier Head LLC extension	29	0.53	440	0.17
Central Docks LLC extension	4	0.07	10	0.01
Total	*73*	*1.33*	*776*	*0.31*
Staffordshire-type and other slipwares				
Countryside Neptune site	69	1.26	726	0.28
Mann Island LLC extension	6	0.11	56	0.02
Pier Head LLC extension	6	0.11	86	0.03
Central Docks LLC extension	0	0	0	0
Total	*81*	*1.48*	*868*	*0.33*
White salt-glazed stonewares				
Countryside Neptune site	15	0.27	195	0.08
Mann Island LLC extension	28	0.51	310	0.12
Pier Head LLC extension	19	0.35	187	0.07
Central Docks LLC extension	3	0.05	15	0.01
Total	*65*	*1.18*	*707*	*0.28*
Porcelain				
Countryside Neptune site	30	0.55	198	0.08
Mann Island LLC extension	22	0.4	199	0.08
Pier Head LLC extension	28	0.51	180	0.07
Central Docks LLC extension	1	0.02	46	0.02
Total	*81*	*1.48*	*623*	*0.25*

Table 4: The fabrics within the assemblage

Fabric	No fragments	Percentage total assemblage	Weight (g)	Percentage total assemblage
Agate wares				
Countryside Neptune site	19	0.35	112	0.04
Mann Island LLC extension	16	0.29	360	0.14
Pier Head LLC extension	1	0.02	22	0.01
Central Docks LLC extension	0	0	0	0
Total	*36*	*0.66*	*494*	*0.19*
Creamware				
Countryside Neptune site	723	13.2	6566	2.55
Mann Island LLC extension	202	3.69	2615	1.01
Pier Head LLC extension	522	9.53	13,078	5.07
Central Docks LLC extension	53	0.97	460	0.18
Total	*1500*	*27.39*	*22,719*	*8.81*
Pearlwares				
Countryside Neptune site	173	3.16	1600	0.62
Mann Island LLC extension	24	0.44	544	0.21
Pier Head LLC extension	75	1.37	734	0.28
Central Docks LLC extension	3	0.05	103	0.04
Total	*275*	*5.02*	*2981*	*1.15*
White earthenwares				
Countryside Neptune site	137	2.5	1638	0.64
Mann Island LLC extension	36	0.66	421	0.16
Pier Head LLC extension	148	2.7	2246	0.87
Central Docks LLC extension	7	0.13	36	0.01
Total	*328*	*5.99*	*4341*	*1.68*
Industrial slipwares				
Countryside Neptune site	69	1.26	717	0.28
Mann Island LLC extension	26	0.47	486	0.19
Pier Head LLC extension	23	0.42	306	0.12
Central Docks LLC extension	3	0.05	42	0.02
Total	*121*	*2.2*	*1551*	*0.61*
Other minor fabrics				
Countryside Neptune site	91	1.66	2112	0.82
Mann Island LLC extension	13	0.24	827	0.32
Pier Head LLC extension	70	1.28	2014	0.78
Central Docks LLC extension	2	0.04	156	0.06
Total	*176*	*3.22*	*5109*	*1.98*
Black-glazed redwares				
Countryside Neptune site	473	8.64	31,986	12.4
Mann Island LLC extension	334	6.1	35,384	13.72
Pier Head LLC extension	467	8.5	47,746	18.52
Central Docks LLC extension	34	0.62	3762	1.46
Total	*1308*	*23.86*	*118,878*	*46.1*

Table 4: The fabrics within the assemblage (cont'd)

Fabric	No fragments	Percentage total assemblage	Weight (g)	Percentage total assemblage
Self-glazed redwares				
Countryside Neptune site	71	1.3	3871	1.5
Mann Island LLC extension	43	0.79	1230	0.48
Pier Head LLC extension	10	0.18	566	0.22
Central Docks LLC extension	4	0.07	408	0.16
Total	*128*	*2.34*	*6075*	*2.36*
Stonewares, brown				
Countryside Neptune site	117	2.14	8274	3.21
Mann Island LLC extension	21	0.38	1272	0.49
Pier Head LLC extension	41	0.75	2707	1.05
Central Docks LLC extension	8	0.15	186	0.07
Total	*187*	*3.42*	*12,439*	*4.82*
Stonewares, grey *etc*				
Countryside Neptune site	19	0.35	3250	1.26
Mann Island LLC extension	0	0	0	0
Pier Head LLC extension	0	0	0	0
Central Docks LLC extension	0	0	0	0
Total	*19*	*0.35*	*3250*	*1.26*
Sugar wares				
Countryside Neptune site	719	13.13	37,954	14.72
Mann Island LLC extension	153	2.79	13,803	5.35
Pier Head LLC extension	201	3.67	23,712	9.2
Central Docks LLC extension	25	0.46	1568	0.61
Total	*1098*	*20.05*	*77,037*	*29.88*
Grand Totals	**5476**	**100**	**257,848**	**100**

Table 4: The fabrics within the assemblage (cont'd)

There is a single example of a large cup with trailed and combed decoration, and a band of spots around the rim (Pl 165), a style at its most popular between *c* 1700 and 1720 (*op cit*, 15). Most, however, are from press-moulded dishes, current well into the mid-eighteenth century (Poole 1995). Although most of this type of pottery was probably made in the Staffordshire area (*p 182*), there is limited evidence to suggest that some was made in or around Liverpool or more generally in south-west Lancashire. For instance, finds of slip-decorated pottery from excavations at Shaws Brow (*Ch 3, p 47*) in 1967 give some reason to believe that local potters there were producing in the same style (Smith 1970, 1), and excavations in Manchester Dock produced similar material, thought to be Lancashire products (J Speakman *pers comm*).

There is also a small amount of other slipware (27 fragments; 443 g), made in different fabrics, but probably falling into the same date range. Some of this might well derive from Buckley, in Clwyd (Pl 166), which supplied North Wales and the North West, but not, it seems, Liverpool in any quantity, until the early eighteenth century, when its products became confined to a more local market (Barker 1993, 12; Longworth nd). It must be noted, however, that press-moulded dishes continued to be made in some small potteries into the nineteenth or even the twentieth century (Brears 1971, 111; Barker 1993, 30-1). Sherds from both the Mann Island and Pier Head sections of the LLC extension were present in reclamation material, a possible chamber pot from the latter coming from nineteenth-century reclamation deposits to the north of river wall *3801* (*Ch 4, p 127*).

The effective absence of contemporary Black-glazed redware tablewares (only three sherds, including a cup rim, all from the Countryside Neptune site) may be significant. This type of pottery forms a very significant proportion of the ceramics used close to Liverpool Castle (Davey and McNeil 1985) and in assemblages from the period of the Civil Wars and later seventeenth century from across the region, such as those from Beeston Castle (Noake 1993),

Plate 166: Slipware chamber pot

Plate 165: Early eighteenth-century Staffordshire slipware cup

Norton Priory (Brown and Howard-Davis 2008), and Bewsey Old Hall (Lewis *et al* 2011), all in Cheshire, and Speke Hall (Higgins 1992), Merseyside. This may, therefore, indicate that the early slip-decorated pottery from Liverpool's waterfront sites is largely or entirely residual.

Blackwares would undoubtedly have been freely available to Liverpudlians of the day, being produced in some quantities in outlying towns such as Prescot and possibly Rainford. In addition, there is evidence that they were made in Liverpool, albeit at a later date, at the Park Lane pot-house (*Ch 3, p 47*; Fig 16), where 'Jackfield'-type blackwares were being produced by the mid-eighteenth century (Smith 1970, 10). Black-glazed redware coarsewares, widely used in the kitchen and for storage, and made by the same potteries, were in use from the late seventeenth century at least, and continued as late as the twentieth century. These are well-represented in the assemblage from the Countryside Neptune site, which strongly suggests that they were freely available. In general terms, however, the finer tablewares, especially cups,

had fallen into serious decline by the last quarter of the eighteenth century (Philpott 1985).

Imported stoneware

A few fragments of Westerwald stoneware (Pl 167) were recovered from the Countryside Neptune site and the Pier Head section of LLC extension. These are probably of early eighteenth-century date (Hurst *et al* 1986, 222), and the rim form of one suggests that it derives from a chamber pot, a vessel

Plate 167: Imported German stoneware

form commonly imported from *c* 1710 (Noël Hume 1969, 148) until the 1760s, when the market was taken over by English producers (*ibid*).

Tin-glazed wares
Tin-glazed ware, originally imported from Holland, was first made in London in any significant quantity during the early seventeenth century, with production spreading to Brislington and Bristol in the 1640s (Ray 2000, 4). Although never cheap (*op cit*, 5), it was swiftly and increasingly popular, and was made in quantity in Liverpool from 1710, when a group of potters was sent north from Southwark (Longworth nd) to set up production at the Lord Street pottery (Smith 1970, 2; *Ch 3, p 47*). The production of tin-glazed ware relies on imported light-firing clays, notably from Belfast and Carrickfergus, which Liverpool, already with a thriving Irish trade (Farrer and Brownbill 1911), was ideally situated to receive in large amounts (*ibid*). Such was its success in the town that by 1750 there were nine producers, making some of the best wares available (Ray 2000, 5). Their arrival marks the opening days of Liverpool's eventual eighteenth-century domination of pottery production in England, being described by 1756 as 'where the Earthen ware manufacture is more extensively carried on than in any other town in the Kingdom' (Boney 1957, 4).

Like the other early eighteenth-century fabrics, it is not present in large quantities (73 fragments, weighing 776 g; Table 4), which again reflects the likelihood that most of the pottery was dumped in the second half of the eighteenth century, or later. It is difficult to differentiate tin-glazed wares on the basis of their fabric (Cotter 2000, 229), but it seems reasonable to suggest that this group is probably all a product of Liverpool, being made, in general terms, between 1710 and the 1780s (Hildyard 2005, 118). Most fragments derive from flatwares with blue-and-white decoration (Pl 168), from undecorated hollow-ware vessels, or from small, probably undecorated, bowls with upright, slightly out-turned rims, perhaps ointment jars. They are clearly not from the best-quality vessels, often made for display or as commemorative pieces, at which Liverpool excelled (Ray 2000, 5), or from specialist vessels such as apothecary jars, but were rather intended for ordinary domestic use (*ibid*), and were presumably largely utilitarian items, used in middling households.

Fragments of several tin-glazed vessels were recovered from the Pier Head section of the LLC extension. These include a small, probably undecorated, bowl, with an upright, slightly out-turned rim, from a deposit associated with late eighteenth-century land reclamation to the north of wall **3504** (*Ch 3, p 78*); the base of a cylindrical tankard from an early nineteenth-century pottery and glass dump north of river wall **3801** (*Ch 4, p 127*); and fragments of a plain chamber pot from early nineteenth-century reclamation material located to the east of river wall **5513** (*Ch 4, p 127*). In contrast, the sherds from the Countryside Neptune site and other sections of the canal extension are all worn and relatively fragmentary, perhaps suggesting that these, along with the small amounts of other early fabrics, represent a largely residual element in the assemblage; several of these were recovered from reclamation layers west of eighteenth-century river walls **7304** and **7325** (*Ch 3, pp 59, 63*). A single biscuit-fired fragment from the Countryside Neptune site presumably represents production debris from Liverpool's thriving eighteenth-century tin-glaze industry, and reflects other wasters seen in material from Chavasse Park (J Speakman *pers comm*).

Manganese-mottled wares
Manganese-mottled wares are broadly contemporary with the main period of tin-glaze production (Kelly and Greaves 1974), but only seven fragments (104 g) are present, all from the Countryside Neptune site. Although principally made in Staffordshire, evidence suggests that they were also made locally at Prescot (McNeil 1989; Davey 1991, 135), and at Buckley, Clwyd, where they have been assigned to the period 1690-1720 (Amery and Davey 1979). It is likely that production elsewhere continued into the late eighteenth century, as excavations at the Greatbatch pottery site in Fenton, Staffordshire, have produced fragments of manganese-mottled ware dating to between 1765 and 1775, and probably as late as 1782 (Barker 1984).

Agate wares
Agate wares, popular from the 1750s to the 1770s (Barker and Halfpenny 1990), also form a small element of the assemblage (36 fragments, 494 g; Table 4). A fragment of a dish, from the Mann Island section of the LLC extension, is probably a Staffordshire product, with rouletted slip decoration similar to that present on a vessel illustrated by Noël Hume (1969, fig 49), dating to *c* 1760. The pottery itself remained in production into the 1790s (Erickson and Hunter 2003). A single tankard

Plate 168: Tin-glazed plate rim

0   50mm

Plate 169: Agate-ware tankard

base (Pl 169) was recovered from early nineteenth-century reclamation deposits behind river wall **5513** (*Ch 4, p 127*), where it appears amongst a group of other, effectively contemporary, material, including a small glass phial of typically seventeenth- or eighteenth-century design (*p 211*).

White salt-glazed and other fine stonewares
Only a small amount of white salt-glazed stoneware (65 fragments; 707 g; Table 4) was recovered, mostly from land-reclamation deposits. It represents only 1.18% of the total assemblage (0.28% by weight), which again suggests that the principal period of deposition post-dated the widespread use of this fabric, regarded as typical of the first three-quarters of the eighteenth century (Jennings 1981, 222). This fabric was made in great quantities from *c* 1730, mainly in Staffordshire, when the use of porous moulds for casting was introduced, allowing production on an industrial scale (Sempill 1904, 21).

Small quantities were recovered during excavations on the Pier Head and Central Docks section of the LLC extension (21 fragments; 202 g). The fragments are mostly from flatwares, with some derived from material contemporary with the construction of river wall **3544** in the 1780s (*Ch 3, pp 76-8*), and also from deposits laid down during the process of land reclamation around Chester Basin (*Ch 4, p 122*). Slightly more (43 fragments; 505 g) came from the Countryside Neptune site. Again, these are mostly from plates, with either plain or decorated rims

0   50mm

Plate 170: White salt-glazed stoneware rims, exhibiting mid-eighteenth-century designs

187

Plate 171: *A possible second from Mann Island, suggesting the manufacture of white salt-glazed wares nearby*

(Pl 170), all dating to after 1740, when dinner services in this fabric first became popular (Hildyard 2005, 42), and probably to the 1750-60s, when a wide range of rim designs were in use (*op cit*, 44), although production continued into the 1770s. A few fragments are decorated in the scratch-blue style, introduced in the 1720s, most popular from 1745-55 (Savage 1952), but continuing in production in a debased form until *c* 1790 (Noël Hume 1969, 118). Two small fragments are polychrome enamelled, a technique not used widely until the 1750s (Hildyard 2005, 46), and one fragment from a chamber pot has a medallion bearing the cipher of George III (1760-1820).

One example, a plate with very poor-quality moulding (Pl 171), is of bad enough quality to suggest that it might have been sold as a second. Another plate fragment, from late eighteenth-century reclamation deposits behind a slip wall (*7325*; *Ch 3*, *p 63*), has broken along the line of a large crack with vitrified edges, which would have rendered it unusable, and is thus likely to be a waster. Both pieces suggest that some, at least, of the Mann Island white salt-glazed stonewares were locally made, particularly as seconds tend to be sold at a reduced price, usually close to their place of production. Although well known from documentary sources (Smith 1970, 5), Liverpool's white salt-glazed stoneware production sites have not been explored archaeologically (*op cit*, 49). White salt-glazed stoneware wasters have, however, been found in Prescot (Holgate 1989), suggesting that production occurred there as well.

Red stonewares were made sporadically by a number of producers from the seventeenth century, throughout the eighteenth and into the early nineteenth century (Poole 1995, 68). Two fragments were recovered during the excavations at the Countryside Neptune site, one being a cast handle from a mug or small jug, the other a sherd from a teapot. There were also two fragments of tea-wares in black basalt, or Egyptian Black, an unglazed black stoneware made after 1750 by Josiah Wedgwood, and continuing in production by other potters throughout the eighteenth century (Noël Hume 1969, 121). Both fragments came from buildings on Nova Scotia. The greyish appearance of the fabric might suggest that they are from the Herculaneum pottery, which is known to have produced such wares between 1796 and 1810 (Hyland 2005, 74).

Tin-glazed tiles

Tin-glazed tiles were another staple of Liverpool's eighteenth-century ceramic industry, being sold widely, and were especially used for decorative fireplaces, following the Dutch tradition. In all, 42 fragments of tin-glazed tile were collected during the excavations. Liverpool was a well-known eighteenth-century production centre (Ray 1973), with tiles produced from as early as 1716 (Honey 1969, 49). In 1756, Liverpool entrepreneurs developed the transfer-printing technique, effectively moving tile production onto an industrial scale (*ibid*). Subsequently, production in Liverpool appears, to a degree, to have specialised in cheaply made tiles printed with designs in black.

The majority of the fragments recovered are hand-painted, rather than printed, most in blue and white (Pl 172), though one fragment from the Countryside Neptune site is decorated in pale mauve, presumably manganese. Although they are fragmentary, designs depicting rural landscapes are evident on several of the tiles, and two joining fragments (Pl 173), from nineteenth-century deposits immediately east of

Plate 172: *Tin-glazed wall tile, with a typical hand-painted landscape design*

0   50mm

Plate 173: Tile utilising the 'Fazackerley' palette

George's Dock Passage (*Ch 3, p 71*), are decorated with carefully drawn polychrome flowers in the so-called 'Fazackerley palette', which is closely associated with Liverpool producers (Poole 1995). In addition, a small fragment from late eighteenth-century land-reclamation deposits adjacent to river wall **7583** (*Ch 3, p 78*) seems to have been decorated using a technique known as 'bianco-sopra-bianco', which was popular in the mid- to late eighteenth century (Honey 1969, 45). A polychrome, yellow-and-green, rather than a blue-and-white, fragment was also recovered from these deposits, and the black outlines of the design could well have been transfer-printed, dating it to after the introduction of this technique in 1756 (Savage 1952, 152).

Liverpool's ceramic heyday: the mid-/late eighteenth century to the closure of the Herculaneum Pottery in 1840

During the latter half of the eighteenth century and early part of the nineteenth century, pottery production in Liverpool reached its peak and, significantly, the port also continued to export large quantities of Staffordshire-derived wares. The mid- to late eighteenth-century town contained numerous pot-houses, which had been largely built along its eastern and southern fringes (*Ch 3, p 47*). However, these were eclipsed in 1796, when Samuel Worthington established the Herculaneum Pottery to the south of the town, which, until its closure in 1840, would

represent Liverpool's most important pottery. From the early nineteenth-century, however, the Liverpool pottery industry fell into a steep and rapid decline. Herculaneum produced a range of different wares, including earthenwares and stonewares, though it is best known for its porcelain production, which rivalled that being produced by the Staffordshire potteries (Hyland 2005).

Porcelain

It is possible that small amounts of Chinese porcelain are present in the assemblage, although it is not generally well-represented in Liverpool assemblages (J Speakman *pers comm*). This presumably echoes the large-scale eighteenth-century importation of Chinese tea-wares by the East India Company, which ended abruptly in 1791 (Hildyard 2005, 123) when English production had significantly reduced its economic worth as an import. These fragments were recovered from unstratified deposits in the Central Docks section of the LLC extension, and also from late eighteenth-century reclamation layers to the west of slip wall **7325** (*Ch 3, p 63*), in the vicinity of Chester Basin (*Ch 3, p 87*), and next to river wall **3544** (*Ch 3, pp 76-8*). They would, perhaps, have been originally used in well-to-do households although, by the end of the eighteenth century, Chinese imports had become accessible to a much greater portion of the pottery-buying public and/or had been passed down the social scale as second- or third-hand goods (Staniforth 1996; Wang 2011).

The remainder of the porcelain came from a variety of different contexts spanning a wide range of dates. It seems likely that most was manufactured in Liverpool, particularly as the second half of the eighteenth century saw a flowering of porcelain production in the city (*cf* Boney 1957; Smith 1970; Hildyard 2005, 123). A biscuit-fired waster was found within a demolition layer associated with a warehouse at Nova Scotia (**7339**; *Ch 4, p 147*) and three similar wasters came from nineteenth-century reclamation deposits in the Pier Head section of the LLC extension. These are good evidence for the local production of soft-paste porcelain, as it seems unlikely that unmarketable pottery waste would have been transported far from its production site. In addition, a small plate fragment associated with clay-pipe kiln dump **7382**, in the Mann Island section of LLC extension (*p 197*), might represent a product of Pennington and Partners, as its shows their typical fisherman-style design (*cf* Godden 1974, 272, pl 323).

Creamwares and Pearlwares

Although Creamware and Pearlware fabrics were developed successively, there was a considerable overlap in their use. The Herculaneum Pottery, for

189

instance, produced both ware types in its early days, often using the same body and moulds for both, the only distinction being in the glazes used (Hyland 2005, 52-3). Moreover, the considerable exchange of workers between Staffordshire and Liverpool at this time must mean that often identical techniques and designs were used by the two industries, on occasion by the same workers (Smith 1970).

Creamwares form an important part of the assemblage, with 1500 fragments (22.719 kg), representing 27.39% of the total by fragment count but, as it is a relatively light fabric, only 8.81% by weight. They were current from the mid-eighteenth century to the early nineteenth century, by which time, especially at the high end of the market, they had largely been replaced by Pearlwares (Noël Hume 1969, 125; Hyland 2005, 50). Most would have been brought from Staffordshire to Liverpool for export (Smith 1970), or for finishing with printed decoration before export (Drakard 1993). However, it is likely that some, at least, are local products, as many of the Liverpool potteries produced this type of vessel (Smith 1970; Hyland 2005), including Herculaneum, at the very end of the eighteenth century, although little of it is marked (Smith 1993).

The Creamwares, which comprised, by fragment count, the largest element of the entire assemblage (Table 4), are not particularly varied in form, being mainly plain flatwares, chamber pots, and tureens or strainers, with only a few fragments hinting at more decorative vessels. Although only one small fragment is marked (Pl 174; from the Countryside Neptune site), it is quite possible that many, or all, were products of the Herculaneum Pottery. The style of back-stamp used suggests a date between 1796 and 1810 (Smith 1970, 108). It must, however, be borne in mind that vast amounts of Creamwares from Staffordshire passed through the port, and breakages en route could well have been dumped in the reclamation backfills in large quantities.

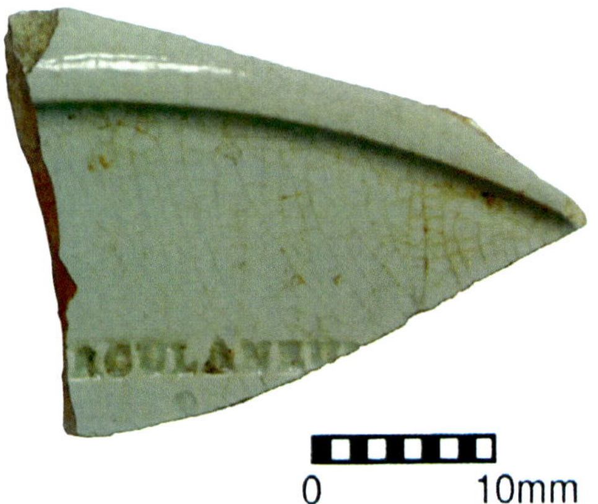

Plate 174: Herculaneum back-stamp

The greatest concentrations of Creamwares were recovered from late eighteenth-century reclamation deposits west of river wall **7638** (158 fragments; *Ch 3, p 62*), west of wall **7325** (99 fragments; *Ch 3, p 63*), and north of Chester Basin (300 fragments). The uniformity of the forms seen in the latter (undecorated plates with plain rims, introduced at Herculaneum *c* 1805; Hyland 2005, 59) seems to set them apart, indicating that these had been dumped as a group, probably as industrial waste, the absence of kiln debris perhaps identifying them as vessels broken in transit, during finishing, or in storage (for decorated examples in this form, see Hyland 2005, fig 39).

Most of the vessels represented are plates and shallow dishes with a variety of rim patterns (the following terminology is after Noël Hume 1969), but mainly the Royal pattern, very similar to examples made at Herculaneum in its early days (*cf* Hyland 2005, fig 27, made *c* 1800), and feather edge, but including spearhead, as well as shell-edged plates, mainly in blue, but with a few green-edged examples. The latter have their origins in the later eighteenth century (*ibid*), and such plates were certainly amongst the slightly later Herculaneum Pearlware repertoire (*op cit*, fig 11).

From the 1750s, Liverpool was an important centre for undertaking transfer-printed decoration on pottery (Poole 1995, 74). Several baluster-shaped jugs from the Countryside Neptune site bear the typically black, over-glaze transfer-printing associated with Messrs Sadler and Green of Liverpool, who decorated a range of Staffordshire products (*ibid*) in the years between 1763 and the 1790s, although production probably continued at Herculaneum as late as the 1830s (Hyland 2005, 58). In addition, glazing faults are also present on several fragments from the Pier Head section of the LLC extension and, whilst not major, could point to them being wasters. Substantial parts of two jugs from the Countryside Neptune site bear Masonic iconography (Pl 175), and smaller fragments show nautical (Pl 176) and related themes (Pl 177), which seem to have been popular as souvenirs (*ibid*). Furthermore, this site produced a coffeepot- or teapot lid printed in brown, again commonly used on Creamwares.

Several hand-painted examples are also present. These include a closed vessel, which is painted with swags of green-ivy leaves, and a plain plate whose rim is edged with painted-brown lines, both from the Central Docks section of the LLC extension. Other painted vessels were recovered from early nineteenth-century reclamation layers associated with river wall **5513** (*Ch 4, p 127*). These include plates and dishes, all decorated with brown-painted lines on the rim, or edge, and free-hand painted leaves in a distinctive

Plate 175: Transfer-printed Creamware jug with Masonic iconography

Plate 176: Jug fragment printed with nautical scene and probably intended as a souvenir

Plate 177: Fragments of jugs printed with nautical scenes and probably intended as souvenirs

Plate 178: Creamware painted with a distinctive floral style in brown

'dotty' style (Pl 178). The remaining painted vessels from these reclamation deposits comprise a small bowl, possibly a tea bowl, painted with a swag of narrow green leaves (in the style shown on a plate from Herculaneum, made in *c* 1805; *op cit*, fig 25), and a rather crudely painted teapot- or coffeepot lid.

Pearlwares, produced from 1779 (Coysh and Henrywood 1982), if not earlier, comprised 5.02% of the assemblage by fragment count (275 fragments), and 1.15% by weight (2.981 kg), which is a surprisingly small amount (Table 4). The largest group was recovered from the Countryside Neptune site (173 fragments; 3.16% by fragment count), where it was scattered over 36 separate contexts. Again, much of it could have been produced or decorated by the Herculaneum Pottery, with most of the latter coming from Staffordshire. It comprises, for the most part, tableware and tea-wares, painted or transfer-printed with mainly, but not exclusively, Chinese-influenced designs, including willow pattern, which post-dates 1792 (Noël Hume 1969, 130). There are also shell-edged plates, and a complete small, straight-sided cup, with a blue-glazed rouletted band at the rim.

Refined white earthenwares
Later refined white earthenwares, dominating the market by *c* 1820 (*ibid*), are also present, forming 5.99% of the assemblage by fragment count (328) and 1.68% by weight (4.341 kg; Table 4). The proportions and range of forms are almost identical to those of the Pearlware, though the largest proportion of this material was recovered from the excavations along the Pier Head section of the LLC extension (148 fragments; 2.7% by fragment count). Most of the vessels bear blue underglaze transfer-printed decoration, in a range of designs, mostly Chinoiserie, but one fragment includes a vignette of a young woman playing a

harp (Pl 179), whilst others bear exotic scenes, both Indian and European. Occasional fragments are transfer-printed in brown or pink, whilst fragments from the Countryside Neptune site are printed in black and green, colours which appeared in the late 1820s (Neale 2004, 138). One of the few vessels bearing a maker's mark also came from the Countryside Neptune site and is attributable to W H Grindley (Pl 180), working in North Staffordshire during the late nineteenth and

Plate 179: Plate showing a young female harpist

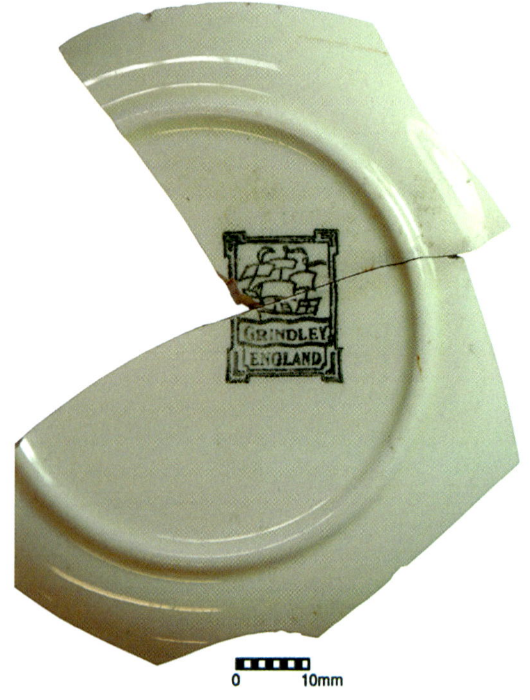

Plate 180: Back-stamp attributable to the North Staffordshire pottery of W H Grindley, dating to c 1936-54

Plate 181: Almost complete industrial slipware tankard

twentieth centuries (Birks nd). The particular mark was in use in *c* 1936-54 (*ibid*). When considering the white earthenwares and Pearlwares together, these two fabrics are still far out-represented by Creamwares, perhaps suggesting that the peak period of deposition, at least for fine tablewares, lay in the late eighteenth century, although it clearly continued well into the twentieth century.

Industrial slipwares
While not strictly fine tablewares, industrial slipwares represent a small element of the assemblage (121 fragments; 2.2% by fragment count; Table 4). Decorative, but somewhat utilitarian in nature, these late slipwares appeared in the late eighteenth century (*c* 1770), initially made in Creamware and then in Pearlware. They remained popular through the nineteenth, and on into the twentieth, century (Rickard 2006). Mocha-type decoration can be seen on some fragments, a form with a long life, possibly from the 1780s until the eve of World War II (*op cit*, 46). Pieces with decoration applied with a multi-chambered slip trailer are probably of nineteenth-century date (*op cit*, 13).

Forms present include dishes, tankards, and chamber pots, and some notable examples, probably dating to the eighteenth century, were recovered from the Mann Island section of the LLC extension. These include the base of a tankard, decorated with brown and yellow marbling, reminiscent of similar wares produced at the Herculaneum Pottery (Hyland 2005, 190) but also widely produced in Staffordshire, and a second tankard fragment imitating agate wares has sprigged decoration, a technique introduced in the 1780s (Hildyard 2005, 172). A fine lathe-turned black-and-white-chequered chamber pot also came from this area. Lathe-turning was introduced in 1782 (*ibid*) and again it seems likely that this vessel can be dated to the late eighteenth century. During excavation along the Pier Head section of the LLC extension, a small tankard (Pl 181) was found in a layer of rubbish in the small warehouse excavated on the northern side of the Chester Basin (*Ch 4, p 129*). The inferior quality of its decoration might point to it being a poorly fired second.

Lustreware
Lustreware was developed at the very end of the eighteenth century (Cotter 2000), though most dates to the nineteenth century, with painted designs most popular from *c* 1815 to the 1860s (Hughes 1968). During the excavation at the Countryside Neptune site, 29 fragments (336 g) of pink lustreware were

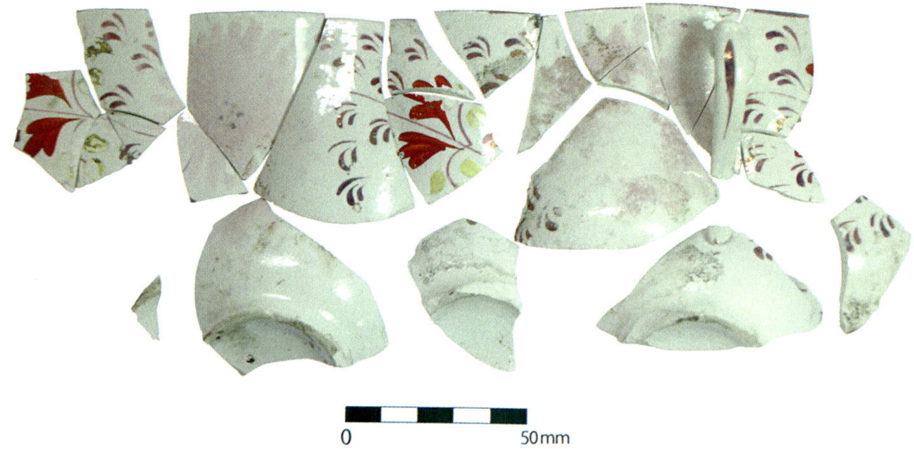

Plate 182: Hand-painted lustreware

recovered. These represent three vessels: a small bowl; a jug; and the lid of a serving dish. Two almost complete, identical, copper lustreware jugs, probably dating to the nineteenth century (Bosanko 1916; Bagdade and Bagdade 2004, 158) came from a layer of rubbish in the small warehouse on the north side of Chester Basin (*Ch 4, p 129*), along with a rather bizarrely decorated cup, with pink lustre detail (Pl 182).

Other minor fabrics
A single rim fragment (44 g), in an unusual, fairly soft, micaceous fabric, came from a late demolition deposit excavated at the Countryside Neptune site, where it was almost certainly residual. Two similar fragments (264 g), with splashes of glaze, were recovered from a pottery dump within an early nineteenth-century reclamation deposit next to river wall *3421* (*Ch 4, p 127*). Another was found during earlier excavations at South Castle Street, coming from an early eighteenth-century context (Innes and Philpott 1985, fig 42.314). They clearly came from large, globular vessels, ostensibly unglazed, and most likely to be amphora-like jars, which contained olive oil, and were imported from Spain from the medieval period to as late as the nineteenth century (Ashdown 1972). Although in different fabrics, an unglazed handle and a thick wall fragment, from the excavations at the Countryside Neptune site, could also be from large storage vessels.

A single large fragment (134 g) from a North Devon Gravel-tempered-ware jug was also recovered from the same site, which is likely to be of eighteenth-century date (Noël Hume 1969, 133; Allan 1984). North Devon Gravel-tempered ware has also been found in small quantities at other sites in Liverpool (*cf* Davey and McNeil 1985).

Coarse kitchen and storage wares
Black-glazed redwares
Black-glazed storage vessels comprise 23.86% of the assemblage by fragment count (1308 fragments) and,

as might be expected from their substantial nature, considerably more, 46.1%, by weight (118.878 kg; Table 4). Although these vessels were recovered from a wide range of contexts, marked concentrations were present at the Countryside Neptune site. More specifically, concentrations of these vessels were recovered from late eighteenth-century reclamation deposits between walls *7304* and *7325* (*Ch 3, pp 59, 63*), and in the demolition material in the basement of a warehouse on Nova Scotia (*7202; Ch 3, p 84*). The former contained 137 fragments, whilst there were 62 from the latter. Another concentration (136 fragments) was associated with an early nineteenth-century pottery dump contained in reclamation deposits to the north of wall *3801* (*Ch 4, p 127*).

Made from the local red-firing boulder clays, black-glazed redwares are difficult to assign to a particular source, and still more difficult to date with any precision. There is, however, much similarity between the fabrics seen in this group and those from the Prescot kilns (Philpott and Davey 1989, especially fabric 6), and other South-West Lancashire potteries, known to have been major suppliers of black-glazed wares to Liverpool in the eighteenth century (Davey 1991, 135). Buckley, in Clwyd, also supplied Liverpool, especially in the earlier part of the eighteenth century, exporting many of its products to America via the port (Noël Hume 1969, 133), but few of the black-glazed wares in this group show the lamination of red-and-yellow-firing clays regarded as characteristic of this pottery, and it is not well-known from other excavations in Liverpool (J Speakman *pers comm*).

This fabric group shows a very restricted range of forms, being dominated by only two utilitarian vessel types. These consist of tall, more-or-less cylindrical, storage vessels with horizontal-lug handles similar to those seen at Prescot (Philpott and Davey 1989, figs 10.7.5, 10.8.10, 10.8.16), and in excavations in

194

South Castle Street, Liverpool (Davey and McNeil 1985), and large pancheons and/or bowls, again comparable to those from Prescot (Philpott and Davey 1989, fig 10.11.29), and the South Castle Street excavations (*ibid*). Given these similarities, it is likely that most were supplied from Prescot (*cf* McNeil 1989), although several other South-western Lancashire potteries would have produced similar vessels. Within the material from the Countryside Neptune site, and the Mann Island and Pier Head sections of the LLC extension, there are a few thinner-walled sherds, perhaps deriving from jugs or tankards. Other vessel forms represented by rims include shallow dishes, a more globular storage vessel, with a rim seated for a lid, whilst some of the bases also suggest more globular or tapering vessels, including relatively small globular-bodied jugs. Several sherds from the Mann Island and Pier Head sections of the LLC extension also suggest that some of the vessels were seconds, as occasional very large inclusions had caused large blisters or cracks in vessel walls and bases, a phenomenon also seen in sugar wares (*p 208*).

Self-glazed redwares
A small group of self-coloured coarseware vessels is present within the assemblage (Table 4), and is closely related to the black-glazed material, being in the same red-firing fabrics. Again, they can be paralleled with material from Prescot (*ibid*). Where their form can be reconstructed, these are all shallow bowls and dishes, although other vessel forms cannot be ruled out.

There are also a few fragments in speckled wares, current in the late seventeenth and eighteenth centuries (Barker and Halfpenny 1990), and, where the form can be determined, these too are from dishes and bowls. In addition, a single unstratified mottled redware dish was recovered from the Central Docks section of the LLC extension, and is probably in a similar fabric to the black-glazed vessels. Its deliberately heavily ridged profile probably had a specific purpose, but this has not been determined.

Brown stonewares
Brown stonewares, made in a number of different pottery centres, and in Liverpool from the late eighteenth century (Hildyard 2005, 38), form a relatively small element of the assemblage (Table 4), with the largest proportion recovered from the Countryside Neptune site. Types present comprise a range of utilitarian storage vessels, mainly small bottles, with smaller amounts of kitchenwares. There are several fragments of large globular bottles with narrow necks (Pl 183), possibly dating to after 1785 (Green 1999, 151). Most of the more recent vessels are small bottles, often labelled as containing blacking,

0   50mm

Plate 183: One of several large brown stoneware bottles, probably of late eighteenth-century date, from the Countryside Neptune site

a type mass-produced from *c* 1800 (Hildyard 2005, 35). Smaller storage or cooking vessels, some of them Nottingham stonewares, were also recovered from an early nineteenth-century pottery dump located to the north of wall **3801** (*Ch 4, p 127*), whilst the upright rim of a thin-walled possible jug came from the Central Docks section of the LLC extension. The unusual, highly blistered, appearance of this rim raises the possibility that it is a waster, or at best a second, from a local pottery.

Late stonewares of other colours were only recovered from the Countryside Neptune site and make up 0.35% (19 fragments) of the overall assemblage by fragment count and 1.26% by weight (3.25 kg). These are, again, utilitarian forms, including straight-sided 2 lb (0.9 kg) jars and flat lids. A vessel with an unusual square neck came from a modern drain to the east of George's Dock Passage and, as it bears a stamped registration mark, it can be dated with some precision to after 1876, the design having been registered on 28 December of that year (Coysh and Henrywood 1982, 299). A bottle from the base of the pit for one of the Pumping and Ventilation Station fans (*Ch 5, p 171*) bears the legend '*F Metcalf and sons. Fine spirit and porter merchants. South Shields*', and is thus one of the few indisputable imports which reached Mann Island.

195

In addition to the pottery, there is evidence from the Countryside Neptune and LLC extension sites for two other important Liverpool industries: clay tobacco pipe manufacture and sugar refining. The first relied, like the finer pottery manufacture, on imported clays coming into the port, whilst the other depended on imports of sugar and molasses from the West Indies (Sheridan 2000).

Clay tobacco-pipe industry
David A Higgins

The excavations produced a very large clay tobacco-pipe assemblage, some 41,700 fragments, dating, for the most part, to the end of the eighteenth century. Most of it (*c* 40,800 fragments) came from the Countryside Neptune site and the Mann Island elements of the LLC extension, with much smaller amounts (897 fragments) from the Pier Head and Central Docks section of the LLC extension. It comprises primarily production waste, dumped from local workshops, the names of which could be identified by the presence of distinctive stem stamps. First appearing during the second half of the eighteenth century (Higgins 2008, 132), these stamps comprise a long, single-line mark containing the maker's name and place of work (in this case Liverpool) in relief lettering.

The largest dumps, from the Countryside Neptune site and the Mann Island section of the LLC

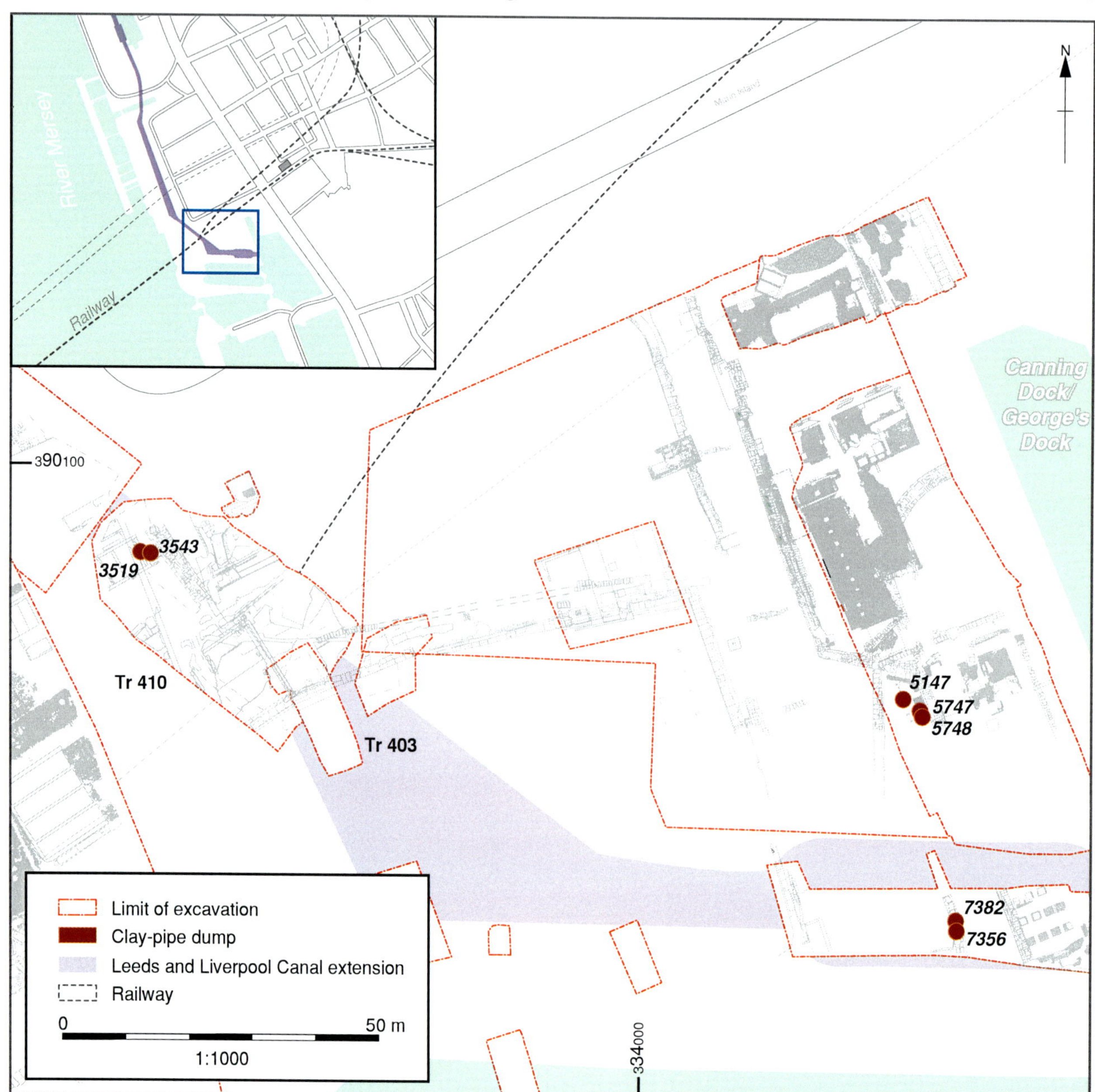

Figure 74: The locations of the clay tobacco-pipe kiln dumps (© Crown copyright 2014 Ordnance Survey 100005569)

extension, were subject to detailed analysis, the results of which will appear in a separate volume concentrating on the finds from the docks (Philpott in prep). The methodologies adopted for this study and the rationale behind them are found within the project archive (Higgins 2011a; 2011b; 2012). These dumps are the first from the city to have been studied in detail, providing an important step in defining the range of pipes produced, and some insight into the dynamics of, and interaction between, individual workshops.

The dumps from reclamation associated with the construction of Manchester Basin

Five tobacco-pipe kiln dumps (*7382, 7356, 5147, 5748,* and *5747;* Fig 74) were recovered from reclamation deposits, which were associated with the creation of Manchester Basin in the last decades of the eighteenth century (*Ch 3, p 78*). Two of the dumps (*7382* and *7356*) fell within the Mann Island section of the LLC extension, producing 5830 fragments, along with very large quantities of other production debris. One of them (*7382*) produced only stamps belonging to William Morgan, but the other (*7356*) included those of both William Morgan and Thomas Hayes, two prominent makers at the end of the eighteenth century (Higgins 2012). The dumps had many mould types in common, suggesting that they were not only related, but also contemporary. The remaining three dumps (*5147, 5747,* and *5748*) were recovered from the Countryside Neptune excavations, and all derived from William Morgan's workshop. The vast majority of the material (33,500 fragments, out of a total of 33,708) were derived from dump *5747*, however.

The kiln dumps of late eighteenth-century date come from a period when Liverpool had an internationally important pipe-making industry, and was rapidly eclipsing Chester both as a port and a pipe-production centre (Higgins 2008, 138). While the stems of this period changed little in form and are, therefore, difficult to date, the bowl forms, maker's marks, and decorated pieces, all provide reliable evidence, suggesting that the land reclamation containing this material did not take place until after *c* 1780 (*Ch 3, p 78*).

Kiln dump 7382
The assemblage (640 bowl fragments, 1527 stems, and 102 mouthpiece fragments) included 41 marked stem fragments, representing at least 20 different pipes. As the name stamps are exclusively those of W Morgan (Pl 184), the entire group has been attributed to his factory. There are, however, two documented pipe-makers of this name, who worked between 1767 and 1822 (*eg* Gore 1767; 1823), but the context suggests that this group dates from the 1780s, and can thus be attributed to the earlier of them, William (I). This dating is reinforced by the fact that many of the mould types are duplicated in the second kiln group (*7356; p 199*), which also produced the marks of Thomas Hayes (II), who was working from *c* 1780-1800 (Gore 1787; 1790; 1796; 1800).

In total, 14 mould types were identified (Types A-I, K-O), but there may well have been more, as some

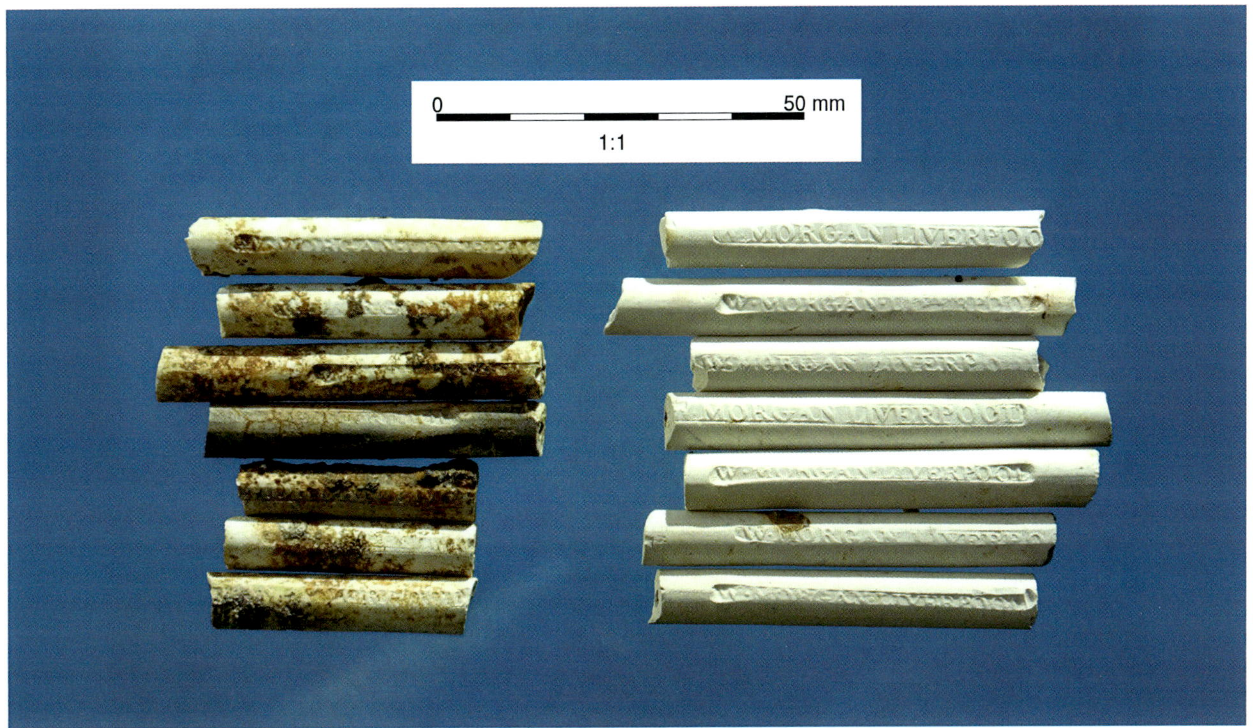

Plate 184: Stamped-stem fragments of W Morgan of the 1780s, before cleaning with EDTA, and after

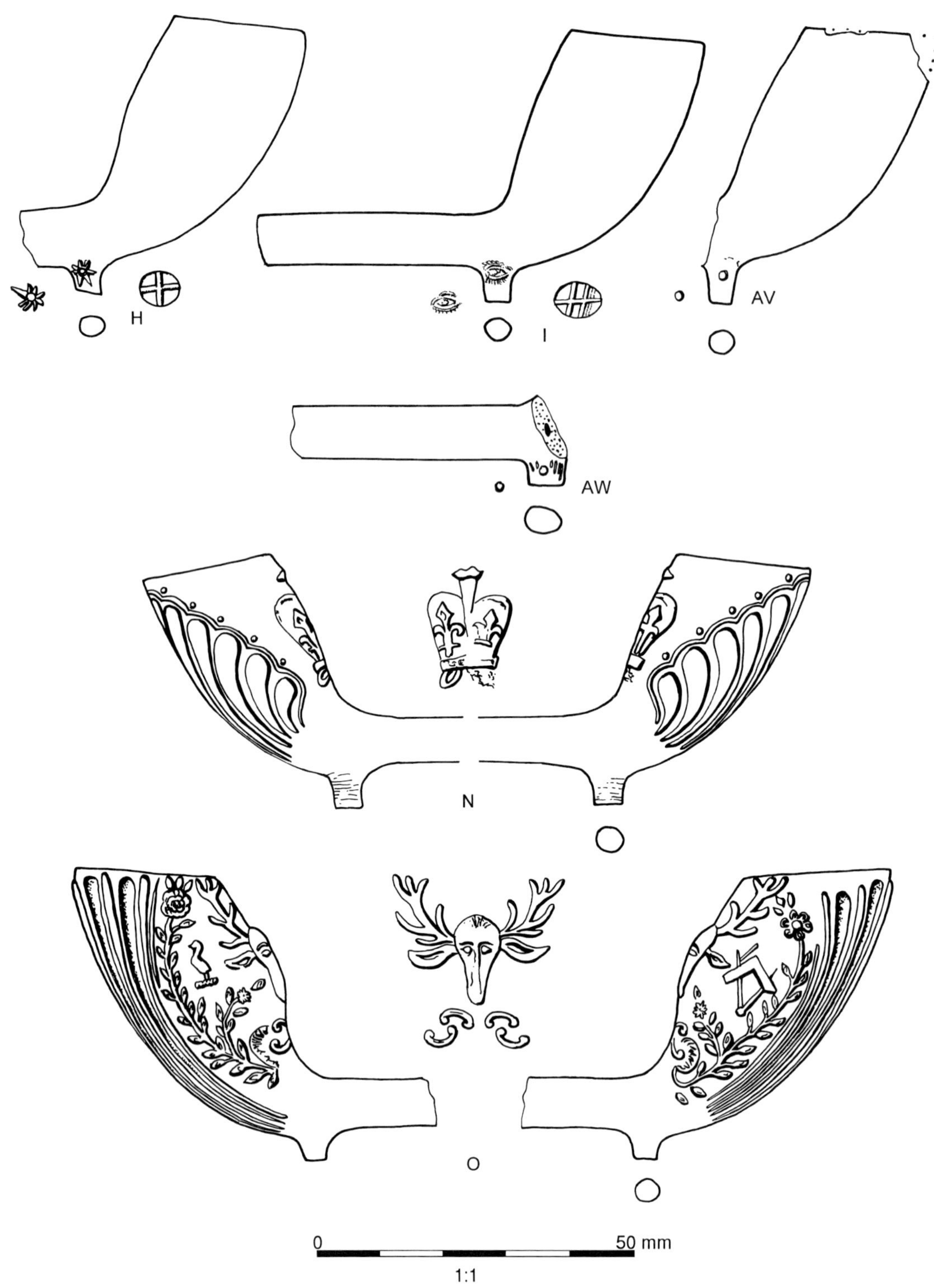

Figure 75: Clay tobacco-pipe bowls produced by William Morgan in the 1780s

fragments were too small for detailed identification. Evidence from another of the dumps (**5747**; *p 201*) confirms that all of them were produced by Morgan's workshop, but also adds at least three, and possibly as many as seven, more (Types AQ-AW).

Most of Morgan's forms (19 of the 21 defined) are plain, with three of them (A-C) being heel-less export types. These were not used in England until the middle of the nineteenth century (*cf* Atkinson and Oswald 1969) and thus the fact that this dump is of substantially earlier date makes it clear that Liverpool makers were producing for the specific requirements of the export trade, and not just for home markets. Ships from Liverpool were heavily involved in the slave trade, and the much larger export-style pipes (forms A and B) were almost certainly produced as trade goods to be used in bartering for slaves, as well as for sale in the Caribbean and North American markets (Higgins 1995).

The other plain forms represent a range of sizes and styles that would have been intended for both the home and the export markets. Several have internal bowl crosses and four have relief-moulded marks on the sides of the heel: a star (Type H); an 'all-seeing eye' motif, drawn from Masonic iconography (Type I); a single dot on each side of the heel (Types AV and AW; Fig 75). Two of the mould types are highly decorated, one with scalloped decoration and a crown facing the smoker (Type N), and the other with a range of motifs, including a Liver Bird on the left-hand side of the bowl, a square and compasses on the right-hand side, and a stag's head facing the smoker (Type O). The fluted decoration is particularly distinctive on this type, comprising alternating concave and convex flutes, a style particularly associated with the Liverpool area, and only used towards the end of the eighteenth century (*pers obs*). The bowl form itself is also typical of the time and place, being characterised by a very slender base to a large, relatively thin-walled bowl, with the rim dipping slightly back towards the smoker.

The presence of nine glazed mouthpieces shows that William Morgan (I) was producing glazed tips, and provides the earliest firm evidence for this practice from the Liverpool area. The colour of the glaze varies, but the majority are pale green or yellowish/light brown. It is not certain whether all the pipes had glazed tips or whether it was confined to certain types, as most of the pipes in the dump are likely to have been discarded after their initial firing, and the glazed tips were most probably applied as a secondary process. Indeed, it would not be surprising if this, at the time, innovative, finishing technique was reserved for the better-quality and/or more-expensive types.

Kiln dump **7356**
Although somewhat larger than **7382** (684 bowl fragments, 2669 stem, and 208 mouthpieces), the two dumps are clearly related, as nine of the 15 mould-types present in **7382** are duplicated in this group. Whilst apparently contemporary, it is unusual in producing stem marks from two different makers, with 13 stamped fragments attributable to William Morgan (I), and 62 to Thomas Hayes (II). Analysis suggests that around three-quarters of the identifiable pipes are attributable to Hayes, and further, that nine of the mould types which appear in both dumps can be attributed to Morgan, whilst the new types can probably all be attributed to Hayes.

Thomas Hayes (II) is only recorded in trade directories from 1787-1800 (*eg* Gore 1787; 1790; 1796; 1800),

although it is likely that he was running the nearby Strand Street factory from *c* 1780. It is, therefore, almost certain that this dump can be dated to the last two decades of the eighteenth century. If the group represents, as seems likely, an early phase of Hayes' production, then a date of *c* 1780-90 can be suggested, which matches that of dump **7382** (*p 197*). As documentary evidence suggests that there was probably a family connection between Hayes and Morgan (*p 206*), it seems reasonable to suggest a partnership of sorts, which would explain why their waste was dumped together.

As the maker's marks are often poorly impressed or broken, it is very hard to separate individual die types, but there seem to be minima of four types for Hayes and two for Morgan. The number of different dies represented must therefore imply that these were significant manufactories, with several different workers producing pipes.

There are 17 mould types unique to this dump, all of which have been attributed to the workshop of Thomas Hayes (II) (Types P-AF). They reflect a similar range of products to those of William Morgan, with two decorated and 17 (probably) plain forms. The two decorated forms (Types P and Q; Fig 76) are very similar to each other, and also to one, produced by Morgan, that includes the use of alternate concave and convex flutes (Type O; Fig 75). The bowl forms produced by Hayes are, however, generally less slender at the base, and the rim angle sometimes dips away from, rather than towards, the smoker (Fig 77). This style is probably slightly later than that used by Morgan, although they were obviously in contemporary production. The plain forms are also similar to Morgan's, including an export style (Type R; Fig 76), as well as a range of other forms, both large and small. The main difference between the two producers lies not so much in the range, but in emphasis, with Hayes apparently producing a larger number of smaller forms, but fewer export types.

Several of the pipes attributed to Hayes have internal bowl crosses, and five have moulded marks; two are stars (Types W and X), two others are probably intended as an 'all-seeing eye' (Types Z and AA), and one (Type AB) appears to be the initials TH, for Thomas Hayes. The use of moulded initials is very rare in the North West (*pers obs*), and, in addition, the initials appear on the heel in an unusual upright orientation. The mould-maker appears to have had trouble engraving the letters, with the H apparently cut twice in different orientations, leaving a grid-like mark, which is possibly superimposed on a T underneath. One of the few parallels in the North West is a fluted bowl of *c* 1770-90 in the Grosvenor

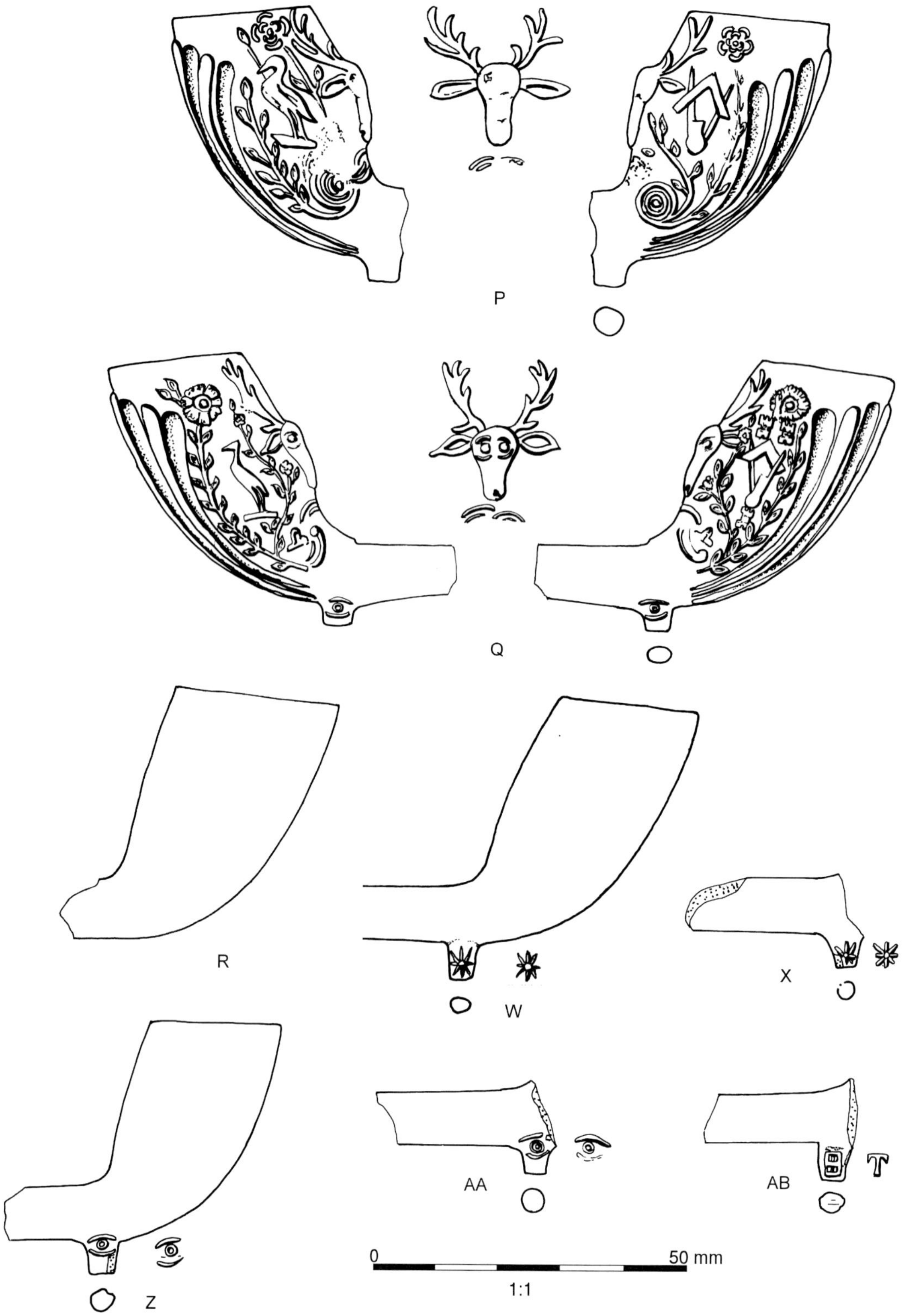

Figure 76: Clay tobacco-pipe bowls produced by Thomas Hayes

Museum, Chester (GVS 84-5), with the upright initials IH on the spur, most likely for John Hall of Chester, working *c* 1750-1818 (Rutter and Davey 1980, 241). One of the star designs is only represented by a broken-off spur, but it can be matched with a complete example from excavations in Poole, Dorset, which retains its T Hayes stem stamp (*pers obs*).

One of the mould types is of particular interest, in that it occurs in two distinct forms, albeit clearly from the same mould, which has distinctive flaws on the sides of the heel. One version is much taller than the other (Types Ya and Yb), and it is clear that the mould has been modified by cutting down its rim, thereby producing a shorter bowl with a more compact appearance.

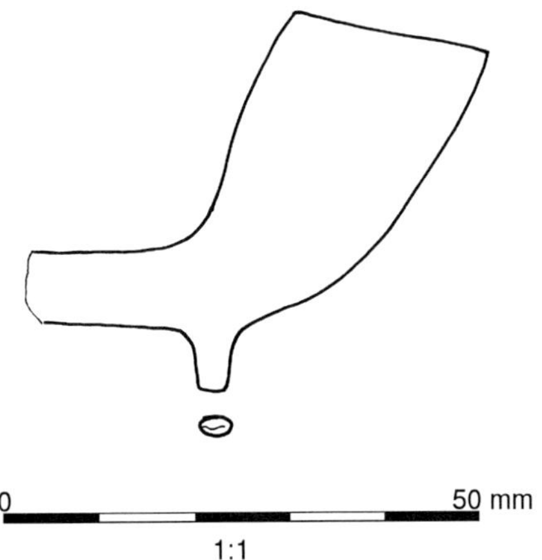

Figure 77: Clay tobacco-pipe bowl produced by Thomas Hayes in the 1780s

There is, again, evidence for glazed tips, with ten mouthpieces and 53 stems having glaze on them. The colour was mainly a vivid dark green or a range of browns. During the nineteenth century, a 'tipping muffle' was used to glaze stems (Peacey 1996, 183), but a piece of kiln debris (a roughly triangular-sectioned, applied clay strip, with glaze runs and broken stems adhering) from this dump suggests that an earlier method, whereby the tips were glazed in the main kiln rather than in a separate tipping muffle, had been used by Hayes. This is probably the earliest evidence from the entire country for how the pipes were tipped, and represents a technique somewhat different from that which became the norm (*pers obs*).

There were, in addition, tens of thousands of fragments of kiln debris, clearly showing that both Morgan and Hayes appear to have been using developed muffle kilns of the type that had become fairly standard by the end of the eighteenth century (Peacey 1996). Some pieces of the slag/stem laminate include stamped stems, confirming that the waste did indeed come from the factories of Morgan and Hayes.

Kiln dump 5147
The small group comprising dump *5147* contained 29 bowls. None had been smoked, and many of the stems are over-fired or encrusted with clay or slag from having been used in muffle construction. Other fragments of kiln debris were present, so that it is clear that this is kiln waste.

Again, the material can be attributed to William Morgan (I), with nine of the stems stamped with a single-line maker's mark, reading 'W. MORGAN LIVERPOOL', and at least two different dies are represented. Although none of the seven cut mouthpieces is glazed, there are three stem fragments with yellowish-green glaze on them, showing that some of the pipes had glazed tips. The bowls are rather fragmentary, but eight different

mould types can be identified, all matched by those in dump *7382* (*p 197*), implying that this is another contemporary deposit.

Kiln dump 5748
Dump *5748* was found close to dump *5747* (*see below*). It contained 179 pieces of clay tobacco pipe, with 31 unsmoked bowls, and three fragments of kiln-waste. The material can, again, be attributed to William Morgan (I), as all of the identifiable examples can be matched with those in dump *7382* (*p 197*). There are 22 plain bowl fragments, including two with moulded marks (one with stars and one with 'all-seeing eyes'; Types H and I; Fig 75; *p 199*), and nine mould-decorated fragments (eight of type N and one of type O).

Kiln dump 5747
Dump *5747* is by far the most important of those encountered, being the largest from Liverpool yet to be studied. In total, it is estimated that it comprised some 33,500 pipe fragments (*c* 6800 bowl fragments, 25,700 stem, and 1000 mouthpieces), as well as more than 1000 fragments from kiln supplements used during the firing process. Again associated with William Morgan (I), it dates from the 1780s, and was deposited during land reclamation associated with the construction of the Manchester Basin (*Ch 3, p 78*).

It is well-known that pipe makers at this period would have produced a range of different pipe styles for different markets, including the export trade (Jackson and Price 1974, 84), and the large size of this group probably ensures that a full range of products has been identified. It produced multiple examples of 14 (Types A-O) of the 15 mould types seen in dump *7382*, confirming their identification as Morgan products. The only form not represented was Type J, which suggests that this stray spur was from a pipe produced elsewhere, or that it was intrusive. As well as the 14 bowl forms, there are at least three, and possibly as many as seven, more of Morgan's types in this dump (Types AQ-AW), bringing the total number of forms recognised to between 17 and 21, at least three of which were specifically for export (*p 199*). Three of the new mould types are represented by multiple examples (Types AQ-AS), but the four others (Types AT-AW) are only represented by one or two examples each, and thus cannot be attributed with complete confidence. As they do not appear to have been smoked, however, and as two of them seem to be wasters, there is a strong case for their having been made by Morgan. All seven had plain bowls, four having internal bowl crosses (Types AR-AU), and two having moulded dot marks on the spur sides (Types AV-AW).

The group produced about 550 marked stem fragments (representing *c* 230 complete marks) of at least two different stamp types, all of which can be attributed

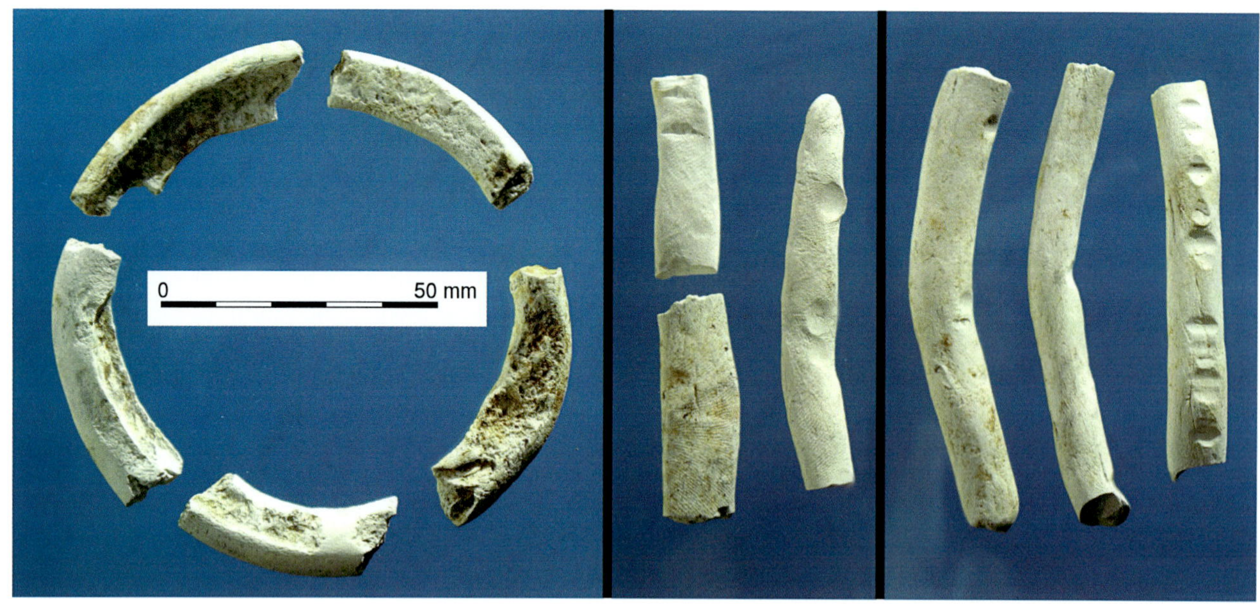

Plate 185: Examples of ring wads, applied strips, and rolls

to William Morgan (Pl 184), demonstrating that this is a large and uncontaminated group. The estimated number of complete marks is much smaller than the number of pipes indicated by the presence of 1000 mouthpieces, possibly suggesting that only 20-25% of the pipes produced at the factory were stamped.

Several of the stems and/or mouthpieces were glazed (*c* 190 fragments), in order to prevent the dry clay of the pipe sticking to the smoker's lips. This was still a relatively new introduction in the 1780s, with the earliest recorded use in this country coming from Staveley Hall in Derbyshire, where examples occur in a house-clearance group dating from the second quarter of the eighteenth century (*pers obs*). The Staveley group is, however, unusually early, and comes from a high-status household. In contrast, the Morgan factory was clearly producing an everyday range of pipes, typical of Liverpool products of the period, which suggests that it was common practice in Liverpool by this date, and making this the earliest firm evidence for any widespread use of the technique. The glazes used ranged in colour from dark green, through pale limes and yellows, to dark browns.

Kiln dump **5747** did not produce any evidence for the nature of the kiln itself, or any of the furniture that would have been used within it. There was, however, a good sample of supplements, including 'ring wads', 'applied strips', and 'rolls', (Pl 185), which were used to bed the kiln furniture and support the pipes during firing within the kiln. All of the historical accounts and illustrations of the firing process show pipes stacked in the kiln with the bowl downwards, and the ends of the stems resting on a central mushroom support (Peacey 1996; Fig 78).

There were also copious amounts of 'slag/stem laminate', which illustrate the commonly seen use of previously fired pipe stems to provide the framework for a layer of clay, ash, and horse manure, that was used to seal the top of the muffle chamber during firing (*op cit*, 168-71). The mixture

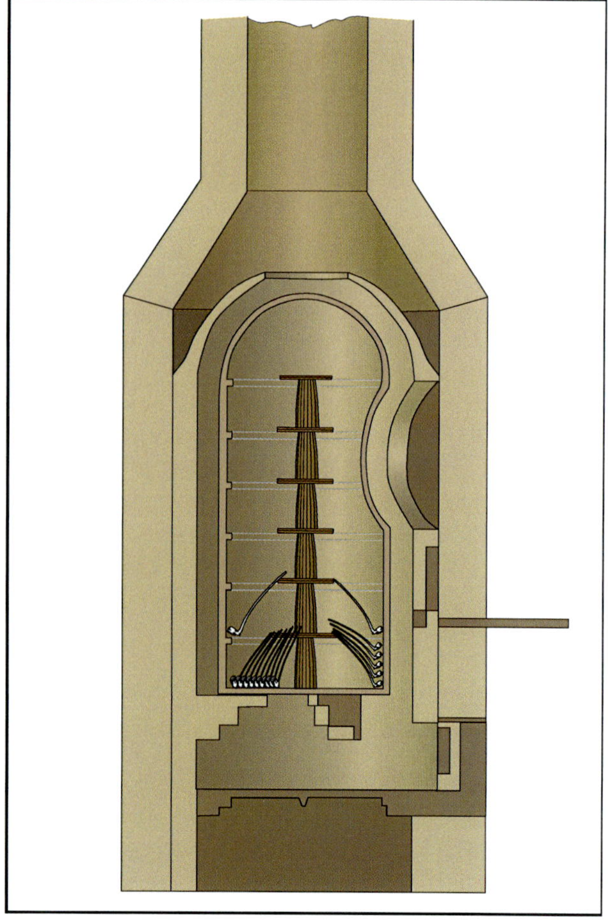

Figure 78: Section through a clay-pipe kiln

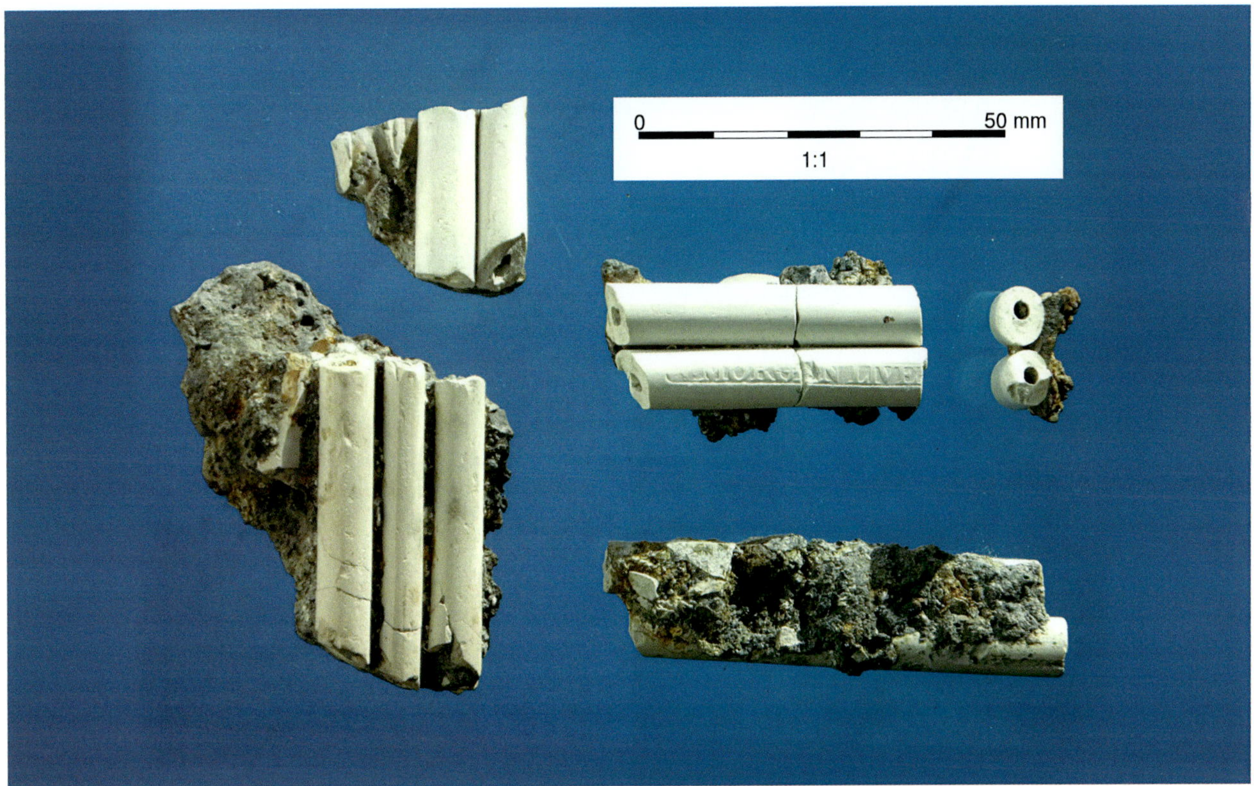

*Plate 186: Slag/stem laminate from the W Morgan kiln dump, **5747**, of the 1780s, including a stem with part of a 'W.MORGAN LIVERPOOL' stamp surviving*

became slaggy during the firing and fused to the pipe-stem framework. Many of the waste stems from **5747** have slaggy deposits adhering, and there are several chunks containing multiple stems, showing that this technique was being used by Morgan in the 1780s (Pl 186), probably some 40 years earlier than the earliest previously recorded use (*op cit*, 171).

Hayes' later dumps from between Chester Basin and the Manchester Dock

The Pier Head excavations on the LLC extension produced another 866 pipe fragments, ranging in date from the mid-eighteenth to the mid-nineteenth century. This included material from two small, late eighteenth-century dumps (**3519** and **3543**; Fig 74), derived from the Thomas Hayes (II) workshop, both dating to *c* 1795.

Kiln dump **3519**

Dump **3519** was found within reclamation deposits in Tr 410, west of river wall **3544** (*Ch 3, p 78*), which were probably laid down in *c* 1795. It comprised a small group of seven bowls, 62 stems, and 12 mouthpieces. As all of the bowls are unsmoked, and one has a piece of clay sheet from the kiln adhering to its rim, these have been identified as kiln waste. The bowls are all plain, and several have trimmed heels, a finishing technique that went out of use around 1800 (*pers obs*).

Three stem stamps were noted (from three different pipes), all of which appear to be marks used by Thomas Hayes (II), who was working *c* 1780-1800 (*p 197*). Four mould types are represented (Types AH, AL, AM, and AP), the first three duplicating types in dump **3543** (*see below*); the fourth is a spur bowl. As the stem marks also duplicate those from **3543**, the two deposits are clearly very closely related. The 12 mouthpieces are all unglazed, with simple cut ends, although there was a stem fragment with splashes of yellowish-brown glaze.

Kiln dump **3543**

Dump **3543** lay very close to **3519**, and is probably contemporary. It produced 125 bowl fragments, 531 stems, and 50 mouthpieces. Again, all of the 20 marked stem fragments can be attributed to Thomas Hayes (II), being inscribed with a long, single-line stamp. At least two different die types are represented, one of which is also seen in dump **3519** (*see above*). The second is unique amongst the dies, in having a numeral, in this case '2', added to the end of the die, so that it reads 'T.HAYES.LIVERPOOL.2'.

Neither the stamp types, nor the mould types, correspond to those seen in the earlier Hayes' workshop material from Mann Island (dump **7356**; *p 199*), which was dated to the 1780s, perhaps suggesting that the pipes in **3543** might be later. Indeed, some of the decorated pipes would normally

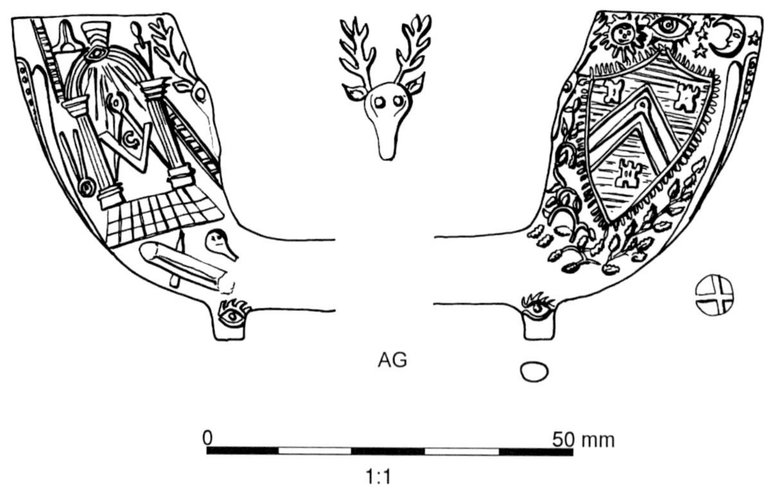

0   50 mm

1:1

Figure 79: Decorated clay tobacco-pipe bowl produced by Thomas Hayes in c 1795

be regarded as nineteenth-century types and, as Hayes had died by 1803 (Gore 1803), this allows the group to be placed at the very end of the eighteenth century.

There are no spurless export-style pipes in this dump, but the group is too small to determine whether this reflects a change in fashion, or a particular production batch. A few of the bowls, all from a single mould type (Type AG), are highly decorated, their sides covered with a wide range of Masonic motifs (Fig 79). Similar pipes from dump *7382* bore depictions of the Liver Bird and stags' heads (*p 199*), but this new design has a rather more upright bowl style, and it would appear that the earlier designs had fallen out of use. The fluted decoration and stags' heads are still present, however, but the other decorative motifs have been expanded to cover almost all the bowl's surface.

The majority of the forms from this group are plain, appearing in a range of sizes and styles (Types AH-AM). There are also two forms with simple leaf-decorated seams (Types AN-AO), a type of decoration that became very widely used from the early nineteenth century onwards (*pers obs*). Only one of the 50 mouthpieces is glazed (a translucent pale lime green/yellow), but there are stem fragments with traces of a similar colour glaze. This low incidence suggests either that glaze was rarely used at this point, or that this dump comprised waste from the actual firing process, rather than any secondary tipping process.

There is also a small amount of a range of waste characteristic of that from a developed muffle kiln (Peacey 1996, fig 94). The fuel used was clearly coal, as small fragments survive, as do large quantities of ash and cinder.

Other pipes
In addition to the well-defined kiln dumps, numerous other fragments of clay tobacco pipe

were recovered, offering a rare opportunity to study some of Liverpool's post-medieval trading connections. Most date from the mid-eighteenth to the late nineteenth or early twentieth century, but there are also a few residual seventeenth-century fragments.

A spur bowl with Masonic decoration, dated to *c* 1770-1810, came from cellar floor *5708* (*Ch 3, p 87*). Although Masonic motifs were commonly used in the Liverpool area (*p 199*), this example is in a Yorkshire style (White 2004, 567), and is thus presumably imported. Other imports include a late seventeenth-century bowl manufactured in London (Fig 80), and a stem of Dutch origin. Pipes from the Netherlands are generally very rare in the UK and, when they do occur, they are most frequently encountered in ports, where they probably reflect casual loss by sailors, rather than trade (Higgins 2009, 43).

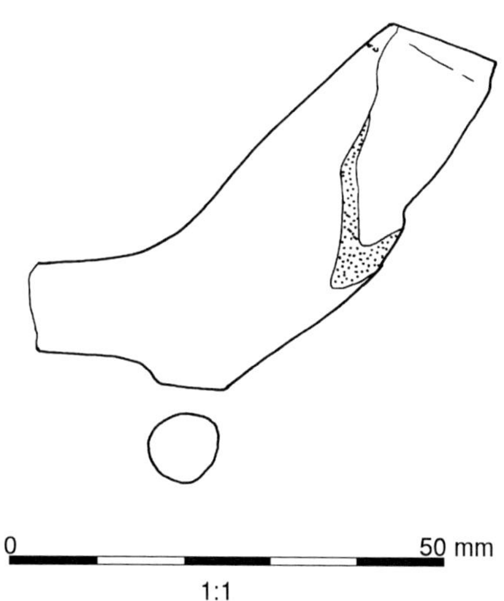

0   50 mm

1:1

Figure 80: Late seventeenth-century clay tobacco-pipe bowl, manufactured in London

204

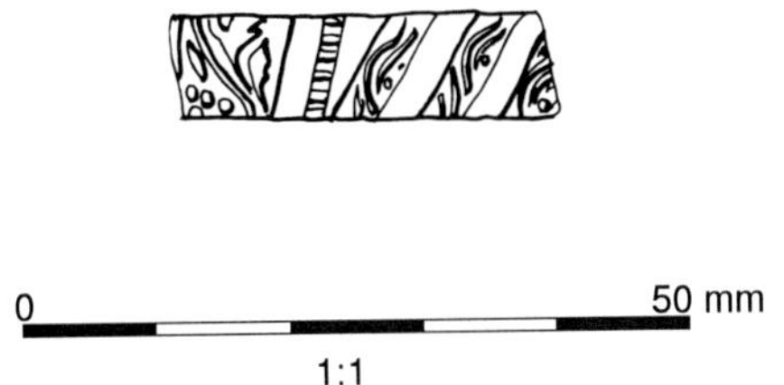

Figure 81: *Elaborately decorated eighteenth-century clay tobacco-pipe stem*

Fragments from the Countryside Neptune site included 39 that were marked with the maker's name. Other notable examples include an elaborately decorated eighteenth-century stem (Fig 81) from *5122*, backfill overlying a cobbled area of the quayside at Nova Scotia (*Ch 3, p 80*). Its tendril border and decorated stem twist are characteristic of pipes produced in Chester in *c* 1720-80 (Rutter and Davey 1980). Similar pipes with ornately decorated stems were also produced in Rainford (Dagnall 1987) and production might be expected in Liverpool as well, where the pipe makers would have been in direct competition with those from Chester, especially for overseas orders.

The group also includes a range of distinctive decorated pipes produced in the Liverpool area, all of which employ particular motifs, such as a stag's head facing the smoker, Masonic emblems, the Liver Bird, and flower/foliage motifs. They include a particularly unusual example from a demolition layer, which has a stag's head facing the smoker, and flutes on the opposing side. The right-hand side of the bowl is largely missing, but has traces of Masonic decoration, but, unusually, the left-hand side depicts the Glasgow Arms (a bird sitting on a tree with a bell and fish; Fig 82). It dates from *c* 1780-1810, is the earliest known example of the Glasgow Arms being used to decorate a pipe, and it seems likely that this is a Liverpool product, intended for export. The design is shown in various early twentieth-century trade

catalogues (*cf* Jung 2003, 390) and has been seen on late nineteenth-century pipes, but never before on anything earlier than *c* 1860 (*pers obs*).

There are also some slightly later pipes (*c* 1820-50), which are typically decorated with a panel containing a variety of motifs above fluted decoration and, sometimes, a shield, with the maker's initials, facing the smoker. An example, marked EM in a shield (Fig 83), can be attributed to Elizabeth Morgan (working 1816-39; Gore 1816; 1839). There are not many late nineteenth- to early twentieth-century pipes, but a few provide evidence for the kinds that were being used in the waterfront areas at that time. They include examples marked with pattern names, such as 'LONDON' or 'DUBLIN PIPE' (Fig 84), as well as makers' marks from firms in other areas. These include McDougall's of Glasgow, which was in operation from 1846 to 1967 (Anon 1987, 356), and

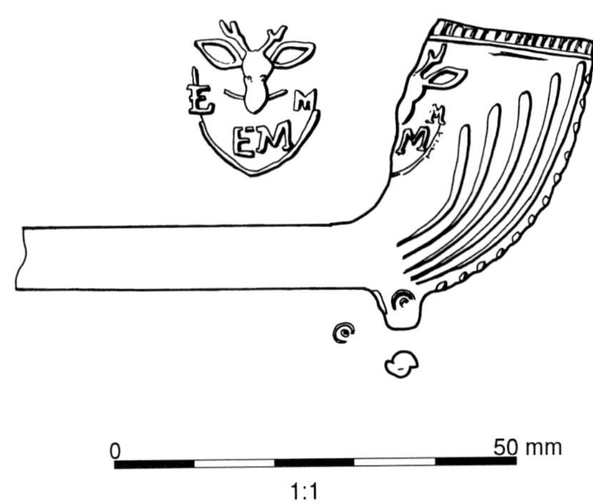

Figure 83: *Decorated clay tobacco-pipe bowl, marked 'EM'*

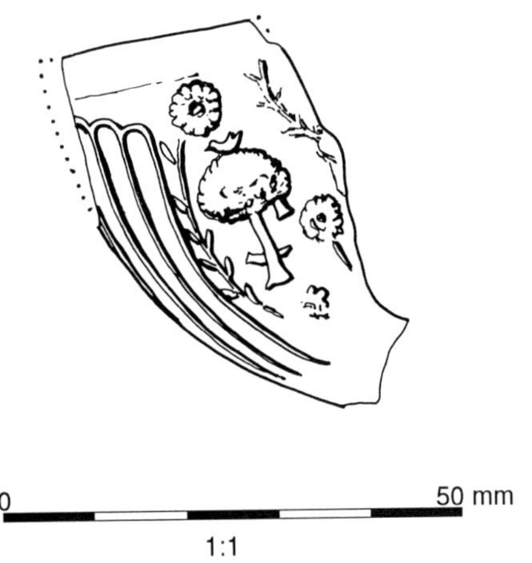

Figure 82: *Clay tobacco-pipe bowl decorated with the Glasgow Arms*

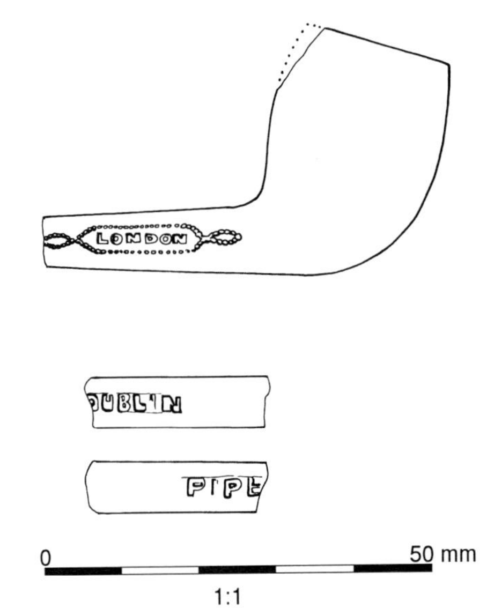

Figure 84: *Clay tobacco-pipe bowl, marked 'LONDON', and a stem marked 'DUBLIN PIPE'*

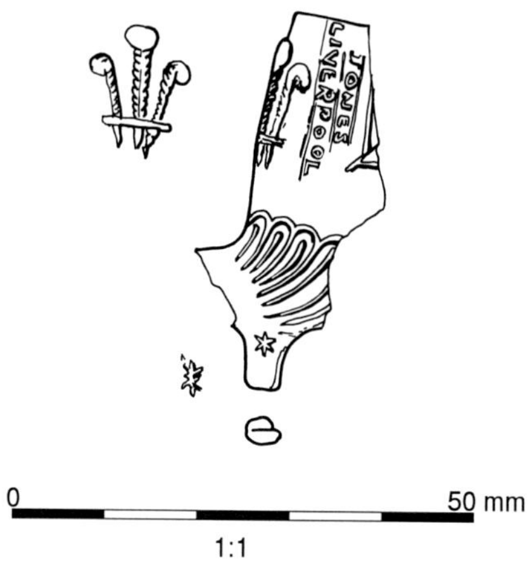

Figure 85: Clay tobacco-pipe bowl marked with 'JONES/ LIVERPOOL'

Southorn's of Broseley, both of whom had agents in Liverpool during the second half of the nineteenth century, and were shipping their products out of the port (*eg* Gore 1874; 1882; 1892). These came from a fairly large assemblage (five bowls, 132 stems, and 14 mouthpiece fragments), from the backfill (**5116**) of the cellar (**5114**) of a late eighteenth-century warehouse (*Ch 3, p 83*). The lack of bowl fragments, and the extensive burning, suggests that they were from a domestic deposit, rather than being kiln waste, with the most likely date of deposition being the 1850s.

Another bowl, with enclosed flutes at the base, the Prince of Wales feathers facing the smoker, and a small star on each side of the spur, is marked 'JONES/ LIVERPOOL' in relief on the right-hand side (Fig 85). The lettering is in an unusual location, being upright, and running from top to bottom of the bowl. It has no known parallels, but was made by either John Jones (father), or John George (son), of Liverpool, who only worked on their own from *c* 1835-57 (*eg* Gore 1835; 1857).

Discussion

Despite its pre-eminence as a maritime port, and the concomitant access to world-wide export markets, the eighteenth- and nineteenth-century pipe producers of Liverpool, who would have serviced those markets, are not well-known, even though, by the 1830s, Lancashire (which then included Liverpool) contained no less than 17.4% of all English pipe makers (Higgins 2008, 138). More than 350 pipe makers have been documented as working in the city, and pipes bearing Liverpool marks or designs are well-known from Canada to the Caribbean, and from Africa to Australasia. Despite this, there has been almost no publication of pipes or of kiln waste from the city, which presently makes it almost impossible for researchers to identify and date Liverpool pipes.

The assemblage was dominated by production and kiln waste dumped by two related manufacturers, who clearly worked closely together in the last quarter of the eighteenth century, perhaps sharing workers and/or premises, as well has having possible familial links (*see below*). Analysis has allowed their products to be much better understood, with their form, decoration, and, importantly, the maker's stamps and dies fully recorded, and dated with some precision.

Stem stamps identified the two manufacturers as William Morgan (I) and Thomas Hayes (II). William, the son of a tailor, was born in Liverpool in 1743 (LVRO 283 SMW/1/4). It is not clear when he began to make pipes, but, from 1767 onwards, when he was 23 or 24 years old, he appeared regularly in the early trade directories (*eg* Gore 1767). He could have set up his business before this, but it is unlikely that he would have been working independently before his 21st birthday in 1764. He moved between several different addresses during his career: in 1796 he was in Gradwell Street (Gore 1796), with a second manufactory in Parliament Street. This is the only reference to William having a Parliament Street address, but, between 1816 and 1839, later members of the family are recorded as having a pipe warehouse and/or manufactory there (Gore 1816; 1821; 1823; 1825; 1827; 1832; 1834; 1835; 1837; 1839), presumably on the site established by him. William Morgan died in 1804, aged 61, and was described in the burial register as a pipe maker (LVRO 283 NIC/1/8). Evidence suggests that he might have retired around 1800, as a directory entry for 1803 lists a 'William Morgan Junior' in Gradwell Street (Gore 1803), presumably indicating that a son of the same name had taken over the business.

There is less documentary background for the career of Thomas Hayes (II). He is only recorded in directories in the period 1787-1800 (Gore 1787; 1790; 1796; 1800), but it is likely that he was running the nearby Strand Street factory from 1780, when he married Lydia (née Banner), the widow of pipemaker Johnathan Hutchinson, who had previously occupied the site (LVRO 283 PET, 3 October 1780; Gore 1777). Interestingly, the parish registers of St Nicholas (LVRO 283 NIC/1/6), recording the death of William Morgan's daughter Kitty in 1794, note the maiden name of his wife as Mary Hayes. This raises the possibility that she came from the prominent Hayes family of pipe makers, and so could have been a close relative of Thomas Hayes, which would explain the close collaboration between the two men.

The range of forms seen in the waste dumps also shows that they were producing pipes in a number of styles, including spurless export pipes (probably with short stems), plain and decorated pipes with large bowls (probably with long stems), and plain pipes with smaller bowls (medium-length stems). There was also some evidence for the rapid evolution of bowl forms and decorative styles, with Morgan's decorated forms looking slightly outdated in comparison to those used by Hayes, which, in turn, could be seen to evolve between dumps dating from the 1780s and *c* 1795. Although his visit to the Liverpool pipe factories in the 1750s is somewhat earlier in date, the Swedish industrial spy, John Julius Angerstein, records a similarly wide range of products, noting that 'pipes sold for 9 pence to 30 pence per gross' (Berg and Berg 2001, 311), showing that the best pipes were selling for more than three times the cost of the cheapest.

Documentary research has allowed the production periods to be defined quite closely, and analysis of the kiln debris (Higgins in prep) has established that both manufacturers were using developed muffle kilns to produce their wares, of the type that had become fairly standard by the end of the eighteenth century (Peacey 1996). There were, however, idiosyncrasies, and it seems that mouthpieces were glazed within the main kiln, rather than in a separate 'tipping muffle', as was the case in the nineteenth century.

The assemblages also give some indication of the scale of late eighteenth-century production. Evidence shows that William Morgan was using at least 17-21 different moulds during the 1780s, and Thomas Hayes produced at least 17 pipe types during the 1780s and ten during the 1790s. Assuming that each maker had all their mould types in simultaneous use (*ie*, with some 10-20 moulding benches being used in any given factory), then the workshops would have been capable of producing at a scale comparable with the enormous numbers of pipes known to have been shipped from the city at that time. For example, the shipping records for 1770 show that some 5535 gross (797,040 pipes) were exported in that year alone (Higgins 2008, 138).

The sugar-refining industry

Sugar refining has been associated with Liverpool since the seventeenth century, when the first sugar house was set up by Richard Cleaveland and Daniel Danvers (Brown 1993, 16), and by 1756 there was a pottery factory (the Mould Works, near the Infirmary) making, among other things, sugar moulds and drips and, significantly, selling them 'on the same terms as for Prescot, Sutton and other places' (Smith 1970, 5), which were also undoubtedly supplying Liverpool's sugar-refining needs. By 1773, there were eight sugar houses in the town (Brown 1993, 16), which probably would have had a huge and increasing requirement for the moulds and syrup jars used in refining. Furthermore, in the period 1785-1810, the sugar trade through Liverpool increased by 277% (Hyde 1971, 26), leading to a concomitant need for moulds and refining jars.

Plate 187: The rim of a syrup jar

Sugar wares (sugar-loaf moulds and syrup-collecting jars) comprise a significant element of the pottery assemblage (1098 fragments; 20.5% by fragment count and 29.88% by weight; Table 4) and several deposits were identified which contained considerable amounts. At the Countryside Neptune site, these included two dumps from eighteenth-century land-reclamation deposits to the east of river wall **7638** (*Ch 3, p 62*). One of these dumps contained 309 fragments, whilst the other produced 138 fragments. In addition, during excavation on the Mann Island section of the LLC extension, vessel fragments were particularly concentrated in two late eighteenth-century reclamation layers west of slip wall **7325** (*Ch 3, p 64*); the earlier layer contained 72 fragments, whilst the later contained 42 fragments. Another concentration (78 fragments) was present in the early nineteenth-century pottery dump located to the north of river wall **3801** (*Ch 4, p 127*).

There are large numbers of rim fragments from relatively large-diameter sugar-loaf moulds (Pl 187), and variations in the rim profiles make it clear that there are numerous moulds present. Several of the fragments appear to have rows of small holes running across them, which does not seem to be a normal feature, and might point to a more specialised use, or a specific manufacturer, or could, perhaps, have served to bear supporting bands used round some moulds (J Speakman *pers comm*). In addition, the assemblage contains the basal apertures from several moulds (Pl 188), and glazed rim fragments from a number of syrup jars, as well as three small pinched feet in a fabric similar to the loaf moulds, which could also derive from syrup jars.

These vessels almost certainly originate from the local sugar-refining industry, and were made in Liverpool, or perhaps Prescot, where it has been established that sugar wares were also produced during the early eighteenth century (McNeil 1989), in fabrics

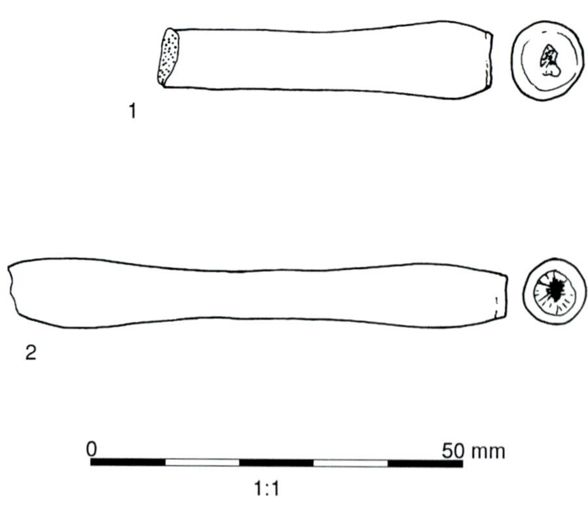

Figure 86: Pipe-clay hair curlers

Plate 188: The perforated base of a sugar-loaf mould

effectively identical to those from these excavations. Interestingly, syrup-collecting jars at Prescot are described as over-fired to vitrification, and a high proportion of fragments in the Mann Island/Pier Head assemblage have been similarly over-fired, with large inclusions, and they are frequently blistered. There is no doubt that sugar wares were also made in Liverpool, and it has been suggested that, as several potters had interests in both production centres, a split was made between finewares, which relied on imported clays brought to Liverpool by sea, and so were most economically made in Liverpool, and coarsewares, which used clays from the coal-measures, made in Prescot, where they were locally abundant (Davey 1991).

Other Materials

Pipe-clay hair curlers
David A Higgins
Two pipe-clay hair curlers were recovered from the Pier Head section of the LLC extension (Fig 86). Both have probably been shaped by rolling the clay over some type of former, but the first is more neatly finished, with the end formed with a single cut, leaving just a small central dimple from rolling (Fig 86.1). The second is less neatly finished and the end has just been allowed to form a conical hollow where the clay has run off the end of the former (Fig 86.2). There seems to be a line near one end that presumably marks the edge of the former and the position where the end should have been trimmed (the other end is chipped off).

Both examples are of slender eighteenth-century forms, and may well date from late in the century, since one was associated with pipe stems attributed to Thomas Hayes II, who was working *c* 1780-1800 (*p 197*). These curlers were almost certainly manufactured as a sideline by the local pipe-makers.

Ceramic building material
During the excavations on Mann Island, a representative sample of 128 bricks was retained from a range of contexts. Of these, 122 were from the Countryside Neptune site, with some deriving from the floors of the numerous cellars, while others came from the foundations and walls of buildings on Nova Scotia and north of Canning Dock. They all appear to be of late eighteenth- or early nineteenth-century date, and comprise examples of slop-moulded and, possibly, pallet-moulded bricks (Ryan 1996, 92), by unknown makers. The majority are handmade, and most of these, and also the machine-made bricks, fit into the range of 220-240 x 105-115 x 60-90 mm, reflecting the thicker standard that prevailed in the north of England at the time (Brunskill 1997, 38). The remaining 16 bricks, all of which appear to be of late eighteenth-century date, came from the Mann Island section of the LLC extension and are again by unknown makers. They were from a number of contexts representing the foundations, walls, and surfaces associated with a mid-nineteenth-century warehouse (*7339; Ch 4, p 197*).

Metalwork
In total, 450 fragments of metalwork were recovered during the combined programmes of excavation. This assemblage is composed of copper-alloy objects, ironwork, and a small quantity of lead.

Copper-alloy objects
Coins and tokens
Some 19 copper-alloy coins were recovered, with 17 coming from the Countryside Neptune site, the

other two from the Mann Island and Central Docks sections of the LLC extension respectively. Size suggests that most of the coins are halfpennies or farthings, small denomination coins, which might not have been sought for particularly assiduously when lost or dropped. All but two are in extremely poor condition, and most have proved unidentifiable, except on size grounds.

One of the two firmly identified examples is a well-preserved penny of 1799 (Pl 189), which was from the cobbled floor (**5708**) of a small single-room cellar dwelling on Mann Island (*Ch 3, p 87*). The other is a halfpenny, probably of George III, and most likely to have been struck in 1806 or 1807 (Brooke 1966, 221).

Two other coins from the Countryside Neptune site can also be relatively confidently identified as issues of George III, probably the third or fourth of his reign (Spink and Sons Ltd 2010), dating to 1799 and after 1806 respectively. These came from the fill of a small brick-built chamber that had probably been constructed in the late eighteenth century against the west-facing elevation of river wall **5707** (*Ch 3, pp 57-9; Fig 24*). A third coin from the same context is a penny of George IV, second issue, dating from 1825-30 (*ibid*).

Two half-penny tokens came from backfill of the late eighteenth-century warehouse cellars between Irwell Place and Murray Place (*Ch 3, p 82*). One is an issue of the Associated Irish Mine Company, or AIMC (Dalton and Hamer 1915, token 428), which had an agent and offices in Liverpool. This bears the coat of arms of the AIMC, a windlass over a shield decorated with the company's coat of arms: two spades; three picks; and a horn of gunpowder for

*Plate 189: Well-preserved penny of 1799, from the cobbled floor (**5708**) of a late eighteenth-century cellar dwelling at the Countryside Neptune site*

blasting. The inscription around the shield reads 'ASSOCIATED IRISH MINE COMPANY 1789'. On the opposite side of the token, in reference to the Irish heritage of the company, is the image of St Patrick, shown in profile and surrounded by the words 'CRONEBANE HALF PENNY'.

The other token is a so-called Portsea halfpenny of 1794. It appears to bear the arms of the City of Liverpool, and has some resemblance to tokens issued for Thomas Clarke during the period 1791-4 (National Maritime Museums nd).

Buttons
There were only five artefacts associated with personal appearance, all buttons. Two of these came from demolition material within a mid-nineteenth-century warehouse (**7339**) at Nova Scotia (*Ch 4, p 147*). Both are flat and round, 23-24 mm in diameter, with a wire loop to the rear; one is decorated with a simple pattern of radiating lines. Their size suggests that they derive from outer garments, such as an overcoat or cloak, and they could easily have been lost in day-to-day activity. Although not precisely dated, they would not be out of place in a late eighteenth- or early nineteenth-century context.

The remaining three buttons were from a deposit of decayed wood against a late eighteenth-century river wall (**5505**) near Pier Head (*Ch 3, p 89*). All are quite small (*c* 12-16 mm in diameter), two having sub-hemispherical caps, the third being flat; none appears to be decorated. Again, these could easily have been lost from garments in the course of day-to-day activity and may date to the late eighteenth or early nineteenth century, although they remain in production to the present day.

Nails
There are, in all, 19 small copper-alloy nails, all 24-40 mm in length, of a type that was widely used in ship-building, since they are relatively resistant to saltwater corrosion. Four of them came from the Mann Island section of the LLC extension, from reclamation material west of river wall **7325** (*Ch 3, p 63*), and from a demolition layer associated with the warehouse on Nova Scotia (**7339**; *Ch 4, p 147*). Excavation at Pier Head produced the remaining 15 examples, of which six were from decayed wood lying against the west face of river wall **5505** (*Ch 3, p 89*), five from a later construction deposit, whilst the remainder were from mixed later layers.

Other objects
In addition, the excavations produced several other copper-alloy objects. These were a small L-shaped hook, probably intended to be screwed into wood, and resembling a modern cup-hook, and a small,

perforated, rectangular plate, which was probably also used in carpentry, from Mann Island. There are also three small fragments of sheet metal and an unidentifiable fragment (all from the warehouse demolition material), whilst an angular chunk of material is probably copper ore of some kind.

The remaining objects came from the Pier Head excavations, and appear relatively modern in date. They include an oval door handle from Tr 410, perhaps from a cupboard or cabinet door, and a short length of piping from construction trenching for one of the air-raid shelters (*Ch 5, p 177*), which may have been associated with the supply of water.

Ironwork

Ironwork forms the largest component of the metalwork assemblage (401 fragments). Most objects are badly corroded, but the majority appear to be large, hand-forged nails, which are a long-lived type used to secure timber structures. In addition, the assemblage contains other fastenings, such as iron bolts, again used in large-scale woodwork, and modern small hooks and pins.

Identifiable objects from the Pier Head excavations include a barrel hoop and a curving piece of ironwork, which is either from another stave-built vessel, or forms the poorly preserved remains of a small cast wheel, perhaps from a winch or other dockside machinery. Backfill to the rear of river wall *3544* (*Ch 3, p 78*) also produced a large hollow object, perhaps intended as a reinforcement for a large pile, but as it appears to have been subjected to intense heat, its surfaces bubbled, and streaked with green deposits (copper alloy?), it could be the base of a relatively small crucible.

In addition, the Mann Island excavations produced three probable tools from the basement of warehouse *7339* (*Ch 4, p 147*); part of a blade; a cold-chisel; and what appears to be part of a tanged file. These could have been used in a wide range of circumstances, but the flaring shape of the chisel might suggest that it is, in fact, a caulking iron, used to insert oakum between ships' planking, in order to make the seams watertight.

Lead

Only two relatively small fragments of lead were recovered, during the Pier Head excavations. This, perhaps, reflects its easily recyclable nature and resale value, which would have meant that large-scale dumps, such as those for land reclamation, would have been turned over and scavenged on a regular basis. A short length of lead strip, perhaps flattened piping, came from one of the cobbled surfaces laid down following the backfilling of

Manchester Dock (*Ch 5, p 147*), and a large curving offcut, with numerous chisel marks, was from a late levelling layer.

Glass

In all, 1726 fragments of glass were recovered, of which 1577 were from a limited range of blown and moulded vessels, and 149 were small fragments of window glass. All are in relatively good condition, although some vessels, especially those from earlier contexts, have iridescent weathering and some flaking of surfaces. In general, the fragments are large, with the more robust parts of vessels, like bases and necks, often surviving complete.

The majority of the glass comprises bottles of various forms and types of manufacture. Most of the bottle assemblage (1313 fragments, *c* 83%) consists of dark-green wine and beer bottles, with 604 fragments from this group (*c* 46%) being the distinctive dark olive-green wine bottle or 'English' bottle. These were used as containers for a number of liquids, including mineral water (Hurst Vose 2008, 368), from the late seventeenth century onwards, throughout the eighteenth, and into the early nineteenth century (*op cit*, 367). The bottles within the assemblage, however, particularly the taller cylindrical forms, date from the mid- or late eighteenth century onwards.

Eighteenth-century vessels
Dark-green bottles
Some 228 fragments, from dark-green 'English' wine/beer bottles, came from an early nineteenth-century dump of pottery and glass to the north of river wall *3801* (*Ch 4, p 127*). Most of these are tall, cylindrical bottles of similar size (Pl 190), with bases 80-90 mm in diameter and a high-domed kick, many of them having a distinct pontil mark. All are probably mould-blown, and are most likely to date to the late eighteenth or early nineteenth century, their form suggesting the period 1790 to *c* 1820 (Jones 1986).

Other late eighteenth-century dark-green glass vessels were represented by several fragments from square or polygonal-sectioned bottles (Pl 191), one from a late eighteenth-century reclamation layer west of river wall *7638* (*Ch 3, p 62*), and another from the glass and pottery dump to the north of river wall *3801* (*Ch 4, p 127*). Part of the rim of a very thick-walled vessel with an applied string rim, possibly a demijohn, was also recovered during the Countryside Neptune excavations.

Colourless vessels
Two complete colourless pharmaceutical phials were recovered, along with a fragmentary base, from the Countryside Neptune site. In addition, a complete

Plate 192: Pharmaceutical phial, from the construction
cut for a warehouse on the north quay of Chester Basin

free-blown phial, with a tooled everted rim, in bluish-
colourless metal (Pl 192), came from a construction
cut for the warehouse on the north quay of Chester
Basin (*Ch 4, p 129*), whilst the colourless neck and rim
from a phial were associated with backfill behind the
north wall of Chester Basin (*Ch 4, p 128*). Though in
use by the seventeenth century (*cf* Gooder 1984), these
simple vessels usually appear in colourless metal
from the mid-eighteenth century (Noël Hume 1969,
74), and their cylindrical form suggests a date after
1780. However, it is possible that the second phial is
machine blown, and thus of nineteenth-century or
later date.

Nineteenth-century vessels
Dark-green bottles
Two backfill deposits, contained within the cellars
of the late eighteenth-century warehouses between
Irwell Place and Murray Place (*Ch 3, pp 82-3*),
produced 160 and 628 fragments of dark-green
bottles respectively, the latter containing at least
37 bottles. These fragments were all from narrow-
diameter (76-78 mm) mould-blown bottles, with a
distinctive embossed four-pointed star on the base.
These are unlikely to be any earlier than the mid-
nineteenth century and could be considerably later.
Four comparable mould-blown bottles, dating to
after the 1820s, were also recovered from the fill of a
construction cut for a warehouse on the north quay
of Chester Basin (*Ch 4, pp 129-30*).

Colourless bottles
A further 122 fragments are from bottles in colourless
or almost colourless metal. All are from mould-blown
or machine-blown vessels, and are likely to be no
earlier than the mid- or late nineteenth century.

Plate 190: Late eighteenth- or early nineteenth-century
bottle, one of many recovered from Tr 414 in the Pier
Head section of the Leeds and Liverpool Canal extension

Plate 191: Shattered base of a late eighteenth-century
case bottle

Plate 193: Early nineteenth-century wine glass, from a cellar on Nova Scotia

Tablewares
Fine tablewares are restricted to a group of four wine glasses from the cellar of one of the late eighteenth-century warehouses between Irwell Place and Murray Place on Nova Scotia (*Ch 3, p 82*). All are in a colourless leaded metal, and are identifiable as 'rummers' (Pl 193), a style of glass introduced into England in the last quarter of the eighteenth century, which was most popular in the early nineteenth century, and remained popular until *c* 1830 (Noël Hume 1969, 195). Two heavy bases in good-quality leaded glass, from the Countryside Neptune site, are probably drinking beakers; one, clearly blown, has the pontil-mark polished away. An insufficient amount remains of either vessel to allow them to be dated, although they are almost certainly of nineteenth-century or later date.

In addition, the bowl and stem of a small colourless, plain wine glass with a baluster stem was recovered from the early nineteenth-century glass and pottery dump to the north of river wall **3801** (*Ch 4, p 127*). Although not closely datable, it is presumably contemporary with other vessels from this deposit. This very marked lack of tablewares might add to the suggestion that material in this dumped layer was not of directly domestic origin, but was, in great part, from other sources, including producers.

Miscellaneous fragments
A group of 50 fragments of thin colourless glass from a late eighteenth-century cellar between Irwell Place and Murray Place (*Ch 3, p 82*) appears to have come from a lamp glass of some kind, and can be dated to the later nineteenth century. Two fragments of mould-blown cobalt blue glass from the same cellar have been tentatively identified as being from a glass fire grenade, a method of fire-fighting in use from about 1870 into the early twentieth century (London Fire Brigade nd).

Window glass
Window glass represents only 8.6% of the total glass assemblage. Most fragments are relatively small, mid-pane, in slightly greenish, slightly bluish, and colourless metals, and cannot be closely dated, although they are probably not earlier than the late eighteenth or nineteenth century, as cast glass was not produced in England until 1773, when the British Plate Glass Company was opened in St Helens (Barker and Harris 1994, 112). Only six small fragments are likely to be earlier, being thin, greenish, probably muff-blown glass of late seventeenth- or early eighteenth-century date. These all came from the Countryside Neptune site, from a deposit closely associated with clay pipe-kiln dump **5747** (*p 201*), and some from late eighteenth-century land-reclamation material west of the river wall **7638** (*Ch 3, p 62*).

Gunflint
A single blade, almost square, gunflint was recovered from late backfill at Pier Head. It is approximately 25 mm long, and made from an opaque dark grey flint. Although not datable with any precision, it conforms to Lotbiniere's (1984, 207) 'common gunflint' type and is unlikely to pre-date the introduction of the platform technique of manufacture from France in 1775. Gunflints of this form continued to be made into the 1950s (*ibid*).

Animal Bone and Molluscs

In total, some 460 fragments of animal bone were recovered from various backfill and levelling layers. The assemblage was, however, too small and fragmentary to draw any meaningful conclusions, particularly given the context of its disposal.

There was also 9.159 kg of marine shell from the Pier Head and Central Docks sections of the LLC extension. The assemblage consists of 435 more or less complete individual valves, the overwhelming majority of which were from the edible oyster, all of a size suitable for consumption, indicating that they represent food waste. Only a few other species were present: the scallop; the edible cockle; the limpet; and a variety of clam. The numbers of these, however, are so small as to have no significance.

Conclusions

The finds from these excavations clearly make a significant contribution to an understanding of the late eighteenth- and nineteenth-century development of Liverpool's dockland. The nature of the deposits, being predominantly reclamation dumps, has, however, resulted in an interesting dichotomy. Pottery, clay pipe, and bottle glass all appear in large amounts, undoubtedly being discarded industrial waste, brought in to aid the reclamation process. Thus, rather than illustrating life around the docks, these materials provide evidence of some of Liverpool's great industries. In contrast, some finds, for instance the ironwork, especially the nails, presumably derive from buildings on and around the docks, with, perhaps surprisingly, very few reflecting the maritime nature of the area. Other classes of finds appear in far smaller quantities, and offer often more intimate glimpses of the life and work of individuals on, or about, the waterfront, with only a handful of coins and tokens, a single gunflint, and perhaps most personal of all, two ceramic wig-curlers reflecting the fashionable preferences of late eighteenth-century individuals.

7

ARCHAEOLOGY AT THE WATERFRONT

Richard A Gregory and Christine Howard-Davis

The Evolution of the Port-settlement

By virtue of its maritime links, Liverpool for much of its history can be classified as a port-settlement, functioning as 'a central place of economic and cultural interchange' (Hoyle and Pinder 1981, 1). Significantly, being a port-settlement has meant that Liverpool has had a different urban trajectory when compared with those settlements within its hinterland, and many of its inhabitants, particularly its entrepreneurs, have perhaps possessed a more global and less parochial outlook. Indeed, when compared with the settlements in its hinterland, Liverpool appears unique, and it can be argued that its historical growth and morphology are more akin to other major British and European seaports, which developed from the medieval and early post-medieval periods onwards (Hoyle 1988, 9; Milne 2006, 257).

The apparent similarities between the major British and European seaports and their associated settlements has long been recognised, and has resulted in the formulation of several theoretical models, which chart the idealised historical growth of a port. The more well-known of these include Bird's (1963) 'Anyport' model (Fig 87), which focuses on the development of port facilities, and Hoyle's (1988) 'Cityport' model, which considers both the port and the associated urban settlement. These two geographical models appear applicable to the development of the majority of British and European ports and therefore provide a convenient framework

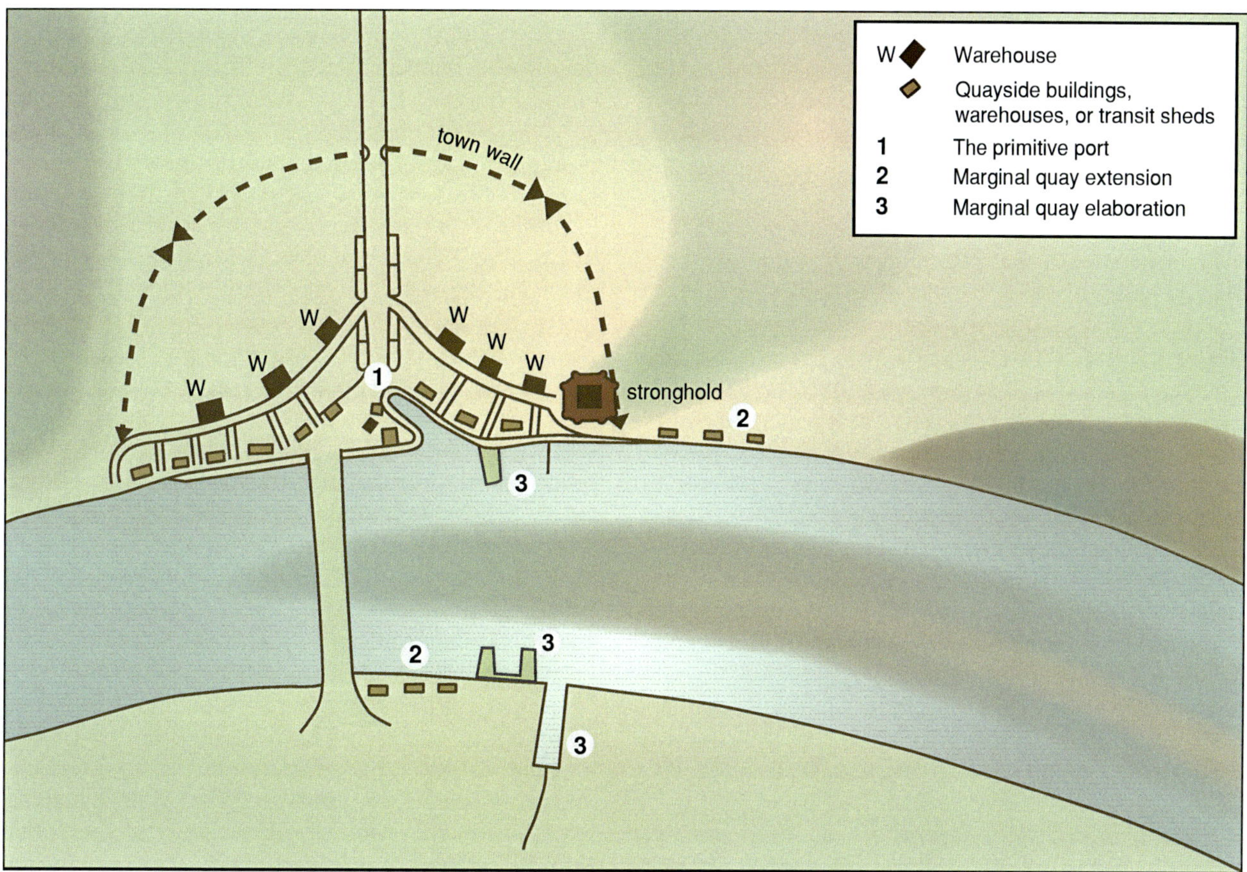

Figure 87: James Bird's 'Anyport' model: the first four eras of development

215

within which to slot the archaeological remains uncovered along Liverpool's waterfront.

The first stage of both Bird's (1963, 27-8) and Hoyle's (1988, 7) models relates to the establishment of a 'primitive port', which has a close spatial and functional association with an adjacent settlement (Fig 87). The establishment of the port-settlement was normally at a coastal location that afforded some physical advantages for trade, which might include a suitable land site; a convenient water site, such as a natural harbour; a suitable water situation, with approaches from the sea; and proximity and access to a developing hinterland (Bird 1963, 27). Within the primitive port-settlement, the waterfront forms the focus, and the functional characteristics of the settlement are also strongly conditioned by maritime trade, notably the provision of merchant stores, and other maritime activities, such as provisioning, careening, and shipbuilding. In terms of urban morphology, Bird (*op cit*, 28) suggests that the primitive port will possess a main road at right-angles to the waterfront, which also forms the major route used to transport goods to inland markets. The idealised primitive port also has a line of quays extending along the waterfront, though, prior to the fifteenth century, small vessels using the port could be safely grounded on its foreshore at low tide (*ibid*). Following its establishment, Bird (*op cit*, 28-9) then suggests that the primitive port may experience a phase of 'marginal quay extension', which often extends outside the settlement nucleus. This is then followed by 'marginal quay elaboration', which involves making cuttings into the riverbank or extending piers out into the water (*op cit*, 30).

Liverpool closely follows this postulated sequence, with the establishment of its thirteenth-century primitive port being a result of external political factors, specifically the speculative policy of King John, who may have wished to create his own west-coast port, separate from Chester (*Ch 2, p 23*). The site of John's new town lay on a sandstone promontory, adjacent to a tidal creek, and together these created a suitable land site for a primitive port-settlement. This location could be easily accessed from the Irish Sea, which initially formed the focus of Liverpool's maritime interests (*Ch 2, p 27*), and hence it possessed a suitable water situation. At low tide, ships could be either beached within the tidal creek or on the gently sloping foreshore, areas that effectively functioned as the primitive port's 'quays'. Indeed, the beaching of ships on these areas would only become more hazardous after the fifteenth century, once ships had increased in size, and had acquired two or more masts (*ibid*).

In terms of urban morphology, the focus of Liverpool's primitive port was Water Street/Dale Street, which formed the main route linking the settlement with its hinterland, and also the parallel route of Chapel Street/Tithebarn Street (*Ch 2, p 25*). Both of these streets ran down to the primitive port's waterfront, which was dominated by the chapels of St Mary del Key (*Ch 2, p 25*) and St Nicholas (*Ch 2, p 26*), during the medieval period, and also the Tower from the fifteenth century (*Ch 2, p 28*). Significantly, these routes, along with a transverse route to the castle (*Ch 2, p 25*), would form the nucleus of the primitive port up until the eighteenth century, and would greatly influence Liverpool's expanding urban morphology during the late seventeenth century (*Ch 2, p 31*). During the sixteenth century, Liverpool also experienced 'marginal quay extension' through the construction of a breakwater at the mouth of the Pool, and the installation of sluice gates on the stream feeding it, which provided a means of scouring out accumulations of silt (*Ch 2, p 29*). This was then followed by 'marginal quay elaboration' during the seventeenth century, which involved the construction of a quay on the Mersey foreshore (*Ch 2, p 34*).

Knowledge of the archaeology of Liverpool's primitive port is, at present, extremely limited and it is likely that, as with the North West's other large urban settlements, much of the pre-eighteenth-century archaeology has been destroyed or severely truncated by later features, most notably nineteenth- and twentieth-century basements. Therefore, the archaeology of the early port is probably contained within a series of detached 'islands', falling between these areas of deep disturbance. To date, the remains identified include riverine deposits forming parts of the Pool (*Ch 2, p 26*) and the early foreshore of the Mersey (*Ch 2, p 25*), and land-reclamation deposits relating to seventeenth-century encroachment into the Pool (*Ch 2, p 35*). To these may be added several boundary ditches, soil horizons, and a small collection of medieval and early post-medieval artefacts (*Ch 2, p 27*), which, as with the riverine and reclamation deposits, provide comparatively little insight into the form and functioning of Liverpool's early settlement.

It became increasingly clear by the close of the seventeenth century that the Pool and foreshore, which together formed Liverpool's port (*see above*), were defective, particularly given the increases in trade and the number of larger ships entering the primitive port, alongside the increasing levels of industry/economic growth in Liverpool's immediate hinterland (*Ch 2, p 34*). This understanding resulted in Liverpool entering into another phase of development, common to most large port-settlements. This is associated with 'dock elaboration' (Bird 1963, 30) and an 'expanding cityport', which in most instances resulted in separation between the 'city' and 'port' (Hoyle 1988, 9). In terms of Bird's 'Anyport' model during this phase of dock elaboration,

'A site for the first commercial dock may well be found by demolishing an outdated part of the port nucleus. If this is impracticable, it is necessary for *Anyport* to break new ground, preferably downstream by excavations in the river's floodplain. If the river is sufficiently wide, an alternative is to build a dock on land more palpably reclaimed from the river – a water-encroaching site. *Anyport's* dock is equipped with a tidal basin to lock in a number of sailing vessels at any one time. This may not be *Anyport's* first dock, but previous docks were used for shipbuilding and ship repairing. In Britain this era usually occurs in the first half of the nineteenth century, with further docks provided as trade increases, each larger than the previous and built progressively downstream and further from the nucleus. Lengthening landward communications back to the port distribution centre are dealt with by the railway. These earlier docks have elaborate outlines, either by means of branch docks or jetties within one dock. Dock engineers wished to have the maximum convenient length of quay for a given water area. Such docks are equipped with transit sheds and warehouses if their trade is predominantly general cargo' (Bird 1963, 30).

Whilst port development at Liverpool typified those events postulated at 'Anyport', it also represents the first of Britain's primitive ports to enter this phase of dock elaboration, which resulted in the opening of the Old Dock in 1715 (*Ch 2, p 36*). Although this was not the country's first impounded wet dock, as two earlier examples had been built on the Thames, at Blackwall in *c* 1660 and Howland between 1697 and 1700 (Pl 194), whilst one had been created at Sea Mills on the Avon in *c* 1710, the example at Liverpool represents the world's first commercial wet dock (Jackson 1983, 43-5). It was therefore not solely designed, as with the earlier wet docks, for the laying up of ships, but was provided with a quayside and a Custom House to enable it to function as a commercial entity, which was securely linked to maritime trade. Following its construction, Liverpool's phase of dock elaboration continued unabated until 1927, finally ending with the opening of Gladstone Dock (Bird 1963, 278; *Ch 5, p 159*). Significantly, this resulted in the creation of

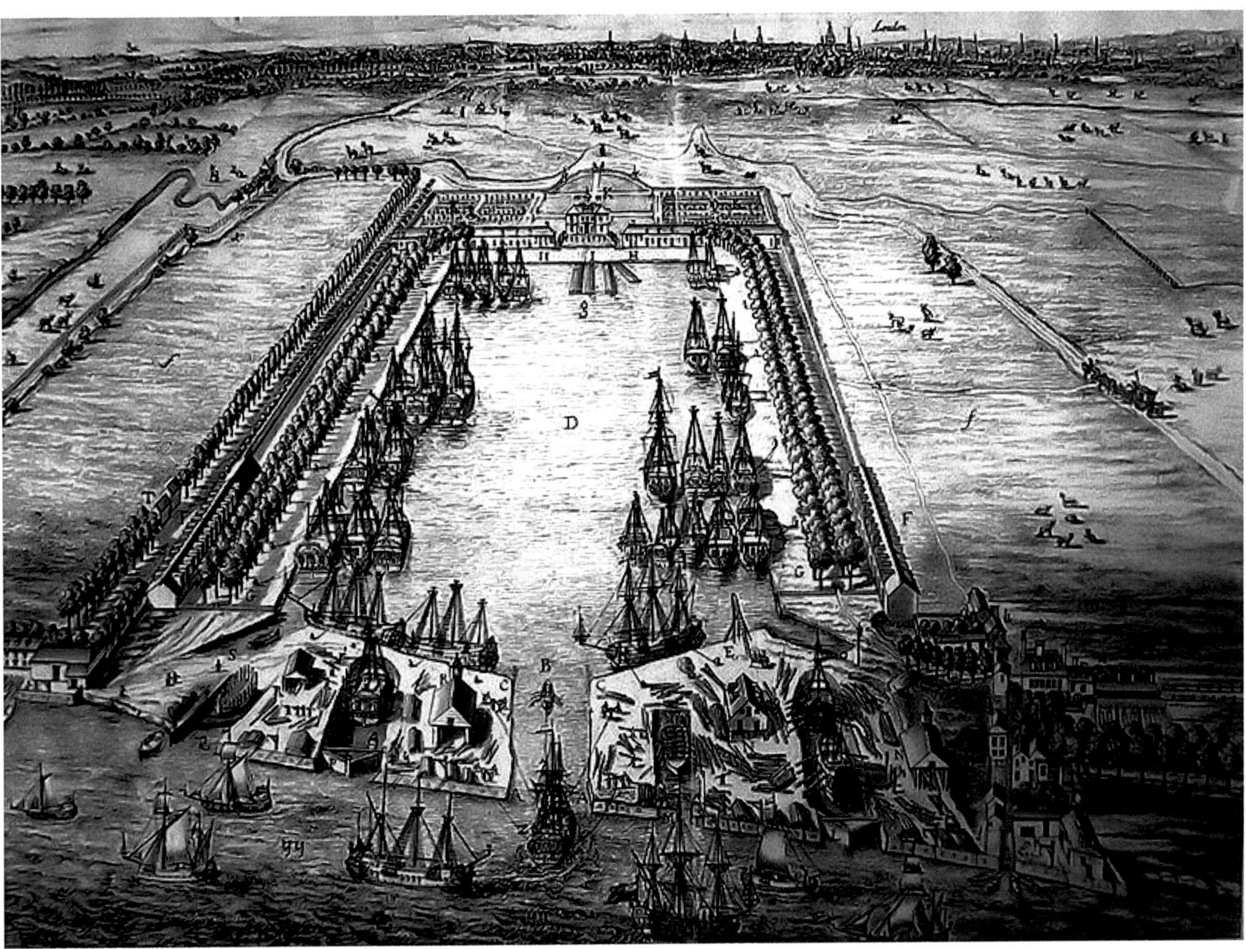

Plate 194: Howland Great Wet Dock, *as drawn by T Badslade and engraved by J Kip for* Supplement du Nouveau Theatre de la Grand Bretagne

docks designed to serve both inland and ocean-going vessels, involved in the transportation of both goods and people, and during this protracted period of dock elaboration, three docks (Alexandra, Gladstone, and Canada) were also established which were supplied with extensive quaysides. In the 'Anyport' model, these extensive quays are termed 'simple lineal quayage', and they were designed to accommodate the largest of the late nineteenth-century sea-going vessels (*op cit*, 30, 278). In essence, dock elaboration, and the later provision of several extensive quays, was the only way that Liverpool's port could cope with the dramatic expansion in trade between the eighteenth and early twentieth centuries. This therefore resulted in the progressive creation of the 9 km-long line of docks, ancillary features, and the substantial swathe of reclaimed land, which emanated from the nucleus of the primitive port (*Chs 3-5*).

Significantly, the extent, scale, variety, and date, of the features associated with Liverpool's dock elaboration have resulted in the creation of a comparatively rich and varied archaeological resource, which allows some insight into the development of one of the world's more significant eighteenth- and nineteenth-century ports. These remains form the body of evidence recorded during the various campaigns of archaeological work along Liverpool's historic waterfront (*Ch 1*). They include eighteenth- and nineteenth-century dock and sea walls (*Chs 2 and 3*), and contemporary land-reclamation deposits, many of which were associated with dumps of pottery, clay tobacco pipe, and other fragments of artefacts (*Ch 6*). Furthermore, the archaeological resource includes remains relating to eighteenth- and nineteenth-century quayside technology, warehouses, commercial properties, and public buildings, as well as domestic occupation within a small portion of Liverpool's 'Sailor-town'. In addition to the eighteenth- and nineteenth-century evidence, both above- and below-ground remains were recorded during the archaeological investigations that hold significance for its early twentieth-century history. These relate specifically to the infilling and modification of pre-existing docks, the construction of the MRC tunnel, and the later use of some of the quayside areas.

According to Hoyle's (1988, 7) model, following dock elaboration and the expansion of the city port, a process that ended at Liverpool during the early twentieth century, many of Europe's modern port-settlements then passed through three further stages of development. These took place between the mid-twentieth century and the present day, and they relate to the decline and reuse of an idealised port's historic waterfront. The earlier of these stages relates to the creation of the 'modern industrial cityport', during the mid-twentieth century, which led to the establishment of separate facilities, principally for oil refining, though parts of the historic docks were still utilised, albeit in a modified form. At Liverpool, the creation of the Dingle Oil Jetty forms part of this phase of port evolution. Hoyle (*ibid*) then suggests that this stage is followed by retreat from the older areas of the port, following changes in maritime technology. In the case of Liverpool, this relates to the emergence of containerisation and the construction of the Royal Seaforth Dock, and the abandonment of the historic waterfront (*Ch 5, pp 159-60*). In archaeological terms, it was during this, and also the preceding, phase that many features of Liverpool's historic waterfront were abandoned, modified, or destroyed, which included the infilling of several of the historic docks. Hoyle's (*op cit*, 13) final stage of port-city development encompasses the redevelopment of abandoned areas of the historic waterfront, which ultimately leads to urban renewal of the port's original core for residential, commercial, and/or recreational use. Liverpool is currently still in the midst of this process, which was initiated in the 1980s (*Ch 5, p 153*), and significantly, it is a process that has enabled the archaeology of the waterfront to be examined in some detail.

Dock Building and Land Reclamation

Along the waterfront, some of the more significant archaeological remains uncovered during the various campaigns of excavation relate to eighteenth- and early nineteenth-century dock building and land reclamation. These remains take three principal forms: dock/basin walls; river walls; and land-reclamation deposits. Whilst these features are commonly found at other British ports, by virtue of Liverpool being the first of Britain's port-settlements to begin the process of 'dock elaboration' (*p 216*), which led to the creation of the world's first mercantile dock system, these remains hold particular importance, as they reflect pioneering features in the history of dock building.

Dock and basin walls were critical to the success of 'dock elaboration' and in order for them to function successfully, they needed adequate foundations, which could support their weight. In addition, the dock/basin wall also had to be strong enough to resist the pressures of water within the dock and the weight of backfilled material to its rear (Ritchie-Noakes 1984, 103). The archaeological evidence from excavations at the Old Dock (*Ch 2, pp 37-9*) indicates that Liverpool's earliest dock walls, dating to the second decade of the eighteenth century, were largely experimental in nature, as indeed was the dock, as no clear precedent existed for successful dock-wall construction at this time. These pioneering walls were generally *c* 1.25 m thick and were constructed entirely of handmade brick,

Plate 195: The walls of the Old Dock, built directly on the bedrock

capped with sandstone blocks, which was quarried either from St James's Mount or Brownlow Hill, or was reused stone that had been removed from the nearby medieval castle (*op cit*, 19; *Ch 2, p 25*). The archaeological investigations indicated that the wall was constructed at a slight angle and rested either directly on cut bedrock foundations, which had a gently curving profile (Pl 195), or on large sandstone blocks. To the rear was a backing of redeposited clay and brick rubble and, in order to resist the pressure of the backfill, horizontal timbers seem to have been employed to tie the dock wall into this backing.

These walls are unique, particularly as they are almost entirely constructed in handmade brick. This certainly created problems, seemingly as a result of the choice of brick as a building material and the use of lime mortar as a bonding agent, as this type of mortar is not a particularly effective hydraulic cement. The use of lime mortar would therefore have made the walls susceptible to collapse and it appears that these were sufficiently insubstantial that they could easily be demolished by eighteenth-century shipbuilders wishing to launch vessels into the dock (*op cit*, 19, 21). In all, this meant that this style of construction was not adopted in subsequent dock building.

The other eighteenth-century dock/basin walls examined during the archaeological investigations

date to the 1730s, late 1760s, and late 1770s, forming part of the Dry Dock (*Ch 3, p 55*), George's Dock Dry Basin (*Ch 3, p 70*), and Manchester Basin (*Ch 3, p 74*). Although the putative wall of Manchester Basin had been largely removed during an early nineteenth-century scheme of modification (*Ch 4, p 103*), and the wall of George's Dock Dry Basin had probably been extensively repaired in the 1820s, it appears that all three of the eighteenth-century dock/basin walls were of comparable design. They were all, for instance, constructed of yellow sandstone blocks which, following the inadequacies of the walling used at the Old Dock (*see above*), had replaced handmade brick as the preferred medium for dock-/basin-wall construction. This comparatively soft sandstone was probably acquired from Brownlow Hill (Ritchie-Noakes 1984, 37), and it had been cut into large rectangular- and smaller square-sized blocks, which were generally laid in an irregular fashion. In two instances, at the Dry Dock and George's Dock Dry Basin, the eighteenth-century dock/basin walls also became wider at their bases, which was achieved by progressively stepping out the masonry blocks on the rearward side of the wall. This allowed for greater structural strength and was a technique that was extensively employed during the mid-nineteenth century by Jesse Hartley during his campaign of dock construction (*op cit*, 109-11). Although the complete vertical extent of

219

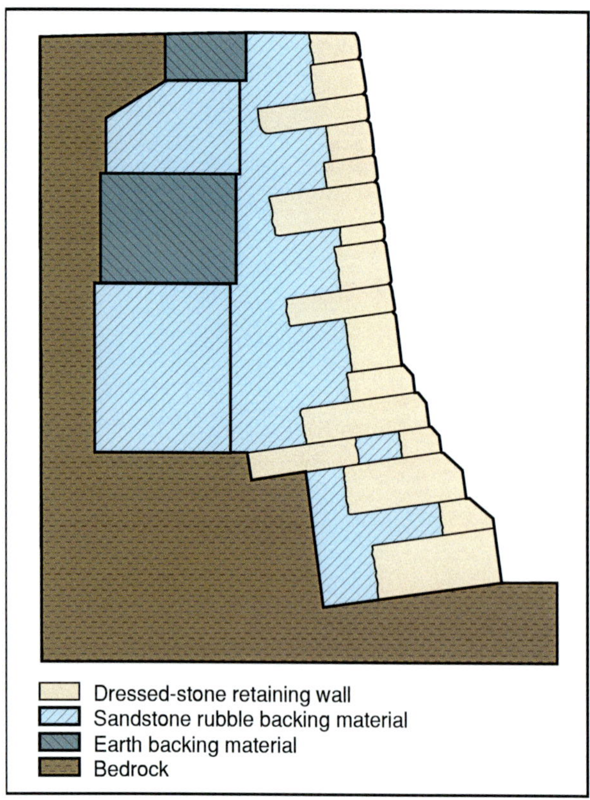

Figure 88: Idealised section across an early nineteenth-century dock wall (after Ritchie-Noakes 1984, 109)

the eighteenth-century dock/basin walls was not established, it is possible that, as with the known profiles of the early- and mid-nineteenth-century dock walls, these curved outwards towards their bases, and were supported by timber piles, or lay directly on the bedrock (Fig 88).

There was also some evidence for the use of a lime-based mortar to bond the masonry within the eastern and northern walls of the Dry Dock. Significantly, siliceous material had been added to the mortar, which would have presumably made it more waterproof, and also enabled it to set more quickly in damp conditions (*op cit*, 103). This may therefore represent an early attempt in the use of a water-resistant bonding agent, prior to the more widespread use of pozzolanic-type mortars, which, in Liverpool, were employed from the late eighteenth century onwards (*ibid*). Apart from these dock walls, the western side of George's Dock Passage was also uncovered, which linked the Dry Dock with George's Dock (*Ch 3, p 74*). This wall was probably constructed in 1775, and it was of comparable design to the eighteenth-century dock walls, though its upper courses had been replaced at a later date. It was constructed of large yellow sandstone blocks, which, in this instance, were coarsely hewn, and it is possible that some of these might have been recycled from an earlier graving dock, constructed in 1746, that lay at this location (*Ch 3, p 74*).

River walls were essentially of similar construction to the dock/basin walls, in that they needed to possess adequate foundations and also had to resist the pressures of both water on one side and backfilled material on the other. The archaeological excavations exposed two different types of eighteenth- and early nineteenth-century river walls. The first type was designed as a permanent feature, acting as a retaining wall for a specific pier/quay that projected into the Mersey. Several examples of this, dating from the eighteenth century, lay immediately west of the Dry Dock and they defined the progressive limits of the area of reclaimed land, which became known as Nova Scotia and Mann Island (*Ch 3, pp 60, 74*). Of these, one was contemporary with the construction of the Dry Dock (**5707/7304**; *Ch 3, pp 58-9*), whilst another (**7638**; *Ch 3, p 62*) was constructed at a slightly later date, in the early 1740s, in order to extend the area of reclaimed land northwards. This latter area lay to the north of a graving dock, which was attached to the Dry Dock in *c* 1746, and the cartographic evidence suggests that it sloped downwards to the river. To the west of this area, two further river walls (**3504** and **3544**; *Ch 3, p 76*) were identified, which were established between the mid-1770s and 1785. One of these bounded a narrow finger of reclaimed land that lay immediately north of Manchester Basin, whilst the other had been constructed to extend this quay further northwards, perhaps in the early 1780s.

In addition to the eighteenth-century walls, a comparable river wall (**233/235**; *Ch 4, p 107*) was also uncovered at Mann Island, which dates to *c* 1803. This relates to a phase of early nineteenth-century land reclamation, which was designed to extend the western limits of Manchester Basin's northern quay. However, archaeological excavation indicated that it was never completed, probably because of a decision to extend this quay further westwards as a part of a new scheme of work, which occurred between 1805 and 1806. More specifically, this work was designed to provide Manchester Basin with an entrance lock and convert it into a half-tide dock (*Ch 4, p 111*). To the north of Manchester Basin, another section of permanent river wall (**5505**) was uncovered which, in this instance, was constructed in *c* 1795 to extend the western quay of George's Dock (*Ch 3, p 89*). This also defined a projecting pier on the southern side of George's Dock Dry Basin, which represents a modification of an earlier pier that had been built in 1779 (*Ch 3, p 71*). Elements of this earlier pier included two parallel dry-stone walls (**5520** and **5521**), which probably functioned as supporting buttresses (*Ch 3, p 72*).

All of these permanent river walls were essentially similar in form, and were also comparable to the eighteenth-century walling that had been used in dock/basin construction after the opening of the Old

Dock (*Ch 2, p 35*). All had been constructed in yellow sandstone, generally laid either irregularly or in a more regular bond. It also appears that some of these walls were of dry-stone construction, as there were instances where no evidence for mortar was present. The riverward side of these walls, where visible, was constructed to a comparatively high standard, consisting of well-tooled stonework with a near-flat finish. This contrasted with the landward side, which, in all cases, was rougher in character. The profile of one of the river walls (*5707/7304; Ch 3, p 57*) was examined close to the Dry Dock, and this was essentially similar to the dock/basin walls in that it had a trapezoidal shape, with a wider base created by progressively stepping out the stonework on the landward side of the wall. This stepping also created a rudimentary and continuous counterfort. The wall defining the quayside of George's Dock in *c* 1795 had also been provided with a horizontal timber fender, which suggests that vessels were sometimes moored alongside this pier.

The other type of eighteenth- and early nineteenth-century river wall was designed as a temporary feature, which had been erected during the process of land reclamation. Four examples of this were exposed. The earliest of these was associated with late eighteenth-century land reclamation to the north of George's Dock Dry Basin (*7583; Ch 3, p 78*). This was a dry-stone wall, composed of yellow sandstone blocks, which may have marked the limit of a season's work. However, once land reclamation proceeded to its west, this wall was no longer required. It was therefore partially dismantled, and it is probable that its stonework was then reused to create another river wall. The other examples date to the early nineteenth century, and were associated with the scheme of land reclamation which led to the creation of the enlarged early nineteenth-century quayside immediately west of George's Dock. Two of these dry-stone walls (*3801* and *3421; Ch 4, p 127*) were aligned perpendicular to the waterfront and appear to mark a temporary stage in this scheme, which occurred between 1803 and 1815. Moreover, one of these (*3421*) was composed of recycled masonry derived from a high-status building, map evidence indicating that this river wall was probably built between 1803 and 1805, forming the northern side of a narrow wharf which projected into the Mersey. The other temporary wall in this area (*5513; Ch 4, p 127*) may have marked an interim westward point reached during this scheme of reclamation. Although only a small section of this wall was uncovered, it too was constructed of unmortared yellow sandstone blocks.

The documentary and archaeological evidence indicates that, although yellow sandstone was used in dock/basin wall and permanent river-wall construction from the 1730s until the beginning of the nineteenth century, these walls were prone to failure and required rebuilding in the early part of the nineteenth century. This certainly appears to have been the case with the excavated sections of George's Dock Dry Basin (*Ch 3, p 72*) and George's Dock Passage (*Ch 3, p 74*), as both showed evidence for later rebuilding. The reasons for the failure of the early stone dock/basin walls might reside in the inadequacy of their foundations, the use of dry-stone construction, or the application of an inferior bonding mortar. The choice of a yellow sandstone derived from Brownlow to construct the walls might also have contributed to their failure, as this was a comparatively soft and friable type. Indeed, the inferior qualities of the Brownlow sandstone had certainly been identified by the late eighteenth century, and this resulted in the switch in the early part of the nineteenth, under the tenureship of the dock engineer John Foster, to the use of pink sandstone, derived from quarries at Runcorn (Ritchie-Noakes 1984, 37). Indeed, the use of this sandstone appears to have been an integral part of Foster's 'special relationship' with the quarry firm of Hetherington and Grindrod (Jarvis 1991b, 38).

Following its adoption, pink sandstone was used up until the late 1820s, along with yellow sandstone, to construct the core of the river and dock walls, and was also used to face their waterside elevations. The archaeological excavations along the historic waterfront exposed several examples of this type of walling. The earliest examples were the dock walls constructed in *c* 1803, which later formed part of Manchester Dock (*Ch 4, p 107*), as well as the walls used in the construction of this dock's entrance lock, which dates to *c* 1807, and the wall forming part of Rochdale Basin, which may date to 1805-10 (*Ch 4, p 131*). Significantly, these may well represent some of the earliest of Liverpool's dock walls to use this type of stone, and their constructional composition was certainly mirrored in other early nineteenth-century dock walls. At Manchester Dock, for instance, the walls were faced with pink sandstone ashlar masonry, bonded with lime-based mortar, and their landward sides were composed of pink and yellow sandstone. In the case of this latter material, this may have been recycled from the earlier walls of Manchester Basin. The walls of Manchester Dock were also wider at their base, in order to provide additional support, and these were perhaps built upon a series of vertical timber piles. Horizontal timbers had also been used to tie one of the walls of the entrance lock into its backing material.

Another comparable early example of this type of wall was exposed immediately to the north. This was probably constructed between 1805 and 1806, initially as a river wall, though it later formed the southern side of Chester Basin, again constructed of pink sandstone (*Ch 4, p 125*). The wall defining the northern side of Chester Basin was also exposed. This was again constructed between 1803 and 1805 and was similarly faced with pink sandstone, whilst its landward side was composed of a mix of yellow and pink sandstone ashlar, intermixed with rougher masonry blocks (*Ch 4, p 125*). A further dock wall, constructed between 1807 and 1815, was located to the north of Chester Basin, forming an element of George's Ferry Basin (*Ch 4, p 129*). However, this wall differed slightly from those to the south in that it was faced with both yellow and pink sandstone blocks.

Other early nineteenth-century dock walls examined during the archaeological work dated to a slightly later period, and included small sections of Prince's Dock, which was constructed between 1810 and 1821 (*Ch 4, p 137*), and those walls dating to the 1820s which formed part of the modifications made to the Dry Dock, resulting in the creation of Canning Dock (*Ch 4, p 135*). The section of wall forming part of Prince's Dock had a pink and yellow sandstone core and was faced with pink sandstone ashlar blocks. A similar style of construction was also apparent within the excavated section of wall that defined the western side of Canning Dock, though this had been provided with a supporting buttress, and contained several niches that may have secured the scaffolding used during its construction. It also appears that this wall had directly replaced the earlier wall of the Dry Dock, which had seemingly been dismantled during the construction works associated with the creation of Canning Dock. However, in contrast, excavation indicated that the lower sections of the Dry Dock's eastern retaining walls had been kept, whilst the upper courses had been rebuilt. This rebuilt section of walling was constructed of pink sandstone blocks, bonded with a hard grey mortar, though it also contained patches of brick, bonded with lime mortar.

In the late 1820s, the materials employed in dock- and river-wall construction changed once again, following the appointment of Jesse Hartley as dock engineer. Hartley, who trained as a stone mason, preferred to use harder-wearing granite and limestone, instead of sandstone, in his expansive scheme of dock building (Ritchie-Noakes 1984, 97, 104). Significantly, in utilising these materials, Hartley also introduced cyclopean-style construction, whereby the river and dock walls were composed of large granite headers surrounded by smaller pieces of granite rubble, separated by thin mortared joints. These cyclopean walls were normally backed by courses of sandstone rubble, and the mortar was a water-resistant pozzolanic-type composed of lime, sand, and ash (*op cit*, 106). In addition, Hartley's dock and river walls utilised square counterforts, which were bonded into the

rear of the dock wall, in order to provide additional strength (*ibid*).

Clarence Dock, which opened in 1830, was the first of Liverpool's docks to have a granite wall, with this material deriving from a quarry at Craignair, in Kirkcudbrightshire, south-west Scotland, which was leased by Hartley in 1826 (*op cit*, 87; Sharples 2004, 96). In 1830, the supply of granite was obtained from the Kirkmabreck quarry, also in Kirkcudbrightshire, which was leased by the Dock Board's trustees (Ritchie-Noakes 1984, 87). However, at certain times, it appears that this quarry could not supply the total quantity of granite required for Hartley's ambitious scheme of dock building. This, therefore, forced Hartley to construct some of his dock and river walls as composite structures, which utilised both pink sandstone and granite in their designs (*op cit*, 106; Sharples 2004, 96). The excavations along the waterfront uncovered two such composite dock walls, one forming part of Trafalgar Dock and other part of Victoria Dock, which both opened in 1836 (*Ch 4, p 139*). Both of these walls were faced with pink sandstone, bonded with pozzolanic-type cement, and backed by sandstone rubble and clay. Both also had square counterforts, which were bonded into the rear of the dock walls. These, as with the other walls, were constructed of pink sandstone. However, both dock walls were capped with granite coping stones that were maintained in alignment by diamond-shaped locking stones. These were used extensively by Hartley to secure and align the coping stones capping the dock walls, comparable examples being visible at Albert Dock (Pl 196).

The final type of feature associated with the construction of dock/river walls that was examined during the archaeological investigations was the material used to reclaim land. These deposits were exposed during the work on Mann Island

Plate 196: Diamond-shaped locking stones at Albert Dock

Figure 89: The progressive scheme of land reclamation leading to the formation of Mann Island and Nova Scotia (© Crown copyright 2014 Ordnance Survey 100005569)

and along the LLC extension, associated with eighteenth- and nineteenth-century reclamation. Significantly, the actual process of backfilling, leading to the creation of new land, probably remained comparatively unchanged throughout the eighteenth and nineteenth centuries. It was, for example, undertaken by hand, even though mechanisation became an increasing feature of nineteenth-century dock building (Jarvis 1996, 144). It was also not undertaken as a single operation, but instead normally occurred over an extended period of time, which allowed the backfill time to settle adequately (*ibid*). Indeed, following the widespread application of pozzolanic-type hydraulic mortars, it was not advisable to place too much weight on those walls bonded with this agent until it had set and strengthened, which could take anything up to a year (*ibid*). In these circumstances, if backfilling was undertaken too quickly, 'the fill would impose an overturning load on the wall before the mortar was fully cured, resulting in distortion or even collapse of the masonry' (*ibid*). Moreover, land reclamation was also dependent on obtaining suitable sources of material, and the problems in obtaining it may

also have led to the gradual, rather than rapid, accumulation of backfill to the rear of the dock and river walls in some parts of the dock estate.

The earliest of the reclamation deposits excavated was adjacent to the Dry Dock, and had been dumped during its construction and that of a river wall, which lay to its west, in order to create land later known as Nova Scotia (*Ch 3, p 60*; Fig 89). They included layers of sand, silty clay, and crushed pink sandstone which, given the known chronology of dock construction, were probably dumped during the late 1730s. Significantly, these had been dumped from the east and some of the lower layers may therefore represent spoil generated during the construction of the Dry Dock itself. This potential source might also explain the apparent absence of associated artefacts. However, other sources of backfill probably included ballast derived from the ships entering the port. Indeed, this is confirmed by entries in the minutes of the Common Council, dating to July 1738, which indicate that orders were issued for ships to dump their ballast at the outside wall of the intended Dry Dock (MDNB/MP/25, 50). Ships of this period were capable of carrying over 50 tons of ballast (Hahn 1981) and this may well have resulted in the fairly rapid build-up of land across this relatively shallow area, which was probably no deeper than 6.2 m. Again, the use of ballast might also explain the sterile character of these reclamation deposits.

Other mid-eighteenth-century land-reclamation deposits related to the extension of Nova Scotia, dumped to the rear of a river wall (*7638; p 220*) that probably dates to the 1740s. These deposits were similar in character to those associated with the initial formation of Nova Scotia (*p 223*) and, again, it is possible that some of this material represents ships' ballast that was dumped fairly rapidly across this area. However, in addition, waste derived from nearby industries was also used as backfill, as evidenced by the discovery of a sizable dump of sugar wares (*Ch 6, p 207*). The use of industrial waste as backfill appears therefore to have been initiated during this period and would set a precedent for its use in future schemes of land reclamation (*see below*).

The other eighteenth-century land-reclamation deposits examined in some detail were associated with the creation of Manchester Basin and the portion of land to its north that would become Mann Island, as depicted on Charles Eyes' map of 1785 (*Ch 3, pp 74-5*). The documentary and artefactual evidence indicate that the creation of this area of reclaimed land may have extended over a ten-year period, perhaps beginning in the mid-1770s and continuing into the 1780s (Fig 89). The materials employed immediately to the east of Manchester Basin included quarry waste and/or ships' ballast, which sloped gently downwards from east to west, indicating that it was probably carted from other areas in the docks and dumped from the landward side of the waterfront. Significantly, this material also contained comparatively large quantities of industrial waste, which included five large clay tobacco-pipe dumps (*Ch 6, pp 197-203*). These date to the 1780s and, given that the initial creation of this reclaimed land began in the mid-1770s, they indicate that, in this instance, backfilling was a fairly long and drawn-out process. The presence of industrial waste also suggests that the process of land reclamation offered a convenient mechanism for the disposal of industrially produced detritus. However, it is quite possible that local industries were encouraged to surrender their waste, particularly as one persistent problem during this period was the procurement of adequate supplies of backfill (Ritchie-Noakes 1984, 103).

Other late eighteenth-century reclamation deposits examined lay to the north of Manchester Basin and were associated with the extension of Mann Island into an area immediately to the north of a narrow parcel of land that originally defined the northern side of Manchester Basin (*Ch 3, p 80*; Fig 89). These deposits probably date to the 1780s and were largely comparable to those located at the eastern edge of the basin, though none contained industrial waste. Immediately to the west, slightly later land-reclamation deposits were examined, which had been deposited during the creation of Chester Basin, and probably date to *c* 1795 (*Ch 3, p 89*). As with the other eighteenth-century land-reclamation deposits, this material comprised quarry waste, ballast, and industrial waste, and included two sizable clay tobacco-pipe dumps, which probably date to the mid-1790s (*Ch 6, pp 203-4*).

To the west, other reclamation deposits were examined, which had been dumped, between 1805 and 1806, to extend Manchester Basin's northern quayside further west, intimately connected with the decision to convert the basin into a half-tide dock (*Ch 4, p 113*). As with the earlier land-reclamation deposits surrounding Manchester Basin/Dock (*see above*), the materials employed appear to have included ships' ballast and quarry waste, and also a large quantity of industrial waste and other detritus, indicated by the substantial assemblage of artefacts. A proportion of this material was dumped from the landward side, and this would have been carted from the surrounding docks, whilst other materials appear to have been transported to this area by boat and dumped from the riverward side of the waterfront. A proportion of the spoil might have been derived from a contemporaneous phase of work occurring to the south, which entailed the deepening and widening of King's Dock (Ritchie-Noakes 1984, 37), and in addition, other materials, such as deposits of sterile white sand, may have been derived from river dredging. However, during this period, material obtained by such dredging was expensive and difficult to acquire, not becoming a cheap and plentiful source until the advent of steam dredging, which was first employed at Liverpool in 1818 (A Jarvis *pers comm*). Comparable early nineteenth-century backfill deposits, containing quantities of industrial waste, as well as organic and timber debris, were also located to the north. In this case, these had been deposited to create the extended early nineteenth-century quayside to the west of George's Dock (*Ch 4, p 128*).

Two areas of nineteenth-century reclamation were exposed within the footprint of the LLC extension. One of these areas was adjacent to Prince's Dock (*Ch 4, p 137*), whilst the other was sandwiched between Victoria and Trafalgar Docks (*Ch 4, p 139*). In both instances, this backfill differed from the material used in the schemes of late eighteenth- and early nineteenth-century reclamation to the south (*see above*), as it contained a marked absence of industrial waste and other detritus. One potential reason for this was that these two docks lay some distance from the heart of the early- and mid-nineteenth-century town, though it is also probable that backfilling occurred at a much faster rate, and did not extend over several years. It is also probable that, during the construction of these docks, a greater quantity of suitable material was available for backfilling. At Prince's Dock, the character of the backfill suggested that it represented quarry waste derived from the actual excavation of the dock basin whilst, at Victoria and Trafalgar Docks, the material appeared to include quarry waste from the dock basins, as well as materials that were probably dredged from the Mersey.

Warehouses and Transit Sheds

The archaeological investigations along the waterfront uncovered the remains of numerous eighteenth- and nineteenth-century quayside buildings. A proportion of these were small warehouses/transit sheds that were integral to the functioning of the historic docks. Some of the earliest examples were two buildings which had been established at Nova Scotia during the mid-eighteenth century (*Ch 3, pp 67-8*). Only fragments of these buildings survived, comprising short sections of walling which formed their southern gable ends. However, it is clear from these remains that their walls were constructed of yellow sandstone and that this may have been partly derived from a nearby, defunct eighteenth-century river wall (*5707/7304; Ch 3, pp 57-8*). Although the function of these buildings is difficult to ascertain, the cartographic and archaeological evidence indicates that the westernmost had a linear form and was constructed directly adjacent to the mid-eighteenth-century waterfront, using a river wall as its foundation course. The cartographic evidence also indicates that this building was directly associated with Bird's Slip, a small embayment, that was probably owned by Joseph Bird, an important mid-eighteenth-century local landowner and entrepreneur (*Ch 3, p 61*). This might therefore suggest that it functioned as a small warehouse, where goods or other materials transported along the slipway could be stored, and the adjacent building might have performed a similar function.

In terms of the construction of these buildings, the use of yellow sandstone was not particularly unique, as other buildings dating to this, and a slightly earlier, period also appear to have utilised this material in their design. This was particularly evident from the excavations at the Old Dock and Chavasse Park (*Ch 1, p 9*), where yellow sandstone had been used to construct eighteenth-century street frontages and other supporting walls (OA North 2009a). Furthermore, it was also employed in the construction

of a large building with timber foundations on the Old Dock's southern quay (*Ch 2, p 39*). This building was constructed in the second decade of the eighteenth century and may well have functioned as a private warehouse. The use of sandstone in those early to mid-eighteenth-century buildings, directly adjacent to the waterfront and surrounding the Old Dock, appears therefore to confirm Defoe's (1726, 541) descriptions, that during this period brick was only employed to construct the more 'handsome' and affluent dwellings in the expanding town.

Both of the mid-eighteenth-century buildings excavated at Nova Scotia were demolished and replaced by 'new' buildings in the latter part of the eighteenth century, which formed parts of a swathe of properties on either side of George's Dock Passage. The remains of these later buildings were examined archaeologically, which confirmed that several had clearly functioned as private warehouses. The remains of five such warehouses were present to the west of George's Dock Passage (*Ch 3, p 80*). Of these, one faced the Passage, at the corner of Irwell Place and Nova Scotia, and was a five-storeyed building, whilst three were conjoined and formed major elements within the block of properties that was sandwiched between Irwell Place and Murray Place. Later map evidence indicates that these were warehouses with four, five-and-half, and seven-and-half storeys. Significantly, all of these warehouses were composed of handmade bricks, indicating that this building material was now widely used within the late eighteenth-century town. They also possessed fairly substantial brick-floored cellars, designed for the storage of goods, and the cellars of two of the properties also produced evidence, in the form of access wells, for the use of hoists. Hoists were a common feature of Liverpool's late eighteenth-century warehouses, the pulley being normally housed beneath the gable of the warehouse, often covered by a cathead (Sharples 2004, 205).

Other features that were normally associated with late eighteenth-century warehouses included stairs, loading doors, that were set above each other on the central bay of the building, and a pedestrian access (Giles and Hawkins 2004, 26). All of these features were positioned at the front of the building (Pl 197), whilst to the rear was the warehouse's storage space (*ibid*). During the late eighteenth century, it was also normal for the merchant owning the private warehouse to live close by, often in an attached house, and it is tempting to speculate that some of the smaller properties at Mann Island and Nova Scotia were occupied by the owners of the warehouses. The remaining warehouse, to the west of George's Dock Passage, lay at the eastern limit of Manchester Basin's northern quay. This building is depicted as

Plate 197: The front elevation of a private warehouse, at 20-2 College Lane, typical of those dating to the late eighteenth and early nineteenth centuries

a north/south-aligned range on Horwood's map of 1803, though only part of its far southern end survived in the excavated area (*Ch 3, p 86*).

The fragmentary remains of a warehouse were also uncovered to the east of George's Dock Passage. This building is also plotted on Horwood's map, as a fairly large rectangular property facing the Dry Dock, and elements of its north-western and south-eastern external walls were evident as below-ground features (*Ch 3, p 86*). However, in contrast to those warehouses to the west, it was not provided with a basement and its external walls were constructed in pink and yellow sandstone. The presence of pink sandstone is, perhaps, important, as this might suggest that the stone was initially employed to construct specific late eighteenth-century buildings, prior to it being utilised in the construction of dock and river walls at the turn of the eighteenth and nineteenth centuries (*p 221*).

The remains of several warehouses, dating to the first half of the nineteenth century, were also exposed during the various campaigns of archaeological excavation. In total, six examples were uncovered, three within Nova Scotia and the others adjacent to Manchester Dock and Chester Basin. One of the former had been built on the western side of George's Dock Passage, between 1803 and 1836, and appears to

have replaced, or probably modified, an eighteenth-century property (*Ch 4, p 147*). Although this building was comparatively small in size, with three-and-half storeys, its design was comparable to the other late eighteenth-century private warehouses in this area (*see above*), in that it contained a brick-floored cellar and also an access well, suggesting that it had a hoist. However, a Goad's Insurance Plan (1890) indicates that by the late nineteenth century this property had ceased to function as a warehouse and was instead used by a mast maker. The two other warehouses in Nova Scotia were slightly later in date and were constructed at some point between 1836 and 1850, having two and one-and-half storeys respectively (*Ch 4, p 147*). The remains of these were partial and fragmentary, though they did indicate that the floor of the one-and-half storey warehouse was supported by a series of handmade brick piers.

The remains of another early- to mid-nineteenth-century warehouse/shed were exposed on the northern quay of Manchester Dock. These consisted of fragmentary handmade brick footings, the positions of which tally with a range depicted on Gage's map of 1836. This warehouse/shed was probably erected by the Mersey and Irwell Navigation Company, which owned the northern quay during the early nineteenth century (*Ch 4, p 121*).

Another warehouse associated with Manchester Dock stood at its eastern end (*Ch 4, p 120*. This was probably erected in 1841, again by the Mersey and Irwell Navigation Company, and was designed to attract and serve independent traders (Ritchie-Noakes 1984, 35). It was, however, different in form from many of the other mid-nineteenth-century warehouses in the dock estate, in that it was designed to overhang the eastern end of the dock, and had three covered loading bays. This allowed flats and other smaller vessels using the dock to unload their cargoes directly into the warehouse. In this respect, it was comparable to the grain warehouse at Duke's Dock, constructed in 1811, which was provided with internal loading docks, known as 'barge holes', and also several other inland canal warehouses, which possessed similar features (Ritchie-Noakes 1984, 31; Nevell 2003). The archaeological remains relating to this warehouse, although limited, included a counterbalance to secure its overhanging framework, and several shaped pitch-pine timbers with iron fittings. These timbers projected up from Manchester Dock and formed the structural supports for the overhanging and covered loading bays. The remains of the sixth mid-nineteenth-century warehouse lay immediately north of Chester Basin (*Ch 4, p 130*). This was one of the smaller warehouses located in the dock estate, and was originally a two-storeyed building. It was also unpretentious in character, possessing handmade brick walls and sandstone foundations, with little architectural elaboration.

In addition to the late eighteenth- and early- to mid-nineteenth-century warehouses, the below-ground remains of late nineteenth-century warehouses/transit sheds were uncovered, whilst an examination was also made of an extant early twentieth-century transit shed. One late nineteenth-century warehouse was at Duke's Dock, where an archaeological watching brief identified one of its walls (*Ch 5, p 160*). The other warehouse/shed of this date was located on Manchester Dock's northern quay (*Ch 5, p 165*), its remains consisting of brick and concrete footings. These related to a building depicted on an 1872 plan (MMMMAL 107/1/5) and 1873 architectural drawing (MMMMAL 184/52/45), which was adjacent to the northern quayside, and possessed two lucams projecting out over Manchester Dock. The presence of external brick-built walls indicate that the form of this building was therefore comparable to the larger transit sheds built by the dock engineer George Lyster during the late nineteenth century, which possessed similar external walls (Ritchie-Noakes 1984, 139). Given this, it is also probable that its internal supports, which are visible on the architectural drawing of the shed, were in fact cast-iron columns, which were also a common feature of Lyster's transit-shed design (*ibid*). This type of construction was also evident in the standing early twentieth-century transit shed recorded (*Ch 5, p 173*), which possessed brick-built external walls. However, in this example, steel trusses and bracing were present to support the roof.

Late Eighteenth-/Early Nineteenth-century Domestic Buildings

Apart from the warehouses, several other late eighteenth-century quayside buildings were excavated along the historic waterfront. Within Nova Scotia, these consisted of three properties that may have partly functioned as cellar dwellings (*Ch 3, pp 83, 87*). This supposition was based on the presence of fireplaces within the cellars, suggestive of domestic occupation, and also the recovery of domestic artefacts from them. All of these potential cellar dwellings were contained in properties fronting the street named Nova Scotia on late eighteenth-century mapping, which was parallel with the Dry Dock and George's Dock Passage. More specifically, one of the properties lay within a building contained within the block of properties between Murray Place and Irwell Place. However, this property had been heavily modified in the early part of the nineteenth century, and was functioning as a pubic house by 1850 (OS 1864b); hence it was difficult to discern the original form of this potential dwelling.

The other potential cellar dwellings lay to the south, within two separate properties at the far northern end of a range of single-depth terraces. The cellars

within these properties had been subdivided into two separate areas, *c* 3.8 m square, and it is quite possible that these represent four separate dwellings. These singled-roomed dwellings may well have housed a single family and would have offered a cramped, dark, and dank domestic environment. Moreover, the size of this living area is comparatively small, particularly when compared with those cellar dwellings that have been examined within the City of Manchester (*cf* Gregory 2007; Miller 2007, 30-1). In Manchester, archaeological excavation has uncovered a selection of possible cellar dwellings dating to the late eighteenth and early nineteenth centuries, most examples generally containing a room measuring around 4.2 x 4.5 m, with the smallest room recorded, at Loom Street, Ancoats, of only *c* 4 x 4 m (Gregory 2007). Another notable feature of the potential cellar dwellings excavated at Nova Scotia was the apparent absence of stairs leading into the cellars. This might suggest that access was via a ladder leading down from a trapdoor, which opened at ground-floor level. The life of these cellar dwellings may have been short-lived, however, as the trade directories indicate that, by 1800, both properties functioned as public houses. Furthermore, by 1836, these potential squalid and insalubrious properties had been demolished and were later replaced by a row of warehouses (*Ch 4, p 147*).

Miscellaneous Nineteenth-century Quayside Buildings

In addition to the warehouses and domestic buildings, the excavations also uncovered remains associated with several miscellaneous structures adjacent to the docks, which had a range of different functions. The earliest of these were those associated with George's Baths, which lay at Pier Head, on the western quay of George's Dock (*Ch 4, p 123; Pl 198*). These remains were

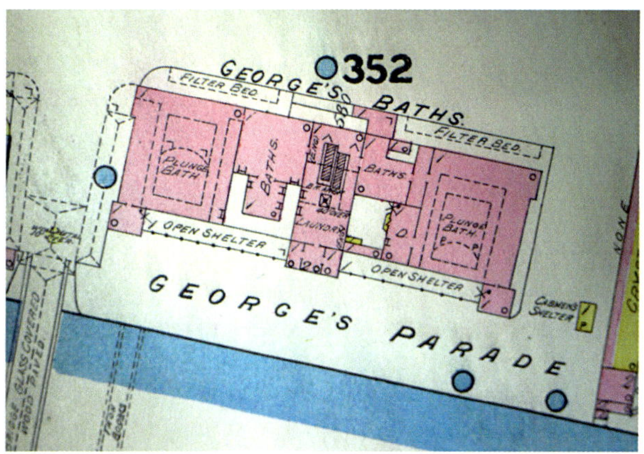

Plate 198: George's Baths, as depicted on an 1890 Goad's Insurance Plan

fairly limited, but included parts of a small rectangular room, or annexe, at the far north-western end of the building, a culvert, and also the tiled walling of one of the baths at the centre of the bathhouse.

In the area to the east of George's Dock Passage, a fairly dense collection of nineteenth-century remains was present, associated with a selection of miscellaneous buildings. The earliest of these remains were the stone steps of a fairly grand dockside building, designed by Jesse Hartley and constructed in 1834, which functioned as the Dock Police and Marine Surveyor's Offices (*Ch 4, p 144*). Immediately to the south-east of these offices, the complete ground plan of an unusual, perhaps unique, mid-nineteenth-century dock-side building was also uncovered. This lozenge-shaped building, perhaps also designed by Jesse Hartley,

was constructed of finely tooled pink sandstone and functioned as the 'Foreman Sweeper's Office' (*Ch 4, p 145*). It may well, therefore, have housed those responsible for maintaining the order and cleanliness of the quays and wharves around Mann Island and also perhaps the surrounding environs. This office adjoined an earlier rectangular building, which functioned as a police station, the eastern wall of which was present within the excavated area to the east of George's Dock Passage. Other nineteenth-century remains were also present in this area, and formed part of the George's Dock Pumping and Ventilation Station (Pl 199). This served the MRC tunnel and was constructed between 1881 and 1886 (*Ch 5, p 167*). The surviving below-ground remains related to two separate buildings, one of which housed the pumping gear, whilst the other contained two fans, which ventilated two sections of

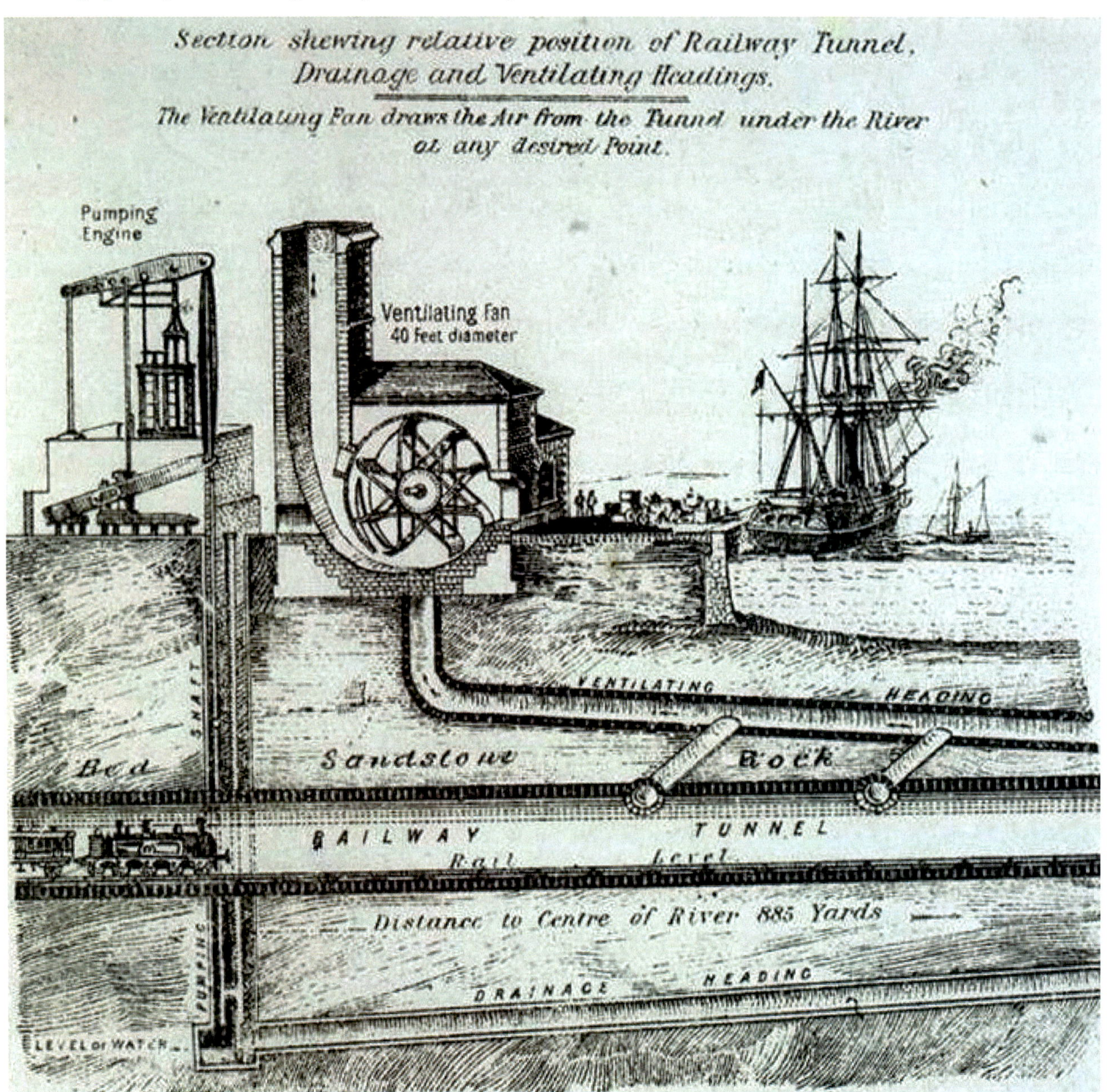

Plate 199: *Engraving produced in January 1886 by the Mersey Railway Company, showing the ventilation and pumping stations associated with the Mersey Railway Tunnel*

the railway tunnel. Those remains within the pumping-station building formed elements of the boiler room and included the setting for one of the boilers, which powered the steam pumps. The remains within the ventilation station building were more complete and included the housing for the two fans, brick walling defining air drifts and locks, and also the probable base of a horizontal steam engine, which drove one of the fans (*Ch 5, pp 171-3*).

Dock-ancillary Features

In order for the docks to work effectively, aside from the storage areas provided by warehouses and transit sheds, they also required a series of ancillary features, which were either joined or were within the docks, or alternatively were directly adjacent to the quayside. Several such features were uncovered during the archaeological work, including slipways, cranes, swing bridges, and also lock gates.

Two slipways were examined, both of which relate to the eighteenth-century use of Nova Scotia and Mann Island. Slipways formed a vital element of the early docks, as they enabled access to moored vessels and also the movement of goods onto the quayside, at all levels of the tide. Generally, prior to the nineteenth century, cargo handling was a manual operation and goods would have been contained in casks or packages, which could be easily carried by hand (Jarvis 1996, 165). One of the eighteenth-century slipways examined formed an element of Bird's Slip, a small private embayment, which is marked on late eighteenth-century mapping and is also mentioned in 1749 (*Ch 3, p 61*). This slip was defined by two separate sections of yellow sandstone walling, one of which abutted an eighteenth-century river wall (*Ch 3, p 63*), and it allowed access to the eighteenth-century warehouses on the quayside at Nova Scotia. It also seems likely that, prior to the construction of this slipway, mooring at this location was aided by a line of vertical timber posts, which had been placed between the river wall and the later wall defining the slipway (*Ch 3, p 66*).

The other slipway examined lay to the north of Bird's Slip, which appears to have joined with the quayside at the far south-western corner of George's Dock (*Ch 3, p 66*). It is possible that it was constructed in *c* 1772 by Henry Berry, and related to the establishment of a quay which functioned as a coal wharf. This was comparable in form to Bird's Slip, in that it was defined by a sloping sandstone wall, parallel with an eighteenth-century river wall. This slip was also associated with a line of sandstone blocks, and it is possible that they were used as supports for a temporary roadway, allowing

safe access out onto a nearby graving bank at low tide, where ships could be careened for repair.

The remains of five nineteenth-century quayside cranes were also discovered during the various campaigns of archaeological excavation. One of these was uncovered close to Prince's Dock, though its remains were limited and piecemeal in nature, comprising a brick and concrete platform with a complex arrangement of recesses (*Ch 4, p 138*). The remaining four cranes lay on the northern quay of Manchester Dock. Three of these were probably manually operated derricks, and the earliest of these (*Ch 4, p 121*) dates to between *c* 1807 and 1841. This was positioned on the eastern quay of Manchester Dock and its surviving elements consisted of several sandstone blocks which secured its base (Pl 200). The other two manually operated cranes (*Ch 5, p 163*) probably date to the late nineteenth century and the remains in each case comprised a metal fitting set within a brick-lined recess, with a concrete base. Both were located within an open shed and stacking area that formed an element of the 1841 warehouse erected by the Mersey and Irwell Navigation Company, which overhung the eastern end of Manchester Dock (*Ch 4, p 120*).

Plate 200: The sandstone base for the manual crane at Manchester Dock

Plate 201: The in situ *lock gates at Manchester Dock*

The third crane on Manchester Dock's northern quay was much larger in scale and comprised an hydraulic crane at the north-eastern end of the river lock. Hydraulic cranes were used at Manchester Dock during the late nineteenth century (*Appendix 2*) and the excavated crane dates to 1891. Its surviving remains included its concrete and brick-built base, as well as hydraulic fittings and pipes (*Ch 5, p 164*). In addition, close to this crane base, two chambers were discovered, which were probably associated with an hydraulic pump mechanism, that may have supplied this crane with the required hydraulic power.

Apart from the remains of the hydraulic crane and chambers, an engine house, dating to 1875, was excavated on the southern quay of Manchester Dock (*Ch 5, p 165*). This was integral to provide hydraulic power to those cranes on this quayside that were operated by the GWR. The settings for two boilers within this engine house were uncovered, which would have powered steam pumps contained within this building. These, in turn, supplied high-pressure water to an accumulator, which was then piped to a crane and used as a source of power (*Appendix 2*). Other features relating to hydraulic power were also present immediately to the west, though the fragmentary nature of these makes precise interpretation difficult (*Ch 5, p 166*).

Another set of important ancillary features at Manchester Dock comprised the lock gates, associated with the inner river lock (Pl 201; *Ch 4, p 115*). Although

this lock was the first of the two river locks to be gated, in *c* 1807, enabling Manchester Dock to function initially as a half-tide dock, it is likely that the *in situ* lock gates represent replacements. The reasoning for this is that they were made of tropical hardwood, Guyanese Greenheart (*Ocotea rodaei*), which is a type of timber that was only utilised in lock-gate construction from the 1830s onwards (Jarvis 1996, 197). However, this said, they are probably the earliest surviving lock gates yet examined within the Liverpool docks, and they may well date to the middle decades of the nineteenth century.

In design, they possess many of the common features associated with nineteenth-century lock gates. For example, aside from the choice of timber, these gates were mitred and fixed to heel posts, which were set within the masonry recesses on either side of the lock gates. Furthermore, they had a slight frontward curve, known as a rise, which allowed them more effectively to resist the pressure of the water, which at times was higher on the inside of the dock than on the outside (*op cit*, 193). The gates were also opened using the four-engine system, identified through the discovery of four winch chambers, placed as pairs on either side of the river lock. Although this arrangement was commonly employed at several of Liverpool's other nineteenth-century docks, it is possible that the four-engine system uncovered at Manchester Dock is one of the earliest of this type of opening/closing system yet recorded in Liverpool (*op cit*, 201).

Plate 202: The extant swing bridge-operating mechanism at Albert Dock, showing the cruciform handle

The swing bridge formed a final dock-ancillary feature that was recorded during the excavation work. These bridges spanned the entrance locks to the docks and they appear to have been introduced to Liverpool in the early years of the nineteenth century, and followed a design that was produced by the engineer John Rennie in *c* 1805 for a swing bridge spanning the Wapping entrance of London Dock (*op cit*, 212; Ritchie-Noakes 1984, 163). They replaced earlier timber drawbridges, which were used throughout the eighteenth century, and probably first appeared at Prince's Dock, forming original elements of its design (Jarvis 1996, 212). Following their use at Prince's Dock, numerous swing bridges, based on Rennie's earlier design, were then constructed across the waterfront by the dock engineer Jesse Hartley, and the remains of two examples were partially examined at Mann Island (*Ch 4, p 146*) and the entrance lock to Queen's Dock (*Ch 4, p 148*). In both instances, the remains probably formed part of the housings for comparable double-leaf iron swing bridges, though that at Mann Island dates to the early 1840s, whilst the Queen's Dock bridge was probably constructed between 1851 and 1852.

The remains relating to these bridges were largely comparable in that they comprised arcing pink sandstone walls, which formed the housings for the running gear, which enabled the bridges' respective leaves to be swung 'open' when access was required through the passage/entrance lock (*op cit*, 213).

However, the remains at Queen's Dock were slightly more extensive in that they included the setting for a manually operated engine used to move the northern leaf of this bridge. This engine was probably comparable to the surviving example at Albert Dock and, if so, it would have had cruciform handles (Pl 202), which would have used bevel gears to drive a vertical shaft (*op cit*, 215). At the base of the vertical shaft would have been a pinion which would have engaged with a cast-iron rack (Pl 203). This rack would, in turn, have moved the leaf on its roller track. At Queen's Dock, a ramp was also present, sloping down to the running gear. Such ramps are another common design feature of swing-bridges (*ibid*), and allowed easy access to the running gear.

Plate 203: The extant swing bridge-operating mechanism at Albert Dock, showing the pinion

Material Culture

During the OA North excavations at the Countryside Neptune site and along the LLC extension, a large assemblage of finds was recovered (*Ch 6*). These were mostly from extensively redeposited contexts, which, under normal archaeological circumstances, might be regarded as of minimal significance to interpretation. However, in this instance, it has been possible to use these finds to begin to build an impression of Liverpool's growing industry and its

Plate 204: View of the Herculaneum Pottery in the late eighteenth century, by W G Herdman (1878, pl XXIX; by courtesy of the University of Liverpool Library SPEC Y87.5.41v1)

trading contacts throughout the eighteenth, and on into the nineteenth, century. This can be placed alongside other sources of evidence to illustrate the development of the river front and its increasing adaptation to service Liverpool's vast maritime trade. There seems little doubt that the dumps of pottery, clay tobacco pipes, and glass reflect both local products and the type of goods that came to the port destined for export, much of it to the West Indies and to North America. Unfortunately, the stage of pottery production at which this material was dumped has proved difficult to define, as Liverpool had its own substantial pottery-making industry during the eighteenth and early nineteenth centuries (Pl 204), and it also decorated and shipped a vast amount of the output of the Staffordshire and other potteries. The clay-tobacco pipe-making waste dumps, however, have added much-needed, and internationally significant, detail of late eighteenth-century clay-pipe manufacture in Liverpool, and, on occasion, was able to supply information on exports as well as pipes intended for consumption in the UK.

No doubt, Liverpool's pre-eminence as a clay-pipe manufacturer was closely linked with its role as a major entry port for tobacco, and the amount of sugar-refining pottery also illustrates its substantial importance to the import of sugar from the West Indies, a position it held well into the twentieth century. The absence of personal items does perhaps emphasise the fact that the material used for land reclamation was not, for the most part, domestic waste in any sense, little of it being rubbish dumped directly from individual households, when a greater number of lost personal items might have been expected, or reflecting the clearance of larger midden sites. There is little doubt that the various phases of reclamation used large amounts of industrial waste, presumably brought in by the various manufactories of the town, and this directly reflects the importance of such deposits for comprehending the growth and development of Liverpool's industries and trading life.

Conclusion

The existence of the world's first mercantile-dock system dating to the early eighteenth century, and the subsequent expansion of this during the eighteenth and nineteenth centuries, has largely secured Liverpool's importance in world history. During this period, this expansion allowed Liverpool to function as one of the world's premiere general-cargo ports, and also a port that was intimately linked to the mass migration of Europeans to North America. This importance has been internationally recognised, and Liverpool's waterfront now forms one of the 28 WHS sites within the UK and its overseas territories (UNESCO 2014). Furthermore, it was noted by UNESCO that Liverpool represents the supreme example of a commercial port at a time of Britain's greatest global influence (Liverpool City Council 2013).

Naturally, the archaeology associated with the port holds similar international significance and the recent and ongoing redevelopment of the waterfront provides important opportunities for the identification, excavation, and recording of these highly significant remains. Moreover, across this area, archaeological investigation, when allied with detailed historical research, allows for a fuller understanding of the processes and outcomes of historic dock building, and also the use and operation of the adjacent quaysides. In essence, the practice of archaeology along the waterfront forms an important technique for uncovering the nuances of an area that was both integral to the rise and success of Liverpool, and which also continues, and will continue, to exert a significant sway on Liverpool's cultural and economic identity.

APPENDIX 1: MERSEY FLATS

Michael Stammers

Flats

Mersey flats were a distinctive type of sailing barge, which were different in hull shape, construction, rig, and operation from other regional types of barge, such as the Thames barge or the Severn trow. All, however, had a common purpose: to deliver and collect cargoes from inland or coastal places, from deep-sea ports to smaller ones, and *vice versa*. In the case of the Mersey flat, this might be to or from Liverpool, either inland or along the Irish Sea coast. The flat varied in cargo capacity. The earliest carried about 20 tons while some early twentieth-century craft could carry as much as 250 tons (Stammers 1993).

The flats seem to have been adapted from the small, single-masted 20-ton vessels that plied the coast and

the Irish Sea in the sixteenth and seventeenth centuries (Stammers 1995, 92). Some idea of the form of these eighteenth-century vessels, specifically those used on the Mersey and Irwell Navigation (*Ch 3, p 50*), are provided by John Harris, who depicts two such vessels in his view of eighteenth-century Manchester. This appears on Casson and Berry's map of 1745 (Pl 205). The flats depicted have square sails and the 'apple-cheeked' round bow, which was typical of this period (Stammers, 1993, 16). Their sheer (hull profile) was also much greater than the later versions, which suggests a coastal origin. The rig was changed to the more versatile sloop rig, probably before 1750, which consisted of a triangular foresail, fastened on the fore stay, and a main sail supported on upper and lower spars, a gaff, and a boom. This remained the standard rig to the present. 'Inside' flats, working the inland waters, had masts that could be lowered to pass under fixed bridges, whilst some coastal or

Plate 205: Two mid-eighteenth-century Mersey flats, depicted by John Harris, at the Mersey and Irwell Navigation Company's quay at Manchester (extract from Casson and Berry's 1746 map of Manchester and Salford)

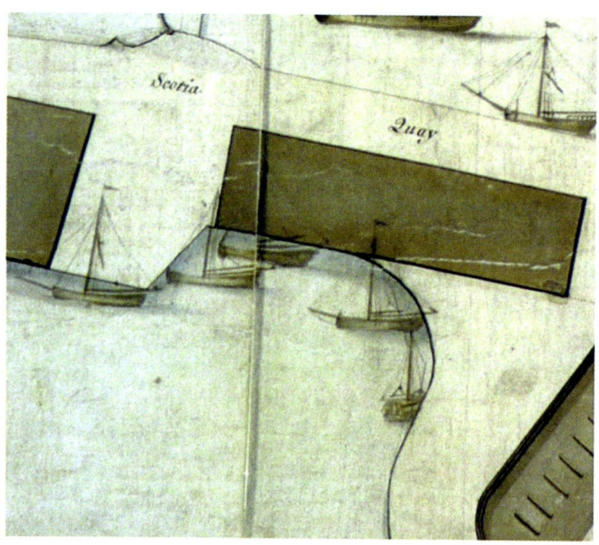

Plate 206: Extract from Lightoller's plan of 1765 of Liverpool (© Trustees of National Museums Liverpool), showing Mersey flats next to the Nova Scotia quay

'outside' flats had extra sails, and a larger two-masted version known as a 'jigger' flat was built in the late nineteenth century (*ibid*).

The dimensions of the flat used on the Mersey and Irwell Navigation were dictated by the depth of water and the dimensions of its eight locks, which measured 68 ft (20.7 m) long by 17 ft 6 in (5.3 m) beam (Paget-Tomlinson 1978, 191). The *Friend's Goodwill* was typical of these vessels, and traded on the Weaver Navigation (*Ch 3, p 50*), having been built at Northwich in 1750, and measuring 50 ft (17.7 m) long by 14 ft 6 in (4.4 m) beam, with a depth of 5 ft 4 in (1.62 m; Stammers 1993, 20). This remained more or less the standard size of flat for the rest of the century (*ibid*). The Mersey and Irwell Navigation flats were probably of a similar size, and could load a cargo of about 30-40 tons: Timothy Lightoller's manuscript plan of 1765 shows the quayside next to Nova Scotia with five sloop-rigged flats (Pl 206). This suggests that they were around the size of the *Friend's Goodwill*; the two with bowsprits may have been coastal traders.

William Strickland's Report for the *Pennsylvania Society for the promotion of internal improvement* of 1826 included a plan of a Mersey and Irwell flat (LVRO Hf 320 STR), as he recommended this as a model for an efficient inland carrier, and he believed that such a vessel could reach Liverpool from Manchester in 15 hours. This vessel measured 59 ft (18 m) in overall length, by 13 ft (4 m) beam, and 6 ft depth (1.83 m). In 1833, the directors of the Mersey and Irwell Navigation Company settled on a new design of flat, which had a third more capacity than its predecessors, and, to test their efficiency, one was ordered to be built in wood and another in iron. The latter was so successful that a further eight were ordered in 1833-4 (Kavanagh 2004,

29). Iron did not catch on as a building material for flats, however, and although it was sometimes used for framing the hull, wood remained the predominant material used. This may simply have been because these were the cheapest to build, though. For example, in 1887, the Shropshire Union Railways and Canal Company (SURCC) decided to order four steel flats, at a cost of £700 each, against £570 for a wooden one (BM D6919). Flats increased in tonnage for the rest of the nineteenth century, demonstrated by a sample from the Liverpool Shipping Registers between 1850 and 1875, which suggests an average registered tonnage (not cargo capacity) of 69.4 tons, rising to 76.2 tons from 1875 to 1900 (Stammers 1993, 20).

The flats belonging to the Ellesmere Canal Company and the Chester Canal Company and their successors, the Ellesmere and Chester Canal Company (established 1813), and the SURCC (established 1845), which utilised Chester Basin (*Ch 3, p 87*), followed a similar development in size. The 56-ton *Ann* was registered at Chester in 1796, the year after the canal was opened (Kavanagh 2006, 59). The *Mossdale* (formerly *Ruby*) is a surviving SURCC dumb flat, built in 1867, which measures 72 ft (22 m) by 14 ft 3 in (4.3 m), with a depth of 5 ft 6 in (91.7 m), and could carry 64 tons of grain on a draught of 4 ft 3 in (1.3 m; *pers obs*). This vessel is currently sunk at the National Waterways Museum, Ellesmere Port. Rochdale Canal flats, which also used Chester Basin (*Ch 3, p 87*), were different from the typical flat, in that they were more bluff in the bow and were fitted with four rubbing strakes. Their builders may have been influenced by the design of the inland Yorkshire keels (Stammers 1993).

Flats were built mainly of oak, possibly with an elm keel. They had a flat bottom, rounded bilge (where the sides meet the bottom), and round bow, with a square or round stern. They were heavily framed, with floor timbers as much as 10 in (254 mm) deep, and top timbers 7 x 6 in (177 x 152 mm). This 'skeleton' was planked on the outside in oak, 2.5 in (66 mm) thick, and on the inside by pine or oak planking, 2 in (51 mm) thick. There was a massive keelson running down the centre line, which could be as much as 13 in (330 mm) wide and 26 in (660 mm) deep (Howard 1999, 13-15). This 'girder' was essential to the structural strength of a hull, which might have to sit on the mud, and which also had a structural weakness because of its large hold openings (for easy access to the cargo).

The layout below the deck was simple. In the bow, there was a small store and bunk space for a third hand; then there was the hold, with a hatch on either side of the mast for a sailing flat, or a single hold for a mast-less 'dumb' or 'cut' flat; and abaft the hold was the main cabin for the usual crew of two (Stammers

1993). On deck, there was a powerful anchor windlass in the bow, which had a smaller winch, carrying the barrel line. This was a length of rope that could be used to move the flat around a dock by fastening one end to a bollard. The two hatches were covered with curved hatch boards and tarpaulins. Aft, there were low rails to protect the crew, a heavy wooden pump, an access hatch to the cabin, a water barrel, and a long tiller to move the big rudder. There was also a small boat known as a 'cock boat', which was either carried on the main hatch or towed astern (*ibid*).

The state of the tide was critical in entering and leaving a dock or basin. The depth of water would depend on whether it was a spring or neap tide, since the lock gates could only be opened when the water levels were equal in the river and the dock. The depth of water over the sill was also critical for a fully loaded vessel, hence the positioning of a depth gauge in the lock, such as that recovered during the excavation of Manchester Dock's entrance lock (*Ch 4, p 115*). Flats would have shortened sail before entering the dock, as to sail in under full canvas would have risked damage to the vessel and other craft (*ibid*).

The entry sequence would probably have been to 'scandalise' the mainsail (that is to drop its gaff to take the drive out of the sail), drop the foresail, and allow the flat's forward momentum to carry it into the lock. The crew would get a line ashore as quickly as possible, and then use that to warp the flat into its berth. When in dock, the crew would have used the barrel line attached to a bollard on the quay to winch the flat to a new berth. If this was on the other side of the dock, the cock boat would be sculled across, using a single oar over the stern to take the line over to any convenient bollard. At low water, the whole of the foreshore would dry out, as would Chester Basin. The flat's flat bottom, however, enabled it stay upright when the water receded (*ibid*).

Given the turbulent character of the Mersey, there were accidents and collisions. For example, the SURCC's *Herbert* sank with 70 tons of general goods in 1902, and in the same year, the *John* was damaged in a collision with a 'mast' flat off Manchester Dock (BM D6919). There were also collisions in dock, for instance, when the steam flat *Sea Swallow* squashed the flat *Belgrave* inside Chester basin in 1873 (*ibid*).

In the early nineteenth century, steam tugs were also used to tow the flats, which meant that deliveries were less dependent on wind and tide. Steam towage of flats between Liverpool and Runcorn had started in 1824 (Stammers 1993), and in 1831, the Mersey and Irwell Navigation Company ordered two tugs and started to convert an old flat into a third one. They intended to keep two in service and one in reserve, to assist sailing flats on the tideway. These tugs were small wooden paddle steamers, which were highly manoeuvrable but low on power. By 1832, the sails and masts of ten of their flats had been removed and they were towed by tugs on the Mersey, and by horses on the section above the tidal limit, from Runcorn to Manchester (Kavanagh 2004, 29). The Mersey and Irwell Navigation Company's take-over by the Trustees of the Bridgewater Canal in 1844 reduced their fleet to one tug by 1854, the 47-ton *Tower* (Marwood 1855, 250).

The Ellesmere and Chester Canal Company (*Ch 3, p 52*) also took to steam towage. In 1836, having acquired the flats of Messrs Fairhurst, Tilston & Co, the chief carriers on the Chester run, they hired tugs from the Steam Tug Company of Liverpool at a rate of £3 for towing three flats. In 1838 and 1839, they had powerful 117-ton paddle tugs (the *Clive* and *Earl of Powis*) built for their river traffic (Kavanagh 2006, 65), although their replacements seem to have been screw propelled: the *Magnet*, built at Chester in 1864; and a second *Lord Clive*, built by Bowdler and Chaffer at Seacombe in 1875. This latter vessel was converted to a dumb barge in 1889 and continued to carry cargo until broken up at Preston in 1967. The SURCC took over these vessels, and replaced them in 1903 with three 173-ton twin-screw tugs, built by John Jones's & Co at Tranmere, Birkenhead. They were dual purpose, as they towed flats and carried passengers (*ibid*). One of the trio, the *Daniel Adamson* (formerly the *Ralph Brocklebank*), is being restored at Liverpool (*pers obs*).

Tugs worked from the up-river terminals of Runcorn (up to 1871) or Ellesmere and Birkenhead, and might tow as many as 16 flats. These would be 'breasted up' together in pairs. Tugs would not enter the dock or the basin but would drop their tows outside in the river (Leathwood 2005, 33), and the flats had sufficient way (momentum) either to go alongside the river wall, or straight into the open lock. Flat crews would use the barrel lines to work the flat to the quay, whilst outward-bound flat crews would warp their craft out to the river wall, where the tug could pick them up.

The Rochdale Canal Company owned ten steamer flats and one motor barge when they were operating out of Chester Basin (Clarke 2008, 8-10). The first three were second-hand and reduced the time for delivery to Rochdale from 29 hours by horse boat to 17 hours. In 1891, the Rochdale Canal Company had new steel steamers built that were fitted with 25 hp compound steam engines, and these could carry 45 tons of cargo, and tow two flats to and from Liverpool (*ibid*).

Cargo

Cargoes delivered and collected by the Mersey flats varied considerably. By 1801, there was a daily service of 32 flats between Liverpool and Manchester (Moss 1801, 42), which at Liverpool would have used Manchester Dock and Chester Basin. The variety of cargo was reflected in the rates advertised in the *Manchester Mercury* of 4 September 1810: timber, lead, clay, bricks, grain, tallow, soap, provisions, hides, rope, flour, meal, clog soles, coffee, tobacco, horns, oak bark, cotton, wool, bale goods (*ie* textiles), linen, tea, hops, glass, oil, and spirits. A list from 1860 contained about 80 individual items, ranging from ale and porter for export to cotton for four Manchester firms, to pig iron and railway wheels delivered to Liverpool (BM D512). Cotton was the most important cargo for the Mersey and Irwell Navigation Company and, as early as 1815, Liverpool was responsible for 63% of the total import of British cotton (Hall 2001, 69). However, it is unclear how much cotton was loaded over-the-side from deep-sea vessels and how much was actually loaded at Manchester Dock. Rochdale Canal flats were nicknamed 'bale boats', because they carried large quantities of cotton bales on deck, and, in turn, they had wider side decks than the other flats. Their

Date	Tons
1753	9360
1766	16,380
1771	23,000
1791	33,800
1799	44,600
1808	40,497
1825	37,800
1839	211,663

Table 5: Estimated volumes of cargo transported by the flats using Manchester Dock between 1753 and 1839 (based on Kavanagh (2004, 19, 27), Langton (1983, 8, table 1), and Hadfield and Biddle (1970, 96, 123))

steam flat *Humber* loaded 48 tons of grain in her hold and 7 tons of cotton on her first trip in 1891 (Clarke 2008, 9). There seems to be no record of what cargoes were delivered to Liverpool from the hinterland, but presumably manufactured items, especially textiles, would have been the main items.

Although the volume of cargo moved by the flats between the mid-eighteenth and mid-nineteenth century is difficult to ascertain, some estimations can be made as to the combined tonnages for Manchester Dock (Table 5). These estimations are derived from Kavanagh's (2004, 19, 27), Langton's (1983, 8, table 1), and Hadfield and Biddle's (1970, 96, 123) data and are based on the known number of flats trading, multiplied by an average cargo of 32.5 tons, with the resultant figure being multiplied by 36, which represents the average number of cargoes moved by each flat per year (*cf* Langton 1983, 8). Between 1753 and 1839, it is therefore clear that there was a rising tonnage, which clearly justified the capital improvements made at Manchester Dock (*Ch 4, p 103*). Moreover, after 1839, the volume of cargo continued to rise until about 1848, and it has been estimated that the annual average tonnage was about 200,000 tons between 1838 and 1848 (Hayman 2003, 70). After this date, and following the takeover of the Mersey and Irwell Navigation Company by the Bridgewater Trustees in 1844 (*Ch 4, p 106*), tonnages declined, as cargoes were mainly despatched from Duke's Dock (Ritchie-Noakes 1984, 34).

Unfortunately, there are no cargo figures for the flats of the Ellesmere Canal Company and the Chester Canal Company that used Chester Basin. However, an estimate for 1836 claimed that 49,600 tons annually passed out of the Ellesmere and Chester Canal into the Mersey (Herson 2010, 27). The overall traffic was almost certainly less than that entering Manchester Dock, however, particularly as Chester Basin handled different commodities. During the first half of the nineteenth century, this included pig iron from Shropshire, pottery from Staffordshire, and agricultural produce, all of which entered Liverpool, with return cargoes including salt, timber, flax, and oats (*op cit*, 29).

APPENDIX 2:
THE HYDRAULIC CRANES AT MANCHESTER DOCK

Adrian Jarvis

Hydraulic techniques were intended to transmit power from a central point to the point of use, which might include a selection of hydraulically powered machines (*cf* Phillips 1983; Jarvis 1985). However, in the case of Manchester Dock, hydraulic power appears to have been used solely to power several cranes lining the dock, and as yet no records have been found of any other types of hydraulic machinery that were being used there.

In essence, during the late nineteenth century, the system utilised to achieve hydraulic power comprised a boiler, which powered steam pumps, and these, in turn, supplied high-pressure water (typically about 700 lbs/in²) controlled by an accumulator. From the accumulator, a pipe carried the supply, via a quayside stop valve, to the crane. The typical steam engine used to drive the pump developed fairly rapidly from about 1850, then during the 1860s reached a mature form, being a 90° two-cylinder horizontal affair, with the steam cylinders at one end and the crankshaft at the other (Jarvis 1985). In between were the hydraulic pumps, which simply consisted of solid cylindrical iron rams, that were forced into a cylinder containing water under the modest pressure of a header tank.

The forcing stroke lifted a non-return valve and drove water into the accumulator; at the end of the stroke, the valve closed under the back-pressure so that withdrawal of the ram refilled the cylinder from the tank. This general arrangement of the pumps can be seen at The Boat Museum, Ellesmere Port. Strictly speaking, the pump did not normally have pistons which 'pushed' the water, but rams which displaced it, so that the only part requiring (expensive) accuracy was the cylinder neck and its gland, which both guided and sealed the ram. The whole of the rest of the cylinder could remain roughcast, and the rams, while needing to be smooth, did not require dimensional precision. This arrangement did have the drawback that a displacement ram does not lift well, so the engine house needed to have a fairly large header tank and a town's water supply, or a float-controlled auxiliary pump, to fill it, providing the main pumps with a constant positive head. This was also the point at which any recirculated water was introduced.

Starting the main pumps would raise the pressure in the accumulator, a cylinder sunk in the ground with a large neck gland and ram, and with up to 100 tons of 'kentledge' (ballast) in a bin running on vertical guiderails, the weight of which was supported on the ram. The rise in pressure lifted the ram, which automatically stopped the pumps when full working pressure was reached. Drawing off power by working a crane caused the pressure, and the accumulator, to fall, which automatically restarted the pumps (it was to avoid getting the steam cylinders 'dead-centred' and refusing to start that the 90° crankshaft was adopted).

At the crane end of the system, when power was demanded by opening the stop valve, a ram resembling those in the pumps was displaced from its cylinder, lifting the crane hook and its load. In most cases, there were 'multiplying sheaves' on both cylinder and ram. These worked like a simple block and tackle in reverse, the force of the ram moving the sheaves apart. Round the sheaves ran a chain, and the larger the number of passes the chain made round the cylinder and ram, the smaller the force acting on the hook, but the longer its travel. Typically, a small quayside crane might have a ram travel of 6 ft (1.82 m) or 8 ft (2.43 m), with a multiplication of six, multiplying the lift at the hook by six, but also dividing the force at the hook by rather more than six, because of the greater frictional losses. Surviving examples may be seen elsewhere in Liverpool, in Albert and Edward Pavilions, and at the Colonnades, all at the Albert Dock (*pers obs*).

The hydraulic crane was a brilliantly simple device; because it worked on static pressure, any attempt to overload it simply caused it to stop. It may be significant that the only crane failure recorded at Manchester Dock was of a steam crane under test load (MMMMAL MAL/B/LHPC 172). On the other hand, it was possible briefly to draw more power than the pumps produced by running down the accumulator. Lowering a load was achieved by releasing the water in the cylinder to waste (or for recycling). Lowering the hook and chain with no load on required a spherical or cylindrical weight on the chain, just above the hook, to expel the exhaust water and overcome the friction in the cylinder gland.

The Hydraulic Machinery at Manchester Dock

Although the MDHB supplied services to some of its tenants and customers, there is no record of hydraulic power being supplied from its system to any of the various occupants of Manchester Dock. In about 1875, a pump house and an engine were built just to the south-east of the lock (MMMMAL MAL/B/LHPC 172; *Ch 5, p 162*). These appear to have been of similar general layout to the machinery formerly fitted in the Pump House public house at the opposite corner of Canning Half-tide Dock, with boiler(s) at ground level, but with the machinery floor elevated to create space below for the heavy pipework. Several sources, including the MDHB Works Committee Minutes (12 March 1875), refer to this simply as a steam engine and a 10-ton crane to be erected by the GWR (MMMMAL MDHB 17/1/35). However, in 1919, the railway company found it was cheaper to close down its own system and buy power from the public system of the Liverpool Hydraulic Power Company (LHPC). This company's enabling Act required an inspection and report by the LHPC's Chief Engineer on each of eight machines newly connected to the company's system, and in every case, the report notes that the machine was previously connected to the GWR supply, the pressure of which '...was approximately the same...' as their own (*ibid*). It seems unlikely that all those that were not newly built were bought second-hand in or about 1919, and it is more likely that the original engine and crane were in fact part of a system which also included at least two Vulcan cranes built in 1875 (MMMMAL MDHB/116). In short, the evidence suggests that there was a fully fledged hydraulic power system in use on the site by GWR between 1875 and 1919.

The 1919 changeover also required a new 3 in (76 mm) main to be run along the length of Irwell Street. Unfortunately, the LHPC's set of 10 ft : 1 mile OS plans (MMMMAL, MAL/B/LHPC), with mains and major appliances drawn on, had such heavy use during their working life that they are largely illegible, and two relevant sheets are completely missing. This wear and tear may be indicative of further alterations to the system as yet unknown, including possible repairs or alterations following the fire of 1890 (*Ch 5, p 162*). The 3 in (76 mm) main, which is also mentioned in MDHB records (MMMMAL MDHB/116), was authorised by the LHPC Engineer for use on 14 March 1919, and is one of the few parts of the system still clear on these OS plans.

What remained of the GWR system at the time of connection to the LHPC was something of an assortment, manufactured at different dates by different makers. All but one were platform cranes, installed at 'platform height' (in this case the height of a 'wagon dock') with the machinery below, leaving an unobstructed working area. All these had power slew and fixed rake; most had a 30 cwt Safe Working Load (SWL). Exceptions included an Armstrong machine for 1 ton SWL, dating from 1859, and a new 5 ton SWL Vulcan (*ibid*). Undated drawings survive, referring to appliances numbered up to 15. Among those not transferred to the new system were some dual-power cranes and some of very high (for a barge dock) lift; crane No 4 reached 55 ft (16.76 m), a height which could only have been beneficial in its ability to plumb the hold of a boat about three or four boats' width from the quay, suggesting that this was a busy place. All appliances inspected employed multiple sheaves, up to eightfold. Two completely different arrangements were shown as well, namely No 1, a roof jigger, and No 2, a wall crane, neither of which was reconnected in 1919. It should be recalled that hydraulic machines were extremely simple and reliable and, with anything like careful maintenance, would certainly last several decades, and withstand several removals. The whole original installation probably resembled, albeit on a much smaller scale, that installed in the Paris and Lyons Railway Goods station by Sir William Armstrong's company, and carefully described by him (Armstrong 1868).

APPENDIX 3:
WATERFRONT TIMELINE 1715-1972

Dates of opening/modification of docks, basins, and select ancillary features

1715	Old Dock opened
1739	Dry Dock (later Canning Dock) opened
1746	Graving dock added to the north-western corner of Dry Dock (later converted to George's Dock Passage in 1771)
1753	South Dock (later Salthouse Dock) opened
1756	Graving dock added to western side of Dry Dock
Late 1760s	Canning Graving Docks Nos 1 and 2 added to western side of Dry Dock
1767	Charles Roe's Basin opened
1771	George's Dock, Basin, and Passage opened
1772	Duke's Dock opened
Late 1770s	Manchester Basin created
1788	King's Dock opened
1795	Chester Basin completed
1796	Queen's Dock opened
1796-1803	New retaining walls added to Manchester Basin
1802-10	King's Dock widened and deepened
1805-6	Manchester Basin converted into half-tide dock
1805-10	Rochdale Basin opened
1805-15	Chester Basin extended George's Ferry Basin opened
1810-15	Enlargement of George's Dock
1813	Lengthening of Dry Dock graving docks
1816	Union Dock opened

c **1820**   Duke's Dock modified

1821   Prince's Dock and Basin opened
              Seacombe Ferry Basin opened

1823   South Ferry Basin opened

1825   Manchester Dock converted into fully impounded wet dock
              Completion of rebuilding and enlargement of George's Dock
              Clark's Hole opened

1826   Old Dock closed and backfilled

1829   Canning Dock opened (formerly known as the Dry Dock)

1830   Clarence Dock, Half-tide Dock, graving docks, and graving-dock basin opened

1832   Brunswick Dock, Half-tide Basin, and two graving docks opened

1833   Floating Landing Stage built

1834   Waterloo Dock opened

1835   Victoria Dock opened
              Trafalgar Dock opened

1836   Rebuilding of Brunswick Dock

1837-40   Toxteth Dock built
              Egerton Dock built
              Harrington Dock and Harrington Dry Basin built

1840   Coburg Dock created (involved modifying Brunswick Basin)

1842   Salthouse Dock rebuilt
              Canning Dock deepened
              Canning Half-tide Basin opened
              New river entrance and half-tide basin constructed at Duke's Dock
              Canning Graving Docks Nos 1 and 2 created (involved modifications to the graving docks that
              were originally attached to the Dry Dock)

1843   Trafford Dock built

1845   Albert Dock opened

1847   George's Landing Stage opened

1848   Stanley Dock opened
              Salisbury Dock opened
              Collingwood Dock opened
              Nelson Dock opened
              Bramley-Moore Dock opened
              Clarence Graving Dock Basin enlarged

1850   Wellington Dock and Half-tide Basin opened

1851   Sandon Dock and Basin opened

| 1852 | Huskisson Dock opened |

1852   Huskisson Dock opened

1853   Clarence Half-tide Dock enlarged

1855   Wapping Dock and Basin opened
        Salthouse Dock enlarged

1856   Queen's Half-tide Dock opened
        Queen's Dock reopened following rebuilding and deepening

1857   Prince's Landing Stage opened

1858   Canada Dock, Basin, and Lock opened
        Joining and enlargement of Coburg and Union Docks (renamed Coburg Dock)
        Widening and enlargement of passages to Brunswick and Queen's Docks

1861   Huskisson Branch Dock No 2 opened

1862   Canada Half-tide Basin (later renamed Brocklebank Dock), and North and South Carriers' Docks opened

1863   Landing stage off Harrington Dock opened

1866   Herculaneum Dock opened

1868   Prince's Half-tide Dock opened
        East Waterloo and West Waterloo Docks opened

1871   Brocklebank Dock enlarged
        George's Dock Basin backfilled and George's-Prince's Passage converted into graving dock

1872   Huskisson Branch Dock No 3 opened

1874/5 Floating Landing Stage destroyed by fire, rebuilt and named George's Landing Stage

1876   Graving dock No 3 opened at Herculaneum Dock
        Floating Bridge opened
        Prince's Landing Stage extended

1878   Brunswick River Craft Dock opened

1879   Langton Dock opened

1880   Alexandra Dock opened

1881   Herculaneum Dock deepened and branch dock opened

1883   Harrington Dock opened

1884   Hornby Dock opened

1888   Toxteth Dock opened

1889   Union Dock opened

1895   Canada Dock river lock modified

1896	Canada Dock enlarged Canada Branch Dock No 1 opened Alterations to Huskisson Dock Rebuilt Prince's Landing Stage opened
1897	Alterations to Huskisson Dock Widening of Hornby Passage Partial backfilling of Stanley Dock
1900	Alterations to Huskisson Dock Widening of Trafalgar-Victoria Passage George's Dock closed and backfilled
1901	Queen's Dock enlarged Queen's Branch Dock No 1 opened
1902	Huskisson Branch Dock No 1 opened Sandon Half-tide Basin opened Fourth graving dock opened at Herculaneum Dock
1903	Canada Branch Dock No 2 opened Brocklebank graving dock opened Brunswick North and South Locks opened
1905	Queen's Branch Dock No 2 opened
1906	Canada Branch Dock No 3 opened Brocklebank Branch Dock opened King's Branch Docks Nos 1 and 2 opened
1913	Gladstone Graving Dock opened
1922	Dingle Oil Jetty opened Prince's Landing Stage extended
1927	Gladstone Dock opened
Late 1920s	Closure of Manchester and Chester Basins
1950-70s	Waterloo, Langton, and Canada Docks provided with new entrances Victoria Dock remodelled New berths built at Langton Dock Prince's Dock graving dock converted into branch dock Canada Dock Basin rebuilt Passage between Canada and Brocklebank Dock widened
1972	Royal Seaforth Dock opened

BIBLIOGRAPHY

Cartographic Sources

Austin, H, 1836 *Liverpool and its environs, including the Cheshire coast*, LVRO and Liverpool Libraries P & SP Collection

Anon, 1729 *Plan of Liverpool in the year 1729*, reproduced as an inset in the map produced by the Society for the Diffusion of Useful Knowledge (1833)

Bartholomew, J, 1855 *Plan of the town and borough of Liverpool with Birkenhead, Tranmere, Seacombe, New Brighton etc*, LVRO and Liverpool Libraries P & SP Collection

Bennison, J, 1848 *Liverpool from an actual survey*, LVRO and Liverpool Libraries P & SP Collection

Casson, R, and Berry, I, 1745 *A plan of the towns of Manchester and Salford in the County Palatine of Lancaster*

Chadwick, J, 1725 *The mapp [sic] of all the streets, lanes and alleys within the town of Liverpool*, LVRO and Liverpool Libraries P & SP Collection

Eyes, C, 1785 *Plan of the town and township of Liverpool*, LVRO and Liverpool Libraries P & SP Collection

Eyes, J, 1765 *Plan of Liverpool surveyed in June 1765*, LVRO and Liverpool Libraries Local P & SP Collection

Eyes, J, 1768 *Plan of the town of Liverpool, with its docks, streets, lanes, and alleys laid down to the 29 September 1768*, LVRO and Liverpool Libraries P & SP Collection

Gage, M A, 1836 *Map of the town and port of Liverpool*, MMMMAL, Drawer Z/F3

Goad, C E, 1888 Insurance Plan, Liverpool, **1**, sheet 7, LVRO and Liverpool Libraries, Hf 368.00034 GOA

Goad, C E, 1890 Insurance Plan, Liverpool, **2**, sheet 32, LVRO and Liverpool Libraries, Hf 368.00034 GOA

Gore, J, 1796 *Plan of Liverpool*, LVRO and Liverpool Libraries P & SP Collection

Gore, J, 1806 *Plan of Liverpool*, Richard Hawes collection

Horwood, R, 1803 *Plan of town and township of Liverpool shewing [sic] every house*, MMMMAL, Drawer Z/F3

Jones, W, and Woodward, C, 1805 *Plan of Liverpool*, produced for *The picture of Liverpool; or, stranger's Guide* (Jones and Woodward 1805), the University of Liverpool Library, SPEC J24.43

Kaye, T, 1810 *Plan of Liverpool*, produced for *The stranger in Liverpool* (Kaye 1810), LVRO and Liverpool Libraries P & SP Collection

Kaye, T, 1815 *Plan of Liverpool*, produced for *The stranger in Liverpool* (Kaye 1815), LVRO and Liverpool Libraries P & SP Collection

Kaye, T, 1829 *Plan of Liverpool*, produced for *The stranger in Liverpool* (Kaye 1829)

Lightoller, T, 1765 *A plan for the new intended dock, Liverpool*, MMMMAL, M/D/1

Ordnance Survey, 1850a 6":1 mile, Lancashire Sheet 113, surveyed 1846-8

Ordnance Survey, 1850b 6":1 mile, Lancashire Sheet 106, surveyed 1848-9

Ordnance Survey, 1864a 5 ft: 1 mile Liverpool Sheet 28, surveyed 1848, first published 1850, new railways, landing stage, *etc* inserted 1864

Ordnance Survey, 1864b 5 ft: 1 mile Liverpool Sheet 29, surveyed 1848, first published 1850, new railways, houses, *etc* inserted 1864

Ordnance Survey, 1864c 5 ft: 1 mile Liverpool Sheet 34, surveyed 1847, first published 1849, new railways, houses, *etc* inserted 1864

Ordnance Survey, 1893a 25":1 mile, First Edn, Lancashire Sheet 106.14, surveyed 1890

Ordnance Survey, 1893b 25":1 mile, First Edn, Lancashire Sheet 113.2, surveyed 1889-90

Ordnance Survey, 1893c 25":1 mile, Lancashire Sheet 106.9, surveyed 1890

Ordnance Survey, 1893d 25":1 mile, First Edn, Lancashire Sheet 106.10, surveyed 1890

Ordnance Survey, 1894a 6":1 mile, Lancashire Sheet 106 NW, resurveyed 1890

Ordnance Survey, 1894b 6":1 mile, Lancashire Sheet 113 NW, revised 1892

Ordnance Survey, 1910a 6":1 mile, Lancashire Sheet 106 NW and Cheshire, parts of Sheet 7, 1910 Edn, revised 1906-7

Ordnance Survey, 1910b 6":1 mile, Lancashire Sheet 106 SW and Cheshire, parts of sheets 7 and 8, 1910 Edn, revised 1906

Ordnance Survey, 1910c 6":1 mile, Lancashire Sheet 113 NW and Cheshire, parts of Sheets 13 and 14, 1910 Edn, revised 1906

Ordnance Survey, 1927 25":1 mile, 1927 Edn, Lancashire Sheet 106.14, revised 1924

Ordnance Survey, 1955 25":1 mile, Plan SJ 39

Perry, G, 1769 *Plan of the town and port of Liverpool*, LVRO and Liverpool Libraries, Mapcase 6

Sherwood, W S, 1821 *A plan of the town and township of Liverpool, with the environs*, LVRO and Liverpool Libraries Local P & SP Collection

Society for the Diffusion of Useful Knowledge, 1833 *Liverpool*, LVRO and Liverpool Libraries Local P & SP Collection

Stockdale, J, 1795 *Plan of Liverpool*, LVRO and Liverpool Libraries P & SP Collection

Tallis, J, & Co, 1851 *Liverpool*, LVRO and Liverpool Libraries, Mapcase 24

Troughton, T, 1807 *Plan of Liverpool*, LVRO and Liverpool Libraries, Mapcase 13a

Walker, J, and Walker, A, 1823 *A plan of Liverpool and the environs containing the latest improvements*, LVRO and Liverpool Libraries, Mapcase 15

Primary Sources

Boat Museum (BM), Ellesmere Port (now National Waterways Museum)
D512 Rates of freight on the Bridgewater Canal and the Mersey Irwell Navigation, November 1860

D6919 T Kavanagh's transcripts of the Shropshire Railway and Canal Co's minutes and reports

Liverpool Record Office (LVRO)
283 NIC/1/6 St Nicholas Church burial registers

283 NIC/1/8 St Nicholas' Church burial registers

283 PET St Peter's Church Parish registers

283 SMW/1/4 St Mary's Church, Walton-on-the-Hill, early register

Hf 320 STR Strickland, W, 1826 *Report for the Pennsylvania Society for the promotion of internal improvement*

Hf 352 CEM 1/17/2 Liverpool Municipality, 1886 St Thomas's Churchyard, inscriptions of grave stones

Hf 942.72 GRA, 1877 Engraving of the grain warehouses at Waterloo Dock

Mersey Maritime Museum, Maritime Archives and Library (MMMMAL)
Mersey Docks and Harbour Board (MDHB) records
MDHB 17/1/35 Minutes of the Mersey Docks and Harbour Board Committee of Works, 1858-1949

MDHB/116 Mersey Docks and Harbour Board records, hydraulic machinery 1874-1920

MDHB/2211/M38 Mersey Docks and Harbour Board records

MDHB/2901/L88 Mersey Docks and Harbour Board records

MDHB/JH/117 Mersey Docks and Harbour Board records

MDHB/M51 Mersey Docks and Harbour Board records

MDHB/MP/25 Minutes for the Common Council of Liverpool Docks from 1699

MDHB/MP/82 Mersey Docks and Harbour Board records

Plans and architectural drawings
105/7/52 Untitled and undated plan of the Harbour Master's Office and its immediate environs

107/1/5 Liverpool, Manchester Dock premises – block plan, 7 November 1872

182/1/2 Untitled plan with the caption 'This plan so far as regards the alterations of George's Dock and George's Dock Basin is approved and ordered to be carried into immediate execution. Dock Committee of 21 May 1822'

184/5/no ref Architectural plans and elevations of the 1834 Dock Police and Marine Surveyor's Offices designed by Jesse Hartley

184/5/1-42 Architectural plans and elevations of the Police Station designed by Jesse Hartley, with modifications by George Lyster

184/52/45 Manchester Dock–Liverpool–Shropshire Union Company's shed

689 Pumping station buildings – George's Dock Liverpool – west elevation, Grayson & Ould Architects

691 Pumping station buildings – George's Dock Liverpool – ground plan, Grayson & Ould Architects

694 Pumping station buildings – George's Dock Liverpool – north elevation – south elevation, Grayson & Ould Architects

MAL/B/LHPC Liverpool Hydraulic Power Company plans

no ref Blueprint of a hydraulic crane at Manchester Dock, 10 February 1891

Parliamentary Acts and Bills

HL/PO/PU/1807/47G3sIn60 Public General Act, 47, George III, session 1, An Act for the Abolition of the Slave Trade, 25 March 1807

HL/PO/JO/10/8/685, the Liverpool and Manchester Railroad Bill, Session 1825

Trade directories

Gore, 1766 *Liverpool directory*, Liverpool

Gore, 1767 *Liverpool directory*, Liverpool

Gore, 1769 *Liverpool directory*, Liverpool

Gore, 1774 *Liverpool directory*, Liverpool

Gore, 1777 *Liverpool directory*, Liverpool

Gore, 1781 *Liverpool directory*, Liverpool

Gore, 1787 *Liverpool directory*, Liverpool

Gore, 1790 *Liverpool directory*, Liverpool

Gore, 1796 *Liverpool directory*, Liverpool

Gore, 1800 *Liverpool directory*, Liverpool

Gore, 1803 *Liverpool directory*, Liverpool

Gore (Kelly), 1816 *Directory of Liverpool and environs*, Liverpool

Gore (Kelly), 1821 *Directory of Liverpool and environs*, Liverpool

Gore (Kelly), 1823 *Directory of Liverpool and environs*, Liverpool

Gore (Kelly), 1825 *Directory of Liverpool and environs*, Liverpool

Gore (Kelly), 1827 *Directory of Liverpool and environs*, Liverpool

Gore (Kelly), 1832 *Directory of Liverpool and environs*, Liverpool

Gore (Kelly), 1834 *Directory of Liverpool and environs*, Liverpool

Gore (Kelly), 1835 *Directory of Liverpool and environs*, Liverpool

Gore (Kelly), 1837 *Directory of Liverpool and environs*, Liverpool

Gore (Kelly), 1839 *Directory of Liverpool and environs*, Liverpool

Gore (Kelly), 1850 *Directory of Liverpool and environs*, Liverpool

Gore (Kelly), 1857 *Directory of Liverpool and environs*, Liverpool

Gore (Kelly), 1874 *Directory of Liverpool and environs*, Liverpool

Gore (Kelly), 1882 *Directory of Liverpool and environs*, Liverpool

Gore (Kelly), 1891 *Directory of Liverpool and environs*, Liverpool

Gore (Kelly), 1892 *Directory of Liverpool and environs*, Liverpool

Gore (Kelly), 1900 *Directory of Liverpool and environs*, Liverpool

Newspapers

Liverpool Chronicle and Marine Gazetteer 12 June 1757

Manchester Mercury 4 September 1810

Secondary Sources

Adams, M H, 2006 *An archaeological watching brief on land at the former King's Dock, Liverpool*, Unpubl rep

Adams, M H, 2007 *An archaeological watching brief on land at Duke's Dock, Liverpool*, Unpubl rep

Allan, J P, 1984 The post-medieval pottery, in J P Allan, *Medieval and post-medieval finds from Exeter, 1971-1980*, Exeter Archaeol Rep, **3**, Exeter, 98-226

Amery, A, and Davey, P J, 1979 Post-medieval pottery from Brookhill, Buckley, Clwyd (Site 1), in S Sell (ed), Medieval and later pottery in Wales, *Bull Welsh Medieval Pottery Res Group*, **2**, 49-85

Anon, 1706 *A trip to Leverpoole by two of fate's children in search of fortunatus's purse: a satyre, by a gentleman of Lincoln's Inn*, London

Anon, 1848 *The Parliamentary gazetteer of England and Wales*, **3** (1845-6), London

Anon, 1987 Alphabetical list of pipemakers in Scotland, in P J Davey (ed), *The archaeology of the clay tobacco pipe X*, BAR Brit Ser, **178**, Oxford, 337-50

Armstrong, W G, 1868 On the transmission of power by water pressure, *Proc Inst Mech Eng*, **19**(1), 21-41

Ashdown, J, 1972 Oil jars, in R Middlewood, Mewstone Ledge wreck, *Int J Nautical Archaeol*, **1**, 147-53

Ashpitel, A, 1851 *Observations on baths and wash-houses*, 2nd edn, London

Atkins, T, and Hyde, D, 2000 *GWR goods services: an introduction*, Didcot

Atkinson, D, and Oswald, A, 1969 London clay tobacco pipes, *J Brit Archaeol Ass*, 3 Ser, **32**, 171-227

Atkinson Ward, G, 1842 *Journal and letters of the late Samuel Curwen; an American refugee in England 1775 to 1784*, New York

Aughton, P, 1993 *Liverpool: a people's history*, Preston

Badeslade, T, Winstanley, H, Harris, J, and Kip, J, 1728 *Supplement du nouveau theatre de la Grand Bretagne*, London

Bagdade, S, and Bagdade, A, 2004 *Warman's English and Continental pottery and porcelain*, 4th edn, Wisconsin

Baines, T, 1852 *History of the commerce and town of Liverpool*, London

Barker, D, 1984 Eighteenth and nineteenth century ceramics excavated at the Foley Pottery, Fenton, Stoke-on-Trent, *Staffordshire Archaeol Stud*, **1**, 63-86

Barker, D, 1993 *Slipware*, Princes Risborough

Barker, D, and Halfpenny, P, 1990 *Unearthing Staffordshire*, Stoke-upon-Trent

Barker, R, 2011 *The rise of an early modern shipping industry: Whitby's golden fleet, 1600-1750*, Woodbridge

Barker, T C, and Harris, J R, 1954 *A Merseyside town in the Industrial Revolution: St Helens, 1750-1900*, London

Belchem, J, 2006 Celebrating Liverpool, in J Belchem (ed), *Liverpool 800: culture, character and history*, Liverpool, 9-57

Belchem, J, and MacRaild, D M, 2006 Cosmopolitan Liverpool, in J Belchem (ed), *Liverpool 800: culture, character and history*, Liverpool, 311-91

Berg, T, and Berg, P, 2001 *R R Angerstein's illustrated travel diary 1753-55*, London

Bird, J, 1963 *The major seaports of the United Kingdom*, London

Birks, S, nd *A-Z of Stoke-on-Trent potters*, http://www.thepotteries.org/allpotters/472.htm

Boney, K, 1957 *Liverpool porcelain of the eighteenth century and its makers*, London

Bosanko, W, 1916 *Collecting old lustreware*, London

Brears, P C D, 1971 *The English country pottery: its history and techniques*, Newton Abbot

Brooke, G C, 1966 *English coins*, 3rd edn, London

Brown, E M, 1993 Liverpool – the city and its industries, in E M Brown and T A Lockett, *Made in Liverpool: Liverpool pottery and porcelain 1700-1850*, Liverpool, 12-20

Brown, F, and Howard-Davis, C L E, 2008 *Norton Priory: monastery to museum, excavations 1970-87*, Lancaster Imprints, **16**, Lancaster

Brunskill, R W, 1997 *Brick building in Britain*, London

Canney, D L, 1998 *Lincoln's navy: the ships, men and organization, 1861-65*, London

Ching, F, 2011 *A visual dictionary of architecture*, Chichester

Clarke, M, 1993 Thomas Steers, in A Jarvis and P Rees (eds), *Dock engineers and dock engineering: papers presented at a research day school organised by National Museums and Galleries on Merseyside and the University of Liverpool*, Liverpool, 5-17

Clarke, M, 2008 The Rochdale Canal and its carrying department, *Waterways J*, **8**, 5-19

Clarkson, T, 1830 *Abolition of the African slave trade by the British parliament*, Augusta

Collard, I, 2001 *Mersey ports: Liverpool and Birkenhead*, Stroud

Collins, G, 1693 *Great Britain's coasting pilot*, London

Colvin, H M, 1954 *Biographical dictionary of English architects 1660-1840*, London

Cossons, N, and Jenkins, M, 2011 *Liverpool: seaport city*, Surrey

Cotter, J, 2000 *Post-Roman pottery from excavations in Colchester, 1971-85*, Colchester Archaeol Rep, **7**, Colchester

Coysh, A W, and Henrywood, R K, 1982 *The dictionary of blue and white printed pottery, 1780-1880*, **1**, Woodbridge

Dagnall, R, 1987 More Chester pipes in Rainford, *Soc Clay Pipe Res Newsletter*, **16**, 14-17

Dalton, R, and Hamer, S H, 1915 *The provincial token-coinage of the eighteenth century*, Bristol

Davey, P J, 1977 South Castle Street 1976: interim report, *J Merseyside Archaeol Soc*, **1**, 13-15

Davey, P J, 1991 Merseyside: the post-Roman pottery, in P Tomlinson and M Warhurst (eds), The archaeology of Merseyside, *J Merseyside Archaeol Soc*, **7** (1986-7), 120-42

Davey, P J, and McNeil, R, 1985 Excavations in South Castle Street, Liverpool, 1976 and 1977, *J Merseyside Archaeol Soc*, **4** (1980-1)

Davis, R, 1962 *The rise of the English shipping industry in the seventeenth and eighteenth centuries*, Newton Abbot

Deane, P, and Cole, W A, 1962 *British economic growth 1688-1959*, Cambridge

Defoe, D, 1726 *Tour through the whole island of Great Britain*, London

Delano-Smith, C, and Kain, R J P, 1999 *English maps: a history*, London

Drakard, D, 1993 Herculaneum, in E M Brown and T A Lockett, *Made in Liverpool: Liverpool pottery and porcelain 1700-1850*, Liverpool, 39-42

Ekwall, E, 1922 *The place-names of Lancashire*, Manchester

Emery, G (ed), 2005 *The old Chester Canal: a history and guide*, Chester

English Heritage, 1991 *Management of archaeological projects*, 2nd edn, London

Erickson, M, and Hunter, R, 2003 Swirls and whirls: English agateware technology, *Ceramics in America 2003*, 87-110

Farnie, D A, 1992 The cotton towns of Greater Manchester, in M Williams with D A Farnie, *Cotton mills in Greater Manchester*, Preston, 13-47

Farrer, W, and Brownbill, J A, 1911 *The Victoria history of the county of Lancaster*, **4**, London

Fergusson, C B, 1967 *Place-names and places of Nova Scotia*, Halifax

Fox, F, 1886 *The Mersey railway*, Minutes Proc Civil Engineers, **86**, London

George, D, and Brumhead, D, 2002 The Mersey Irwell Navigation: the Old Quay at Manchester, in R McNeil and D George (eds), *Manchester: archetype city of the Industrial Revolution: a proposed World Heritage Site*, Manchester, 22-4

Giles, C, and Hawkins, B, 2004 *Storehouses of empire: Liverpool's historic warehouses*, Swindon

Godden, G A, 1974 *English porcelain: an illustrated guide*, London

Gooder, E, 1984 The finds from the cellar of the Old Hall, Temple Balsall, Warwickshire, *Post-medieval Archaeol*, **18**, 149-250

Green, C, 1999 *John Dwight's Fulham Pottery, excavations 1971-79*, Engl Heritage Archaeol Rep, **6**, London

Greene, J P, 1995 A study of the 1830 warehouse at Liverpool Road Station, Manchester, *Ind Archaeol Rev*, **17** (2), 117-28

Greenhill, B, 1980 *The ship: the life and death of the merchant sailing ship, 1815-1965*, London

Gregory, R A, 2007 *Loom Street, Ancoats, Manchester: an archaeological excavation of late eighteenth- and nineteenth-century workers' housing*, Unpubl rep

Griffiths, D, Philpott, R A, and Egan, G, 2007 *Meols: the archaeology of the north Wirral coast. Discoveries and observations in the 19th and 20th centuries with a catalogue of collections*, Oxford Univ Sch Archaeol Monog Ser, **68**, Oxford

Hadfield, C, and Biddle, G, 1970 *The canals of north west England*, **1**, Newton Abbot

Hadfield, C, and Skempton, A W, 1979 *William Jessop, engineer*, Newton Abbot

Hahn, H M, 1981 *The colonial schooner 1763-1775*, Greenwich

Hall, N, 2001 The emergence of the Liverpool raw cotton market, *Northern Hist*, **38**, 65-81

Harthen, D, and Adams, M, 2005 *An archaeological desk-based assessment of the proposed Museum of Liverpool*, Unpubl rep

Hayman, A, 2003 The Bridgewater canal and Mersey and Irwell docks at Liverpool, *Waterways J*, **5**, 61-71

Hellier, J, nd *Policing in nineteenth-century Liverpool*, http://liverpoolcitypolice .co.uk/#/19th-century-policing/4554835006

Herdman, W G, 1856 *Pictorial relics of ancient Liverpool, accompanied with descriptions of the antique buildings etc. Compiled from original evidences, private muniments, and unpublished collections: subscriber's copy*, Liverpool

Herdman, W G, 1878 *Pictorial relics of ancient Liverpool: with seventy-two plates produced in permanent autotype photography by Brown, Barnes and Bell*, **1**, Liverpool

Herson, J, 2010 A canal in its context: transport in the Chester area in the early nineteenth century, *Waterways J*, **12**, 25-36

Higgins, D A, 1992 Speke Hall: excavations in the west range, 1981-82, *J Merseyside Archaeol Soc*, **8**, 47-84

Higgins, D A, 1995 Clay tobacco pipes: a valuable commodity, *Int J Naut Archaeol*, **24** (1), 47-52

Higgins, D A, 2008 Merseyside clay tobacco pipes, *c* 1600–1750, *J Merseyside Archaeol Soc*, **12**, 125-60

Higgins, D A, 2009 Country summary – England, *J Académie Internationale de la Pipe*, **2**, 41-9

Higgins, D A, 2011a The clay tobacco pipes, in OA North 2011a, 23-30

Higgins, D A, 2011b The clay tobacco pipes, in OA North 2011c, 26-30

Higgins, D A, 2012 The clay tobacco pipes, in OA North 2012, 61-73

Higgins, D A, in prep, The clay tobacco pipes, in R A Philpott, in prep

Higham, N J, 2004 *A frontier landscape: the North West in the Middle Ages*, Macclesfield

Hildyard, R, 2005 *English pottery 1620-1840*, London

Holgate, R, 1989 Excavations at Prescot, December 1980-January 1981 (Sites A-E), *J Merseyside Archaeol Soc*, **5** (1982–3), 11-21

Honey, W B, 1969 *English pottery and porcelain*, 6th edn, London

Howard, F, 1999 Fieldwork on the Mersey flats *Bedale* and *Sir R Peel*, in M K Stammers (ed), *Mud flats: archaeology in intertidal and inland waters around the Mersey estuary*, Liverpool, 10-25

Hoyle, B S, 1988 Development dynamics at the port-city interface, in B S Hoyle, D A Pinder, and M S Husain (eds), *Revitalising the waterfront*, London and New York, 3-19

Hoyle, B S, and Pinder, D A, 1981 Seaports, cities and transport systems, in B S Hoyle and D A Pinder (eds), *Cityport industrialization and regional development*, Oxford, 1-10

Hudson, B, 2006 *Irish Sea studies 900-1200*, Dublin

Hughes, G B, 1968 *Victorian pottery and porcelain*, London

Hurst, J G, Neal, D S, and van Beuningen, H J E, 1986 *Rotterdam Papers VI: a contribution to medieval archaeology: pottery produced and traded in north-west Europe 1350-1650*, Rotterdam

Hurst Vose, R, 2008 Glass vessels, in Brown and Howard-Davis 2008, 358-70

Hutchinson, C R, 1978 The docks, in Liverpool Heritage Bureau, *Buildings of Liverpool*, Liverpool, 1-17

Hyde, F E, 1971 *Liverpool and the Mersey: the development of a port 1700-1970*, Newton Abbot

Hyde, R, 1994 *A prospect of Britain; the town panoramas of Samuel and Nathaniel Buck*, London

Hyland, P, 2005 *The Herculaneum Pottery*, Liverpool

Innes, V, and Philpott, R, 1985 Unglazed earthenwares, in Davey and McNeil 1985, 116–21

Jackson, G, 1983 *The history and archaeology of ports*, Tadworth

Jackson, R, and Price, R, 1974 *Bristol clay pipes - a study of makers and their marks*, City Bristol Mus Art Gallery Res Monog, **1**, Bristol

Jarvis, A, 1985 *Hydraulic machines*, Princes Risborough

Jarvis, A, 1991a *Liverpool Central Docks 1799–1905*, Stroud

Jarvis, A, 1991b *Prince's Dock: a magnificent monument of mural art*, Liverpool

Jarvis, A, 1996 *The Liverpool dock engineers*, Stroud

Jarvis, A, 2001 *Glory days: transport in Liverpool*, Hersham

Jarvis, A, 2003 *In troubled times: the port of Liverpool, 1905-1938*, Newfoundland

Jarvis, A, 2011 Appendix 3: the context in which Manchester Dock was constructed: negative influences, in Philpott *et al* 2011, 27-8

Jennings, S, 1981 *Eighteen centuries of pottery from Norwich*, East Anglian Archaeol, **13**, Norwich

Jones, O R, 1986 *English wine and beer bottles 1735-1850*, Stud Archaeol Architect Hist, Ottowa

Jones, W, 2006 *Dictionary of industrial archaeology*, Stroud

Jones, W, and Woodward, C, 1805 *The picture of Liverpool, or, stranger's guide*, Liverpool

Joyce, J, 1983 *Roads, rails, and ferries of Liverpool, 1900-1950*, London

Jung Jr, S P (ed D A Higgins), 2003 *Pollocks of Manchester: three generations of clay tobacco pipemakers. The archaeology of the clay tobacco pipe XVII*, BAR Brit Ser, **352**, Oxford

Kavanagh, T, 2004 Flats and flatmen of the rivers Mersey and Irwell, *Waterways J*, **6**, 19-36

Kavanagh, T, 2006 Sailing flats of the Chester and Ellesmere Canals, *Waterways J*, **8**, 55-71

Kaye, T, 1810 *The stranger in Liverpool; or an historical and descriptive view of Liverpool and its environs*, 2nd edn, Liverpool

Kaye, T, 1815 *The stranger in Liverpool; or an historical and descriptive view of Liverpool and its environs*, 4th edn, Liverpool

Kaye, T, 1829 *The stranger in Liverpool; or an historical and descriptive view of Liverpool and its environs*, 9th edn, Liverpool, LVRO and Liverpool Libraries P & SP Collection

Kelly, J H, and Greaves, S J, 1974 *The excavation of a kiln base in Old Hall Street, Hanley, Stoke-on-Trent, Staffordshire*, City Stoke-on-Trent Mus Archaeol Rep, **6**, Stoke-on-Trent

Kermode, J, Hollinshead, J, and Gratton, M, 2006 Small beginnings: Liverpool 1207-1680, in J Belchem (ed), *Liverpool 800: culture, character and history*, Liverpool, 59-111

Lancashire Online Parish Services, nd *The district of Liverpool, central Liverpool*, http://www.lan-opc.org.uk/Liverpool/Liverpool-Central/indexst.html

Lancaster University Archaeological Unit (LUAU), 2001 *The Old Dock, Canning Place, Liverpool: evaluation report*, Unpubl rep

Langton, J, 1983 Liverpool and its hinterland in the late eighteenth century, in B L Anderson and P J M Stoney (eds), *Commerce, industry and transport: studies in economic change on Merseyside*, Liverpool, 1-25

Leathwood, W, 2005 A 1930s journey by a tug towing flats on the River Mersey, *Waterways J*, **7**, 21-34

Lewis, D, 2001 *The churches of Liverpool*, Liverpool

Lewis, J, Heawood, R, and Howard-Davis, C L E, 2011 *Bewsey Old Hall, Warrington, Cheshire: excavations 1977-81 and 1983-5*, Lancaster Imprints, **17**, Lancaster

Lewis, S, 1831 *A topographical dictionary of England*, London

Lindsay, J, 1979 *The Trent and Mersey Canal*, Newton Abbot

Liverpool City Council, 2005 *Maritime mercantile city, Liverpool: nomination of Liverpool – maritime mercantile city for inscription on the World Heritage List*, Liverpool

Liverpool City Council, 2013 *Welcome to Liverpool world heritage*, http://www.liverpoolworldheritage.com/

Liverpool Museums, nd *Trading places: Mersey docks*, http://www.liverpoolmuseums.org.uk/nof/docks/access/theme10.html#bbk

London Fire Brigade, nd *Our history*, www.london-fire.gov.uk

Longmore, J, 2006 Civic Liverpool: 1680-1800, in J Belchem (ed), *Liverpool 800: culture, character and history*, Liverpool, 113-69

Longworth, C, nd *Buckley sgraffito: a study of a seventeenth-century pottery industry in North Wales, its production techniques and design influences*, intarch.ac.uk/journal/issue16/1.html

Lotbiniere, S de, 1984 Gun flint recognition, *Int J Nautical Archaeol*, **13**(3), 206-9

McCarron, K, and Jarvis, A, 1992 *Give a dock a good name*, Liverpool

McCarthy, M, 1985 The iron hull – a brief history of iron ship building, in M McCarthy (ed), *Management of iron vessels and steam shipwrecks: iron ships and steam shipwrecks*, Perth, 219-23

McCarthy, M, 2002 *Iron and steamship archaeology: success and failure on the SS Xantho*, London

MacLeod, K, 1982 *The Old Dock: Merseyside docklands history survey*, Unpubl doc

McNeil, R, 1985 The 1977 excavations, in Davey and McNeil 1985, 20-32

McNeil, R, 1989 Excavation of an eighteenth century pottery in Eccleston Street, Prescot (Site F), *J Merseyside Archaeol Soc*, **5** (1982–3), 49-94

McNeil, R, and Newman, R, 2006 The post-medieval resource assessment, in M Brennand (ed), *The archaeology of north west England: an archaeological research framework for the North West region*, Archaeol North-West, **8**, Manchester, 145-64

Malet, H, 1977 *Bridgewater, the canal duke, 1736-1803*, Manchester

Marriner, S, 1982 *The economic and social development of Merseyside*, London

Marwood, T, 1855 *Annual directory, shipping register and commercial advertiser*, Sunderland

Maund, T B, 2002 The steam era on the Mersey Railway 1886–1903, *Railway Archive*, **2**, 2-19

Mayer, J, 1855 On Liverpool pottery, *Trans Hist Soc Lancashire Cheshire*, **7**, 178-210

Merseyside Archaeological Service (MAS), 2006 *An archaeological watching brief at Prince's Dock, Liverpool*, Unpubl rep

Merseyside Passenger Transport Executive (MPTE), 1986 *Mersey Railway centenary 1886-1986*, Liverpool

Metcalfe, R, 1877 *Sanitas sanitatum et omnia sanitas*, London

Miller, I, 2007 Ancoats: the development of a new industrial townscape, in I Miller and C Wild, *A & G Murray and the cotton mills of Ancoats*, Lancaster Imprints, **13**, Lancaster, 25-32

Milne, G J, 2000 *Trade and traders in mid-Victorian Liverpool: mercantile business and the making of a world port*, Liverpool

Milne, G J, 2006 Maritime Liverpool, in J Belchem (ed), *Liverpool 800: culture, character and history*, Liverpool, 257-309

Moore, E, 1899 *Liverpool in King Charles II's time*, W F Irvine (ed), Liverpool

Moss, L, and Stammers, M, nd *Liverpool's South Docks: an archaeological and historical survey*, Liverpool

Moss, W, 1796 *The stranger's guide to Liverpool*, Liverpool

Moss, W, 1801 *Guide to Liverpool*, Liverpool

Mountfield, S, 1965 *Western gateway: a history of the Mersey Docks and Harbour Board*, Liverpool

Mowl, T, and Earnshaw, B, 1988 *John Wood, architect of obsession*, Bath

Murden, J, 2006 City of change and challenge: Liverpool since 1945, in J Belchem (ed), *Liverpool 800: culture, character and history*, Liverpool, 393-485

National Maritime Museums, nd *Collections online*, http://www.nmm.ac.uk/collections

Neale, G, 2004 *Collecting blue and white pottery*, London

Nevell, M, 2003 The archaeology of the canal warehouses of north-west England and the social archaeology of industrialisation, *Ind Archaeol Rev*, **25** (1), 43-57

Nicholson, S M (ed), 1981 *The changing face of Liverpool 1207-1727*, Liverpool

Noake, B, 1993 The post-medieval pottery, in B Ellis (ed), *Beeston Castle, Cheshire: a report on the excavations 1968-85 by Lawrence Keen and Peter Hough*, Engl Heritage Archaeol Rep, **23**, London, 191-210

Noël Hume, I, 1969 *A guide to the artifacts of colonial America*, New York

North Western Society for Industrial Archaeology and History (NWSIAH), 1982-4 *Proposed maritime museum: an archaeological site survey*, Unpubl rep

Oxford Archaeology North (OA North), 2005a *31 Hanover Street, Liverpool: fabric survey, interim report*, Unpubl rep

Oxford Archaeology North (OA North), 2005b *20–22 College Lane, Liverpool: fabric survey, interim report*, Unpubl rep

Oxford Archaeology North (OA North), 2005c *The Stanley Buildings, Hanover Street, Liverpool: fabric survey, interim report*, Unpubl rep

Oxford Archaeology North (OA North), 2005d *The Strand sludge pipe, Liverpool, Merseyside: archaeological investigation*, Unpubl rep

Oxford Archaeology North (OA North), 2005e *Canning Dock, Liverpool: watching brief and evaluation report*, Unpubl rep

Oxford Archaeology North (OA North), 2005f *Canning Dock, Liverpool, Phase 2: archaeological evaluation*, Unpubl rep

Oxford Archaeology North (OA North), 2005g *Land at St Paul's Square, Liverpool: archaeological evaluation report*, Unpubl rep

Oxford Archaeology North (OA North), 2006a *The Eagle Public House, Paradise Street, Liverpool: fabric survey, interim report*, Unpubl rep

Oxford Archaeology North (OA North), 2006b *15–17 Hanover Street, Liverpool: fabric survey, interim report*, Unpubl rep

Oxford Archaeology North (OA North), 2006c *Canning Place Fire Station, Liverpool: fabric survey, interim report*, Unpubl rep

Oxford Archaeology North (OA North), 2006d *Nautical Catering College, Canning Place, Liverpool: fabric survey, interim report*, Unpubl rep

Oxford Archaeology North (OA North), 2006e *Mann Island, Liverpool: archaeological evaluation, project design*, Unpubl doc

Oxford Archaeology North (OA North), 2006f *Mann Island: archaeological mitigation recording, project design*, Unpubl doc

Oxford Archaeology North (OA North), 2006g *Liverpool Canal Link: archaeological evaluation and mitigation recording, project design*, Unpubl doc

Oxford Archaeology North (OA North), 2006h *Liverpool Canal Link - Mann Island section, Liverpool: archaeological mitigation recording, project design*, Unpubl doc

Oxford Archaeology North (OA North), 2006i *St Paul's Square, Liverpool: archaeological watching brief*, Unpubl doc

Oxford Archaeology North (OA North), 2008 *Ferry Terminal, Liverpool, Merseyside: archaeological evaluation report*, Unpubl rep

Oxford Archaeology North (OA North), 2009a *The Old Dock and Chavasse Park and environs, Liverpool: post-excavation assessment report*, Unpubl rep

Oxford Archaeology North (OA North), 2009b *St Paul's Church, Liverpool: archaeological watching brief*, Unpubl rep

Oxford Archaeology North (OA North), 2010 *Mann Island, Liverpool, Merseyside: archaeological post-excavation assessment report*, Unpubl rep

Oxford Archaeology North (OA North), 2011a *Mann Island Canal Link, Merseyside: archaeological excavation report*, Unpubl rep

Oxford Archaeology North (OA North), 2011b *Central Docks Canal Link, Merseyside: archaeological excavation and watching brief report*, Unpubl rep

Oxford Archaeology North (OA North), 2011c *Pier Head Canal Link, Merseyside: archaeological excavation report*, Unpubl rep

Oxford Archaeology North (OA North), 2012 *Mann Island, Merseyside: archaeological excavation report*, Unpubl rep

Paget-Tomlinson, E W, 1978 *The complete book of canal and river navigations*, Albrighton

Peacey, A, 1996 *The development of the clay tobacco pipe kiln in the British Isles: the archaeology of the clay tobacco pipe XIV*, BAR Brit Ser, **246**, Oxford

Peel Ports, nd *Port of Liverpool*, http://www.peelports.co.uk/port-of-liverpool/

Percy, C M, 1905 *The mechanical equipment of collieries*, Manchester

Phillips, N, 1983 *Quayside and warehouse fixtures in Liverpool's south docks*, Liverpool

Philpott, R A, 1985 Mottled ware, in Davey and McNeil 1985, 50-62

Philpott, R A, in prep *Archaeology at the waterfront 2: finds from Liverpool's historic docks*, Liverpool

Philpott, R, Adams, M, Ahmad, C, Jones, H, Speakman, J, and Pevely, S E, 2011 *An archaeological watching brief on the site of the Museum of Liverpool, Mann Island (centred at NGR SJ 3394 9004): interim assessment report*, Unpubl rep

Philpott, R A, and Davey, P J, 1989 Sampling excavations in Prescot, 1983-4 (Sites 6-26), *J Merseyside Archaeol Soc*, **5**, 39-48

Picton, J A, 1873 *Memorials of Liverpool historical and topographical, including a history of the dock estate*, 1st edn, London

Pike, W T, 1911 *Liverpool and Birkenhead in the twentieth century*, Brighton

Poole, J E, 1995 *English pottery*, Fitzwilliam Mus Handbooks, Cambridge

Pooley, C G, 2006 Living in Liverpool: the modern city, in J Belchem (ed), *Liverpool 800: culture, character and history*, Liverpool, 171-255

Quick, M, 2001 *Railway passenger stations in Great Britain: a chronology*, Oxford

Ray, A, 1973 *English Delftware tiles*, London

Ray, A, 2000 *English Delftware in the Ashmolean Museum*, Oxford

Reed, C, 1992 *Gateway to the west: a history of Riverside Station, Liverpool*, Potters Bar

Rees, P, 1991 *A guide to Merseyside's industrial past*, Birkenhead

Rennie, J, 1846 *Report on the sewerage of the town of Liverpool in the year 1816*, Liverpool

Rideout, E H, 1928 *The custom house, Liverpool*, Liverpool

Rickard, J, 2006 *Mocha and related dipped wares, 1770-1939*, Hanover and London

Ritchie-Noakes, N, 1984 *Liverpool's historic waterfront: the world's first mercantile dock system*, London

Roberts, J, 1993 'A densely populated and unlovely tract': the residential development of Ancoats, *Manchester Region Hist Rev*, **7**, 15-26

Rutter, J A, and Davey, P J, 1980 Clay pipes from Chester, in P Davey (ed), *The archaeology of the clay tobacco pipe III*, BAR Brit Ser, **78**, Oxford, 41-272

Ryan, P, 1996 *Brick in Essex from the Roman conquest to the Reformation*, Colchester

Savage, G, 1952 *Eighteenth-century English porcelain*, London

Scholfield, S A, and Smith, K, 1999 The cardinal role of Liverpool's dock gates in the port's engineering history, in A Jarvis and K Smith (eds), *Albert Dock, trade and technology*, Liverpool, 53-60

Sempill, C, 1904 *English pottery and china*, London

Sharples, J, 2004 *Liverpool*, New Haven and London

Sheridan, R B, 2000 *Sugar and slavery: an economic history of the British West Indies 1623-1775*, Kingston

Slaughter, M, 1869 *Railway intelligence*, **15**, London

Smith, A, 1970 *The illustrated guide to Liverpool's Herculaneum Pottery 1796-1840*, London

Smith, A, 1993 Herculaneum, in E M Brown and T A Lockett, *Made in Liverpool: Liverpool pottery and porcelain 1700-1850*, Liverpool, 43-6

Spink and Sons Ltd, 2010 *Coins of England and the United Kingdom: standard catalogue of British coins*, 45th edn, London

Stammers, M K, 1993 *Mersey flats and flatmen*, Lavenham

Stammers, M K, 1995 What's in a picture? Pictorial evidence for ships and harbours, in P Carrington, *Where Deva spreads her wizard stream: trade and the port of Chester*, Chester, 90-4

Stammers, M K, 1999 *Images of England: Liverpool Docks*, Stroud

Stammers, M K, 2007 *The industrial archaeology of ports and harbours*, Stroud

Staniforth, M, 1996 Tracing artefact trajectories: following Chinese export porcelain, *Bull Australian Inst Maritime Archaeol*, **20** (1), 13-18

Stewart-Brown, R, 1930 The Pool of Liverpool, *Trans Hist Soc Lancashire Cheshire*, **82**, 88-135

Stewart-Brown, R, 1932 *Liverpool ships in the eighteenth century*, London

Trinder, B, 1982 *The making of the industrial landscape*, London

Troughton, T, 1810 *The history of Liverpool, from the earliest authenticated period down to the present time*, Liverpool

Tyrer, F, 1970 *The great diurnal of Nicholas Blundell of Little Crosby, Lancashire, Volume 2, 1712-19*, Rec Soc Lancashire Cheshire, **112**, Chester

UNESCO, 2014 *United Kingdom of Great Britain and Northern Ireland: properties inscribed on the World Heritage List*, http://whc.unesco.org/en/statesparties/gb

UKIC, 1984 *Environmental standards for the permanent storage of material from archaeological sites*, London

Wang, N, 2011 A comparison of Chinese and British tea culture, *Asian Cultur Hist*, **3** (2), 13-18

Wardell Armstrong, 2003 *Liverpool Canal Link: archaeological and cultural heritage/architectural impact assessment*, Unpubl rep

Wardell Armstrong, 2006 *Mann Island: environmental statement*, Unpubl rep

Welbourn, N, 2008 *Lost lines: Liverpool and the Mersey*, Hersham

White, S D (Davey, P J, and Higgins, D A (eds)), 2004 *The dynamics of regionalisation and trade: Yorkshire clay tobacco pipes c 1600-1800. The archaeology of the clay tobacco pipe XVIII*, BAR Brit Ser, **374**, Oxford

Williams, G, 1897 *History of the Liverpool privateers and letters of marque, with an account of the Liverpool slave trade*, Liverpool

Wilson, E A, 1975 *The Ellesmere and Llangollen Canal: an historical background*, Phillimore

Wilson, J M, 1870-2 *Imperial gazetteer of England and Wales*, London

INDEX